A Guide to the Birds of
TRINIDAD AND TOBAGO

A GUIDE TO THE

BIRDS OF TRINIDAD and TOBAGO SECOND EDITION

Richard ffrench

Plates and drawings by
JOHN P. O'NEILL

Portraits by
DON R. ECKELBERRY

Comstock Publishing Associates

A DIVISION OF *Cornell University Press*

ITHACA, NEW YORK

Second edition published 1991 by Cornell University Press.

First edition published 1973 by Livingston Publishing Company. Revised editions published 1976, 1980 by Harrowood Books.

Library of Congress Cataloging-in-Publication Data

Ffrench, Richard.
   A guide to the birds of Trinidad and Tobago / Richard Ffrench ; plates and drawings by John P. O'Neill ; portraits by Don R. Eckelberry. — 2nd ed.
       p.   cm.
   Includes bibliographical references (p.   ) and index.
   ISBN 0-8014-2567-0 (cloth : alkaline paper). — ISBN 0-8014-9792-2 (paper : alkaline paper)
   1. Birds—Trinidad and Tobago. 2. Birds—Trinidad and Tobago—Identification. I. O'Neill, John Patton, 1942–   . II. Eckelberry, Don R. III. Title.
QL688.T8F47   1991
598.2972983—dc20   91-6396

Printed in the United States of America.
Color section printed in Hong Kong.

⊗ The paper in this book meets the minimum requirements
of the American National Standard for Information Sciences—
Permanence of Paper for Printed Library Materials, ANSI Z39.48-1984.

In memory of Jonnie Fisk
with warm affection

Contents

Illustrations and Tables

xii   ILLUSTRATIONS AND TABLES

PLATES, *following page 236*

Foreword to the Second Edition

For countless bird-watchers and for many professional ornithologists, a visit to Trinidad and Tobago has been their introduction to the amazingly rich South American avifauna. The two islands might almost have been designed for the purpose. Here, in beautiful country and within a comparatively small area, members of nearly all the families of South American birds are to be found. The number of species is not so overwhelming as on the nearby mainland, but there are plenty, and those that are present are in many cases much more abundant and easily seen than on the mainland.

There was no satisfactory guide to the birds of Trinidad and Tobago until the publication of Richard ffrench's book in 1973. It had the great merit that it not only served as a thoroughly practical identification guide by an expert who knew the birds in the field better than anyone, but it also summarised existing knowledge of the ecology and behaviour of the birds, with full references, which made it an invaluable introduction to the biology of the avifauna and a source of information to research workers in other parts of tropical America. In this it set a pattern that has been followed with great advantage by later authors covering other parts of the region.

Knowledge of the birds of Trinidad and Tobago has steadily advanced since 1973, so much so that a thoroughly revised edition has become necessary. It will doubtless prove as useful in the coming decades as the first edition has been for the past eighteen years.

DAVID W. SNOW

Preface

As interest in birds continues to increase throughout the world, so too arises the need for adequate books to enable people first to identify the birds of an area and second to become more thoroughly acquainted with the lives of the different species. A possible consequence is that students of birds may, by discovering in a book what is not known about a species, be encouraged to try to fill in the gaps and thus add significantly to our knowledge of bird life.

To identify the areas of our ignorance has been the chief aim of this book, which attempts to summarise and present in a handy and readable form all that is known about the birds of Trinidad and Tobago, taking also into account information on the same species which may have been collected outside these islands. Trinidad in particular possesses, for its size, an extremely rich avifauna. It is quite a small island, in which most areas are reasonably accessible, while the facilities of civilisation remain available. Its birds, therefore, have been fairly thoroughly studied, compared with those of the rest of South America. It has thus proved to be an excellent place in which to find the material for such a book.

Ever since I first visited Trinidad and Tobago in April 1956, and came to live here in 1958, I have kept detailed notes on my observations of bird life. I have become familiar with some 350 species in the field. These notes form the basis of my work, especially where field identification and the distribution of species are concerned; but I have used many other sources of information. Originally I planned to co-author this book with David W. Snow, who studied the birds of Trinidad, principally in the Northern Range, during 1957–61. On his departure from Trinidad Dr. Snow felt he could not adequately give his attention to the project; but he generously allowed me the use of his unpublished notes, and his publications have been one of my principal sources of information. I have benefited too from personal contacts with many other people, who have contributed their observations and helped in many ways. They include T. H. G. Aitken, E. Alefounder, P. R. Bacon, M. Baird, W. C. Baker, J. Bond, O. M. Buchanan, C. T. Collins, I. Darnton, J. P. de Verteuil, T. Davis, J. J. Dinsmore, W. G. Downs, R. Eades, A. Fell-Smith, Erma J. Fisk, R. G. Gibbs, M. Gochfeld, D. R. Griffin, T. Hake, P. J. Hamel, F. Haverschmidt, D. S. Heinzelman, R. Krebs, D. Lack, I. Lambie, A. Lill, T. E. Lovejoy, G. F. Mees, R. Meyer de Schauensee, F. Nottebohm, J. P.

O'Neill, J. C. Ogden, R. A. Pallant, W. H. Phelps, P. C. Petersen, R. C. Rosche, J. Satterly, J. B. Saunders, P. Schwartz, P. Slud, B. Smith, B. K. Snow, A. L. Spaans, E. H. Stickney, E. S. Tikasingh, A. Wetmore, S. L. Wilcox, R. H. Wiley and C. B. Worth. Since the publication of the first edition I have also been provided with observations and helped in various other ways by B. Andres, R. Andrews, E. J. Bitterbaum, G. Blidberg, D. Buch, B. Cassie, J. Cudworth, J. Danzenbaker, M. D. England, P. Feinsinger, D. Finch, D. J. Fisher, R. Forster, G. Gomes, C. Green, P. Hall, S. Higgin-botham, A. James, C. James, T. Keeler-Wolf, G. M. McHugh, T. D. Mano-lis, R. D. Morris, W. L. Murphy, R. Neckles, F. Oatman, W. Peterson, V. Quesnel, S. Quinn, D. Raby, J. and R. Ramlal, B. Richardson, N. R. Rogers, D. Rooks, D. Simon, A. Small, C. R. Smith, M. Stewart, C. L. Stoute, G. Upton, R. van Halewyn, G. White and J. Wunderle. In the species accounts those who provided me with personal observations are cited by surname in parentheses.

In addition, I have received useful information on the local vernacular names of birds in Trinidad from R. Boodoo, L. Calderon and R. S. W. Deane, and in Tobago from E. James.

I have studied important collections of birds from Trinidad and Tobago in various museums. Principally, I worked in the American Museum of Natural History in New York, with financial help from the Frank M. Chapman Memorial Fund. D. Amadon, E. Eisenmann, W. E. Lanyon, C. O'Brien and J. Bull were of great assistance to me there. K. C. Parkes and the staff of the Carnegie Museum, Pittsburgh, also facilitated my work greatly. At the British Museum J. D. Macdonald and D. W. Snow were also very helpful. In Trinidad at the Regional Virus Laboratory, Port of Spain, I received every assistance from the staff.

The text of the book has benefited extensively from the critical comments of E. Eisenmann and D. W. Snow, with further comments from O. M. Buchanan, Erma J. Fisk and J. P. O'Neill. I am also grateful for the remarks of J. B. Saunders and my wife, Margaret.

The illustrations are the work of two outstanding bird artists, Don R. Eckelberry and John P. O'Neill. The latter prepared the identification plates, using his wide experience as a field ornithologist in South America and drawing upon his personal knowledge of birds in Trinidad and Tobago. I am especially grateful to Don Eckelberry, who made available to me his superb portraits of individual species, painted from living birds in Trinidad. I feel most honoured that such talented artists should be associated with my text. In this connection I must thank Dean Amadon of the American Museum of Natural History in New York, Emmet R. Blake of the Field Museum of Natural History in Chicago and George H. Lowery of the Louisiana State University Museum of Zoology in Baton Rouge for their willingness to send specimens for the artists to use.

My thanks go also to the Trinidad Water Resources Survey for providing rainfall data on Trinidad and Tobago, to the Bird-Banding Laboratory of the

U.S. Fish and Wildlife Service for providing band recovery data, and especially to the following banders for permission to publish their data: B. Adams, O. L. Austin, D. A. Beimborn, J. L. Dusi, R. S. Kennedy, J. N. Rice, W. E. Savell, I. S. Sturgis, L. Tyler, W. T. van Velzen, S. L. Wilcox, Florida Audubon Society, Massachusetts Audubon Society, U.S. Fish and Wildlife Service and Minnesota Department of Natural Resources. I am also extremely grateful to J. B. Saunders for allowing me the use of his habitat photographs, and to R. A. Pallant for drawing the maps of Trinidad, Tobago and the Caribbean area.

In the preparation of this second edition I have received valuable editorial assistance from Helene Maddux and Robb Reavill of Cornell University Press and from Melinda Conner, for which I am most grateful.

Final acknowledgments go to two people. Erma J. ("Jonnie") Fisk championed the cause of this book from the beginning and in countless ways assisted in its progress. It is difficult for me to express adequately my appreciation for all that she did. My wife, Margaret, too, has been a moving spirit throughout, encouraging, criticising, correcting, typing the manuscript and helping in innumerable ways. To her and to all the others mentioned (or perhaps inadvertently omitted) go my most grateful thanks.

RICHARD FFRENCH

Gloucester, England

A Guide to the Birds of
TRINIDAD AND TOBAGO

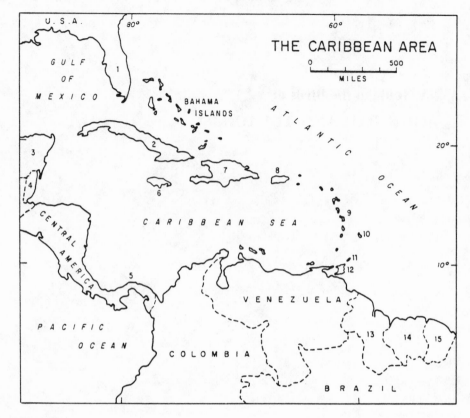

Map 1

1. Florida
2. Cuba
3. Mexico
4. Belize
5. Panama
6. Jamaica
7. Hispaniola
8. Puerto Rico

9. Lesser Antilles
10. Barbados
11. Tobago
12. Trinidad
13. Guyana
14. Surinam
15. French Guiana

Introduction

History of Ornithology in Trinidad and Tobago

The first ornithologists in the islands were mainly collectors, but with some notable exceptions their collections were made in a somewhat haphazard manner. Some of the earliest specimens still extant today in museums are of hummingbirds bearing the label "Trinidad" and no other data. These include certain species not to be found now in Trinidad or in neighbouring Venezuela. Clearly many of these skins originated from the millinery trade, which flourished in the early nineteenth century. Trinidad formed a collecting centre for skins obtained from various countries in South America, and the skins were then forwarded to destinations in Europe. Unfortunately, in discounting the validity of this material as originating from Trinidad, we have to ignore some specimens which are in all probability genuine.

Apart from a short article on the birds of Tobago by Jardine (1846), the first important literary references are from Taylor (1864) and Léotaud (1866). The former collected widely in Trinidad from December 1862 to March 1863, but much of the collection, which went to the British Museum, appears to have been dispersed. Léotaud, a Trinidadian resident, made a remarkable collection which is well documented in his interesting book. Most unfortunately, this collection, including some unique specimens, was totally destroyed by a fire in Port of Spain in March 1920.

In Tobago a local naturalist, James Kirk (1883), made a list of the local and migratory birds, and collected specimens, some of which reached the British Museum. It is a pity that his nomenclature is confused and inconsistent, for no other ornithologist before or since has had an equal opportunity to make a comprehensive survey of Tobago's birds. Other collections from Tobago were by W. W. Brown, reported by Cory (1893), Ober in 1878 (Kelso 1936) and de Dalmas (1900), but not all these specimens can be found today. A little later Klages collected a few specimens, now in the Carnegie Museum at Pittsburgh.

In Trinidad a major collection was made by F. M. Chapman (1894, 1895) and another by Andre and his associates (Hellmayr 1906). Most of these specimens found their way to the American Museum of Natural History in New York. Smaller collections were made by Finsch (1873) and Cherrie (1906, 1908). In 1909 Carriker made a moderately large collection for the

1

Carnegie Museum. Later collections include those of Roberts for the Academy of Natural Sciences in Philadelphia, Plowden-Wardlaw, who collected mostly swamp and savannah species for Yale University's Peabody Museum in 1950–51, and Mees, who collected widely in both islands in 1953–54 for the Leiden Museum in Holland. A few other specimens have been contributed by various people to different museums, but the only other sizeable collection is that held at present by the Trinidad Regional Virus Laboratory in Port of Spain, and contributed mainly by Downs.

Apart from scattered remarks accompanying the lists of specimens in the early accounts by Léotaud, Chapman and others, the first article dealing with other aspects of ornithology is by Williams (1922), who in his very useful paper recorded the stomach contents of many species and gave precise nesting details on several, especially hummingbirds. More useful data on stomach contents came from Vesey-Fitzgerald (1936). Roberts (1934) published a list of Trinidad birds, adding interesting notes on the moult and breeding of some species. Next, in a series of six articles Belcher and Smooker (1934–37) described the nidification of the birds of both islands, referring also to other aspects of their lives. These articles were the result of many years of research, mainly in Trinidad and principally by Smooker, and afford an extremely valuable and, for the time, remarkably detailed account of the nesting of Neotropical birds. Unfortunately, some of their data are not very definite, nor are they adequately documented by modern standards. In addition, it appears that their searching for nests mainly took place at the time when they expected them, so that in many cases the limits they give to the breeding seasons are too narrow. Nevertheless, much of their work contains valuable information and it remains an extremely important contribution to the ornithology of Trinidad and Tobago.

Mees' extensive collection was well documented (Junge & Mees 1958), with tables of measurements, some interesting field notes and short descriptions of each species; the position of Trinidad and Tobago in the zoogeography of the region is also briefly discussed. The work ranks with that of Belcher and Smooker as one of the most valuable additions to the literature.

For many years no author (apart from Léotaud, whose book, written in French, had a very limited distribution) provided full descriptions of the birds of Trinidad and Tobago. After a short pamphlet by Devas (1950) appeared, which treated informally a very limited number of species, Herklots' standard work was published in 1961; to this I and some others contributed some notes, mostly on status. This has proved quite valuable to the field-worker, particularly to one handling birds. The very full descriptions of species, however, have not always made the work adequate as a field guide, while the illustrations, though admirable in themselves, do not measure up to the high standards of modern professional artists. I have found Herklots' remarks on distribution and status to be somewhat limited. Nevertheless, the book has filled a real need, and many visitors to our islands have found it indispensable.

Various naturalists, both professional and amateur, have studied different aspects of ornithology in Trinidad since the days of Belcher and Smooker. These include Johnson (1937), Chenery (1956), Brown (1947), Quesnel (1956), Gilliard (1959b) and Darnton (1958). Dinsmore (1972) and Bond (1970) spent some considerable time on Tobago. Popular articles on the more spectacular aspects of bird life have been contributed by Johnson (1956–57), Saunders (1956, 1957) and Eckelberry (1964, 1967). There is no doubt that the interest generated by such articles spreads the knowledge of and interest in birds very widely.

A major source of research has emanated from the New York Zoological Society's tropical field station at Simla in the Arima Valley, established by William Beebe in 1950. Much of it comes from D. W. Snow and B. K. Snow, who have published extensively on the results of their wide-ranging field-work (see Bibliography). Valuable contributions have also come from Collins, Lill, Feinsinger, Keeler-Wolf, Manolis and others. Scientists working with the Trinidad Regional Virus Laboratory—notably Downs, Aitken and Worth—have also made useful and interesting contributions to the islands' ornithology.

During the years from 1970 onwards there has been increasing interest in bird-watching, with many hundreds of birders coming individually or in groups, principally from North America, to enjoy the wealth of bird life in Trinidad and Tobago. The establishment of the Asa Wright Nature Centre in 1967 has certainly facilitated and promoted this interest. One result of the influx has been the discovery of many more rarities and species hitherto unrecorded from the islands. It has to be pointed out, however, that on the one hand, many visiting birders are completely or comparatively inexperienced with Neotropical avifauna, so their sight records must be treated with proper caution. On the other hand, it is now necessary that an adequate system of recording unusual species be established locally to replace the hitherto haphazard arrangement. In my view, the logical body to collate and record these aspects of Trinidadian ornithology is the long-established Trinidad and Tobago Field Naturalists' Club, and it is my hope that a proper system will shortly be established.

My own contributions, apart from concentrated work on the Dickcissel, Scarlet Ibis, Pearl Kite and Brown Noddy, have been somewhat scattered and general, although I have also spent much time and effort on attempts to foster local appreciation of birds and other wildlife, believing that only this can lead to an interest in conservation. There is still a seemingly limitless amount of basic research into life-histories to be done, such as can be performed even by amateurs with limited time at their disposal.

The Environment

TRINIDAD

Geographical position. The island of Trinidad, politically one of the West Indies, was separated only in geologically recent time from the continent of

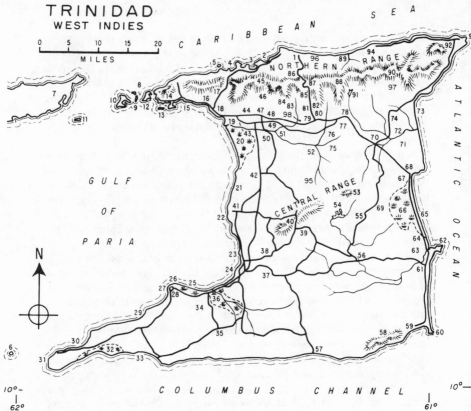

Map 2

South America. It is situated between latitudes 10° and 11° north and spanning longitude 61° west (Map 1); its greatest length from north to south is fifty-five miles and its average width is forty miles. Distances of about ten miles separate its north-western and south-western peninsulas from Venezuela. In the north-west this distance is shortened by the intervening islands of the Bocas. The total area of Trinidad, which is roughly rectangular in shape with the two projecting peninsulas, is 1754 square miles.

Apart from Tobago, twenty-six miles away to the north-east, the nearest West Indian island is Grenada, one of the Windward Islands, which is ninety miles to the north. Geologically, Trinidad and Tobago are not connected with the Windward and Leeward islands. A few million years ago Tobago was probably connected to Trinidad, for even during the Pleistocene, while the gap between the two islands was undoubtedly smaller, deep channels must still have separated them, while Trinidad's separation from Venezuela must have taken place only about eleven thousand years ago.

Physiography. The island of Trinidad may be conveniently divided into three regions of hills running roughly east to west, divided by belts of lowlands (Map 2). The mountains of the Northern Range, a prolongation of the coastal cordillera of Venezuela, form the most conspicuous region, rising to over 3000 feet in the peaks of Cerro del Aripo and El Tucuche. Above 1500 feet the slopes are quite steep and there are no high plateaux. Formed of phyllite, quartzite and some limestone, these mountains have a rather poor soil on the whole.

South of the Northern Range lies the Caroni plain, mostly less than 100 feet above sea level, and drained by the Caroni River to the west and the Oropouche River to the east. Much of the soil is sandy.

Running roughly as a belt across the middle of Trinidad is the Central Range, a fairly low range of hills, rising gradually to Mount Tamana, 1009 feet, at the eastern end. South of this is gently undulating country with narrow ridges, ranging generally between 50 and 200 feet above sea level.

Finally, the Southern Range flanks the south coast, but its height rarely reaches 500 feet, except in the south-east, where the highest of the Trinity Hills is 997 feet high; this is the range after which Columbus named the island Trinidad.

There are various swamps: the Caroni, South Oropouche and Cedros being open to tidal influx from the Gulf of Paria on the west; the Nariva and North Oropouche, facing east, and Erin in the south are enclosed by sand-bars.

Apart from the various islands of the Bocas in the north-west, two small islets are to be found off the coasts of Trinidad. Just off the coast north of Port of Spain is Saut d'Eau Island, and a few miles west of Icacos Point in the south-west is tiny, isolated Soldado Rock (Fig. 1). Both provide nesting grounds for seabirds.

Climate and rainfall. In such a small island it is strange to find any considerable variation in climate; nevertheless, this is so. The trade wind from

Figure 1. Soldado Rock, a wildlife sanctuary, is a large limestone boulder located six miles west of Icacos Point, two acres in extent and 117 feet high. Sparse vegetation of tussocky grass and low-growing *Plumbago* provide nests for thousands of Sooty Terns. The Brown Noddy nests on the cliffs and raised platform surrounding the rock. Gray-breasted Martins commonly nest in the rock crevices.

the east blows fairly constantly throughout the year, particularly during the dry season, but the rainfall varies according to the height of the locality and its distance from the east coast.

Thus in the higher mountains in the east of the Northern Range annual rainfall may exceed 150 inches, while farther west the Arima Valley at 500 feet averages 80 inches. However, the farthest island of the Bocas, Chacachacare, averages only 40 inches a year. On the east coast itself the rainfall reaches only 60 inches along a narrow belt, affected by the constant, strong wind across the sea. (See Map 3.)

Moreover, there is considerable variation annually, and the vegetation is probably most affected by the amount of rainfall in the driest months. In a very dry year there may well be a drought; the vegetation becomes extremely parched and bush fires are common. The breeding of many species of birds is inhibited at such times. During the wet season very heavy rains occasionally fall, as much as 14 inches being recorded in a single day, and nests may be destroyed or flooded out by heavy storms.

Trinidadians refer to the annual climate broadly as the "dry season", from January to April, and the "wet season", from late May to December. There is, however, a break in the wet season, occurring in September or October, locally referred to as the "petit carême". Naturally these seasons are variable at their beginning and end, and the most reliable annual phenomenon is the onset of heavy rains in late May, at the start of the main wet season.

The temperature in Trinidad ranges generally between 70°F and 86°F, with a drop below 70° during night-time in the dry season, especially in hilly areas. Very occasionally in the wet season the temperature may reach 90°F or more at midday.

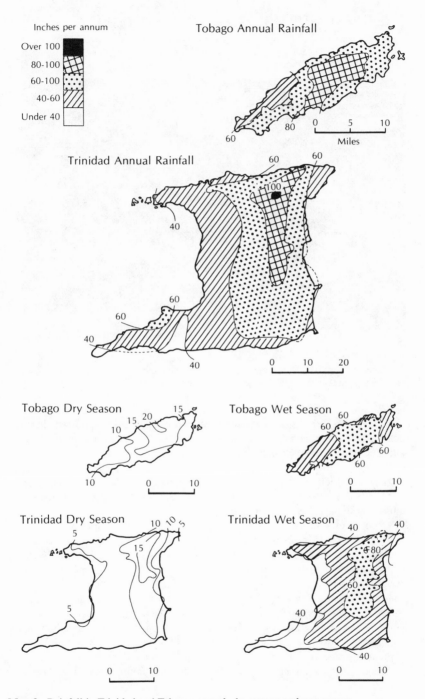

Map 3. Rainfall in Trinidad and Tobago: annual, dry season and wet season

Figure 2. Tropical rain forest in the Northern Range stretching from sea level to about 2000 feet above Balata Bay. Steep slopes and ridges with a closed canopy at about 80 feet are typical.

Humidity is very high, reaching saturation point at night, and remaining near 90% during much of the day in the wet season. It may drop to near 50% during the dry season at midday.

Vegetation. The extremely varied natural vegetation of Trinidad has been admirably described by Marshall (1939) and Beard (1946). I present here only a broad summary, based upon their categories.

Tropical rain forest covers large parts of the island, especially in the Northern Range (Fig. 2) and in various other areas, principally in the east and south (Fig. 3). In this forest there are several tiers of vegetation, interlaced with lianas and vines, while epiphytic orchids, bromeliads and ferns are common. The tallest trees may reach 150 feet or more, though the main canopy is usually lower than this, being formed by the subdominants, while owing to the steep ridges and slopes the canopy itself is often not continuous, letting light penetrate to the lower levels. Though deciduous species exist commonly in this forest, and in fact Beard prefers to call it seasonal forest, the general impression is of an evergreen, luxuriant vegetation.

Among the most typical plant species to be found among tropical rain forest

Figure 3. Tropical rain forest in the Trinity Hills looking west towards Moruga. Extremely steep slopes of the terrain (with underlying sandstone) and remote location provide an important location for the Trinity Hills Sanctuary.

in many parts of Trinidad are the crappo (*Carapa guianensis*), silk cotton (*Ceiba pentandra*), hog plum (*Spondias monbin*), wild chataigne (*Pachira insignis*), guatecare (*Eschweilera subglandulosa*) and yellow poui (*Tabebuia serratifolia*) among the dominants; among the subdominants the bois mulatre (*Pentaclethra macroloba*) is outstanding; in the understory are such common plants as the cooperhoop (*Brownea latifolia*) and various species of Myrtaceae. Generally ground vegetation is sparse where the canopy is dense, but where light permits, small palms, ferns and various species of *Heliconia* may abound.

In the higher reaches of the Northern Range a slightly different association is found, with the mahoe (*Sterculia caribaea*) prominent among the dominants and wild debasse (*Licania biglandulosa*) and bois charbon (*Diospyros ierensis*) among the subdominants. The forest is less luxuriant at higher altitudes. There are fewer epiphytes and lianas, although tree ferns and several species of small palms become more abundant.

At the top of Cerro del Aripo is a small area of elfin woodland with an almost pure consociation of the mountain mangrove (*Clusia intertexta*). Various other plants, including a terrestrial bromeliad, seem to be confined to these high altitudes (Fig. 4).

Another common type of forest is the freshwater swamp forest, found mainly in flat areas west and south of the Nariva swamp and west of Sangre Grande. This has a dense closed canopy formed mainly by the lower-story

Figure 4. Montane vegetation south of the summit of Cerro del Aripo. A landslip has exposed the forest to sunlight. High rainfall accounts for the dense vegetation. Tree ferns, bromeliads, lianas and mosses are prominent.

vegetation; palms of various species, principally the spiny roseau or pic-moc (*Bactris major*), carat (*Sabal mauritiiformis*) and cocorite (*Maximiliana caribaea*), along with the bloodwoods (*Pterocarpus* spp.) are prominent.

One notable type of forest, found extensively in east Trinidad, especially near Matura and Mayaro, is mora forest, dominated very largely by the gregarious *Mora excelsa* (Fig. 5). This large evergreen often reaches a height of 150 feet. A characteristic of this forest is its open nature above a dense undergrowth 6–8 feet high, formed by thousands of small *Mora* saplings.

All the above might be termed different types of rain forest, so before proceeding to describe other natural vegetation in Trinidad, I should indicate some of the effects that humans have produced on them.

A great deal of forest in Trinidad has been changed by humans. Apart from a considerable area of the Northern Range east of Morne Bleu, which is more untouched than any other, the forest has been significantly affected by logging; the larger and more valuable timber trees have been removed, albeit under proper control, even from parts of the forest reserves (which themselves total 30% of the land area of Trinidad). Roads, trails and clearings open up the forest in many areas, especially in the oil-producing districts of the south, while agricultural activities encroach gradually upon the lower slopes of the Northern Range and much of the lowland areas of the east and south.

Up the valleys of the Northern Range, often as high as 1800 feet, cocoa, coffee and citrus are grown in plantations characterised by the predominance

Figure 5. A cleared track through mora forest at Matura. Tall, straight mora with prominent buttresses are often found in single-species forest in lowland areas of east and south Trinidad. Other species thrive where clearings permit.

of the introduced mountain immortelle (*Erythrina poeppigiana*), a shade tree, which flowers conspicuously between November and February. Since cocoa is a crop of economically variable value, it is not unusual to find abandoned cocoa estates, the trees festooned with vines and epiphytes.

The presence of *Erythrina* is particularly significant for nectar-feeding birds, since during its flowering season the availability of nectar is at its height (Feinsinger & Swarm 1982). At other times of year nectar resources drop considerably, reaching a low point from September to early December, when some nectar-feeding species are forced to disperse elsewhere.

Where natural second growth fills in the gaps caused by humans, fast-growing species quite different from the original plants take over. These include the trumpet tree (*Cecropia peltata*), balsa (*Ochroma pyramidale*) and *Vismia* species. The cocorite palm, which withstands the effect of fire, is often prominent in second growth, while on damp clay soils may be found dense clumps of the banana-like *Heliconia bihai*. The introduced bamboo has also become very common in some areas.

Undoubtedly forest fires have taken their toll of Trinidad's forests, especially on the slopes and ridges of the Northern Range. Though some may be genuinely accidental, it is certain that most are the products of "slash and burn" agriculture. This shifting cultivation practised by farmers has led to large areas of second growth.

An entirely different kind of natural vegetation is found in the tropical semi-deciduous forest, found mostly in the north-western peninsula and on the Bocas Islands (Fig. 6). This forest is much more open, owing to the lack of a proper canopy, the greater proportion of deciduous trees and the smaller number of large trees. Mosses and epiphytes are much less common, and one gets an overall impression of dryness, the rainfall being in fact very low in the

Figure 6. Semi-deciduous forest at Pointe Gourde, looking west towards the Bocas Islands with Venezuela in the distance. Very dry conditions produce a forest or scrub with low trees, leafless for most of the dry season.

dry season (see Map 3). Prominent trees in this area include the savonette (*Lonchocarpus punctatus*), naked Indian (*Bursera simaruba*), saltfishwood (*Machaerium robinifolium*) and bread-and-cheese (*Pithecellobium unguiscati*). Several species of cactus and the tall century plant (*Agave evadens*) are also common on these islands (Fig. 7).

In the foothills of the Northern Range, especially the area north and east of

Figure 7. Xerophytic vegetation on one of the Bocas Islands, including several species of cactus and tall *Agave evadens*. The Paria peninsula of Venezuela is in the background.

Figure 8. Mangrove forest in the Caroni swamp with channel leading out to open lagoon. The most common species here is the stilt-rooted *Rhizophora mangle.*

Port of Spain, may also be found a slightly different semi-deciduous forest, with the cypre (*Cordia alliodora*) and the yellow poui prominent. This area, of course, has been much changed by man.

On the wind-blown east coast a rather characteristic vegetation is found. It is low-growing and varies from creeping herbs to a low bushy forest composed mainly of the hardy sea grape (*Coccoloba uvifera*), poisonous manchineel (*Hippomane mancinella*) and the seaside mahoe (*Pariti tiliaceum*), while coconut palms are cultivated extensively.

The very specialised mangrove forest covers significant areas of Trinidad, particularly the Caroni and South Oropouche swamps, and is very important as a bird habitat, with nearly 100 species recorded breeding in or regularly visiting mangroves (Fig. 8). Depending on brackish water conditions, several genera and species of mangroves occur in Trinidad, principally *Rhizophora mangle,* which reaches a height of 80 feet along the eastern side of the Nariva swamp, but is elsewhere smaller (Figs. 9 and 10), *Avicennia nitida,* which is only found away from the sea, and *Laguncularia racemosa. Conocarpus erecta* is less widely distributed, being common only near Cedros.

Bordering the mangroves are often extensive freshwater marshes, where grasses, reeds and sedges abound. Where drainage permits, rice and water-melon are cultivated, and in the drier areas sugarcane and vegetable crops of various kinds are grown. As a result of drainage schemes in the Caroni, South Oropouche and Nariva marshes, much land has become cultivable within the

Figure 9. Mangroves and open brackish lagoons in the Caroni Swamp Wildlife Sanctuary. Northern Range in background. Extensive mudflats at low tides provide important feeding areas for many water-birds. A former nesting area of the Scarlet Ibis, centre right.

last forty years and the habitat suitable for water-birds correspondingly reduced.

The Nariva swamp is the largest freshwater, herbaceous swamp in Trinidad. It is usually underwater except in dry years, and is very difficult of access. The vegetation is largely the tall *Cyperus giganteus,* which forms a canopy about 10 feet above the water-level. The fern *Acrostichum aureum* and the aroid *Montrichardia arborescens* are also found extensively, the former mostly in brackish conditions.

In Aripo Savannah, south-east of Arima, a very specialised vegetation is found, growing on an extremely acid soil with poor drainage. On the open savannah are found the grass *Paspalum pulchellum* and the sedge *Lagenocarpus tremulus,* with scattered shrubs of *Byrsonima crassifolia* and *Chrysobalanus icaco.* Here too are the insectivorous *Drosera capillaris* and various *Utricularia* species.

Alongside such savannahs and also at the edge of the Nariva swamp are found palm "islands" (Fig. 11), where the tall moriche palm (*Mauritia setigera*) is common, along with the manac (*Euterpe oleracea*), and in Nariva the cabbage palm (*Roystonea oleracea*). Below the palms a dense bushy undergrowth is formed, very difficult to penetrate.

There remains only the portion of Trinidad, especially in the west and south,

Figure 10. Tall mangroves flanking the Nariva River at its mouth. Coconuts have been planted along the extensive sand-spit. Several species of seabirds often rest on the beach.

which has been extensively altered by humans for agricultural, industrial and dwelling purposes. Here much sugarcane is grown, small gardens and farms abound and housing estates sprawl increasingly. In the well-kept estates of large industrial and agricultural companies (Fig. 12), large areas of short grass, surrounded by large shade trees, attract a rather specialised bird popula-

Figure 11. Freshwater swamp at Nariva with palm "islands" amidst tall *Cyperus giganteus,* and aroid *Montrichardia arborescens,* which normally grow in several feet of water. The rare Limpkin and a few macaws are found here.

Figure 12. Housing estate and freshwater reservoir at Pointe-a-Pierre. This is a typical semi-open area with extensive gardens and cover from ornamental trees. Cormorants, grebes and river terns frequent the reservoirs; close-cut lawns encourage species like mockingbirds and the Saffron Finch.

TOBAGO

Map 4

1. The Sisters
2. Parlatuvier
3. Plymouth
4. Grafton
5. Buccoo Reef
6. Pigeon Pt.
7. Bon Accord
8. Crown Point Airport

9. Friendship
10. Rockly Bay
11. Scarborough
12. Mason Hall
13. Hillsborough Dam
14. Smith's I.
15. Pembroke
16. Roxborough

17. Pigeon Peak
18. Speyside
19. Little Tobago
20. Charlotteville
21. Man O'War Bay
22. St. Giles Is.

tion, and may well have assisted in the spread of certain recently arrived species, such as the Tropical Mockingbird and Saffron Finch.

TOBAGO

Physiography. Politically linked to Trinidad since 1888, Tobago lies some twenty-six miles to the north-east, forming the final link in the chain of mountain ranges extending eastwards from the Venezuelan coastal cordillera (Map 1). It is on the very edge of the continental shelf, for while comparatively shallow water separates it from Trinidad, depths of several hundred fathoms divide Tobago from Grenada and Barbados.

The island is twenty-six miles long and seven and a half miles broad at its widest point. The dominant feature is the Main Ridge (Map 4), running like a backbone along the northern part of the island and reaching a height of 1890 feet, though there is no well-defined peak. Steeply broken ridges and gullies

Figure 13. St. Giles Islands Wildlife Sanctuary and rocks off north-east Tobago. At the edge of the continental shelf, an upwelling of deep water provides a good feeding area for pelagic birds. The Magnificent Frigatebird, Red-footed Booby and Red-billed Tropicbird breed on St. Giles.

adjoin the mountainous area, and the land gradually flattens out at the south-west end into what is called "The Lowlands". Small islets are to be found scattered off the coast, especially at the north-east end, where the St. Giles Islands and Little Tobago are significant features (Fig. 13). The total area of Tobago is 114 square miles.

The northern part of the island including the Main Ridge is formed of metamorphic rocks of sedimentary origin, rather similar to the Northern Range of Trinidad, while much of the rest of Tobago is constituted of igneous rocks, shattered to a considerable depth, which yield excellent soil. In the lowlands there are Tertiary beds, mainly coral limestones rising in a series of flat terraces.

Climate and rainfall. The climate of Tobago resembles that of the Lesser Antilles more than that of Trinidad, with a noticeably more invigorating effect. The steadily blowing north-east trade winds and lower humidity remind one of conditions at Toco in Trinidad, where the temperature is similar.

The rainfall of Tobago, too, resembles that of the Lesser Antilles. Though adequate records for the whole island are lacking, annual means range from about 56 inches in the west to 93 inches in the east; but this varies considerably, since amounts of 31 inches and 130 inches have been recorded in the west, with 68 and 132 in the east. In the higher parts of the Main Ridge rainfall may well reach 150 inches in a year. Generally the first five months of the year form the dry season, and the last seven the wet season, with November the wettest month. In Tobago the "petit carême" is not as noticeable as in Trinidad.

Vegetation. Since large portions of the island have been converted to agricultural use, the natural vegetation of Tobago, well described by Beard (1944), is found mostly in the Main Ridge Forest Reserve and adjoining Crown Lands, forming less than one quarter of the island's area. In addition there are a few small swamps in the south-west and some littoral scrub and semi-deciduous forest, mostly in the north-east.

The tropical rain forest of the Main Ridge is subdivided by Beard into three categories. Most of it is lower montane rain forest, found largely from 800 feet up, where there are the lowest temperatures, the highest rainfall and the greatest exposure to wind. This is a luxuriant, evergreen forest, with some lianas and many epiphytes, especially the bromeliads *Aechmaea dichlamydea* and *Gravisia aquilega.* The dominant trees are the rosewood (*Byrsonima spicata*), wild cocoa (*Licania biglandulosa*) and redwood (*Ternstroemia oligostemon*). Subdominants include palms (*Euterpe* spp.) and Myrtaceae spp., and at the shrub level many species of Melastomaceae are found. The ground vegetation is very sparse, including a few ferns.

To the north of the Main Ridge is lowland rain forest, ascending only to 1200 feet and mostly outside the forest reserve. This has a closed canopy at about 120 feet, with many large trees, especially the crappo (*Carapa guianensis*) and angelin (*Andira inermis*). In this forest wild cocoa is a subdominant, and again the *Euterpe* palms are very common at lower levels.

South of the Main Ridge on shallow igneous soil above 800 feet is a formation Beard describes as xerophytic rain forest. Here rainfall is quite high, as is exposure to wind, but little moisture is retained in the soil, and the general appearance of this forest is dry. The trees have very shallow root systems and long, thin trunks and give an appearance of poor growth. The canopy is at about 50 feet, with solitary emergent trees rising to 100 feet. These trees are evergreen, many with thick, fleshy leaves, and several shed their bark in large papery strips. There are no lianas and few epiphytes, and in any gap caused by a windfall razor grass grows abundantly. The emergent trees of this forest are gooseberry (*Manilkara bidentata*) and galba (*Calophyllum lucidum*). At lower levels blue copper (*Guettarda scabra*) is very common, along with *Roupala montana* and various Myrtaceae.

On Little Tobago, St. Giles Islands and the adjoining coast the vegetation resembles that of the Bocas Islands in many ways, though Beard prefers to call this deciduous seasonal forest. Here the canopy is at about 45 feet, and dominant trees include naked Indian (*Bursera simaruba*), dogroot (*Lonchocarpus domingensis*) and the fan palm (*Coccothrinax australis*). Though many of the dominant species are deciduous, the understory is mostly evergreen, with *Eugenia* spp. and San Maria (*Mayepea caribaea*) prominent. At ground level the aroid *Anthurium hookeri* is abundant.

Near the windward coasts the canopy becomes lower and the vegetation gradually planes off. Various species of cactus are found along with low herbs such as *Plumbago scandens* and the succulent *Batis maritima.*

Though the rest of Tobago has largely been converted to agriculture, and much second growth similar to that in Trinidad exists where farms have been abandoned, there remain a few areas of mangrove swamp, mostly in the west of the island. Some of this has recently been reclaimed. Along the coasts may be found patches of littoral woodland, with dwarfed trees showing distorted and gnarled branches; the components are the same as on Trinidad's east coast.

Hurricanes. Though both Trinidad and Tobago are normally considered to be outside the "hurricane belt", occasional storms occur. Some of these are only locally violent, such as one which occurred over south Trinidad in June 1933. But in September 1963 Hurricane Flora devastated Tobago, causing widespread damage and altering radically the natural environment.

The vegetation was extensively destroyed by the wind, especially at higher altitudes, where many trees were blown down or decapitated, and any remaining leaves were scorched. Up to 100% loss of the natural forest was recorded in many areas of the Main Ridge, and the canopy, of course, disappeared. In the last twenty-five years I have witnessed a gradual regeneration. At first a preponderance of vines and razor grass covered the tangled mat of fallen trees; second growth sprang up with such species as *Cecropia peltata* common. Many palms (*Euterpe* spp.) survived, and the large truncated trees produced new growth. In 1990 I estimated the average canopy height of this forest at 55 feet. Foresters estimate that it may take 50–100 years for the Main Ridge forest to regenerate. In the meantime, as a result of the changed habitat some very interesting ecological observations may be made (e.g., Keeler-Wolf 1982).

There was a noticeable change in the bird life of Tobago's Main Ridge after the hurricane. The White-tailed Sabrewing hummingbird at first seemed to have been almost completely extirpated (there being no records between 1963 and 1972), and there was a greater scarcity of Collared Trogons, Plain Antvireos and White-necked Thrushes. A number of lower-altitude species normally inhabiting second growth and open areas correspondingly increased, including several finch species, the Tropical Mockingbird, the Rufous-vented Chachalaca, the White-lined Tanager and several flycatchers.

From 1975, however, the situation has very gradually returned to something nearer the pre-hurricane situation. Sabrewings were located in a few less disturbed spots, and since 1988 breeding has been recorded. Most of the other species typical of Main Ridge forest are also once again flourishing. Nevertheless, the understory in 1990 is still dense and comparatively impenetrable, whereas before 1963 one could walk with little difficulty under the forest canopy.

Ecology and Distribution of Species

Some remarks are necessary to amplify the section on environment and to explain the terms I have used in the text under Habitat.

Especially in Trinidad the word *forest* may be used to cover habitats of several different kinds, e.g., mountain forest, swamp forest, semi-deciduous forest. I have already remarked that considerable areas of forest in Trinidad have gradually been affected by humans, through roads and trails, logging and shifting cultivation, with the result that second growth is sometimes inter-mingled with true primary forest. In addition, the steep slopes of the mountain ridges cause the forest trees to be steeply tiered, and the light penetrating in many places produces a more open type of woodland with luxuriant under-growth and many lianas and epiphytes. Although a canopy is formed, it is rarely as complete as that found in the lowland forests of the mainland.

In addition, the comparatively depauperate fauna of Trinidad, to be ex-pected in an island community, albeit of only a few thousand years' experi-ence, includes several species that have been able through lack of competition to spread into habitats where they are unknown in mainland populations. Thus the Long-billed Gnatwren and Golden-fronted Greenlet, restricted to open woodland, second growth and forest edges on the mainland, are found in primary forest at the top of El Tucuche in Trinidad, in addition to those habitats they frequent on the mainland. Similarly, on Tobago a number of species are found in forest habitat, although on Trinidad or the mainland they are typical second-growth birds. These include the Rufous-vented Chachalaca, Copper-rumped Hummingbird and Barred Antshrike, all of which show a tendency towards generalist foraging techniques (Keeler-Wolf 1982).

A few species are highly specialised in their choice of habitat, and it is not surprising that they are rare in Trinidad, sometimes verging on extinction. These include the Band-tailed Pigeon, Scaled Antpitta, Orange-billed Nightin-gale-Thrush and Blue-capped Tanager, all inhabitants of the higher mountain forest; in mangrove forest the Straight-billed Woodcreeper and Dark-billed Cuckoo are only occasionally found; on the eastern savannahs and palm islands bordering the Nariva swamp those species rarely seen elsewhere include the Red-bellied Macaw and Moriche Oriole.

Another group of species profits by the activities of humans, and their numbers have increased in consequence. The first species to move into newly cleared land are the Ruddy Ground-Dove and Blue-black Grassquit. Shiny Cowbirds and Giant Cowbirds also seem to have increased, the latter being a recent arrival in Tobago. The Tropical Mockingbird, once apparently re-stricted in Trinidad to the St. Augustine area, is now common in western Trinidad and is gradually making its way up the valleys of the Northern Range. Another species to profit from the spread and maintenance of gardens in south-west Trinidad is the Saffron Finch, which feeds on close-cut grass pastures. Little need be added here about the success of the Cattle Egret, first recorded in Trinidad in 1951 and now the most numerous member of the heron family in the island.

The development of endemic races on the two islands may be of interest, though opinions differ widely on whether those populations regarded here as separate races really show significant morphological differences. As I explain later, I merely follow the traditional treatment here, without becoming involved in controversy. Of the 246 species known to breed in Trinidad, 23 (9%) are represented by endemic races. The majority of these have been separated on grounds of plumage differences. Of the 87 species known to breed in Tobago, 27 (31%) have endemic races, 6 being common to both islands. Of Tobago's endemic races, 17 (63%) have been separated because of their larger size. It is to be expected, of course, that Tobago would contain more endemic forms than Trinidad, since its separation from the mainland took place so much longer ago.

The total number of species recorded for the two islands is 433, of which 411 are recorded for Trinidad and 210 for Tobago. I have also mentioned in the book several other species of very dubious status; I have given my reasons elsewhere for rejecting these (ffrench 1973). The list for Trinidad includes 246 known breeding species, 140 migrants and 25 of doubtful status (some of which may well breed in Trinidad). Tobago's list (see Appendix I) comprises 87 known breeding species, 97 migrants and 26 of similarly doubtful status. Most of Tobago's birds are also known in Trinidad, but I list in Appendix II 22 species from Tobago, including 12 breeding species, not recorded on the island of Trinidad. Interspecific competition seems the most likely factor to account for the absence of the majority of these species from Trinidad, especially since 2 or 3 of them are to be found on the small Bocas Islands, where their probable competitors are absent. In the case of the Red-billed Tropicbird, the absence of suitable nesting habitat, combined with different feeding conditions, has probably prevented it from colonising Trinidad.

On the other hand, apart from its smaller size, in Tobago the paucity of different habitats plainly restricts the number of species by comparison with Trinidad. Tobago has no extensive marshes and swamps, no swamp forest and no mountain forest over 2000 feet. Keeler-Wolf (1982) found that by comparison with lower montane rain forest on Trinidad the Main Ridge forest of Tobago provides significantly lower food resources, resulting in lower density and diversity in the avifauna. Also, Tobago's separation from the mainland at a much earlier time than Trinidad's must have resulted in the elimination of certain species from Tobago by competition.

In a recent analysis of the relationship of the Trinidad and Tobago avifauna to that of Sucre, the nearest Venezuelan state to the west of Trinidad, Snow (1985b) points to the close connection between Andean elements of the two regions, as compared with the affinities between the montane species of Sucre and those of the Venezuelan mountains farther west. Snow also shows that the Amazonian-Guianan elements on the islands are not only proportionately more numerous than in Sucre, but in several cases exhibit considerable subspecific differentiation from populations on the mainland. This poses interesting questions regarding the origins of the local avifauna, the isolation of such species as the Blue-backed Manakin and the nature of climatic and vegetational changes in northern South America during the Pleistocene and earlier.

In addition, other interesting problems of bird distribution present themselves. There are no representatives in Trinidad of the corvid family, the barbets or the puffbirds, all widespread on the mainland. Is there no jay in Trinidad because of competition from the larger and abundant Crested Oropendola, or possibly from the smaller but aggressive Great Kiskadee? Both these species share a diet similar to the jays', and both are pre-eminently successful in Trinidad. Is the absence of puffbirds due to the lack of the specialised nesting habitat of several species—a sandy, porous soil in which to dig their sloping nest tunnels, which are thus protected from rain? Has the presence of several nest and brood parasites, such as the Giant and Shiny cowbirds, the Piratic Flycatcher and the Striped Cuckoo, had the effect of cutting down the number of competing species on the islands, so that the less resilient species have died out? Trinidad's position as a comparatively recent island gives rise to several speculations such as these, providing many opportunities for valuable field-work.

Breeding

At least 246 species of birds are known to have bred in Trinidad, and 87 in Tobago, 73 species being common to both islands. Many species have been studied in detail, an outstanding contribution being the Snows' quantitative survey (1964) of the land birds of Trinidad, while Belcher and Smooker's study (1934–37) provided much useful information, especially on savannah and marsh species.

There is some breeding going on in every month of the year, but most species have a well-defined peak, sometimes two. Of the 123 species of land birds listed by the Snows, the following are the numbers of species breeding in each month:

I	II	III	IV	V	VI
42	51	62	64	75	76

VII	VIII	IX	X	XI	XII
72	52	34	26	32	31

Evidently the availability of food affects the breeding season significantly. Hummingbirds and the Bananaquit breed mostly in the dry season, when nectar is most available from the flowering trees and herbs which they favour. Finches and seedeaters nest especially from May to September, when the seeding of grasses is at its height. Manakins and tanagers reach a peak of nesting activity from April to June, when there is the greatest abundance of fruits and insect life, following the onset of heavy rains.

For many species with long breeding seasons two peaks of activity are apparent, the first in May and a smaller one about November, when flowers and fruits also reach a minor peak of abundance, and when insects are again available after the "petit carême".

Swamp and marsh species mostly nest in the latter half of the year, when the rains often produce flood conditions in low-lying areas. Invertebrates undoubtedly increase in the swamps as the water level rises; conditions are not at all conducive to breeding during the dry season when many marsh areas dry out.

The seabirds breeding on the coasts of Tobago and the islets off Trinidad nest mainly in the early months of the year, the gulls and terns being somewhat later than the others. The exposed sites of their open nests are especially vulnerable to heavy rains, and early storms in April sometimes annihilate whole colonies, as happened to the Sooty Terns on Soldado Rock in 1966. The breeding cycles of seabirds in this area appear to be annual, though the cycles of one or two species, such as the Brown Booby (which in the South Atlantic has an eight-month cycle), require further study.

That the breeding activity of land birds is allied to climatic changes seems to be obvious when one notes the immediate flurry of nest-building which follows the onset of heavy rains after a long dry period. If the rains ease off in late May, to start again after two or three weeks' drought, breeding activity likewise slackens off and recommences later. However, undoubtedly other factors are of importance, such as the abundance of food and even the availability of certain nest materials.

Breeding activity itself, therefore, seems to be somewhat variable in our islands, stimulated by certain factors and inhibited by others. The most reliable annual phenomenon is the onset of the main adult moult, which in the great majority of cases reaches a peak about August and September. I have therefore recorded in the text the months when this is known to occur for each species. Certain species show some irregularity in their moult schedule, some breeding and moulting simultaneously, others stopping their moult in the middle and recommencing later. Further studies on the moult schedule of these species should shed much light on the correlation of breeding and moult in tropical birds.

Of the species whose breeding has been studied in detail, the majority make two, even up to four, nesting attempts in a year. Though clutch size is low, compared with that in temperate regions, breeding success is heavily affected by a high rate of predation, especially in forested areas. The chief predators are probably snakes, though few examples of actual predation are ever witnessed. Other possible nest-robbers include squirrels, bats and other small mammals, one or two species of birds and even, in rare cases, crabs and large spiders.

One cannot help being impressed by the variety of nest types to be found in our islands. While the majority of species build the "traditional" cup-shaped nests, using an enormous variety of materials and utilising many different sites, many others build dome-shaped nests with side entrances, thus gaining extra protection from the weather and from predators (D. W. Snow 1978). More unusual nests include the long bags of the Crested Oropendola, the hollow tube of the Lesser Swallow-tailed Swift, the large mound of the Oilbird, the flimsy hammocks of the hermit hummingbirds and the huge, complicated structures of the spinetails.

Table 1. Species that visit Trinidad and/or Tobago regularly and have a local population (usually breeding)

From the north	
Brown Pelican	Wilson's Plover
Snowy Egret	Common Snipe
Little Blue Heron	Roseate Tern
Tricolored Heron	Royal Tern
Green-backed Heron	Sandwich Tern
Broad-winged Hawk	Gray Kingbird
From the south	
Scarlet Ibis	Fulvous Whistling-Duck
Fork-tailed Flycatcher	Blue-and-white Swallow

Migration

Trinidad (and to a lesser extent Tobago) is situated in a very interesting position from the point of view of bird migration. It is on one of the main routes of migrants travelling south down the chain of the Antilles from North America (T. C. Williams et al. 1977, T. C. Williams 1985). Certain Antillean species join this stream on the way to "wintering" grounds in South America. Another group of species travels north from southern South America to escape the austral winter. A few of these spill over from the continent into Trinidad, rarely Tobago.

Some species that breed in Trinidad or Tobago are increased by members of other populations from north or south. Others migrate out of our islands in some numbers, leaving some of the population behind. There is plainly a great deal to be discovered about local migration and dispersal to the continent. Unfortunately, we are not likely to amass much data until regular trapping and banding stations can be set up in the area; this is not likely to happen for some time yet. Meanwhile, almost any information on local movements is worth recording.

I have tabulated the various categories of migrants (see Tables 1–4). Ade-

Table 2. Species that breed locally and migrate overseas or disperse to the mainland (sometimes only partially)

Audubon's Shearwater	Laughing Gull	White-tailed Goldenthroat
Red-billed Tropicbird	Bridled Tern	Pied Water-tyrant
Red-footed Booby	Sooty Tern	Piratic Flycatcher
Great Egret	Brown Noddy	Crested Doradito
Swallow-tailed Kite	Eared Dove	Caribbean Martin
Plumbeous Kite	Ruddy Quail-Dove	Chivi Vireo
Ornate Hawk-Eagle	Lesser Nighthawk	Red-legged Honeycreeper
Yellow-headed Caracara	Nacunda Nighthawk	Swallow-Tanager
American Kestrel	White-necked Jacobin	Sooty Grassquit
Caribbean Coot	Black-throated Mango	Lesson's Seedeater
Collared Plover	Ruby-topaz Hummingbird	Yellow-bellied Seedeater
Black-necked Stilt		

Table 3. Migration of regular non-breeding visitors

From the north						Months						
	I	II	III	IV	V	VI	VII	VIII	IX	X	XI	XII
Leach's Storm-Petrel	R	O	R	R	R			O		O	R	R
Great Blue Heron	R	R	R	R	R	R	R		R	R	R	R
Blue-winged Teal	R	R	R	R	O							R
American Wigeon	R	R	R	R	O							R
Osprey	R	R	R	R	O	O	O	O	O	R	R	R
Peregrine Falcon	R	R	R	R						O	R	R
Merlin	R	R	R	R					O	R	O	R
Sora	R	R	R	R	R	R	R					R
Black-bellied Plover	R	R	R	R	R	R	R	R	R	R	O	R
Lesser Golden Plover	O	O			O				R	R	R	O
Semipalmated Plover	R	R	R	R	R	R	R	R	R	R	R	R
Ruddy Turnstone	R	R	R	R	R	R	R	R	R	R	R	R
Upland Sandpiper			O	O				O	R	R		
Whimbrel	R	R	R	R	R	R	R	R	R	R	R	R
Lesser Yellowlegs	R	R	R	R	R	R	R	R	R	R	R	R
Greater Yellowlegs	R	R	R	R	R	R	O	R	R	R	R	R
Solitary Sandpiper	R	R	R	R	O	O	R	R	R	R	R	R
Spotted Sandpiper	R	R	R	R	R	R	R	R	R	R	R	R
Willet	R	R	R	R	R	O	O	R	R	R	R	R
Short-billed Dowitcher	R	R	R	R	O	O	R	R	R	R	R	R
Red Knot					O		O	O	R	R		
Sanderling	R	R	R	R	R	R	R	R	R	R	R	R
Semipalmated Sandpiper	R	R	R	R	R	R	R	R	R	R	R	R
Western Sandpiper	R	R	R	R	R		O	R	R	R	R	R
Least Sandpiper		R	R	R	O	O	R	R	R	R	R	
White-rumped Sandpiper			R	R	O			R	R	R	R	
Pectoral Sandpiper		O			O		O	R	R	R	R	R

Species												
Stilt Sandpiper	R					O		O		O		
Buff-breasted Sandpiper	O											
Black Tern	R	R	R			O		R	R	R	R	R
Gull-billed Tern	R	R	R	R	R	R	R	R	R	R	R	R
Common Tern	O	R	R	R	O	R	R	R	R	O	R	R
Least Tern		O	O	O	O	O		R		R		R
Yellow-billed Cuckoo	R	R	R	R	R							
Belted Kingfisher	R	R	R	R	R					R		R
Olive-sided Flycatcher	R	R	R	R	R							
Barn Swallow	R	R	O	R	R	R	R		R		R	R
Black-and-white Warbler	R	R	R	R							R	R
Prothonotary Warbler	R	R	R						O	R	R	R
Yellow Warbler	O	O	O	O							O	
Blackpoll Warbler	R	O	O	O					R	R	O	R
Northern Waterthrush	R	R	R	R	R	R		O	R	R	R	R
American Redstart	O	O	R			O		R				O
Summer Tanager	O	O		R							O	O
Dickcissel	R	R	R	R	O	R						R

From the south

Species												
Olivaceous Cormorant	R	R	R	R	R	R	R	R	R		R	
Anhinga	R	R	R	R	R	R	O	R	R		O	
White-necked Heron	R	R	R	R	R	R	O	R	R	R	O	R
Roseate Spoonbill								R		R		
Large-billed Tern	O		R	R	R	R	R	R	R	R	R	R
Yellow-billed Tern	O	O	O	R	R	R	R	R	R	R	R	
Black Skimmer	O	O	O		R	R	R	R	R	R	R	R
White-collared Swift	O					R	R	R	R	R	R	O
Swainson's Flycatcher	O				R	R	R	R	R			

R signifies regular recorded occurrence; O signifies occasional occurrence.

Table 4. Occasional visitors (mostly non-breeding)

From the north

*Bulwer's Petrel
*Cory's Shearwater
*Manx Shearwater
 White-tailed Tropicbird
 Masked Booby
*Gray Heron
*Little Egret
*Western Reef-Heron
 Reddish Egret
 Snow Goose
 Green-winged Teal
 Northern Shoveler
 Lesser Scaup
 Ring-necked Duck
 Swainson's Hawk
 American Coot
 American Oystercatcher
*Ringed Plover
 Snowy Plover
 Killdeer
*Common Greenshank
*Spotted Redshank
 Baird's Sandpiper
*Ruff
 Eskimo Curlew
 Hudsonian Godwit
 Marbled Godwit
 American Avocet
 Pomarine Jaeger
 Parasitic Jaeger
 Herring Gull
*Lesser Black-backed Gull
 Ring-billed Gull

Common Black-headed Gull
Sabine's Gull
Caspian Tern
Black-billed Cuckoo
Common Nighthawk
Black Swift
Bank Swallow
Cliff Swallow
*White Wagtail
Gray-cheeked Thrush
Veery
Yellow-throated Vireo
Black-whiskered Vireo
Red-winged Blackbird
Northern Oriole
Bobolink
Golden-winged Warbler
Northern Parula
Magnolia Warbler
Cape May Warbler
Yellow-rumped Warbler
Blackburnian Warbler
Black-throated Blue Warbler
Black-throated Green Warbler
Prairie Warbler
Chestnut-sided Warbler
Bay-breasted Warbler
Ovenbird
Common Yellowthroat
Hooded Warbler
Scarlet Tanager
Rose-breasted Grosbeak
Indigo Bunting

From the south

Great Shearwater
Wilson's Storm-Petrel
Chestnut-bellied Heron
Jabiru Stork
Wood Stork
White Ibis
Glossy Ibis
Greater Flamingo
White-faced Whistling-Duck
Southern Pochard
Comb Duck
Muscovy Duck
King Vulture
Snail Kite
Rufous Crab-Hawk
Black-collared Hawk
Black Hawk-Eagle

Crested Caracara
Orange-breasted Falcon
Aplomado Falcon
Paint-billed Crake
Azure Gallinule
Double-striped Thick-knee
Southern Polar Skua
Fairy Tern
Scaled Dove
Scarlet-shouldered Parrotlet
Ringed Kingfisher
Amazon Kingfisher
White Bellbird
Variegated Flycatcher
Small-billed Elaenia
Orange-fronted Yellow-Finch

*Old World species.

quate information is lacking on those species representing more than one population, so I merely list them, as I do also the occasional or accidental visitors, which make up the largest category. I am well aware that the data I present here are extremely sketchy.

One phenomenon deserves comment, namely, the number of species of northern visitors of whom substantial numbers remain in this area during the "summer" months. Some of these are probably first-year birds that have not yet attained breeding status. I have banding evidence, however, showing that at least some northern sandpipers may remain in the tropics for as long as three years, although it is possible that some of these may have migrated north and returned to the same winter quarters (cf. Thomas 1987). Ample opportunities for research in this most rewarding field await future students of birds in Trinidad and Tobago.

The Species Accounts

General family headings. At the beginning of each family the common characteristics of its members are briefly summarised, with respect to appearance, habitat and habits. At the end of the paragraph the number of species in the family recorded for Trinidad and Tobago is given in parentheses. In this second edition I have not departed far from the Wetmore order and arrangement of families that I followed in the first edition (1973) and the two revised editions (1976, 1980). Although I am aware that radical changes have recently been proposed in familial classification, I agree with those other authors of major works on Neotropical avifauna (e.g., Ridgely & Tudor 1989, Stiles & Skutch 1989) that since classification is presently in a state of flux, it would be premature to adopt major taxonomic changes, which may well themselves be revised within the next few years. My decision will at least facilitate comparison between this edition and previous ones.

Nomenclature. I have almost invariably followed the standard English and scientific names in Meyer de Schauensee's *Species of Birds of South America* (1966). Below the main designation I have included any English names used by Herklots (1961), the AOU Check-list (1957) and various other works, as well as alternative scientific names and local vernacular names when I have reason to believe these are still in use; the latter are in quotation marks, as in some cases they are misleading.

Habitat and status. For each species the range of habitat within Trinidad and Tobago is given, with altitude where this is significant (see my remarks above on overlapping habitats); precise localities are only given where records are few. The status is summarised for each form in both islands (omitting mention of one island if the form occurs only on the other). For migrants, dates of occurrence are given, including earliest and latest when these are precise. For rare species, details of dates and names of observers or collectors are included.

The whereabouts of collected specimens is summarised by abbreviations for the major collections as follows:

AMNH   American Museum of Natural History, New York
ANSP   Academy of Natural Sciences, Philadelphia
CM   Carnegie Museum, Pittsburgh
YPM   Yale University Peabody Museum, New Haven
FSM   Florida State Museum, Gainesville
LSUM   Louisiana State University Museum of Zoology, Baton Rouge
BM   British Museum
LM   Leiden Museum, Holland
TRVL   Trinidad Regional Virus Laboratory, Port of Spain (now CAREC)
PSM   Port of Spain Museum

Apart from species represented by extant specimens, I have also considered as accepted species those collected and documented with measurements by Léotaud (1866), whose collection was destroyed by fire. I have also included those species supported only by sight records if they are easily identified species reported by responsible observers under good conditions. When the sight records are of easily confused species, e.g., wood warblers, or when there is any doubt about the validity of the record, even though it may be likely, the species name is enclosed in square brackets.

Banding status. When information from the U.S. Fish and Wildlife Service is available on the banding of birds, it is summarised.

Range and subspecies. The range of the species is outlined, followed by that of the subspecies to which the Trinidad and Tobago populations have been assigned (if this has been determined). As I am not a taxonomist I have not attempted to determine subspecific identifications myself. In general, I have followed the opinions of Hellmayr and Conover's *Catalogue of Birds of the Americas* (1942 and later) or the later volumes of Peters' *Checklist of the Birds of the World* (1931 and later). Since it may be felt that some of their distinctions hardly warrant subspecific separation, I have attempted to summarise these distinctions without, however, becoming involved in controversy. In general I have followed Meyer de Schauensee in treating closely related forms, recognised by some as separate species, as separate races of the same species.

Description. The average length is given in inches. Then the race (or races) of the species known in Trinidad and Tobago is described briefly, essentially for field use, though occasionally, for confusing species, I have added details useful only to someone examining a bird in the hand. Features given in italic type are diagnostic. Soft parts are described only if these are significant for field identification. For sexually dimorphic species male and female are

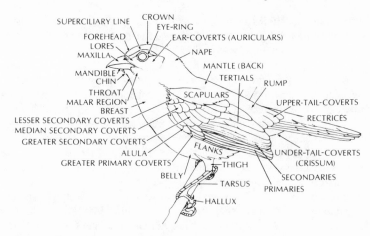

Figure 14. Topography of a bird

treated separately, and immature plumages are treated separately or with the
female if similar. So little is known of downy plumage that I have not normally
included this.

Measurements. Wing measurements in millimeters are given for the distance from the carpal joint to the tip of the longest primary (unflattened) in a
non-moulting bird. Sample size, range, average (in parentheses) and sometimes standard deviation for large samples are included. Sexes are separated
and data from unsexed birds are given when there is significant variation or
when too little information on sexed birds is available. The sources of these
data are the Trinidad and Tobago specimens in some of the major collections,
Junge and Mees (1958), D. W. Snow and Snow (1963a) and the work of
several people, especially Erma J. Fisk, Charles T. Collins, Alan Lill and
myself with trapped birds. Weight in grams is similarly tabulated. The sources
here are mainly Snow and Snow and my own data. Junge and Mees' material is
used only when other data are unavailable and is distinguished in the text by an
asterisk. This is because Mees' specimens were weighed after they had been
frozen for some time, involving a significant loss of weight, especially for
smaller species. Occasionally, when no Trinidad or Tobago data are available,
I have used data from South America, from the same subspecies, specifying
the source.

Voice. The known call-notes and song of Trinidad and Tobago forms are
described. The sources are Snow's or my notes, unless otherwise stated.

Food. I have summarised the available information, from Trinidad and
Tobago if possible; when this is not local, the source is stated. I have only been

specific about food items in instances in which special studies have been made, e.g., Williams (1922), Vesey-Fitzgerald (1936), Snow and Feinsinger (various papers) and Keeler-Wolf (1982).

Nesting. I have presented a summary of the range of the breeding season, giving where possible the number of nest records per month according to when the first egg was known or calculated to have been laid. The months when birds undergoing wing-moult have been recorded are also stated. Then follow descriptions of the nest and eggs, including average measurements of a sample of eggs and the sample size (in parentheses). The role of the parents and the development of the young are described when known. The incubation period is calculated from the laying of the last egg to the hatching of the last young. The fledging period is the time from hatching to leaving the nest. The sources of the data are mostly local. Apart from my own work, I have drawn heavily on D. W. Snow and Snow (1964) and Belcher and Smooker (1934–37). The latter are used principally to corroborate other data; where they alone provide the information I have designated it B/S, since their work is not invariably explicit (e.g., range of breeding seasons) and some of their conclusions have been shown to be wrong.

When life-history material is not available from Trinidad or Tobago but is published elsewhere (even for different races, as, for example, in Central America by Skutch), I have briefly summarised it, noting the source.

Behaviour. This is treated very generally, giving the common and conspicuous habits, such as flocking. Details of display are only mentioned when special studies have been made.

Notes. I have included under this heading any matters which do not fit in under the other sections, and especially information relating to conservation in Trinidad and Tobago. I make no apology for referring repeatedly under individual species to a general topic, namely, over-exploitation by humans. In this area such a subject cannot be emphasised too much.

When a species is only known to have occurred a very few times in Trinidad or Tobago, I have confined the text to status, range, description, and voice (if a significant field mark), and measurements if specimens are available.

Details are not given of the nesting of species not known (or suspected) to nest in Trinidad or Tobago, though I have occasionally mentioned literature which refers to the little-known nesting of some mainland species.

Conservation

Trinidad and Tobago are fortunate in possessing at this time a most enlightened law relating to the protection of wild birds, the Conservation of Wild Life Act of 1980. Under this law all bird species are protected, except for those listed and classified as game-birds, cage-birds and vermin. The first category, including most ducks, certain herons and waterfowl and large pigeons, may be hunted during the open season from November to March (also October outside swamp areas). Certain finches, the two commoner euphonias and the Green-rumped Parrotlet may be trapped for cages from October to March. The Orange-winged Parrot and Crested Oropendola are classified as agricultural vermin and may be hunted at any time by the owners of private land on their property.

In addition there are bag-limits on certain swamp birds, a number of areas set aside as wildlife sanctuaries and limitations on the methods of hunting and trapping. The Forest Division of the Ministry of Agriculture maintains a permanent staff of wildlife wardens, and a committee of specialists (on which I sat as ornithologist from 1963 until 1985) advises the minister on matters relating to wildlife. Certain anomalies in the law remain to be remedied, and it is to be hoped that an even better law may result in the not too distant future.

Unfortunately, there is a very wide gap between the theory and the practice of the law. Enforcement is extremely difficult with the very small (and largely untrained) band of wardens, and cooperation from forest rangers, police and the general public is at a very low level. Infringements of the law, especially relating to birds, which in the eyes of many people "don't count" as wildlife, very often go undetected and unpunished. Ignorance of the law is widespread, and a general apathy exists in the minds of the majority concerning wildlife. It is difficult to persuade politicians and other authorities to take much interest in the problems of wildlife when other troubles, more serious to them, also require attention.

Meanwhile, it is important that conservation matters be publicised as much as possible. Films, books and treatment by the mass media are fortunately becoming more and more available. A recently growing awareness of environmental problems should benefit wildlife as people turn their attention to the beauty of their surroundings. Educational literature on the wildlife of this region is still sadly lacking, but a demand for it is growing, and it will undoubtedly be provided soon.

The most satisfying aspect of conservation in Trinidad and Tobago is the stability of the habitat, especially by comparison with areas of Latin America which have been devastated by social and agricultural demands. Although some forest areas have been cleared in Trinidad (a few most unfortunately, since they offer little agricultural profit), and some swamps and marshes have been reclaimed, thus reducing water-bird habitats, by and large there are still considerable areas of unspoilt natural vegetation. With their wide variety of habitats Trinidad and Tobago should remain as areas of exceptional interest for students of Neotropical birds for some time to come.

SPECIES ACCOUNTS

TINAMIDAE: Tinamous

These birds are superficially like partridges, short-legged with rounded wings and very short tails. They are generally cryptic in coloration. In Trinidad the one species inhabits only forests and second growth, living almost entirely on the ground and rarely flying. (1)

Little Tinamou: *Crypturellus soui*
Pileated Tinamou; "Caille"   **Figure 15**

Habitat and status. A common resident in Trinidad, inhabiting forests and particularly second growth; essentially terrestrial. (Specimens: AMNH, LM.)

Range and subspecies. Mexico S to Peru, Bolivia and Brazil; *C. s. andrei* (Brabourne & Chubb) occurs in Colombia, Venezuela and Trinidad.

Description. 8.5 in. Generally chestnut brown with dark gray crown and pale throat; a dumpy, "tail-less" bird.

© John P. O'Neill-1990

Figure 15. Little Tinamou

37

Measurements. Wing: 4 males 124–129mm (126); 6 females 132–137mm (134.2). Weight: 1 female 279gm*.

Voice. A melancholy, long-drawn-out, slightly tremulous whistle, sliding up and then down in pitch. Also a series of whistles of similar quality, each one higher in pitch and volume than the preceding, but diminishing in length, and ending abruptly. Heard most frequently at dusk, also during day and night.

Food. Seeds and terrestrial insects.

Nesting. B/S reported breeding peak in May, but the Snows (1964) found nests in almost every month from February to November. Usually 2 glossy purplish brown eggs laid on ground amidst a few leaves, av. 41 × 32mm (8). In Brazil (Pinto 1953) *C. s. albigularis* eggs were incubated by males only, as is apparently general in tinamous. The incubating bird sits very tight. In Costa Rica (Skutch 1963a) *C. s. modestus* sat for a long period each day, taking only one recess early in the day. The chicks leave the nest less than 24 hr after hatching; their dark downy plumage is conspicuously marked about the head with a black-and-tawny pattern; a juvenile plumage, with blackish spots on the upperparts, emerges during the second week. A 3-wk-old captive bird (with wing measuring 84mm) could fly a little.

Behaviour. Extremely secretive, but when disturbed flies off with loudly whirring wings, keeping close to the ground and never flying far. It apparently sleeps on the ground.

Notes. It is commonly hunted in Trinidad, in spite of protection under the law.

PODICIPEDIDAE: Grebes

These are small water-birds, inhabiting mainly freshwater areas. Superficially resembling ducks, they have lobed toes and more sharply pointed bills. They are rarely seen to fly, but dive frequently for food and protection. They build nests which appear to float on the water but are usually anchored to the bottom. (2)

Least Grebe: *Tachybaptus dominicus*
Short-billed Grebe; "Diver"; *Colymbus dominicus; Podiceps dominicus*

Habitat and status. A rather uncommon and local resident found in freshwater lakes, reservoirs, ponds and marshes, such as Hollis Reservoir, Caroni marshes, Pointe-a-Pierre and Hillsborough Dam, Tobago. (Specimens: AMNH, BM.)

Range and subspecies. SW USA and Mexico S through Central and South America to Chile and Argentina, also Bahamas and Greater Antilles; *P. d. speciosus* (Lynch Arribalzaga) ranges through South America.

Description. 9 in. Generally dusky grayish brown, paler below, with white wing-patch visible in flight; head and neck gray, the crown and throat black during breeding, the latter white at other times; *iris orange-yellow;* bill thin, *blackish, sharply pointed.*

Measurements. Wing: 2 males 93, 97mm; 1 female 92mm.

Voice. A short, nasal note, like a toot from a toy trumpet; also a high-pitched chattering. Young birds utter a weak, plaintive *peep.*

Food. Fish, aquatic insects, algae. Quantities of feathers are often found in the stomach; the function of these is uncertain.

Nesting. Eight breeding records at Pointe-a-Pierre and Caroni marshes between April and November; one pair had broods in September and November. The nest is a mass of floating vegetation, anchored to the bottom in open water 2–5 ft deep. Clutch is of 3 or 4 eggs (up to 6 in Ecuador: Marchant 1960); the eggs are white, soon becoming stained, av. 34 × 24.5mm (6). Both parents incubate; the period is 21 days (in USA); the young remain near the nest for about 10–14 days, sometimes "riding" on their parents in the water; in downy plumage they have striped crowns.

Behaviour. When feeding, this species remains underwater for about 12 sec on average (Jenni 1969, in Costa Rica) and rarely surfaces near where it dived; it also regularly dives when alarmed, seldom flying. In display birds chatter considerably and chase each other, pattering over the water for usually no more than 30 yd.

Pied-billed Grebe: *Podilymbus podiceps*
"Diver"

Habitat and status. A rather uncommon resident of both islands, found on reservoirs, ponds and marshes. Up to 30 regularly visit Pointe-a-Pierre reservoirs from October to June. Individuals seen at Hillsborough Dam, Tobago, in April and August. (Specimen: AMNH.)

Range and subspecies. Canada S to Patagonia, also the West Indies. *P. p. antarcticus* (Lesson) ranges through most of South America, also Trinidad and Tobago; it is somewhat larger than the nominate race.

Description. 12 in. Dark grayish brown above, whitish below; in breeding plumage the throat is black; iris dark; bill short, stout and *pale,* crossed by black band during breeding season.

Measurements. Wing: 1 female 134mm.

Voice. Usually silent: adult occasionally calls a fairly high-pitched, musical hoot, resembling a gallinule's note; also a low-pitched, rattling *ke-ke-ke-ke.*

Food. Small fish, crustaceans, aquatic insects; in USA (Storer 1961) known to regurgitate pellets including chitin, feathers and algae.

Nesting. Breeds from mid-June to early October (B/S), also in November (1 nest). Nest similar to that of Least Grebe. The clutch is 4–6 eggs, whitish, soon becoming stained, av. 44 × 32mm (12). Both parents incubate, covering the eggs with debris when unattended; incubation period (in USA) is about 23 days.

Behaviour. During the off-season congregates in small flocks of 5–15. Rather shy of people, tending to dive at an approach closer than 50 yd. I have seen an adult rush across the water towards a caiman which was cruising near its nest.

PROCELLARIIDAE: Petrels and Shearwaters

These medium-sized seabirds are usually seen only far out to sea during the day, gliding low over the waves. They breed in burrows on isolated islands and wander great distances outside the breeding season. Some are gregarious in habits. (5)

Bulwer's Petrel: *Bulweria bulwerii*

Habitat and status. An oceanic seabird, accidental in Trinidad (1 record). A bird was found dead on Soldado Rock on 23 January 1961 (ffrench 1963). (Specimen: AMNH.)

Range. Breeds during May–June on islands in E Atlantic (Madeira, Salvage, Canary and Cape Verde islands), also in C and W Pacific Ocean. Ranges outside breeding season to coast of Brazil, but the above is one of the very few records N of the equator in the W Atlantic.

Description. 10 in. Entirely sooty black, with indistinct paler bar on wing-coverts; rather long, wedge-shaped tail; bill stout, black, with double nasal opening; tarsi pale flesh.

Cory's Shearwater: *Calonectris diomedea*
North Atlantic Shearwater; Mediterranean Shearwater; *Puffinus kuhlii; Puffinus diomedea*

Habitat and status. An oceanic seabird, accidental in Trinidad (3 records). Dead or exhausted birds have been found on Manzanilla and Mayaro beaches, 21 June 1955, 19 February 1956 and 29 April 1961. (Specimens: AMNH, TRVL.) A fourth record on 4 April 1957 (Herklots 1961) now seems doubtful (Collins 1969).

Range and subspecies. Breeds on islands of E Atlantic and Mediterranean, ranging the N Atlantic outside the breeding season, though there are a few records from the coasts of North and South America; *C. d. borealis* (Cory) breeds on the Azores, Madeira, Salvage and Canary islands.

Description. 20 in. Generally grayish brown above with *no* contrasting head or rump patches; underparts white; bill *yellow.*

Measurements. Wing: 1 male 379mm.

Great Shearwater: *Puffinus gravis*
Greater Shearwater

Habitat and status. An oceanic seabird regularly occurring in the course of northward migratory movement off Trinidad's E coast. Dead or dying birds have been found, usually in mid-June, between Matura and Mayaro. Observations at an oil-rig 15 miles off Point Galeota in 1982 showed small numbers passing daily between 14 and 17 June. (Specimen: TRVL.)

Range. Breeds on islands of S Atlantic from November to April, migrating north into N Atlantic from April to June, many being seen in May off coast of Brazil (Metcalf 1966); occasional in Caribbean (Bond 1966). Common in N Atlantic until October.

Description. 19 in. Upperparts generally brown, cap black, collar nearly meets on nape; rump white, tail blackish, underparts white; bill black.

Measurements. Wing: 3 males 328, 330, 340mm; 1 female 315mm. Weight: 2 males 385, 447gm.

Manx Shearwater: *Puffinus puffinus*
Common Shearwater

Habitat and status. An oceanic seabird accidental in Trinidad (4 records); an exhausted bird was found inland at Vega de Oropouche on 29 March 1958, and 2 dead birds (not preserved) on Manzanilla Beach on 6 December 1958. (Specimen: AMNH.)

Range and subspecies. Breeds on islands in eastern N Atlantic from April to June; also in Mediterranean Sea and Pacific Ocean. *P. p. puffinus* (Brünnich) is the Atlantic race, wintering in S Atlantic. A bird banded at Skokholm, Wales, on 30 August 1967 was recovered at Manzanilla Beach on 10 November 1968. It seems that in the summer some non-breeders move N from the S Atlantic into the Caribbean area (Post 1967).

Description. 14 in. Upperparts black with somewhat mottled cheeks and sides of neck; underparts, *including* under-tail-coverts, white; tail short; wings longer than in Audubon's Shearwater; legs pale pinkish.

Measurements. Wing: 14 males 224–244mm. Tail: 14 males 74–82mm (Witherby et al. 1952).

Audubon's Shearwater: *Puffinus lherminieri*
Dusky-backed Shearwater; Dusky Shearwater; "Diablotin"

Habitat and status. An oceanic seabird breeding in considerable numbers on islets off Tobago, including St. Giles and Little Tobago. Absent from Tobago in July. Occasionally seen at sea off Trinidad, rarely close to shore, but dead birds found at Manzanilla on 4 April 1957 and 27 March 1969. (Specimens: AMNH, BM, TRVL.)

Banding status. Twenty young and 4 adult birds were banded on Little Tobago in April 1967. No recoveries yet.

Range and subspecies. Breeds on islands from Bermuda S to the Caribbean and Ascension, also in the tropical Pacific Ocean; *P. l. lherminieri* (Lesson) breeds on Bermuda, the Bahamas and the Antilles; it is larger than *loyemilleri* (Wetmore) of Panama and the Venezuelan islands. A few Tobago birds seem too small for the nominate race, and Collins (1969) has suggested that the Tobago colonies may represent an intermediate population.

Description. 12 in. Upperparts *blackish brown, cheeks* and underparts white, but under-tail-coverts *blackish;* bill black; legs flesh. Easily confused in the field with the Manx Shearwater.

Measurements. Wing: 1 male 193mm; 2 females 190, 200mm. 14 unsexed 187–205mm (197). Tail: 10 birds 85–96mm (Witherby et al. 1952). Weight: 2 females 201, 205gm; 15 unsexed 186–234gm (217). A young nestling still growing primaries weighed 249gm.

Voice. A weird caterwauling, heard at the breeding grounds at night.

Food. Fish, planktonic crustaceans and cephalopods, taken at the surface or in shallow dives.

Nesting. Breeds January–April on Little Tobago (many nests, Dinsmore 1972); cycle is apparently annual, though in Galápagos (D. W. Snow 1965a) another race has a 9-month breeding cycle. The nest is usually in a burrow or on a sheltered ledge; frequently the burrows on Little Tobago are constructed beneath large aroid plants. Adults arrive at nests some time before breeding and are often found there during the day. One white egg is laid, av. 51 × 35mm (5). Incubation lasts about 7 wk, depending on food availability (Harris 1969), but an incubating bird may sit up to 10 days without being visited. After hatching, the chick is fed at night, usually soon after sunset. The parent accompanies the chick during the day only for the first week. The fledging period averages 11 wk, but varies from 9 to 14 wk according to the food supply (Harris 1969, in Galápagos).

Behaviour. Flies with rapid wing-beats, gliding less than most other shearwaters. Entirely nocturnal near land, except at Galápagos during the breeding season (Harris 1969); it may often be seen around a brightly lit stationary ship at night. In the burrow the adult sits tight when disturbed, but when handled can deliver a powerful bite. Homing ability is well developed, as was shown when birds released in February 1968 at various distances up to 400 miles returned to their burrows on Little Tobago (Griffin and Hatch, unpub.).

HYDROBATIDAE: Storm-Petrels

Closely related to shearwaters, storm-petrels also are usually seen well out to sea. Smaller in size, they fly close to the waves with an erratic fluttering flight, often landing on the water. Some species follow ships. (2)

Leach's Storm-Petrel: *Oceanodroma leucorhoa*
"Galla Bird"

Habitat and status. An oceanic seabird seen offshore from both islands or found exhausted on the coast, usually during the first 4 months of the year, especially in late April; one was found inland at Bois Neuf on 5 May, another banded in Nova Scotia on 25 October 1981 was found dead at Manzanilla on 22 April 1982. Latest date for live birds is 20 June. (Specimens: AMNH, TRVL.)

Range and subspecies. Breeds on islands in N Atlantic and N Pacific from May to August, wintering southward. *O. l. leucorhoa* (Vieillot) breeds on Atlantic islands and in extreme N Pacific, wintering widely throughout the tropical Atlantic and N Pacific.

Description. 8 in. Generally blackish brown, with pale bar on wings; upper-tail-coverts white, usually divided by dusky central stripe, tail forked; bill and legs black. Flight erratic, rather fast.

Measurements. Wing: 3 unsexed 153, 155, 158mm. Weight: 28gm (1 exhausted bird).

Food. Includes plankton, hence the local name (in Trinidad, plankton is called "Galla").

[Wilson's Storm-Petrel: *Oceanites oceanicus*]

Habitat and status. One seen off Charlotteville, Tobago, on 24 April 1987, possibly on other dates, too (Rooks 1987).

Range. Breeds on subantarctic islands; winters N to Labrador, also in Old World. Some records off coasts of Venezuela and the Guianas (April–July).

Description. 7 in. Very similar to Leach's Storm-Petrel, but white on rump more extensive, and tail square; legs longer with *yellow* webs. Difficult to distinguish in the field except at very close quarters.

PHAETHONTIDAE: Tropicbirds

Tropicbirds are seabirds resembling enormous terns with heavy bills and very long central tail-feathers. Seen both far from land and close to shore, they usually fly high above the sea with strong, rapid wing-beats, and dive, tern-like, for fish. They nest on ledges, often on steep cliffs. (2)

Red-billed Tropicbird: *Phaethon aethereus*
Boatswain Bird; "Booby"

Habitat and status. An oceanic seabird breeding on islets off Tobago, especially Little Tobago (over 300 birds) and St. Giles; also breeds on Smith's Island. Mostly absent at sea from August to November. Rarely recorded off Trinidad, where muddier conditions prevail; one found dead at Manzanilla in February 1987. (Specimens: AMNH, TRVL.)

Range and subspecies. Breeds on islands of the West Indies, Cape Verde Islands, Galápagos Islands and islands from California to Ecuador, also in the S Atlantic and Indian Ocean; *P. a. mesonauta* (Peters) ranges through the West Indies, Cape Verde and eastern Pacific islands.

Description. 40 in. (20 in. without long central tail-feathers). *Adult:* generally white with conspicuous black stripe through eye and fine black bars on upperparts; wings white, with some black on outer primaries; 2 long central tail-feathers white; bill scarlet. *Immature:* has coarser bars, usually a black crescent on nape, lacks long tail-feathers; bill dull greenish yellow.

Measurements. Wing: 1 female 330mm; 2 unsexed 314, 315mm. Weight: 1 female 685gm.

Voice. A high, screaming rattle, *kee-kee-krrt-krrt-krrt-krrt,* delivered in flight or from the nest; also in flight a single, sharp *keek.*

Food. Fish obtained by surface-plunging. On Ascension Island birds feed mainly on small flying-fish and squids (Stonehouse 1962).

Nesting. Breeds apparently annually on islands off Tobago (1956–68), although breeding cycles vary considerably on Ascension (Stonehouse 1962) and Galápagos (D. W. Snow 1965b). Breeding peak December–February, earliest date for egg 20 November, latest 28 April, but an adult was found on a "nest" (? with egg or young) on 2 August. Nest-site is usually a ledge on a cliffside, sometimes a cavity among rocks. One egg is laid, light olive brown with dark brown or red spots, av. 59 × 42mm (20). On Ascension incubation lasted about 43 days, both parents attending egg and chick (Stonehouse 1962). The young fly after about 3 months. At over-crowded colonies competition for nest sites is fierce and nest mortality high; this probably results in an extended breeding season.

Behaviour. Very clumsy at the nest, which they rarely leave when approached; after handling by humans (to which they vociferously object, sometimes biting fiercely) the adults usually settle back calmly on the nest. In an aerial display several birds fly together in close formation, gliding occasionally with wings held high and tails depressed, while they utter their shrill screaming call.

[White-tailed Tropicbird: *Phaethon lepturus*]
Yellow-billed Tropicbird

Habitat and status. The species has been included in previous publications as a breeding resident of islands off Tobago, in place of the Red-billed Tropicbird. In fact *P. lepturus* does not breed near Tobago, and its inclusion was in my view (ffrench 1961) a mistake based on the incorrect identification of a specimen (now apparently lost) mentioned by de Dalmas (1900) as *P. americanus*. However, an adult was seen off Little Tobago on 29 December 1983 (B. Richardson), associating with a number of its congeners.

Range. Breeds in many West Indian islands S to St. Vincent, and is widespread throughout tropical oceans.

Description. 38 in. Very similar to *P. aethereus* but smaller. *Adult:* back pure white, *not barred; black band on inner wing;* bill orange-yellow to orange-red. *Immature:* has *fine* barring on back and *lacks* the black crescent on nape; also lacks long tail-feathers; bill greenish yellow.

Measurements. Wing: 10 males 273–291mm (285); 10 females 271–297mm (282). (Data from Palmer 1962.)

PELECANIDAE: Pelicans

Very large seabirds with long, hooked bills and enormous gular pouches; commonly seen in coastal waters. Pelicans frequently fly in formation with slow, heavy wing-beats and heads retracted. One species is common in our area, and there is a possible sight record of another, the White Pelican (*Pelecanus erythrorhynchus*), seen in December 1963 far outside its normal range (Eckelberry 1964). (1)

Brown Pelican: *Pelecanus occidentalis*
"Bacula"; "Grand Gosier"

Habitat and status. Common on all coasts of Trinidad and Tobago, congregating into flocks of up to 1000 in the Gulf of Paria; least common off E coast of Trinidad. Small breeding colonies on both islands; population fluctuates considerably, but extent of dispersal not known. (Specimens: ANSP [*carolinensis*].)

Range and subspecies. Coastal waters of USA, the West Indies, Central and W South America, also S along the Caribbean and Atlantic coasts of South America to Surinam; *P. o. occidentalis* (Linnaeus) breeds in the West Indies; the larger *P. o. carolinensis* (Gmelin) breeds in SE USA, migrating S at least as far as Trinidad (specimens examined).

Description. 42–54 in.; wingspread 6.5 ft. *Adult:* white crown, back of head and neck chestnut, upperparts and wings silvery gray, edged with black; underparts brown. *Immature:* mainly brown, underparts white.

Measurements. *P. occidentalis,* 1 unsexed bird. Wing: 460mm. Bill: 281mm. Weight: 3000gm. *P. carolinensis,* 4 unsexed birds. Wing: 485–510mm (499). Bill: 300–331mm (316). (Data from birds found dead on Soldado Rock.)

Voice. Usually silent, but occasionally grunts when alarmed.

Food. Small fish, normally caught after a heavy vertical dive with wings folded back. A survey in USA showed that practically no commercially valuable fish are taken. Has been known to catch stingrays (Bostic & Banks 1966), with fatal results.

Nesting. Breeds apparently annually February–April, on Saut d'Eau Island sanctuary and occasionally in Caroni swamp and on remote rocks on Tobago. The size of the Saut d'Eau colony varies according to the degree of molestation by poachers, but 150 nests have been recorded (Brown 1947). Nests there are usually built in trees, often at considerable height, and are rough stick constructions, often grouped together. Eggs usually 2, sometimes 3, white, av. 74 × 48mm (4). Incubation period about 28 days (in USA); both parents incubate. Young fly after about 9 wk, but still depend on parents for some time after that.

Behaviour. Pelicans are gregarious, forming both small and large groups. About a dozen often fly together, quite low over the water, alternately flapping their wings and gliding almost in unison. When not fishing, birds occasionally soar high in the air. They frequently fish in company with boobies, gulls and terns, the latter taking advantage of the pelicans' comparative clumsiness by seizing fish even out of their pouches. They roost communally, as in Caroni mangroves and on Soldado Rock, where they have often been observed flying about at night.

Notes. Commonly hunted for food, both at nesting places, roosts and at sea, in spite of legal protection. Some birds may live to a considerable age; one banded bird in USA was 31 yr old.

SULIDAE: Boobies

These large seabirds have cigar-shaped bodies, long, pointed wings and stout, sharp bills. Often seen in groups, they glide low over the water and obtain their food by diving into the sea. They breed on remote islands and outside the breeding season may be seen well out to sea. (3)

Masked Booby: *Sula dactylatra*

Habitat and status. A single record of an adult seen at close quarters and photographed in 1988 at an oil-rig platform 12 miles off Trinidad's E coast (I. Lambie).

Range. Tropical oceans around the world; breeds in the West Indies S to the Grenadines.

Description. 33 in. *Adult:* similar to white phase of Red-footed Booby, but larger, with more extensive black on flight feathers and scapulars, also *tail mainly black;* facial skin dark; bill yellowish; legs blackish.

Red-footed Booby: *Sula sula*

Habitat and status. Fairly common nesting bird (perhaps 1500 birds) on St. Giles Islands, Tobago, but rarely seen elsewhere off Tobago or Trinidad, though reported off Trinidad (B/S). Oceanic outside breeding season. (No specimens, but collected by Léotaud.)

Range and subspecies. Tropical oceans around the world; the nominate race occurs in the West Indies, tropical Atlantic, and on the coast of British Honduras.

Description. About 28 in. *White phase:* generally white, tinged with buff, primaries and tips of secondaries black. *Brown phase:* generally brown with slightly darker wings; abdomen, rump and tail usually white, sometimes gray. In both phases legs and toes red; bill and gular pouch pink and blue, but variable.

Significance of the two phases not yet understood (Murphy 1936); birds breed in both. In Tobago brown birds outnumber white by at least 20 to 1.

Voice. Harsh squawks and barking calls, uttered in display or alarm; the female's voice is deeper and gruffer, the male's more metallic (Nelson 1969).

Food. Fish, including flying fish, which are sometimes caught in the air. Normally the booby dives for fish; most feeding is done far from land.

Nesting. Has been found breeding in all months from August to April, but the timing of the breeding cycle is still obscure (Dinsmore & ffrench 1969). Nests colonially in trees (usually sea grape [*Coccoloba*]); nest is of sticks 8–12 ft above ground. One egg is laid, pale blue covered with chalky deposit, av. 58 × 39mm (5), but size variable. Incubation period 44 days in British Honduras (Verner 1961) and 46 days in Galápagos (Nelson 1969); both parents build the nest and share incubation; the young fly short distances after about 3 months, but extended flight may not be made until 5 months; even after this, young birds return regularly to the nest to be fed. Later large groups of immature birds "club" together for feeding and roosting.

Behaviour. Though relying heavily on wind for take-off, once in the air boobies fly with great agility and ease, frequently gliding; they also soar in updraughts (Verner 1961). At the nest both parents and young flutter their gular pouches, which serves to keep down body temperature in conditions of intense heat. Before taking flight or leaving the nest an adult often flicks its wings half open and closes them again (Nelson 1969). The male attracts the female by pointing his bill vertically upward, thus showing the bright gular colours; there is much aggressive behaviour between the pair.

Notes. Both species of boobies are commonly persecuted at the nest by inhabitants of Tobago, in spite of full legal protection. Without enforcement of the law by an adequate patrol, the future of these seabirds in Tobago remains in jeopardy.

Brown Booby: *Sula leucogaster*
White-bellied Booby

Habitat and status. Breeds on rocky coasts of Tobago and offshore islands, where it is common, less pelagic and more widespread than *S. sula.* Also seen occasionally off Trinidad, commonly in small numbers on Soldado Rock, where, however, it has not yet been found to breed. (Specimen: ANSP.)

Banding status. One adult banded in 1964 on Soldado Rock, and on Little Tobago 1 young bird in 1967, 5 more in 1975.

Range and subspecies. Tropical oceans around the world; *S. l. leucogaster* (Boddaert) is found throughout the Caribbean, also islands in the tropical Atlantic and off the E coast of South America.

Description. 29 in. *Adult:* head, neck, upperparts, tail and upper breast blackish brown, sharply divided from white lower breast and rest of underparts; a broad white stripe on underwings; legs yellow; bill straw yellow, facial skin pale yellow, a prominent dark spot in front of eye (female), much less pronounced or absent in male. *Immature:* brown above and below, but paler brown lower underparts, showing line of demarcation at breast.

Voice. A strident honking or screeching, usually heard only at breeding grounds; male's call quieter than female's.

Food. Fish, usually small (less than 100mm), but including flying fish (at Ascension). Obtained by diving, both vertically and from a shallow angle.

Nesting. Breeding occurs on rocky coasts of NE Tobago, on St. Giles Islands, and Little Tobago. Two peaks of egg-laying on Little Tobago, 103 nests recorded by Dinsmore (1972) and 71 by Morris (1984), centered around July and December–January; laying recorded in all months from June to March. In Ascension the species seemed to have an 8-month cycle (Dorward 1962); the cycle in Tobago is probably 6 months. Usually the nest is little more than a flattened circle of vegetation on a ledge, but sometimes includes extra leaves, grass, stones and feathers. One or 2 chalky white eggs, av. 56 × 39mm (2), but of the 2 chicks normally only 1 survives. Incubation by both parents, about 45 days; young fly after 3–4 months, but leave the nest some time earlier. Nesting success is unfortunately restricted by poaching, even on sanctuaries (Morris 1984).

Behaviour. Not particularly gregarious, though occasionally feeds in flocks. At the nest boobies are frequently fearless of people, but when disturbed may go through a displacement routine, playing with a root or feather. Various displays have been described (Dorward 1962), including pointing the bill at the sky, sparring with bills and turning the bill down or away from another bird.

PHALACROCORACIDAE: Cormorants

These large blackish water-birds are found both on seacoasts and inland waters. Possessing long necks and hooked bills, they are most ungainly on land, but are strong fliers and expert swimmers, diving for long periods and catching their food underwater. (1)

Olivaceous Cormorant: *Phalacrocorax olivaceus*
Neotropic Cormorant; Brazilian Cormorant; "Black Duck"; "Muscovy"

Habitat and status. A regular non-breeding visitor in varying numbers (maximum 2000) to inland reservoirs in S Trinidad; some flocks also on seacoast and Caroni swamp. Regularly present December to August, with stray birds staying through the year. Migration recorded near Cedros in January. Birds in wing-moult at Pointe-a-Pierre from January to May. (Specimen: TRVL.)

Range and subspecies. The whole of South America, Central America, S USA, Cuba and the Bahamas; *P. o. olivaceus* (Humboldt) ranges through South America N to Costa Rica.

Description. 26 in. *Adult:* generally black, but acquiring more glossy plumage just before breeding, including conspicuous white filamentous feathers on the side of the head; iris green; upper mandible black, lower mandible and gular pouch dull orange-yellow, brighter in the breeding stage; legs black. *Immature:* paler than adult, more brownish black.

Measurements. Wing: 1 male 290mm. Weight: 1 male 1350gm.

Voice. A pig-like grunting.

Food. Fish, pursued underwater.

Behaviour. At Pointe-a-Pierre cormorants, when not feeding, sit in groups on convenient perches in and around the reservoirs; they roost on the high branches of bamboos and casuarina trees. After swimming or rain they frequently stretch out their wings to dry. In an aerial display, most common in the evening, two or more birds fly around, circling high over the water. Every now and then one bird makes a sudden dart downwards, changing direction abruptly rather like a nightjar. Breeding displays are seen in Trinidad from late May to August. One or two birds splash vigorously in the water; sometimes one swims towards the other with head and neck submerged; chases are frequent.

Notes. This species may be hunted during the open season, but in fact few birds are shot.

ANHINGIDAE: Anhingas or Darters

Somewhat resembling cormorants in both form and habits, anhingas have very long, slender necks, small heads and long, pointed bills, with which they spear fish. The tail is long and shaped like a narrow fan in flight. Since both primaries and secondaries are moulted simultaneously, these birds become flightless for a while. (1)

Anhinga: *Anhinga anhinga*
American Darter; Snake-bird; "Black Duck"; "Water Turkey"

Habitat and status. Inhabits inland waters of both islands, including swamps, river and reservoirs, especially where bordered by heavy woods; birds are usually found perched in trees on the edge of the water. Recorded breeding for first time at Pointe-a-Pierre in January 1991 (J. B. Saunders). Normally, however, most water-birds breed here between August and November, so the species probably migrates to the mainland to breed. (Specimens: AMNH.)

Range and subspecies. S USA, Cuba, Central and South America S to Argentina; *A. a. anhinga* (Linnaeus) ranges from Panama S, being larger than the northern form and with a broader band on the tail.

Description. 34 in. *Male:* mainly black with white markings on the wings; tail broadly tipped buff. *Female:* brown head, neck and upper breast. Bill yellow, sharply pointed.

Measurements. Wing: 1 male 337mm; 1 unsexed 328mm.

Voice. Various grunting croaks; the male in alarm utters a guttural, growling *karr-karr-karr.*

Food. Fish, including the introduced *Tilapia,* and aquatic insects. The fish are caught underwater, but are sometimes brought out of the water and manipulated in the bill.

Behaviour. On a perch the Anhinga often assumes a statuesque pose with wings and tail spread; sometimes it rocks back and forth waving its wings; the long, snake-like neck moves from side to side as the bird seems to peer about nervously. As he calls his guttural note, the male may extend his orange gular pouch. When alarmed on a perch, the Anhinga dives directly into the water, even from several feet above; when swimming with its head above water it moves with an odd bobbing motion. It may stay submerged for long periods, putting up its head at a vertical angle and withdrawing it with hardly a ripple. Before flying it emerges onto a perch to dry its waterlogged plumage. In the air it glides and soars, with occasional rapid flaps, often circling with outstretched neck and spread tail at a considerable height.

Notes. Though legally protected, the Anhinga is often persecuted by hunters in Trinidad, who "misidentify" it as a "kind of duck".

FREGATIDAE: Frigatebirds

Very large seabirds with narrow, pointed wings, keeping mainly to coastal waters; frigatebirds are usually seen gliding high above the sea, their wings forming a conspicuous shallow W pattern in silhouette. The long tail is occasionally divided into a deep fork; the bill is long and powerfully hooked. They are never seen on the water. The nests are built colonially in trees on remote islands. (1)

Magnificent Frigatebird: *Fregata magnificens*
"Man-o'-War"; "Carite bird"

Habitat and status. Common in coastal waters, especially W and N of Trinidad, and off Tobago, where it breeds on St. Giles Islands. Over 300 birds sometimes roost on Soldado Rock, up to 2000 on St. Giles; hundreds move daily along the windward coast of Tobago, and regularly birds are seen high above Trinidad's Northern Range. (Specimen: ANSP.)

Range. Throughout tropical American waters from Mexico and Florida S to Brazil and Ecuador; also off Gambia and Cape Verde Islands.

Description. 40 in.; wingspread 7 ft. *Male:* all black; gular sac brilliant scarlet in breeding season when inflated into a balloon, at other times dull orange and shrunken. *Female:* black, with breast and sides of lower neck white; pale brown band on wings. *Immature:* head and most of underparts white.

Measurements. Wing: 1 male 625mm; 2 unsexed 620, 622mm.

Voice. Usually silent in flight. Birds settling to roost sometimes make a grating rattle. At the nest various crackling noises are uttered, mainly by the young.

Food. Fish, caught at or near the surface; the bird flies low over the water and snatches the food with a deft backward flick of the sharply hooked bill. Also frigatebirds commonly attack other seabirds, including boobies, gulls and terns, and force them to disgorge their meals. Sooty Tern eggs and chicks and Red-footed Booby eggs are occasionally taken. In harbours frigatebirds are scavengers, feeding on offal and refuse of all kinds.

Nesting. Breeds, probably annually, on St. Giles Islands from December to April; a few nests and eggs also found on Soldado Rock, Trinidad, in February 1973 (Saunders). Nesting is colonial, with several nests in one tree. The nest is of sticks, normally in a treetop, usually about 10 ft above ground. One white egg is laid, av. 69 × 46mm (22). Both parents incubate, for about 6 wk. The young hatch naked but soon acquire white down; they are fed by regurgitation, and fledge after about 5 months.

Behaviour. The most striking form of display is the male's inflation of his gular sac into an enormous scarlet balloon. This is usually seen at or near the nest but is occasionally observed in flying birds. The frigatebird's mastery of flight is stupendous, especially in strong winds. When attacking and robbing other birds, it strikes powerfully with its bill; I once saw a bird force a Brown Booby down to the water, where it continued to harass the smaller bird for over 5 min. The frigatebird itself never settles on the sea, as it quickly becomes waterlogged and is then unable to take off. Observations in Mexico (Kielhorn et al. 1963) show that occasionally frigatebirds bathe in fresh water in the manner of swallows.

Notes. In spite of legal protection, frigatebirds are killed at the nest by local inhabitants; hunting is usually at night with clubs and torches. In some years no young survive to fledging.

ARDEIDAE: Herons

This well-known group of large wading birds is characterised by the long legs, neck and bill; in flight herons normally hunch the head back between the shoulders, and the legs show well beyond the tail. They frequent swamps and other freshwater habitats, whilst some are to be found on the seacoast. Many species nest and roost colonially. (19)

Gray Heron: *Ardea cinerea*
European Common Heron

Habitat and status. Only one record in Trinidad, a bird shot near Fyzabad on 27 August 1959. It had been banded as a nestling in France on 28 May 1958 (Baudouin-Bodin 1960). Another bird banded at the same locality on 26 May 1959 was found dead on Montserrat, West Indies, on 20 September 1959.

Range and subspecies. Europe, Asia and Africa, accidental in Greenland; *A. c. cinerea* (Linnaeus) ranges through Europe, W Asia and much of Africa.

Description. 36 in. Very similar to Great Blue Heron, but smaller and paler, almost lacking in rufous or brown tones. Upper breast white, streaked black; lower breast, abdomen and *thighs white*, sides black; legs brownish.

Measurements. Wing: 12 males 430–470mm (Witherby et al. 1952).

Great Blue Heron: *Ardea herodias*
"Crane"

Habitat and status. A regular visitor to both islands in small numbers, frequenting the seacoast and swamps. Usually a few (up to 8) on mudflats at Pointe-a-Pierre November–July; earliest date 24 October, latest 17 August. (Specimens: TRVL.)

Range. The several races range throughout temperate North America, dispersing after the breeding season S to Central and N South America and the West Indies; immature non-breeding birds often summer in the tropics.

Description. 48 in.; wingspread 6.5 ft. *Adult:* head pale with black sides of crown and plumes (in breeding season). Upperparts grayish blue, wings slate, neck and underparts pale, streaked with black; *thighs rufous;* bill yellowish, legs dark olive. *Immature:* more brownish, with blackish cap. (All-white birds are known in various areas, including some islands off Venezuela.)

Measurements. Wing: 1 unsexed 420mm. Bill: 122mm.

Voice. Usually silent; occasionally, when alarmed, a deep croak.

Food. Mostly fish; also aquatic insects.

Behaviour. Usually solitary, standing motionless in shallow water for long periods. In flight, wing-beats very slow and heavy.

Notes. Occasionally hunted in Trinidad, where it is considered a great prize, for it is a wary bird. Known to live over 20 yr (Owen 1959).

White-necked Heron: *Ardea cocoi*
Cocoi Heron; "Crane"

Habitat and status. A bird of mainly freshwater lakes and swamps, visiting Trinidad in small numbers January–June; regular visitor to Pointe-a-Pierre reservoirs, earliest date 25 November, latest 5 July. One bird seen at Bloody Bay, Tobago, on 16 February. (Specimen: TRVL.)

Range. Throughout South America N to Panama.

Description. 45 in. Similar to Great Blue Heron, but whiter and with more contrasting colours. *Adult:* crown black; wing-coverts whitish gray contrasting with blackish wing-quills; neck, breast and *thighs white*, sides of breast and abdomen black; bill blackish basally, yellow at tip. *Immature:* browner above; underparts almost entirely white with a few black streaks on breast.

Measurements. Wing: 1 male 465mm.

Voice. A deep croak.

Food. Mainly fish; feeds like the Great Blue Heron.

Behaviour. Quite solitary. When 2 birds inhabit the same area, they seem to choose the farthest possible distance from each other.

Great Egret: *Casmerodius albus*
Common Egret; American Egret; Large White Egret; *Egretta alba*

Habitat and status. A fairly common visitor to both islands, known regularly in the Caroni and Nariva swamps from November to August, in flocks up to 100. Occasionally individuals are seen at Pointe-a-Pierre reservoirs and seashore. A few breeding records since 1926. Known to breed on the neighbouring mainland. (Specimens: AMNH, TRVL.)

Range and subspecies. Almost cosmopolitan. *C. a. egretta* (Gmelin) ranges throughout America from S Canada to Patagonia.

Description. 40 in. All white, with *yellow bill* and *black legs*. Considerably larger than the other white egrets, with a more ponderous flight.

Measurements. Wing: 2 males 395, 390mm.

Voice. A harsh *caw*.

Food. Fish, frogs and insects. Known to hunt lizards at a distance from water in Venezuela (Friedmann & Smith 1950).

Nesting. B/S record nesting during late July and August in 1923, 1924 and 1926. The next records after that time were 4 nests found in Caroni swamp during July 1978 (June laying). Likewise nesting in Tobago is not definitely recorded. The nest is a typical heron stick nest; clutch in USA varies from 2 to 5 eggs, 3 being commonest. In Trinidad the clutch was 2 or 3 pale blue eggs, av. 57.5 × 43mm (2). Incubation lasts about 3.5 wk, and like other herons the young leave the nest after about 2.5 wk, before they can fly.

Behaviour. Normally solitary in Trinidad, except at the roost. However, birds do congregate to feed under unusual circumstances; 60 birds were seen at a drying pool in the Nariva swamp in which fish were dying in large numbers. Similarly, 80 birds were grouped at a creek in the Caroni marshes at the very end of the 1960 dry season. Roosting is normally colonial, and in the Caroni swamp up to 100 birds may be seen at a traditional roost near the sanctuary.

Little Egret: *Egretta garzetta*

Habitat and status. An occasional visitor to both islands, either becoming more common recently or previously missed (Murphy & Fried, in press). First recorded on 13 January 1957, when a bird banded as a nestling on 24 July 1956 at Coto Donana, Spain, was shot by C. L. Williams in Caroni swamp (Downs 1959). Recent records of several individuals seen by many people have come from sewage treatment ponds near Trincity and Port of Spain, also Buccoo marsh, Tobago, between November 1989 and March 1990. (Specimen: AMNH.)

Range and subspecies. S Europe, Africa, S Asia and N Australia, *E. g. garzetta* (Linnaeus) ranges through S Europe, Africa and S Asia. Other New World records include birds collected in Newfoundland (8 May 1954), Barbados (16 April 1954), Martinique (6 October 1962) and Surinam (June 1969, banded as a nestling in Spain, June 1968). More recently several birds have been seen in St. Lucia during 1985–87.

Description. 23 in. Very similar to Snowy Egret, but averaging larger. Distinctions: in breeding plumage crest feathers include 2 very long, narrow, tapering plumes; aigrettes on back are straight, *not* recurved; bare lores black to greenish gray, *not* yellow. In non-breeding plumage toes more greenish yellow, base of mandible pale.

Measurements. Wing: 250–295mm. Bill (from feathers): 78–92mm. Tarsus: 100–110mm. (Witherby et al. 1952.)

Western Reef-Heron: *Egretta gularis*

Habitat and status. One record only, of a dark-phase bird seen and photographed at Nariva on 22 January 1986 (Murphy & Nanan 1987). Some uncorroborated reports from Tobago (Murphy 1986). (No specimen.)

Range. Breeds in Africa and SW Asia, mainly in coastal areas. Several recent sight records from St. Lucia and Barbados, also Massachusetts. Considered by some authors conspecific with Little Egret.

Description. 24 in. *Dark phase:* fairly similar to Tricolored Heron, but with prominent white throat, heavier and more down-curving bill with blackish upper mandible, and black legs with yellow feet. There is also a white morph, distinguished from similar species by the heavier, brownish bill.

Snowy Egret: *Egretta thula*
"Aigrette"; *Leucophoyx thula*

Habitat and status. Rather uncommon resident of both islands, frequenting swamps and marshes and more especially saltwater areas. Recorded in all months, but numbers augmented by winter visitors from the north September–March. (Specimens: YPM.)

Banding status. A bird banded as a nestling on 10 August 1968 in New Jersey, USA, was recovered in Trinidad on 18 November 1968.

Range and subspecies. USA S through Central and South America and West Indies; *E. t. thula* (Molina) occurs throughout the range except for W USA.

Description. 23 in. All white; in the breeding season has a conspicuous crest and recurved aigrettes on the back; bill black, bare lores yellow (sometimes reddish when breeding); legs black (greenish posteriorly in immature), toes bright yellow. *Downy young:* dark pink legs, with flesh-coloured feet, pink bill tipped black, and dark brown iris.

Measurements. Wing: 6 males 247–270mm (255); 7 females 237–257mm (241). Bill (from base): 76–84mm (79). Tarsus: 88–102mm (95). (Wetmore 1965.)

Voice. A hoarse *aah,* or *a-wah-wah-wah;* especially vocal at breeding colony.

Food. Small fish, crustaceans, insects and other aquatic creatures. Often seen feeding on exposed mudflats in saltwater swamps and on seashore.

Nesting. Breeds regularly in small numbers in mangrove swamps, nests found mainly from May to August, though B/S have a record for late October. Nests, which are typical heron structures, have always been in a mixed-species colony; clutch varies from 2 to 4 pale blue-green eggs, av. 43.5 × 32.5mm (8). No exact data on incubation or fledging periods, but it is likely they resemble other herons of this size.

Behaviour. A very active feeder, striding about in shallow water with great energy. It also feeds by stirring the water with one foot, seizing any prey which is disturbed. Various forms of display have been described in USA (Meyerriecks 1960), some of them involving the brightly coloured feet and lores and the long ornamental breeding plumes. In the "stretch display" birds point the bill straight up, pumping the head up and down, calling loudly and erecting the plumes. I have seen a Snowy Egret display at a Cattle Egret which landed beside its nest, but I have not found evidence to show that the Snowy Egrets have declined in numbers since the other species arrived in Trinidad.

Little Blue Heron: *Egretta caerulea*
"Blue Gaulding"; "Black Egret"; *Florida caerulea*

Habitat and status. A common resident of both islands, inhabiting swamps, flooded fields and marshes and the seacoast. Numbers increase between October and December, as migrants from the north arrive (Dusi 1967). It is not known how long these visitors stay. (Specimens: AMNH, ANSP, YPM, TRVL.)

Banding status. Between 1933 and 1968 5 birds banded as nestlings in USA were recovered in Trinidad, and 1 in Tobago. Four originated between New Jersey and South Carolina, 2 from Alabama. All were less than 1 yr old when recovered.

Range. S. USA S through Central America, West Indies, N and E South America; on dispersal reaches E USA north to Canada.

Description. 24 in. *Adult:* generally slate blue, the head and neck purplish rufous; bill grayish blue with dark tip, thicker at the base than that of similar species; legs dark or greenish. *Immature:* all white. Older, piebald birds with patches of slate are frequently seen. *Downy young:* has green or yellowish green legs, blackish bill and pale iris.

Measurements. Wing: 1 male 255mm; 1 unsexed 247mm.

Voice. Occasionally a harsh croak.

Food. Remarkably diverse, including fish, crustaceans, snakes, frogs, lizards and insects. Usually hunts alone, in shallow water or on land, stalking prey with deliberate, rather slow movements, but a bird has been seen to catch fish from the surface of the water while in flight (ffrench 1965b).

Nesting. Breeds during all months from February to August (and probably other months) at more or less annual intervals. B/S called its breeding "capricious". Nests colonially, usually in mangrove, but also in bamboo, and amid cactus in Tobago. Mangrove nests are rough stick structures, usually 3–15 ft above high tide (but one found in Caroni was only 1 ft above). Clutch 2–5 plain blue eggs, av. 43.5 × 34.5mm (8). Incubation period about 22 days; both parents incubate and feed the young, which fly after about 1 month, but leave the nest for the outer branches of the tree during their third week. Most breeding adults are in the dark blue plumage, but occasionally white or piebald birds breed.

Behaviour. Sometimes seen in flight with neck outstretched, especially soon after take-off. Roosts colonially in mangrove swamps, often at breeding site. Courtship takes place near the nest, but promiscuous copulation is quite common. During nest-building, the female builds and the male collects material, usually from nearby. I have seen a bird pick a twig up from the surface of deep water with its bill. When the male hands over the twig, both birds raise the plumes on their heads and scapulars. While the female inserts the twig, the male nibbles gently at her back and flanks. There are various other typical heron displays and postures, but very few aerial displays.

Notes. Occasionally hunted, in spite of legal protection.

Tricolored Heron: *Egretta tricolor*
Louisiana Heron; Red-necked Heron; "Trinidad Heron";
Hydranassa tricolor

Habitat and status. A common resident of swamps and adjoining marshes in Trinidad, also frequents coasts; rather uncommonly seen in Tobago. (Specimens: Trinidad, AMNH, ANSP, YPM, LM, TRVL.)

Range and subspecies. South American coast from Brazil and Peru N to West Indies, Central America and S USA. *H. t. rufimentum* (Hellmayr) is confined to Trinidad, being distinguished by its dark chestnut chin and line down the neck. Tobago birds are probably migrants from the north, *H. t. ruficollis* (Gosse), larger and with a white chin; this has been recorded on Grenada and St. Vincent.

Description. 25 in. *Adult:* mainly dark slate gray above, white below; occipital crest and rump white, neck very slender, streaked rufous and white; bill long, yellowish, tipped black; legs yellow. In breeding season bill bluish, legs orange. *Immature:* no crest, generally brownish gray above, neck more chestnut.

Measurements. Wing: 2 males 225, 228mm. Weight: 1 male 295gm*.

Voice. A harsh croak, normally silent.

Food. Mainly fish, crustaceans and insects (in USA); usually feeds by deliberately stalking prey, then striking suddenly.

Nesting. Breeds in all months from February to August; though often found in mixed heronries in mangroves with Cattle and Snowy egrets, Little Blue Herons and Scarlet Ibis, this species often anticipates the others in its building. In 1963 many young were fledged by the end of March, but in 1963–66 eggs were also laid in June and July. The nest is a rough stick structure. Clutch 2–4 blue eggs, av. 40 × 30mm (8). Both adults incubate, for about 3 wk, and the young are fledged within about 5 wk, leaving the nest during the third week. Since the downy plumage is dark above, they are readily distinguished from the downy white of the other 3 heron species with which they associate. In Georgia they were found to be particularly active and expert in climbing (Teal 1965).

Behaviour. Often seen hunting solitarily, but very gregarious at roosts and breeding grounds. Display of North American race shows great similarity to that of other herons (Meyerriecks, in Palmer 1962); but it also combines a "snap and stretch" display, which is unique. The male extends his head out and down, erecting all his plumes; then, raising his bill to the sky, he pumps it up and down, extending his wings and fanning with them. The male attracts the female with these displays, and it is he who selects the nest-site and begins to build.

Reddish Egret: *Egretta rufescens*

Habitat and status. Three records only, of 4 birds in Caroni swamp in January 1973 (D. Simon), 1 at Mucurapo in October 1976 and 2 at Pointe-a-Pierre (D. Fisher, ffrench 1977). Possibly overlooked owing to similarity with Little Blue Heron. Found in coastal mudflats and mangrove swamps.

Range. Southern states of USA and Mexico S to Costa Rica, also N

Colombia and Venezuela with offshore islands, Bahamas and Greater Antilles. Breeding range recently found to extend S to Bonaire, so records on Trinidad may be part of a pattern of range extension.

Description. 30 in. *Dark phase:* head and neck reddish brown, appearing shaggy in the field, otherwise slaty gray sometimes tinged reddish; bill pinkish with the distal part black; legs dark blue. *White phase:* all white; bill as in dark phase. Commonly forages very actively in shallow water, rushing erratically about, often with outstretched wings.

Green-backed Heron: *Butorides striatus*
Striated or Green Heron; *Butorides virescens;* "Chuck"; "Gaulin"   **Plate 1(1)**

Habitat and status. A common resident on both islands, frequenting freshwater swamps, mangroves, streams, anywhere close to water; northern migrants increase the numbers from October to March. (Specimens: AMNH, YPM, ANSP, LM, TRVL.)

Range and subspecies. S Canada south to South America, also Africa, Asia, Australia and the Pacific islands; the nominate race ranges through South America from Paraguay and Argentina N to Panama, Venezuela and Trinidad; *B. s. virescens* (Linnaeus) breeds in E North America and Mexico, wintering S to Panama and Venezuela; it is longer-winged than *B. s. maculatus* (Boddaert) which breeds in the West Indies S to Tobago and in Central America.

Description. 17 in. *Adult:* crown blackish, sides of head, neck and breast gray (*striatus*) or chestnut (*virescens* and *maculatus*); loral streak greenish, white stripe from chin to breast, mid-breast spotted with black; back and wings greenish slate, abdomen grayish brown; legs orange or yellow. *Immature:* generally duller; sides of head and neck and underparts streaked brown and white; pale edges to wing-coverts; legs greenish yellow.

Measurements. *B. striatus.* Wing: 1 female 160mm; 2 unsexed 162, 164mm. Weight: 1 unsexed 135gm*. Tobago birds. Wing: 4 males 177–183mm (179); 4 females 170–180mm (175). Weight: 1 female 184gm*. At least some of these specimens seem to be the longer-winged *virescens.*

Voice. An explosive *kyow.*

Food. Frogs, fish, crustaceans, spiders and insects.

Nesting. Recorded in every month of the year (Trinidad) with a peak from July to October; in Tobago recorded in March. On Barro Colorado Van Tyne (1950) also found a long breeding season. The nest is typically a smallish structure of sticks placed in a tree or bush near water, usually fairly low, but recorded as high as 25 ft. Clutch is 2–4 pale greenish blue eggs, measuring 35.7 × 27.4mm (1). In North America both parents share incubation for about 20 days and the young fly after about 3 wk, having left the nest and climbed about in the tree for the last few days prior to flight; they are still dependent on their parents for several days afterwards.

Behaviour. Normally a solitary bird, frequently seen stalking stealthily along the banks of a river or marsh, adopting at intervals a hunting posture which it keeps for long periods, bill and body thrust forward almost horizontally. When alarmed it frequently flicks its short tail and raises its prominent crest. Its display includes stretching forward with open bill, holding the head and neck vertically, swaying, bill-snapping and a circular flight display, in which the bird flies with its neck in a curiously kinked position with crest erect and legs dangling (Meyerriecks 1960). This species also adopts the attitude typical of bitterns: a frozen posture with head and bill thrust skyward and neck elongated.

Chestnut-bellied Heron: *Agamia agami*
Agami Heron   **Plate 1(6)**

Habitat and status. A rare visitor to Trinidad, frequenting rivers or pools within or bordering lowland forest; also recorded in August and September in Caroni swamp. Not recorded this century, except for sight records (Herklots) of individuals seen in October 1956 at Caroni, in January 1958 at Nariva and at Laventille swamp in August 1961. (Specimens: AMNH.)

Range. Mexico S to Peru, Bolivia and Brazil.

Description. 28 in. *Adult:* mainly dark green above, scapulars, sides of neck and lower underparts chestnut; crown and sides of head black, long plumed crest bluish; breast grayish; bill very long and narrow, mostly yellowish; legs greenish, rather short. *Immature:* mainly dark brown above, streaked brown and white below.

Measurements. Wing: 2 males 277, 280mm.

Cattle Egret: *Bubulcus ibis*
Buff-backed Heron; *Ardeola ibis;* "Tick Bird"

Habitat and status. A very common resident in Trinidad, inhabiting savannahs and marshes by day, and roosting in swamps, usually mangroves. Rather rarely feeds in saltwater areas and mudflats. First recorded in Trinidad in 1951, fairly common by 1955, now the commonest, most conspicuous heron in the island. Fairly common in SW Tobago, where it first appeared in the early 1960s. (Specimens: TRVL.)

Banding status. Sixty-five nestlings were banded in July 1964 in Caroni swamp. To date 3 of these have been recovered, all in 1966–67, 1 nearby, the other 2 near San Fernando 30 miles to the south.

Range and subspecies. S Europe, Africa, Asia, Australia and America from Brazil N to SE Canada; *B. i. ibis* (Linnaeus) ranges from S Europe and W Asia through Africa; it was first reliably reported in the New World in the 1930s (though there is evidence that it may have been noticed first in the late nineteenth century); it spread from Surinam and Guyana through N South America and the West Indies, and is now established through E North America. No one can be sure how it first reached the New World, but the recent occurrence in the West Indies of several herons banded in Europe makes it probable that the Cattle Egret arrived by natural means.

Description. 21 in. White with conspicuously *yellow bill;* legs vary from yellow to olive to blackish. At the beginning of the breeding season the crest, breast and back plumes are buff or salmon-coloured, the bill becomes carmine red, tipped yellow, and legs bright yellow or reddish. Has a stouter-necked appearance than the other white herons. *Downy young:* has dark gray legs with green or yellowish undersurface and toes; bill blackish tipped yellow, and iris pale gray.

Voice. Usually silent, but a harsh croak is often uttered at the roost or nest, and occasionally by aggressive birds when feeding.

Food. In Trinidad mainly insects, especially grasshoppers and crickets, also spiders, frogs and lizards. Nearly all feeding is in freshwater areas. There is little evidence that ticks form an important part of the diet. In USA there are rare instances of predation on exhausted small birds.

Nesting. Breeds regularly in large mixed colonial heronries in the mangroves of Caroni and South Oropouche swamps. Main nesting period is soon after the start of the "wet season" in June, but breeding recorded in all months from November to August. Two seasons in one year have been found in Guyana (Lowe-McConnell 1967); this may well be happening in Trinidad, though not necessarily with the same individuals. Colonies sometimes contain over 1000 nests. The nest, built mainly by the female with material supplied by the male, is typical for herons, built from a few to 30 ft above water. Known to use abandoned Scarlet Ibis nests. The clutch is 1–5 (usually 3) plain blue eggs, av. 43.4 × 33.4mm (103 Florida eggs); incubation, by both sexes, lasts about 24 days. The young hatch consecutively. I have never found more than 3 chicks in a nest, and one of these is always considerably smaller and weaker. Chick mortality is high, especially in the early stages after leaving the nest. First flights are made after about 1 month. Birds have been known to breed when 1 yr old (Siegfried 1966).

Behaviour. Characteristically feeds beside cattle, obtaining insects disturbed by the grazing animals, perhaps twice as many as when not associated with cattle (Heatwole 1965). The egrets accompany the animals singly or in groups, occasionally even perching on their backs. I have seen an egret balancing precariously on the head of a goat! Sometimes, however, egrets will feed in large groups without cattle, taking advantage of an abundant food supply, often following ploughs or mowing machines. They roost and nest mainly in mangrove, usually in brackish areas. Even so, food obtained in freshwater savannahs has to be carried a mile or more to the nestlings in the brackish swamps. In the Roussilac swamp I have seen a colony of 200 nests in mangrove on the sea-edge. The birds fly to their roost in the evening after assembling into sizeable flocks up to 200.

Courtship display mainly resembles that of other herons, including bill-snapping, twig-shaking, neck-stretching and erecting all plumes. While the male performs these aggressive displays, the female approaches him from behind, lands on his back and subdues his aggression through repeated blows on the head (Lancaster 1970). Sometimes 2 females subdue 1 male and a polygamous bond is formed, but these do not last; the eventual pair bond is maintained by both birds performing the aggressive displays. The birds are much less wary of humans at the nest than other heron species, returning rapidly after disturbance. This is very noticeable at the Caroni colonies, after low-flying aeroplanes have passed.

Notes. Anxiety has been expressed in Trinidad over the Cattle Egret's phenomenal success, that the species may adversely affect indigenous species such as the Scarlet Ibis and Snowy Egret. But the Cattle Egret is not a serious competitor with any of these large wading birds. Only at the nesting site do its requirements overlap those of the other species; but in fact they are more aggressive than it is, as I have noted many times, losing ground by their greater shyness and consequent absence from the nest. The Cattle Egret's food demands are unique among herons in Trinidad, and incidentally of great benefit to agriculture.

Black-crowned Night-Heron: *Nycticorax nycticorax*
"Crabier Batali"

Habitat and status. A fairly common resident in mangrove swamps in Trinidad, less common in Tobago. Mainly nocturnal, moving out at dusk to feed in the swamps and adjacent marshes. (Specimens: AMNH.)

Range and subspecies. Cosmopolitan, except for Australia; *N. n. hoactli* (Gmelin) ranges through North America and Central and N South America.

Description. 25 in. *Adult:* a chunky, short-legged heron, with mainly black crown and back, gray wings, lower back and tail, and white forehead, occipital plumes and underparts; bill short and black. *Immature:* grayish brown, streaked and spotted with white (see also Yellow-crowned Night-Heron).

Measurements. Wing: 2 males 285, 293mm; 2 females 280, 300mm.

Voice. An explosive *quock* or *wok-wok*.

Food. Small fish, crustaceans and insects (in USA); also frogs, rodents and the young of other birds, especially herons and terns.

Nesting. Has been found breeding in all months from April to September in the Caroni swamp. The nest is a more bulky structure of twigs than those of other herons; it is situated in mangrove 3–25 ft above water, usually several nests together. Clutch is 2 or 3 pale blue-green eggs, av. 50.25 × 35.5mm (5). Incubation is by both sexes (in USA) for about 25 days. Young will leave the nest when disturbed, at about 3 wk, but are inclined to stay and defend it vigorously (Teal 1965). They finally fly at about 6 wk.

Behaviour. Birds are prone to disturbance during the day at their roosting grounds in the Caroni Sanctuary. They fly off, calling loudly, and disappear into the mangroves. Threat and courtship displays at the nest include a low crouch with horizontal bill, erection of plumes and bill-snapping; also stretching the head and neck up, forward and down, finishing with an odd call which sounds like a snap and a buzz.

Notes. Although not common, the two night-heron species may be hunted during the open season (with a bag limit of 5 per person per day).

Yellow-crowned Night-Heron: *Nyctanassa violacea*
"Crabier à Croissant"; *Nycticorax violacea*

Habitat and status. A fairly common resident in Trinidad, usually frequenting mangrove swamps, also found by reservoirs and rivers. (Specimens: AMNH, BM) Also resident in Tobago, not uncommon in swamps, by streams and reservoirs; also along the seacoast and on offshore islands. (Specimens: AMNH, YPM, LM, BM.)

Range and subspecies. USA S through Central America to Peru and Brazil, also West Indies and Galápagos Islands. *N. v. cayennensis* (Gmelin) ranges from Panama through coastal areas of N and E South America, including Trinidad; it is darker than the nominate race. *N. v. bancrofti* (Huey) ranges through the West Indies S to Tobago, also the Pacific coast to Mexico and Baja California; it is paler, with a heavier bill. The nominate race, fairly dark and with a slender bill, may also occur on Tobago, having been recorded in several West Indies islands S to Barbados and the Grenadines.

Description. 25 in. *Adult:* generally pale gray; head black with pale crown, occipital plumes and cheek patch. *Immature:* much like immature Black-crowned Night-Heron, but darker brown, spots on back smaller and legs longer; in flight some shank shows beyond the tail. Generally a less chunky bird.

Measurements. Wings: *cayennensis*, 2 males 289, 292mm; 1 female 295mm; *bancrofti*, 2 males 273, 279mm; 3 females 272, 275, 290mm. Weight: *bancrofti*, 1 female 662gm*.

Voice. A hoarse *quak*, higher-pitched than the call of the Black-crowned Night-Heron.

Food. Mainly crustaceans, including fiddler crabs.

Nesting. In Trinidad breeds in mangrove; nests found in April, May and August (B/S), 2–3 light blue eggs, av. 47.5 × 35mm (5). Nests in Tobago have been in forest bordering fresh water, several found in March; av. 50 × 36mm (2). Generally nests are harder to find than those of other herons, so breeding biology is not well known.

Behaviour. More diurnal than *Nycticorax*, birds being often seen feeding at low tide in Caroni swamp, especially between 5 P.M. and dusk. More solitary than gregarious, though I once saw 12 individuals scattered over a single large mudflat.

Rufescent Tiger-Heron: *Tigrisoma lineatum*
Tiger Bittern; Banded Tiger-Heron   **Plate 1(4)**

Habitat and status. A rare inhabitant of lowland swampy forest in Trinidad, such as Bush-Bush Forest, Nariva swamp, Vega de Oropouche, also recorded in Caroni marshes. Probably resident; recent sight records from November to January, also June and August. (Specimens: YPM, PSM.)

Range and subspecies. Central America S from Honduras to Paraguay and Argentina; *T. l. lineatum* (Boddaert) ranges S to Peru and Amazonian Brazil.

Description. 27 in. In shape resembles a bittern. *Adult:* head, neck and sides of breast chestnut, barred black (though this barring is absent in older individuals); upperparts blackish with buff vermiculation; underparts white with broad brown streaks. *Immature:* neck, upperparts and sides of breast coarsely barred and spotted with black and tawny; mainly whitish below.

Voice. A loud, deep *quok-quok*, like the call of a night-heron; Friedmann and Smith (1950) describe it as "a loud, explosive *bao*"; it is said to resemble the call of a jaguar or the lowing of cattle.

Food. Fish and aquatic insects.

Nesting. Léotaud found the species common enough to be considered a probable resident, and B/S believed it the owner of 2 bluish white eggs found in a Caroni reed-marsh in September. But their measurements are far smaller than authentic eggs of this species found by Haverschmidt (1962b) in Surinam, where 2 bluish white eggs, spotted pale violet, averaged 56.75 × 43.2mm. Three clutches each contained 1 egg or chick. The nests were flimsy stick structures placed high in immortelle trees.

Behaviour. Léotaud believed this heron to feed at night. Certainly Blake (1950) found it very furtive in Guyana, avoiding flight over open water. When disturbed it would "freeze", but without elevating the bill. Birds I disturbed in Nariva swamp flew off into thick cover. W. G. Downs noticed a habit of nervously flicking its tail up and down. Friedmann and Smith in Venezuela found that "when approached the bird customarily extends its neck straight out, compressing all its feathers". When flushed it called loudly.

Stripe-backed Bittern: *Ixobrychus involucris*
Variegated Bittern; "Small Chuck"   **Plate 1(5)**

Habitat and status. An uncommon and local resident in Trinidad, recorded only in Caroni marshes and Oropouche Lagoon, favouring reed-beds and sedge. (Specimens: ANSP, YPM, TRVL.)

Range. Throughout most of South America.

Description. 12 in. Generally yellowish buff with black coronal streak; back striped with black and rufous; wings brown with chestnut tips to primaries. Paler than Least Bittern.

Food. Small fish, crustaceans and insects.

Nesting. Breeding recorded from July to September (B/S), moult in January. The nest is small, made of reeds and weed stems placed among reeds just above water level. The clutch is 3 bright yellowish green eggs, av. 31.0 × 24.5mm (6).

Behaviour. I have found this species hard to flush. When disturbed it adopts the "freezing" bittern posture with elongated neck and bill skyward. Flight weak and invariably short.

Least Bittern: *Ixobrychus exilis*
"Small Chuck"; "Susianna"

Habitat and status. A fairly common resident of swamps and marshes, mostly freshwater, in Trinidad. (Specimens: AMNH, YPM, TRVL.)

Range and subspecies. Through most of America from S Canada to Paraguay and N Argentina; *I. e. erythromelas* (Vieillot) ranges from Panama and Colombia through E South America to Argentina; it differs from the nominate northern form by having the side of the head chestnut instead of buff.

Description. 11 in. *Adult male:* generally blackish above, but nape, cheeks and greater wing-coverts chestnut, other coverts buff; underparts pale buff with a V-shaped black patch across breast; bill, lores and legs yellow. *Female:* as male, but dark brown above, streaked with buff below. *Immature:* as female, but with short, dark markings on breast and wing-coverts; feathers of upperparts tipped buff.

Measurements. Wing: 2 males 106, 113mm; 2 females 108, 113mm; 1 unsexed 115mm. Weight: 1 male 78.5gm.

Voice. Most commonly a churring *woh*, also in alarm a loud *kock;* various other calls recorded in USA.

Food. Mainly fish and crustaceans (in USA).

Nesting. Breeds from July to October in Caroni swamp. B/S found all nests in reeds, but 2 of 4 found by me were placed in the low fork of mangroves and constructed of twigs. The normal clutch is 3 eggs, buffy white, av. 32.0 × 24.5mm (6). Incubation, by both parents, lasts about 17 days. Young leave the nest temporarily after only a few days, but return during first 2 wk.

Behaviour. Though usually skulking in cover, birds are very prone to fly a short way when disturbed. At other times they will adopt the usual bittern stance, with bill pointed to the sky, and not move until almost touched. One bird I approached near its nest displayed threateningly at me with opened wings, bowing and stretching. When I released a captured bird on the ground, instead of flying off, it attacked me with its bill three times before backing away.

Pinnated Bittern: *Botaurus pinnatus*
Plate 1(7)

Habitat and status. A rather uncommon resident of Trinidad, inhabiting dense reed-beds and freshwater marshes. (Specimens: AMNH, ANSP.)

Range. Throughout Central and South America from tropical Mexico to Argentina.

Description. 25 in. Generally dark brown, finely barred with buff and black; crown black, neck, wings and lower back barred buff and blackish; upper back mottled black, buff and rufous; underparts pale with rufous streaks; bill thick, yellowish.

Measurements. Wing: 1 male 323mm.

Voice. Known to "boom" in the nesting season; in alarm a deep croak.

Food. Fish, amphibians, snakes and insects (in Surinam, Haverschmidt 1968a).

Nesting. Breeds during July to October (B/S). The nest is situated in reed-beds or grassy swamps, just above the water level. Clutch 2 or 3 olive eggs, av. 49.5 × 36.25mm (5).

Behaviour. When feeding or adopting a protective pose, this bittern much resembles European and North American members of this genus; nearly vertical bill posture is often seen. Herklots (1961) observed a bird creeping along with its body extended horizontally. Rather slow to flush.

Notes. Although fully protected by law, the bittern is sometimes hunted. Hunters regard it as "a kind of crabier or night-heron".

COCHLEARIIDAE: Boat-billed Herons

The only species in this family somewhat resembles a Black-crowned Night-Heron, but it has an enormously wide, flat bill, used more as a scoop than a spear. Its habits are largely nocturnal, for which its large eyes are well adapted. Many authors merge this family with the Ardeidae. (1)

Boat-billed Heron: *Cochlearius cochlearius*
"Crabier Bec Plat"   **Plate 1(2)**

Habitat and status. A rather rare and local resident of mangrove swamps in Trinidad; not often seen except at nests; mainly nocturnal, roosting colonially by day. (Specimens: AMNH, TRVL.)

Banding status. Three nestlings were banded in Caroni swamp in October 1965, and one nearly adult bird at Pointe-a-Pierre in November 1965. No recoveries to date.

Range and subspecies. Mexico S to Peru and Argentina: *C. c. cochlearius* (Linnaeus) is the South American form, ranging from E Panama south and east.

Description. 21 in. *Adult:* crown, long, rather bushy crest and upper back black; forehead, throat and breast white; lower back and wings pale gray; lower underparts rufous with black flanks; bill black, very broad. *Immature:* no crest; upperparts generally chestnut brown, underparts whitish tinged brown. *Downy young:* upper bill black, lower yellow, with greenish yellow legs.

Measurements. Wing: 3 males 274, 274, 288mm; 1 female 275mm; 1 unsexed 280mm.

Voice. A deep croak; also a high-pitched *pee-pee-pee*.

Food. Fish, crustaceans and insects.

Nesting. Breeding recorded from June to October (14 nests). The frail nest of twigs is situated in mangroves 6–25 ft above the water. Nesting is frequently colonial; I have found up to 6 nests together. The clutch is 1–3, usually 2, bluish white eggs, sometimes faintly spotted with red at the thicker end, av. 49.7 × 35.9mm (10). Both parents incubate. At the age of 2–3 wk young birds will move from the nest if disturbed, but not far.

Behaviour. Feeds entirely by night; if disturbed during the day it will immediately conceal itself amidst dense vegetation. At the nest displaying adults nibble at each other's heads or necks, erecting the crest feathers (Lowe-McConnell 1967). A captive bird in Brazil performed a "forward stretch display" (Rand 1966), with the crest spread out like a fan and strong contrast showing between the black bill, crest and flanks and the white forehead and neck. When approached near the nest young birds make a curious popping sound with their bills as they snap at the intruder.

CICONIIDAE: Storks

These are very large wading birds with long necks and legs. Unlike herons they always fly with neck extended and in flight alternately flap and glide. They frequent swamps and savannahs. (2)

Jabiru Stork: *Jabiru mycteria*

Habitat and status. A single record, of an adult seen at Buccoo, Tobago, between May and October 1988 (D. Rooks et al.).

Range. Mexico S through the Neotropics to Argentina, but local in distribution. Not normally found in the West Indies, but a vagrant has reached Grenada (Fr. Devas).

Description. 4.5 ft. *Adult:* Huge, all-white stork with bare black head and neck, the lower neck bright red; grotesquely shaped bill and legs black. *Immature:* brownish gray.

Wood Stork: *Mycteria americana*
American Wood-Ibis

Habitat and status. Formerly an occasional visitor from July to October to swamps and marshes in Trinidad. Not recorded since 1942. (No specimen, but collected by Léotaud.) Mentioned by Kirk for Tobago, but this may refer to the Jabiru Stork.

Range. Intermittently from SE USA and the Greater Antilles through Central America to Peru and Argentina.

Description. 3.5 ft. All white with black flight feathers and tail; head and upper neck bare and dark; bill long, thick, decurved.

Voice. Usually silent; hisses at the nest.

Food. Reptiles, according to Léotaud, but in USA and Venezuela mainly small fish.

Behaviour. Gregarious in small flocks, often soaring like vultures or perching in trees. A study in Florida (Kahl & Peacock 1963) has shown that Wood Storks feed by probing in muddy water with their bills. When the lower mandible touches the prey, the bill can be closed within 0.025 sec. They also use foot-stirring to drive fish out of cover.

THRESKIORNITHIDAE: Ibises and Spoonbills

Smaller than storks, birds of this family are distinguished by their long, slender, decurved bills. They fly with outstretched neck and are often found in large flocks. They inhabit swamps and marshes. (4)

White Ibis: *Eudocimus albus*

Habitat and status. A casual visitor to Trinidad; there are 6 records, all from Caroni swamp, on 19 July 1964, 17 August 1964, 9 March 1976, 8 November 1977, 20 February 1979 and August 1985. (No specimen.)

Range. Along the coasts of S USA, Middle America, W Greater Antilles and N South America.

Description. 23 in. *Adult:* all white, with 4 longest primaries tipped black; bill, bare face and legs red. *Immature:* almost indistinguishable from immature Scarlet Ibis, but head and neck mottled brown and white.

Notes. Zahl (1950) and Ramo and Busto (1987) have found Scarlet and White ibises interbreeding in the Venezuelan llanos. Hybrids have also occurred in captivity in Florida (Bundy 1965), but it is still not clear whether the two *Eudocimus* species should be considered separate or merely colour phases which are almost entirely segregated geographically.

Scarlet Ibis: *Eudocimus ruber*
"Flamingo"; "Flamant"   **Plate 29(4)**

Habitat and status. Resident for much of the year in the Caroni swamp mangroves in some thousands; also known in the mangroves of Oropouche, Roussilac and Los Blanquisales, rare in Nariva swamp. Considerable changes have taken place during the last 30 yr, and ibises no longer nest at Caroni, as they did between 1953 and 1970; and breeding birds migrate to Venezuela (approx. March–August). Outside the breeding season the ibises feed on mudflats, amongst the mangroves and occasionally in freshwater marshes; at night they congregate at traditional mangrove roosts. (Specimens: AMNH, YPM, TRVL.)

Banding status. Fifty-four nestlings were banded in Caroni swamp in 1963, 77 in 1965. Two recoveries were recorded, one still in the Caroni swamp 5 months later, the other 1 yr later on the coast of the Gulf of Cariaco, NE Venezuela, 170 miles W of the Caroni swamp.

Range. N South America from Colombia to NE Brazil, especially in Venezuelan llanos (Luthin 1984); casual in Ecuador, Central America, S USA (where also recently introduced in small numbers), Jamaica, Grenada and Tobago.

Description. 23 in. *Adult:* brilliant scarlet all over, the 4 longest primaries tipped black; legs, bill and bare face pink, the bill usually blackish in the breeding season. In captivity, deprived of carotenoids, adults usually lose the brilliance of their scarlet plumage and fade to a dull pink. *Immature:* grayish brown above, with white rump and underparts (locally known as Black or Gray Ibis). Between 6–12 months the plumage gradually changes to pink (locally "Tawodé") and then scarlet.

Measurements. Eight males: wing: 260–275mm (266); weight: 710–770gm (741). Thirteen females: wing: 231–262mm (246); weight: 505–640gm (588). The male's bill and legs are also significantly longer than the female's.

Voice. A light, high-pitched, squeaky *tior-tior,* plaintive but more musical than herons' calls. Only heard at the nest, roost or when disturbed. Young birds call a faint, shrilling *ssiu.*

Food. Small crustaceans, usually fiddler crabs (whose larger claw they discard if too large), small fish, spawn, insects and algae. Birds usually probe for food in the mud; when caught, the food is gradually worked up the bill from the tip.

Nesting. Formerly bred colonially in Caroni swamp for 2–3 months between April and October, moult in October and November. Start of nesting season varied considerably since protection of the breeding colony began in 1953 (ffrench & Haverschmidt 1970). About 2500 nests were counted in 5 acres in June 1963. The nests, often built in groups a few feet apart, are frail structures of dry twigs placed on mangrove forks, or where 2 branches cross, usually 8–35 ft above ground; occasionally a nest is built on mangrove roots a few inches above high-tide level. The eggs are 2–3 (rarely 4), dull grayish olive with brown spots and splotches, av. 55.3 × 37.6mm (14). Incubation, by both sexes, takes about 23 days. I have hardly ever found more than 2 chicks in a clutch to survive. At about 12 days they begin moving away from the nest and congregate in the upper branches where they are fed. They use wings as well as bills and feet as levers to assist them in climbing. First flights occur between 4 and 6 wk.

Behaviour. Extremely gregarious when feeding, nesting or at the roost. Commonly associates with herons at the roost, tending to perch higher in the mangroves than the latter. At the nest birds are wary and if disturbed will not return for perhaps half an hour. Low-flying aircraft sometimes cause a disturbance. In the Caroni swamp the roost site varies little, and flocks of up to 200 assemble after 5 P.M. flying to the roost in an irregular V-formation.

Notes. The Scarlet Ibis was formerly hunted in Trinidad, but in 1953 it received legal protection during the breeding season and a sanctuary was created for the species in the Caroni swamp. Since 1965 it has been totally protected by law. Many theories have been put forward to explain why the ibises abandoned the nesting colony in Trinidad, including ecological change, pollution, poaching, etc., none of them yet proven. My own view is that this wary species is most likely to have been disturbed from the nest-site by excessive and often noisy tourist traffic. The roost, where some birds are present throughout the year, has constituted a great tourist attraction, and not without reason. As each flock glides in, travelling at considerable speed, the observer receives the impression of the birds' vivid, almost luminous, scarlet contrasted sharply with the green mangroves or the blue sky. The roosting flock is gradually increased, then occasionally some alarm causes the entire gathering of some thousands to rise up, wheel slowly in the air, perhaps several times, and settle again. It is an unforgettable sight, rivalling for sheer spectacle the mass movement of any other species in the world. At independence in 1962 the Trinidad government chose the Scarlet Ibis to be the national bird of Trinidad, and it is figured on the country's coat of arms.

Glossy Ibis: *Plegadis falcinellus*
"Black Ibis"

Habitat and status. An occasional visitor in small numbers to Caroni swamp and other wetlands along Trinidad's W coast, also recorded at Buccoo, Tobago. (No specimen.)

Range. This species has long bred in extreme SE USA and in the tropical and warm temperate zones of the Old World. In the past several decades it has had a great breeding expansion along the E coast of USA and the West Indies; individuals considered migrants or wanderers have been recorded in Costa Rica, Panama, Colombia, Venezuela and Guadeloupe, and the species is now apparently breeding in Venezuela.

Description. 21 in. *Adult:* head, neck, mantle and underparts dark chestnut, appearing black at a distance; rest of upperparts glossed dark green and purple. In post-breeding plumage head and neck streaked whitish. Bill dark brown; iris brown; in breeding season facial skin slaty blue with pale bluish white border (slaty thereafter); legs gray. (Note: in the closely related *Plegadis chihi*, the White-faced Ibis, which has been suspected as present in Venezuela, in the breeding season facial skin is all *red* bordered by a white line of feathers, iris red, legs reddish to pinkish gray.) *Immature:* blackish brown with little gloss, head and neck streaked whitish.

Roseate Spoonbill: *Ajaia ajaja*

Habitat and status. A regular visitor in very small numbers (up to 16) to Caroni swamp in Trinidad from April to September, earliest April 8, latest September 23; recorded at Pointe-a-Pierre reservoirs in May. There are two recent records from Buccoo, Tobago. (Specimens: AMNH.)

Range. Throughout N and E South America, the Greater Antilles, Central America and extreme S USA.

Description. 30 in. Mainly pink with carmine patch on wing and tail; neck and upper back white; head and throat bare, greenish yellow; bill pale gray, long, broad and flattened at the tip. *Immature:* pale pink with white head and neck, head becoming bare as age increases.

Measurements. Wing: 1 male 350mm; 1 female 345mm.

Voice. A gentle quacking when disturbed.

Food. Mainly fish and crustaceans, also large beetles in Venezuela (Friedmann & Smith 1950).

Behaviour. Occasionally very tame, feeding alone or in small groups. Flies in formation. When feeding, the birds move their heads vigorously from side to side with a sweeping motion. They roost communally, favouring a particular mangrove clump in the Caroni Swamp Sanctuary.

PHOENICOPTERIDAE: Flamingoes

This family of birds with extraordinarily long necks and legs and distinctive, thick, decurved bills is distributed locally in both the New and Old worlds. They frequent seacoasts and brackish areas, feeding on tiny marine organisms. (1)

Greater Flamingo: *Phoenicopterus ruber*
American Flamingo

Habitat and status. Only three records from Trinidad, of immatures at Balandra beach on 12 April 1980 (G. White) and at Brickfield mudflats on 29 May and 20 August 1990 (G. Gomes). Previous reports of the species may have been confused by the local name for the Scarlet Ibis. (No specimen.)

Range. In the New World from Bahamas, Yucatan and Greater Antilles S to Colombia, Venezuela, the Guianas and N Brazil, also Galápagos and other islands off South America. Also locally distributed in Europe, Africa and W Asia.

Description. 4 ft. *Adult:* unmistakable, generally rosy pink with black-tipped wings. *Immature:* grayish white, with some brown. Distinguished from Scarlet Ibis by colour, bill shape and much longer neck and legs.

ANHIMIDAE: Screamers

These birds are heavy-bodied with large feet and small heads and bills. They frequent marshes and savannahs, nesting on the ground and feeding on grasses. They are sometimes seen soaring at a great height and resembling vultures. (1)

Figure 16. Horned Screamer

Horned Screamer: *Anhima cornuta*
"Wild Turkey"   **Figure 16**

Habitat and status. Formerly a resident in Nariva swamp in Trinidad, but records sparse since 1910. Individual birds, including immatures, were reported in 1936 and again in 1964, but these require confirmation. Definitely extirpated now. (No specimen, but known to Léotaud.)

Range. Through most of South America S to Peru, Bolivia and Brazil.

Description. 26 in. A very heavy turkey-like bird, black with crown and nape speckled white; white patch on wing-coverts, lower underparts and underwing white; a 2–3 in. horn-like quill projects from forehead, and there are sharp spurs on the wings.

Voice. A loud, far-carrying *mo-hoo-ca.*

ANATIDAE: Ducks

The general shape and habits of ducks are similar all over the world. In Trinidad they inhabit swamps and marshes, but of the following list most species are visitors, several of them accidental. With constant persecution by hunters, both in and often out of season, and a gradual programme of marsh-draining, it seems unlikely that the few breeding species will be permitted to survive. It may be of interest to add that additional species reported to me by hunters, with very varying degrees of reliability, include Orinoco Goose, Northern Pintail, Gadwall, and a "merganser". (16)

Fulvous Whistling-Duck: *Dendrocygna bicolor*
Fulvous Tree-Duck; "Wichichi"; "Ouikiki"

Habitat and status. An occasional visitor in variable numbers to Trinidad swamps, sometimes breeding. Flocks of up to 400 birds occur some years; usually smaller numbers are seen. A single bird seen at Bloody Bay, Tobago on 5 May 1975 (H. Beegel). (Specimens: ANSP.)

Range. S USA, Mexico and South America, now extending its range into Cuba and the Greater Antilles; casual in Panama and Central America; also Africa and S Asia.

Description. 19 in. Head and underparts rich brown, nape and upperparts black, mantle barred with rufous; bill and legs bluish gray. All tree-ducks have longer necks and legs than other ducks.

Voice. A high-pitched, rather raucous, double whistle.

Food. Aquatic vegetation.

Nesting. Occasionally breeds in marshes during wet season; the nest is made of dead leaves and situated on the ground. The clutch is up to 6 white eggs, av. 52.5 × 42.0mm (2).

Behaviour. Pairs and single birds are commonly seen during the breeding season; non-breeding birds tend to gather into large flocks.

White-faced Whistling-Duck: *Dendrocygna viduata*
White-faced Tree-Duck; "Ouikiki"; "Wichichi"   **Figure 17**

Habitat and status. Formerly resident in Trinidad swamps, now a rare visitor. A few recent records, possibly affected by the captive breeding programme at Pointe-a-Pierre. (No specimen, but collected by Léotaud.)

Range. Costa Rica and Panama irregularly S through South America; casual in West Indies; also Africa.

Description. 17 in. *Adult:* face and neck white, nape and a band across throat black; upper back and breast chestnut; wings, tail, lower back and abdomen black; sides barred black and white; bill dark gray with pale band. *Immature:* head largely gray, with some rufous on face; upperparts as adult, underparts light gray with dark bars.

Voice. A thin, clear, high-pitched whistle, 2 or 3 notes together.

Food. Aquatic vegetation; Friedmann and Smith (1950) record seeds.

O'Neill
72

Figure 17. White-faced Whistling-Duck

Nesting. B/S record breeding from August to October. Nests are made of dead leaves and situated on marshy ground. Clutch is up to 9 white eggs, tinged with cream, av. 47 × 37mm. No other details.

Black-bellied Whistling-Duck: *Dendrocygna autumnalis*
Black-bellied (or Grey-breasted, or Red-billed) Tree-Duck; "Wichichi"; "Ouikiki"

Habitat and status. Resident locally in swamps and marshes such as Caroni, Nariva and Oropouche, also Buccoo, Tobago; some local migration evident; commonest during wet season. (Specimen: AMNH.)

Banding status. Between January 1967 and September 1975, 243 young birds were reared in captivity at the Pointe-a-Pierre Wildfowl Trust, banded and released; 11 others were released at Speyside, Tobago. To date 6 Trinidad birds have been recovered, 1 from Biche, 1 from Oropouche and 2 from Caroni swamp; 1 of the Tobago birds was recovered at Charlotteville.

Range and subspecies. S USA and Middle America S through South America to Argentina; *D. a. discolor* (Sclater & Salvin) is the South American race, ranging S from Colombia.

Description. 21 in. *Adult:* crown brown, sides of head and neck, lower breast gray; upper breast, nape and back rufous brown, lower back, abdomen, flight feathers and tail black, large white patch on wing-coverts; bill coral red;

legs pink. *Immature:* similar but rufous is replaced by grayish brown; abdomen grayish; bill and legs duller.

Measurements. Wing: 1 male 233mm; 1 unsexed 220mm. Weight: 1 unsexed 410gm.

Voice. Typically a high sandpiper-like series of whistles, like the Fulvous and White-faced whistling-ducks, *weeiss-chi-chi.*

Food. Aquatic vegetation; they also feed in ricefields, where some damage is done.

Nesting. Formerly bred regularly (B/S), now occasionally in Caroni and Nariva swamps during the "wet season". Recently nested during November in the Oropouche Lagoon ricefields. Nest is on the ground or in a treestump. Clutch is up to 14 white eggs, av. 48 × 37mm (10). Incubation period about 28 days; both parents incubate and attend the young, which in downy plumage are striped brown and yellow.

Behaviour. This species, like *D. bicolor* and *D. autumnalis,* frequently perches in trees, usually in small groups, also flocks on water. Much of its feeding is done at night. Haverschmidt (1947) describes how a parent bird in Surinam with newly hatched young showed "injury-feigning" when approached. It splashed in the water as though crippled. When in danger both adults and young dive.

Notes. Some years ago, when this duck was common in Trinidad, most hunters disdained smaller ducks, such as Blue-winged Teal. When large flocks did damage to the ricefields NW of the Nariva swamp, hunters were requested by the government to assist in ridding the country of the "pest". Thus with increased opportunities for hunting and the marsh drainage programme this duck, among others, became quite scarce. As a conservation measure aviculturists at Pointe-a-Pierre bred a number of whistling-ducks in captivity, the original wild birds being captured as ducklings in about 1953. Some of their descendants now live in captivity at Pointe-a-Pierre, while a proportion were regularly released, totalling about 350 young birds between 1967 and 1981.

Snow Goose: *Chen coerulescens*

Habitat and status. An adult white-phase bird was recorded at Caroni in December 1975 (C. Green et al.), and four immature blue-phase birds were seen in nearby marshes on 30 December 1984 (many observers). There had been earlier, somewhat unreliable, reports of geese shot by hunters in Oropouche Lagoon. (No specimen.)

Range. Breeds across arctic North America, wintering S to Mexico and the Gulf states, casual in Belize and West Indies. Although the species is popular in collections, I have been unable to trace any record of "escapes" locally to account for the above records, which I am treating as of truly wild birds.

Description. 30 in. *White phase:* all white with black primaries. *Blue* *phase: adult:* Head and neck white, upperparts and most of underparts gray, with white upper- and under-tail-coverts, and wing-coverts paler gray; bill and legs pink. *Immature:* as adult, but generally browner, head and neck dusky; bare parts darker.

[Mallard: *Anas platyrhynchos*]

Habitat and status. Possibly a rare visitor to Trinidad and Tobago. Herklots (1961) states without details that birds were "seen and shot in Caroni Swamp in 1958." I have heard from hunters that the "Mallard" occurs. Kirk (1883) records it for Tobago. There may be confusion between this species and the Northern Pintail (*A. acuta*). I consider the present evidence to be unsatisfactory, especially in view of the species' known range.

Range. Through North America, wintering S to Mexico, rarely Cuba, casual in Panama, Bahamas, Puerto Rico and Virgin Islands; also Europe and Asia.

Description. 24 in. *Male:* glossy green head and neck, white collar, dark chestnut breast, rump black; violet-blue speculum on rear of wing, bordered by 2 white bars; otherwise grayish; bill greenish yellow. *Female:* generally brown, mottled; wing as male, tail whitish; bill orange and dusky, legs orange.

Voice. The male calls a thin raspy *weep-weep;* the female quacks.

Green-winged Teal: *Anas crecca*

Habitat and status. A rare winter visitor from the north to swamps in Tobago; 1 filmed at Friendship Estate in early 1958 (Darnton), and 1 seen at Bon Accord in February 1969 (M. Baird). Kirk mentions the species, but it is perhaps significant that he does not list the much commoner Blue-winged Teal. (No specimen.) There have been reports from hunters of its occurrence in Trinidad.

Range. Breeds in N temperate zones of America, Europe and Asia, wintering S into tropical areas; *A. c. carolinensis* (Gmelin) breeds in N North America, wintering S to Honduras and the West Indies, casual in Colombia.

Description. 14 in. *Male:* head rufous brown with broad green stripe behind eye; generally gray with vertical white mark on body in front of wing; green speculum on rear of wing; underparts pale. *Female:* mottled brown with green speculum. Both teals can be distinguished from larger ducks by their extremely rapid flight as well as their size.

American Wigeon: *Anas americana*
Baldpate; "White-belly"; "Canvasback"; *Mareca americana*

Habitat and status. A regular winter visitor from the north to swamps of both islands, some years occurring in quite considerable numbers. A large flock of up to 144 birds wintered on Pointe-a-Pierre reservoir from January to April 1959. Earliest date early December, latest 2 May. (Specimens: AMNH, TRVL.)

Range. Throughout North America, wintering S to Colombia, Venezuela and the West Indies.

Description. 20 in. *Male:* generally brown, with white crown, green patch on sides of head, and large white patch on fore part of wing; breast dark, contrasting with white abdomen. *Female:* generally ruddy brown with gray head; wing patches pale.

Measurements. Wing: 1 male 252mm.

Voice. A shrill triple whistle.

White-cheeked Pintail: *Anas bahamensis*
Bahama Pintail   **Figure 18**

Habitat and status. An uncommon resident in swamps of both islands, occurring sometimes in flocks of 20–30 birds, as at Buccoo, Tobago. (No specimen but sight records numerous and eggs collected.)

Range and subspecies. Throughout South America, also Bahamas islands and West Indies S to Guadeloupe; this is probably the nominate form, ranging from Bahamas S to Colombia and Brazil.

Description. 17 in. Generally mottled brown, crown dark brown; cheeks and throat white, wing speculum green; tail buff, pointed; bill red at base.

Voice. A rather faint squeak (male); the female quacks.

Food. Aquatic vegetation.

Nesting. Breeds in the Caroni swamp from August to November (B/S), also nests reported from Friendship, Tobago. Nests have been found among mangrove roots, merely a few leaves being added to the site. Clutch is up to 10 eggs, cream, becoming darker with staining; size of eggs 50–54mm × 34–38mm. Incubation period is about 25 days.

Behaviour. In display the male utters a strange, subdued, honking call, accompanied by convulsive movements of the body.

Notes. In view of its rarity, this species is protected by the Conservation Ordinance. A few birds have been bred in captivity at Pointe-a-Pierre.

Blue-winged Teal: *Anas discors*
Blue-wing

Habitat and status. A common winter visitor from the north to both islands, frequenting mainly swamps, but also seen in freshwater marshes,

© John P. O'Neill - 1990

Figure 18. White-cheeked Pintail

reservoirs and on the seacoast; earliest date mid-September, latest 10 May. (Specimens: Trinidad only, AMNH.)

Banding status. Of the 90 birds recovered in Trinidad (and a few in Tobago) from 1920 to 1971 the majority originated in C North America, especially Minnesota, Illinois and Wisconsin; but some were banded as far W as Alberta and Saskatchewan, others as far E as Nova Scotia and the New England states. Most birds were recovered within a year or two of being banded, but one was taken 6 yr after it had been banded as an adult.

Range and subspecies. Breeds in N North America, wintering S to Central America, West Indies, Ecuador and Brazil; most birds in Trinidad are from the nominate form, which breeds in C North America, but it is likely from banding evidence that the darker race, *A. d. orphna* (Stewart & Aldrich), which breeds in NE Canada and USA, also occurs in Trinidad.

Description. 15 in. *Male:* a small duck, generally gray-brown with white crescent mark in front of eye; large, pale blue patch on fore-wing, appearing whitish at a distance; underparts dark. *Female:* generally mottled brown with similar pale blue wing patch.

Measurements. Wing: 3 females 180, 181, 181mm.

Voice. A thin piping; sometimes a light quack.

Food. Aquatic vegetation, in both freshwater and saltwater areas of Caroni swamp.

Behaviour. Travels in considerable flocks, sometimes totalling hundreds of birds. Often feeds among mangrove roots in thick cover.

Notes. The majority appear to arrive in September or October. When the start of the hunting season was moved forward from November 1 to October 1 (for the sake of standardisation), hunters found that many ducks never settled in Trinidad, probably because they were never given the opportunity to find and get used to regular feeding areas. In response to their requests, therefore, the Trinidad government restored the opening of the duck season to November 1.

Northern Shoveler: *Anas clypeata*
Common Shoveler; "Spoonbill Duck"; *Spatula clypeata*

Habitat and status. An occasional winter visitor from the north to swamps in Trinidad. A few recent records. (No specimen, but collected by Léotaud.)

Range. Widely distributed throughout North America, wintering S to Colombia and West Indies; also Europe, Asia and Africa.

Description. 19 in. *Male:* dark green head, middle of back dark, breast and sides of back white, flanks and abdomen dark chestnut; large pale bluish patch on fore-wing; bill long and shaped like a shovel. *Female:* mottled brown with bluish wing patch; resembles female Blue-winged Teal, but is larger with a longer and heavier bill. At rest in the water this duck appears weighted down in front by its ungainly bill.

Southern Pochard: *Netta erythrophthalma*
Figure 19

Habitat and status. Formerly an occasional visitor to Trinidad, according to Léotaud, who collected 1 bird. No records since then. (No specimen.)

Range. Irregularly distributed through South America from Colombia and Venezuela S to Peru and Chile; also in S and E Africa.

Description. 20 in. *Male:* generally brown and black with white patch on wing; back black vermiculated with white, sides chestnut; bill grayish blue with dark tip. *Female:* generally brown with white wing patch; white spots in front of and behind eye.

Lesser Scaup: *Aythya affinis*

Habitat and status. An occasional winter visitor to both islands, frequenting swamps and reservoirs. Recent records have been in November and December. (No specimen, but collected by Léotaud.) Kirk records it for Tobago.

Range. Throughout North America, wintering S to Ecuador, Colombia and Venezuela; rather rare in Lesser Antilles.

Description. 16 in. *Male:* head, neck and breast blackish glossed green or purple, back and sides gray, tail black, abdomen white; wings black with

© John P. O'Neill - 1990

Figure 19. Southern Pochard

broad white wing stripe; bill dark blue. *Female:* generally brown with pale underparts and white wing stripe; white patch at base of bill.

Behaviour. These ducks feed by diving, by which method they also escape when necessary. Unlike the "dabbling" ducks, diving ducks cannot fly straight from the water into the air, but patter along the surface for a little way before taking off.

Ring-necked Duck: *Aythya collaris*

Habitat and status. An accidental visitor to Trinidad swamps; there are 2 records, 1 from October 1956 when C. L. Williams shot a female bird in Caroni swamp, the other when a banded male was taken from a flock of 7 in December 1967 at Oropouche Lagoon by R. Sudial. This bird had been banded in Nova Scotia on 28 August 1967. (Specimen: AMNH.)

Range. Throughout North America wintering S through Central America, casually to West Indies and Venezuela.

Description. 17 in. *Male:* somewhat similar to male Lesser Scaup, but with back black, wing stripe gray and a conspicuous white mark in front of wing; chestnut ring about neck not usually visible in the field; bill dark blue-gray with white band. *Female:* generally brown with gray wing stripe, abdomen white; eye-ring and base of bill whitish, pale band on bill.

Measurements. Wing: 1 female 185mm.

Figure 20. Comb Duck

Comb Duck: *Sarkidiornis melanotos*
Carunculated Duck   **Figure 20**

Habitat and status. A rare visitor to Trinidad, recorded twice; B/S saw 2 males and 1 female in Caroni swamp in August 1932; and R. H. Wiley saw 2 birds in the same area on 3 August 1971; also reported to have been shot by hunters in Oropouche Lagoon. In NE Venezuela Friedmann and Smith (1950) found the species quite common on the larger savannahs, especially in July, when a specimen taken was in breeding condition.

Range. Throughout most of NE South America, where the form is *S. m. sylvicola* (Ihering & Ihering); also in Africa and SE Asia.

Description. *Male:* 30 in. Goose-like. Crown black, head and neck white spotted with black; collar and underparts white, rest of back, wings and tail black, glossed green and purple; bill black with large black wattle or comb at base of upper mandible. *Female and immature:* 23 in. Smaller and without wattle. A male collected in Venezuela weighed over 6.5 lb.

Food. Aquatic vegetation.

Behaviour. A very wary bird, found in small flocks.

O'Nell
72

Figure 21. Muscovy Duck

Muscovy Duck: *Cairina moschata*
Figure 21

Habitat and status. A rare visitor to swamps and marshes in Trinidad; recent sight records in January and August. Typical habitat in Guyana (Davis 1952) was *Mauritia* savannah, of which Nariva swamp contains examples here. (No specimen, but collected by Léotaud.)

Range. Mexico S to Argentina and Peru.

Description. Male 33 in.; female 26 in. A very large goose-like duck, all black, glossed green, with prominent white wing patches; bare face black with red warts; bill black with 2 bluish white bands.

Notes. Protected by the Conservation Ordinance. This species is the source of the domestic Muscovy, commonly reared in tropical America. In many parts of South America feral domestic birds mix with true wild stock.

Masked Duck: *Oxyura dominica*
White-winged Lake-Duck

Habitat and status. A rather uncommon and local resident in Trinidad, frequenting mainly freshwater marshes and ricefields, also mangrove swamps. Most recent records are in the first half of the year, when marshes are more accessible to observers. (Specimens: AMNH.) Reported by Kirk for Tobago.

Range. Throughout South America, N to Mexico and West Indies; occasional in S USA.

Description. 14 in. *Male:* generally rufous brown, the back spotted and streaked with black; front of head black; conspicuous white wing patch; tail black, fan-shaped, often held erect (hence the name "Stiff-tail"); bill pale blue. Goes into a duller eclipse plumage after breeding. *Female:* brown above, spotted with buff; head buff with two horizontal black stripes, underparts mainly pale; wings and tail similar to male. *Downy young:* black with yellow lower underparts and 4 yellow spots on back; head striped black and yellow; tail rather long with stiff feathers.

Measurements. Wing: 1 male 146mm; 1 female 133mm. Weight: 2 day-old ducklings weighed 32gm each.

Voice. Clucks like a hen.

Food. Aquatic vegetation, including seeds; feeds on the surface, sometimes "tipping up"; also dives for food, length of 16 diving times averaged 21 sec (Jenni 1969).

Nesting. Present data are confusing (Wetmore 1965). B/S describe September nests (2) placed among rushes in marshy land, with clutches of 3 and 4 eggs; these were buffy white with granulated shells, av. 60 × 46mm (4). These measurements, seemingly over-large for a small duck, were also those of a clutch of 4 similar eggs found in a Caroni ricefield in November 1967. These latter unquestionably belonged to this species—3 ducklings hatched and were carefully examined. Bond (1958, 1961), however, describes Cuban eggs of this species as considerably smaller and smoother-shelled, with clutches of 8–18 eggs.

Behaviour. This small species is easily overlooked as it skulks amidst water hyacinth and similar marshy vegetation. When approached it often submerges silently, but sometimes it flies a short distance, rising easily from the surface or (less often) pattering along for a few yards to gain momentum.

CATHARTIDAE: American Vultures

These are very large birds with relatively small, nearly naked heads. They are usually seen soaring at a considerable height and are distinguishable from hawks by their small heads and, sometimes, by the greater dihedral of their wings. They feed largely on carrion and often congregate at garbage dumps and other places where waste is available. (3)

King Vulture: *Sarcoramphus papa*
Plate 2(8)

Habitat and status. A rare visitor to Trinidad, usually seen over forest;

recent records in January, April–June, August and December. (Specimens: AMNH, BM, PSM.)

Range. Through Central and South America from Mexico to Argentina.

Description. 30 in.; wingspread 6.5 ft. *Adult:* mainly creamy white, with lower back, tail, rear edge of wings and primaries black; gray ruff; head and neck bare, brightly coloured with orange, yellow and blue; large wattle at base of bill. *Immature:* dark brown below, with some white on underparts and under-wing-coverts. Distinguished by very large broad wings and square-ended tail.

Measurements. Wing: 1 unsexed 516mm. In USA a captive female weighed 3kg (Conway 1962).

Food. Carrion. The only record for Trinidad is of several birds seen eating a dead snake (Taylor 1864).

Behaviour. A well-known attribute of this species is its dominance over other American vultures, in particular the Turkey Vulture, which shares its habitat. Blake (1950) recorded that a single King Vulture could always disperse a number of Turkey Vultures feeding at a refuse heap in Guyana.

Black Vulture: *Coragyps atratus*
"Corbeau"

Habitat and status. A common resident in Trinidad, frequenting mainly open country and towns, also over forest. Particularly abundant about refuse dumps near towns and on seashores. Known on all the islands off Trinidad, but not recorded from Tobago (though a few individuals, released from captivity in 1959, were seen near Little Tobago up to 1972). (Specimen: AMNH.)

Range and subspecies. S USA through Central and South America to Chile and Argentina. Not in the West Indies. *C. a. brasiliensis* (Bonaparte) is the smaller, tropical race, ranging from S Mexico southwards. Eisenmann (1963) and Skutch (1969a) suspected a migratory movement of the species late in the year southward through Costa Rica and Panama, but in Trinidad it seems sedentary enough.

Description. 25 in.; wingspread 4.5 ft. All black with whitish bases to primaries, forming a pale patch clearly visible from below; square, short tail; wings relatively broader and more rounded than in other American vultures; head and upper neck bare, blackish.

Voice. Normally silent, but when alarmed on the ground utters a choking gasp.

Food. Mainly carrion, offal and refuse of all kinds. Food is located by sight, either directly or through observation of other vultures. Birds also congregate at heaps of opened coconuts, feeding on the remains of the nut, and are known to feed on avocados (Wetmore 1965) and the fruits of a palm (Pinto 1965). They occasionally attack live animals, especially the newborn, including hatchling leatherback turtles (Mrsovsky 1971).

Nesting. Breeding recorded from November to February (6 nests). The "nest" is usually made on the ground at the foot of a large tree in the forest or light woodland. Two eggs are laid, dull white, sometimes spotted red-brown, av. 70 × 51mm (8) but size very variable. In Ecuador Marchant (1960) found the incubation period to be about 5 wk and the fledging period 10–11 wk.

Behaviour. The Black Vulture is frequently seen in characteristic situations: a large number spiralling together in the high funnel of a hot air current, sitting with wings outstretched and drying after a rain shower, feeding in a pack on the carcase of a dead dog by the roadside, or clustering on the beaches where fishermen unload their catch. Marchant (1960) points out that birds are often seen in pairs, except during the breeding season, when one is attending the nest. This suggests pairing for life. When disturbed at the nest a parent bird stays close at hand.

Notes. Attracting, as it does, mixed feelings of respect and disgust in the Trinidadian, it is rather surprising that this species may be hunted during the open season according to law. This appears to be a safety valve for occasions when it becomes a nuisance at poultry runs and on rooftops. Generally, it is regarded as an invaluable scavenger of road-killed carcases and left strictly alone. At Pointe-a-Pierre I have occasionally found it so tame around kitchen-drains that one could walk amongst the birds as amongst domestic chickens!

Turkey Vulture: *Cathartes aura*
Red-necked Turkey-Vulture; "King Corbeau"; "Red-head Corbeau"

Habitat and status. A common resident in Trinidad, frequenting mainly forested areas but also other parts of the countryside. Rarely seen near towns. (No specimen.)

Range and subspecies. S Canada through North, Central and South America, including Greater Antilles; this is probably *C. a. ruficollis* (Spix), which ranges from Panama and Colombia S to Uruguay and Argentina. Large numbers of vultures from Middle America migrate late in the year into NW South America.

Description. 30 in.; wingspread 6 ft. Generally brownish black, the underside of the flight feathers pale gray, contrasting with the dark coverts; head and neck bare, mainly red, but in this race with several yellow bands on nape, sometimes giving the impression of a whitish stripe. Head of immature blackish. In flight readily distinguished from Black Vulture by longer tail, longer, narrower wings and by its manner of flight. The wings are tilted upwards at an angle, giving a dihedral effect, and it soars with a swinging movement, tilting unsteadily as if with precarious balance; only rarely does it flap, then with long, slow wing-beats. The Black Vulture soars smoothly, but quite frequently gives several quick flaps.

Voice. Usually silent, but occasionally gives a coarse hiss.

Food. Carrion, with a preference for smaller animals, snakes, toads, etc., rather than the larger carrion eaten by the Black Vulture. Food is located by smell (Stager 1964) with the aid of its well-developed olfactory lobes. This species, unlike the King and Black vultures, is rarely known to attack living animals. Also eats coconuts and, in Brazil, the ripe fruit of an oil-palm (Pinto 1965).

Nesting. Breeds from November to March (B/S), 1 or 2 eggs, cream with dark red markings, av. 69 × 46mm (8). In Colombia a "nest" was on bare ground from which leaves had been cleared (Miller 1947). Soon after the egg had hatched the adult had to be pushed off the nest; later it feigned injury as a distraction display.

Behaviour. Most commonly the Turkey Vulture is seen systematically coursing fairly low above the forest, quartering an area rather like a harrier. Like the Black Vulture, it is often seen perching with wings spread after a rain shower, presumably drying them. But McKelvey (1965) also describes Turkey Vultures in USA bathing in the rain with wings spread. In hot weather they cool themselves by panting and by excreting onto their legs (Hatch 1970). Although normally not a gregarious species, the Turkey Vulture performs a stylized courtship dance in groups (Loftin & Tyson 1965). In USA birds have been seen gathering on a cleared area; with lowered head and outstretched wings one bird hops towards another, which in turn hops towards a third and so on. Apparently the group forms a circle during this operation.

[Lesser Yellow-headed Vulture: *Cathartes burrovianus*]

Habitat and status. No satisfactory record from Trinidad, although sight records have been published (B/S, Herklots), and some observers have reported possible occurrences. It seems certain that confusion exists over the identification of this species and *C. aura ruficollis*.

Range. Mexico S through Middle and South America; in Venezuela the nominate race is fairly common on open savannah or marsh, rarely over forest.

Description. 25 in. Much like the Turkey Vulture but smaller, the head looking wholly yellow at a distance, though it has patches of red on the forehead and blue on the crown, and is otherwise orange and yellow; in some birds the base of the primaries appear paler from above, the quills being white. Tail shorter than that of Turkey Vulture; legs whitish.

ACCIPITRIDAE: Kites, Hawks and Eagles

These birds of prey, ranging in size from the Kiskadee-sized Pearl Kite to the very large eagles, are more usually seen in flight than at a perch. For identification their silhouettes are in many cases more diagnostic than colour characteristics, for some species have several phases, and juvenile plumages are frequently most confusing. I have accordingly often found it impossible to be sure of the identification of many raptors seen in Trinidad, especially since the current check-list is most unlikely to be comprehensive for this family, with the mainland so close at hand.

Most kites can be distinguished from hawks and eagles by their smaller, lighter build, more pointed wings and longer tails; both hawks and eagles have rather broad wings and (in most cases) broad, rounded tails, but eagles are considerably larger, their wings proportionately longer and their tails fairly long. The immatures of many species are generally brown, with streaked underparts. In most birds of prey the females are distinctly larger than the males. (23)

White-tailed Kite: *Elanus leucurus*
Black-shouldered Kite

Habitat and status. Formerly considered a rare visitor, now established as an uncommon resident, especially in Nariva, Caroni and Oropouche Lagoon. The improvement in status began in the early 1970s. (Specimen: ANSP.)

Range and subspecies. S USA and Middle America S throughout South America; *E. l. leucurus* (Vieillot) ranges through South America. There has been a sudden population explosion and range extension in USA (late 1950s) and in Middle America (1960s), probably due partly to increased habitat following irrigation and agricultural development (Eisenmann 1971).

Description. 16 in. *Adult:* generally pale gray, with white underparts, head and tail; conspicuous black patch at bend of the wing; wings pointed, tail long. *Immature:* similar, but tinged brown above and with rufous streaks on breast; tail pale gray.

Measurements. Weight: 3 males 250, 272, 297gm; 1 female 307gm. (Haverschmidt 1962b, in Surinam.)

Voice. A soft, plaintive mewing.

Food. Principally small rodents.

Nesting. A breeding pair was found in Nariva swamp in June 1976, and another in the Caroni marshes in April 1982. Haverschmidt (1962b) reported that in Surinam 2 broods are sometimes raised in a yr.

Behaviour. Rather solitary or in pairs, though a number of birds may appear at a suitable feeding area. When feeding, the bird hovers like a Kestrel, with wings held horizontally. As it dives for its prey the wings are stretched upwards, the tips almost touching.

Pearl Kite: *Gampsonyx swainsoni*
Swainson's Pearl Kite   **Plate 3(7)**

Habitat and status. A rare resident in Trinidad, not known to breed locally until 1970; favours savannah edges bordering deciduous woodland, especially on E coast, and usually in the vicinity of coconut palms. (Specimens: TRVL, PSM.)

Range and subspecies. South America from Colombia and Venezuela S to Bolivia and N Argentina, also Nicaragua; *G. s. leonae* (Chubb) is found in Nicaragua and South America N of the Amazon and E of the Andes; it differs from the nominate southern form by its rufous flanks.

Description. 9 in. *Adult:* crown, lores, upperparts, wings and tail generally black, collar white edged rufous; forehead and sides of head orange-buff, flight feathers, wing-coverts and tail edged and tipped white; underparts white with short black bar at the sides of breast; flanks and thighs chestnut; bill black; legs bright yellow. *Immature:* as adult but back and wings tipped with chestnut and whitish, collar pale buff; underparts white with more or less buff on breast, flanks and under-tail-coverts.

Measurements. Wing: 145, 159mm. Weight: 93gm (2 unsexed birds).

Voice. A high-pitched, musical series, *pip-pip-pip,* etc., sometimes a disyllabic *kitty-kitty-kitty,* given by both sexes but more usually the male; during breeding the female usually calls a soft but plaintive, drawn-out, single note, reminiscent of an elaenia's whistle; also both sexes utter a kingbird-like chatter consisting of a shrill whistle followed by a series of rapid, descending notes.

Food. Mostly lizards, especially *Anolis;* also occasionally small birds, e.g., *Volatinia, Mimus* nestlings; and insects, including cockroaches.

Nesting. Breeding recorded at Pointe-a-Pierre, Piarco and Chaguanas (14 nests) in January–March, May and October (ffrench 1982); moult April–June. One pair was double-brooded for 4 consecutive years. The nest is a fairly deep cup of sticks placed in a fork 60–80 ft high in a casuarina tree. The clutch is 2–4 eggs, white marked irregularly with brown spots, measuring 29.5 × 24.3mm (1). Both adults build the nest and incubate, though the female sits most of the time and always at night. Incubation period 34–35 days. Food for the young and the female is brought by the male, but only the female feeds the young until they leave the nest. Fledging period is about 5 wk, and the young remain in the vicinity of the nest for about another month.

Behaviour. Usually sits on high perches, from which it swoops down onto its prey. It also sometimes soars at a considerable height. In an apparent courtship display the male glides near the nest, sometimes fluttering his wings slowly and calling in an excited manner, while the female follows him from above, diving down occasionally as if in pursuit. When not nesting a pair frequently roost side by side in a tall tree. I have sometimes been struck by the species' apparently fearless curiosity, as it has approached within a few feet of me.

Notes. With its rather falcon-like proportions the species had been considered by many authors a member of the Falconidae. Its skeleton and moult schedule, however, place it clearly among the Accipitridae.

Swallow-tailed Kite: *Elanoides forficatus*
"Scissors-tail"

Habitat and status. A fairly common breeding visitor to Trinidad, regularly recorded from March to August, occasional records from October, December and February. One sight record (ffrench & ffrench 1966) of 2 birds in Tobago 12 April 1963. Usually seen over forest, sometimes in considerable flocks of up to 50 birds. (Specimen: AMNH.)

Range and subspecies. C USA south through Middle and South America to N Argentina; *E. f. yetapa* (Vieillot) ranges through South America N to Mexico; it is distinguished by its dark green (rather than dark blue) upper back and scapulars from the nominate northern form; the latter migrates S into South America (a Florida-banded bird having been taken in SE Brazil), but its migration route is uncertain.

Description. 24 in.; wingspread 4 ft. Head, neck and underparts white; upperparts blackish green, flight feathers and long, forked tail black.

Measurements. Wing: 1 unsexed 417mm. Weight: (data from Haverschmidt in Surinam, 1962) 2 males 390, 407gm; 4 females 372–435gm (399).

Voice. A high *quee-quee-quee*.

Food. Heterogeneous, including insects (mostly taken in the air, but also from treetops), lizards, treefrogs, snakes and nestlings. Skutch (1965) describes how in Costa Rica kites robbed a thrush's nest without alighting, clinging to the twigs and flapping their wings; sometimes a whole nest was carried away.

Nesting. Breeding in Trinidad suspected previously (B/S), but first nest found 17 April 1965 in a large bromeliad near the top of a 100-ft tree at Andrew's Trace. Other birds seen in forested areas with nest material in April 1965, April 1969 and May 1972. Four nests in Costa Rica (Skutch 1965) were similarly situated, being made mainly of sticks lined with lichen or some other soft material. The sticks are broken off by the birds without their alighting. Both parents incubate and feed the young, the intervals between feeding being rather long. The fledging period for birds of the northern race is about 5.5 wk.

Behaviour. Typically Swallow-tailed Kites are sociable; rarely is a single bird seen, the commonest size of a group being 5–9. The birds sail with a languid grace, occasionally turning at a sharp angle, which displays the deeply forked tail. Mostly these kites are seen either high in the air or at treetop level. Once, however, in the Moruga forest, a bird swooped from its high perch to take a dragonfly a few yards from me close to the ground. On other occasions several birds were seen drinking water from the Hollis Reservoir, taking it on the wing like Fork-tailed Flycatchers. I have several times seen these kites attacking other hawks, usually driving them off; but they in turn, like other raptors, are themselves harried by kingbirds.

Gray-headed Kite: *Leptodon cayanensis*
Cayenne Kite   **Plate 3(1)**

Habitat and status. Rather uncommon in woodland and swamp forest in Trinidad, probably resident. Records throughout the year from Northern and Central ranges and from the south. (Specimen: LM.)

Range. Mexico S through Central and South America to Peru, Bolivia and Argentina.

Description. 19 in. *Adult:* head gray, upperparts black, the tail with 2 or 3 whitish bands; underparts white, sometimes faintly tinged gray, underwings barred black and white; bill black, mandible pale blue, legs pale gray. *Immature: (light phase)*: crown, eye-stripe and upperparts blackish, rest of head, neck and underparts white; tail barred; bill black, cere and legs yellow. *Immature: (dark phase)*: head, neck and upperparts blackish; underparts pale buff streaked with dusky; the streaking varies considerably from fine shaft streaks to heavy, coarse marks, the latter especially on throat and breast. Intermediate individuals are found (Foster 1971).

Measurements. Wing: 1 male 310mm; 1 unsexed 315mm. Weight: 1 male 524gm* (notably more than an average of 446gm for 3 males in Surinam recorded by Haverschmidt [1962b]).

Voice. A cat-like *keow;* from Costa Rica Slud (1964) also records calls reminiscent respectively of a trogon and a hawk-eagle.

Food. Apparently mainly insects, but also snakes, frogs, birds' eggs and (Herklots 1961) birds.

Nesting. Léotaud believed it to breed in Trinidad, but no nest has ever been recorded. However, eggs reputedly from Trinidad (Schönwetter 1961) were whitish, some of them lightly marked with reddish brown, av. 53.8 × 43.9mm (3) (Brown & Amadon 1968).

Behaviour. Usually seen at a high perch; when flying, it moves deliberately, flapping its wings a few times, then gliding. Found singly or in pairs.

Hook-billed Kite: *Chondrohierax uncinatus*
Red-collared Kite   **Plate 3(3)**

Habitat and status. Formerly considered "not rare" in Trinidad by Léo-taud (who collected it), but now rare; recent records include a pair at Valsayn in April 1978, one near Bush-Bush in February 1982 and a pair with two immature birds at Aripo Savannah in July 1989; in other parts of its range it is sedentary and usually found in swampy forests.

Range. Mexico S to Argentina, also Cuba, Grenada and (rarely) Texas.

Description. 16 in. Plumage variable. *Adult male:* upperparts dark slate to dark brown, tail barred white; underparts gray, banded finely with white, buff or cinnamon, underwings barred black and white. *Female:* blackish above with rufous or white collar, underparts broadly banded brown and white. *Immature:* brown above, with collar and sides of head whitish or buff; under-parts whitish with brown bars, throat indistinctly spotted. *Other phases:* all slate gray with unbarred underparts; also all blackish (sometimes with white on nape) with 1 broad white tail-bar. Both wings and tail are rather long. Bill large and strongly hooked; lower mandible yellowish green, bare facial area greenish or bluish; iris white; legs yellow.

Voice. A musical whistle.

Food. Mainly land snails, which are extracted from their shells.

Nesting. No authentic record from Trinidad, though 2 eggs reputed to be of this species (Schönwetter 1961) were white with brown markings, av. 53.6 × 40.5mm. In Surinam, however, (Haverschmidt 1968a) 2 authentic eggs aver-aged 45.0 × 37.0mm. Two nests were found about 30 ft up in immortelle trees. Both parents shared nesting duties.

Behaviour. All observers agree on the sluggish disposition of this species, which, when found on a branch, tamely allows a close approach.

Double-toothed Kite: *Harpagus bidentatus*
Double-toothed Hawk   **Plate 3(8)**

Habitat and status. A rather uncommon resident of forested areas in Trinidad, both Northern and Central ranges, also Bush-Bush Forest. Most records are from January to June, so possibly it migrates to the mainland. (Specimens: AMNH, TRVL.)

Range and subspecies. Mexico S to Bolivia and Brazil; *H. b. bidentatus* (Latham) ranges from Colombia and Venezuela south; it is less barred below than the northern form.

Description. 12 in. A small kite, shaped rather like an accipiter. *Adult:* upperparts and head slate, browner on back, tail banded white; underparts mainly chestnut, barred on abdomen with gray and white, throat white with narrow black central stripe; under-tail-coverts white, underwings barred black and white; toothed bill black, cere greenish; iris yellow; legs orange yellow. *Immature:* brown above, whitish below streaked with brown, throat with central stripe.

Measurements. Wing: 3 males 180, 192, 201mm; 1 female 213mm; 4 unsexed 178–200mm (186).

Voice. A thin *tsip,* repeated several times.

Food. Bats, insects and lizards; known to associate with monkeys (in Panama, Greenlaw 1967), feeding on insects flushed by them.

Nesting. Breeding recorded twice at Springhill in April 1975 and June 1988. One nest was of sticks in the fork of an immortelle at 60 ft. The female incubated, attended by the male, and she fed the two young birds, mainly on pieces of large lizards brought by the male. Downy plumage is white.

Behaviour. Usually seen on high, open perches or flying at or just below treetop level, occasionally soaring. In Bush-Bush Forest birds were caught in mist nets set 60 ft up below the canopy (Brooke Worth).

Plumbeous Kite: *Ictinia plumbea*
Plate 3(2)

Habitat and status. A fairly common breeding visitor to Trinidad, frequenting mainly lowland forests, second growth and savannah, especially in the south and east. Regularly present March–August; earliest date 11 February, latest 5 October. Birds seen in the south during mid-August are often in large flocks of up to 17 birds, presumably on migration. (Specimens: AMNH, ANSP, YPM, TRVL.)

Range. Mexico S through Central and South America to Peru, Bolivia and Argentina. Distribution during northern winter not well known.

Description. 14 in. *Adult:* generally slate gray, the head paler; inner webs of primaries rufous; tail square-ended with narrow white bars; bill black; iris red; legs orange. When bird is perched the long wings extend beyond the tail. *Immature:* head and underparts gray, streaked with white; upperparts blackish, wings without rufous; tail barred.

Measurements. Wing: 3 males 293, 295, 300mm; 3 females 292, 315, 325mm. Weight: 5 males 190–267gm (239); 5 females 232–272gm (255). (Weight data from Haverschmidt 1962b in Surinam.)

Voice. A sharp, high-pitched *si-see-oo,* quite musical; the second syllable longer than the first and fading into the third.

Food. Usually only insects of many kinds, mostly caught in the air with the feet; but Chapman (1894) reported it swooping down after wounded birds.

Nesting. Breeding recorded from February to June, mostly in March and April. I found 2 pairs building nests in forest near Rio Claro on 13 June, and another pair copulating on a high branch on 4 June. The nest is a flimsy structure of sticks lined with leaves, placed on a branch 20–60 ft high. The clutch is 1 or 2 pale bluish white eggs, av. 40.75 × 34.5mm (3). Downy young are white.

Behaviour. Characteristically this kite perches high up on bare or dead branches, preferring the semi-open forests of the oilfields to the denser growth of the Northern Range. In flight it is rather slow, gliding frequently. Even when hunting insects it is more often than not rather languid, catching its prey almost casually in its feet and bringing it up to the bill while in flight. When a swarm of termites takes to the air, several kites assemble to exploit the feast. Only the larger insects cause the birds to move with more alacrity, and these are usually eaten at the perch.

Snail Kite: *Rostrhamus sociabilis*
Everglade Kite

Habitat and status. A rare visitor to freshwater marshes in Trinidad; only a few records since Léotaud's day, from Nariva swamp, Caroni marshes and Pointe-a-Pierre reservoirs, records spread through the year. (No specimen, but collected by Léotaud.)

Range and subspecies. Mexico S through Central and South America to Uruguay and Argentina, also S Florida and Cuba; *R. s. sociabilis* (Vieillot) ranges from Nicaragua to Argentina; it is apparently smaller than the other races.

Description. 17 in. *Adult male:* generally dark slate with prominent white on rump, under-tail-coverts, base and tip of tail. *Female:* dark brown, heavily streaked with buff below; superciliary stripe whitish, rump and under-tail-coverts white; bill black, long, slender, strongly hooked; cere, lores, legs orange to red; tail long. *Immature:* as female, but upperparts edged rufous.

Voice. "Like the bleat of a goat, a guttural rasp, or a very dry, creaking rattle" (Slud 1964, in Costa Rica).

Food. Snails of the genus *Pomacea*. They are extracted from their shells with the hooked bill, and the shells are discarded below feeding perches.

Behaviour. A sluggish bird which can scarcely be disturbed from its low perch. Normally a sociable species. In Surinam Haverschmidt (1954a) has described large numbers gathering to roost in the evening.

White-tailed Hawk: *Buteo albicaudatus*
White-tailed Buzzard

Habitat and status. A rather rare resident in Trinidad, recorded over swamp and savannah (its typical habitat in South America), and also over forest, especially in the south of the island. (Specimens: AMNH.)

Range and subspecies. Texas S with rather scattered distribution through Middle and South America to Argentina, also islands off Venezuela; *B. a. colonus* (Berlepsch) ranges from E Colombia and Venezuela through Trinidad and the Guianas to N Brazil; it is smaller and paler than other races.

Description. 22 in. *Adult:* generally slate gray above, with rufous wing-coverts and white rump and tail, the latter with a broad, black subterminal band; underparts, including underwing, white except for black tips of flight feathers; flanks barred black; legs yellow. *Immature:* upperparts blackish brown, underparts mottled brown and white. There is also a dark phase, entirely slate gray except for the white tail with black band.

Measurements. Wing: 2 males 388, 395mm; 1 female 430mm. Weight: 1 female 585gm (from Surinam, Haverschmidt 1948).

Voice. A series of high, whistled notes, *kee-kee-kee,* rapidly repeated (Friedmann & Smith 1950).

Food. Small mammals, lizards, snakes, birds (including poultry) and insects.

Nesting. Has bred during March and April (B/S), the nest being of sticks and grass, situated in a tree. A low nest in a tree on a Venezuelan savannah contained many parrot feathers. Clutch size is 1 or 2 dull white eggs, spotted and streaked with rust brown, av. 58.75 × 42.25mm (3).

Behaviour. Usually seen soaring, singly or in pairs. Commonly sits on a low perch, or even perches on the ground. Occasionally stoops from a height, but usually hunts from a hovering position. Friedmann and Smith (1950) describe how it follows immediately behind the flames of a savannah fire, preying on disabled reptiles and insects.

Zone-tailed Hawk: *Buteo albonotatus*
Small Black Buzzard   **Plate 29(5)**

Habitat and status. An uncommon resident in Trinidad; nearly all records are from the forested areas of the Northern Range, especially the dry seasonal forest of the north-west and Bocas Islands. (No specimen, but collected by Léotaud.)

Range. Sporadically from USA S to Panama, Colombia to Paraguay, Bolivia and Brazil.

Description. 20 in. *Adult:* generally black, but with 2 or 3 tail bands, gray above, whitish below, only the lower one broad; bill black, cere and legs yellow. In flight superficially resembles a Turkey Vulture, with similar wing dihedral. *Immature:* more brownish black; back and underparts spotted with white, tail with several narrow whitish bands.

Voice. A whistled scream.

Food. Reptiles, birds and mammals.

Nesting. Very little information. B/S believed a nest found on 2 March at Diego Martin, 30 ft up in a tree, to be of this species. It contained 2 eggs, pale bluish white, av. 55.75 × 43.5mm. A definite nest in NE Venezuela (Friedmann & Smith 1955) was 40 ft up in a tree in deciduous woodland and contained 1 large young on 1 May.

Behaviour. This species is normally seen in flight, quartering its territory at a low altitude very like a Turkey Vulture. When it sees its prey it makes a sudden dash for it, only occasionally stooping from a height. Willis (1963, 1966) has suggested that it mimics the attitude, appearance and flying style of the Turkey Vulture so that its potential prey do not take evasive action at its approach. Since it makes only a shallow dive, brushing the treetops as it snatches its victim, other potential prey do not notice the kill or become accustomed to avoid it.

Broad-winged Hawk: *Buteo platypterus*
"Chicken Hawk"; "Cabbage Hawk"

Habitat and status. A fairly common resident of Tobago, seen in all months of the year mainly over forested areas, but also elsewhere. Sometimes in sizeable flocks (41 individuals over Little Tobago on 2 May [Dinsmore 1972]), presumably migrants. Occasional records from Trinidad, including one collected at Vega de Oropouche in December 1957. (Specimens [*antillarum*]: Tobago, AMNH, LM; Trinidad, AMNH.)

Range and subspecies. Canada and USA, also West Indies; *B. p. antillarum* (Clark) breeds on the islands from St. Vincent to Tobago, also recorded on Trinidad; it has tawny breast markings and averages smaller than the nominate northern form; the latter is migratory, wintering S from Florida and Mexico to Peru and Brazil, and may well occur on our islands.

Description. 15 in. A small *Buteo*, dark brown above, paler below, barred brown; broad tail banded with black-and-white bands of equal width; base of bill and legs yellow. *Immature:* tail banded more finely, underparts streaked.

Measurements. Wing: 3 males 257, 258, 259mm; female: av. 267mm (Brown & Amadon 1968). Weight: 1 male 392gm*.

Voice. A high, plaintive whistle.

Food. Insects, mammals, reptiles and sometimes birds.

Nesting. No definite breeding record from Tobago, though its presence throughout the year leads one to suspect it breeds, probably in the dry season.

In USA builds a fairly large stick nest lined with moss, bark, etc. Clutch is 2–3 grayish eggs heavily spotted with dark brown.

Behaviour. In Tobago it is commonly seen soaring above forest and cocoa plantations, but its normal method of hunting is the "still hunt"; the bird waits silently on a perch for the appearance of a victim close by. Only occasionally does this hawk stoop.

Notes. Like many other hawks, particularly those of the genus *Buteo*, this species has a largely undeserved reputation for preying on chickens. Only recently have ornithologists been able to accumulate enough evidence to show that the benefit done to farmers by these hawks in their removal of rats, snakes, insects and other vermin far outweighs the damage they do by taking the odd pullet. But the bad tradition dies hard, and most farmers in the West Indies still instinctively reach for their guns when they see the "Chicken Hawk". All these hawks are legally protected.

Short-tailed Hawk: *Buteo brachyurus*

Habitat and status. A fairly common species in Trinidad, recorded breeding once on Chacachacare. Numerous sight records throughout the year, mainly over the Northern Range, also from Trinity Hills, Nariva swamp and Central Range. One sight record from Tobago (Eckelberry 1964). Its omission from check-lists prior to Herklots (1961) probably due to misidentification. (No specimen.)

Range. Through South America S to Bolivia, Paraguay and Argentina; also known in Florida, Mexico, Costa Rica and Panama.

Description. 15 in. *White phase:* blackish above, also sides of head; forehead, underparts, including undertail, white. Considerably smaller than other hawks with white underparts. *Dark phase:* generally blackish, but forehead white and underwings whitish. Most birds seen in Trinidad have been white phase.

Voice. In Costa Rica a long-drawn-out nasal *keeer* (Slud 1964).

Food. Birds, including ground-doves and Dickcissels; also rodents, reptiles and insects (in other parts of its range).

Nesting. The only record is of a nest in a tree in the dry seasonal forest on Chacachacare in March 1942 (Abbott, in Herklots 1961).

Behaviour. Almost always seen soaring, or stooping sharply for its prey.

[Swainson's Hawk: *Buteo swainsoni*]

Habitat and status. Two records only, of adults seen at Little Tobago on 27 January 1989 (D. Finch) and on 22 March 1990 (B. & S. Andres and W. Haag).

Range. Breeds in W North America, migrating S in winter through Central America to S South America. Very few records from NE South America.

Description. 21 in. *Pale-phase adult:* dark brown above, whitish below with brown band across chest. In flight the pale under-wing-coverts contrast with the dark flight feathers; tail brown with numerous dark bars, the outermost widest. There is a rare dark phase. This long-winged hawk soars with its wings in a shallow dihedral.

Gray Hawk: *Buteo nitidus*
Shining Buzzard-Hawk; *Asturina nitida*   **Plate 29(6)**

Habitat and status. A fairly common resident in Trinidad, widespread in open country and forest edges, also in all Bocas Islands. A few recent sight records for Tobago. (Specimens: Trinidad, ANSP, YPM, TRVL.)

Range and subspecies. SW USA and Mexico S through Middle and South America to Bolivia and Argentina; *B. n. nitidus* (Latham) ranges from Colombia and Venezuela to the Guianas and N Brazil.

Description. 16 in. *Adult:* generally pale gray, underparts finely barred with white; tail black with 3 white bands; bill black, cere yellow; legs orange. *Immature:* head and neck buff streaked with dark brown, upperparts dark brown with rufous edges; underparts creamy white with scattered, dark brown, tear-shaped spots; tail dark brown with several pale bands. A noticeably short-winged species.

Measurements. Wing: 1 male 252mm. Weight (from Surinam, Haverschmidt 1962b): 5 males 430–497gm (465); 2 females 516, 592gm.

Voice. A shrill, high, flute-like whistle, *kleee-oo.*

Food. Mainly lizards and snakes, but also occasionally small birds, frogs and mammals.

Nesting. Breeds during February to April, the stick nest being situated high in a tree, 2 separate clutches of 1 egg av. 48.4 × 40.5mm, pale bluish white with a few fine red markings. Clutches of 2 known in USA. Fledging period about 6 weeks (Gibbs & Gibbs 1975).

Behaviour. This species, though quite commonly seen soaring, usually hunts from a perch or while gliding from a low altitude. In USA Stensrude (1965) found it to behave like accipiters, flying among trees with great dexterity and picking lizards off trees without slackening speed. Sometimes, after a few short wing-beats, it would glide a long distance to pick up its prey off the ground. Stensrude also describes a possible courtship flight, in which the pair would climb together to over 1000 ft, diving rapidly downwards again. Copulation occurred on a tree. Other hawks were driven from the nesting territory, but Turkey Vultures were ignored.

White Hawk: *Leucopternis albicollis*
White-collared Hawk; White Snake Hawk   **Plate 2(2)**

Habitat and status. A fairly common resident in Trinidad, frequenting mainly forest in the Northern Range, but also seen over wooded areas elsewhere. (Specimens: CM, BM.)

Range and subspecies. S Mexico south to Peru, Bolivia and Brazil; *L. a. albicollis* (Latham) ranges from E Colombia and Venezuela S to Brazil; it is smaller than the northern races and has more extensive black on the tail.

Description. 18 in. *Adult:* generally pure white with black wings and black spots on upper back; tail black with broad white band. From below appears all white with black edges to wings and base of tail. Bill black; legs yellow. *Immature:* as adult, but more black on upperparts; head and neck white.

Measurements. Wing: 1 male 360mm; 1 female 365mm. Weight: 1 male 600gm (from Surinam, Haverschmidt 1948).

Voice. A plaintive but hoarse mewing, *ker-wee.*

Food. Mainly lizards and snakes, including coral snakes. Also insects and mammals in Central America and Ecuador (Slud 1964, Wolfe 1962, Brosset 1964).

Nesting. The only definite record is that of Abbott (in Herklots 1961), who found a nest of twigs on a bromeliad 80 ft up in a tree in March 1943. There was one egg, pale bluish white with brown markings.

Behaviour. Usually seen soaring high over forest. A "still hunter", settling on a perch within the forest along a streambed or at forest edges, it is often seen with a reptile dangling from its talons as it flies up to a feeding place. In a spectacular aerial display (observed in May 1973) mated birds clutch talons and cartwheel down for hundreds of feet towards the ground.

Black-collared Hawk: *Busarellus nigricollis*
Fishing Hawk (or Buzzard)

Habitat and status. A rare and local species in Trinidad, possibly breeding in Nariva swamp, where all records up to now have been in the Bush-Bush area (Eckelberry 1964). I had a close view of an adult there on 13 June 1982, sitting low in a moriche palm, eating a fish. (No specimens.)

Range. Mexico S to Bolivia, Brazil and Argentina.

Description. 19 in. *Adult:* head and neck creamy white, large black patch on lower throat, otherwise bright rufous with black primaries and tail banded black; bill black; legs gray. *Immature:* as adult, but streaked with dusky on upper- and underparts; upper breast buffy, streaked indistinctly with dusky. Wings broad, tail quite short.

Voice. A hoarse screech, or a heron-like croak.

Food. Mainly fish; also crustaceans and aquatic insects.

Behaviour. Perching low over water, it dives awkwardly for fish. Sometimes it circles overhead like an Osprey.

Savanna Hawk: *Heterospizias meridionalis*
Red-winged Hawk   **Plate 2(5)**

Habitat and status. A rather uncommon resident in Trinidad, frequenting savannahs and swamp edges in the east of the island and at Waller Field; a significant increase has followed the expansion of cattle ranching in C and E Trinidad over the last 25 years. (Specimen: ANSP.)

Range. Panama and Colombia S to Bolivia, Argentina and Uruguay.

Description. 21 in. *Adult:* generally rufous, mottled with gray above, and finely barred with black below; wing quills tipped black, tail black with white band and tip; legs yellow. *Immature:* duller and darker above than adult, with pale buff forehead and superciliary stripe; paler below with coarser blackish barring. The species has noticeably long legs and long, broad wings.

Voice. A loud, mewing scream, descending in pitch.

Food. Small mammals, insects, lizards, toads and snakes, taken from the ground; also fish, crabs and roots recorded in Brazil (Schubart et al. 1965).

Nesting. Breeds in the early months of the year; most nests are built at the base of the leaves of cocorite palms on open savannahs, of sticks, lined with grass. Definite clutches are of 1 egg, white, unmarked, av. 55.1 × 46.2mm (2). (B/S also mention some larger, spotted eggs which they suspect are of this species.)

Behaviour. Usually seen singly or in pairs. From its perch in a tree overlooking the savannah it plunges awkwardly down to the ground to catch its prey.

Common Black Hawk: *Buteogallus anthracinus*
Black Hawk; Crab Hawk; "Chicken Hawk"   **Plate 2(4)**

Habitat and status. A fairly common resident of Trinidad, being found both in mangrove swamps and forests; occasional in Tobago. (Specimens: AMNH, YPM, TRVL.)

Range and subspecies. SW USA and Mexico S to Panama, the Pacific and Caribbean coasts of South America S to Peru and Guyana, Cuba and some Lesser Antilles; *B. a. anthracinus* (Deppe) occurs throughout the range except for Cuba and the Pacific coast from Mexico to Peru.

Description. 22 in.; wingspread 4 ft. *Adult:* all black, tail crossed by *one* broad white band and white tip; bill black, but base, cere and legs orange or yellow. *Immature:* upperparts dark brown, spotted and streaked variously; underparts whitish to buff, heavily streaked with dusky; primaries pale at base, forming "windows"; tail with a number of irregular black-and-whitish bars. Wings broad, shaped rather like those of Black Vulture.

Measurements. Wing: 1 male 362mm; 1 female 373mm.

Voice. A rapid series of several high-pitched "spinking" notes, repeated quite frequently; by far the best field mark for this species.

Food. In Trinidad exclusively crabs, so far as I can discover, though Herklots (1961) lists other items, e.g., snakes, frogs, insects, possibly taken in other parts of its range.

Nesting. Breeds from March to July (B/S), though breeding display has been observed in early January. Nests—stick structures lined with leaves— are placed in mangroves and other trees. The clutch is 1 pale bluish egg, some marked with red-brown blotches; of 6 eggs attributed to this species by B/S, 5 av. 61.3 ($\pm$1.1) $\times$ 46.7 ($\pm$0.9)mm; the other 55.25 $\times$ 44mm.

Behaviour. When soaring high in the air, this species often betrays its identity by an occasional lazy flap or by uttering its ringing call. In courtship display 2 birds soar together, then, as one flies above the other, the lower bird rolls over and both touch talons momentarily; the call is repeated many times. I have several times seen it in rather casual conflict with other hawks or the Black Vulture, and it is itself harried by the larger flycatchers, though not, I suspect, because it preys on birds. It is sometimes seen on a forest path or by a stream, feeding on the red mountain crabs, and the shells of the latter strew a feeding place. Similarly, this species feeds on rock crabs (*Grapsus*) and mangrove crabs; though I have seen it amidst a Scarlet Ibis nesting colony, I am sure it does not prey on eggs or young ibis. I very much doubt whether its appellation of "Chicken Hawk" is justified.

Rufous Crab-Hawk: *Buteogallus aequinoctialis*

Habitat and status. A few records only, one at Pointe-a-Pierre on 5 June 1976, and others at the eastern edge of Nariva swamp in early 1982 and since then (D. Fisher, J. Ramlal). A very sedentary bird, usually confined to mangrove swamps. (No specimen.)

Range. Coastal areas of NE South America from Venezuela to Brazil.

Description. 18 in. Smaller than Common Black Hawk, which it resembles except for rufous edges to the upperparts, chestnut flight feathers and barred underparts; the white tail-band is narrow and obscure.

Great Black Hawk: *Buteogallus urubitinga*
Brazilian Eagle   **Plate 2(3)**

Habitat and status. An uncommon resident in both islands, possibly increasing in Tobago, inhabiting both forests and swamps; there is considerable confusion amongst observers over the identification of this and the Common Black Hawk, which is much more common. (No specimen but collected by Léotaud and Kirk.)

Range. Mexico S through Middle and South America to Peru and Argentina.

Description. 26 in.; wingspread 5 ft. *Adult:* all black except for *white basal half of tail* and tip; bill black; cere, bare preorbital area and legs yellow. *Immature:* upperparts dark brown; below buff with dark tear-drop spots; thighs and under-tail-coverts barred; tail barred with numerous irregular black and brownish gray bands. See also Common Black Hawk.

Measurements. Weight: 2 males 1250, 1306gm (Haverschmidt 1962b in Surinam).

Voice. A high-pitched, rather even scream, *ooeeeee,* quite different from call of Common Black Hawk. Also in Venezuela a rapidly repeated Osprey-like whistle (Friedmann & Smith 1955).

Food. Frogs, lizards, snakes, large insects and carrion.

Nesting. B/S found a nest in a mangrove in Caroni swamp during May. The 1 egg, pale blue spotted with red-brown, measured 57.5 × 47mm, somewhat smaller than 5 eggs of the Common Black Hawk, a smaller species. I feel this record must remain suspect. Also, on 30 March 1981 an adult was seen with nest material near Bloody Bay, Tobago.

Behaviour. A rather sluggish species, usually seen soaring.

Ornate Hawk-Eagle: *Spizaetus ornatus*
Crested Hawk-Eagle (Eagle-Hawk); Mauduyt's Hawk-Eagle;
"Chicken Hawk"   **Plate 2(6)**

Habitat and status. Rather uncommon but widespread, occasionally breeding, known mainly from hill forests of both islands, especially Northern Range. Hill farmers claim to know the species well as a poultry-stealer. (Specimen: AMNH; also collected by Kirk.)

Range and subspecies. Tropical Mexico S to Peru and Argentina; *S. o. ornatus* (Daudin) ranges from Colombia south and east.

Description. 24 in. *Adult:* upperparts and crown blackish, with long pointed crest; hindneck, sides of head and sides of breast rufous, throat white, bordered by black band; rest of underparts, including feathered legs, barred black and white; tail barred brown and black; bill black. *Immature:* head, crest and underparts generally white, upperparts brown; barring restricted to sides, legs and underwings. Hawk-eagles have broad wings, long, rounded tails and legs feathered to the base of the toes.

Measurements. Wing: 1 female 395mm.

Voice. A series of high-pitched notes, *whee-oo, whee-oo,* etc.; also a loud, ringing *ca-leee-oo,* dying away, and followed by an accelerating series of chuckling notes; also a Limpkin-like *qu-ouw.* In Costa Rica Slud (1964) reports a hunting call that resembles a cat's snarl.

Food. Probably mainly birds; known to prey on chickens, and Friedmann and Smith (1955) in Venezuela found one to have taken an adult guan. Also known in Central America to take snakes.

Nesting. Several nests recorded in Arima Valley since 1985, mostly in February and March. The large stick nest is placed high in the fork of a forest tree, the site being sometimes re-used in subsequent years. The breeding cycle covers several months, with adults bringing sticks as early as November, and young which hatch in March still present near the nest in August.

Behaviour. In its normal perching stance the bird appears to be leaning forward ready to fly. When excited its crest is raised vertically. Slud (1964) describes what may be a courtship manoeuvre in the air: "Calling in a very excited manner the bird falls with folded wings, then opens them at the bottom of the dip; sometimes it completes a perfect loop". I have also seen the aerial display in which, as the pair glide in small circles, the male approaches the female from above and behind, then she rolls onto her back with extended feet, while he makes a grab at her talons, occasionally touching them.

Black Hawk-Eagle: *Spizaetus tyrannus*
Tyrant Hawk-Eagle   **Plate 2(7)**

Habitat and status. A very rare visitor to Trinidad, seen occasionally over lowland forest, once in Arena Forest in early 1965, also near Moruga in April 1977 and August 1978. (No specimen, but collected by Léotaud.)

Range. C Mexico south to Peru and N Argentina.

Description. 27 in. *Adult:* generally black with a prominent dark crest; white barring on underwings, thighs and under-tail-coverts; tail black with 4 broad grayish white bars; bill black. *Immature:* mainly sooty brown, with white streaks on head and white barring on lower underparts and tail. In silhouette the wings appear narrower (or "pinched in") at the base than those of the Ornate Hawk-Eagle.

Voice. Rather similar to that of Ornate Hawk-Eagle, but with the short, chuckling notes *preceding* the loud, high scream, e.g., *whi, whi, whi, wheer;* almost constantly calls while soaring.

Food. Birds, mammals and reptiles.

Behaviour. Soars much like Ornate Hawk-Eagles, but more often in the open; also perches low on trees.

Long-winged Harrier: *Circus buffoni*
Circus brasiliensis   **Plate 2(1)**

Habitat and status. An uncommon breeding species in Trinidad, recorded locally in freshwater marshes; may move about considerably outside breeding season, but records from all months December–August. Reported from Tobago (Kirk) but this may refer to the northern migrant Marsh Hawk. (Specimen: Trinidad, ANSP.)

Range. Colombia E and S to Chile, Brazil, Argentina and Uruguay.

Description. 20 in. *Adult male:* upperparts generally blackish brown, with white rump and some white on the head; wing-coverts silvery gray; below whitish with a broad dark band across the upper breast; tail grayish with several dark bands; legs yellow. *Adult female:* similar to male, but browner above and underparts streaked with brown. *Dark phase:* generally blackish with whitish barring on wings and tail. *Immature:* upperparts brown, paler below and heavily streaked with brown; some have chestnut thighs and under-tail-coverts. Though the plumages are complicated, this long-winged, long-tailed species can easily be recognised as it courses low over the marshes in a typical harrier attitude.

Measurements. Weight: 2 males 391, 430gm; 2 females 580, 645gm (Haverschmidt 1962b, in Surinam).

Voice. In alarm, a fairly rapid series of similar, high-pitched notes, like the call of a sandpiper in tone.

Food. Mainly small mammals and reptiles, but also birds' eggs and small birds.

Nesting. Known to breed in Caroni marshes during June (B/S), a nest being made on the ground among rushes. Two pale bluish white eggs av. 47.7 × 36.25mm.

Behaviour. When hunting this harrier quarters the marshes, flying very slowly and buoyantly up and down, frequently hovering low over the ground, before it pounces on its victim. Friedmann and Smith (1955) describe a bird which unsuccessfully chased a large lapwing (*Vanellus*) over a Venezuelan savannah.

PANDIONIDAE: Osprey

This species, the only one in the family, is distinguished from most other birds of prey by its dependence on water, where it dives feet-first for fish. Mainly white below, it flies with a pronounced bend in the long wings, forming a shallow W. Though nesting has been suspected in Trinidad and Venezuela, there is no definite record of breeding farther south than Belize. (1)

Osprey: *Pandion haliaetus*
Fish Hawk

Habitat and status. A fairly common visitor to both islands, seen over reservoirs, waterways and seacoasts especially from October to April; immature birds are also present in the other months. At least 8 individuals seen together at Pointe-a-Pierre in December 1958; usually only isolated birds found May–September. (Specimens: AMNH, TRVL.)

Banding status. Three birds banded as nestlings in USA have been recovered in Trinidad, one from Long Island aged 7 yr, the other two from Maryland and Virginia within a few months of leaving their nests.

Range and subspecies. Almost cosmopolitan; *P. h. carolinensis* (Gmelin) breeds in North America, wintering S to Chile and Argentina; it is smaller than the nominate Old World form, but larger than a form resident in islands of the N Caribbean.

Description. 23 in.; wingspread 6 ft. Head and neck buffy white, feathers tipped black; distinctive black streak through eye; rest of upperparts dark brown, tail banded; underparts white; bill black; legs bluish.

Measurements. Wing: 1 male 450mm; 1 female 488mm; 1 unsexed 465mm.

Voice. A series of high-pitched, mewing notes, *chyeep-chyeep,* etc.

Food. Fish, including some up to 18 in. long. At Pointe-a-Pierre the introduced *Tilapia* is often taken.

Behaviour. When not perching on a high point overlooking water, or on a stump, buoy or marker in the sea, the Osprey may be seen flying with powerful wing-beats, usually at some considerable height above water. Occasionally soaring or gliding, it hovers for several seconds before diving perhaps a hundred feet with a tremendous, untidy splash into the water. If successful, it emerges quickly from the water, shakes itself and makes off with the fish held head-foremost in its strong talons. Normally it flies straight to its perch and eats the fish there, but occasionally a bird carries a fish for quite some time, circling meanwhile. The Osprey is frequently mobbed by terns or skimmers, as well as the pugnacious kingbirds; once I saw an Osprey in a group of three attacking another, descending upon it with open outstretched talons and uttering its piercing call.

FALCONIDAE: Caracaras and Falcons

This group of raptors includes the true falcons, distinguishable by their long, pointed wings and fairly long, comparatively slim tails, and the broader-winged caracaras and forest-falcons. The former fly with rapid wing-beats, rarely soaring, though occasionally hovering; many feed on birds caught in the air. The caracaras found in Trinidad tend to feed on the ground, mainly on carrion or invertebrates. (8)

Yellow-headed Caracara: *Milvago chimachima*
Northern Carrion Falcon   **Plate 3(6)**

Habitat and status. Formerly a rare visitor to Trinidad, but more common in recent years, clearly benefiting from the increase in cattle-ranching. Breeding recorded since 1984; first seen on Tobago in November 1987 (D. Rooks). A bird of savannah, swamp and forest edges. (No specimen.)

Range. Panama S through South America.

Description. 16 in. *Adult:* head and underparts pale creamy buff; black streak behind eye; upperparts brown with very distinctive pale patch on base of primaries; tail with several bars of cream and brown. *Immature:* mottled below. Wings rather broad, tail fairly long.

Voice. A high scream, *shreee-oo*.

Food. Almost omnivorous. Recorded to have taken carrion, fish, birds' eggs and young, snakes, lizards, insects, corn and even bread from a bird feeding-table. I watched one in Caroni feeding on a dead caiman which was extremely putrid.

Nesting. Breeding first recorded at Waller Field in early 1984 (J. Ramlal). On the mainland nests of sticks have been placed in palm trees; 1 or 2 buff eggs marked with brown.

Behaviour. On the continent this bird is called "tickbird", owing to its being frequently seen perched on the backs of cattle, feeding on various external parasites, including ticks.

Crested Caracara: *Polyborus plancus*
Savannah Kite; Southern Caracara; *Caracara plancus*

Habitat and status. A rare visitor to Trinidad, 5 sight records in February, April and October; normally a savannah or open-country bird, it has been seen near Caroni marshes and in Nariva swamp. (No specimen.)

Range. S USA south through Middle and South America, also Cuba.

Description. 22 in. *Adult:* crown black with short crest, white hindneck, rest of upperparts blackish, mantle barred buff; white area across middle of primaries forms conspicuous whitish patch in flight; sides of head, neck and breast white, abdomen blackish; tail pale buff with several black bars and a wide, black subterminal band; bare face red; bill pale; legs yellow. *Immature:* similar but mainly brown above; breast and upper abdomen dark brown, streaked and spotted with white. This species has conspicuously long legs.

Voice. A harsh cackling, also a rattling note.

Food. Mainly carrion of all kinds, also lizards, mammals, young turtles, fish, young caimans, insects and other invertebrates.

Behaviour. Flies smoothly, often soaring and sailing. Though it sometimes perches in trees, it is most commonly seen walking on the ground, often in ploughed fields. It reaps the advantages of burned savannahs and modern highways by feeding on the corpses of animals killed on them.

Peregrine Falcon: *Falco peregrinus*
Duck Hawk

Habitat and status. A regular winter visitor to both islands, seen mainly over coasts, swamps and open country. Recorded in all months November–April, most records being of birds on passage in November. Earliest date 21 October, latest 27 April. (Specimen: AMNH.)

Banding status. One female was banded at Port of Spain in February 1985. An adult bird banded in October 1956 in Virginia was recovered in Trinidad 3 months later.

Range and subspecies. Cosmopolitan, with many recognised races. *F. p. anatum* (Bonaparte) breeds in North America, migrating S to Chile and Argentina; it is darker than the nominate form, with more rufous wash on the underparts. If the recently described subspecies *tundrius* (C. M. White) of arctic North America is accepted, most of our birds are likely to be of this highly migratory population. A southern form (*cassini*) with heavier markings below migrates occasionally N to Colombia and might occur here in the middle of the year.

Description. 15–20 in.; wingspread 3.5 ft. *Adult:* head and upperparts slate blue, tail banded black with white tip, blackish "moustache"; throat, breast and ear-coverts white, rest of underparts banded black and white; legs yellow. *Immature:* upperparts brown, underparts streaked, brown moustache.

Measurements. Wing: 1 unsexed 313mm.

Voice. A hoarse *kak-kak-kak*.

Food. Birds, especially terns and sandpipers; seen chasing bats.

Behaviour. This magnificent falcon is well known for its superb dash and verve, and its ferocity is such that it sometimes kills more than it can eat. A typical peregrine-killed corpse has all the head and body cleaned out, with the wings mostly untouched. On one occasion a Peregrine made for a mist net I had set up, in which 2 or 3 Western Sandpipers were caught. Just in time the falcon saw the net and stalled abruptly out of its 50 m.p.h. charge. I have also seen Peregrines mobbing a Black Vulture and a Common Black Hawk, without, however, causing serious damage.

Orange-breasted Falcon: *Falco deiroleucus*
Temminck's Falcon   **Plate 3(4)**

Habitat and status. A very rare visitor to Trinidad forests, possibly breeding; since Léotaud's day seen by B/S (no details), on 11 August 1965 in Arena Forest by P. J. Hamel and party, by P. C. and M. L. Petersen in June 1971 in Arima Valley and by M. Stewart and R. Dunn in April 1975 near Blanchisseuse. (No specimen, but collected by Léotaud.)

Range. South America from Colombia to Peru and Argentina, also spottily in Central America north to S Mexico.

Description. 14 in. *Adult:* head and upperparts black, the tail with 3 white bars; throat white, breast, under-tail-coverts and thighs rufous, abdomen black spotted with rufous; bill yellow, tipped black; legs orange. *Immature:* sooty brown above, buff below in place of rufous.

Measurements. Weight: 1 female 654gm (Guatemala, Smith & Paynter 1963).

Food. Birds; in Costa Rica a parakeet (Slud 1964), and in Brazil a ground-dove (Schubart 1965).

Nesting. Two Trinidad nests were ascribed to this species by Smooker (Coltart 1951), dated 21 April 1930 and 28 March 1937; they were situated in tree hollows 30–40 ft above ground; the clutches were 2 and 3 yellowish eggs, marked with smears and blotches of reddish brown, av. 41.4 × 34.8mm (5). The small size of these eggs, compared to the size of the bird, has led to doubts as to their authenticity.

Bat Falcon: *Falco rufigularis*
White-throated Falcon; *Falco albigularis*   **Plate 3(5)**

Habitat and status. A rather uncommon resident in Trinidad, mainly in forested areas, also found in more open country. No definite records for Tobago (where observations attributed to me by Herklots [1961] were probably cases of misidentification). (No specimen, but collected by Léotaud.)

Range and subspecies. Mexico S to Bolivia and N Argentina; the nominate race ranges over N South America from E Colombia and Venezuela to Bolivia and N Brazil.

Description. 11 in. *Adult:* generally slaty black above, throat and upper breast buffy white to cinnamon, lower breast and abdomen black narrowly barred with white to cinnamon, under-tail-coverts and thighs chestnut. *Immature:* similar, but throat buffier and under-tail-coverts barred black and cinnamon.

Measurements. Weight: 11 males 108–148gm (129); 6 females 177–242gm (202; Haverschmidt 1962b, in Surinam).

Voice. A liquid, high-pitched series, *kiu-kiu-kiu-kiu*, etc.

Food. Bats, including fruit bats (*Carollia*); also small birds, mammals and insects.

Nesting. Breeding recorded during February (B/S), the nest being made of twigs, lined with fibres and built in a tree-hole fairly high up. The clutch is 2 eggs, cream with profuse dark brown blotches and spots, av. 40.2 × 31.3mm (4).

Behaviour. Partly crepuscular, when bats are hunted. Also seen frequently by day, when this fierce little falcon can be found perched on high trees, from which it makes forays after small birds or insects. Often seen in pairs, apparently with a definite territory. Its flight is either direct, with steady, fast wing-beats, or soaring in circles, or in a series of quick wing-beats followed by a glide—and this repeated.

Aplomado Falcon: *Falco femoralis*
Falco fusco-caerulescens

Habitat and status. A rare visitor to Trinidad savannahs, recorded breeding by B/S; recent records since then from Waller Field, December and March (D. W. Snow), Nariva in October (G. Gomes), Oropouche in January and Caroni in July and November. (No specimen, but collected by Léotaud.)

Range. SW USA south through Middle and South America to Argentina.

Description. 16 in. *Adult:* generally dark gray above, the tail with several white bands; conspicuous face pattern, black "moustache" and ear-coverts, pale buff superciliary meeting behind crown; throat and breast whitish to buff, sides and band across abdomen black, lower underparts cinnamon. *Immature:* similar but blackish brown above; upper breast heavily streaked with black.

Voice. The only recorded note is a scolding *ee-ee-ee-ee* (Friedmann & Smith 1950).

Food. Birds, bats, mice, lizards, fish and insects. I watched one chasing Dickcissels and bats in the Oropouche Lagoon, while Friedmann and Smith (1950, 1955) in Venezuela recorded plovers, sandpipers, pigeons, doves, nighthawks and hummingbirds among its prey.

Nesting. Breeding recorded near Caroni by B/S during April, the nest made of sticks high in a bamboo clump. Clutch is 1 or 2 eggs, bluish or cream with heavy red brown blotches, av. 40.1 × 33mm (2), 45.5 × 36.5mm (1).

Merlin: *Falco columbarius*
Pigeon Hawk

Habitat and status. A regular winter visitor in small numbers to both islands, frequenting mainly open areas and cultivated lands; present October–April, earliest 24 September, latest 22 April. (Specimens: YPM, LM.)

Banding status. Four birds were banded near Princes Town in 1963–64. No recoveries to date.

Range and subspecies. Widespread in both Old and New worlds; *F. c. columbarius* (Linnaeus) breeds in Canada and N USA east of the Rocky Mountains, wintering S to Ecuador, Peru, Colombia, Venezuela and West Indies. One specimen, taken on 15 December 1950, is the rather paler *bendirei* type (not recognised as a valid race by some authors, e.g., Temple (1972); *bendirei,* also recorded from Panama, nests in C North America north into parts of Alaska.

Description. 12 in. *Male:* generally slate blue above, with several paler bars on tail, pale superciliary; underparts buffy white streaked dark brown; bill bluish gray, cere and legs yellowish. *Female:* like male but dark brown above.

Measurements. Wing: 5 females 208–220mm (212). Weight: 2 females 185*, 224gm.

Voice. No call recorded in winter quarters.

Food. Principally birds, also lizards, insects and small mammals, including bats. The staple diet for some individuals in Trinidad is Dickcissels, but I have also seen a bird attack a White-rumped Sandpiper, and one in Tobago hunting bats.

Behaviour. The Merlin's favourite perch and feeding place seems to be near the top of a large tree on a savannah. From this base it flies out with fast, steady wing-beats, making wide, sweeping searches after its prey. On many occasions I have seen it hunting Dickcissels (ffrench 1967b) as they approached or left their roosts in canefields. Sometimes the Merlin dived into a large flock, often emerging with no victim. More often it sped along the paths close to the ground, snatching a stray Dickcissel as it crossed the open ground. Below the feeding tree disgorged pellets were found, containing only the remains of Dickcissels. There almost always seemed to be 1 or 2 Merlins at the Dickcissel roosts, and it is likely that they follow the latter even on migration journeys.

American Kestrel: *Falco sparverius*
American Sparrow Hawk

Habitat and status. Occasionally found in N Trinidad, especially near Chaguaramas; formerly a rare resident of swamps and marshes. On the mainland of Venezuela it is abundant on the edge of deciduous forest and on savannahs, especially where telephone poles provide perches. First Tobago record in February 1991 (W. L. Murphy). (No specimen.)

Range. Most of North and South America, also the West Indies, but largely absent from heavily forested areas of South America and parts of Middle America.

Description. 10 in. *Male:* top of head gray with chestnut crown-patch, throat and cheeks white, 2 black moustachial streaks and black ear-spot; back rufous, barred black; tail rufous with a wide, black subterminal band; wings gray; underparts buff to cinnamon, spotted black; cere and legs yellow. *Female:* as male, but wings and tail rufous brown, barred black, underparts streaked.

Voice. A shrill, rapid *killi-killi-killi.*

Food. Venezuelan birds take lizards and insects (Friedmann & Smith 1950, 1955). Also reported in USA to eat mainly insects but also occasionally small birds and bats (Mayr 1966).

Nesting. B/S record a nest found during May in a hole in an immortelle tree. Clutch was 4 cream eggs, blotched with red-brown, av. 34.1 × 26.75mm. Recorded breeding at Chaguaramas in 1988 (D. Buch). In Venezuela Friedmann and Smith (1950, 1955) found nests in hollowed-out termite nests, also under the eaves of a house. Only the female was seen to incubate.

Behaviour. Characteristically hovers while looking for prey; also perches frequently on wires and poles.

CRACIDAE: Guans and Chachalacas

This family of large turkey-like birds inhabits dense forest and thick scrub. Their flight is heavy and awkward, and they are most often seen in trees or, occasionally, on the ground feeding on fruits and seeds. (2)

Rufous-vented Chachalaca: *Ortalis ruficauda*
Red-tailed Guan; Rufous-tailed Chachalaca; "Cocrico"   **Figure 22**

Habitat and status. A fairly common but local resident in Tobago, frequenting hill forest but also thick scrub down to sea level. (Specimens: BM.)

© John P. O'Neill - 1990

Figure 22. Rufous-vented Chachalaca

Range and subspecies. Venezuela, including Margarita Island, Colombia and Tobago, also introduced on the Grenadines; *O. r. ruficauda* (Jardine) ranges from E Colombia through N Venezuela to Tobago.

Description. 22 in. Upperparts generally olive brown with gray head and neck; long, broad tail bronze, outer feathers broadly tipped rufous; underparts gray, flanks and under-tail-coverts rufous; legs and orbital ring dark blue, bare throat red. *Downy young:* chestnut head with central black stripe.

Measurements. Wing: 1 female 215mm.

Voice. A loud, grating, 4-syllabled phrase, *ka-ka-ra-ka,* with stress on the first and last syllables. Often the birds duet, and if several pairs are together the din is indescribable. Softer calls include a higher-pitched phrase, *ka-ka-ka-creeoo,* and a variety of clucks.

Food. Fruits, especially of the palm *Euterpe,* flowers, berries, seeds and leaves. I have also seen semi-wild birds persuaded to take soaked bread at a feeding table.

Nesting. Breeding scattered through the year (14 nests). Four nests in NE Venezuela during May and June were built at levels from the ground to 10 ft up, all in forest at the edge of savannah, not the normal habitat (Friedmann & Smith 1955). The flimsy nest is made of sticks and leaves. The clutch is 2–4 pale yellow, rough-shelled eggs, av. 66.3 × 44.1mm (3). The female incubates for about 26 days, guarded by the male (Lapham 1970). Eggs have been hatched under domestic fowl, and the young, which are precocial, raised in captivity. One captive bird flew short distances the day after hatching.

Behaviour. Mostly arboreal, about 10–20 ft above ground, but also seen on the ground, where dust-bathing takes place. Seemingly most active at dawn and dusk, when the calls are most frequently heard. Birds roost in trees in flocks, and to a certain extent these flocks stay together during the day, keeping communication with each other by a soft peeping or clucking. A semi-wild flock at Grafton in September consisted of at least 6 adults and 1 nearly full-grown young bird. The immature bird pecked at food in the bills of both its parents, and they transferred food to each other and to it. In a threat display the adult raises its crest. One April on Pigeon Peak I watched 3 adults displaying at each other with much raucous calling and wing-flapping.

Notes. Cocrico is the name known to all inhabitants of Trinidad and Tobago, and it has been chosen as Tobago's national bird, adorning the country's coat of arms along with Trinidad's Scarlet Ibis. Although the bird has been legally protected for many years, it is considered a delicacy and is often shot for food, some farmers claiming (on conflicting and confused evidence) that it attacks certain crops. After a recent increase in its numbers the Cocrico was proclaimed an agricultural pest, although the only authentic study (by A. Diamond) found that it was unlikely to affect agricultural lands that were adequately tended. Without doubt those who wish to eat the bird have found it convenient to label it a pest. As its habitat comes under increasing pressure from development, it is likely that this rather unwary species may soon become threatened on Tobago unless greater efforts are made to protect it.

Common Piping-Guan: *Aburria pipile*
White-headed, Blue-throated or Trinidad Piping-Guan; *Pipile pipile*
"Pawi"; "Wild Turkey"   **Plate 29(3) and Figure 23**

Habitat and status. A rare resident of dense forest in Trinidad, confined to remoter areas of the Northern Range and Trinity Hills, mainly above 1500 ft altitude. Recent study (James & Hislop 1988) reveals that small numbers still exist but are threatened by illegal hunting. (Specimens: AMNH, FMNH.)

Range and subspecies. Formerly considered an endemic species, the nominate race is endemic to Trinidad, being glossed purple rather than green, and with largely black crown feathers edged with white. Other races inhabit South America from Colombia and Venezuela S to Bolivia and Paraguay.

Description. 24 in. Generally blackish with a green or purple gloss; large crest blackish brown edged white; conspicuous white patch on wing-coverts. Bill black, cere and orbital ring blue, bare throat and wattle dark blue, legs red. Stiff outer primaries cause a noticeable swishing sound in flight.

Measurements. Wing: 2 males 360, 363mm; 2 females 345, 350mm.

Voice. A thin piping. Also, in display makes a rattling whirr with its wings.

Figure 23. Common Piping-Guan

Food. Fruits and berries of a variety of forest trees, including *Ocotea, Ponteria, Bursera, Didymopanax* and *Erythroxylum* (James & Hislop 1988); also seen feeding in second growth at black sage (*Lantana*) near Waller Field (J. Ramlal).

Nesting. Only the vaguest information has been gleaned from a number of sources, but these indicate breeding in the early dry season. "Nest is said to be a platform of sticks placed quite near the ground within a tangle of vegetation" (B/S).

Behaviour. Largely arboreal, but some hunters claim to have seen guans foraging on the ground beneath trees. Gregarious; flocks of up to 50 reported by the older hunters (perhaps exaggerated). Notably indifferent to gunfire, so that several birds of a flock may be shot one after the other, while the survivors fly only a few feet, keeping together. Most active in the early morning, when it is usually seen on the main branches of forest trees.

Notes. Still hunted, despite official protection. People in the remote districts neither obey nor are forced to obey the game laws. Knowing of a flock of 12 guans, they will claim that the species is "quite common" in that area. Unless a sizeable portion of remote forest is set aside as a reserve, and suitable enforcement of the law provided, this species will become extirpated long before education will affect the attitude of those who hunt it. Recent efforts in this respect by personnel of the Forestry Division are quite encouraging.

ARAMIDAE: Limpkins

This family, represented by a single species, lives in freshwater marshes and swampy woodland. Looking rather like ibises, Limpkins are related to cranes and rails. In flight they can be distinguished from ibises by their crane-like wing action, a slow downbeat and a jerky upward stroke, bringing the wings above the body level. (1)

Limpkin: *Aramus guarauna*
"Crao" or "Carau"

Habitat and status. A rather uncommon but widespread resident of fresh-water marshes in Trinidad, most frequently seen in the Nariva swamp area. (Specimen: PSM.)

Range and subspecies. SE USA and Middle America S to Peru and Argentina, also Greater Antilles; *A. g. guarauna* (Linnaeus) ranges through most of South America from Panama to Argentina.

Description. 26 in.; wingspread 3.5 feet. Generally dark bronze brown, with white streaks all over, especially on hindneck and mantle; long yellowish bill, slightly decurved at tip; legs dark. Flies with outstretched neck.

Voice. A loud, wailing scream, *krraow;* also various other notes, including a heron-like croak and a soft repeated *tchup.*

Food. Mainly molluscs, which are extracted from the shell before being eaten. Also recorded for this species are frogs, lizards and insects.

Nesting. Breeds during the wet season, nests being recorded from August to November. The nest is a platform of twigs and leaves amid vegetation 1–8 ft above water. Clutch is 3–6 eggs, cream with brown blotches and spots, av. 58.75 × 43.75mm (10).

Behaviour. Most active at dawn and dusk, when its calls are most often heard, although I have seen or heard birds at all times of day and in the night. Rather unwary; perches awkwardly in the open on low bushes when alarmed, and flies rather short distances when approached. When feeding it walks on the ground, deliberately but with a jerky motion, flicking its tail like a rail.

Notes. The species is still hunted, despite legal protection. It is now more or less confined to swampy areas where few people go.

RALLIDAE: Rails, Gallinules and Coots

These marsh and swamp dwellers, collectively known locally as "water-hens", are mostly difficult to observe as they skulk amidst the thick vegetation, rarely flying. Only the gallinules are commonly seen. Consequently the distribution and life-histories of this family are very imperfectly known. Most species have fairly long bills, very long toes adapted to walking on floating vegetation, and frequently flick their short, upturned tails. (14)

Clapper Rail: *Rallus longirostris*
"Mangrove Hen"; "Long-beak"; "Dahoe"

Habitat and status. A fairly common resident in Trinidad, frequenting mangrove swamps in various parts of the island. (Specimens: AMNH, YPM.)

Range and subspecies. South American coast from Colombia S to Peru and Brazil, also in North America from USA to Mexico and British Honduras; in the N West Indies S to Guadeloupe. *R. l. pelodramus* (Oberholser) is found only in Trinidad, differing from the nominate form by its heavier black markings above.

Description. 13 in. Head gray-brown, back and wings warm brown broadly streaked with black, sides of breast, flanks and abdomen dark, vertically barred with white; throat white, mid-underparts pale brown, under-tail-coverts white; long, nearly straight bill, mainly orange-red; legs reddish. *Downy young:* all black.

Measurements. Wing: 4 males 129–138mm (135); 2 females 127, 136mm.

Voice. A loud, grating series, *kek-kek-kek*, etc., also a snarling note. During the breeding season birds call vociferously in chorus as they display.

Food. Mainly fiddler crabs, which the bird runs down.

Nesting. Breeding recorded from April to December (B/S), but I have found most nests in May and June. The nest of twigs is usually placed among mangrove roots, very near the water level. Clutch is 3–7 pale buff eggs, spotted and blotched with deep purple, av. 42 × 29.5mm (7). Young precocial. Adult sits very tight while incubating. In USA incubation period is 14 days.

Behaviour. Though a shy species occasionally, it is not uncommon for one of these birds to approach to within a few feet of an observer, seeming not to notice him. Once as I approached in a boat an individual on an open mudflat, it flew a short way across the stream, fell in the water and swam a little before flying out onto the bank and into cover.

Spotted Rail: *Rallus maculatus*
Plate 4(2)

Habitat and status. A rather rare and local resident in Trinidad, found in freshwater marshes; a few fairly recent records, including several in 1965 (Gochfeld 1973). Also collected by Kirk on Tobago. (Specimens: Trinidad, AMNH, YPM, TRVL; Tobago, BM.)

Range and subspecies. Mexico, British Honduras, Costa Rica, Cuba and Colombia S to Peru and Argentina; *R. m. maculatus* (Boddaert) is found in the South American range.

Description. 11 in. *Adult:* generally black, the upperparts edged with brown and spotted and streaked with white; lower underparts barred black and white, under-tail-coverts white; bill yellowish green, red at base; legs red. *Immature:* upperparts browner; in some birds the white barring on the underparts is lacking.

Measurements. Wing: 3 males 124, 126, 130mm.

Voice. In Costa Rica a call given by disturbed birds was a 4-note whistle, the first longer and the next three shorter and slightly lower in pitch (Birkenholz & Jenni 1964). Cuban birds make a deep grunting and an accelerating clucking (Bond 1960).

Food. In Costa Rica beetles and earthworms were taken.

Nesting. Breeding recorded in June and August (3 nests); an open rush nest was placed just above water level. Clutch is 2–7 pale buff eggs, marked mainly at the thick end with dark purple, av. 35 × 25.5mm (7).

Behaviour. The Costa Rican birds referred to above appeared to have definite territories, 8 or 9 occupying a marsh of about 50 acres. This rail is extremely secretive, keeping to cover except when flushed and then flying only a short way. When the grass-cover grows long, they can hardly be flushed at all.

Gray-necked Wood-Rail: *Aramides cajanea*
Cayenne Wood-Rail; "Killicow"   **Plate 4(5)**

Habitat and status. A widespread, though not common, resident of Trinidad, inhabiting mangrove swamps, freshwater marshes and moist lowland forest. Also known in scrub and second growth bordering reservoirs at Pointe-a-Pierre. (Specimens: AMNH.)

Range and subspecies. Most of South America S to Bolivia and Argentina, and N to tropical Mexico; the nominate race ranges N to Costa Rica.

Description. 14 in. Head and neck gray, most of upperparts olive, remiges rufous; breast pale rufous, flanks and lower underparts black; bill yellowish, red at base; legs red.

Measurements. Wing: 1 unsexed 170mm. Weight: 1 male 408gm; 1 female 462gm (Haverschmidt 1948, 1952, in Surinam).

Voice. A loud, fowl-like cackling, variously rendered. The call often appears to be antiphonal, with at least 2 birds taking part, *ko-kirri-ko-kirri-ko-kirri-ko-ko-ko.* Various other clucking noises have been recorded.

Food. Insects and worms.

Nesting. Breeding recorded from May to August (B/S); the nest is a deep bowl of twigs lined with leaves and fibres, situated in a tree or vine 3–20 ft above ground or water. The clutch is 3–7 eggs, pale cream with spots and blotches of rich brown, sometimes also with scrawls and lines, av. 46 × 33.5mm (6).

Behaviour. Though generally wary and skulking, keeping close to thick cover and nervously stealing across open places, this wood-rail is occasionally seen in the open under unexpected circumstances. Once at Pointe-a-Pierre a bird emerged from a thicket onto an open gravelled track a few yards from me. Possibly not seeing me, it ran boldly down the road for fully 10 yd before turning off into the cover again. Calling is particularly prevalent at dusk, and during the breeding season I have heard birds calling at night as well as at all times of day.

Rufous-necked Wood-Rail: *Aramides axillaris*
Venezuelan Wood-Rail   **Plate 4(6)**

Habitat and status. A rare resident, possibly no longer extant, in Trinidad proper, but fairly common on all the Bocas Islands and Saut d'Eau Island (ffrench 1965a, 1967a, 1969a). In Trinidad known only from mangroves (T. Manolis), but on the islands it is found in deciduous forests. (Specimens: AMNH.)

Range. Mainly along the coasts from Mexico S to Ecuador and Surinam.

Description. 13 in. Head, neck, breast and remiges chestnut to rufous brown, mantle gray, back and wing-coverts brownish olive, rump, tail and under-tail-coverts black; bill yellowish; legs red.

Measurements. Wing: 1 male 157mm; 4 females 162–168mm (166).

Voice. An incisive, loud series, *pik-pik-pik,* or *pyok-pyok-pyok,* repeated about 8 times and often antiphonal, the whole series reminiscent of the style of *A. cajanea.* Though I have heard this call on many occasions, also a cluck and *kik* in alarm, I have never heard the soft, low *boop-boop-boop* attributed to this species by Herklots (1961).

Food. Probably insects and worms, as birds' tracks were often found in the soft mud beside streams and swampy patches.

Nesting. Breeding recorded in July and October (B/S). Nest and eggs are reported to be indistinguishable from those of *A. cajanea.*

Behaviour. Most active at dawn and dusk, when the calls of this species are invariably heard. It is a shy and secretive bird, rarely flying and keeping mostly to thick undergrowth.

Sora: *Porzana carolina*
Carolina Rail; Sora Crake

Habitat and status. A winter visitor to swamps and marshes in both islands, locally distributed, perhaps rare but probably fairly common (Gochfeld 1973). B/S suspected a local resident form, but to my mind on inconclusive evidence. Regular dates December–April, earliest 17 November, latest 9 May. (Specimens: YPM.)

Range. Breeds in North America S to Pennsylvania, California and Mexico, wintering through West Indies, Central and South America as far as Venezuela, Guyana and Peru.

Description. 8.5 in. *Adult:* upperparts brownish olive, mottled with black, streaked with white; head and breast gray, the male with black crown line, front of face and throat; lower underparts white, flanks barred brown and white; bill short, yellow; legs green. *Immature:* browner rather than gray, no black head markings.

Voice. A high-pitched whinny, descending in pitch; also a plaintive *er-ee,* with a rising inflection.

Food. Mostly seeds; also insects, small molluscs and crustaceans.

Behaviour. Skulking and usually silent in winter quarters, but responds to hand-clapping and other disturbances. It is fairly easy to flush, but flies only a short distance.

Ash-throated Crake: *Porzana albicollis*
White-necked Crake   **Plate 4(1)**

Habitat and status. A rare species, possibly resident, in Trinidad, frequenting freshwater marshes (B/S). No recent records. (No specimens, but collected by Léotaud and Taylor.)

Range. Colombia S to Argentina and Brazil.

Description. 8 in. Generally olive above, broadly streaked with black, wings browner; sides of head and underparts blue-gray; throat whitish; flanks

120 R A I L S , G A L L I N U L E S , C O O T S

barred black and white; bill short, greenish; legs brown. Rather similar to
Sora, but lacks black face pattern.

Voice. Undescribed.

Nesting. Probably breeds in wet season, July–October. In Guyana both
Beebe and Davis recorded breeding in the wet season. Nests and eggs recorded
by B/S are probably those of *Laterallus exilis,* a considerably smaller species.

Yellow-breasted Crake: *Porzana flaviventer*
Plate 4(3)

Habitat and status. Numbers difficult to assess because of its secretive
habits, but locally common and possibly widespread, probably breeding, in
freshwater marshes bordering Caroni swamp and Oropouche Lagoon (Gochfeld 1973, ffrench & Manolis 1983, G. White). (Specimens: YPM.)

Range and subspecies. Patchy from Mexico S to Paraguay and Argentina,
also Greater Antilles; *P. f. flaviventer* (Boddaert) ranges from Colombia to the
Guianas.

Description. 5.5 in. Upperparts buffy brown, the feathers with broad black
centres and whitish streaks, crown black, conspicuous white superciliary,
black eye-streak; throat and breast yellowish buff, abdomen whitish, sides and
under-tail-coverts barred black and white; bill short, blackish; legs and long
toes yellow.

Voice. A high-pitched *tee-di,* accented on the first syllable.

Food. Seen pecking small insects and probably other organisms from pond
surface amongst water hyacinth; in Costa Rica recorded taking tiny snails
(Orians & Paulson 1969).

Nesting. No nests recorded in Trinidad. In Antilles (Bond, 1960) the nest is
loosely built in a water plant. Clutch 5 eggs, sparsely spotted.

Behaviour. Extremely skulking, rarely flies, and is very hard even to flush.
The flight is very weak, little more than a flutter with dangling feet. Even when
the bird ventures into the open from the side of a pond, it steals quickly from
plant to plant as if avoiding exposure. Often seen in pairs during May, which
may indicate breeding then.

Gray-breasted Crake: *Laterallus exilis*
Temminck's Crake   Plate 4(4)

Habitat and status. A rather uncommon resident of marshland in Trinidad,
perhaps more numerous than it seems. (Specimens: YPM.)

Range. Patchy distribution from Honduras S to Panama, and in South
America to Ecuador, Peru and Brazil.

Description. 5.5 in. *Adult:* upperparts generally olive brown with some fine white barring on rump and wing-coverts; head, neck and breast gray, (darker in *male*); chestnut band on nape and mantle; throat and mid-abdomen white, flanks barred with black; bill short, upper mandible blackish, lower green; legs dull orange yellow. *Immature:* lacks the chestnut band.

Voice. A rapid, high-pitched piping series of 5–6 notes.

Nesting. Breeding recorded in July (B/S); one nest was spherical with a side entrance, made of grass and situated near the root of sugarcane; the clutch is 3 eggs, cream with dark brown spots mainly at the thicker end, av. 31.1 × 23mm (3). Other nests found by B/S and probably attributable to this species were in July, August and September. Seven similar eggs averaged 32.75 × 25.5mm.

Behaviour. Skulking and a weak flier. Haverschmidt (1974) found that in Surinam many crakes were congregated in a dry area of tall grass adjoining a housing estate, where they were only detected when the grass was mown.

Paint-billed Crake: *Neocrex erythrops*

Habitat and status. A single record only, of a bird found dead on a roadside near Cumuto on 9 September 1987 (White 1987). Frequents marshes, grassy areas and thickets. (Specimen preserved.)

Range. Through South America from Colombia and Venezuela to Bolivia and Argentina; known to be a wanderer in Venezuela.

Description. 7.5 in. Upperparts brownish olive, sides of head and underparts slate gray, throat white, flanks and under-tail-coverts barred dark brown and white; bill greenish yellow, the *basal half red,* legs reddish brown.

Voice. A frog-like croak.

Common Moorhen: *Gallinula chloropus*
Florida Gallinule; "Red-seal Coot"; "Water-hen"

Habitat and status. A common resident of swamps and marshes in both islands. (Specimens: Trinidad, AMNH, YPM, TRVL; Tobago, AMNH.)

Range and subspecies. Almost cosmopolitan; *G. c. galeata* (Lichtenstein) is found from Venezuela and Trinidad S to Bolivia, Argentina and Uruguay; its back is more olive than the grayish brown of *G. c. cerceris* (Bangs), which occurs throughout the West Indies S to Tobago.

Description. 13 in. Generally slate gray, back tinged brownish, white on flanks and sides of under-tail-coverts (forming an inverted horseshoe pattern); bill and frontal shield bright red, the former tipped yellow; legs greenish, toes very long. A duck-shaped bird with a chicken-like bill. *Downy young:* black with red bill.

Measurements. Wing: *galeata,* 4 males 165–175mm (171); *cerceris,* 1 male 178mm; 2 females 163, 173mm.

Voice. A variety of querulous clucks, cackles and screams.

Food. Mainly vegetable, seeds and leaves of water plants. Also aquatic insects, worms and tadpoles.

Nesting. Breeding from July to December (B/S). Nests are built of rushes and grass among water plants, usually roofed over, or of twigs among mangroves up to 5 ft above water level. The clutch is 3–7 eggs, varying greatly in size and markings; usually grayish white to deep buff, spotted and blotched with deep red-brown, with underlying pale purple markings, av. 45.2 × 32.2mm (17). Both sexes incubate. Incubation period of European race about 3 wk. Young are precocial, leaving nest after a few days.

Behaviour. Much less secretive than the rails and crakes, often seen swimming in open water, its head pumping backwards and forwards as it moves. When disturbed it will fly to cover, pattering off along the water with a laboured start, but flying well once started. When walking over waterlilies it moves with a jerky nervous action, cocking its tail and stepping high with its enormous feet. If sufficiently alarmed it will dive, and is known to expose its head only, grebe-like, when it surfaces. There is speculation as to whether it anchors its normally buoyant body by grasping underwater plants with its feet. Various forms of display have been studied in the European race; these include certain postures such as pointing the bill to the feet, tilting the tail sideways, bowing and preening. In the water birds dive or rapidly duck head and neck. The male also pecks and chases the female.

Purple Gallinule: *Porphyrula martinica*
"Blue Waterfowl"

Habitat and status. A fairly common resident in freshwater marshes and waterways of both islands, perhaps less frequent in Tobago. (Specimens: AMNH, ANSP, YPM, TRVL.)

Range. S USA south through Central America and the West Indies into most of South America to N Chile, Argentina and Uruguay. Some migration takes place, vagrants being found in Europe and Africa.

Description. 13 in. *Adult:* generally brilliant dark blue, glossed with violet; mid-back greenish blue; under-tail-coverts all white; frontal shield pale blue; bill red, tipped yellow; legs yellow, toes very long. *Immature:* generally dull brownish, under-tail-coverts white, bill and shield dingy.

Measurements. Wing: 2 males 178, 183mm; 1 female 178mm. Weight: 2 females 179, 213gm.

Voice. Squawks and reedy cackles very similar to those of the Common Gallinule; also a Limpkin-like howl.

Food. Mainly vegetable: leaves, flowers and seeds of water plants, especially water hyacinths; also aquatic insects, tadpoles and molluscs. Occasionally fruit (see Notes below).

Nesting. Breeding from April to December. The nest is a roofed structure of rushes placed near or in water up to 4 ft above water level. The clutch is 3–7 eggs, creamy to deep buff, with small spots of rich brown and pale purple mainly at the thick end, av. 42 × 30.1mm (6). Nestlings leave the nest 1 or 2 days after hatching.

Behaviour. Generally a noisier, more excitable bird than the Common Gallinule, which it otherwise resembles in behaviour. It swims infrequently, but walks on water plants and climbs readily on reeds and small bushes. In short flights it typically dangles its legs, and the white under-tail-coverts are very prominent. Display patterns studied in USA (Meanley 1963) are basically similar to those of the Common Gallinule. In an additional posture a bird bends forward with outstretched neck and wings held at right angles to the body, bent at the wrist. Standing thus the bird sways slowly, also lifting its feet alternately. Birds also strut in front of each other like barnyard roosters.

Notes. In Trinidad this species is hunted, along with the other larger Rallidae, during the open season. In Tobago, however, an anomalous situation resulted when at one time the Agriculture Department gave away free cartridges as a bounty to people shooting Purple Gallinules at any time of the year, even when they were "protected" during the close season. It was claimed that the birds ate farmers' crops, bananas, maize, cocoa, pigeon peas, etc.! The bird has, in fact, been proved to eat fruit on occasions, but probably very rarely. On investigation it was discovered that no competent official examined the carcases of "Purple Gallinules" brought in exchange for cartridges, that wildly fluctuating numbers of free cartridges were distributed in any one year (ranging from 100 to over 5000!) and that the unfortunate Purple Gallinule was the scapegoat for all farmers' losses, meanwhile being the excuse for obtaining free ammunition at government expense.

Azure Gallinule: *Porphyrula flavirostris*

Habitat and status. First recorded in Trinidad at edge of Nariva swamp on 2 July 1978 (S. Quinn et al.) and subsequently seen by many people, mostly near Bush-Bush. Its apparent absence before that time (in spite of much field-work near Bush-Bush during the 1960s) indicates a recent range extension. A bird of freshwater marsh, where it skulks in vegetation. (No specimen.)

Range. NE South America from Colombia S through Venezuela in patchy distribution to Argentina and Paraguay.

Description. 10 in. *Adult:* smaller than Purple Gallinule, whose immature form it resembles, but sides of head, neck and breast *pale blue;* wing-coverts blue; bill, frontal shield and legs *yellow. Immature:* browner.

Behaviour. Occasionally emerges from thick marsh vegetation to climb to the top of a bush; flies short distances with dangling feet.

Caribbean Coot: *Fulica caribaea*
Plate 4(7)

Habitat and status. A rare visitor to marshes in both islands, possibly breeding occasionally; recent Tobago records in January of 1987 and 1988. (No specimen, but collected by Léotaud.)

Range. Through most of the West Indies, N Venezuela and offshore islands.

Description. 15 in. Generally sooty gray, blacker on the head and neck; under-tail-coverts white, and white rear edge to wing; bill and frontal shield white, very prominent, appearing to reach up to the crown (unlike the smaller shield of the American Coot [*F. americana*]).

Measurements. Wing: 1 male 193mm; 1 female 183mm (Voous 1957, in Curaçao).

Voice. Various clucking notes.

Nesting. B/S found 3 nests in June and August, well-cupped amidst rushes just above water level. The clutch is 4–6 eggs, pale gray with small brownish black spots and underlying markings in pale lilac gray, av. 47.8 × 34.7mm (5).

[American Coot: *Fulica americana*]

Habitat and status. A casual visitor, recorded at Buccoo marsh, Tobago, 21 January 1985 (D. Fisher). Possibly confused with Caribbean Coot. (No specimen.)

Range. Breeds virtually throughout North and Central America, W South America and N West Indies; casual visitor as far S as Grenada and Barbados, but unrecorded in Venezuela.

Description. 14 in. Similar to Caribbean Coot, but white of frontal shield *much reduced,* so as to be inconspicuous, in some birds dark chestnut; short, thick bill is white.

HELIORNITHIDAE: Sungrebes

This little-known family is represented in the New World by only one species. Slightly suggesting grebes in possessing lobed toes, they are not related to that group, and they have long tails. When not in the water they may be found at a low perch just beside a stream or pond bordered by dense forest. (1)

Figure 24. Sungrebe

Sungrebe: *Heliornis fulica*
American Finfoot   **Figure 24**

Habitat and status. A very rare species in Trinidad, being known only from 1 specimen collected by Léotaud and various reports, the most recent being a sight record of a bird at the Valencia Reservoir in January 1966 (L. Calderon). Normally a bird of heavily forested streams and rivers. (No specimen.)

Range. Mexico S through Central and South America to Bolivia, Paraguay and Argentina.

Description. 12 in. Upperparts olive brown, appearing almost black in the field, underparts white; crown, nape, streak behind eye and another on sides of neck black; superciliary and streak bordering the nape white; long, fan-shaped tail tipped white. In breeding condition *female* has a rufous cheek stripe. Bill fairly long, yellow to red; legs yellow, feet (with lobed toes) banded yellow and black.

Measurements. Weight: 1 male 110gm (Haverschmidt 1948, in Surinam); 1 female 132gm (Smithe & Paynter 1963, in Guatemala).

Voice. A loud *wak-wak-wak* or *kow-kow-kow;* also *chip-chip* (Slud 1964).

Food. Insects, molluscs and crustaceans.

Behaviour. Frequently seen swimming; when disturbed it flies low, pattering on the water at takeoff, or dives. It perches in low trees or shrubbery overhanging water, and is reported to nest in such vegetation. While it swims, it pumps its head backwards and forwards like a gallinule. Observations (Alvarez del Toro 1971) in Mexico have confirmed the nineteenth-century belief that the male of this species carries the newly hatched young in flight. In a pocket under the wing, formed by a pleat of skin and feathers, the male parent protects the naked, helpless young, which hatch after a short incubation period of 10–11 days. The female parent does not possess this pocket of skin.

JACANIDAE: Jacanas

These small rail-like marsh-dwellers are characterised by their long legs and toes, with which they walk easily on lily leaves and other aquatic vegetation. The Trinidad species possesses wattles above and beside the bill and a sharp spur on the bend of the wing. (1)

Wattled Jacana: *Jacana jacana*
South American Jacana; "Spurwing"; "Lily-trotter"   **Figure 25**

Habitat and status. A common resident of freshwater marshes in Trinidad; since 1974 established and breeding on Tobago. (Specimens: AMNH, ANSP, YPM, TRVL.)

Range and subspecies. Panama and Colombia S to Bolivia, Argentina and Uruguay; *J. j. intermedia* (Sclater) ranges from E Colombia to NE Venezuela and Trinidad. There is disagreement as to whether this species is conspecific with *J. spinosa* of Central America and the Antilles, which has considerable differences in the colour and form of the frontal plate.

Description. 10 in. *Adult:* head, neck, breast and upper back black; rest of upperparts dark chestnut, but flight feathers greenish yellow, tipped dark brown (only noticeable in flight); bill yellow, bare wattled forehead and rictal lappets red; legs and very long toes nondescript grayish. *Immature:* brown above, white below, with long black streak from eye to hindneck, white superciliary. Yellow obvious in open wing.

Measurements. Wing: 3 males 113, 118, 128mm; 2 females 120, 131mm.

Voice. A noisy, hysterical rattle, descending in pitch.

Food. Fish, molluscs, insects and vegetable matter.

Nesting. Breeding from June to March (many nests). Certainly at least double-brooded. The nest is a floating platform of weed stems amidst aquatic

© John P. O'Neill - 1990

Figure 25. Wattled Jacana

vegetation. The clutch is 3–5 eggs, olive brown to deep buff, covered with crisscross blackish lines, av. 31 × 22.75mm (4). One very large egg was 34 × 24mm. Incubation and parental care done wholly or largely by male. Female believed to be polyandrous. Young precocial, leaving nest after a few days.

Behaviour. Rather gregarious, sometimes indulging in a kind of communal display, flying about and landing together like shorebirds. Also commonly seen is wing-waving, when the prominent yellow wing-patches are displayed. Normally when landing a jacana holds its wings aloft for a moment before folding them. It is extremely adept at moving about on floating vegetation and rarely swims or dives, though it does in emergency. The parent is very attentive to the small young, which have an extraordinary capacity for camouflaging themselves. On occasions of danger the adult puts on an excited distraction display, sometimes crouching down with wings flopping in apparent helplessness while it keeps up a continuous, noisy chatter.

Notes. This species is frequently hunted, though technically it is fully protected, not being one of the Rallidae. Hunters are somewhat wary of the bird's sharp spur, with which it is known to wound dogs. The function of this spur is not entirely understood. Presumably it has some use in hostile behaviour towards other members of the species.

HAEMATOPODIDAE: Oystercatchers

These are large, thickly built shorebirds, black and white or all black with long, stout, bright orange-red bills. Inhabiting rocky or sandy shores, they feed largely on bivalve molluscs; the call is a clear, insistent piping. (1)

American Oystercatcher: *Haematopus palliatus*

Habitat and status. A rare visitor to both islands; recent records from Blanchisseuse in December 1988 (J. Ramlal) and from Tobago in August 1982 and February–March 1986 (D. Rooks). (No specimen, but collected by Léotaud.)

Range. Known along the coastlines of all the Americas from California and New Jersey S to Chile and Argentina, also in the West Indies. It is sometimes regarded as a race of the Old World *H. ostralegus*.

Description. 17 in. Head, neck and upper breast black; rest of upperparts brown with white rump and wing-bar; rest of underparts white; bill red, thick and straight; legs flesh-coloured, rather short.

BURHINIDAE: Thick-knees

Also known as stone-curlews, these large, long-legged birds resemble plovers with their short bills, but the large eyes well suit their nocturnal habits. Inhabitants of open, dry savannahs, they walk or run easily, and frequently crouch unobtrusively on the ground. They feed mostly at night on frogs, lizards and invertebrates. (1)

Double-striped Thick-knee: *Burhinus bistriatus*

Habitat and status. A single record only, of a bird seen on Port of Spain savannah on 24 June 1983 (Rooks 1983). (No specimen.)

Range. Mexico S to Colombia, Venezuela and N Brazil, also Hispaniola and islands off Venezuela.

Description. 18 in. Head, breast and upperparts brown streaked with buff; a prominent broad white eyebrow bordered by black above; lower underparts white. In flight shows a white wing-stripe. Bill short, legs long.

CHARADRIIDAE: Plovers

This family comprises long-legged, short-billed birds which frequent both seashores and inland grassy areas and pools, especially in the wet season.

Running swiftly over sand and mud, they feed on insects and small aquatic creatures. Most species in our area are migrants. (9)

Southern Lapwing: *Vanellus chilensis*
Cayenne Lapwing; *Belonopterus chilensis*   **Plate 1(3)**

Habitat and status. First recorded on Trinidad in 1961, and on Tobago in 1974, rapidly increasing with the extension of cattle ranching; by 1990 well established as resident in marshy savannahs on both islands, especially at Waller Field, Caroni plain, Oropouche Lagoon, Nariva marshes, Buccoo marsh. (No specimen.)

Range. Colombia (and occasionally Panama), Venezuela and the Guianas S to Tierra del Fuego.

Description. 13 in. Most of head, upper breast and upperparts pale buff, wings bronze-green with black primaries and much white on wing-coverts; forehead and throat black, bordered by white; lower breast and long occipital crest black; rump and base of tail white, rest of tail black, narrowly tipped white; bill blackish, short; legs long, reddish brown; iris red. The only crested plover recorded in Trinidad.

Voice. A penetrating series of high-pitched notes, often uttered in flight and heard both day and night.

Nesting. Breeding first recorded at Waller Field in June 1976 (J. Ramlal); has since occurred in various months of the year, as early as March. The "nest" is a mere scrape on the ground; the eggs are olive brown marked with black; chicks precocial.

Behaviour. Friedmann and Smith (1950) describe some of this species' display during May to July, the breeding season in NE Venezuela. On open savannahs, the typical habitat, small groups flew about calling continuously. Pairs displayed with spread wings, stiffly erect postures and crouching, sometimes with one wing raised.

Black-bellied Plover: *Pluvialis squatarola*
Grey Plover; "Ploward"; *Squatarola squatarola*

Habitat and status. A regular visitor to mudflats and coasts of both islands. Occurring mainly on passage from the north from August to October, some birds winter in Trinidad, and flocks of up to 50, mostly in immature plumage, have remained on Pointe-a-Pierre mudflats from April to July. (Specimens: YPM, TRVL.)

Range. Throughout the Western hemisphere, breeding in the arctic and wintering from S USA south to Chile and Argentina; also found in Europe, Africa, S Asia and Australia.

Description. 11 in. *Winter plumage:* stocky, gray-brown with white forehead and superciliary, white rump and barred tail, and black axillaries, very noticeable in flight; indistinct white wing-bar. *Summer plumage (adult):* most of underparts black, lower abdomen white, sides of head and neck bordered by white. In summer *immature* birds in Trinidad resemble adults in winter. Bill shortish, black, legs gray. Has a hind-toe.

Measurements. Wing: 1 male 190mm; 1 female 175mm.

Voice. Typical call given in flight a plaintive, trisyllabic whistle, *klee-oo-ee,* the last syllable pitched highest.

Food. This species feeds on exposed mudflats or sand rather than in shallow water. Foods include gastropods and small crustaceans.

Behaviour. Generally more wary than other shorebirds in Trinidad. Occurs individually or in straggling flocks.

Lesser Golden Plover: *Pluvialis dominica*
American Golden Plover; "Ploward"

Habitat and status. A fairly common winter visitor to savannahs and coasts of both islands, frequenting especially fields with close-cut grass, golf courses and airports. Numbers greatest mid-September to late October (earliest date 3 September, latest 12 February). Records at Pointe-a-Pierre show that most birds stay for about 6 wk before moving on south. Adults arrive before immatures. Only spring record is of 2 birds on 11 May. (Specimen: LM.)

Banding status. Five birds have been banded at Pointe-a-Pierre, in 1960, 1961 and 1965. No recoveries.

Range and subspecies. *P. d. dominica* (Muller) breeds in arctic America, wintering S to Argentina. Another race breeds in N Asia.

Description. 10 in. *Winter plumage:* much like Black-bellied Plover, but generally browner rather than gray above, no white on wing or rump, and axillaries nondescript gray, *not* black. *Summer plumage:* resembles Black-bellied Plover, but upperparts speckled with yellow; underparts all black, bordered by white on sides of head and neck. Many adult birds in Trinidad are in a transitional stage, showing patches of black below. Bill and legs black. No hind-toe.

Measurements. Wing: 5 unsexed 171–174mm (173). Weight: 3 unsexed 114, 119, 126gm.

Voice. A harsh, shrill whistle, *queedle* or *kleee,* also a musical trilling.

Food. Mainly small insects, also worms.

Behaviour. When found on the seacoast they usually keep in compact flocks of 20–40 birds; these may have been birds on passage. In contrast, those individuals spending several weeks on Pointe-a-Pierre golf course form loose flocks of rarely more than 15 birds. In this bird sanctuary they become fairly tame. Hostile behaviour towards others of the same species has been frequently observed among feeding birds.

[Common Ringed Plover: *Charadrius hiaticula*]

Habitat and status. One record only, of a bird trapped on Pointe-a-Pierre mudflats on 31 October 1962. It was examined by J. B. Saunders, my wife and myself most carefully before being banded and released. Separation in identity from the Semipalmated Plover was based on the comparative absence of webbing between the toes. Another bird, trapped on 4 September 1960, was suspected to be this species.

Range. Breeds in N Europe and Asia, also in Greenland and Baffin Island, wintering S to Africa and S Asia; one previous West Indies specimen from Barbados (1888).

Description. 6.5–8 in. In winter plumage hardly distinguishable from the Semipalmated Plover, though head markings are darker, pectoral bands generally broader and blacker, and wings longer. Web between inner and middle toes indistinct, that between middle and outer toes not quite up to the first joint.

Measurements. Wing: 12 males 128–140mm; 11 females 130–139mm. (Data from Britain, Witherby et al. 1952.) The Trinidad bird was moulting flight feathers. Weight: 1 unsexed 45gm.

Semipalmated Plover: *Charadrius semipalmatus*
American Ringed Plover; "Ring-neck"

Habitat and status. A very common visitor to coasts and marshes of both islands, most frequent from August to April, but many (possibly immature) birds are present May–July on Pointe-a-Pierre mudflats and other localities. (Specimens: AMNH, ANSP, LM.)

Banding status. Forty-one birds were banded at Pointe-a-Pierre 1959–62; 1 bird banded on 29 December 1959 was retrapped at Pointe-a-Pierre on 17 November 1960.

Range. Breeds in arctic America, wintering S to Chile and Argentina.

Description. 6–7.5 in. Head and upperparts generally dark brown with blackish eye-streak, fore-crown and cheek-patch; forehead, wide collar, throat and underparts white, with broad blackish breast-band; tail dark, bordered with white; white wing-bar; bill short, tipped black, orange at the base; legs orange-yellow. Web between inner and middle toes halfway up to first joint, that between middle and outer toes up to first joint. *Immature:* has browner breast-band and a white superciliary stripe. See also Collared and Thick-billed plovers.

Measurements. Wing: 26 unsexed 116–126mm (120). Weight: 7 unsexed 42–46gm (44).

Voice. A plaintive, rather musical double note, *tu-ee,* the second syllable higher-pitched and more accented.

Food. Molluscs, crustaceans, worms and insects.

Behaviour. Though I have occasionally found several hundred of these plovers scattered over the mudflats, they do not form unified flocks like the small sandpipers with which they commonly associate. Individuals will sometimes join the sandpiper flocks, but generally they are found in small groups, except that various flocks combine when roosting. The bird feeds in typical plover fashion, standing motionless with head erect, running swiftly in a straight line to stop, pick up food with a rapid tilt of the body and look up again.

[Snowy Plover: *Charadrius alexandrinus*]

Habitat and status. One sight record only from Tobago, where my wife and I saw one bird on the sandy beach at Roxborough Bay on 22 August 1968. (No specimen.)

Range. Almost cosmopolitan. In America northern birds winter S to Panama (casual) and the Antilles; also known to breed on Curaçao and Bonaire, and in W South America; recorded on Margarita Island.

Description. 5.5 in. Resembles Semipalmated Plover but smaller and very pale gray above, with incomplete breast-band restricted to black patches on sides of breast; indistinct, grayish eye-streak; bill black; legs dark.

Collared Plover: *Charadrius collaris*
South American Ringed Plover; Azara's Ringed Plover   **Figure 26**

Habitat and status. A fairly common resident of both islands, found on sandy beaches, mudflats and savannahs. It is likely that some migration takes place outside the breeding season, for almost all records are from May to November only (16 February, Satterly). (Specimens: ANSP, LM, YPM.)

Range. Mexico S through Central and South America, also some of the Lesser Antilles and S Caribbean islands.

Description. 6 in. Rather similar to Semipalmated Plover, but slightly smaller; upperparts paler, sandy brown, *some rufous on nape* and often on back, no white in wing, black breast-band narrower; bill slightly longer, all

Figure 26. Collared Plover

black; legs flesh pink. Generally the markings about head and breast are more distinct and the bird has a dapper-looking appearance.

Measurements. Wing: 1 male 92mm. Weight: 1 male 26.5gm*.

Voice. A light *peet,* sometimes repeated.

Food. Insects and small crustaceans.

Nesting. Recorded only at Caroni, Trinidad, in June and July (B/S). The nest is a mere scrape in the ground with a few twigs; the clutch is 2 eggs, cream, spotted and blotched with dark brown, av. 30.5 × 22mm (4).

Behaviour. Though this species associates freely with the other ringed plovers, it does not normally flock. I have often found it in pairs on the long beaches of the SW and E coasts; as one approaches, the bird runs off with twinkling feet, flying only as a last resort. It bobs frequently in alarm and is extremely wary. Though I have often tried to trap it with the other shorebirds, I have invariably failed.

Killdeer: *Charadrius vociferus*

Habitat and status. An uncommon but regular winter-passage migrant on both islands, recorded between 8 November and 21 January. Usually occurs in small groups on open savannahs or coastal mudflats. (No specimen.)

Range. Breeds in North America, wintering south to N South America; there are also resident races in the Greater Antilles, Chile and Peru.

Description. 10 in. A large "ringed" plover. Upperparts brown with orange-rufous rump and tail; underparts white with 2 complete black breast-bands; tail longer than those of smaller ringed plovers.

Voice. A plaintive, mewing double note, *dee-ee.*

Food. Mainly insects (in USA); also worms and crustaceans.

Wilson's Plover: *Charadrius wilsonia*
Thick-billed Plover

Habitat and status. A rather uncommon inhabitant of mudflats, swamps and beaches in Trinidad. (Specimens: AMNH.)

Banding status. Four adults banded at Pointe-a-Pierre, one on E coast, 1959–64. No recoveries.

Range and subspecies. USA S to Peru and Brazil; *C. w. cinnamominus* (Ridgway) ranges from Colombia to the Guianas, also islands in the S Caribbean as far N as the Grenadines, being distinguished by the rich rufous on head and breast-band; the nominate race breeds in North America and the Greater Antilles, wintering S to Brazil; it probably visits Trinidad and Tobago in winter.

Description. 7.5 in. *Breeding plumage:* rather similar to Semipalmated Plover, but crown and cheeks somewhat rufous with a distinct white superciliary, black breast-band fairly broad and tinged rufous (especially in female); thick all-black bill, noticeably longer and heavier; grayish pink legs. Birds in winter plumage (of either race) lack the rufous; the races are then practically indistinguishable. Distinguished from Collared Plover by larger size, heavier build, broader breast-band and thick bill.

Measurements. Wing: 5 males 114–121mm (116); 5 females 110–118mm (112); 4 unsexed 119–124mm (122). Weight: 2 unsexed 59, 67gm.

Voice. An incisive *wheet,* sharper than the call of the Collared Plover.

Food. Crustaceans, molluscs and insects.

Nesting. Although breeding in Trinidad had been suspected before by B/S and Herklots, the first recorded nest on the island was found by me at Pointe-a-Pierre on 26 May 1960. A second nest was found on 14 June. They were both on the bare ground, with a few leaves and shells nearby, bordering mudflats. The clutches were 2 and 3 eggs, grayish white heavily spotted with dark brown, av. 36.5 × 27mm (4). Incubation period about 24 days. The young are precocial, leaving within 24 hr. The parents showed particular anxiety nearby soon after laying and hatching but at other times were conspicuously absent or at some distance from the nest.

Behaviour. Always seen in small numbers in Trinidad. More confiding than Collared Plover. Though I have never witnessed it here, the species is well known in USA for its distraction display.

SCOLOPACIDAE: Sandpipers and Snipe

This family of long-winged shorebirds is mainly cryptic in colour, with long, slender bills and, usually, long legs. All except the snipe are migrants from the north, many spending the winter months here, while several species are also found in the summer. Extremely gregarious, they frequent mudflats and estuaries, marshes and coasts, while a few are found on inland savannahs and waterways. (26)

Ruddy Turnstone: *Arenaria interpres*

Habitat and status. A winter visitor in small numbers to both islands from the north, but some individuals stay through the summer; recorded in every month; frequents mudflats and rocky coasts, but also occasionally flooded savannahs. (Specimens: AMNH, ANSP, TRVL.)

Banding status. Seven birds were banded 1960–62 at Pointe-a-Pierre and on the E coast. No recoveries.

Range and subspecies. Almost cosmopolitan; *A. i. morinella* (Linnaeus) breeds in arctic America, wintering S to Argentina and Chile.

Description. 9 in. *Winter plumage:* a stocky bird with black-and-brown-patterned head, upperparts and upper breast; rest of underparts white. In flight the extensive white on wings, rump and tail shows a harlequin effect. Legs orange; bill black, rather short and slightly upturned. *Summer plumage:* head white, patterned with black; upperparts rufous, not brown; legs red. Most birds summering here only show traces of the breeding plumage.

Measurements. Wing: 6 unsexed 142–154mm (147). Weight: 2 unsexed 96, 122gm.

Voice. A hoarse, but not loud, cackling, *katakak*.

Food. Mainly molluscs, crustaceans and insects; known to break and eat tern eggs.

Behaviour. The Turnstone is often found in small flocks but also forages individually. Its name is derived from its habit of turning over or removing small objects on the stony shore in order to find its prey. I have often found them on Soldado Rock, where they may be seen busily rooting about not only on the shoreline among rocks but also on the ridge among the nesting Sooty Terns 100 ft above sea level.

Solitary Sandpiper: *Tringa solitaria*

Habitat and status. A fairly common visitor to both islands, frequenting freshwater areas of all kinds, even streams and mud volcanoes in dense lowland forest. Not seen on the coast. Recorded in all months from July to April, earliest date 21 July, latest 4 May. (Specimens: YPM, LM, TRVL.)

Range and subspecies. Breeds in N North America, wintering S to Bolivia and Argentina; *T. s. solitaria* (Wilson) breeds in Canada and N USA; the larger and paler *T. s. cinnamomea* (Brewster), which breeds in Alaska and NW Canada, has also been recorded in Venezuela on migration and may well occur here.

Description. 8 in. Blackish brown above, spotted and streaked with white on head and neck; prominent pale eye-ring; outer tail barred black and white, underparts white; bill black; legs dark green. It does not teeter constantly like the Spotted Sandpiper, but nods its head sharply, more like a Yellowlegs.

Measurements. Wing: 3 males 129, 129, 131mm. Weight: 3 males 39, 46, 48gm*.

Voice. A sharp *peet*, sometimes given 3 times, usually when flushed.

Food. Mainly aquatic insects, crustaceans and molluscs.

Behaviour. Never seen in flocks, though occasionally 2 or 3 birds associate. I once found 10 birds feeding at a mud volcano near Guayaguayare. On 19 April 1959 I watched a breeding display at Pointe-a-Pierre; one bird rose up to about 4 ft above another and hovered, spreading its tail and calling a long series of notes, *tee-tee-tee*, etc., before eventually descending. In flight the Solitary Sandpiper is quite distinctive, for it changes direction as rapidly as a swallow. Sometimes on landing it holds its wings aloft for a moment.

Lesser Yellowlegs: *Tringa flavipes*

Habitat and status. A common winter visitor to both islands, frequenting swamps, coastal mudflats and flooded pastures. Though numbers are highest from August to November, birds are present in considerable numbers throughout the year. (Specimens: AMNH, ANSP, YPM, LM, TRVL.)

Banding status. Nineteen birds were banded at Pointe-a-Pierre in 1959–61. One of these birds, banded on 24 August 1960, was found dead at Plankinton, South Dakota, USA, on 1 May 1965.

Range. Breeds in arctic America, wintering S to Argentina and Chile.

Description. 10 in. Upperparts dark brown lightly spotted with white; rump white; tail white, barred brown; wings dark, no wing-bar, underparts white, some streaking on breast and flanks; bill black, straight, fairly long; legs bright yellow.

Measurements. Wing: 15 unsexed 148–161mm (156). Weight: 8 unsexed 69–93gm (82).

Voice. A light but penetrating whistle, *kiu* or *kiu-kiu*, rather plaintive. Also frequently a light *kip*. I once heard a prolonged honking call in Caroni swamp.

Food. Crustaceans, molluscs and insects. Frequently feeds in shallow water, as well as above the shoreline.

Behaviour. Associating commonly with many other species of shorebirds, the Lesser Yellowlegs is often found in sizeable flocks, especially in flight. When feeding, the flocks spread out considerably. I have found that the large numbers present during the autumn move about a good deal on the W coast of Trinidad, for according to the state of the tide they feed on the mudflats or further inland in swamps and marshes. The species is well known for its habit of bobbing its head and tilting its body, this being particularly noticeable when the bird is alarmed. Once in late April I observed several birds hovering together just above the ground and calling an unusual series of short notes; this was presumably a display, possibly connected with breeding, though at this date it would be expected that these were first-year birds.

Greater Yellowlegs: *Tringa melanoleuca*
"Pika"

Habitat and status. A common winter visitor to both islands, slightly less numerous than the Lesser Yellowlegs; found in much the same habitat, but occasionally seen well inland near water, even along rivers some way up wooded valleys. Most numerous from August to October, but recorded throughout the year. (Specimens: ANSP, LM, TRVL.)

Banding status. Six birds were banded at Pointe-a-Pierre in 1959–62. No recoveries.

Range. Breeds in arctic America, wintering S to Chile and Argentina.

Description. 13 in. Much like the Lesser Yellowlegs but noticeably larger, although the two are hard to identify separately. Bill also longer and slightly upturned towards the tip.

Measurements. Wing: 5 unsexed 179–205mm (188). Weight: 5 unsexed 124–166gm (149).

Voice. Usually a 3-syllable call (sometimes 4-syllable), *kiu-kiu-kiu,* clearer and more strident than that of the Lesser Yellowlegs.

Food. Small fish, crustaceans, molluscs and insects. Frequently feeds up to its breast in water.

Behaviour. Less gregarious than the smaller species. In other respects very similar.

Notes. Along with various other shorebird species, the Greater Yellowlegs is commonly hunted in Trinidad, as in most West Indian islands. Since the open season for hunting does not begin until after most shorebirds have passed through the island, they would seem to be adequately protected. Considerable illegal hunting takes place, however, in the latter part of the closed season, most of it directed against shorebirds.

[Common Greenshank: *Tringa nebularia*]

Habitat and status. Recorded on Tobago at Buccoo on 7 July 1977 (Bull 1978), also in early 1987 at Waller Field, Trinidad (J. Ramlal), in each case beside a pond on a flooded savannah. Accidental visitor to the New World. (No specimen.)

Range. Breeds in N Europe and Russia, wintering S to Africa, Asia and Australia; regular in Aleutians and Pribilofs.

Description. 13 in. Similar to Greater Yellowlegs but less heavily streaked. In flight shows dark wings and *white streak* up the middle of the back; bill long, slightly upturned; *legs green.*

Voice. A ringing *tew-tew-tew,* rather similar to Greater Yellowlegs.

[Spotted Redshank: *Tringa erythropus*]

Habitat and status. A single record only, of a bird at Bon Accord, Tobago, on 13 February 1983 (D. Fisher). Accidental visitor to the New World. (No specimen.)

Range. Breeds in N Europe and Russia, wintering S to Africa and Asia; rare visitor to Aleutians and Pribilofs, and known as rare vagrant on Barbados in March and October (Bond 1985).

Description. 12 in. *Winter:* mainly brownish gray above, wing-coverts brown fringed with white; eyebrow white; below white, grayish on breast and flanks; in flight shows white line on lower back, tail barred; bill long and thin, with slightly drooping tip, and reddish at base; legs orange. *Summer:* mainly black, spotted with white; legs dark red.

Voice. A loud *tu-eet,* reminiscent of Semipalmated Plover.

Spotted Sandpiper: *Actitis macularia*

Habitat and status. Very common winter visitor to both islands, frequenting coasts, swamps, forest streams and ditches. Always present from late July to May, earliest date 12 July, latest 5 June. (Specimens: AMNH, ANSP, YPM, LM, TRVL.)

Banding status. Seventy-six birds were banded in 1959–62, mostly at Pointe-a-Pierre but also at Shark River near Matelot, Waterloo, and in a Tobago river valley. No recoveries, but 2 birds were retrapped after intervals of 4 and 6 wk respectively.

Range. Breeds in N North America, wintering S to Peru, Brazil and Bolivia.

Description. 7.5 in. *Winter plumage:* upperparts olive brown, white eye-stripe and narrow white wing-bar; outer tail barred black and white; underparts and shoulder-mark white; bill blackish, lower mandible yellow at base; legs dark. *Summer plumage:* upper parts barred with blackish, underparts conspicuously spotted with black. (These spots are usually present from April to September.)

Measurements. Wing: 41 unsexed 96–111mm (104). Weight: 25 unsexed 29–42gm (36).

Voice. Usually a plaintive double whistle, *weet-weet,* the second syllable lower in pitch; also a longer series, similar in tone.

Food. Crustaceans, insects and small fish; usually a solitary feeder.

Behaviour. A distinctive species in various ways. One of its most noticeable characteristics is its constant teetering as it walks or rests, moving the entire body in this action. In flight it differs from other Trinidad shorebirds by its short, stiff wing-beat, several quick beats being followed by a glide with wings bowed below the horizontal. Several writers in USA have described its ability to swim and dive when in danger. Though it is not otherwise a gregarious species, I have found it in sizeable roosts in the mangroves of Caroni swamp. Fifty or more birds may gather in the low branches of a small mangrove clump.

Willet: *Catoptrophorus semipalmatus*

Habitat and status. A rather uncommon winter visitor to both islands, frequenting mainly coasts and mudflats, occasionally also inland swamps. Largest numbers (flocks up to 50) found from September to November, but recorded in every month. (Specimens: AMNH, YPM.)

Banding status. Eleven birds (*semipalmatus*) were banded at Pointe-a-Pierre in 1960–61. No recoveries. But on 11 August 1978 I saw a colour-banded bird at Buccoo, Tobago, which had been banded as a nesting adult male in coastal Virginia on 18 May that year.

Range and subspecies. Breeds in North America S to Los Roques, wintering S to Peru, Bolivia and Brazil; *C. s. semipalmatus* (Gmelin) breeds from E North America south to Los Roques, wintering S to Brazil and Bolivia; it is commoner in Trinidad than *C. s. inornatus* (Brewster), which is paler and larger and has longer bill and tarsus; this race breeds in Western North America, winters S to Peru, and has been recorded also in Venezuela and Surinam.

Description. 15 in. Generally gray-brown above, white below; in flight it shows a very distinctive wing-pattern: a broad white bar across the base of the primaries and secondaries separating black wing-coverts and black wing-tips; in repose the species resembles the Greater Yellowlegs but is grayer, has bluish gray legs, and the bill is thicker at the base.

Measurements. *C. s. semipalmatus* (11 unsexed). Wing: 171–193mm (185). Bill: 48–58mm (55). *C. s. inornatus.* Wing: 1 male 203mm; 1 female 200mm. Bill: 1 male 62mm; 1 female 59.5mm.

Voice. Variable, but usually noisy and rather unmusical calls, including *whee-er,* dropping in pitch on the second syllable, and a trisyllabic *whe-whe-whe.*

Food. Insects, crustaceans, molluscs; frequently feeds in deeper water than other shorebirds.

Behaviour. Usually solitary, except for small flocks which frequent the mudflats at Pointe-a-Pierre. Here it commonly associates with Whimbrels. It nods and bows less than the Greater Yellowlegs and seems less wary.

Red Knot: *Calidris canutus*
American Knot; Knot

Habitat and status. A rather uncommon migrant from the north, frequenting the coasts and mudflats of Trinidad. Records mainly August–October, but a flock of over 60 birds, mainly in summer plumage, spent most of May 1959 at Pointe-a-Pierre; otherwise earliest date 26 August, latest 27 October. (Collected by Léotaud.)

Banding status. Three birds were banded at Pointe-a-Pierre in September 1960 and September 1962. No recoveries.

Range. Breeds in arctic America, wintering S to Argentina and Chile; other races are found in the Old World.

Description. 10.5 in. A rather stocky sandpiper. *Winter plumage:* feathers of upperparts generally gray, edged with blackish; a noticeable white wing-bar, rump and tail pale gray, not white, vaguely barred; underparts white; bill dark, shortish, rather thin; legs greenish. *Summer plumage:* upperparts mottled darker, underparts rufous.

Measurements. Wing: 3 unsexed 156, 162, 169mm. Weight: 2 unsexed 93, 96gm.

Voice. Usually silent; sometimes gives a nondescript *krrt.*

Food. Crustaceans, molluscs and insects.

Behaviour. Gregarious when present in sufficient numbers.

Least Sandpiper: *Calidris minutilla*

Habitat and status. A regular visitor to both islands, but occurring in much smaller numbers than the other small sandpipers. It is found both on the coast and on flooded savannahs and ditches inland, also in the marshes. I have definite records for February–May and late July–November, but it may well occur throughout the year. (Specimens: AMNH, TRVL.)

Banding status. Fifteen birds were banded at Pointe-a-Pierre in 1959–60. No recoveries.

Range. Breeds in arctic America, wintering S to Chile and Brazil.

Description. 5.5 in. Resembles the Semipalmated Sandpiper, but is smaller, with a short, thin bill, and yellowish green, not black, legs. General colouring of upperparts browner than Semipalmated, and streaking on upper breast more pronounced.

Measurements. Wing: 5 unsexed 87–89mm (88).

Voice. A thin, rather weak *peep.*

Food. Mainly aquatic insects.

Behaviour. Less gregarious than the other small sandpipers, it is often very tame and will allow an extremely close approach.

White-rumped Sandpiper: *Calidris fuscicollis*
Bonaparte's Sandpiper

Habitat and status. A regular visitor to both islands in small numbers, frequenting coastal mudflats, marshes, flooded savannahs and reservoirs. Recorded March–June, and August–December, but probably present in all months. Most common in September and October. (Specimen: PSM.)

Banding status. Eighteen birds were banded at Pointe-a-Pierre in 1959–64. No recoveries.

Range. Breeds in arctic America, wintering S to Peru, Argentina and Brazil.

Description. 7.5 in. Resembles Semipalmated Sandpiper but larger; upperparts streaked grayish brown, with white rump, conspicuous in flight; white superciliary stripe very noticeable; legs dark.

Measurements. Wing: 11 unsexed 115–123mm (121). Weight: 4 unsexed 33–46gm (40).

Voice. A light *jeep,* resembling call of Western Sandpiper.

Food. Aquatic insects, molluscs and seeds.

Behaviour. Associates freely with small sandpipers, but rarely found in large enough numbers to form a flock of its own species.

[Baird's Sandpiper: *Calidris bairdii*]

Habitat and status. Two records only for Trinidad; one bird seen at Waller Field on 2 September 1976 (A. Small et al.), the other at Port of Spain sewage ponds on 17 November 1989 (Murphy, in press). Prefers pools and flooded savannahs. (No specimen.)

Range. Breeds in the far north, wintering S in the New World to S South America. Rare on migration in the West Indies, but recorded casually from Venezuela, Puerto Rico and Barbados.

Description. 7.5 in. Head and upperparts brown, the feathers of back and wings darker with pale edging, with a *scaly appearance;* breast buff brown, rest of underparts white; *dark rump* distinguishes it clearly from White-rumped Sandpiper; bill rather short; legs black.

Pectoral Sandpiper: *Calidris melanotos*

Habitat and status. A fairly common visitor to both islands, frequenting mainly flooded savannahs and ricefields but also found on the coast and in marshes. Present in considerable numbers early August–November, isolated records on 21 February, 2 May and 28 July. (Specimens: LM, TRVL.)

Banding status. Nineteen birds were banded at Pointe-a-Pierre in 1960–61, and 2 in 1970. No recoveries.

Range. Breeds in arctic America and Siberia, wintering S to Chile and Argentina.

Description. 9 in. A medium-sized sandpiper, upperparts streaked brown, dark line along rump and tail, bordered by white; no wing-bar; breast streaked brown, sharply contrasted with white lower underparts; legs greenish yellow. Size varies considerably within a flock owing to difference between the sexes.

Measurements. Wing: 9 unsexed 122–135mm (130). Weight: 2 unsexed 48, 49gm.

Voice. A sharp, single chirping note, lower-pitched than most sandpiper calls; mostly given in alarm.

Food. Insects, including caterpillars, beetles and grasshoppers, and molluscs and seeds.

Behaviour. Extremely gregarious, frequenting the golf course and playing fields at Pointe-a-Pierre in flocks up to 100, in company usually with Lesser Golden Plover. It seems to be less nervous than most other sandpipers, standing motionless and silent in the grass as people approach, and eventually taking off suddenly in a flock. When feeding, birds sometimes show hostile behaviour towards others of the same species.

Semipalmated Sandpiper: *Calidris pusilla*
"Sanderling"; "Plover"

Habitat and status. A very common visitor to both islands, found mainly on the coasts but also in inland marshes, flooded savannahs and beside reservoirs. Present in large numbers throughout the year, but most numerous from August to April. (Specimens: AMNH, ANSP, TRVL.)

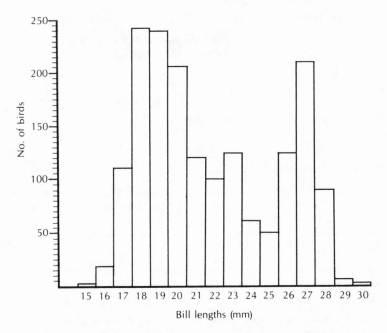

Figure 27. Proportions of Semipalmated and Western Sandpipers

Banding status. From 1959 to 1964 a total of 1749 small sandpipers were banded, nearly all at Pointe-a-Pierre. Of these, 963 were identified as Semipalmated, 638 as Western Sandpipers, and 148 could not be determined between the two species, either from measurements or plumage. Apart from numerous retraps at Pointe-a-Pierre, 1 Semipalmated Sandpiper was recovered shot at Caroni 1 wk after being banded. Among the retrapped birds were some caught 3 yr after being banded.

Range. Breeds in arctic America, wintering S to Chile, Brazil and Argentina.

Description. 6 in. Upperparts grayish brown, the dark centres of many feathers giving a mottled or streaked effect; eye-stripe pale; central tail blackish, flanked by white; underparts mainly white; legs black, bill short, black. See also Western Sandpiper.

Measurements. Figure 27 shows the proportions of birds of this and the Western Sandpiper (measured in Trinidad) with differing bill lengths (measured from the feathers to the tip). There is some overlap at 21–22mm between female Semipalmated and male Western. Females of both species are larger and have longer bills. Of birds with bills 15–20mm, 111 unsexed had wings 89–102mm, av. 95.7, S.D. 2.26; 50 unsexed weighed 17–30gm, av. 22.8, S.D. 3.28.

Voice. A rather nondescript single note, *djjt;* also a light chittering.

Food. Molluscs, crustaceans, aquatic insects and algae, mostly taken just above the tide line. Feeds mostly by pecking at the surface of mud.

Behaviour. Extremely gregarious, especially in flight, when very large flocks wheel and manoeuvre in unanimous movements. On Pointe-a-Pierre mudflats shorebirds are much dependent on the state of the tide, and a great deal of movement goes on as it rises and falls. The birds feed by night as well as by day.

Western Sandpiper: *Calidris mauri*

Habitat and status. A very common visitor to both islands, found mainly on the coastal mudflats, occasionally in inland marshes. Present in large numbers throughout the year, but especially from September to April. More common than the Semipalmated Sandpiper October–December. (Specimens: AMNH, LM.)

Banding status. See Semipalmated Sandpiper. Many Western Sandpipers have been retrapped at Pointe-a-Pierre, some nearly 3 yr after the original banding.

Range. Breeds in Alaska, wintering S to Peru, Colombia, Venezuela, the Guianas and the West Indies.

Description. 6 in. Almost indistinguishable in the field from Semipalmated Sandpiper; however, the bill is noticeably longer in most birds, especially females, is thinner at the tip and droops slightly so that the Western Sandpiper appears somewhat over-balanced and tipped forward. Moreover, some birds, especially in summer and early fall, have considerable rufous markings on the upperparts, mainly on the scapulars.

Measurements. See Figure 27. Of birds with bills 25–30mm (possibly mostly females) 111 unsexed had wings 92–104mm, av. 97.6, S.D. 2.03; 50 unsexed weighed 22–32gm, av. 27.3, S.D. 2.44.

Voice. A sharp *jeep,* quite distinct from call of Semipalmated Sandpiper.

Food. Molluscs and aquatic insects. Feeds mostly by probing in wet mud, often in shallow water.

Behaviour. Essentially similar to that of Semipalmated Sandpiper, with which it associates commonly.

Sanderling: *Calidris alba*

Habitat and status. A fairly common visitor to both islands, being found in flocks of up to 40 on the sandy beaches of E and SW Trinidad and W Tobago, also occasionally on Pointe-a-Pierre mudflats. My records cover September–

May, but some birds are probably present throughout the year. (Specimens: LM.)

Range. Breeds in the Arctic, wintering S in America to Chile and Argentina; also found in all other continents.

Description. 7.5 in. *Winter plumage:* upperparts gray, spotted and streaked black; a very distinct white wing-bar noticeable in flight; underparts white; bill and legs black. I have never seen birds in summer plumage.

Measurements. Wing: 2 males 121, 124mm; 1 unsexed 124mm. Weight: 2 males 49gm each*; 1 unsexed 43.5gm*.

Voice. A sharp, single note, *kit.*

Food. Molluscs and aquatic insects.

Behaviour. Of all the sandpipers in Trinidad this species is the most consistent both in habitat and habits. It is almost invariably found in small flocks running about on sandy beaches just above the waterline, chasing the retreating waves to their limit in search of prey and hurrying back before the new ones advance.

Notes. The name "Sanderling" is generally used in Trinidad to denote any small shorebird.

Stilt Sandpiper: *Calidris himantopus*

Habitat and status. A regular visitor to coastal mudflats, lagoons and swamps in Trinidad, recorded in small numbers at Pointe-a-Pierre from July to October, also in April and May; most records occur in September and October. Recorded on passage through Tobago in 1974 (M. Archer). Birds have been recorded throughout the summer in Surinam (Haverschmidt) and on islands off Venezuela (Voous). (Specimens: TRVL.)

Banding status. Ten birds were banded at Pointe-a-Pierre in 1960–62. No recoveries.

Range. Breeds in arctic America, wintering S to Bolivia and Argentina.

Description. 8.5 in. *Winter plumage:* resembles a small Lesser Yellowlegs with dark upperparts and wings, no wing-bar, and white rump and underparts; legs greenish yellow; bill a little longer than Lesser Yellowlegs, tapering and slightly drooping at the tip. *Summer plumage:* white superciliary stripe above chestnut cheek-patch, underparts buffy, barred blackish. Birds seen in April, May and up to 20 September showed varying degrees of summer plumage; others were in winter plumage from 5 August onwards.

Measurements. Wing: 10 unsexed 126–134mm (131). Weight: 3 unsexed 42, 49, 52gm.

Voice. A plaintive single note, *kiu.*

Food. Aquatic insects, molluscs and crustaceans, often taken in water by the bird wading up to its breast and submerging its head.

Behaviour. Usually associates with Dowitchers and Lesser Yellowlegs, but frequently feeds apart in deeper water.

Ruff: *Philomachus pugnax*
Reeve (female)

Habitat and status. A rare vagrant to both islands; 3 records from Trinidad include individuals seen in Caroni swamp from 30 April to 2 May 1965, also on 1 May 1982, and at St. Augustine on 4 October 1971; also recorded at Buccoo, Tobago, in August 1974, 2 birds in December 1981, and others on 28 January 1982 and in mid-January 1989. (No specimen.)

Range. Breeds in N Europe and Asia, wintering S to Africa and S Asia; vagrants regularly recorded on Barbados and in E USA.

Description. 12 in. *Winter plumage:* resembles Lesser Yellowlegs but slightly larger; distinctly browner upperparts, boldly patterned with buff; throat and breast also buff, lower underparts white; white oval patches on either side of dark central tail, prominent in flight; bill straight, shorter than that of Yellowlegs and thicker at base; legs greenish yellow to orange. *Transitional plumage:* (males) upperparts, throat and breast often distinctively marked with black or buff splotches and mottling. (In breeding plumage male Ruffs display various combinations of colours with prominent ruffs and ear-tufts.) Female some 2 in. smaller than male.

Food. Crustaceans, molluscs and insects.

Buff-breasted Sandpiper: *Tryngites subruficollis*

Habitat and status. A rare visitor to both islands, probably on passage. Most recent records are of individuals seen on one day only, at Pointe-a-Pierre golf course and mudflats and Nariva River mouth; 1 record (Gibbs) is of 12 birds on a flooded savannah at St. Augustine, several of which stayed for a few days. All records are between 11 September and 16 October. (No specimen, but collected by Léotaud and Kirk.)

Range. Breeds in arctic America, wintering S to Uruguay and Argentina.

Description. 8 in. A plover-like sandpiper, upperparts brown mottled with black, head and neck buffish brown, not streaked, underparts uniform pale buff; bill rather short; legs yellowish.

Voice. A low *chwup,* or a trilled *prrreet* (from Bent 1929). I have never heard the call.

Food. Insects.

Behaviour. When feeding, this species associates mostly with Lesser Golden Plovers and Pectoral Sandpipers. Its plover-like attitudes enable it to be readily distinguished from the latter species, even at a distance. On 11 September 1960, when I was attempting to trap shorebirds and terns on the sandy beach at the Nariva River mouth, a Buff-breasted Sandpiper flew up and landed close to the mist net. After inspecting the net carefully it walked under the lowest section and flew on its way.

Upland Sandpiper: *Bartramia longicauda*
Upland Plover; Bartram's Sandpiper

Habitat and status. An uncommon passage migrant through both islands, inhabiting savannahs, golf courses and flooded pastures. Regular records in Trinidad of a few birds in September and October, earliest date 26 August, latest 22 October. A few records for March and April. No Tobago records since Kirk (1883). (Specimen: AMNH.)

Banding status. One bird was banded at Pointe-a-Pierre in September 1960. No recoveries.

Range. Breeds in arctic America, wintering through South America from the Guianas (Haverschmidt 1966) to Argentina.

Description. 12 in. Upperparts and breast dark brown, streaked buff; crown-stripe whitish; central tail blackish; rest of underparts white; bill yellowish, rather thin and short; legs pale yellow. Somewhat resembles Golden Plover, but distinguished by small head, long neck and long, pointed tail.

Measurements. Wing: 1 male 155mm.

Voice. In alarm, a light *kip-ip-ip-ip*.

Food. Almost entirely insects.

Behaviour. Occurring only in small flocks or individually, this species gives the impression more of a plover than a sandpiper both in its demeanour and in its choice of habitat. It prefers to run rather than fly when disturbed, is more wary than most sandpipers and often, on alighting, keeps its wings aloft for a moment. It also occasionally perches on posts.

Whimbrel: *Numenius phaeopus*
Hudsonian Curlew; "Crook-bill"

Habitat and status. A fairly common winter visitor from the north to both islands, frequenting mudflats and swamps. Recorded in Trinidad during all months, but mainly August–November. There have also been 3 sight records of the white-rumped Eurasian subspecies: at Caroni on 6 July 1975 (J. Danzenbaker) and 14 February 1984 (R. Forster), and at Buccoo, Tobago, on 7 July 1977 (Bull 1978). Vagrants of this race have been recorded on Barbados. (Collected by Léotaud.)

Banding status. Three birds were banded at Pointe-a-Pierre 1960–62. One of these, banded on 8 October 1960, was recovered in Surinam on 18 August 1961.

Range and subspecies. Almost cosmopolitan, breeding in the N of America, Europe and Asia and migrating S in winter; *N. p. hudsonicus* (Latham) breeds in arctic America, wintering S to Argentina and Chile. The nominate race breeds in N Europe and Siberia, wintering mainly in Africa and India.

Description. 17 in. Upperparts generally grayish brown, mottled with whitish buff; pale buff crown-stripe and superciliary; rest of crown and eye-stripe dark brown; underparts white, streaked and barred with brown; long, decurved bill (3–4 in.); legs bluish gray.

Measurements. Wing: 3 unsexed 226, 234, 249mm.

Voice. A series of rapid, piping whistles, *whee-whee-whee-whee*.

Food. Molluscs, crustaceans and insects.

Behaviour. Usually found in small flocks. In flight the birds often fly in single file, occasionally in V-formation.

Eskimo Curlew: *Numenius borealis*

Habitat and status. Formerly a passage migrant from the north through both islands. Léotaud had a specimen taken in September on a dry savannah, and Kirk recorded it in Tobago. No records this century. Recently considered on the verge of extinction, this species was occasionally seen in S USA in the early 1960s, and a specimen was taken in Barbados in September 1964.

Range. Breeds (or bred) in arctic America, wintering S to Argentina.

Description. 13 in. Rather similar to Whimbrel, but smaller and with a shorter, only slightly curved bill (about 2 in.). Head not conspicuously striped, underparts buffy, distinctly lighter than upperparts; undersurface of wings noticeably cinnamon; legs dark greenish.

Voice. A sharp squeak, also a twittering series (hence one of its West Indian names, "Chittering Curlew").

[Long-billed Curlew: *Numenius americanus*]

Habitat and status. Recorded by Kirk for Tobago, under the name *N. longirostris*. It is most likely that this record refers to the Whimbrel.

Range. Breeds in C Canada and USA, wintering south to S USA, Mexico and Guatemala, casually to Panama.

Description. 23 in. Much larger than the Whimbrel, lacking the head-stripes; underwings bright cinnamon; bill very long (up to 7 in.), decurved.

Voice. A harsh *cur-lee*, rising in pitch.

Hudsonian Godwit: *Limosa haemastica*

Habitat and status. A rare winter visitor to Trinidad mudflats and savannahs; records include birds seen at Pointe-a-Pierre, Fishing Pond, St. Augustine and Port of Spain sewage ponds between 18 September and 22 January, also on Tobago in November (J. Cudworth); these records are of individuals or small groups to a maximum of 15 (seen in mid-October at Pointe-a-Pierre). (Specimens: PSM; collected by Léotaud.)

Range. Breeds in arctic America, wintering S to Chile and Argentina.

Description. 15 in. *Winter plumage:* a large, gray sandpiper, resembling on the ground a Willet, but with long, slightly upturned bill, pinkish towards base, and blackish legs. In flight shows a very noticeable white rump and black tail, also a narrow white wing-bar. *Breeding plumage:* more blackish above, rusty below with dusky barring.

Voice. A low chattering; usually silent.

Food. Molluscs, crustaceans, worms and insects.

Behaviour. Though considered a wary species, the individual which spent more than a week at Pointe-a-Pierre in October 1965 was almost always to be found on the close-cut lawn surrounding a large office building, often feeding a few yards from it. It appeared to favour a certain spot with especially soft soil, for it fed there a great deal, thrusting its long bill deep into the ground and extracting worms. So constant was the godwit's attention at this place that I set a clap-net close by and twice just failed to catch it. It is a very sedate bird, never bobbing and tilting like the Yellowlegs.

Notes. Hagar (1966) has shown that the species breeds in large numbers in the Hudson Bay area and is not so rare as has been thought for many years. One reason for its reputation is the scarcity of records of migrant birds. Even in Barbados, where such a large shorebird would never escape the notice of hunters, records are regular but very few. Hagar suggests that this godwit normally makes its landfall farther south in South America, after an oversea journey from the New England coast.

Marbled Godwit: *Limosa fedoa*

Habitat and status. Recently recorded on passage in Trinidad; 4 birds at Pointe-a-Pierre on 27 September 1980, and others there and at Port of Spain savannah in October 1984. (Collected by Léotaud, but no extant specimens.) Kirk recorded it for Tobago, but his records may refer to the Hudsonian Godwit.

Range. Breeds in W Canada and NW USA, wintering mainly down the W coast of America S to Peru and Chile.

Description. 18 in. Larger than the Hudsonian Godwit; generally buff-brown with a marbled pattern on back and wings; underparts barred; no distinctive tail markings; bill long, slightly upturned, pinkish towards base.

Voice. A harsh single syllable.

Short-billed Dowitcher: *Limnodromus griseus*
Eastern Dowitcher; Common Dowitcher

Habitat and status. A common visitor to both islands, frequenting mainly mudflats but also freshwater swamps and flooded pastures. Largest numbers (flocks of over 250) are present from late August to mid-October, but fair numbers are present through the winter and a few have been recorded in all summer months. (Specimens: TRVL.)

Banding status. At Pointe-a-Pierre from 1959 to 1964 144 birds were banded, the majority in 1960. Two of these, banded in August and September 1960, were recovered on the coast of Guyana in October 1960. Another, banded on 20 September 1960, was shot in the Oropouche Lagoon on 9 October 1960. Other birds were retrapped at Pointe-a-Pierre after intervals of 5–8 wk.

Range and subspecies. Breeds in Canada and Alaska, wintering S to Brazil and Peru; *L. g. griseus* (Gmelin) breeds in NE Canada, wintering S from the Caribbean to Brazil. Measurements of trapped birds suggest that the larger *L. g. hendersoni* (Rowan) is also present in winter; it breeds in NW Canada, wintering south to N South America.

Description. 11 in. *Winter plumage:* generally gray-brown above, streaked and barred with blackish and buff; rump and a narrow V up the lower back white; tail barred black and white; prominent whitish superciliary; underparts mainly white. *Summer plumage:* generally rufous above, paler below. Bill long, straight and black; short legs dark greenish. Females are larger than males.

Measurements. Wing: 127 unsexed 130–152mm (143). Bill: 139 unsexed 47–68mm (57). Weight: 49 unsexed 59–124gm (92). To a certain extent this wide range in weights is correlated with wing lengths, but it is more probably due to the fact that some birds were trapped soon after arrival, others after a stay of several weeks. One bird weighing 87gm on 18 September 1962 weighed 122gm when retrapped on 14 November 1962.

Voice. A sharp triple call, *tew-tew-tew*, reminiscent of Yellowlegs but more rapid, usually given in flight.

Food. Molluscs, aquatic insects and worms; it feeds very like a snipe, jabbing its long bill deep into soft mud, sometimes feeding in shallow water.

Behaviour. This snipe-like shorebird is particularly remarkable for its extreme tameness, at least in Trinidad, where this quality may be accentuated by fatigue after a long migratory journey. Of the larger shorebirds they have been by far the easiest to trap in mist nets, and the same flock will return to the net several times, even when some of their number have already been taken. In flight the Dowitcher is extremely gregarious, and its erratic flight is characteristic.

Notes. In spite of its small size, the Dowitcher is often hunted, usually illegally in the closed season. A hunter reporting the recovery of a band referred to this species as "Spikers or Ploward", showing that considerable confusion exists over the identification of this bird, yellowlegs and plovers.

Common Snipe: *Gallinago gallinago*
Wilson's Snipe (*delicata*); South American or Brazilian Snipe (*paraguaiae*)

Habitat and status. Frequents swamps and marshes of both islands, breeding locally in Trinidad; recorded in every month except September, northern migrants being especially common in January; records from May to July very few. (Specimens: TRVL [*delicata*]; PSM [*paraguaiae*].)

Range and subspecies. Almost cosmopolitan; *G. g. delicata* (Ord) breeds in North America, wintering S to Colombia, Venezuela and Surinam; it is a little larger than *G. g. paraguaiae* (Vieillot), which also has white (*not* buff) under-tail-coverts barred with brown. The latter ranges throughout most of South America.

Description. 11 in. Head and upperparts generally dark brown, the back and wings streaked and barred with buff; a prominent whitish superciliary and narrow crown-stripe; tail rufous, tipped black; breast mottled brown, abdomen white; under-tail-coverts buff or white barred with pale brown; bill long, straight, horn-coloured; legs very short, grayish green.

Measurements. Wing: *delicata,* 1 male 120mm.

Voice. A short rasping *tssk,* usually given when flushed (northern race).

Food. Worms, insects, seeds and algae.

Nesting. Four nests of *paraguaiae* recorded at Aripo Savannah and Caroni in May, September and October. The nest is a mere depression in a tuft of grass. The clutch is 2 buff eggs with blackish markings, av. 40.6 × 29.4mm (8). The incubation period of *delicata* in North America is about 19 days, both sexes incubating. The young are precocial. Barlow (1967) describes a parent's distraction display with dragging wings in Uruguay.

Behaviour. When flushed, a snipe characteristically flies off with an erratic, zigzag course, rising high in the air before circling to drop back to the ground not far away. Although I have not witnessed it in Trinidad, the species is well known for its aerial courtship manoeuvres, during which it dives steeply down from a considerable height, producing a resonant "drumming" or "winnowing" sound for 2 or 3 sec with the vibrations of its spread outer tail-feathers and half-closed quivering wings.

RECURVIROSTRIDAE: Stilts and Avocets

This family of shorebirds is characterized by very long legs, sharply contrasting black-and-white plumage and long, thin bills, in the Avocet noticeably upturned. They inhabit swamps and lagoons of both fresh and salt water, and are often seen in small flocks. (2)

Black-necked Stilt: *Himantopus mexicanus*
American Stilt

Habitat and status. A rather uncommon inhabitant of mangrove swamps in Trinidad, probably migrating to the continent outside the breeding season, but recorded in all months (White 1987). Also 2 adults seen at Buccoo, Tobago, on 7 February 1990. (No specimen, but recorded by Léotaud.)

Range and subspecies. Throughout the warmer temperate and tropical zones of America; the nominate race breeds from USA S through Middle America, West Indies and South America to Bolivia and Brazil; an allied race is known in S South America.

Description. 14 in. Crown, nape, patch behind eye, upperparts and wings black; forehead, eye-ring, underparts, upper-tail-coverts and tail white; bill black, long, thin; legs very long, pink.

Voice. A sharp nasal note, *peent,* repeated at intervals.

Food. Mostly insects and molluscs obtained by probing.

Nesting. Breeding recorded between March and June at Caroni, Cedros and Port of Spain sewage ponds. The shallow nest of sticks and roots is placed on the bare earth, sometimes below mangroves. The clutch is 3–4 olive-buff eggs, blotched and spotted with black, av. 44 × 32mm (4). Young precocial.

Behaviour. These are noisy, excitable birds, often found in flocks of up to 30. They wade in shallow water and are one of the first species to notice any intruder; they bob repeatedly like sandpipers. In July 1959 I saw some birds, probably breeding, in the mangroves bordering the Beetham Highway. One bird allowed me to approach to within 10 yd, when it flew close over my head, landed and promptly sat down on the bare ground, effectively distracting my attention from a nest, which I never found! Other forms of injury-feigning known for *mexicanus* are limping and helpless wing-flapping.

American Avocet: *Recurvirostra americana*

Habitat and status. The only record is that of Kirk for Tobago, which in this case seems authentic. It has been recorded as an accidental visitor to other

West Indian islands, including Barbados. (No recent records and no specimen.)

Range. Breeds in W Canada and USA, wintering from S USA south to Guatemala.

Description. 18 in. Mainly white with scapulars and wings black and white; bill long, thin, noticeably upturned; legs very long, bluish. In breeding plumage head and neck tinged brownish.

Voice. A repeated, sharp *wheek*.

Behaviour. Feeds in shallow water with a spoonbill-like action, sweeping its bill from side to side searching for insects and other prey.

STERCORARIIDAE: Skuas and Jaegers

These large, powerful seabirds breed in the cold regions of the world, wintering in the more temperate climates. Larger than most gulls, they obtain their food mostly by piracy, pursuing and robbing other birds. (3)

Pomarine Jaeger: *Stercorarius pomarinus*
Pomarine Skua

Habitat and status. An uncommon visitor to coastal waters off Trinidad. Good sight records of 12 birds: 1 off Pointe-a-Pierre on 15 January, 4 off Galeota Point on 5 March and 7 off Toco on 2 January. Other jaegers seen may have been this or Parasitic Jaeger. (No specimen.)

Range. Breeds in the Arctic, wintering at sea in the Atlantic S to the Caribbean and off W Africa, occasionally off N South America; also in other oceans.

Description. 22 in. Rather similar to Parasitic Jaeger, but larger and heavier. Central tail-feathers of adult longer, blunt-ended and twisted. *Immature:* all dark brown or mottled and barred, without elongated tail-feathers.

Parasitic Jaeger: *Stercorarius parasiticus*
Arctic Skua

Habitat and status. A rather rare visitor to coastal waters off both islands. Of 18 jaegers recorded between 1958 and 1982, covering the months of December, January and April–July, most were immature birds and only 6 can definitely be referred to this species. On 30 December 1988 a light-phase adult was seen inland over Waller Field (W. Peterson et al.). (No specimen.)

Range. Breeds in the Arctic, wintering in the Atlantic S to the latitude of the Straits of Magellan, also in other oceans. Casual records from Curaçao, Barbados and the Grenadines.

Description. 17–18 in. *Light-phase adult:* black cap, dark brown upperparts and wings, with white primary quills showing as a white flash in flight, whitish cheeks, neck and underparts; tail wedge-shaped, the central feathers elongated by up to 3 in.; bill black, hooked. *Dark phase:* nearly uniform dark brown. Many intermediate forms occur with a dark breast-band and barred flanks. *Immature:* generally barred and mottled dark brown and whitish, with pale bases to primaries. Central tail hardly elongated.

Behaviour. Very like a falcon in flight. It pursues and harries other seabirds, especially terns, until they disgorge their most recent meal (usually fish), which the jaeger then catches in the air. I have also seen it resting like a gull on the sea.

[South Polar Skua: *Catharacta maccormicki*]

Habitat and status. One light-phase bird seen at Icacos Point, Trinidad, on 13 July 1980 (Manolis 1981). Another large skua seen off Tobago on 7 March 1986 (Rooks 1987) may have been this species, or possibly the Great Skua (*C. skua*), which breeds both in the Antarctic and in the far north.

Range. Breeds in the Antarctic, wintering (from May to November) in the N Atlantic and Pacific, mostly well out to sea. Also known from Puerto Rico, Îles des Saintes and Barbados.

Description. 22 in. Generally dark brown with bold white bar at base of primaries; bill heavier than in jaegers; tail broad and short. Light-phase birds have paler gray head, neck and underparts. A heavy-set, powerful bird.

Behaviour. Often pursues smaller seabirds, robbing them of their prey.

LARIDAE: Gulls and Terns

These are the most commonly seen seabirds, frequenting mainly coastal waters but also rivers and lakes. Most species are mainly white or gray. Gulls have slightly hooked bills; terns have more sharply pointed ones. Terns also have narrower wings and dive for their food, while most gulls feed while swimming or walking on the shore. (20)

Herring Gull: *Larus argentatus*

Habitat and status. A rare visitor to Trinidad; one bird banded as a nestling on 11 July 1958 in Michigan, USA, was caught in a fishing net off Chaguanas on 15 October 1959; other immature birds were seen at Pointe-a-Pierre on 3 October 1976 and 19 February 1982.

Range. Breeds in northern parts of both hemispheres, wintering S into temperate and tropical zones; *L. a. smithsonianus* (Coues) has been recorded occasionally as far south as Panama, Aves Island and Barbados.

Description. 23 in. *Adult:* generally white; upper back and wings pale gray, outer primaries black; bill yellow with red spot near tip of lower mandible; legs flesh pink. *Immature:* grayish brown, wings and tail blacker. Bill dark. Gradually acquires white on head, rump and underparts in first 3 yr.

Voice. A loud, clear scream.

Lesser Black-backed Gull: *Larus fuscus*

Habitat and status. A rare visitor to both islands, with 4 records of adults near Pointe-a-Pierre between 25 August and 11 October, and a single record (D. Fisher) from Buccoo, Tobago, on 14 January 1988. (No specimen.)

Range. An Old World species, recently increasing along Atlantic coast of North America and the Caribbean.

Description. 21 in. *Adult:* head and underparts white, back and wings *slate gray;* bill and legs yellow. *Immature:* plumages (first 3 yr) are mottled brown, with black bill and pink legs, gradually showing more signs of adult plumage.

Ring-billed Gull: *Larus delawarensis*

Habitat and status. Several isolated records for both islands; 7 records from Pointe-a-Pierre of individuals seen in every month except July; in Tobago seen at Pigeon Point in December (B. Richardson) and at Buccoo in January 1988. All birds accompanied flocks of Laughing Gulls. (No specimen.)

Range. Breeds in Canada and N USA, wintering S to Panama and Cuba; casual records from Jamaica, Martinique and Barbados.

Description. 19 in. *Adult:* generally white, with gray back and wings, primaries tipped black with white spots; bill yellow, with a conspicuous black ring; legs yellowish or greenish. *Immature:* back and wings brown, head paler, tail white with narrow, black subterminal bar; underparts mottled grayish white; bill and legs dark. Noticeably larger than Laughing Gull.

Laughing Gull: *Larus atricilla*
"Booby"; "Sea-gull"

Habitat and status. Found on the coasts of both islands in all months, but most common from March to November, when flocks of up to 2000 birds have been seen at Pointe-a-Pierre. Absent from many areas of coast December–March, but flocks of 500 have been recorded in December and February at Pointe-a-Pierre, and 200 in January at Port of Spain. Breeding recorded on Little Tobago, but not on Trinidad (or its offshore islands). (Specimens: AMNH, ANSP, YPM, TRVL.)

Range. Breeds on the coasts of USA, Central America and Caribbean islands, wintering S to Peru and Brazil.

Description. 16 in. *Adult (breeding)*: head blackish gray, back and wings gray, outer primaries black, rear edge of wing white; underparts white. Bill and legs dark red. *Adult (non-breeding)*: as above, but head white with mottled black markings; bill black. *Immature:* generally brown above, with white rump and dark band on tail; breast dark; bill and legs black. Many adult birds are in breeding plumage from April to August.

Measurements. Wing: 5 males 275–310mm (297); 3 females 276, 277, 299mm.

Voice. A high scream, often repeated, *kah-kah-kah,* etc.

Food. Mainly fish and crustaceans, also offal, flying termites and fruit of the manjack tree (*Cordia collococca*).

Nesting. Breeding recorded on Little Tobago from April to June (Dinsmore 1972, Morris 1984), moult in July and August, probably also breeds on St Giles Islands and N coast of Tobago. The nest is a slight hollow, sometimes lined with grass, on the ground of the steep, vegetation-covered hillside. The clutch is 1–3 buff eggs, blotched and spotted with dark markings. Of 4 eggs, 3 measured exactly 54 × 35.5mm, the fourth 48.5 × 34.5mm. In USA incubation lasts for about 20 days. A few days after hatching the chicks leave the nest but stay close by it. They do not fly until some weeks later.

Behaviour. I have found these gulls extremely gregarious, particularly in the evenings when they gather from their feeding grounds to form a large raft on the sea, or assemble on the mudflats just above the tide. During the day they feed in more scattered groups, except that they join the gatherings of terns fishing over a shoal. In feeding they exploit every opportunity. Thus they are often seen about ships, seizing the scraps of offal, or clustered about pelicans, sometimes sitting on their backs and helping themselves greedily to whatever they can glean from the pelicans' catch. I have also seen them hawking for flying termites near the shore. In each case the gull approached the insect from below, and with a short upward glide snapped it up. Most unusual of all, in Tobago I watched a flock of about 20 gulls feeding on the berries of a manjack tree 400 ft above sea level and about a mile from the shore. The birds took the fruit on the wing, hovering beside the branches in a rather ungainly fashion.

Common Black-headed Gull: *Larus ridibundus*

Habitat and status. A regular, but fairly rare, visitor to both islands, apparently increasing since first recorded in 1976 (Fisher 1978), especially on W coast of Trinidad, reservoirs and sewage ponds, and off Turtle Beach, Tobago. (No specimen.)

Range. An Old World species, recently expanding its range in the New World, especially on N Atlantic coast, where nesting has been recorded (Holt et al. 1986). A Russian-banded bird was recovered on Barbados.

Description. 16 in. *Adult (non-breeding)*: differs from Laughing Gull mainly in much paler gray back and wings, showing prominent white wedge on upper leading edge of wing, contrasting with dark area below; head white with dark ear-spot. *Breeding adult:* chocolate-brown hood, less extensive than Laughing Gull's, and red legs.

Notes. Greater interest and expertise amongst ornithologists with regard to seabirds has led to the recent discovery of previously unsuspected species far from their known ranges. One such possibility is a sight record of the Patagonian Brown-hooded Gull (*L. maculipennis*) at Store Bay, Tobago, by English ornithologist N. Rogers (in litt.) on 22 August 1987. This S Atlantic species, considered by some a race of *L. ridibundus,* has hitherto only been known to range as far north as 10° S off the Brazilian coast during the austral winter, some 2500 miles distant from Tobago. In my view the record remains doubtful.

[Sabine's Gull: *Xema sabini*]

Habitat and status. A single record only, of an immature bird seen and photographed at an oil-rig off Galeota Point, SE Trinidad, on several occasions between 2 and 21 March 1982 (D. Raby).

Range. Breeds in the Arctic, wintering S in Pacific and Atlantic oceans; the only other Caribbean record is from Cuba in December 1954.

Description. 13 in. *Adult* (winter): head, underparts, rump and shallow *forked tail* white, with dark band behind crown; back and upperwing gray, outer primaries black, inner primaries and secondaries white; bill black, tipped yellow. Breeding birds have dark gray heads. *Immature:* as adult, but back and upperwing brownish, and tail tipped black.

Black Tern: *Chlidonias niger*

Habitat and status. A regular but rather uncommon passage migrant on the coasts of Trinidad, where occasionally large numbers have been seen in September and October; earliest date 26 June, latest mid-January. A few spring records. (Specimens: TRVL.)

Range and subspecies. *C. n. surinamensis* (Gmelin) breeds in Canada and USA, wintering S to Chile and the Guianas; the nominate race breeds in Europe, Africa and W Asia.

Description. 9.5 in. *Adult (breeding)*: head, neck and underparts black, and white under-tail-coverts; back and wings gray; tail shallow-forked, rather short. *Adult (non-breeding) and immature:* back and wings gray; head and underparts white, with blackish patch over ear-coverts and dark hindneck. All the birds I have seen have been in the latter plumage, or in intermediate plumage with mottled head and underparts.

Measurements. Wing: 1 male 210mm.

Voice. A sharp *keea* or *krik*.

Food. Small fish; in the breeding season largely insects.

Behaviour. Flocks of up to 200 birds have been recorded resting on the beach at the Nariva River mouth; at intervals they all fly off to feed over the sea. On passage this species does not seem to frequent inland lakes, marshes and rivers, which are its normal habitat in the breeding season. At sea near Soldado Rock I encountered many Black Terns on 30 September. Most were sitting on the rafts of floating water hyacinth (*Eichornea*) which are brought into the Gulf of Paria from the Orinoco.

Large-billed Tern: *Phaetusa simplex*
Great-billed Tern   **Figure 28**

Habitat and status. A fairly common visitor, occasionally breeding, to the W coast, reservoirs and freshwater marshes of Trinidad, regularly recorded from March to October, earliest date 11 January, latest 17 November. (Specimens: AMNH, ANSP, TRVL.)

Range and subspecies. South America from Colombia to Argentina and Uruguay; *P. s. simplex* (Gmelin) ranges S to Peru and Brazil.

Description. 15 in. Crown black, mantle and short, almost square, tail dark gray, wing-coverts and secondaries white, primaries dark brown, underparts white; legs olive; massive bill bright yellow. In the latter months of the year the head is mainly white, with a black ear-patch. No other tern shows this "harlequin" pattern on its upperparts.

Measurements. Wing: 2 males 278, 297mm; 3 females 270, 283, 292mm.

Voice. An extremely raucous call, almost goose-like in tone; also a more subdued cluck. The noisy cry is often heard from several birds together as they pursue each other.

Food. Mainly fish, obtained by surface-plunging. Also frequently seen hawking for termites inland.

Nesting. Breeding recorded only by B/S during May in the freshwater area of the Caroni marshes. The nest was a depression on the ground amidst rushes. The clutch is 2 eggs, pale gray with brown spots and blotches, av. 46.25 × 33.5mm (4). (Cherrie [1916] recorded this species breeding in the Orinoco region from December to February.)

Behaviour. I have frequently seen this tern flying up and down the coast or over Pointe-a-Pierre reservoirs in small bands of 5 or 6 birds. At rest on the mudflats, however, it forms quite large flocks of 50 or more. It also perches on old treestumps along the shore. It seems to be a bird of an excitable and

© John P. O'Neill - 1990

Figure 28. Large-billed Tern

energetic temperament, often indulging in wild chases involving from 2 to 6 birds, the significance of which I have not yet understood. It is quite aggressive towards other water-birds, and I have seen a single bird attacking an Osprey.

Gull-billed Tern: *Sterna nilotica*
"Pillikins"; *Gelochelidon nilotica*

Habitat and status. A regular winter visitor in small numbers to Trinidad, frequenting the W and S coasts, also found inland over freshwater marshes and ricefields. Recorded from August to December, but also on 12 May, 19 June and 28 July, latest date 18 December. No Tobago record yet. (Specimen: ANSP.)

Range and subspecies. Almost cosmopolitan, except for the colder regions; *S. n. aranea* (Wilson) breeds in S USA, Mexico, Bahamas and the Virgin Islands, wintering S to Peru and Argentina; recorded throughout the year, but not breeding, in the Guianas.

Description. 15 in. *Adult (breeding)*: crown black, upperparts pale gray, underparts white; tail moderately forked, rather short; bill short, black, noticeably thicker than that of other terns; legs dark. *Adult (non-breeding) and immature:* head nearly all white, with small dark ear-patch. Flies with a rather leisurely wing-beat.

Voice. A rather dry call, *kerreck.*

Food. Fishes and crustaceans, including crabs; also frequently insects taken in freshwater areas, and sometimes small reptiles and mammals.

Behaviour. Rather distinctive in feeding. Flying with comparatively slow wing-beats, it does not direct the bill and head downwards as do the diving terns, but swoops suddenly to the surface of the ground or water, where it deftly picks up its prey. Associates freely with other gulls and terns.

Caspian Tern: *Sterna caspia*

Habitat and status. A rare visitor to Trinidad; the single record is of a bird banded as a nestling at Parry Sound, Ontario, in June 1951 and recovered in Caroni swamp on 15 November 1953. (It is of interest that another bird banded by the same bander in the same area in June 1955 was recovered in Panama in November 1955, constituting the only record for the species in Panama.)

Range. Cosmopolitan in temperate and tropical zones, except for South America; New World birds breed locally in Canada and USA, wintering S to Mexico and Greater Antilles, and are regularly recorded in Colombia.

Description. 21 in. Resembles Royal Tern but is larger, has a less deeply forked tail, darker wing-tips (from below) and a heavier, *red* bill. In winter the crown, forehead and sides of head are black streaked with white.

Voice. A loud, harsh *kaark,* deeper than call of Royal Tern.

Common Tern: *Sterna hirundo*
"Pillikins"; "Sea Swallow"

Habitat and status. A common visitor to the coasts of Trinidad, especially west and south, recorded in every month. Non-breeding birds are present in large numbers April–July; also recorded off Tobago from May to July (Dinsmore). (Specimens: Trinidad, AMNH, YPM, TRVL.)

Banding status. Between 1920 and 1971 there have been 376 recoveries from Trinidad of birds banded in USA, the great majority being birds banded as nestlings in Massachusetts or New York. A few were banded in the Great Lakes area, one as far west as Minnesota. The great majority were taken in their first 2 yr of life, but 2 individuals were at least 14 and 15 yr old respectively. Recovery dates were well distributed through the year, with smallest totals in August, September and December. Also, one bird recovered in 1970 had been banded in Finland.

Range and subspecies. Cosmopolitan; in the New World the nominate race breeds in North America, the Antilles and islands off Venezuela, wintering S to Peru and Argentina.

Description. 14 in. *Adult (breeding)*: black cap, pale gray back, rest of plumage white, except for black edges to outer primaries; tail deeply forked; legs reddish; bill reddish orange with black tip. *Adult (non-breeding) and immature:* fore-crown white, black patch from eye across nape; black mark on "shoulder" of wing, noticeable in flight; bill blackish.

Measurements. Wing: 2 females 231, 248mm; 1 unsexed 245mm. Weight: 89 unsexed birds 99–104gm (102.2). Erwin et al. (1986) point out that these weights, low compared with those of adults on breeding territory, may result from a variety of factors, e.g., migration stress, local food shortage, the effects of moult or slight oil contamination, or because many were "inexperienced" immature birds.

Voice. In alarm an excited *kee-yarr;* also a high-pitched *kik-kik-kik.*

Food. Mainly small fish, especially *Sardinella,* obtained by surface-plunging, also by following fishing-boats, attending at the landing of seine nets and general scavenging at the shore-line (Blokpoel et al. 1984).

Behaviour. Extremely gregarious, both at rest on mudflats and when fishing over shoals. When feeding, terns of this genus typically fly with fast wing-beats, head and bill pointed downwards, sometimes hovering with spread tail; at the sight of prey they dive with partly closed wings, splash into the sea and emerge almost immediately, shaking off the water.

Notes. Difficulty has been experienced here, as in other countries, in distinguishing this and the Roseate Tern, especially at a distance in non-breeding plumage. Examination of the bird in the hand is the most certain method, and without this check I have often been content to designate birds simply as "white" terns, pending further study of their status and movements. I have therefore only included data which could be referred with reasonable certainty to one or the other species. Needless to say, the local names "Pillikins", "Booby", "Sea-gull", etc., refer to all terns indiscriminately.

Roseate Tern: *Sterna dougallii*

Habitat and status. A fairly common visitor on coasts of both islands; definite records for Tobago April–November (also breeding); large numbers off Trinidad in September, also recorded in most other months from May to February; confusion with Common Tern precludes a more definite status. (Specimen: Trinidad, ANSP.)

Banding status. Between 1927 and 1970, 17 birds banded, mostly as nestlings, in Massachusetts were recovered in Trinidad. Recovery dates were confined to October, November, January, February, May and June; the 6 birds taken in the latter 2 months were all less than 2 yr old.

Range and subspecies. Breeds in temperate zones of both hemispheres; in the New World. *S. d. dougallii* (Montagu) breeds in E USA, the West Indies and S Caribbean islands, wintering S to Venezuela.

Description. 15 in. Very similar to Common Tern, but upperparts whiter and in breeding plumage outer tail-feathers longer; wings shorter. In breeding season adult has a slightly rosy breast; bill black, with some red at base; legs red. Non-breeding birds have a black bill. Immature birds have dark edgings to the pale gray feathers of upperparts and wings. Different call-notes are probably the best diagnostic feature.

Voice. A rasping, guttural note, *kaarr,* a single, light *kik,* and a soft *kirrik,* rather resembling call of the Semipalmated Plover.

Food. Small fish.

Nesting. First authentic nests found near Buccoo in May 1983, also in 1986 and 1987 at Charlotteville (D. Rooks); earlier Dinsmore found a breeding colony of "white" terns on the N coast of Tobago in May 1966. Also many birds frequently seen during April carrying fish and indulging in various courtship activities; in August recently fledged birds still being fed by adults. The eggs of this race are greenish gray finely spotted and flecked with black, and rather variable in size, nearly 200 av. 43 × 30mm.

Bridled Tern: *Sterna anaethetus*

Habitat and status. A rather uncommon tern, frequenting the rocky coasts of Tobago, where it breeds, from March to September; also occasionally found off Trinidad; Soldado records March–August. Absent from both islands October–February. (Specimen: Tobago, AMNH.)

Range and subspecies. Tropical oceans of both hemispheres; *S. a. recognita* (Matthews) ranges throughout the West Indies, including S Caribbean islands, casually on the South American mainland; it is pelagic outside the breeding season.

Description. 14 in. *Adult:* resembles Sooty Tern; generally dark above, white below, but back gray rather than black, a whitish collar separating the back from the black crown; white superciliary stripe extends from forehead to *behind* eye; out of the breeding season the black crown is streaked with white and the dark upperparts are tipped with whitish spots. *Immature:* crown and upperparts dark brown, streaked and edged with white, underparts white. Not at all like immature Sooty Tern.

Measurements. Wing: 1 male 271mm; 1 female 263mm; 1 unsexed 259mm.

Voice. A single, rather musical note, *yerk.*

Food. Small fish and molluscs.

Nesting. Colonial breeding recorded in July 1958 on Smith's Island off Tobago (D. W. Snow), also from April to June on Little Tobago (Dinsmore). The nest-site is on the ground amidst cactus and other vegetation, often on steep cliffsides. The single egg is creamy white, finely spotted with brown, av. 46.3 × 33.3mm (24), but showing considerable size variations (i.e., 40.6–49.6 × 31.2–35.5mm). Both sexes incubate, each sitting for about 24 hr in turn. The chicks are semi-precocial, leaving the nest after a few days.

Behaviour. I have always found Bridled Terns rather wary at their nests, compared with the Sooty and Noddy terns with which they commonly associate in the breeding colonies. They leave their nests some time before an observer can surely locate it, and as a result frequently escape detection. In a crowded Sooty Tern colony the few Bridleds keep rather to themselves, gliding quietly about in the vicinity of their nests. Murphy (1936) recorded their habit of sitting in flocks on the water, which Sooty Terns hardly ever do.

Sooty Tern: *Sterna fuscata*
Wideawake Tern; "Booby"; "Pillikins"

Habitat and status. Common offshore and breeding on islands off Trinidad and Tobago, including Soldado Rock (5000), Little Tobago (2000), Smith's Island (1000) and St. Giles Islands. Largely pelagic outside breeding season, recorded from March to August at breeding grounds, occasional individuals seen September–January. (Specimens: ANSP, TRVL.)

Banding status. Between May 1960 and March 1982, 783 birds were banded on Soldado Rock, most of them nestlings (ffrench 1989). To date the only bird recovered elsewhere was banded as a nestling on 16 June 1963 and found dead on Martinique on 1 July 1966. Seven birds banded between 1962 and 1970 at the Dry Tortugas off Florida, 6 of them nestlings, have been recovered in Trinidad from September to December, 4 in their first year, 2 in their second year. (Banding data have revealed that birds of this species may live for 30 yr.)

Range and subspecies. Pantropical; *S. f. fuscata* (Linnaeus) breeds on islands in the Gulf of Mexico and Bahamas S through the Caribbean and tropical Atlantic to St. Helena and Martin Vas, wintering at sea in the tropical Atlantic.

Description. 15 in. *Adult:* black above, white below; a white V from the top of the bill to *just above* the eye; outer edges of tail white; bill black; tail deeply forked. (See also Bridled Tern.) *Immature:* dark brown all over, with pale buff speckling on the back and wings. Distinguished from Brown Noddy by its forked tail.

Measurements. Wing: 3 males 280, 288, 290mm; 1 female 271mm. Weight: 59 unsexed birds in April 157–220gm (187); 36 unsexed in June 147–195gm (168).

Voice. A harsh, high-pitched *ke-wakka-wa,* a single *kik,* and various other similar calls, usually heard in confused chorus at the breeding grounds.

Food. Mainly small fish, usually about 2–3 in. long, including *Anchoviella perfascita* and *Sardinella sardina,* which are caught at the surface of the water; the terns often follow a shoal which is being simultaneously attacked by big fish from below.

Nesting. Breeds colonially from February to June in an apparently annual cycle, but few eggs are laid after early June. Even these may well be replacements for lost eggs or young. Morris (1984) found an extremely low reproductive success on Little Tobago, possibly related to poor food availability. This may account for the variation in the timing of nesting. Moult recorded in August and September. No nest is made; the birds lay on the bare ground in a slight scrape, preferring a location next to a projecting rock or bush. On Soldado Rock and Little Tobago the rugged terrain forces many birds to use ledges on the steep hillsides. On Smith's Island the birds nest amidst cactus and long tussocky grass, which is thus honeycombed with tunnels. The single egg is of varying shape and colour, being greenish to light brown with dark red spots and blotches mainly at the larger end, av. 52.6 × 37.1mm (16; max. 56 × 38mm, min. 49 × 35.5mm). Occasionally 2 eggs are found together in the same scrape, one perhaps having rolled to the other. Incubation by both sexes lasts for about 29 days, and the young can fly at the age of about 6 wk (Ashmole 1963, Robertson 1964).

Behaviour. Sooty Terns are extremely gregarious, both when feeding and at their breeding grounds, where they are excitable and noisy, keeping up a constant clamour by day and practically throughout the night. On the wing they are graceful yet powerful fliers, expertly using the updraughts to hang motionless in the air above their nests on the rocky islets. They are hardly ever seen in the water, being liable to waterlogging; when feeding they descend to the surface of the sea, snatching their prey deftly without alighting. Often at the breeding grounds the entire colony performs a peculiar group action (sometimes called a "dread"), in which normal activity is suddenly interrupted; following a particular harsh cry the birds all leave their nests and fly out in silence over the sea, sweeping round, gathering together and gradually returning to their places, where normal activity recommences. At the "nest" the parent is fiercely protective and can occasionally be caught while defending an egg or chick. During the heat of the day the adult provides shade for these, adopting a characteristic pose with wings drooping forward and panting. The chicks soon gather into clusters, sometimes straying as far as 30 yd from their hatching place, as they search for shade.

Notes. Colonial nesters like the Sooty Tern are especially subject to predation, and its predators here include frigatebirds (of eggs and young), Peregrine Falcons, humans and possibly iguanas and rats (*Zygodontomys*). The major colonies all exist on wildlife sanctuaries, but in the past this has not deterred

© John P. O'Neill-1990

Figure 29. Yellow-billed Tern

poachers, for the islands' very inaccessibility has prevented adequate supervision by the authorities. As transportation problems decrease with progress, it is essential that proper steps be taken to safeguard the colonies from both poachers and sightseers. One can foresee that uncontrolled exposure to tourists could lead to serious damage in the colonies, where eggs and young are scattered so close together on the ground that it is difficult to avoid stepping on them.

Yellow-billed Tern: *Sterna superciliaris*
Amazon Tern   **Figure 29**

Habitat and status. A regular visitor in small numbers to freshwater reservoirs and lakes in S Trinidad, where recorded annually from April to November; earliest date 21 March, latest 26 November. Also possibly on the E coast, as in Surinam (Haverschmidt 1972). (Specimen: AMNH.)

Range. Through South America E of the Andes from Colombia to Peru, Argentina and Uruguay. Breeds in Surinam at the end of the year (Haverschmidt 1968a, 1972).

Description. 10 in. *Adult:* resembles Least Tern, but tail shorter, wings longer, and *4* outer primaries mainly dark gray; bill all yellow; legs dull yellow. *Immature:* head mainly white, streaked with black on nape and around eye. Bill yellow, tip horn-coloured.

Measurements. Wing: 1 unsexed 176mm. Bill: 30.5mm. Weight: 11 males 40–57gm (47); 18 females 42–57gm (46). (Weight data from Surinam, Haverschmidt 1972.)

Voice. A light *chit,* or *kirrik.*

Food. Small fish and crustaceans.

Behaviour. Found in small flocks resting on the mudbanks of reservoirs at Pointe-a-Pierre, but feed individually much like Least Tern. I once saw one aggressively chasing a Spotted Sandpiper, but at rest they associate freely with Neotropic Cormorants, Skimmers and other larger terns.

Least Tern: *Sterna albifrons*
Little Tern

Habitat and status. Rather uncommon on the coast of Trinidad, where it is recorded from April to December and in February. A fairly large flock is usually present at the Nariva River mouth in September and October. Also seen off Tobago in April and November. Some confusion in identification of this and the Yellow-billed Tern may occur. (Specimens: ANSP.)

Banding status. A bird banded as a nestling in New Jersey, USA, on 29 June 1961 was recovered in Trinidad on 15 October 1961.

Range and subspecies. Cosmopolitan; *S. a. antillarum* (Lesson) breeds in E North America, West Indies and S Caribbean islands, wintering S to Brazil.

Description. 9 in. *Adult (breeding):* black cap, white forehead, generally pale gray above, white below, 2 outer primaries blackish; legs yellow; bill yellow with black tip. *Adult (non-breeding):* crown whitish, black streak from eye to nape; legs dull yellow, bill mainly black. *Immature:* as non-breeding adult, but dark fore-edge of wing, primaries darker gray.

Voice. A high-pitched *cheet,* sometimes repeated.

Food. Small fish.

Nesting. B/S suspected that birds seen in June were nesting, but these may have been Yellow-billed Terns. However, breeding has been recorded in Curaçao, Aruba and Bonaire.

Behaviour. Less gregarious than larger terns, but flocks of up to 170 have been found resting on E coast beaches. Flight exceptionally buoyant; when feeding this little tern habitually hovers and dives into the water for its prey.

Royal Tern: *Sterna maxima*
Thalasseus maximus

Habitat and status. A fairly common resident and winter visitor from the north, found mainly on leeward coasts of both islands, where it is recorded in all months except October; breeding reported from Tobago (Rooks 1987); many birds in breeding plumage present in April. (Specimens: Trinidad, ANSP.)

Banding status. An adult and a nestling were banded on 15 June 1963 on Soldado Rock; the adult was found dead a few days later on Icacos beach. Three birds banded as nestlings at sites between Virginia and South Carolina were recovered in Trinidad within 1, 2 and 7 yr.

Range and subspecies. In the New World *S. m. maxima* (Boddaert) breeds in S USA, Mexico and West Indies S to Curaçao and Trinidad, wintering S to Peru and Argentina; some birds may breed in Uruguay or Argentina (Escalante 1968). Another race breeds in W Africa.

Description. 18 in. *Adult (breeding)*: black cap with crest at back of head, upperparts pale gray, underparts white, forked tail; massive bill orange; legs black. *Adult (non-breeding) and immature:* forehead white, crown streaked with black; in immature upperparts mottled with brown; legs yellowish.

Measurements. Wing: 1 unsexed 365mm.

Voice. A shrill *keeerr,* also a rather grating squawk.

Food. Mainly fish, up to 6 in. long.

Nesting. Breeding recorded occasionally in May and June on Soldado Rock since 1962 (ffrench & Collins 1965), though all but 1 egg failed to hatch because of interference by humans and rainstorms. The single egg is laid on the bare ground, several being grouped together. The egg is buff, covered with thick black spots and scrawls, av. 64.1 × 42.9mm (6), the size varying somewhat. The young leave the "nest" soon after hatching. In Peru wintering adults were seen to feed young which had been hatched 6 months earlier in USA (Ashmole & Tovar 1968).

Behaviour. Gregarious at breeding grounds and at rest, Royal Terns feed individually or in small groups. They usually fly quite high over the sea, plunging in after their prey with a considerable splash. Compared with Sooty and Noddy terns, they are very nervous at the nest, and their propensity for laying only on the flat ridge of Soldado Rock has led to their nesting failures.

Sandwich Tern: *Sterna sandvicensis*
Cayenne Tern; Cabot's Tern; *Thalasseus sandvicensis*

Habitat and status. A rather uncommon species, frequenting mainly the leeward coasts of both islands, where it is recorded regularly from April to September, also November and December. Breeds occasionally in Trinidad, and probably (but not yet proved) in Tobago. (Specimens: AMNH, ANSP.)

Range and subspecies. Breeds in North, Middle and South America, also Europe and W Asia, wintering in tropical regions; *S. s. eurygnatha* (Saunders) breeds on islands off the E coast of South America from Curaçao to Brazil, wintering S to Argentina. Birds with black bills, tipped yellow, were for some time considered to belong to the northern *S. s. acuflavida* (which has even been recognised by some authors as a different species from *eurygnatha*, the Cayenne Tern); however, Junge and Voous (1955) in Curaçao and Haverschmidt (1968a) in Surinam have found *eurygnatha* with bills showing varying amounts of yellow and black. I am inclined, therefore, to believe that 2 records by Roberts (1934) and 3 by me of birds with mainly black bills should be included under *eurygnatha*, for the birds of N South America and adjacent islands appear to show introgression or hybridization with the northern black-billed birds.

Description. 17 in. Resembles the Royal Tern, but is smaller and slimmer. Bill usually all yellow, but some have varying amounts of black, and a few are all black with yellow tip.

Measurements. Wing: 1 male 289mm; 1 female 270mm.

Voice. A loud, grating *krik,* also *kerrup,* lower in pitch than call of most terns.

Food. Mainly small fish, including *Sardinella,* and molluscs.

Nesting. Recorded breeding on Soldado Rock on 10 June 1962 and again in June 1963 (ffrench & Collins 1965). Courtship feeding observed on Tobago in April 1978. Nest-site on Soldado Rock resembled that of Royal Terns; 4 "nests" each contained a single egg, buff with black-and-gray markings. The lengths of 2 eggs were 51 and 52mm; 45 eggs from islands off Venezuela averaged 50.4 × 35.9mm, though length varied from 44.3 to 56.7mm.

Behaviour. Gregarious; feeding habits much like those of Royal Tern, with which it commonly associates.

Brown Noddy: *Anous stolidus*
Noddy Tern

Habitat and status. Common offshore and breeding on islands off Trinidad and Tobago, including Soldado Rock (3000), Little Tobago (1200), Smith's Island, St. Giles and others. Recorded in all months except November. Most common during breeding season, but up to 1000 roost on Soldado at other times. (Specimens: ANSP, TRVL.)

Banding status. A total of 991 birds, both adults and young, were banded on Soldado Rock during 1960–67 (ffrench 1989). A nestling banded on 16 June 1963 was recovered at Aruba on 10 June 1964, and an adult banded on the same date was shot at St. Lucia on 26 February 1964. Among many recaptured birds, 3 nestlings banded in May 1960 were retaken in April, July and August 1966 and March 1967. An adult banded in August 1960 was recaptured in April 1966. In addition 4 nestlings banded in 1961–63 were found to be breeding in 1966, establishing that the species breeds at the age of 3 yr and upwards.

Range and subspecies. Pantropical; *A. s. stolidus* (Linnaeus) breeds from S USA through the West Indies and islands off Central America to S Atlantic islands as far as Tristan da Cunha, also in the Gulf of Guinea. In the off-season most birds are pelagic near their breeding grounds.

Description. 15 in. *Adult:* dark brown all over with whitish fore-crown; tail wedge-shaped. *Immature:* white on crown less extensive. *Downy young,* in two phases: dark gray or rather dirty white, the dark phase predominating on Soldado.

Measurements. Wing: 2 males 261, 266mm; 1 female 275mm. Weight: 351 unsexed birds 125–205gm, the average varying through the year from 175gm in April (30 birds) down to 147 in June (48 birds), back up to 178 in October (49 birds). Two unfledged young in July each weighed 180 gm.

Voice. Usually silent, but when disturbed at breeding grounds makes a deep, hoarse croak, *kaarr;* also a short cluck.

Food. Mostly small fish, especially *Sardinella sardina* and *Anchoviella perfascita.* The noddy feeds like the Sooty Tern, often catching fish at the surface of the water as they are being attacked by bigger fish from below.

Nesting. Breeds colonially from February to July, some eggs found as late as 9 July, but these are probably replacements. As with the Sooty Tern, this species appears to vary the timing of its nesting, perhaps because of food shortage (Morris 1984). Mostly the nests are on rocky ledges and shallow depressions, both on steep cliffsides and on rocks only just above high-tide level. Often quite an elaborate nest of twigs is made, but in many cases a single feather or piece of seaweed symbolises the "nest". A single egg is laid, pale buff spotted with dark brown mainly at the thicker end, av. 54.6 × 36.7mm (16) (one was only 49mm long). Incubation (by both sexes) and fledging periods are each about 5 wk. The young birds tend to stay at or close to the nest until they fly.

Behaviour. Closely associated at their breeding grounds with Sooty Terns, Brown Noddies are much less excitable, though when danger threatens their nests they show great reluctance to move and become very aggressive if forced off. They are rather erratic fliers, often flying low over the sea with a powerful action. Sometimes a number will settle in a flock on the water like gulls. Out of the breeding season many birds roost on Soldado Rock, arriving noiselessly after dark and leaving before dawn. Various forms of courtship display are known, such as rapid nodding of the head, pointing the bill to the ground or the sky, flicking the head back, gaping and feeding of the female by the male. The pair also display with a special flight in which they ascend rapidly and steeply to a considerable height and then glide gradually down, keeping close together all the time. For details of displays see Moynihan (1962).

Notes. One particularly interesting feature of this population of Brown Noddies is the moult. Unlike the majority of other terns, which moult all their

feathers in the 5 months or so immediately following breeding, Brown Noddies (at least in Trinidad) undergo an exceptionally slow primary moult which
lasts about 10 months (from March to January), the moult process being
apparently little affected by the breeding cycle. Thus the bird's wing maintains
approximately the same degree of efficiency throughout the year, for usually 1
primary feather in each wing is growing at any one time (ffrench 1991).

[Lesser Noddy: *Anous tenuirostris***]**
Black Noddy; White-capped Noddy

Habitat and status. Included for Trinidad by B/S on the testimony of
T. Spencer, who saw a bird and collected an egg on Soldado Rock in May
1928. The egg, however, fits better the size and character of Brown Noddy
eggs, and the described location "on the bare rock", is extremely unlikely for
the Lesser Noddy. I therefore reject this record.

Range. Breeds on islands off Central America and Venezuela (Las Roques),
also in the S Atlantic, Indian and Pacific oceans.

Description. 14 in. Very similar to Brown Noddy, but darker with whiter
forehead and relatively longer bill.

Fairy Tern: *Gygis alba*
White Tern

Habitat and status. A single record only, of a bird seen and photographed
at Store Bay, Tobago, on 16 August 1987 (N. Rogers). It was resting on a
fishing-boat just offshore. (No specimen.)

Range. Tropical oceans around the world. In the S Atlantic breeds N as far
as Fernando de Noronha (about 5° S), rarely recorded N of equator.

Description. 12 in. All white, with large head and conspicuous, large black
eyes; tail forked; bill black; legs bluish gray. Buoyant and graceful in flight.

RYNCHOPIDAE: Skimmers

Resembling large, long-winged terns, skimmers are best distinguished by
their long, grotesque bills, with the laterally compressed lower mandible
considerably longer than the upper. They frequent coastal waters and freshwater habitats, feeding low over the water by ploughing the surface with the
lower mandible. (1)

Black Skimmer: *Rynchops niger*

Habitat and status. A non-breeding visitor in fair numbers, confined to the
W and S coasts of Trinidad, also inland reservoirs at Pointe-a-Pierre. Flocks of

up to 400 are often seen from May to November, but smaller numbers have been recorded in all other months except February. (Specimens: AMNH, YPM.)

Range and subspecies. Throughout most of coastal America from Massachusetts and NW Mexico south to Chile and Argentina; *R. n. cinerascens* (Spix) breeds along the South American coast and large rivers from Colombia to Brazil; it is distinguished from the nominate northern race by its slightly larger size, darker gray under-wing-coverts, darker tail and less white on the tips of the secondaries; *R. n. niger* (Linnaeus) breeds on the North American coast S to Mexico and has been recorded in winter casually from Panama and Venezuela; it may visit our area.

Description. 18 in. Generally blackish brown upperparts, the secondaries and outer tail-feathers narrowly tipped white; forehead, sides of head and underparts white, underwings blackish; non-breeding birds show also a whitish collar; immatures generally browner and mottled above. Base of bill reddish, tip black; legs red.

Measurements. Wing: 2 males 345, 360mm; 1 female 385mm; 1 unsexed 370mm.

Voice. A sharp, repeated *querk,* usually only in alarm.

Food. Small fish and crustaceans, taken from the surface of the water.

Behaviour. Extremely gregarious; when resting on mud- or sandbanks, a flock of skimmers stays close-packed, all the birds facing into the wind. In flight they are very distinctive, especially when feeding. The flock flies low over smooth water with shallow, slow wing-beats, the wings held above the horizontal. Sometimes they glide, all the birds tending to synchronize their movements. As they fly along, the long lower mandible is inserted into the water, cutting it like a knife. As it touches its prey, the mandibles clamp together. The skimmer feeds both by day and by night. It is possible that in tropical waters the phosphorescent organisms disturbed by the skimmer's mandible attract prey, so that the bird gains a distinct advantage by retracing its path. Normally skimmers do not show signs of an excitable nature, but I have seen a few of them chasing an Osprey.

COLUMBIDAE: Pigeons and Doves

Characterised by their plump bodies and small heads, short, rather thick bills and soft plumage, most of this family are generally brown in colour, though often glossed with metallic hues. They are found in forests, swamps and open country, where they feed mostly on fruit and seeds. Some species are largely terrestrial, while others perch only in trees; all, however, fly fast and straight with a rapid wing-action. Call-notes are usually a familiar cooing, varying according to the species in rhythm and tone. Both parents incubate and care for the young. (13)

Band-tailed Pigeon: *Columba fasciata*
White-naped Pigeon   **Plate 5(8)**

Habitat and status. A rare resident of upper hill forest in Trinidad. B/S mention several records in the mid-1920s. I have seen the species on 2 occasions at the summit of El Tucuche, where other observers have also seen it, January, June and August. (No specimens extant.)

Range. W North America, Central and South America S to Peru and Argentina.

Description. 14 in. Generally dark brownish gray, glossed bronze on mantle; conspicuous white patch on nape; broad tail-band paler brown; bill and legs yellow.

Voice. A 2-syllabled call, *croo-oo*, repeated several times. Also a soft *croo* in flight.

Food. Fruits of forest trees, including (in Colombia) berries of *Conostegia* (Willis 1966c).

Nesting. Breeding recorded in March and April (B/S). The small nest of twigs is placed on a tree at about 20 ft. There are 2 white eggs, av. 41 × 28.2mm (4).

Behaviour. Found singly or in small groups in Trinidad, this species is, in my experience, remarkably tame. Elsewhere in its range large flocks are seen outside the breeding season.

Scaled Pigeon: *Columba speciosa*
Scaly-necked Pigeon; "Ramier Ginga"   **Plate 5(6)**

Habitat and status. A fairly common resident of forests in Trinidad, less common in the south. (Specimens: AMNH, ANSP, CM, YPM, PSM.)

Range. Mexico S to Ecuador, Argentina and Brazil.

Description. 12 in. *Male:* generally dark brownish purple, the mantle, neck and underparts having a scaled appearance, the dark feathers being edged or spotted with white or pale green; lower underparts whitish edged with purple; eye-ring red; bill bright red, tipped whitish; legs reddish. *Female:* as male, but dark brown rather than purple; generally a little smaller than male.

Measurements. Wing: 8 males 183–198mm (191); 3 females 184, 185, 188mm. Weight: 1 male 325gm; 2 females 335, 335gm; 3 unsexed 332, 342, 360gm.

Voice. A deep cooing in 2 syllables, *croo-kuk*, or in 4 syllables, *cuck-a-loo-oo*, the accent on the penultimate.

Food. Fruits and seeds of forest trees, especially the hog-plum (*Spondias monbin*).

Nesting. Breeding recorded in March and April (B/S), moult in May. A stick nest is built fairly high in a forest tree. The clutch is 2 white eggs, av. 39.0 × 29.7mm (4).

Behaviour. Usually seen singly or in small numbers feeding in the tops of tall forest trees. Flight is rapid and normally at a considerable height above the canopy. I have found them to approach ground level only when crossing a ridge or peak. An extremely wary species which is hunted in the open season.

Pale-vented Pigeon: *Columba cayennensis*
Blue Pigeon; Rufous Pigeon; "Ramier Mangle"   **Plate 5(9)**

Habitat and status. A fairly common resident of both islands; in Tobago frequents hill forest and secondary scrub at lower altitudes (especially during July–September), but in Trinidad is known only in mangrove swamps, woods bordering savannahs and low-lying forests. (Specimens: AMNH, ANSP, BM, TRVL.)

Range and subspecies. Mexico S to Bolivia and Argentina; *C. c. pallidicrissa* (Chubb) ranges from Mexico to N Colombia, N Venezuela and our islands.

Description. 12 in. *Male:* head, breast and upperparts generally dull purple, glossed coppery on nape; lower back and tail dark gray; lower underparts pale gray; bill blackish; legs red; iris and orbital area red. *Female:* slightly duller above.

Measurements. Wing: 5 males 171–190mm (180); 3 females 177, 179, 186mm. Weight: 1 unsexed 262gm.

Voice. A variable cooing, 3–6 syllables, emphasis being given to every second or third syllable, e.g., *kuk-kuk-croo-oo.*

Food. Small fruits, berries and seeds, including those of *Byrsonima, Solanum* and *Miconia.*

Nesting. Breeding recorded February–May in Trinidad (B/S), and in March, May, June and November in Tobago (Dinsmore); I also found nests with eggs on St. Giles Islands in August. Moult in Tobago recorded in July and August. The nest is a slight structure of twigs 6–15 ft above ground in a small tree. One white egg is laid, av. 38.1 × 28.2mm (3).

Behaviour. Usually fairly solitary, but sometimes found feeding in sizeable flocks. After the 1963 hurricane Tobago birds were often seen in flocks invading poultry-runs near sea level. Normally they are wary, being hunted for food.

Eared Dove: *Zenaida auriculata*
Violet-eared Dove; Wine-coloured Dove; Zenaida Dove;
"Wood Dove"   **Plate 5(7)**

Habitat and status. A fairly common local resident on both islands, but the species almost certainly migrates in some numbers. In Trinidad mainly confined to mangroves and neighbouring swampy savannahs, but August and September records at Toco and Soldado Rock indicate some migration at that time. In SW Tobago fairly common, especially in and near mangroves or on savannahs, and numbers increase in August, apparently from an influx of migrants. Details of this migration remain unclear (see below). The fact that no mention of this species occurs in Léotaud, Kirk or the early collections probably indicates that it is a recent arrival in our islands. (Specimens: ANSP, YPM, LM.)

Range and subspecies. Throughout South America from Colombia in Argentina and Chile; *Z. a. stenura* (Bonaparte) ranges from E Colombia and Venezuela to the Guianas and N Brazil, also on offshore islands from the Grenadines southward.

Description. 9 in. *Adult male:* crown gray, upperparts olive brown, with conspicuous black spots on wing-coverts; black streak behind eye, and a patch below ear-coverts black, glossed blue; tail graduated, tipped broadly with cinnamon buff; underparts vinous; bill black; legs dark red. *Adult female:* as male, but duller. *Immature:* generally much duller, grayish brown, and barred with paler markings.

Measurements. Wing: 1 male 133mm; 1 female 132mm. Weight: 6 males 102–125gm (112); 1 female 95gm*.

Voice. A soft, low *oo-ah-oo.*

Food. Mainly seeds, taken on the ground; also known to take soaked bread from feeding tables after the 1963 hurricane.

Nesting. Breeding recorded in December and January (Bond) and from March to September (B/S), a small twig nest being built from a few to 50 ft above ground in a mangrove or other small tree. The clutch is 2 white eggs, av. 28.4 × 21.1mm (9). In the Ecuadorian race the eggs were laid at 24-hr intervals, and incubation lasted about 14 days (Marchant 1960), but in NE Venezuela (Friedmann & Smith 1950) the whole cycle from nest-building to fledging was completed within 21 days, incubation lasting less than 12 days.

Behaviour. While often seen in pairs or singly, this species is gregarious at times, forming flocks of 50–100 birds. Such behaviour may be associated with migration, for flocking is more noticeable in August, especially in the Crown Point area of Tobago. The bird is most usually seen on the ground, but often perches in low trees, fences and bushes. Roosting appears to be communal, for I have seen considerable numbers gathering into the Caroni mangroves in the evening. In a typical breeding display a bird flies steeply upwards from a perch to about 100 ft, then glides down and round in a semi-circle to its starting point. Billing has also been noticed.

Notes. Though legally protected, this dove is subject to persecution from hunters, especially in SW Tobago, where they are shot at the time when they most tend to flock. The excuse given is that the species is a "type of Ramier" (i.e., *Columba* sp.), which may be shot in the open season. In view of this persecution it would seem worthwhile to investigate the particulars of its migration by trapping and banding birds as they flock in Tobago. Recoveries should soon be forthcoming.

Common Ground-Dove: *Columbina passerina*
Scaly-breasted Ground-Dove   **Plate 6(3)**

Habitat and status. A fairly common but local resident in Trinidad, frequenting the drier parts of savannahs, also the fairly open scrub in the northwest and on Chacachacare, and the more open parts of the foothills of the Northern Range. (Specimens: ANSP, YPM, LM, BM, TRVL.)

Range and subspecies. S USA and Mexico S to Costa Rica, also West Indies and in South America from Colombia and Venezuela S to Ecuador and N Brazil; *C. p. albivitta* (Bonaparte) ranges from N Colombia and Venezuela and offshore islands E to Margarita and Trinidad.

Description. 6.25 in. *Male:* crown pale gray, upperparts generally gray-brown, underparts gray suffused with pinkish; feathers on neck and breast with dark centres, giving a scaly effect; primaries and underwing bright chestnut; some dark spots on wing-coverts; outer tail mainly blackish; bill red or yellowish, tipped darker. *Female:* as male, but without pink flush.

Measurements. Wing: 21 males 78–86mm (82.4); 27 females 77–85mm (81.9). Weight: 4 males 32–37gm (34.7); 3 females 30.5–42gm (35.0).

Voice. A soft musical, double note, *oo-woo.*

Food. Small seeds, mainly of grasses.

Nesting. Breeding recorded from January to November (B/S), with an evident peak in May and June. Most nests are in small trees, from a few to 30 ft above ground, but some are on the ground. (On the mainland of South America nests are usually on the ground [Young 1928, Cherrie 1916].) The nest varies in structure from a few roughly placed pieces of grass to a large cup of twigs. Clutch usually 2, sometimes 3, white eggs, av. 21.7 × 16.3gm (15).

Behaviour. Usually seen in pairs or small groups, this very small dove forages exclusively on the ground but perches frequently in trees and bushes. With its very short legs it walks with a scarcely perceptible bobbing motion, flying up suddenly when approached.

Plain-breasted Ground-Dove: *Columbina minuta*
Grey Ground-Dove   **Plate 6(2)**

Habitat and status. Rather uncommon, but widely distributed in savannahs throughout Trinidad; in the south definitely more common than *C. passerina.* (Specimens: ANSP, LM, BM, TRVL.)

Range and subspecies. Mexico S to Peru, Brazil and Paraguay; *C. m. minuta* (Linnaeus) occurs in the South American range.

Description. 6 in. Very similar to Common Ground-Dove, but upperparts paler gray-brown, and no scaled appearance on neck and breast; only inner webs of primaries chestnut. Female duller than male. Bill gray.

Measurements. Wing: 6 males 73–78mm (76). Weight: 5 males 29–35gm (31.5)*.

Voice. A soft, cooing, single note, repeated about once a second.

Food. Seeds, mostly of grasses.

Nesting. Breeding recorded from March to September; B/S cite June as the principal month. Nest-site and nest similar to those of *C. passerina,* but generally nest is smaller and contains a pad of feathers. The clutch is 2 white eggs, av. 20.3 × 15.3mm (6), but size is variable and overlaps measurements of *C. passerina.* The incubation period is about 13 days.

Behaviour. I have only found this species in pairs or singly.

Ruddy Ground-Dove: *Columbina talpacoti*
Rufous-winged Ground-Dove; Talpacoti Ground-Dove   **Plate 6(1)**

Habitat and status. Very common and widely distributed in open and semi-open cultivated or waste areas of both islands; one of the first species to move into newly cleared forest land. (Specimens: AMNH, ANSP, LM, CM, YPM, BM, TRVL.)

Range and subspecies. Mexico S to Bolivia and Argentina; *C. t. rufipennis* (Bonaparte) ranges through Middle America to Colombia, Venezuela and Trinidad and Tobago; it is distinguished from the nominate race by the greater amount of cinnamon (rather than black) on the undersurface of the wing.

Description. 7 in. *Male:* head and neck pale gray; upperparts reddish brown, with black spots on wing-coverts; outer tail black; underparts paler brown, under-wing-coverts black; bill gray, tipped black. *Female:* browner than male, less reddish.

Measurements. Wing: 41 males 85–92mm (87.5; S.D. 1.8); 40 females 82–88mm (85.5; S.D. 1.7). Weight: 38 males 40–56gm (48.1; S.D. 3.5); 36 females 35–51gm (44.8; S.D. 3.3).

Voice. A rhythmic disyllabic series, *cur-woo, cur-woo,* etc., with emphasis on the second syllable, which at a distance is the only syllable heard.

Food. Seeds.

Nesting. Breeding recorded in all months, peaks occurring in several months since breeding appears stimulated by local conditions, which vary considerably within Trinidad (D. W. Snow & Snow 1964); 133 breeding records are divided among months as follows:

I	II	III	IV	V	VI
7	14	14	6	4	8

VII	VIII	IX	X	XI	XII
18	18	22	4	10	8

Moult recorded in all months; several instances of "arrested" moult have been found, indicating that birds were induced to breed before completion of the moult cycle. The parents often use the same nest for a second or third brood, intervals between broods varying from 2 to 33 days; once a nest was used for 5 consecutive broods. The nest is a small but solid cup of twigs or grass situated in a bush or tree in a fork or among clusters of leaves from a few to 35 ft above ground. The clutch is usually 2 white eggs, av. 23.2 × 17.1mm (35). The incubation period is 12–13 days. In Surinam Haverschmidt (1953a) found that the female sat on the empty nest for a day before laying the first egg. She also incubated at night, the male relieving her from about 10 A.M. to 4 P.M. The young are fledged after 12–14 days. After leaving the nest they are still dependent on their parents for some days, and they all roost together, the young birds sandwiched between the adults.

Behaviour. A very sociable species, often seen in pairs and small groups, and feeding in groups often of a considerable size. Roosting also appears to be at least partly communal. Though it frequently perches in trees and low bushes, it habitually feeds on the ground, where I have often seen 30 or 40 birds feeding together, all facing in the same direction and moving gradually along. Fighting and quarrelling is often seen, the male's wings, which are employed vigorously in a fight, nervously twitching as he perches beside the female. In an evident courtship display the male flies up at a steep angle from his perch, claps his wings audibly once or twice and glides back down. This often precedes copulation, which may take place on the ground, in a tree or even on a telephone wire! Wing-flicking is always seen in these birds when excited. Among mutual displays billing and allopreening are commonly seen.

Blue Ground-Dove: *Claravis pretiosa*
Blue Partridge-Dove; "Ortolan Bleu"   **Plate 6(7)**

Habitat and status. A rather rare resident of Trinidad, but widely distributed at forest edges, especially bordering savannahs; not uncommon on Monos. (Specimens: AMNH, ANSP, LM.)

Range. Mexico S through Central and South America to Bolivia, Argentina and Paraguay.

Description. 8 in. *Male:* generally bluish gray, paler below; black spots on wing-coverts; outer tail black. *Female:* generally olive brown, with chestnut bars or spots on wing-coverts; reddish brown rump and central tail, abdomen grayish. Bill gray, legs pink.

Measurements. Wing: 4 males 109–119mm (112); 2 females 107, 109mm. Weight: 10 males 52–72gm (65); 5 females 65–77gm (72).

Voice. A musical, cooing series, *poop-poop-poop,* etc., uttered with a rising inflection.

Food. Seeds.

Nesting. Breeding recorded from June to August (B/S); the nest is of small twigs lined with fine grass and situated about 20 ft up in a palm or other tree. The clutch is 2 white eggs, av. 24.3 × 17.4mm (6). In Costa Rica (Skutch 1959) both adults co-operate in nest-building, the male bringing the material. Two days separate the laying of the 2 eggs. The incubation period is 14–15 days, and the fledging period 13–14 days.

Behaviour. In Trinidad the species seems very wary, being found singly or in pairs, and seen only when it leaves thick cover for a short, swift flight, which is usually higher above the ground than that of the other ground-doves. It feeds mainly on the ground but often perches in trees, preferring the cover of leafy trees. In other parts of its range it is sometimes found in sizeable flocks when feeding, but this has not been found here.

Scaled Dove: *Scardafella squammata*
Ridgway's Dove

Habitat and status. One record only of 2 birds seen by G. D. Smooker at Toco in October 1929. These may be identical with 2 specimens from Trinidad at the British Museum.

Range. Colombia and Venezuela (including Margarita Island), and in French Guiana, Brazil, Paraguay and N Argentina.

Description. 8.5 in. Above pale brown, each feather edged and tipped black, giving a scaled appearance; below whitish, similarly tipped black; tail long and pointed, the outer feathers black, broadly edged white.

Voice. *Tuc-a-tuuu,* the accent on the last syllable (Friedmann & Smith 1950, in Venezuela).

White-tipped Dove: *Leptotila verreauxi*
White-fronted Dove; Rusty Dove; Verreaux's Dove;
"Mountain Dove"   **Plate 6(4)**

Habitat and status. A common resident in both islands, widely distributed in semi-open country, secondary forest, scrub and the edge of true forest. Common on Bocas Islands. (Specimens: Trinidad, AMNH, ANSP, LM, TRVL; Tobago, LM.)

Range and subspecies. Mexico S to Peru, Argentina and Uruguay; *L. v. verreauxi* (Bonaparte) ranges from Nicaragua S to Colombia, N Venezuela and the offshore islands from Curaçao to Trinidad; *L. v. tobagensis* (Hellmayr & Seilern) is found only on Tobago, differing by its paler underparts, more extensive white on throat and lack of copper sheen on nape.

Description. 11 in. Forehead pinkish gray, rest of head and neck gray with green-and-purple iridescence on nape and mantle; upperparts and wings generally brown, the tail broadly tipped white; underparts whitish, breast tinged pink; bare eye-ring blue; iris brown; bill black, legs red.

Measurements. *L. v. verreauxi*. Wing: 14 males 135–142mm (137.5); 8 females 130–140mm (134). Weight: 3 males 132, 136, 138gm*; 2 females 129*, 148gm; 7 unsexed 123–168gm (149). *L. v. tobagensis*. Wing: 2 females 131, 140mm. Weight: 2 females 109, 122gm*; 34 unsexed 96–157gm (134).

Voice. A low, muffled *oooo* or double *ooo-woo*, sometimes preceded by 2 or 3 soft, rolling churrs, only heard at close quarters.

Food. Mainly seeds; also insects, including caterpillars and moths. After the Tobago hurricane individuals fed on bread at feeding tables.

Nesting. Breeds in all months of the year; out of 68 nests 47 were recorded between March and July; moult recorded in August. The nest is a fairly substantial cup of twigs, lined with grass and situated in a tree from 6 to 25 ft high. The clutch is normally 2 (rarely 1) creamy white eggs, av. 29.2 × 21.6mm (17) (*verreauxi*); 5 eggs of *tobagensis* av. 30.25 × 21.05mm. The second egg is laid somewhat more than 24 hr after the first; incubation lasts 14 days, and the fledging period is about 15 days.

Behaviour. Usually found singly, in pairs or in small groups. This dove feeds essentially on the ground, where it may be seen walking busily about wherever the vegetation is bare enough. When flushed it flies off with a clatter of wings, to perch not far away low in a tree.

Notes. Owing to its comparative tameness and accessibility the "Mountain Dove" is a favourite target for hunters—not the authentic hunters, who consider such a bird too easy game and too small to be worth a cartridge, but boys and young men, who with airguns and catapults indulge in the "sport" of potting at animals and birds of all kinds on the outskirts of urban districts. With these inexpert methods more birds are maimed than killed, but although by law the species is fully protected, rarely are offenders brought to justice. The situation is not likely to change unless public opinion can be influenced to condemn such hunting.

Gray-fronted Dove: *Leptotila rufaxilla*
"Mountain Dove"; "Tourtuelle"   **Plate 6(6)**

Habitat and status. A common resident in forested parts of Trinidad, confined mainly to true forest, but sometimes found overlapping on forest edges with previous species. (Specimens: AMNH, ANSP, LM, CM, YPM, TRVL.)

Range and subspecies. South America from Colombia S to Bolivia, Argentina and Uruguay; *L. r. hellmayri* (Chapman) is found only in Trinidad, except for a few individuals which have occurred on the eastern tip of the Paria peninsula, Venezuela; this race is distinguished by the paler forehead and darker, more rufous upper breast.

Description. 11 in. Very similar to White-tipped Dove, but forehead and crown conspicuously pale bluish gray, lores and bare skin around eye red and not blue; iris pale straw.

Measurements. Wing: 2 males 141, 145mm, 2 females 142, 146mm. Weight: 2 males 158, 164gm*; 1 female 132gm*; 3 unsexed 161, 163, 180gm.

Voice. Very similar to White-tipped Dove, a far-carrying *oooo*, often preceded by a much lower roll, *crrr, crrr,* but this is only heard at close quarters.

Food. Seeds and probably insects, taken from the forest floor; also once seen taking *Costus* fruit perched on the inflorescence.

Nesting. Breeding recorded in all months except September and October; 19 of 25 nests recorded from March to July; moult recorded June–September, also December and April. The nest, a platform of twigs, is situated in a low bush or tree, 3–25 ft above ground. The clutch is 1 or 2 creamy white eggs, av. 29.6 × 21.5mm (6).

Ruddy Quail-Dove: *Geotrygon montana*
Red Ground-Dove; Partridge Dove   **Plate 6(5)**

Habitat and status. A not uncommon resident of forests in Trinidad, where actually recorded only in the Northern Range. Some migration or dispersal evidently occurs, since I trapped a male on Soldado Rock on 1 October. Bond (1979) points out that this dove is a successful colonizer of islands and has often been recorded at sea. (Specimens: ANSP, LM, TRVL.) Tobago records require substantiation.

Range and subspecies. The nominate race ranges from Mexico S through Central and South America to Bolivia and Brazil, also in the Greater Antilles; another race is found in some of the Lesser Antilles from Guadeloupe S to Grenada.

Description. 9 in. *Male:* head, nape and upperparts reddish chestnut, the mantle glossed with purple, a buffish streak from chin to ear-coverts, below this a chestnut streak from throat to sides of neck; breast buff tinged vinous, lower underparts paler; tail short; orbital skin red; bill and legs dark red. *Female:* as male, but upperparts olive brown. The bill is held angled downwards in a very noticeable way.

Measurements. Wing: 3 males 135, 135, 141mm; 2 females 133, 140mm. Weight: 4 males 85–116gm (101); 1 female 99gm*. (In Guatemala 3 males weighed 136, 141, 150gm; 3 females 122, 136, 152gm [Smithe & Paynter 1963]. The difference seems rather striking.)

Voice. A deep, booming *coo,* repeated at intervals. Once 7 calls were given within 20 sec.

Food. Seeds and small fruits taken from the forest floor. Known to take seeds regurgitated by manakins at display grounds.

Nesting. Eight nests recorded between February and July, 4 of them in May. The nest, of twigs lined with leaves, is placed on a treestump, on a low branch or amidst tangled undergrowth up to 8 ft from the ground. The clutch is 2 warm buff eggs, av. 28.2 × 21.5mm (6). Incubation period is 10 or 11 days, and the fledging period is about 10 days. The young are fed regularly and often at first, but a week after hatching receive only about 3 meals a day (cf. Skutch 1949, 1964c).

Behaviour. The species' cryptic coloration and its habit of walking on dark forest floors make it difficult to observe; it is usually found singly or in pairs. When flushed it flies low and with a loud clattering of wings. A mated pair were seen billing and mutually preening just before copulation on the ground (Lill 1969). A parent bird sometimes gives a distraction display on leaving the nest.

Lined Quail-Dove: *Geotrygon linearis*
"Mountain Dove"   **Plate 6(8)**

Habitat and status. In Trinidad much like Ruddy Quail-Dove, but found only in forest at higher elevations; also occurs on Tobago. (Specimens: Trinidad, AMNH, CM, LM; Tobago, FMNH.)

Range and subspecies. Colombia and Venezuela; *G. l. trinitatis* (Hellmayr & Seilern) is found in Trinidad, Tobago and NE Venezuela.

Description. 11 in. Upperparts generally dark purplish brown, glossed on mantle with green; forehead rufous; a long dark-gray streak above eye, broad buff streak below eye, with a conspicuous black streak below, stretching from chin to below ear-coverts; underparts rufous, paler below; bill black; legs dark red.

Measurements. Wing: 5 males 143–152mm, av. 148; 6 females 138–146mm, av. 142. Weight: 1 male 284gm*; 3 females 233, 233, 230gm*.

Voice. "A deep, hollow, pigeonlike *ooouk* at 15–20 sec intervals" (in Colombia, Hilty & Brown 1986).

Food. Similar to Ruddy Quail-Dove.

Nesting. One nest with eggs was found in February (B/S). It was a fairly deep cup of small twigs lined with dead leaves, situated in the horizontal fork of a tree 12 ft above ground. The clutch was 2 rich cream eggs, av. 33.8 × 25.0mm.

Behaviour. Much like Ruddy Quail-Dove. I have only found single birds or pairs, always on the ground in dark forest.

PSITTACIDAE: Macaws, Parrots and Parakeets

This well-known family is distinguished by the short, strongly hooked bill, large head and short neck. The size ranges from the large, long-tailed macaws down to the tiny parakeets. Most species fly fast and direct, usually in groups ranging from a pair to flocks of considerable size. Frequenting mainly forests, they are also found in swampy woodland and mangroves, where they feed on fruit, leaves and seeds. Calls vary from a shrill chattering to a harsh screaming, all of them unmusical. Some species can be taught to imitate the human voice with remarkable accuracy. (7)

Blue-and-yellow Macaw: *Ara ararauna*
Plate 7(2)

Habitat and status. Formerly confined to the vicinity of Nariva swamp in Trinidad, probably now extinct. Small numbers were seen up to 1970; since then only escaped captives are found, also on Tobago. (Specimen: TRVL.)

Range. Panama S through South America to Bolivia, Paraguay and Brazil.

Description. 33 in. Upperparts blue, underparts orange-yellow; very long tail; bill black; bare facial skin white, streaked with lines of black feathers.

Measurements. Wing: 1 unsexed 345mm. Weight: 1040–1286gm (Haverschmidt 1968a, in Surinam).

Voice. A deep, raucous *raaa,* often given in flight.

Food. Fruit and seeds, including those of palms and the sandbox tree (*Hura crepitans*).

Nesting. Breeds in the dry season (January–May), the nest being in a hole in a palm. In Surinam Haverschmidt (1968a) records white eggs, measuring 48.3–50.5 × 35.3–37.4mm.

Behaviour. Almost invariably found in small flocks or pairs. They fly quite high with slow wing-beats, most unlike those of the smaller parrots, uttering at intervals their deep-throated cries. In Surinam large numbers were found gathering at a roost (Haverschmidt 1954a).

Notes. The precarious status of this beautiful macaw in Trinidad was due in no small measure to the illegal taking of young birds from their nests. Birds may be imported under proper licence from South American countries, but illegal traffic continues, especially from Venezuela via S Trinidad fishing villages. Unless the government can adequately enforce the law relating to the caging of parrots and finches, they are all likely to become extinct in Trinidad within a very short time.

[Scarlet Macaw: *Ara macao*]

Habitat and status. There are 2 sight records only of this very conspicuous species: 2 birds were seen in Nariva swamp in October 1934 (B/S), and 5 were seen near Waller Field in May 1943 (Abbott). Recent reports of individuals from Granville probably refer to escapees from captivity. (No specimen.)

Range. Mexico S through Central and South America to Peru, Bolivia and Brazil.

Description. 36 in. Generally scarlet all over, but lower back blue, and wings dark blue with bright yellow coverts; bare face white to buffy pink.

Red-bellied Macaw: *Ara manilata*
Small Red-bellied Macaw   **Plate 7(4)**

Habitat and status. Fairly common local resident in Trinidad in Nariva swamp and the vicinity of Aripo Savannah, especially where the moriche palm (*Mauritia flexuosa*) abounds. (Specimens: TRVL.)

Range. N South America from Colombia to Peru and C Brazil.

Description. 20 in. Predominantly green, with blue forehead and upper wings; breast blue-gray edged green, abdomen red; underwings and undertail dull yellow; bill black, bare face yellow. Long tail distinguishes this from parrots of similar size. *Immature:* has paler, yellowish bill.

Measurements. Wing: 1 male 253mm. Weight: 2 males 358, 360gm (from Haverschmidt 1952, in Surinam).

Voice. A loud scream, usually heard in chorus, higher-pitched than the call of *Amazona,* and shrill rather than raucous.

Food. Fruit and seeds of palms, especially the moriche or ité palm and the cabbage palm (*Roystonea oleracea*).

Nesting. Breeding recorded in February especially (Nottebohm), but also in September; nests are in hollows of dead palm trees, often using nest-sites of Amazon parrots after the latter have finished nesting.

Behaviour. Extremely gregarious, flocks of up to 100 being recorded frequently. The birds feed primarily in the early morning and evening, and at these times flocks are very conspicuous as they travel from one feeding place to another. They roost communally.

[Red-shouldered Macaw: *Ara nobilis*]
Hahn's Macaw

Habitat and status. An extremely unsatisfactory sight record is cited by B/S for October 1934, of 2 birds in Nariva swamp. No other records exist, and a specimen in the British Museum, said to come from Trinidad via the London Zoo, is not adequately documented. One (probably escaped) bird was seen at Pointe-a-Pierre in October 1968, and two others in 1978.

Range. Venezuela, the Guianas and Brazil.

Description. 12 in. Generally green with blue forehead; shoulder, bend of wing and underwings red; abdomen green (*not* red); undertail yellowish; bare face whitish.

Green-rumped Parrotlet: *Forpus passerinus*
Blue-winged Parrotlet (or Parrakeet); "Parrakeet"; "Lovebird"
Plate 7(8)

Habitat and status. A widely distributed resident of Trinidad, occurring in mangroves, lowland forest, semi-open savannahs and suburban areas; unknown to Léotaud, and not recorded before 1916. In Tobago a few specimens were recently introduced, and numbers are rapidly increasing. (Specimens: ANSP, YPM, LM, BM, TRVL.)

Range and subspecies. NE South America from Colombia to the Guianas and Brazil; *F. p. viridissimus* (Lafresnaye) occurs in Venezuela, occasionally in Curaçao, and in Trinidad and Tobago; it differs from the nominate race by being generally darker green, with the male's wings more strongly tinged bluish.

Description. 5.5 in. Generally bright green with very short tail and pale pinkish bill. *Adult males:* greater-wing-coverts brilliant blue. *Female:* more or less yellow on forehead.

Measurements. Wing: 1 male 86mm; 2 females 79, 82mm. Weight: 1 female 24gm*.

Voice. A sibilant chattering or twittering, often a fairly lengthy, squeaky series of notes.

Food. Seeds, including those of grasses and the shrub sorrel (*Hibiscus sabdariffa*).

Nesting. Breeding recorded in most months between February and August. The nest of twigs is constructed in some sort of hole in a dead tree, termite nest, base of palm frond, even in hollow pipes such as clothesline supports or flagpoles. The eggs are almost round and white. One clutch of 2, av. 17.9 × 15.2mm.

Behaviour. This extremely gregarious species is almost always found in flocks. Indeed, when they are seen in pairs, this is usually an indication of breeding. During the day small flocks of about 10 birds commonly associate whilst feeding, and these are very conspicuous as they move noisily from one feeding place to another, flying with long undulating swoops like finches. In the evening the flocks assemble at a roost, usually in casuarina trees at Pointe-a-Pierre. At this time they cluster very close together and the chattering of the gathering can be heard at quite a distance. Immature birds in captivity have been known to rest and preen while hanging upside down from a perch. Mutual preening was also seen (Buckley & Buckley 1968).

Lilac-tailed Parrotlet: *Touit batavica*
Seven-coloured Parrakeet   **Plate 7(5)**

Habitat and status. A common resident in forested areas of Trinidad, but I suspect migration (or at least local dispersal) also occurs, since a large flock of *Touit* sp. was seen flying eastwards high over Chacachacare on 1 September. Also seen flying over Oropouche Swamp and Waller Field. (Specimens: CM, AMNH, ANSP, BM.)

Range. Venezuela and the Guianas.

Description. 6 in. Head green with yellow forehead, upperparts blackish with broad yellowish green band across wing-coverts; tail lilac with black band; underparts bluish green, fore-edge of underwing red; bill yellowish gray. When seen at a distance this bird appears black and green with a pale wing-band.

Measurements. Wing: 5 males 104–114mm (109); 5 females 102–110mm (106). Weight: 9 unsexed 52–59.5gm (55).

Voice. A high-pitched screaming, usually heard in confused chorus from a passing flock; more like a parrot and quite unlike the chattering of the Green-rumped Parrotlet.

Nesting. Breeding recorded January–March, but the season is probably more extensive; early moult recorded in late May. The nest is made in a hole either of a tree or in a large termite nest. The clutch is 5 or 6 white eggs, av. 22.0 × 19.3mm (6).

Behaviour. Extremely gregarious, both when feeding and at the roost. The species is most commonly seen in the forest passing high overhead in a rather widely extended flock, from which the high screaming call is constantly heard. Flight is rapid and without undulations.

Scarlet-shouldered Parrotlet: *Touit huetii*
Huet's Parrot   **Plate 7(6)**

Habitat and status. Classified by Léotaud as an occasional visitor to forests in Trinidad. Flocks were seen by R. G. Gibbs in July 1974 and August 1975 at

Aripo Savannah, also by T. Manolis at Carapo in March 1980. (Specimen: BM.)

Range. Colombia, Venezuela, Guyana, Ecuador, Peru and Brazil.

Description. 7 in. *Male:* head and upperparts generally green, with dark blue upper-wing-coverts and blackish primaries; narrow black band on forehead, cheek-patch blue; underparts yellowish green; underwing, including shoulder, bright scarlet; tail deep lavender, with black subterminal band, tipped green. *Female:* as male, but tail green with black band.

Voice. A high *witch-witch,* quite distinct from Lilac-tailed Parrotlet.

Blue-headed Parrot: *Pionus menstruus*
Red-vented Parrot   **Plate 7(1)**

Habitat and status. A common and widely distributed resident of forests and semi-open cultivated areas in Trinidad. (Specimens: AMNH, TRVL.)

Range and subspecies. Costa Rica S to Bolivia and Brazil; *P. m. menstruus* (Linnaeus) ranges from E Colombia and Venezuela south.

Description. 10 in. Head, neck and upper breast blue; upperparts and rest of underparts green, except for golden tinge to wing-coverts and red undertail-coverts and base of tail. *Immature:* less blue about the head. Wing-beat deeper than that of *Amazona.*

Measurements. Wing: 2 males 178, 183mm; 2 females 166, 177mm. Weight: 1 female 213gm.

Voice. Quite distinct from *Amazona;* the call has a lighter, squeakier quality, but is still unmistakably a parrot's scream, usually heard in chorus. Individuals in flight sometimes call a light *"wick".*

Food. Fruit and seeds, including those of the sandbox tree (*Hura crepitans*) and of the introduced teak tree (*Tectona grandis*); also eats corn (*Zea mays*) and the flowers of the mountain immortelle (*Erythrina*).

Nesting. Breeding recorded in March and October. The nest is in a hole in a tree, one clutch of 4 white eggs av. 31.4 × 25.0mm. In Venezuela Cherrie (1916) recorded breeding in February; at least 4 days separated the hatching of the oldest and youngest in a clutch of 3 eggs.

Behaviour. Gregarious, seen in groups of up to 30 birds.

[Yellow-crowned Parrot: *Amazona ochrocephala*]
Plate 7(3)

Habitat and status. Status obscure, owing to the number of introduced cage-birds, some of which escape; small groups of feral birds exist in suburban areas near Port of Spain, etc. It is probable that wild residents inhabit forests bordering swamps in Trinidad, but the species is certainly at least rare. (No authentic specimens.)

Range and subspecies. Honduras S to Peru and Brazil; the nominate race occurs in Colombia, Venezuela, the Guianas and N Brazil.

Description. 14 in. Generally green with yellow forehead; rest of head green, but with a conspicuous whitish eye-ring; wing speculum and bend of wing red; outer tail red at base.

Voice. A varied vocabulary, but the commonest call-note is a repeated *ker-wow, ker-wow.*

Food. Fruit and seeds, including that of the small savannah tree *Curatella americana* and of cactus.

Nesting. No authentic breeding records in Trinidad, but 3 eggs laid in captivity were white, av. 41.8 × 30.9mm. In NE Venezuela Friedmann and Smith (1950, 1955) found the species breeding early in the year; nests were built in hollowed-out termite nests; of a tame pair the female alone incubated, being fed through regurgitation by the male. In the early morning and late afternoon the pair flew in circles around the nest site, calling loudly.

Orange-winged Parrot: *Amazona amazonica*
Common Amazon Parrot; "Green Parrot"   **Plate 7(7)**

Habitat and status. A common resident in both islands, frequenting forests and semi-open country of both lowland areas and the Northern Range in Trinidad, especially abundant in the east of the island, but in Tobago more confined to hill forest and cultivated slopes, the latter especially during July–September. (Specimens: AMNH, ANSP, CM, BM, TRVL.)

Range and subspecies. Colombia S to Peru and C Brazil; *A. a. tobagensis* (Cory) is known only from Trinidad and Tobago, being larger than the nominate race, while the orange in the wing is more extensive.

Description. 13 in. Generally green, with blue forehead and lores; a variable amount of yellow on crown and cheeks; wing speculum orange; some orange in tail, mostly hidden in flight; no eye-ring.

Measurements. Wing: 3 males 197, 205, 205mm; 3 females 195, 200, 205mm.

Voice. Extremely noisy; the shrill scream is usually heard in a confused chorus, and the vocabulary is so varied as to defy description.

Food. Fruit, seeds and flowers. Known to feed on fruits of palms, e.g., *Euterpe,* hog-plum (*Spondias monbin*), *Sloanea, Richeria* and *Byrsonima,* the flowers of the mountain immortelle (*Erythrina poeppigiana*), and occasionally on cocoa pods, for which reason it is deemed an agricultural pest.

Nesting. Breeding recorded January–June (many nests), but most eggs are laid in late February (Nottebohm); in Tobago moult recorded in August. The nest is situated in a hole in a dead tree, often a cabbage palm; the clutch is 5 white eggs, av. 42.3 × 29.7mm (7). Incubation lasts about 3 wk, and the young fly at about 2 months of age.

Behaviour. Extremely gregarious, especially at the roost, which may be high in a group of palms, bamboos or other trees. In flight this species is almost always seen in pairs, and even a large flock of 100 birds may be seen to be constituted mainly of many pairs. Flight is usually at a considerable height, and the species' extremely shallow, but rapid, wing-action, together with its tendency to fly in pairs, makes it recognisable at a distance.

Notes. This species is classified as a pest by the Conservation Ordinance because of its reputation for attacking cocoa plantations. In fact this tendency seems rather rare and may well be manifested only at times of unusual scarcity of food (Keeler-Wolf 1982). In January 1964, after the hurricane of September 1963 had stripped all the *Erythrina* trees of leaves, these parrots in Tobago turned their attention to cocoa, to which they did considerable damage. More commonly, however, it is hunted for its value as a cage-bird, the young being removed from the nest and reared in captivity. The Yellow-crowned Parrot, however, has a better reputation than the present one as a talker.

CUCULIDAE: Cuckoos

This family forms a rather varied group, but all its members in Trinidad and Tobago are quite large birds, with stout, slightly decurved bills and long tails; most of them are mainly reddish brown and white. They are found mostly in trees, where they feed largely on insects and lizards; several species frequent mangrove swamps, but others are more widely distributed. The anis, which form a highly specialised group, have a complex social organisation in which nesting duties are shared amongst the group. The only parasitic species is also quite different in being mainly terrestrial. (9)

Black-billed Cuckoo: *Coccyzus erythrophthalmus*

Habitat and status. One bird recorded by Léotaud (specimen) in September. No recent records.

Range. Breeds in E North America, migrating S through Central America to Peru, Venezuela and Colombia; accidental in Argentina.

Description. 12 in. Generally brown above, outer tail tipped white, but less so than in Yellow-billed Cuckoo, and without any rufous on wing; underparts white; bill black; narrow red ring around eye. Lacks the gray cap and buff underparts of Dark-billed Cuckoo.

Yellow-billed Cuckoo: *Coccyzus americanus*

Habitat and status. A regular passage migrant in small numbers through both islands; of 25 records, 22 occurred in various localities between 5 October and 17 December, the other 3 on 23 April, 4 May and 24 May. There is no evidence that the species spends the northern winter in our islands. (Specimens: Trinidad, AMNH; Tobago, TRVL.)

Range and subspecies. Breeds in North America and the Greater Antilles, migrating S to Bolivia and Argentina; the nominate race is the eastern form.

Description. 12 in. Generally brown above with rufous on inner webs of primaries only visible in flight; prominent white tips to outer tail-feathers; underparts white; upper mandible dark, lower orange-yellow. A slim, graceful bird in flight.

Measurements. Wing: 1 male 145mm; 1 female 140mm. Weight: 1 emaciated male 30gm.

Voice. Seldom heard from migrants, it is a low, rather harsh series, *cow-cow-cow,* etc.

Food. Insects, especially caterpillars; also small lizards.

Behaviour. Rather solitary and not easily seen when in the cover of a tree, where it may perch motionless for some time; much more conspicuous, however, when it flies, not very fast, over open ground.

Mangrove Cuckoo: *Coccyzus minor*

Habitat and status. A rather rare resident of mangrove swamps in Trinidad, also recorded in secondary forest on Monos. There are 3 sight records for Tobago. (Specimens: ANSP, LM, BM.)

Range and subspecies. S USA and Mexico S to Panama, NE South America south to N Brazil, and various Caribbean islands; the nominate race ranges from E Colombia, Venezuela and Trinidad S to Brazil.

Description. 12 in. Upperparts uniform brownish gray, throat whitish, becoming buff on rest of underparts; broad blackish ear-patch; long tail black, broadly tipped white; upper mandible blackish, lower orange.

Measurements. Wing: 2 females 130, 135mm. Weight: 2 females 62.5, 69gm*.

Voice. A low grating series, *ke-ke-ke-ke-ka-ka-ka.*

Food. Insects, including grasshoppers and caterpillars.

Nesting. Breeding recorded in July (twice) and September. A slight stick nest is built, lined with a few leaves and situated 8–10 ft above water level in a mangrove tree. The clutch is 3 bluish green eggs, varying somewhat in size, av. 30.6 × 23.3mm (6).

Behaviour. A skulking, secretive bird which keeps mainly to the low branches of mangroves. Occasionally it flies quite rapidly from one clump to another.

Dark-billed Cuckoo: *Coccyzus melacoryphus*
Dark-headed Cuckoo   **Plate 5(3)**

Habitat and status. A rare resident in the mangrove swamps of Trinidad, also seen (B/S) in countryside near the swamps. I have only 2 records, in Caroni swamp during June and July. (No specimens, but collected by Léotaud.)

Range. Most of South America from Colombia S to Bolivia, Argentina and Uruguay.

Description. 10 in. Fairly similar to Mangrove Cuckoo but smaller. Crown and nape dark gray, upperparts gray-brown, throat grayish grading to rufous buff on lower underparts; tail black, tipped white; both mandibles of bill *black*.

Measurements. Wing: 118–119mm. Weight: 3 males 45, 47, 48gm; 4 females 44, 45, 50, 63gm. (Data from Colombia and Surinam.)

Voice. A soft, guttural series, very like the Mangrove Cuckoo.

Food. Insects, particularly grasshoppers, caterpillars, stick-insects and beetles.

Nesting. Breeding recorded in October (B/S). The twig nest is situated low in mangroves. The clutch is 2 pale greenish blue eggs, av. 28.7 × 21.5mm (4).

Behaviour. Very like that of Mangrove Cuckoo.

Squirrel Cuckoo: *Piaya cayana*
Chestnut Cuckoo; "Coucou Manioc"   **Plate 5(4)**

Habitat and status. Fairly common resident, widely distributed in forests and semi-open cultivated areas in Trinidad. (Specimens: AMNH, ANSP, LM, CM, YPM, BM, TRVL.)

Range and subspecies. Mexico S through Middle and South America to Bolivia and Argentina; *P. c. insulana* (Hellmayr) is found in NE Venezuela and Trinidad.

Description. 17 in. Head and upperparts rufous; very long tail with black subterminal bar, tipped white; throat and breast pale rufous, lower underparts pale gray; bill and eye-ring greenish yellow.

Measurements. Wing: 8 males 135–143mm (140); 7 females 136–145mm (140). Weight: 2 males 90, 95.5gm*; 2 females 94, 100gm*.

Voice. Various sharp, grating calls; a loud, high-pitched *kik*, repeated at regular intervals, sometimes in flight; a startling *kee-karr;* a grating rattle or churring note; and commonly, perhaps in alarm, a stereotyped 3- or 4-syllabled call, accented on the first and last syllables, *wake-a-curr* or *wake-a-ka-curr.*

Food. Large insects, including caterpillars, cicadas, grasshoppers, cockroaches, beetles, ants and centipedes, and even bees.

Nesting. Breeding recorded in January, May, July (2) and October. The nest is a loose structure of small twigs placed in a tree 15–40 ft above ground; however, in Costa Rica some nests are only 2 or 3 ft above the ground, and large quantities of leaves are occasionally incorporated into the nest (Skutch 1966). The clutch is 2 white eggs, tinged yellowish, av. 33.8 × 26.1mm (4). In Costa Rica the incubation period is about 19 days, both parents sharing the task. They also both feed the young infrequent but substantial meals; towards the end of the fledging period the young may be found near the nest, hopping about in the surrounding branches.

Behaviour. Usually found in pairs, but occasionally in small, loosely associated groups. As it moves about feeding quite high in a tree, the bird hops and darts about with fluid, squirrel-like movements, using its wings sparingly. Upon landing it raises its tail suddenly to balance itself in a characteristic motion. On its short flights it glides most of the way, regaining height by climbing gradually in the branches. In Costa Rica Skutch (1966) saw adult birds feeding their mates; occasionally this immediately preceded copulation, during which both adults kept hold of the insect in their bills together.

Little Cuckoo: *Piaya minuta*
Lesser Chestnut Cuckoo; Lesser Piaya   **Plate 5(2)**

Habitat and status. A rather uncommon resident in Trinidad, found mainly in brackish mangrove swamps, also scrubby woodland near water, such as Waller Field, edge of Nariva swamp and at Pointe-a-Pierre. (Specimens: AMNH, ANSP, YPM, LM, BM, TRVL.)

Range and subspecies. Panama and Colombia S to Bolivia, Peru and Brazil; the nominate race is known from Colombia east and south.

Description. 10 in. *Adult:* resembles a small Squirrel Cuckoo, head and upperparts dark chestnut, tail dark liver brown tipped broadly with white; underparts dark chestnut shading to dark gray abdomen (darker than Squirrel Cuckoo); bill yellow; iris red. *Immature:* generally dark liver brown, glossed purplish; tail even darker with no white tips; bill blackish.

Measurements. Wing: 7 males 102–108mm (106); 4 females 103–110mm (107). Weight: 1 male 38gm; 5 females 37–44gm (39).

Voice. Various harsh clucking monosyllables, such as *tchek* and a nasal *kak* or *kek.*

Food. Insects, including caterpillars and beetles.

Nesting. Breeding recorded only in July (B/S), when a deep nest of small twigs was found 7 ft above ground in a crotch of bamboo. The 2 dull white eggs averaged 23.9 × 18.8mm.

Behaviour. A shy, rather skulking species, which I have always found in pairs or small (family?) groups. Keeps mainly to lower branches, and sometimes forages on the ground.

Greater Ani: *Crotophaga major*
"Gros Merle Corbeau"   **Plate 5(1)**

Habitat and status. A fairly common resident in Trinidad, frequenting mangrove swamps and semi-open woodland near water, also at forest edges. (Specimens: ANSP, YPM, LM, BM, TRVL.)

Range. Panama and Colombia through South America E of the Andes to N Argentina.

Description. 17 in. Generally black with conspicuous blue-green gloss; tail very long; massive bill black, with high ridge on basal half of upper mandible, giving a broken-nosed effect; iris whitish, very conspicuous in the field. *Immature:* dark iris.

Measurements. Wing: 4 males 191–200mm (196); 2 females 194, 204mm. Weight: 4 males 149–174gm (163); 1 female 156gm*.

Voice. Very noisy; various calls include a deep croak, a loud, musical monosyllable, and a prolonged turkey-like gobbling or bubbling, usually made in chorus.

Food. Insects, including grasshoppers, beetles, bugs and caterpillars; occasionally hawks for flying insects, including wasps; also known (in Panama, Wetmore 1968) to take lizards and large seeds of *Euphorbia;* there is evidence that sometimes it takes herons' eggs and nestlings, and also frogs.

Nesting. Breeding recorded August–November (B/S). The nest is a deep cup of twigs lined with leaves and situated 8–15 ft up in a mangrove or other tree near water. Nesting is communal, 3–10 eggs being found in a "clutch". The eggs are rich blue, covered with a chalky white deposit which gradually wears off; they are variable in size, 10 measuring 42.4–49 × 34.8–40mm, av. 45.4 × 36.2mm. I have found 4 adults attending 3 young just out of the nest.

Behaviour. Extremely gregarious, almost invariably found in groups of 4–7 birds, which feed and roost together and hold a definite territory. When a flock proceeds from one tree to another, the birds fly singly or in pairs, never all together; flight is direct with much gliding and is usually higher above the ground than that of the Smooth-billed Ani. The Greater Ani has an excitable temperament, and when alarmed the birds cluster together on a branch and produce their extraordinary communal chorus.

Smooth-billed Ani: *Crotophaga ani*
Common Ani; "Merle Corbeau"; "Old Witch"; "Tick Bird"

Habitat and status. A common resident in both islands, frequenting open and semi-open country and cultivated areas, including urban districts. (Specimens: AMNH, ANSP, YPM, LM, BM, TRVL.)

Range. S Florida, Costa Rica and Panama, the West Indies, and in South America E of the Andes from Colombia S to Argentina, also in Ecuador.

Description. 13 in. Generally black, slightly glossed with purple; tail long; bill black, with upper mandible arched and laterally compressed; iris brown.

Measurements. Wing: 4 males 150–160mm (155); 4 females 145–154mm (148). Weight: 9 males 78–123gm (103); 1 female 98gm*; 17 unsexed 78–116gm (98).

Voice. Most commonly a whining 2-syllable call with upward inflection, *oooleek,* also a variety of querulous whines, chuckles, gasps and grunts. I have also occasionally heard from a feeding group a rather soft, high, musical chirruping, not unlike the subsong of the House Wren.

Food. Mostly insects, including caterpillars, grasshoppers, cockroaches, mole-crickets, beetles and bugs; also spiders, lizards and some seeds and berries. Ticks and other parasites are taken from grazing animals, but these form a small percentage of the diet. Occasionally anis will join other birds hawking for flying termites as high as 100 ft above the ground. Uncommonly they rob the nests of other species of eggs or young. In Guyana a treefrog was recorded in the diet (Young 1928).

Nesting. Breeding recorded in every month, but of 77 nests, 69% were from May to October, with only 1 each in December and January. The nest is a large open cup of sticks, tendrils and grass lined profusely with green leaves. It is situated in a bush or tree 6–45 ft above ground, more usually 8–20 feet up. Often the nest contains eggs in layers separated by leaves. In these cases the lower eggs are usually not incubated and fail to hatch. Nesting is usually communal; several pairs share the nest and the duties of incubation and feeding the young. Smooker found 20 birds building one nest. Often several birds incubate together on the nest, but at a nest in Panama made by 2 females and 1 male, the male incubated at night and all three took turns during the day (Skutch 1966). Each female may lay up to 7 eggs, and as many as 29 eggs have been found in one nest; 40 Trinidad clutches (Snow) varied in clutch size from 3 to 12, with 8 × c/6, 9 × c/7, 7 × c/8. The largest number of young found in one nest was 9. The eggs are blue, covered with a white calcareous deposit, av. 35.25 × 26.7mm (7). The incubation period is from 13 to 15 days. The development of the nestlings is rapid, fledglings being known to leave the nest when disturbed at 6 days old, flying at about 10 days old. Up to 3 broods may be raised in succession, with the young of earlier broods helping to feed the later broods.

194   CUCKOOS

Behaviour. Extremely sociable and usually found in groups of 8–20. Apart from nesting together, the group feeds and roosts together, occupying a definite territory (Davis 1940). When feeding in grass the birds spread out and advance in a loosely extended formation, combing the area for insects. They frequently associate with grazing animals, whose movements disturb the insects. Flight is low and rather laboured, with much gliding, so that in suburban areas anis are often killed by cars. The birds do not fly together but singly or in twos and threes; arriving at a perch they sit side by side, striking grotesque poses with their long tails angled beneath them. They are often seen gaping in hot weather or sunbathing after rain, with their wings extended. When bathing in shallow water they dive right in and flap about excitedly. Their plumage absorbs so much water that they can hardly fly before extensive preening.

Notes. The moult of this species deserves special study; not only are birds found moulting in various months of the year, but the sequence of primary moult is extremely irregular.

[Groove-billed Ani: *Crotophaga sulcirostris*]

Habitat and status. Mentioned without comment by Beebe (1952) as occurring in the Arima Valley. Certainly a mistake for the Smooth-billed Ani.

Range. S USA south through Middle America to Panama, and in Colombia, Venezuela, Guyana, Ecuador and Peru; also islands off Venezuela.

Description. 12 in. Very similar to Smooth-billed Ani but smaller and with grooves and ridges along the upper mandible. Call-note quite distinct, higher-pitched and less whining, *wick,* repeated at intervals.

Striped Cuckoo: *Tapera naevia*
Brown Cuckoo, "Wife-sick"; "Trinity"   **Plate 5(5)**

Habitat and status. A fairly common resident in Trinidad, frequenting mainly the edges of mangrove swamps, open country with scrub and scattered trees, and occasionally larger clearings bordering forest, sometimes well up the Northern Range valleys; also Monos. (Specimens: CM, AMNH, ANSP, YPM, LM, BM, TRVL.)

Range and subspecies. Mexico S to Bolivia and Argentina; the nominate race ranges from Colombia to Ecuador, Brazil and the Guianas.

Description. 10.5 in. *Adult:* upperparts grayish brown streaked with black and buff; crown chestnut and black (often seen as a crest), prominent whitish superciliary streak; bastard-wing black; underparts whitish; tail long, graduated. *Immature:* spotted with rufous on back and wings.

Measurements. Wing: 6 males 103–112mm (108); 7 females 99–106mm (103). Weight: 1 male 40gm; 1 female 41gm.

Voice. A clear musical whistle in a repeated series of usually 2 notes, the second one semi-tone above the first; another call is similar but has 3 notes, the first 2 being of even pitch. Sometimes, also, one note of similar quality and pitch is repeated in a 4- or 5-note call, this sequence occasionally followed by 1 or 2 fainter notes, evenly spaced. The far-carrying 2- or 3-note calls are usually repeated for minutes on end at regular intervals ranging from 5 to 10 sec, and may be heard at any time of night as well as during the day. The crest is raised rhythmically between each call.

Food. Insects, including grasshoppers, dragonflies, caterpillars, cockroaches and bugs, also arachnids.

Nesting. Breeding recorded in March and May–October. Singing also prominent December–April, so the species may well breed throughout the year, as in Surinam (Haverschmidt 1955, 1961). A brood parasite on spinetails (*Certhiaxis, Synallaxis albescens* and *S. cinnamomea*), which build large stick nests, usually near the ground. One egg, occasionally 2, is deposited in the host's nest; the colour varies from white to bluish or greenish, av. 21.8 × 16.5mm (2). Incubation period 15 days, fledging period 18 days. The young spinetails disappear, but it is unknown how this happens.

Behaviour. A rather solitary species, occasionally found in small groups. It usually keeps to the cover of trees and bushes, but when singing often perches on an exposed branch or fencepost. It flies short distances and runs about energetically on the ground, bounding along after grasshoppers. An extraordinary, stylized ritual is also performed on the ground. Raising its crest and flirting its tail from side to side, it half-opens its wings and flicks out the bastard-wing forward and upward in several jerky motions.

TYTONIDAE: Barn Owls

Similar in most respects to typical owls, barn owls have a heart-shaped facial disc and long legs. They are mostly nocturnal and frequent open country with scattered trees. They often nest in buildings with dark attics, where they spend the day. (1)

Barn Owl: *Tyto alba*

Habitat and status. Rather uncommon but widely distributed in the more open country of both islands, including light secondary forest with scattered clearings. (Specimens: AMNH, ANSP, YPM, BM, PSM.)

Range and subspecies. Almost worldwide in temperate and tropical countries, *T. a. hellmayri* (Griscom & Greenway) ranges from Venezuela to the Guianas and N Brazil, and is larger than the forms found on islands off Venezuela and the Lesser Antilles.

Description. 15 in. *Light phase:* upperparts buff, mottled with white and blackish; pale, heart-shaped facial disc; underparts whitish, finely spotted with brown. In the dusk appears all white. *Rufous phase:* underparts more or less rufous.

Measurements. Wing: 2 males 315, 318mm; 1 female 310mm.

Voice. A harsh rasping scream; also a rasping hiss.

Food. Small mammals, including opossums, rats mice and bats; also frogs, lizards and birds, including seabirds on Little Tobago and Dickcissels in Trinidad.

Nesting. Breeding recorded in Trinidad and Tobago from February to April and June (B/S). The nest is in a hole in a tree or in buildings, with 2–4 white eggs laid, av. 42.0 × 35.5mm (8). In Surinam Haverschmidt (1962a) found nests also in dark places under roofs. Clutches varied from 2 to 6, with regular double broods. Breeding occurred throughout the year.

Behaviour. Chiefly nocturnal, but occasionally seen at dusk and dawn, when one, sometimes a pair, hunts about 15 ft above the ground in open country, quartering the area with a wavering but buoyant flight. Many times I watched Barn Owls hunting Dickcissels at their roost in the dusk or at night. The owl would fly low over the canefield where the Dickcissels were roosting in thousands and plunge suddenly into a group of birds. This method of hunting was often unsuccessful, but the owl might persevere from dusk until midnight.

STRIGIDAE: Owls

This family is familiar to most people, the prominent features being the large head, short tail and large eyes directed forward in a facial disc. The bill is short and hooked, and the feet very strong. All the owls in Trinidad and Tobago are generally brown with patterned plumage. Most are strictly nocturnal. The commonest call is some kind of hoot, but various screams are also given. Superstitious people in Trinidad and Tobago, as in many other countries, regard the owl as a bird of ill omen and will attack it out of fear. (5)

Tropical Screech-Owl: *Otus choliba*
Spix's Screech (or Scops) Owl

Habitat and status. A common resident in Trinidad, found in forests, orchards and semi-open country, even on the edge of mangrove swamps. (Specimen: AMNH, YPM, BM, TRVL.)

Range and subspecies. Costa Rica S to Argentina; *O. c. crucigerus* (Spix) ranges from Colombia E to Venezuela, the Guianas, N Brazil and N Bolivia.

Description. 9 in. Short ear-tufts; upperparts grayish brown, streaked and speckled with black and white; white spots on scapulars; facial disc brown, outlined in white; underparts pale gray with fine, dark brown "herringbone" pattern. *Immature:* generally barred with brown. There is also a rufous phase.

Measurements. Wing: 9 males 164–171mm (167); 3 females 160, 160, 167mm. Weight: 3 males 114, 138, 142gm; 3 females 140, 155, 156gm; 1 unsexed 120gm.

Voice. A short, quick series of soft, purring hoots, ending abruptly with a louder single or double note. Also a variety of loud screams, cat-like wails and snarls, which often seem to be given in reaction, perhaps alarm, to the noises of cats, dogs or humans.

Food. Chiefly insects, including grasshoppers, cockroaches, leaf-cutting ants and beetles, also spiders. The bones of bats were found in a nest cavity after the young had left. Captive birds readily take mice.

Nesting. Breeding recorded February–May (6 of 12 records in March). The nest is usually in a tree-hole or other cavity, including the old domed nest of a kiskadee (*Pitangus*). The clutch is 1–3 white, almost round eggs, av. 33.8 × 29.1mm (7).

Behaviour. Strictly nocturnal. Calling heard at all times of year. A bird disturbed from a nest in daylight took up an elongated "alarm" pose, with ear-tufts erect.

Spectacled Owl: *Pulsatrix perspicillata*
Black-breasted Owl   **Figure 30**

Habitat and status. Rather uncommon, but found in dry lowland forest, cultivated estates and rain forest up to 2000 ft at least. (Specimen: AMNH.)

Range and subspecies. Mexico S to Bolivia and Argentina; *P. p. trinitatis* (Bangs & Penard) is found only in Trinidad, differing from the nominate race by its paler buff underparts.

Description. 18 in. Upperparts and patch around eyes dark brown, with whitish superciliary stripe meeting between eyes and prolonged from base of bill below eyes to give "spectacled" effect; throat white below black chin; breast-band dark brown; rest of underparts buff.

Measurements. Wing: 1 male 328mm; 2 females 334, 340mm.

Voice. A rapid series of deep, very soft, breathy hoots, each sounding like *whoof;* occasionally a single pigeon-like *hoop,* repeated every 5–10 sec; also a single, higher-pitched whistled hoot.

Food. Small mammals, birds, frogs, lizards and, to a large extent, grasshoppers and caterpillars (data from other areas).

O'Neill
72

Figure 30.   Spectacled Owl

Nesting. Breeding recorded in January, March (twice) and May. The nest is in a tree-hole; the clutch is 2 white eggs, av. 50.6 × 42.6mm (4).

Behaviour. Usually nocturnal, but occasionally surprised in the open during the day.

Ferruginous Pygmy-Owl: *Glaucidium brasilianum*
"Jumbie Bird"   **Figure 31**

Habitat and status. A common resident in Trinidad, frequenting semi-open country and forests at all levels, also urban districts where there are trees. (Specimens: AMNH, ANSP, YPM, LM, BM, TRVL.)

© John P. O'Neill - 1990

Figure 31. Ferruginous Pygmy-Owl

Range and subspecies. S USA south through Middle and South America to Bolivia and Argentina; *G. b. phaloenoides* (Daudin) is found only in Trinidad, the rufous phase being more rufous and less gray on the upperparts than continental forms.

Description. 6 in. This very small owl without ear-tufts is generally brown above, with white streaks and spots on the crown and wing-coverts; prominent white superciliary streak; dusky patches, resembling eyes at a distance, on back of head; underparts white with brown streaks; short tail barred brown and black. There are two phases, grayish brown and rufous.

Measurements. Wing: 9 males 94–101mm (97); 5 females 94–100mm (97); 2 unsexed 99, 102mm. Weight: 2 females 67, 73gm*; 5 unsexed 66–77gm (72).

Voice. Most commonly a regular series of musical hoots, repeated on the same note 5–30 times, *wup-wup-wup,* etc.; the pitch of the note is usually E flat, but different individuals vary from D to F. Also sometimes a louder rolling double note repeated several times, *churrup-churrup-churrup,* etc. Occasionally I have heard a distinctive variation—an insect-like rattling, continued for up to 5 sec, *tseepeda-tseepeda,* etc. This call seems to be associated with mating. A juvenile begging call is a short rattle, rather like a kingbird's call but lower-pitched and less strident.

Food. Lizards and insects, including caterpillars, moths, grasshoppers and bugs. Only one record exists of this owl taking small birds in Trinidad, but captive birds readily take raw meat.

Nesting. Breeding recorded from February to July, 10 of 14 records in March and April. The nest is in a tree-hole, sometimes in a hollowed-out termite nest, usually 15–20 ft above ground. The clutch is 2–5 white eggs, av. 28.8 × 24.5mm (8).

Behaviour. Mainly nocturnal, but also seen and heard frequently at any time of day. Particularly active at dusk and soon afterwards. Flight rapid and direct with long swoops. Occasionally in conflict with other hole-nesting birds, e.g., Lineated Woodpecker (Kilham & O'Brien 1979). During the day the species is often mobbed by others, especially small passerines. I have seen over 40 individuals of 11 species collect to mob 1 owl; but it is noticeable that while they readily chase it when it moves, they rarely attack seriously if it stays still. The call may easily be imitated by whistling and attracts other owls as well as the smaller birds.

Mottled Owl: *Ciccaba virgata*
Mottled (or Variable) Wood-Owl   **Figure 32**

Habitat and status. A rarely seen nocturnal resident in Trinidad; a few records from Bush-Bush Forest, also from Arima Valley (Buchanan 1971), where it is a regular at the nature centre. (Specimens: AMNH.)

Range and subspecies. Mexico S to Argentina and Paraguay; the nominate race ranges from Panama through Colombia and Venezuela to Trinidad.

Description. 14 in. Upperparts dark brown, mottled with buff; lores and superciliary streak buff; underparts buffy brown boldly streaked with dark brown; tail longish, dark brown with several white bars. There are two phases, dark and light.

Measurements. Wing: 3 males 241, 253, 255mm; 2 females 250, 274mm. Weight: 1 male 238gm; 1 female 248gm.

Voice. A deep guttural hoot, repeated 2 or 3 times at intervals of about 1 sec; also a long, drawn-out, single note with rising inflection, resembling a "whistled-screech" (Buchanan 1971). The latter call is given by both adults and young birds.

Food. Small mammals, including the rodent *Heteromys anomalus;* also, in other areas, snakes, salamanders, insects and spiders.

Nesting. Breeding recorded from March to May (4 records). Nests were 20–25 ft from the ground in tree-holes or the old nest of another species. The clutch is 2 white eggs, av. 39.2 × 32.0mm (4).

O'Neill
78

Figure 32. Mottled Owl

Striped Owl: *Asio clamator*
Streaked Owl; Horned Owl; "Cat-faced Owl";
Rhinoptynx clamator   **Figure 33**

Habitat and status. A rarely seen nocturnal inhabitant of forests and cultivated areas in Tobago, said to be locally common. (Specimens: USNM, BM.)

Range and subspecies. Mexico S to Argentina and Uruguay; *A. c. oberi* (Kelso) inhabits Tobago only; it is larger than the nominate race, and the dark bars on the outer webs of the primaries are broader.

Description. 14 in. Upperparts rufous brown, boldly streaked with dark brown; facial disc white, outlined with black; prominent ear-tufts; underparts pale buff, streaked with dark brown.

Measurements. Wing: 1 unsexed 284mm.

Voice. A series of sharp, low-pitched, barking hoots, about six at a time, *augh, augh, augh,* etc. (B. Smith).

Food. Not recorded in Tobago, but in other areas takes small mammals, treefrogs and large grasshoppers.

Figure 33. Striped Owl

Nesting. Only one record in Tobago, of a nest at Prospect on the ground amidst tall grass on 22 February 1978, with 3 white eggs; 3 Surinam eggs av. 44.6 × 36.1mm (Haverschmidt 1962b).

STEATORNITHIDAE: Oilbirds

This strange species forms a family of its own, showing some resemblance to the nightjars and owls in general appearance but differing in other ways. It is gregarious, living and breeding in dark or pitch-black caves during the day and coming out at night to feed on fruit. (1)

Oilbird: *Steatornis caripensis*
"Guacharo"; "Diablotin"   **Plate 8(1)**

Habitat and status. There are eight known breeding colonies in Trinidad, situated in caves in mountainous country, Oropouche, Aripo, Springhill, or on seacoast, Huevos and La Vache. Five other colonies were recently occupied but are now extinct. Adult numbers estimated 1460 in 1962 (Snow), but some colonies are known to fluctuate considerably. In Venezuela some post-breeding migration or dispersal takes place (Bosque & Ramirez 1988), and this has been suspected also at Springhill. (Specimens: AMNH, ANSP, CM, BM, TRVL.)

Range. Locally from E Panama, Colombia and Venezuela S to Peru and Bolivia.

Description. 18 in.; wingspread 3.5 ft. Generally rich brown with white spots on secondaries and wing-coverts; long, graduated tail; large, hooked bill with prominent rictal bristles; legs short. At rest resembles very large nightjar. Sexes similar, but male is grayer and slightly darker brown, female paler and more rufous.

Measurements. Wing: 9 males 307–333mm (320); 8 females 292–321 (307). Weight: 3 males 405, 410, 480gm; 5 unsexed 375–435gm (404).

Voice. A variety of screams, snarls and clucks are made by the birds when disturbed at the nest or threatened by an intruder; also in flight a short cluck and a series of clicks, which enable the bird to navigate in the pitch dark by echo-location.

Food. The fruits of various forest trees, including palms (especially *Euterpe langloisii*), Lauraceae (especially *Ocotea wachenheimii*) and Burseraceae (especially *Dacryodes*). The birds pluck the fruits in flight, at night, swallowing them whole. The pericarp is digested and the seeds are later regurgitated. Many of these trees are aromatic, and the Oilbirds, which have a well-developed olfactory sense, may find them by smell.

Nesting. Breeding recorded (D. W. Snow 1961, 1962d) December–September, but 89% of 79 recorded nests occurred from December to May. Moult very long, probably overlapping breeding cycle. The nest is a mound about 15 in. wide constructed mainly of regurgitated fruit forming a paste, and situated on a ledge in the cave, often several forming a group. Many nests are used year after year, with fresh material added occasionally. The eggs are laid in a shallow depression, normally 2–4, white but soon stained brown; av. 41.7 × 33.2mm (3), and weighing av. 20.2gm (10). They are laid at an interval of several days. Both parents share incubation for about 33 days. The young hatch naked and grow very slowly, flying 3–4 months after hatching. During this time they become very fat, at 10 wk weighing half as much again as an adult.

Behaviour. Extremely sociable at the colony; also forages in groups. Except when breeding the birds spend all night outside feeding. Little is known about their precise activities during the night, but they may perch in trees when not feeding. At the colony they crouch on or near the nest in pairs, the pair bond being probably permanent once formed (D. W. Snow 1961). One bird sometimes preens its mate's head. The only other courtship display known is a circling display flight by 2 or 3 birds. Oilbirds are completely nocturnal, and most colonies are in the dark. Some colonies are in merely subdued light, and the Aripo Well cave has some nests in normal daylight, possibly even receiving some sunlight.

Notes. In Humboldt's original account of the Oilbird he described how the natives of Venezuela collected the young birds at the peak of their fatness and boiled them down to produce oil for cooking and lighting. More recently colonies have been adversely affected, even extirpated, by habitat alteration and destruction of forests (Bosque 1986). The colonies in Trinidad have been similarly exploited, and protection is hard to enforce, since most of the caves are fairly remote. The small colony at Springhill Estate in the Arima Valley, however, has been safeguarded by the establishment of the Asa Wright Nature Centre, and it is possible that eventually the 2 large colonies at Oropouche and Aripo could be adequately protected if the authorities become convinced of their potential as tourist attractions.

NYCTIBIIDAE: Potoos

Resembling very large, long-tailed nightjars, potoos spend the day perched in an upright position on a post or treestump, their cryptic coloration effectively camouflaging them. At night they hawk for insects like flycatchers, their eyes conspicuously reflecting any bright light. (1)

Common Potoo: *Nyctibius griseus*
Grey Potoo; Giant Nightjar; "Poor-me-one"   **Plate 8(2)**

Habitat and status. A rather uncommon but widely distributed resident of Trinidad, found in lowland forest, cocoa estates, savannahs and mangrove swamps. (Specimens: AMNH, YPM, BM.) Many sight records, including photographs, from Tobago.

Range and subspecies. Mexico S to Bolivia and Argentina, also Greater Antilles; the nominate race ranges from E Colombia and Venezuela to the Guianas and N Brazil.

Description. 15 in. Generally brown, mottled with gray, black and chestnut; black streaks on crown and underparts; tail long; iris orange. There are gray and rufous phases. At night best distinguished from nightjars by the fact that *both* eyes reflect light together, appearing as two large yellow or orange orbs.

Measurements. Wing: 5 males 253–257mm (255). Weight: 1 male 146gm; 1 female 155gm.

Voice. In the distance the call sounds like 5 mournful but musical notes descending the scale, roughly one tone apart. At close quarters 6 or 7 notes can be distinguished, rather rasping and breathy in quality.

Food. Moths, grasshoppers, beetles and bugs, including the large firefly; also termites.

Nesting. Breeding recorded in March (2), April (3), May and July. The "nest" is just a depression on a treestump or broken branch 10–60 ft above ground. One egg is laid, white with lilac spots and streaks, and the size varies considerably; range 35.9–41.5 × 25.0–32.0mm, av. 38.9 × 28.9mm (4). Both adults incubate; Johnson (1937) recorded an incubation period of 30 days and a fledging period of 40 days; the adults brooded the chick alternately for 21 days. The downy young is white.

Behaviour. Usually solitary, but I have seen 2 or 3 Potoos hunting insects together at night. During incubation by day the adult sits upright with head and bill pointed forward. When disturbed it elongates its head and body, opening the bill slightly and almost closing the eyes. It only moves from its position, however, when directly threatened. In its own threat display it opens wide its large eyes and snaps its huge gape. Injury-feigning has also been observed.

Notes. The local name "Poor-me-one" is also used for the dwarf anteater (*Cyclopes*), which for many years used to be considered the author of the Potoo's song.

CAPRIMULGIDAE: Nighthawks and Nightjars

Mainly nocturnal and cryptic in colour, the members of this family are best identified by their calls. They are found in a wide variety of habitats, and some species migrate. They nest and perch on the ground, occasionally sitting lengthwise along a branch. They feed on flying insects, which they catch with their wide mouths. Nightjars hunt by sallying out from a perch, usually on the ground, while nighthawks pursue their prey in the course of a rapid, twisting flight either near or sometimes well above the ground. (6)

Short-tailed Nighthawk: *Lurocalis semitorquatus*
Semicollared Nighthawk   **Plate 8(3)**

Habitat and status. A rarely seen but quite widely distributed species, probably resident in Trinidad; found in forest, both in the hills and lowlands, and at the edge of marshes. Records are distributed throughout the year. (Specimens: AMNH, BM.)

Range and subspecies. Nicaragua S to Peru and N Argentina; the nominate race ranges from Colombia and Venezuela to Guyana and NW Brazil.

Description. 8.5 in. *Male:* generally dark with *no wing-band,* but whitish markings on secondaries and greater-wing-coverts show up in the field as whitish crescents on inner wing; whitish spots on tail; inconspicuous white throat-band; underparts barred rufous and blackish. At rest long wings extend well beyond short, square tail. *Female:* less white on wings.

Measurements. Wing: 1 male 172mm; 1 female 173mm; 3 unsexed 175, 175, 183mm.

Voice. In flight, a light *whit-whit-whit-wiss,* or a clucking *wup-wup-wup.*

Food. Bugs and beetles taken in flight (in Colombia).

Nesting. Herklots found a bird on Aripo Savannah in March incubating 1 egg, measuring 23.5 × 16mm. No other details.

Behaviour. I have seen birds individually and in small bands, hunting low over clearings in the Northern Range in the semi-dark, both at dusk and dawn. Also, small flocks have been seen at dusk hawking low over streams bordering mangroves in the Oropouche Lagoon. The flight is extremely erratic and bat-like.

Lesser Nighthawk: *Chordeiles acutipennis*
South American Nighthawk; Texas Nighthawk

Habitat and status. A common species occurring on savannahs and mangrove swamps in both islands, breeding but probably also migrant. Especially common August–October. (Specimens: ANSP, PSM, BM.)

Range and subspecies. W USA south to Bolivia and Brazil; the nominate race ranges in South America E of the Andes from Colombia to Brazil.

Banding status. One female was banded at Caroni on 22 October 1962. No recovery.

Description. 8 in. *Male:* upperparts dark brown mottled with buff, with chestnut bars on head and scapulars; outer 4 primaries with white bar, very conspicuous in flight; underparts finely barred dark brown and whitish; inconspicuous whitish throat-patch; tail slightly forked with white subterminal bar. *Female:* wing-bar pale buffy rufous, tail without white bar; base of primaries mottled with tawny.

Measurements. Wing: 5 males 156–169mm (162); 5 females 142–162mm (150). Weight: 7 males 39–50gm (46); 3 females 44, 46, 46gm.

Voice. A low *chuck chuck* and a soft guttural trilling (in USA). In breeding season a twanging note (Miller 1947, in Colombia).

Food. Insects, including small beetles and winged ants, dragonflies, bugs and flies.

Nesting. Breeding recorded February–May (B/S); individuals moult in August and October. No nest. One egg is laid among dead leaves on the ground (though elsewhere the species sometimes produces a clutch of 2 eggs); it is whitish marked evenly with brown spots, splotches and lines, av. 26.7 × 20.7mm (10).

Behaviour. Mainly nocturnal, but also seen in the early dusk when it begins to hunt rather low over the savannah. I have several times surprised birds roosting during the day on the low branches of mangroves. Once one of these birds was chased constantly by a party of Carib Grackles until it left the area.

Frequently seen in loosely associated flocks of 20 or more birds. At night they commonly sit on the pitch roads which cross the more isolated savannahs, where a car's headlights show up their eyes in considerable numbers.

[Common Nighthawk: *Chordeiles minor*]
American Nighthawk

Habitat and status. No certain record, but Kirk recorded it in Tobago "from July to October". Possibly a mistake for the Lesser Nighthawk, but this species is known regularly on fall migration through the Lesser Antilles, including Barbados, and casually in Venezuela and offshore islands. (No specimen.)

Range. Breeds in North America and locally S to Panama and Greater Antilles; it has a number of migratory races, being known on migration through Middle and most of South America to Argentina.

Description. 9.5 in. Similar to Lesser Nighthawk but larger; upperparts darker with less buff; both sexes have white wing-bar covering 5 outer primaries and nearer base of feathers, midway across the wing; primaries otherwise completely blackish. Often seen flying quite high above ground, sometimes in broad daylight, though more often at dusk.

Voice. A frequently uttered nasal or buzzy *peent*, given even on migration.

Nacunda Nighthawk: *Podager nacunda*
Plate 8(5)

Habitat and status. Fairly common in savannahs and open areas in Trinidad, apparently breeding occasionally, but dates of most records and behaviour indicate migration to the continent. I have 14 records between 23 June and 23 October, and Léotaud, Williams and others have also noted birds only between June and October. Kirk collected 2 specimens in Tobago, but no recent records there. (Specimens: Trinidad, AMNH, ANSP; Tobago, BM.)

Range and subspecies. Colombia and Venezuela S to Bolivia and Argentina; *P. n. minor* (Cory) ranges south to N Brazil and the Guianas, being smaller than the southern race. See Notes below.

Description. 12 in. Upperparts brown, speckled with white; some black spots on crown and scapulars; white band across base of primaries; throat white, upper breast barred brown, *conspicuously demarcated* from white lower underparts. *Male:* outer tail tipped white.

Measurements. Wing: 1 unsexed 238mm.

Voice. In alarm, a musical *cherk-cherk*, repeated.

Food. Flying insects, including froghoppers (*Tomaspis*), beetles, bugs, especially *Nezara,* and winged ants.

Nesting. B/S record 3 nests during April in the Caroni marshes. Eggs were laid on the ground among dead leaves. The clutch is 1 or 2 eggs, cream with rich brown blotches and lines mainly at the thicker end, av. 36.1 × 26.7mm (4).

Behaviour. Mainly nocturnal but often seen hunting just before dark. During the day they roost in the open, preferring bare ground or thin vegetation, often in sizeable flocks. If disturbed they fly about with a slow wing-action, without zigzagging, before settling again. On the ground they allow quite a close approach, but bob nervously and make their clucking call. On 17 October I watched a close-flying flock of about 25 birds travelling slowly and deliberately across Pointe-a-Pierre in a SSW direction. They resembled gulls in the distance. The date and manner of flight seemed to indicate migration.

Notes. Though specimens collected in Trinidad appear to belong to the smaller northern race *minor,* it is by no means certain that all birds of this species found here are in fact *minor.* A male collected in NE Venezuela was as large as birds of the nominate southern race. In addition, the existence of a small breeding population alongside an apparent influx of migrants during June–October parallels the situation of other visitors from S South America, including *Tyrannus* and *Notiochelidon,* which are represented in Trinidad by both resident and migratory races.

Pauraque: *Nyctidromus albicollis*
White-naped Nightjar   **Plate 8(6)**

Habitat and status. A fairly common resident in Trinidad, generally distributed in light woodland, especially at lower altitudes; at night also found feeding in savannahs bordering forest. (Specimens: AMNH, ANSP, LM, BM, TRVL.)

Range and subspecies. S USA south to Brazil; the nominate race ranges from Guatemala south.

Description. 11 in. A large, long-tailed nightjar, occurring in gray or rufous phase; upperparts gray-brown or rufous mottled with dark brown, and with black streaks on crown and scapulars; ear-coverts chestnut; a prominent white bar on black primaries, pale buff in *female;* white crescent on lower throat; rest of underparts barred blackish and rufous; tail long with outer feathers black, next 2 outer white in *male,* tail barred with buff and outer feathers white-tipped in *female.*

Measurements. Wing: 9 males 145–153mm (148); 3 females 143, 152, 154mm. Weight: 5 males 49–60gm (54); 2 females 50*, 58gm.

Voice. A far-carrying whistle, varying somewhat in tone and number of syllables, but based upon a loud, high note followed by a softer, low one; thus, *ker-whee-oo,* with accent on middle syllable, sometimes rendered "Who-are-you?". Also a lower-toned, nasal *waa-oo,* and a sharp *hip-hip-hip.* Sometimes the short first syllable of the usual call is repeated several times. The call may be repeated for minutes on end, once every few seconds.

Food. Insects, including beetles, grasshoppers, moths and cockroaches.

Nesting. Breeding recorded from February to July (B/S), probably mainly in the dry season. The nest is on the ground among dead leaves in wooded areas. The clutch is 1 or 2 pinkish cream eggs mottled and clouded with reddish brown, sometimes with a few black lines, av. 29.3 × 21.2mm (10). Both parents incubate, only the female at night. In Central America Skutch (1952) found a 2-day interval between laying of 2 eggs, the laying taking place in the evening. The young can move from the nest soon after hatching. Both parents brood and feed the small young.

Behaviour. Nocturnal and generally solitary. If flushed in woodland a bird will flit lightly off to land quite close by, its cryptic colours effectively concealing it on the ground. Sometimes it bobs repeatedly on the ground. Incubating or brooding birds perform a distraction display feigning injury. Often seen at night on or beside minor roads where the yellow-orange eyes reflect the headlights of passing cars. Quesnel (1985) found birds especially common on roads when the moon is full, evidently holding feeding and breeding territories there.

Rufous Nightjar: *Caprimulgus rufus*
Plate 8(7)

Habitat and status. Fairly common, probably resident, among scrub and deciduous woodland in NW peninsula of Trinidad and Bocas islands, where birds have been heard frequently and tape-recorded. No definite records E of St. Augustine. (No specimens, so the race remains undetermined.)

Range. The species, whose relationship to certain other nightjars is not clear (L. I. Davis 1962, Meyer de Schauensee 1966), ranges through most of South America and N to Costa Rica; also the island of St. Lucia.

Description. 10 in. Upperparts rufous brown streaked and vermiculated with black and dark brown; *no* white wing-bar, wings rufous barred with blackish; buff band across throat, rest of underparts barred black and rufous; central tail dark, outer 3 pairs of tail-feathers broadly tipped white on inner webs (in *male*).

Voice. A very distinctive 5-syllabled call, *chuck-wit-wit-wee-oo,* the last 2 syllables sometimes sounding like one syllable, *will.* Call repeated every few seconds.

Nesting. B/S record 4 nests, 1 in each month February–May, which they confidently ascribe to this species. Calls have been heard regularly from April to June, but no later, in the same localities. The clutch is 1 or 2 creamy eggs, blotched with sepia and spotted with pale gray, av. 31.5 × 23.1mm (7).

Behaviour. Apparently completely nocturnal, since no birds were seen during the day on Monos in an area where their calls showed them to be common. Calling began soon after dark at 6:30 P.M. and went on through the night, ending at 5:30 A.M. just before dawn.

White-tailed Nightjar: *Caprimulgus cayennensis*
Cayenne Nightjar; Stenopsis Nightjar   **Plate 8(4)**

Habitat and status. A widespread and fairly common resident on both islands, frequenting semi-open savannahs and large clearings on the edge of forest, even into the foothills of the Northern Range. Also the Bocas Islands and Little Tobago. (Specimens: Trinidad, ANSP, YPM; Tobago, LM, BM.)

Range and subspecies. Costa Rica south to N Brazil and the Guianas, the islands off Venezuela, and Martinique; *C. c. cayennensis* (Gmelin) ranges from E Colombia to Trinidad, the Guianas and N Brazil; *C. c. leopetes* (Jardine & Selby) is restricted to Tobago, being more uniform above with a broader rufous collar.

Description. 8.5 in. *Male:* upperparts dark brown mottled with gray, black, rufous and white; pale rufous collar on hindneck; primaries dark brown, the outer 4 crossed with prominent white bar; breast barred rufous; throat and rest of underparts white; outer tail white with central dark brown bar. *Female:* as male, but wing-bar buff; underparts generally barred and mottled dark brown and rufous; some white markings on throat and upper breast; tail barred dark brown and rufous. Downy young are gray.

Measurements. *C. c. cayennensis.* Wing: 6 males 136–148mm (143). Weight: 4 males 30–38gm (34.5); 3 females 33, 35, 37gm. *C. c. leopetes.* Wing: 2 males 139, 145mm; 1 female 140mm. Weight: 2 males 31, 34gm*.

Voice. A very high-pitched call of 1 short syllable followed by another long-drawn-out note, *chi-peeeeer;* also, in flight, a high *see-see,* irregularly spaced; when flushed, a thin *tic-tic.*

Food. Beetles, grasshoppers and damsel-flies.

Nesting. Breeding recorded in Trinidad during January and March–May (6 nests); in Tobago in February (2), April, May and June (3). The nest scrape is on the ground in the open, in rough grass or on gravel, often with cover nearby. The clutch is usually 2 buffish pink eggs, with purplish brown scrawls and blotches, 6 from Trinidad av. 25 × 19.6mm, 2 from Tobago av. 25.5 × 17.5mm. At 3 days old the young birds can move a few yards. The incubating or brooding female, when disturbed, sits very tight and often feigns injury in a distraction display. I can find no evidence that the male shares in incubation, though he visits the female at the nest.

Behaviour. Mainly nocturnal, but also seen in the half-light at dawn, when I have seen birds flying up and down over low trees. Usually birds perch on the ground, but I have seen one asleep perching across a low branch. At night, in Tobago at least, commonly seen on the roadside.

APODIDAE: Swifts

These birds can be recognized by their rapid, fluttering flight, generally blackish plumage, long, narrow wings appearing curved in flight and streamlined appearance. Superficially resembling swallows, they are never seen perched, except at the nest or roost, but spend most of their time on the wing. Most species nest in small cup-shaped nests attached to a vertical surface, often in some dark locality. Feeding on aerial insects, they may be found over almost any habitat but are most common over hill forests. Known locally as "Rain-birds", flocks of swifts frequently precede squalls and thunderstorms, exploiting the increase in the food supply as insects are swept up in the updraught. (8)

White-collared Swift: *Cypseloides zonaris*
Cloud Swift: *Streptoprocne zonaris*   **Plate 9(4)**

Habitat and status. A regular visitor to Trinidad in small numbers, where it may be seen over all types of country, especially between July and October. Isolated groups seen as late as February, also once each in May and June. Largest flock numbered about 500, in August; one August record from Tobago. (Specimens: AMNH, ANSP, BM, TRVL.)

Range and subspecies. Mexico S to Bolivia and Argentina; *C. z. albicincta* (Cabanis) ranges from Honduras S to Peru, Brazil and Guyana and is also recorded from Grenada.

Description. 8 in. A large black swift with a white collar all round, narrower above than below. *Immature:* white collar reduced.

Measurements. Wing: 3 males 181, 190, 190mm; 1 unsexed 179mm. Weight: 3 males 60, 83, 100gm; 4 females 74–95gm (88); 5 unsexed 63–101gm (89).

Voice. A light but shrill, screaming *chee-chee-chee*.

Food. Flying insects, especially flying ants, also beetles, bees and wasps.

Behaviour. Usually seen in bands of up to 50, these swifts fly fairly low and extremely rapidly across the countryside, disappearing almost as soon as an observer has realised their presence. Sometimes, however, they are found hawking over a concentration of insects, where I have seen them both in the lowlands and at the summit of El Tucuche. One evening in August 1957 D. W. Snow and I watched a great flock of about 500 birds spiralling upwards over the Arima Valley, and we conjectured that these birds might be spending the night on the wing. I have since seen this phenomenon in the evening on other occasions.

Notes. An account of the nesting of the Mexican race (Rowley & Orr 1965) has shown that this swift nests in caves behind waterfalls, where it builds a disc-shaped nest of mud, moss and insect chitin. Certainly such nesting situations are available also in Trinidad, but most of our records indicate that birds visit Trinidad in a post-breeding dispersal, probably from the Venezuelan Andes. Adults were collected here in August just finishing their moult. Alternatively birds may visit Trinidad in the course of avoiding bad weather in Venezuela, for birds of this size and speed of flight might well travel great distances in 1 day.

Chestnut-collared Swift: *Cypseloides rutilus*
Rufous-collared Swift   **Plate 9(3)**

Habitat and status. A fairly common resident in hilly parts of Trinidad, also on N coast, e.g., at Huevos, Saut d'Eau and Blanchisseuse, breeding in caves at all levels, but found foraging only over forest from 500 ft upwards, commonly over summit of El Tucuche, etc. (Specimens: AMNH, FSM.)

Banding status. Thirty-seven birds were banded from 1962 to 1968 in N Trinidad. Many of these have been recaptured, some several times, in the same localities, including birds known to be at least 10 yr old. Collins (1974) found an annual survival rate of at least 83% in an Arima Valley colony.

Range and subspecies. Mexico S to Peru and Bolivia; the nominate race is known only in Colombia, N Venezuela and Trinidad; it has a square-ended tail, and the adult female differs from the male in usually lacking the rufous collar.

Description. 5.5 in. *Male:* generally blackish, with complete rufous collar. *Female:* as male, but usually without rufous collar, or with only a partial collar. *Immature:* partial rufous collar; differs from female by having reddish edge to feathers of crown.

Measurements. Wing: 119–128mm (both sexes). Weight: 24 males 19.25–22.25gm (20.6); 19 females 17.75–24.25gm (19.6).

Voice. A high-pitched, hoarse, chattering series, with a more metallic, buzzing sound than the calls of *Chaetura* swifts, e.g., *chip-chip-chip*, often repeated in aerial chases.

Food. Flying insects, mainly winged ants and termites.

Nesting. Breeding recorded mainly from May to August (70 nests), once in April (B/S once collected eggs, possibly deserted, in November). Moult occurs August–December. Nests are built on rocky walls of mountain gorges, sea caves and under bridges and culverts, all on vertical surfaces, in deep shadow, near water in forested areas up to 1100 ft (D. W. Snow 1962b, Collins 1968a). They are made of soft plant material, e.g., mosses and ferns, mixed with mud and possibly saliva. In shape they resemble truncated cones, or sometimes discs, the eggs being laid in a wide, shallow depression. Normal clutch is 2 white eggs, soon becoming stained, av. 21.9 × 14.7mm (7). The nests are often repaired and used again, and 2 broods in a season are quite common, the interval between them being rather short. Incubation, by both sexes, lasts about 23 days. The young fledge after about 40 days, being brooded almost continuously for the first 10 days. By then they have acquired a down-like semi-plume covering (though hatched naked), which helps to prevent heat loss in their unusually damp and dark nesting site.

Behaviour. This species is usually seen singly or in small parties flying over forested areas at an altitude above ground that is significantly greater than for *Chaetura* species. It sometimes forms mixed flocks with *Chaetura;* large mixed flocks, predominantly of this species, may usually be seen over El Tucuche. At the nest adults feed the young with a compact "food ball" made up of insects collected on somewhat lengthy hunting sessions. Just before flying the young may be seen exercising their wings while still hanging on to the nest rim. After the breeding season small groups of birds gather to roost at the nest site. Although one such roosting flock in Mexico (Rowley 1966) numbered about 300 birds, the largest group observed in Trinidad was only 7 or 8 birds.

[Black Swift: *Cypseloides niger*]

Habitat and status. Sight records of several birds, including those of Smooker, C. B. Worth, D. Lack and myself between 13 June and mid-September (localities: Arima Valley, El Tucuche and Bush-Bush marshes), also of Mr. and Mrs. T. Manolis from Terry Hill, Tobago, on 15 August, indicate a likely post-breeding passage of this species, although its similarity to other species of swifts, especially *Cypseloides*, known from N South America, and even to immature White-collared Swifts, precludes certainty. (No specimen.)

Range. W North America, Central America, and in the West Indies S to St. Vincent. Lesser Antillean birds are thought to migrate to Guyana.

Description. 6.5 in. All black, with some white edges to feathers of forehead and breast. *Cypseloides* swifts differ from *Chaetura* swifts in their relatively longer tails and in having the rump not paler than back and the throat not paler than breast (except in species where it is white or rufous). Their flight is also less erratic.

Chapman's Swift: *Chaetura chapmani*
Dark-breasted Swift   **Plate 9(6)**

Habitat and status. A rather rare resident in Trinidad, found over forests and savannahs, usually in company with other *Chaetura* species. (Specimens: AMNH, BM, TRVL.)

Banding status. Thirteen birds were banded in N Trinidad during 1962–68. No recoveries yet.

Range and subspecies. Panama and Colombia E and S to Peru and Brazil; the nominate race ranges from Panama to the Guianas and NE Brazil.

Description. 5 in. Slightly larger than others of this genus known from Trinidad. Generally blackish, with dark brownish (rather than gray) lower back and rump; underparts uniform dark brown with slightly paler throat. Best identified in company with other swifts. This is the *Chaetura* swift with *least* contrast of paler rump and throat.

Measurements. Wing: 17 males 116–122mm (119); 16 females 116–124mm (120). Weight: 16 unsexed adults 22–28gm (24.7). Immatures weighed on average 2gm less.

Voice. Undescribed.

Food. Insects, including winged ants.

Nesting. The only nest yet identified for this species was found by C. T. Collins near Valencia in April 1963 (Collins 1968b). It was a shallow half-saucer made of small twigs glued together with a salivary secretion and fixed to the vertical wall of a manhole, in which were similar nests of the Short-tailed Swift. Eggs were laid in May. The clutch was 2 (or possibly 3) white eggs. Only 2 eggs survived to hatch, after being incubated for 17 or 18 days, and both young disappeared soon after hatching.

Behaviour. In my experience this species, when foraging, is always associated with one of the other *Chaetura* species. It never seems to occur in large numbers, but instead singly or in small groups. Some birds roost commonly in manholes on Waller Field, up to 6 in one spot. Collins (1968b) describes a wing-clapping display at the roosting site, similar to that of the Chimney Swift.

Gray-rumped Swift: *Chaetura cinereiventris*
Lawrence's Swift   **Plate 9(5)**

Habitat and status. Common, probably resident, in both islands over hill forest; rarely, if ever, seen below 500 ft. (Specimens: both islands, AMNH; Trinidad, ANSP, TRVL.)

Banding status. Sixteen adults were banded on 29 October 1966 and 3 on 27 November 1966, at the head of the Lopinot Valley. No recoveries yet.

Range and subspecies. Costa Rica S to Peru, the Guianas, Brazil and N Argentina; *C. c. lawrencei* (Ridgway) is known in Venezuela, our islands and Grenada.

Description. 4.5 in. Upperparts black with gray triangular rump patch and black tail. Underparts slate gray, less black below than other local *Chaetura* species. A more slender bird than the Short-tailed Swift, with a distinctly longer tail.

Measurements. Wing: 101 unsexed 98–108mm (102.1). Weight: 128 unsexed 11.75–18gm (13.9).

Voice. A light chittering.

Food. Aerial insects, especially flying ants and beetles.

Nesting. No definite nest recorded here, but several birds were trapped in May with incubation patches and weighing 16–18gm. Wing-moult was found only in 31 birds trapped between June and November. Most birds trapped from February to May had no moult or slight body moult. In SE Brazil the nominate race builds nests of small twigs similar to those of other *Chaetura* species (Sick 1959); these are situated on the inside of chimneys, also probably in hollow trees. (D. W. Snow [1962b] suspected nesting in an immortelle tree in Trinidad.) Nesting sites are used again and again. Clutch size up to 4 eggs. Sometimes at night both parents sit on the nest together.

Band-rumped Swift: *Chaetura spinicauda*
Spine-tailed Swift   **Plate 9(8)**

Habitat and status. A common resident in Trinidad, frequenting forested areas both in the hills and the lowlands. (Specimens: AMNH, YPM, BM, TRVL.)

Range and subspecies. Costa Rica S to Colombia, Venezuela, the Guianas and NE Brazil; the nominate race ranges through NE Venezuela, Trinidad and the Guianas.

Description. 4.5 in. Very similar in shape to Gray-rumped Swift. Generally blackish with a distinct whitish (*not* gray) bar across the rump; throat distinctly paler than rest of underparts.

Measurements. Wing: 56 unsexed 98–108mm (102.4). Weight: 68 unsexed 13–20gm (15.2).

Voice. Similar to other *Chaetura* species.

Food. Small flying insects, especially beetles and winged ants.

Nesting. Very little is known about the nesting of this species; in early July D. W. Snow (1962b) saw a pair probably feeding young at a nest in a tree-hole 30 ft above ground. The nest itself could not be seen in the hole. Wing-moult has been found in a number of individuals from early May to late October. The heaviest birds were also found in January and early May.

Behaviour. Found in association with other swift species, also often in loose flocks of up to 50 individuals. This species is often seen feeding just above the ground, especially in forest clearings. Rarely found roosting in manholes on Waller Field with Short-tailed Swifts.

Short-tailed Swift: *Chaetura brachyura*
"Rain-bat"   **Plate 9(7)**

Habitat and status. A common resident in both islands, found at almost all elevations but more plentiful over savannahs, urban areas and forests at lower levels than in mountain districts. (Specimens: AMNH, ANSP, BM, TRVL.)

Banding status. A total of 253 birds, both adults and immatures, were banded in N Trinidad during 1963–66. Of these, 43 have been recaptured in the same localities, up to 41 months later.

Range and subspecies. Panama and Colombia S and E to Ecuador, Peru, Brazil and the Guianas, also in the Lesser Antilles; the nominate race is found throughout the South American range.

Description. 4 in. Generally black, with pale ashy brown lower back, rump and under-tail-coverts. In flight this species can be distinguished from the other *Chaetura* species by its short, chunky body, long wings, noticeably shorter, inconspicuous tail, blackish throat and the fact that the paler patch on the rump does *not* contrast with a darker tail.

Measurements. Wing: 11 unsexed 116–130mm (119.9). Weight: 261 unsexed 15–22gm (18.4).

Voice. A musical, rather excited, chittering.

Food. Aerial insects, mostly 2–4mm long but up to 9mm; prey includes winged ants, termites, flies, beetles and bugs. Mostly feeding is in the open, where birds can sometimes be seen to change direction in order to catch prey. In addition they sometimes flutter briefly near the top branches of tall forest trees, apparently picking insects off the leaves.

Nesting. Breeding has been recorded from April to September, 125 nests distributed as follows:

IV	V	VI	VII	VIII	IX
9	45	29	24	15	3

The start of breeding is evidently influenced by the first heavy rains. Adult moult takes place between August and December. Most nest-sites found have been artificial structures such as manholes, chimneys and even a nest box, but nests have also been found in caves (D. W. Snow 1962b, Collins 1968a). The nest, which is attached to a vertical surface, is a shallow half-saucer made of small twigs glued together with saliva; diameter of the nest is just over 2 in. Clutch size varies from 1 to 7 eggs, 67 clutches av. 3.7, with larger clutches occurring earlier in the season. The eggs are white, av. 18.8×13.1mm (6) and are laid usually every other day. The incubation period is 17–18 days, with both parents incubating and brooding intermittently for the first week after hatching. The young remain in the nest for 3 wk, and near it, without flying, for a further 2 wk. Two broods in a season are not uncommon.

Behaviour. Mainly gregarious during the day, when it is seen in loose flocks of its own species or mixed with other *Chaetura* species. Outside the breeding season birds congregate at night in communal roosts, often at nest-sites, in large numbers (up to 375 recorded together). During the moult period birds remain at the roosts for part of the day, packed together in tight clumps. When disturbed they perform a "wing-clattering" display, slowly raising their wings and clapping them violently down, apparently against the wall to which they cling. Though normal flight is rapid and powerful, the species has been seen hovering when rising vertically out of the manhole nest-sites.

Lesser Swallow-tailed Swift: *Panyptila cayennensis*
Cayenne Swift   **Plate 9(2)**

Habitat and status. A rather uncommon resident in Trinidad but widespread over all types of country, where it is usually seen flying high overhead. The supposed record of Dalmas from Tobago in 1898 refers probably to another species. (Specimens: ANSP, BM.)

Banding status. One bird was banded at a nest in Arima Valley on 31 May 1964. No recovery.

Range. Mexico S through Central and South America to Ecuador and Brazil.

Description. 5 in. Mainly black with wide white collar all round neck and white patches on sides of rump; tail longer than in *Chaetura* swifts and deeply forked, though the fork is only noticeable when turning, otherwise the tail seems sharply pointed. The only small swift with white markings visible from below, in strong contrast to the generally black colour.

Measurements. Weight: 1 male 22gm; 2 females 16, 23gm; 5 unsexed 18.5–28gm (22.1).

Voice. A light *chee-chee-chee*, heard at the nest.

Food. High-flying insects, especially winged ants, termites, bugs and small beetles.

Nesting. Breeding recorded in March and May, but nest-building may last over a long period, even up to 8 months. The nest is usually sleeve-shaped, 1–

2 ft long, made of plant-down, with sometimes several feathers included. It is attached by the top or the side to a tree trunk or branch, occasionally to the ceiling or wall of a house, at heights of 8–50 ft. Most nests have been found on forest trees, but others have been on large trees in the heart of Port of Spain. Both adults build the nest, working the down into a stiff felt by the application of saliva. The entrance is at the bottom, and the eggs are deposited on a small shelf inside the "sleeve", usually near the top. Sometimes several shelves are built in successive years. The clutch is 2 or 3 white eggs, av. 19.7 × 14.4mm (3; av. weight 1.6gm). Both parents incubate and feed the young, which hatch naked and seem to develop slowly (Sick 1958, Haverschmidt 1958).

Behaviour. Usually found singly or in pairs, this swift often accompanies flocks of *Chaetura* swifts when feeding, but is rarely seen foraging at ground level. It flies extremely fast, even when approaching its nest, and the disturbance caused by the parents entering the narrow tube may be the cause of eggs falling off the small incubation shelf. The adults roost in the nest before and after breeding, arriving a few minutes after sunset and leaving before sunrise.

Fork-tailed Palm-Swift: *Reinarda squamata*
Plate 9(1)

Habitat and status. An uncommon resident of savannahs and marshes, known from Nariva, Icacos, Aripo savannah, Santa Cruz and Port of Spain, usually in the vicinity of palms and decidedly local. (Specimens: AMNH, BM.)

Range and subspecies. Colombia, Venezuela, the Guianas, NE Peru and Brazil; the nominate race ranges from N Venezuela and the Guianas to E Brazil.

Description. 5 in. Upperparts greenish black, central underparts whitish but no contrast of colours as in *Panyptila;* tail long and deeply forked. A very slender-bodied species.

Measurements. Weight: 5 males 9.5–9.75gm (9.6); 2 females 9, 10.5gm; 2 unsexed 9, 9gm.

Voice. A slight, short buzz, *dj.*

Food. Aerial insects, including flies, winged ants and beetles.

Nesting. Breeding recorded from April to June (B/S). The nest is a C-shaped structure of plant fibres mixed with feathers and saliva which is attached to the inside of the hanging dead leaf of a moriche palm fairly high up. In the depression at the bottom of the C 3 white eggs are laid.

Behaviour. Usually found foraging in small, scattered bands of 10–30 birds. Feeding is often near ground level and rarely above 30 ft.

TROCHILIDAE: Hummingbirds

This remarkable family is confined to the New World, with most species in the tropics. Many species are extremely small, some not much bigger than a large bumblebee; though frequently appearing black at a distance, most are mainly metallic green above, and at close quarters in bright sunlight many display brilliant iridescent colours, especially on the crown or gorget. Moreover, their agility and speed of flight, combined with a fiercely aggressive temperament, produce an impression of extraordinary power in such small creatures. Apart from their diminutive size, hummingbirds are notable for their long, thin bills, which are straight in most species, curved in others. The female is often different from the male, having generally duller plumage. In addition to their ability to hover, when the rapidly beating wings in some species produce the humming sound that gives them their name, these birds can fly backwards. In some manoeuvres the wings beat incredibly fast—up to 80 beats per sec have been recorded. With their extremely high metabolism hummingbirds require a regular supply of food throughout the day; some species become torpid at night, thereby conserving energy. Hummingbirds feed upon nectar, extracted usually from the flowers by means of their very long tongues, as they hover in front of the plant. Some species, such as hermits, circulate along a regular route visiting the same plants in sequence, in a process known as trap-lining, while others specialise in feeding at particular groups of clumped flowers or forage generally over a wider area (Feinsinger & Colwell 1978). In addition many small insects and spiders are taken from plants, while some are caught in mid air (B. K. Snow & Snow 1972, Feinsinger et al. 1985). Most hummingbirds have a rather limited song with extremely high pitch. Their nests are tiny structures, usually constructed of moss or plant-down, lichens or spider-webs, in which 2 white eggs are laid. The female alone incubates and cares for the young, which fly about 3.5 wk after hatching. Hummingbirds are generally solitary by nature—apart from hermits—and rarely tolerate intrusion by other birds upon their territory; they are known to attack even birds of prey. Like the latter, they often choose a high, exposed branch for a perch. It seems certain that some species migrate seasonally from Trinidad and Tobago, moving presumably to the mainland. These movements appear to be associated with the flowering of certain trees, especially the immortelle (*Erythrina poeppigiana*). Much remains to be discovered, however, about these movements. (17)

Rufous-breasted Hermit: *Glaucis hirsuta*
Hairy Hermit; "Balisier" **Portrait I**

   Habitat and status. A common resident of forest and secondary growth in both islands, occasionally found in the open near forest edges; a bird of undergrowth near streams, rarely seen more than a few feet above the ground. (Specimens: AMNH, ANSP, CM, YPM, LM, BM, TRVL.)

Range and subspecies. Panama S and E to Ecuador, Peru, Bolivia and Brazil; the nominate race ranges from Venezuela through the extreme SE West Indies, and the Guianas to Brazil and Bolivia. Birds from Trinidad, Tobago and Grenada have been separated as *insularum* by Hellmayr and Seilern, but on insubstantial grounds (Berlioz 1962).

Description. 5 in. Head generally dark brown with buff superciliary and moustachial streaks; upperparts bronze-green, underparts pale rufous; tail rounded, tipped white, outer 4 tail-feathers bright chestnut with black subterminal band; bill long, about 1.5 in., strongly decurved; lower mandible yellow, upper blackish (in adult *males* the upper mandible is also streaked with yellow).

Measurements. Wing: 23 males 59–67mm (64, S.D. 1.7); 27 females 55–61mm (58.3, S.D. 1.2). Weight: 37 males 6–8gm (7.3, S.D. 0.54); 37 females 5.5–8gm (6.7, S.D. 0.59); 226 unsexed 5–10.5gm (7.0).

Voice. The flight call is a high-pitched single note, *sweet;* in the hand sometimes gives a plaintive mewing note. The male's song, rarely heard, consists of several flight calls together, followed by a 2–4-sec series of *wee* notes, run together and ending in *weet* (B. K. Snow 1973).

Food. Nectar, insects and spiders. It most commonly feeds at the understory flowers of *Heliconia bihai, Pachystachys coccinea* and *Centropogon surinamensis*. Small invertebrates obtained by searching leaves and twigs form a significant part of its diet.

Nesting. Breeding recorded in all months from December to August. D. W. Snow and Snow (1964) found 392 nests in Trinidad, divided among the months as follows:

I	II	III	IV	V	VI
38	69	46	75	71	58

VII	VIII	IX	X	XI	XII
28	1	—	—	—	6

Moult is recorded from July to January. A few nests have been found in Tobago between December and July. The nest is a flimsy hammock of rootlets attached by spiderwebs to the underside of the leaf (usually *not* the tip) of *Heliconia*, or a fern or small palm, usually beside a forest stream, often overhanging the water at an average height of 8 ft; the nest has a long "tail" trailing down. Both nest-building and egg-laying are done in the morning hours. Six eggs av. 15.7 × 9.3mm. Clutches of 3 eggs probably involve 2 females. Males defend territories with 1–3 females nesting in close proximity, but otherwise do not help at the nest (B. K. Snow 1973). Incubation takes about 17 days. A female may nest 2, 3 or even 4 times in a season; intervals between broods in the same nest varied from 2 to 6 wk. The fledging period is about 23 days. In Trinidad nesting success is low at about 0.17%, the chief predators probably being snakes (D. W. Snow & Snow 1973).

Behaviour. A very aggressive and inquisitive species, often approaching within a few feet of an observer's head. Birds are often seen chasing each other at high speed through the undergrowth in what may be a courtship chase; usually, however, single birds are seen.

Green Hermit: *Phaethornis guy*
Guy's Hermit; "Brin Blanc"   **Plate 10(6)**

Habitat and status. A common resident of hill forests in Trinidad, especially near water; usually keeps to the undergrowth but sometimes emerges to feed in clearings. (Specimens: AMNH, ANSP, CM, LM, BM, TRVL.)

Range and subspecies. Costa Rica and Panama S to Peru, Colombia, N Venezuela and Trinidad; the nominate race is found in NE Venezuela and Trinidad.

Description. 6.5 in. A large hummingbird, green above and gray below, with slightly elongated, white-tipped central tail-feathers; head dark in most *males,* with a rufous superciliary stripe; *females* have pale buff stripes above and below eye, also longer white tail-tips; bill long (1.5 in.) and decurved, the mandible bright red below.

Measurements. Wing: 12 males 60–67mm (63.1); 2 females 61, 63mm. Weight: 9 males 6–7gm (6.4); 3 females 6, 6.5, 6.5gm; 86 unsexed 5.5–8gm (6.3).

Voice. A sharp squeak. Also at their "assembly grounds" (see Behaviour) the males keep up a constant single chirping note, *wartch-wartch,* etc., about 1 per sec.

Food. Plant nectar and small insects; feeds mostly at the same understory plants as the Rufous-breasted Hermit, but also at the bromeliad *Tillandsia fasciculata;* forages for insects less than the Rufous-breasted.

Nesting. Breeding recorded from November to July, most commonly between January and April. Moulting birds have been found between May and October. The males sing throughout the year, except for a period of a few weeks during the moult. The nest resembles that of *Glaucis* but is cone-shaped and lined with plant-down; it is attached to the inside of the tip of a balisier leaf (*Heliconia*), palm or fern, 3–12 ft above ground, usually near or over water. One egg measures 15 × 9.5mm. Incubation period 17–18 days; fledging 21–23 days (B. K. Snow 1974). Males may assist in defending nests.

Behaviour. A restless bird; it flies through the undergrowth at bewildering speed. Though usually solitary when feeding, groups of males are found at traditional "assembly grounds", where they sing throughout the day most of the year. Each male perches on a thin twig a few feet above the ground in a typical attitude with head lifted and long tail bobbing up and down; often he takes part with other individuals in a wild chase through undergrowth or performs an aerial display just above a perch, darting from side to side, uttering a sharp, explosive *tock* and flashing open his bright red gape; sometimes he fans his tail or bends forward in a horizontal posture. Immature males resembling females are also found at these leks (B. K. Snow 1974, 1977). The song perches, which are apparently traditional, are usually only a few yards apart, so that many males may inhabit a quarter of an acre. The females probably visit these leks for mating.

Little Hermit: *Phaethornis longuemareus*
Longuemare's Hermit; "Rachette"   **Plate 10(5)**

Habitat and status. A common resident of forests in Trinidad, sometimes seen in the open at the forest edge, but mostly found in shaded situations and undergrowth. (Specimens: AMNH, LM, BM, TRVL.)

Range and subspecies. Mexico S to Peru and Brazil; the nominate race ranges from NE Venezuela and Trinidad to the Guianas.

Description. 4 in. In shape resembles the Green Hermit, but much smaller and browner. Upperparts bronze-green, rump rufous; head dark with buff streak behind eye, underparts rufous; tail wedge-shaped, central feathers elongated and white-tipped; bill decurved (1 in.), upper mandible black, lower yellowish with black tip.

Measurements. Wing: 7 males 41–43mm (42); 5 females 42–44mm (42.4); 9 unsexed 41–46mm (43.1). Weight: 6 males 3–3.5gm (3.2); 3 females 3gm each; 34 unsexed 2.5–4.5gm (3.2).

Voice. A light squeak made in alarm or while feeding; also at assembly grounds (see Behaviour) the males utter a high-pitched, chittering phrase, usually lasting 1–1.5 sec, which varies considerably in detail but may be generally rendered *ee-wee tiddly weet* (D. W. Snow 1968, Wiley 1971a). The song is uttered about every 2 sec.

Food. Nectar taken from a large variety of plants, mainly below 5 ft above ground; commonly feeds at *Pachystachys* and *Costus spiralis*, also the shrub *Palicourea crocea;* occasionally forages at leaves and twigs for small invertebrates.

Nesting. Breeding recorded from December to June, but 11 of 15 nests were in January and February. Moult is known in July and September, when singing ceases. The nest resembles those of other hermits in location and type, with a long, untidy "tail" and lined with hairy seeds; 2 eggs av. 13.9 × 9.7mm. In Costa Rica Skutch (1964b) found the incubation period to be about 16 days and the fledging period about 21 days. Like other species of *Phaethornis* both the young and the incubating parent sit facing the supporting leaf, with head thrown back and bill pointing vertically upward. Adults incubate for about two-thirds of the daylight hours, and feed the young by regurgitation.

Behaviour. At traditional "singing grounds" the males gather from November to July and spend most of the day singing their short phrases from perches low in the undergrowth. D. W. Snow (1968) found that, though song types vary considerably, birds with neighbouring perches tend to have similar songs, and that the song types persist at individual singing grounds, so that different dialects exist at the various grounds. Various aerial displays are often performed at the end of a song bout. Sometimes the body is held horizontally with head and tail pointing up, as the bird, hovering, moves slowly one way and then another after a rapid turn. It often "flicks" rapidly down towards the perch, making a soft *tock* as it does. This boat-like posture is sometimes held by a bird hovering over another bird, or over a dead leaf or piece of moss. In aggressive encounters birds often wag or fan the tail or gape, which may also be part of the courtship display.

White-tailed Sabrewing: *Campylopterus ensipennis*
Blue-throated Sabrewing   **Plate 10(7)**

Habitat and status. Previously a common resident in hill-forested areas of Tobago. Since Hurricane Flora in September 1963 very rare, but its rediscovery in 1974 indicates a gradually re-establishing population in a small area. (Specimens: AMNH, LM, BM.)

Range. Tobago and NE Venezuela, but unrecorded from Trinidad and the Bocas islands.

Description. 5 in. Generally bright green with dark blue throat and white moustachial streak; outer 3 pairs of tail-feathers mainly white; bill black (1 in.) and slightly decurved.

Measurements. Wing: 7 males 74–78mm (76.4); 3 females 73, 74, 75mm. Weight: 2 males 9.5, 10.5gm*; 2 unsexed 9, 9.5gm.

Voice. A single chirping note with a roll in it, e.g., *crreeet*, repeated at regular intervals from a fixed perch.

Food. Nectar from understory plants; also seen feeding at a flowering bromeliad.

Nesting. Recorded breeding in January and February, also singing in April. The nest is quite large for a hummingbird, over 2 in. wide and nearly 3 in. deep, mostly made of moss, and is saddled on a small branch 6–35 ft above ground. One egg measures 16.2 × 10.4mm. Only 3 complete nests have been recorded from Tobago.

Behaviour. A fearless species, like most of the family; it frequently hovers inquisitively close to an observer.

White-necked Jacobin: *Florisuga mellivora*
Jacobin   Plate 10(2)

Habitat and status. A rather uncommon but widespread inhabitant of forest, mostly at higher elevations, in both islands, being seen usually at a high perch or just above the canopy. Possibly resident in Trinidad, but breeding not recorded. Fluctuation of numbers indicates some local migration, as also the occurrence of an individual on 6 November at Pointe-a-Pierre, far from its normal habitat. (Specimens: Trinidad, AMNH, LM, BM, TRVL; Tobago, AMNH, LM, BM.)

Range and subspecies. Mexico S to Peru, Bolivia and S Brazil; the nominate race is known almost throughout the range, including Trinidad; the larger *F. m. flabellifera* (Gould) is found only in Tobago.

Description. 4.5 in. Fairly large. *Male:* head and breast dark blue, broad white band on nape, rest of upperparts bright green; rest of underparts white; tail all white, tipped and edged blackish. *Female:* generally bronze-green above, throat and breast green, the feathers edged white, giving a scalloped appearance; tail with black subterminal band, tipped white; bill black (0.75 in.) and straight with drooping tip. *Immature male:* resembles female. Occasional females closely approach adult males in appearance.

Measurements. Wing: *mellivora,* 8 males 66–75mm (70); 5 females 65–67mm (65.5); *flabellifera,* 6 males 73–78mm (76.3); 3 females 69, 70, 73mm. Weight: *mellivora,* 3 males 6.5*, 6.5, 7gm; 1 female 9gm; 5 unsexed 6–8gm (6.8); *flabellifera,* 1 male 7.5gm*.

Voice. In flight, a sharp, high-pitched, quickly repeated series, *tit-tit-tit-tit.*

Food. Nectar and insects. Commonly feeds at immortelle (*Erythrina*) blossoms and at the canopy vine (*Norantea guianensis*); also feeds at other trees, e.g., *Bauhinia.* In Tobago known to feed at *Inga* and *Vismia* trees and at pigeon peas (*Cajanus*). Occasionally hawks for insects within the forest 30–40 ft above ground.

Nesting. Recorded in Main Ridge forest, Tobago, in early 1989 (D. Rooks), the cup of moss, lichen and cobweb was moulded to the top of a broad leaf on a shrub 6 ft above ground. In Trinidad there are no firm records, but a female with a brood patch was trapped in the Northern Range on 18 February.

Behaviour. Though the species is usually solitary, small parties of males are often seen indulging in rapid chases high above the canopy, calling excitedly.

Brown Violetear: *Colibri delphinae*
Plate 10(8)

Habitat and status. A not uncommon but rather local resident in the Northern Range forests of Trinidad; seen throughout the year at elevations over 2500 ft, but between November and February often found at lower elevations from 500 ft up, where it frequents more open cultivated areas with flowering immortelles. (Specimens: AMNH, LM, BM.)

Range. Guatemala S to Peru and Bolivia, E to Guyana and Brazil.

Description. 4.75 in. Generally dull brown above, gray below; broad violet patch across cheeks and ear-coverts, white moustachial streak, iridescent green throat with some blue; tail with blackish subterminal band. *Immature:* tail broadly tipped rufous. Bill black and straight (0.75 in.)

Measurements. Wing: 6 males 70–77mm (74.3); 10 unsexed 65–77mm (71.6). Weight: 4 males 5.5–8gm (6.8)*; 3 unsexed 5.5, 6, 6.5gm*.

Voice. A loud, incisive, 5-syllable call, *chip-chip-chip-chip-chip*, delivered from a high perch. The song is repeated throughout most of the day.

Food. Nectar and insects. Often seen at immortelle and other canopy flowers, also a regular attendant at a feeding station in the Aripo Valley. Hawks for small flies at treetop level.

Nesting. Two nests recorded (B/S) in the foothills of the Northern Range during February. They were very small nests of plant-down saddled on twigs 4 ft above ground; 2 eggs av. 13.9 × 9.2mm. The male attends almost constantly at his song perch during the song period, which extends from December to February and occasionally March.

Behaviour. Males evidently establish territories around their individual song perches, for the singer sometimes breaks off to chase an intruder. Each song perch may be 50 yd distant from, but still within hearing of, its neighbour. At P. Rapsey's feeding station in the Aripo Valley a bird appeared to threaten another by hovering close by and briefly raising the bright feathers of the ear-patch at an oblique angle to its head.

Green-throated Mango: *Anthracothorax viridigula*
Plate 10(4)

Habitat and status. A rather uncommon resident of mangrove swamps and marshy savannahs in Trinidad. Sight records of birds in the Northern Range probably refer to the Black-throated Mango. (Specimens: AMNH, YPM, LM, BM, TRVL.)

Range. Also NE Venezuela, the Guianas and N Brazil.

Description. 5 in. *Male:* upperparts bronze-green, outer tail purple tipped black; throat and sides of underparts iridescent green, abdomen black. *Female:* as male, but underparts white with black stripe from chin to abdomen; outer tail tipped white. *Immature male:* as female but sides chestnut. Bill fairly long (over 1 in.), black, slightly decurved.

Measurements. Wing: 7 males 70–73mm (71.1); 5 females 66–70mm (67.8). Bill: 11 both sexes 27–29mm. Weight: 2 males 8.5, 8.5gm*; 1 female (possibly egg-laying) 11gm.

Voice. Undescribed.

Food. Nectar and small insects; seen feeding at swamp immortelle (*Erythrina glauca*).

Nesting. Breeding recorded in January (B/S). The nest is a deep, cone-shaped cup made of silk-cotton, spiderwebs and lichen, and saddled on a thin branch up to 20 ft above ground, occasionally lower; 2 eggs av. 14.2 × 9.6mm.

Black-throated Mango: *Anthracothorax nigricollis*
"Plastron"   Plate 10(1)

Habitat and status. A common resident of both islands, frequenting open country, gardens and the cultivated slopes of the mountain areas. There is some evidence of at least local migration during September–December (ffrench & ffrench 1978, Feinsinger et al. 1985). In Brazil (Ruschi 1967) banded birds are reported to have migrated over a thousand miles. (Specimens: AMNH, ANSP, CM, YPM, LM, BM, TRVL.)

Range and subspecies. Panama E and S through tropical South America to Bolivia and N Argentina; the nominate race is known throughout nearly all the range.

Description. 4.5 in. *Male:* very similar to Green-throated Mango but smaller, and throat black bordered with iridescent blue; outer tail chestnut glossed purple. *Female and immature male:* very similar (indistinguishable in the field) to female Green-throated Mango. *Juvenile:* several head and back feathers tipped pale gray, wing-coverts tipped pale buff; lores and region around eye brown. Bill fairly long (just less than 1 in.), black and slightly decurved.

Measurements. Wing: 15 males 63–69mm (66.6); 14 females 63–68mm (64.9). Bill: 18 both sexes 22–25mm. Weight: 13 males 6.5–9gm (7.3); 12 females 6.5–9gm (7.4); 19 unsexed 6–8.5gm (7.1).

Voice. A sharp, incisive single note, *tsick* or *tiuck,* uttered while feeding. Also in flight a repeated buzzing note (see Behaviour).

Food. Nectar and small insects; usually feeds at large trees, especially the immortelle and yellow poui (*Tabebuia serratifolia*), piercing the corolla-tube at its base, not probing it; also feeds at small trees, vines and garden shrubs, e.g., *Russellia*, ixora, hibiscus; commonly hawks for insects in the open, sometimes more than 50 ft up, also near the ground over a road, stream or mass of fallen fruit; more rarely it forages for insects among foliage.

Nesting. Breeding recorded from January to July, the majority of 43 nests evenly distributed among the first 5 months; moult recorded in June, September and November. The nest is a small cup, 1.5 in. across, made of plant-down decorated with gray lichen; it is usually saddled across a thin branch in an open situation 20–50 ft above ground, rarely lower. The female seems hardly able to fit in the nest. One egg measured 15 × 10mm. Incubation period 16 or 17 days; fledging period usually 24 days; 2 or 3 broods may occur in one season, with recorded intervals between broods of 9–26 days for the same nest, and up to 37 days when a new nest was built.

Behaviour. More wary than other "garden" hummingbirds. The male sometimes displays at a perch with widely fanned tail. In an aerial display flight recorded between November and July the male flies very fast and high from a conspicuous perch, uttering a sharp, rapidly repeated, buzzing note.

Ruby-topaz Hummingbird: *Chrysolampis mosquitus*
Plate 11(8)

Habitat and status. A common resident in open country, gardens and cultivated areas at lower elevations in both islands, frequenting clearings rather than undergrowth; on Tobago, but rarely on Trinidad, also found at higher elevations both in cultivated areas and at forest edges. Largely absent at times of nectar shortage between September and December, or migrates to alternative habitat, probably leaving island (ffrench & ffrench 1978, Feinsinger 1980, Feinsinger et al. 1985). Reported to be long-distance migrant in Brazil (Ruschi 1967). (Specimens: AMNH, ANSP, YPM, LM, BM, TRVL.)

Range. Colombia E and S to Venezuela, the Guianas and C Brazil.

Description. 3.5 in. *Male:* upperparts generally dark brown glossed greenish, crown and nape iridescent ruby red; throat and breast brilliant golden, rest of underparts brown; tail chestnut tipped black. *Female:* upperparts bronzegreen, underparts pale gray with dark stripe from chin to breast; tail mainly chestnut tipped white. *Immature male:* as female but with white spot behind eye; outer tail violet tipped white. Bill straight, black and fairly short (0.5 in.).

Measurements. Wing: 10 males 54–59mm (56.3); 5 females 53–57mm (54.6). Weight: 5 males 4–5gm (4.3); 20 unsexed 4–5gm (4.4).

Voice. A light, rather high-pitched, single note, *tsip.*

Food. Nectar, small insects and spiders; usually feeds at large trees, especially at the samaan (*Samanea*) and *Cordia bicolor;* also at small trees, e.g., wild ixora (*Isertia parviflora*) and *Citharexylum fruticosum,* cultivated crops such as pigeon pea (*Cajanus*) and garden shrubs such as *Russellia;* especially opportunistic on Tobago, visiting a wide variety of flowers, including many not used by its principal competitor, *Amazilia tobaci* (Feinsinger et al. 1982). Rather rarely feeds on insects, sometimes hawking, also searching foliage.

Nesting. Breeding recorded from December to June and once in August; 32 of 36 nests were found from January to May. The tiny cup-shaped nest is made of plant-down decorated with gray lichen and is saddled in the fork of a small branch a few feet from the ground, occasionally up to 15 ft; 2 eggs av. 13.5 × 8.4mm. Incubation period 16 days, fledging period 18 or 19 days.

Behaviour. The male commonly displays at a perch, fanning his tail and showing the bright chestnut colour. He is often aggressive and is known to attack even birds of prey.

Tufted Coquette: *Lophornis ornata*
Plate 11(7)

Habitat and status. A rather uncommon but widespread resident in Trinidad, found mainly in fairly open cultivated areas and forest edges in the Northern Range up to 2000 ft, also in bush savannah; particularly common in pigeon pea cultivation. (Specimens: AMNH, CM, LM, BM, TRVL.)

Range. NE Venezuela, the Guianas and N Brazil.

Description. 2.75 in. *Male:* upperparts bronze-green with pale buff bar across rump, tail dark chestnut edged brown; chestnut crest, rest of head green with long rufous tufts, tipped green, at the sides; throat iridescent golden green. *Female:* lacks crest and tufts; generally greenish above with pale buff rump-bar, rufous below. Bill straight, reddish with black tip, short (less than 0.5 in.).

Measurements. Wing: 5 males 39–40mm (39.6); 4 females 37–39mm (38.5). Weight: 1 male 2.25gm; 2 females 2.75gm each.

Voice. While feeding, a very light, single note, *chik.*

Food. Plant nectar, principally from the orange milkweed (*Asclepias curassavica*), *Stachytarpheta, Lantana camara* and cultivated *Verbena;* also known to feed at pigeon-pea flowers.

Nesting. Breeding recorded in February (B/S). The nest was a small cup of plant-down saddled on a low branch of pigeon pea; 2 eggs av. 12.5 × 9mm.

Behaviour. A solitary but very tame species. In flight the rapidly beating wings give off a high-pitched, almost metallic, buzz, and the bird resembles a large insect as it moves deliberately from plant to plant, hovering motionless for seconds at a time.

Blue-chinned Sapphire: *Chlorestes notatus*
"Saphir"   Plate 11(6)

Habitat and status. A common and widespread resident at all levels in Trinidad, frequenting forests and occasionally cultivated areas with large trees. Some sight records, one with nest (and one unlabelled specimen at BM), from Tobago. (Specimens: AMNH, CM, YPM, LM, BM, TRVL.)

Range and subspecies. Colombia S and E to Peru, the Guianas and Brazil; the nominate race ranges from Colombia east to N Brazil.

Description. 3.5 in. *Male:* upperparts dark green, tail steel blue; upper throat blue, rest of underparts bright green, white thighs. *Female:* as male, but underparts mainly white tipped green, appearing as green spots. Bill straight (0.75 in.), upper mandible black, lower reddish.

Measurements. Wing: 35 males 48–55mm (50.8); 11 females 46–49mm (47.7). Weight: 21 males 3.5–5gm (4.2); 9 females 3.5–5gm (4.1).

Voice. The song is a very high-pitched, metallic series, *sssoo-ssoo-sssoo,* repeated 3–5 times within 3 sec.

Food. Nectar and insects; feeds mostly at trees, both small and large, e.g., *Calliandra guildingii, Ryania speciosa, Eugenia malaccensis, Samanea, Erythrina;* also known to feed at smaller shrubs, herbaceous plants, e.g., *Heliconia wagneriana,* and vines; occasionally hawks for insects but more usually searches foliage.

Nesting. Breeding definitely recorded in February, May and June (6 Trinidad nests). Moult recorded from July to December. The nest is a large, deep cup made of plant-down decorated with lichen and saddled on a horizontal branch usually 6–8 ft above ground; one in a nutmeg tree was 15 ft up. Incubation period 16 days, fledging at 18–19 days.

Behaviour. The species has been observed bathing in the water collected on the leaves of aroids, squatting in it while hovering.

Blue-tailed Emerald: *Chlorostilbon mellisugus*
Carib Emerald; "Saphir-Savanne"   **Plate 11(3)**

Habitat and status. A rather uncommon and local resident in Trinidad, including the Bocas Islands, inhabiting semi-open savannahs and scrub. (Specimens: AMNH, CM, BM.)

Range and subspecies. Colombia S and E to Bolivia, the Guianas and Brazil; *C. m. caribaeus* (Lawrence) ranges from Venezuela to its offshore islands and Trinidad.

Description. 3 in. *Male:* generally brilliant golden green, with white thighs and steel blue forked tail. *Female:* as male, but with blackish ear-patch and short, white superciliary. Underparts grayish white, outer tail tipped white. Bill straight and short (0.5 in.), all black.

Measurements. Wing: 5 males 43–47mm (45); 1 female 44mm. Weight: 1 female 2.5gm.

Voice. A thin pebbly note, *tsip;* also has a twittering song.

Food. Insects and plant nectar; known to feed at garden flowers and flowering trees in Curaçao (Voous 1957).

Nesting. Breeding recorded in May (B/S), moult in June. Nests and eggs resemble those of Ruby-topaz, being tiny cups saddled on branches a few feet above ground. One egg measures 12.75 × 8.25mm. In Curaçao Voous (1957) reported the incubation period to be 13 days and the fledging period 18 days.

White-tailed Goldenthroat: *Polytmus guainumbi*
Shaw's Goldenthroat; "Vert-perle"   **Plate 11(9)**

Habitat and status. A rather uncommon and local resident in Trinidad, frequenting waterlogged savannahs and open areas. Records at Pointe-a-Pierre, almost all between 5 December and 11 August, suggest some seasonal migration after the breeding season. (Specimens: AMNH, ANSP, YPM, BM, TRVL.)

Range and subspecies. Colombia S to Bolivia and Paraguay, and E to the Guianas; the nominate race is known in Venezuela and the Guianas.

Description. 4 in. *Male:* upperparts pale bronze-green, head brownish with white streaks above and below eye; underparts leaf green with whitish abdomen, throat glittering green; outer tail tipped and edged white. *Female:* as male, but facial streaks and underparts tinged rufous. Bill slightly decurved and fairly long (1 in.), black above, reddish below.

Measurements. Wing: 3 males 55, 56, 56mm; 1 female 55mm.

Voice. While feeding, commonly utters a light, sharp *tsip-tsip.* Song a high-pitched 3-syllable squeak, reminiscent of Copper-rumped Hummingbird, delivered from a high perch.

Food. Nectar, insects and spiders; recorded feeding at garden plants, e.g., *Russellia, Bougainvillea,* also at *Heliconia* and flowering trees, e.g., *Lagerstroemia,* usually near water.

Nesting. Breeds during the wet season; 3 nests have been found between June and August at Aripo Savannah. The nest is a cone-shaped cup of plant-down decorated with lichen or seeds and saddled in the fork of a sapling 2 ft above ground (Gibbs). Three eggs av. 13.1 × 8.7mm. In Surinam, Haverschmidt (1962b) found nests (two within a few yards of each other) similarly situated in low shrubbery above deep water in a freshwater swamp.

White-chested Emerald: *Amazilia chionopectus*
White-breasted Emerald   **Plate 11(2)**

Habitat and status. A widespread and common resident in Trinidad, frequenting cultivation and second growth, occasionally clearings and forest edges. (Specimens: AMNH, ANSP, CM, YPM, LM, BM, TRVL.)

Range and subspecies. E Venezuela and the Guianas; the nominate race is found throughout the range except in French Guiana.

Description. 3.75 in. Upperparts brilliant golden green, glossed with bronze, especially on rump and tail; tail tipped purplish black, sometimes with narrow white edging; underparts white with sides green or white spotted with green; bill straight, fairly long (0.75 in.) and all black. Sexes similar.

Measurements. Wing: 8 males 51–53mm (52.1); 7 females 48–52mm (50); 27 unsexed 48–56mm (51.8). Weight: 4 males 4.5–5gm (4.6); 7 females 3.5–5gm (4.4); 45 unsexed 3.5–7gm (4.9).

Voice. Song is variable but basically a churring, grating phrase of up to 5 syllables with a slight break in rhythm after the first note, e.g., *tche, tchu-tche-tche-tche*, the whole phrase lasting about 1 sec and repeated every 5 sec or so; sometimes a 2-syllable phrase, *tizee*, is repeated; also clicks softly while feeding.

Food. Nectar and small insects; usually feeds at large trees, e.g., *Erythrina, Samanea*, less commonly at small trees, e.g., *Calliandra*, or herbaceous plants such as *Pachystachys* and *Heliconia wagneriana;* also forages in vegetation for insects, rarely hawking.

Nesting. Breeding recorded from December to April (8 nests); moult recorded from March to November, especially the last 5 months, during which time song mainly ceases. The nest is a cup of gray plant-fibre decorated with pieces of lichen and saddled on a horizontal branch 3–25 ft above ground. One egg measures 13 × 8.5mm.

[Glittering-throated Emerald: *Amazilia fimbriata*]
Lesson's Emerald   **Plate 11(5)**

Habitat and status. Included for Trinidad only by Herklots (1961), who quotes no authority; presumably a mistake, based perhaps on a nineteenth-century trade-skin. Whereabouts of any specimens unknown.

Range. E Colombia and Venezuela S to Brazil and N Bolivia.

Description. 4 in. Resembles White-chested Emerald, but white only on mid-abdomen, and lower mandible pink, *not* black. *Female:* has outer tail-feathers tipped gray.

Copper-rumped Hummingbird: *Amazilia tobaci*
Common Emerald   **Plate 11(4)**

Habitat and status. Widespread at all levels up to 2000 ft and a common resident in both islands, frequently found near houses; also in open country, second growth, cultivation and even in forest, especially in Tobago, where it is common even during periods of nectar scarcity. (Specimens: Tobago, AMNH, LM, BM; Trinidad, AMNH, ANSP, CM, YPM, LM, BM, TRVL.)

Range and subspecies. Venezuela, Trinidad, Tobago, vagrant to Grenada; *A. t. tobaci* (Gmelin), the larger race, is confined to Tobago, though vagrant to Grenada; *A. t. erythronota* (Lesson) ranges through Trinidad and the Bocas Islands, and is more bronze on the upperparts.

Description. 3.75 in. Upperparts generally bronze-green with pronounced coppery bronze on rump; head and underparts brilliant green, thighs white, tail black; bill straight, fairly long (0.75 in.) and mainly black, the base of lower mandible pinkish.

Measurements. Wing: *tobaci*, 36 unsexed 52–58mm (54.8); *erythronota*, 6 females 48–50mm (49.5); 33 unsexed 46–54mm (51.1). Weight: *tobaci*, 28 unsexed 3.5–5gm (4.4); *erythronota*, 4 males 4–5gm (4.6); 5 females 4–4.5gm (4.2); 103 unsexed 3.5–6gm (4.7).

Voice. While feeding, utters a single chipping note, and in flight an excited, trilling twitter, especially in aggressive encounters. Song from a perch is a high-pitched series of 3 or 4 notes, either *tyee-tyee-tyoo*, the last syllable lower in pitch, or a rather plaintive *tee-tiu-tiu-ti*, becoming fainter towards the end. Occasionally a singing bird will lower its head, crouch and hold up its wings above its back during the song.

Food. Nectar and insects; recorded feeding at a great variety of plants (42 species, B. K. Snow & Snow 1972), including large trees (*Erythrina*, etc.), small trees (e.g., *Calliandra, Isertia parviflora*), herbaceous plants (e.g., *Pachystachys, Heliconia, Costus, Asclepias*), shrubs such as *Palicourea, Hamelia, Lantana,* garden plants such as *Russellia, Ixora,* and vines (e.g., *Gurania spinulosa*). Where competition for nectar is high on Trinidad, primary food-plants are those which match its bill size, but on Tobago in times of shortage it uses flowers of very varied size and shape (Feinsinger & Swarm 1982, Keeler-Wolf 1982).

Nesting. Breeding recorded in most months in Trinidad, 51 nests as follows:

I	II	III	IV	V	VI
9	9	11	4	5	3

VII	VIII	IX	X	XI	XII
3	2	—	—	2	3

In Tobago nests have been found between November and June. The main song period is November–June. Moult takes place between May and September. The nest is a tiny cup of plant-down thickly decorated with gray lichen and saddled on a branch 3–10 (rarely up to 20) ft above ground. Also known to build nests on wires, clotheslines, light-fittings, etc. One egg measures 13 × 8.5mm. Incubation lasts 16 or 17 days and fledging takes place at from 19 to 23 days. There are often 2, occasionally 3, broods in a season, recorded intervals between broods varying from 1 wk to 1 month.

Behaviour. An extremely aggressive species which is often seen to attack and dominate other hummingbirds and much larger species. In gardens this hummingbird frequently appears to lay claim to a certain feeding area, from which it will drive away any other bird, flying at the intruder at high speed, often colliding in mid air, twittering in apparent fury all the while. Sometimes when a large bird is perched in or close to this "territory", this hummingbird attacks it in a series of pendulum-like sweeps, with the victim at the lowest point of each stroke. When bathing, it plunges into a stream and totally immerses itself.

Long-billed Starthroat: *Heliomaster longirostris*
Plate 10(3)

Habitat and status. An uncommon but widespread species in forested country at all levels in Trinidad, being seen usually in clearings, fairly high in trees; also visits gardens in more open suburban areas, especially during the wet season when fewer forest trees are in flower (Quesnel 1977); some seasonal migration is likely. (Specimens: AMNH, LM, BM, TRVL.)

Range and subspecies. S Mexico south to Panama, and Colombia S and E to Bolivia and Brazil; the nominate race ranges from Costa Rica south.

Description. 4.5 in. *Male:* upperparts bronze-green, crown blue, white moustachial streak, outer tail black tipped white; throat reddish purple, rest of underparts gray with mid-abdomen and flanks white, under-tail-coverts black, tipped white. *Female:* as male, but crown greenish; throat black, edged purple; moustachial streak broader; bill long (1.5 in.), black and almost straight.

Measurements. Wing: 4 males 58–60mm (58.8). Weight: 2 males 6.5, 6.5gm; 1 female 7.5gm; 2 unsexed 6, 6.5gm.

Voice. In flight utters short clicks. Song is a regular repeated *weet,* made from a perch.

Food. Nectar and insects. Known to feed in the canopy at *Erythrina* and *Tabebuia,* the vine *Mandevilla hirsuta* and at garden *Ixora;* also hawks for insects like a flycatcher.

Nesting. The only records on Trinidad are of nest-building in early March and a young bird being fed out of the nest in late April. The Mexican race builds a cup-shaped nest situated high or low in a tree; 2 eggs av. 13.2 × 8.6mm.

Rufous-shafted Woodstar: *Chaetocercus jourdanii*
Jourdain's Woodstar   **Plate 11(1)**

Habitat and status. An extremely rare species in Trinidad; recent sight records, mostly at the Nature Centre, were in April 1972, July 1975, May

1986, March 1988, April and June 1989, usually of immature or female birds. (Some undated specimens at AMNH, BM, giving no locality [possibly nineteenth-century trade-skins from Venezuela], and one specimen, no longer extant, taken by Léotaud.)

Range. Colombia and Venezuela.

Description. 2.75 in. A very small, fork-tailed species. *Male:* upperparts bronze-green, throat violet, breast white, abdomen green, tail black, deeply forked. *Female:* upperparts bronze-green, underparts rufous, tail light cinnamon with dark bar. Bill straight (0.5 in.), black.

Measurements. Wing: 4 males 35–36mm; 1 female 35mm.

Food. Seen feeding at flowers of the shrubs *Leonotis neptaefoliae* and vervain (*Verbena*).

TROGONIDAE: Trogons

This family consists of fairly large, brightly coloured birds with long, graduated tails (which often appear square-tipped in the field), short legs and short bills, broad at the base and with curved culmens. The upperparts and breast are usually contrasted in colour with the bright lower underparts. These birds inhabit forest or cultivated areas with large trees, where they perch quietly on the middle branches, calling a monotonous series of hooting notes, often with ventriloquial effect, or occasionally swooping down to flutter in front of a leaf or branch and seize a fruit or insect. Both sexes share in duties at the nest, which is in a hole, often burrowed into an abandoned termite nest. (3)

White-tailed Trogon: *Trogon viridis*
Greater Yellow-bellied Trogon; *Trogon strigilatus*   **Plate 12(3)**

Habitat and status. A common resident of forests and second growth at all levels in Trinidad. (Specimens: AMNH, ANSP, CM, YPM, LM, TRVL.)

Range and subspecies. Panama S to Ecuador, Peru, S Brazil; the nominate race ranges from E Colombia to Peru, Venezuela, the Guianas and NE Brazil.

Description. 11 in. *Male:* head and breast dark blue, upperparts green becoming bluish on rump, wings black; lower underparts golden yellow; outer tail black at base broadly tipped and edged white (*not* finely barred, as in the Violaceous Trogon). *Female:* as male, but head, breast and upperparts dull brownish gray. Eye-ring pale blue, bill pale greenish yellow.

Measurements. Wing: 7 males 134–148mm (141); 4 females 135–144mm (140.2). Weight: 4 males 77–99gm (89.2).

Voice. A deliberate but sometimes hesitant series of about 6–15 notes, ending on 1 or 2 softer notes, variously rendered *kyoh-kyoh-kyoh* or *cow-cow-cow*. Also occasionally utters other clucks, churrs, and a mournful, cat-like *a-rau-ow,* repeated every few seconds.

Food. Small fruits and insects, such as caterpillars; also lizards.

Nesting. Breeding recorded (4 nests) in March, May and July. Nests were in tree-holes or in a termitary, 10–20 ft above ground. There are 2 whitish eggs, av. 31.0 × 25.1mm (4). (In a study of the closely related, possibly conspecific, *T. bairdii* in Costa Rica, Skutch [1962] found that the nest chamber is deep in the wood at the end of an ascending shaft. Clutch is 2 or 3 eggs, laid on wood particles in the unlined nest. Incubation is constant, the male sitting for several hours during the day, the female for the rest of the time. Incubation lasts 16 or 17 days. The young are fed infrequently but with very large portions. Daytime brooding ceases soon after hatching; there is no nest sanitation. The nestlings are fully feathered at 2 wk but may not fly until 25 days old.)

Behaviour. Though usually found singly or in pairs, males of this species are sometimes seen in loose groups of up to 20, calling and swooping from branch to branch in what is probably part of a courtship display. The male sometimes fans his tail-feathers, showing the white portions.

Collared Trogon: *Trogon collaris*
Red-bellied Trogon   **Plate 12(2) and Portrait II**

Habitat and status. Fairly common resident in the forests of the Northern Range of Trinidad; formerly common in forests and second growth at higher levels in Tobago, now recovering gradually from the 1963 hurricane. (Specimens: AMNH, ANSP, CM, YPM, LM, BM.)

Range and subspecies. Mexico S through Central and South America to Bolivia and Brazil; *T. c. exoptatus* (Cabanis & Heine) ranges from E Colombia to Venezuela and Trinidad and Tobago.

Description. 10 in. *Male:* upperparts and breast dark green, glossed bronze; face blackish; wings black vermiculated with white; white breast-band, lower underparts scarlet; outer tail-feathers barred black and white, tipped white; naked eyelid orange; bill yellow. *Female:* brown instead of green; whitish area around eye; lower underparts paler red.

Measurements. Wing: 6 males 119–123mm (121.7); 7 females 117–125mm (120.4). Weight: 1 male 61gm; 5 females 51–62gm (55.4).

Voice. A melancholy yet musical call, rather soft and plaintive. Normally sings 3 or 4 notes, the first loudest, *caow-caow-caow.* Also utters a musical down-scale churring.

Food. Small fruits and insects.

Nesting. Breeding recorded in March and May. The nest is usually made in a termites' nest on a tree trunk, into which the adults burrow a short tunnel.

Two white eggs are laid in the hole. The incubating parent can usually be seen from in front of the tree. In Central America (Skutch 1956b) the fledging period is at least 16 days.

Behaviour. Usually found sitting motionless and upright, like a flycatcher, on a branch quite high in a tree. Apparent courtship behaviour includes raising and lowering the tail while perched, and uttering a churring call.

Notes. The family is not well known to country-dwellers in Trinidad and Tobago; when Collared Trogons were found out of their normal habitat after the 1963 hurricane in Tobago, they were thought to be Birds-of-Paradise!

Violaceous Trogon: *Trogon violaceus*
Lesser Yellow-bellied Trogon; Gartered Trogon   **Plate 12(1)**

Habitat and status. A common resident in Trinidad, frequenting forests, second growth and cultivated areas with large shade trees at all levels. (Specimens: AMNH, ANSP, LM, BM, TRVL.)

Range and subspecies. Mexico S to Peru, Bolivia and C Brazil; the nominate race ranges from E Venezuela to the Guianas and N Brazil.

Description. 8.5 in. *Male:* head and upper breast dark blue, rest of upperparts bluish green, mostly blue on rump; wings black, vermiculated with white; lower underparts golden yellow, outer tail finely barred black and white; eye-ring yellow; bill pale gray. *Female:* upperparts and breast dark gray.

Measurements. Wing: 3 males 120, 121, 125mm; 3 females 115, 117, 118mm. Weight: 5 males 49–55gm (52.1); 6 females 48–53gm (51).

Voice. A longish series of notes, e.g., *kyoo-kyoo-kyoo,* similar in tone and quality to other trogons, but higher-pitched and lighter. Also a rolling churr and a series of soft clucks, reminiscent of the alarm notes of thrushes, accompanied by an upward lift of the tail.

Food. Small fruits, also insects, including caterpillars and grasshoppers, and spiders.

Nesting. Breeding recorded (6 nests) in November, February, March, May and June; moult recorded in July. The season appears to be protracted and ill-defined. The nest resembles that of other trogons; 2 eggs of this race from neighbouring Venezuela were dull white, av. 30.5 × 23.4mm. I have seen an adult male feeding fledged young away from the nest.

Behaviour. Like other trogons this species is usually seen singly among the middle branches of a large tree, where it perches with its tail hanging down for long periods at a time, calling occasionally. Because of the ventriloquial nature of the call (caused by the bird's turning its head) and the bird's habit of sitting quite still, it is often difficult to locate, even when it perches, as often, in an exposed position.

PLATES

by John P. O'Neill

Plate 1: Herons and Lapwing

1. **Green-backed Heron** *Butorides striatus* p. 59
   a. Adult. Small; upperparts slaty, sides of head, neck and breast gray (in Tobago, rufous). Solitary.
   b. Immature. Heavily streaked below.

2. **Boat-billed Heron** *Cochlearius cochlearius* p. 67
   Massive bill, crown and crest black, wings and breast pale, lower underparts rufous. Mainly nocturnal.

3. **Southern Lapwing** *Vanellus chilensis* p. 129
   Large plover; crested, boldly patterned in black and white. Noisy, gregarious.

4. **Rufescent Tiger-Heron** *Tigrisoma lineatum* p. 64
   a. Adult. Large, stocky; head and neck rufous. Solitary, rare.
   b. Immature. Coarsely barred black and tawny.

5. **Stripe-backed Bittern** *Ixobrychus involucris* p. 65
   Very small, secretive; yellowish, streaked black and rufous.

6. **Chestnut-bellied Heron** *Agamia agami* p. 60
   a. Adult. Large; neck and bill very long. Extremely rare. Forest streams.
   b. Immature. Much browner.

7. **Pinnated Bittern** *Botaurus pinnatus* p. 66
   Large, stocky; buffy with fine barring. Flight heavy. Reed-beds.

1a

1b

2

3

4b

5

4a

6a

6b

7

Plate 2: Large Raptors

1. **Long-winged Harrier** *Circus buffoni* p. 104
   a. Male. Slate gray above, chest band black, rump white, tail long.
   b. Female. Browner. Typical harrier flight. Marshes.

2. **White Hawk** *Leucopternis albicollis* p. 99
   Head, neck, underparts, underwings white; tail broadly banded black.

3. **Great Black Hawk** *Buteogallus urubitinga* p. 102
   a. Adult. Black, with basal half of tail white. Forests.
   b. Immature. Blackish brown, heavily streaked; tail with many narrow bands.

4. **Common Black Hawk** *Buteogallus anthracinus* p. 100
   a. Adult. As 3a, but smaller, and white tail-band narrower. Call diagnostic.
   b. Immature. As 3b; tail with fewer bands.

5. **Savanna Hawk** *Heterospizias meridionalis* p. 100
   a. Adult. Conspicuous, rufous, long-legged. Open areas.
   b. Immature. Less rufous than adult; brown mottled with buff.

6. **Ornate Hawk-Eagle** *Spizaetus ornatus* p. 102
   a. Adult. Large with striking crest; sides of neck rufous, underparts barred.
   b. Immature. Head and underparts white. Forests.

7. **Black Hawk-Eagle** *Spizaetus tyrannus* p. 103
   a. Adult. Large, black, with short, shaggy crest; long, banded tail.
   b. Immature. Darker than 6b. Rare.

8. **King Vulture** *Sarcoramphus papa* p. 84
   a. Adult. Huge, broad-winged; white with black tail and flight feathers.
   b. Immature. Blackish; distinguished by size. Rare.

1b

1a

2

4b

3b

4a

3a

5b

6b

6a

5a

7b

8a

7a

8b

Plate 3: Medium-sized and Small Raptors

1. **Gray-headed Kite** *Leptodon cayanensis* p. 91
   a. Adult. Large; rounded wings, longish tail; wing-linings blackish, primaries boldly barred.
   b. Immature (dark phase). Head dark, throat and chest heavily streaked.
   c. Immature (light phase). Mainly white below; banded tail longer than in White Hawk.

2. **Plumbeous Kite** *Ictinia plumbea* p. 93
   a. Adult. Slate gray, inner web of primaries rufous; orange legs.
   b. Immature. Streaked. Common, seasonal visitor.

3. **Hook-billed Kite** *Chondrohierax uncinatus* p. 92
   a. Adult female (rufous). Rufous collar, green facial area. Rare.
   b. Adult male (gray). Slaty above, banded gray and white below.

4. **Orange-breasted Falcon** *Falco deiroleucus* p. 108
   Resembles very large Bat Falcon, but breast orange. Extremely rare.

5. **Bat Falcon** *Falco rufigularis* p. 108
   Small, fast-flying; throat and sides of neck white. Forest edge.

6. **Yellow-headed Caracara** *Milvago chimachima* p. 106
   a. Adult. Head, underparts buffy; primaries with pale "windows".
   b. Immature. Streaked. Open-country scavenger.

7. **Pearl Kite** *Gampsonyx swainsoni* p. 89
   Very small, Kiskadee-sized; face buffy, thighs rufous. Open country.

8. **Double-toothed Kite** *Harpagus bidentatus* p. 92
   a. Adult. Smallish kite; chest rufous, tail narrowly barred.
   b. Immature. Browner, heavily streaked below. Woodlands.

1a 1b 1c 2b 2a 3a 3b 4 5 6b 6a 7 8b 8a

O'Neill
72

Plate 4: Rails and Coot

1. **Ash-throated Crake**   *Porzana albicollis*   p. 119
Medium-sized; olive above, gray below. Resembles Sora without black face. Extremely rare.

2. **Spotted Rail**   *Rallus maculatus*   p. 117
Fairly large; heavily spotted and barred; legs red.

3. **Yellow-breasted Crake**   *Porzana flaviventer*   p. 120
Tiny; yellowish, flanks barred, eye-streak.

4. **Gray-breasted Crake**   *Laterallus exilis*   p. 120
Tiny; upperparts dark brown, nape chestnut.

5. **Gray-necked Wood-Rail**   *Aramides cajanea*   p. 117
Large, relatively conspicuous; head and neck gray. Call diagnostic.

6. **Rufous-necked Wood-Rail**   *Aramides axillaris*   p. 118
Smaller than 5; rufous head and neck. Bocas Islands and NW Trinidad.

7. **Caribbean Coot**   *Fulica caribaea*   p. 124
Large; white frontal shield and bill. Rare.

Plate 5: Cuckoos and Pigeons

1. Greater Ani *Crotophaga major* p. 192
Very large; glossy bluish black; eye white. Gregarious.

2. Little Cuckoo *Piaya minuta* p. 191
Much smaller than 4; generally rufous. Shy.

3. Dark-billed Cuckoo *Coccyzus melacoryphus* p. 190
Similar to the slightly larger Mangrove Cuckoo. Bill all black. Rare and local.

4. Squirrel Cuckoo *Piaya cayana* p. 190
Conspicuous, large cuckoo; lower underparts gray. Forest, second growth.

5. Striped Cuckoo *Tapera naevia* p. 194
Crested, streaked; diagnostic call. Open country, scrub.

6. Scaled Pigeon *Columba speciosa* p. 172
Dark reddish purple; conspicuously scaled neck. Forests.

7. Eared Dove *Zenaida auriculata* p. 174
Medium-sized; wedge-shaped tail, tipped vinous. Open country.

8. Band-tailed Pigeon *Columba fasciata* p. 172
Large; white nape-patch, bill yellow. Rare, mountains.

9. Pale-vented Pigeon *Columba cayennensis* p. 173
As 6, but no scales; lower underparts gray.

Plate 6: Doves and Quail-Doves

1. **Ruddy Ground-Dove** *Columbina talpacoti* p. 176
   a. Male. Rufous with gray head; black wing-linings.
   b. Female. Duller and browner than male; pale head.

2. **Plain-breasted Ground-Dove** *Columbina minuta* p. 176
   a. Male. Gray; head and breast unspotted; rufous wing-linings.
   b. Female. Browner than male.

3. **Common Ground-Dove** *Columbina passerina* p. 175
   Male. As 2a, but head and breast spotted; primaries and wing-linings rufous.

4. **White-tipped Dove** *Leptotila verreauxi* p. 178
   Pale gray below, tail tipped white, eye-ring blue. Scrub.

5. **Ruddy Quail-Dove** *Geotrygon montana* p. 180
   Plump and short-tailed; rufous (female browner), with facial stripes. Terrestrial.

6. **Gray-fronted Dove** *Leptotila rufaxilla* p. 179
   As 4, but crown pale gray; eye-ring red. Forests.

7. **Blue Ground-Dove** *Claravis pretiosa* p. 177
   a. Male. Slightly larger than 1; generally bluish gray.
   b. Female. Olive brown with rufous rump; chestnut markings on wing-coverts.

8. **Lined Quail-Dove** *Geotrygon linearis* p. 181
   Larger than 5; purplish brown; malar stripe black. Terrestrial, rare.

1a

2b

2a

3

1b

4

5

6

7a

7b

8

C Neill
72

Plate 7: Parrots

1. **Blue-headed Parrot** *Pionus menstruus* p. 186
   Medium-sized; green with blue head; red under-tail-coverts. Forests.

2. **Blue-and-yellow Macaw** *Ara ararauna* p. 182
   Very large, unmistakable. Swamps.

3. **Yellow-crowned Parrot** *Amazona ochrocephala* p. 186
   Crown yellow, speculum and bend of wing red; conspicuous whitish eye-ring.

4. **Red-bellied Macaw** *Ara manilata* p. 183
   Long-tailed; bluish green above, underwings yellowish; bare face yellow.

5. **Lilac-tailed Parrotlet** *Touit batavica* p. 185
   Small; green below, black above with yellowish wing-band. Forests.

6. **Scarlet-shouldered Parrotlet** *Touit huetii* p. 185
   Somewhat similar to 5, but underwing scarlet. Rare visitor.

7. **Orange-winged Parrot** *Amazona amazonica* p. 187
   The common large parrot. Wing speculum orange.

8. **Green-rumped Parrotlet** *Forpus passerinus* p. 184
   Tiny; all green (males have blue wing-coverts). Undulating flight.

Plate 8: Oilbird, Potoo and Nightjars

1. **Oilbird** *Steatornis caripensis* p. 202
Unique. Nocturnal cave-dweller. Gregarious.

2. **Common Potoo** *Nyctibius griseus* p. 204
Cryptically coloured; perches erect; large light-reflecting eyes.

3. **Short-tailed Nighthawk** *Lurocalis semitorquatus* p. 205
Small, dark nighthawk; no wing-bar. Bat-like flight.

4. **White-tailed Nightjar** *Caprimulgus cayennensis* p. 210
Small; male grayish, rufous nape, white wing-band and outer tail. Female
(not shown) darker, no white in tail, wing-band buff.

5. **Nacunda Nighthawk** *Podager nacunda* p. 207
Large; contrasting underparts, broad white wing-bar. Open country.

6. **Pauraque** *Nyctidromus albicollis* p. 208
Large, long-tailed, cryptic; white wing-band (buff in female) and outer tail
(only tip in female). Forest edge and roadsides.

7. **Rufous Nightjar** *Caprimulgus rufus* p. 209
Large, rufous; no wing-bar. Bocas islands and NW Trinidad.

O'Neill
72

Plate 9: Swifts

1. **Fork-tailed Palm-Swift** *Reinarda squamata* p. 218
   Slender, low-flying; long, tapering tail, sometimes seen to be forked.

2. **Lesser Swallow-tailed Swift** *Panyptila cayennensis* p. 217
   Black with conspicuous white collar and patch on flank; tail quite long, fork usually held closed. Much smaller than 4.

3. **Chestnut-collared Swift** *Cypseloides rutilus* p. 212
   a. Male. All dark with complete rufous collar.
   b. Female. As male, but rufous collar only partial. Tail longer than in *Chaetura.*

4. **White-collared Swift** *Cypseloides zonaris* p. 211
   Large, powerful flier; conspicuous white collar (in adult). Gregarious.

5. **Gray-rumped Swift** *Chaetura cinereiventris* p. 214
   Small; grayish below, above black with gray rump; tail longer than in 7. Mainly hill forest.

6. **Chapman's Swift** *Chaetura chapmani* p. 214
   Small, but bulkier than 5; generally darker; rump browner. Rare.

7. **Short-tailed Swift** *Chaetura brachyura* p. 216
   Small; noticeably shorter tail than in other *Chaetura;* above and below blackish with grayish brown rump and tail.

8. **Band-rumped Swift** *Chaetura spinicauda* p. 215
   Resembles 5, but mostly dark below with paler throat; whitish rump-bar.

Plate 10: Hermits and Larger Hummingbirds

1. **Black-throated Mango** *Anthracothorax nigricollis* p. 226
Bill slightly decurved. Semi-open areas and cultivation.
   a. Male. Black below, edged blue; tail purple.
   b. Female. White below with black median stripe.

2. **White-necked Jacobin** *Florisuga mellivora* p. 224
Bill nearly straight. Forests; canopy feeder.
   a. Male. Head and breast dark blue; nape, lower underparts and outer tail white.
   b. Female. Green with scaled breast; tail with black band tipped white.

3. **Long-billed Starthroat** *Heliomaster longirostris* p. 233
Bill long, straight. Forests; canopy feeder.
   a. Male. Crown blue, throat purple. Concealed white flank stripe.
   b. Female. Crown green, throat edged purple.

4. **Green-throated Mango** *Anthracothorax viridigula* p. 225
Female as 1b. Male resembles 1a but throat and sides green. Swamps and marshes.

5. **Little Hermit** *Phaethornis longuemareus* p. 222
Small with decurved bill; central tail elongated and white-tipped.

6. **Green Hermit** *Phaethornis guy* p. 221
Much larger than 5. Long, decurved bill.
   a. Male. Superciliary stripe rufous; white central tail tips slightly elongated.
   b. Female. Superciliary stripe pale buff; tail tips considerably elongated.

7. **White-tailed Sabrewing** *Campylopterus ensipennis* p. 223
Bill slightly decurved. Tobago mountain forests. Very rare.
   a. Male. Green with blue throat; outer tail white.
   b. Female. Generally duller; below grayer, less blue.

8. **Brown Violetear** *Colibri delphinae* p. 224
Bill straight. Mountain forests; canopy feeder. Generally brown; ear-patch violet. Loud chipping call.

Plate 11: Smaller Hummingbirds

1. **Rufous-shafted Woodstar** *Chaetocercus jourdanii* p. 233
   Tiny, insect-like; bill short, straight. Forest edge. Very rare.
   a. Male. Tail deeply forked. Gorget violet.
   b. Female. Bronze-green above, rufous below.

2. **White-chested Emerald** *Amazilia chionopectus* p. 230
   Bill straight, all black; upperparts green, glossed bronze; underparts white, sides green.

3. **Blue-tailed Emerald** *Chlorostilbon mellisugus* p. 229
   Bill straight, all black. Local, mostly Bocas islands and NW Trinidad.
   a. Male. All green, thighs white; tail steel blue.
   b. Female. As male, but ear-patch black, and superciliary white.

4. **Copper-rumped Hummingbird** *Amazilia tobaci* p. 231
   Bill straight, black with lower mandible pinkish; green with coppery bronze back and rump; thighs white. Widespread.

5. **Glittering-throated Emerald** *Amazilia fimbriata* p. 231
   Included in error, see text.

6. **Blue-chinned Sapphire** *Chlorestes notatus* p. 228
   Bill straight, black with lower mandible reddish. Widespread in forests.
   a. Male. All green, upper throat bluish.
   b. Female. As male, but underparts whitish edged with green.

7. **Tufted Coquette** *Lophornis ornata* p. 228
   Tiny, bee-like; bill short, straight.
   a. Male. Head and neck ornamented; pale buff rump-bar.
   b. Female. Lacks male ornaments; rufous below; rump-bar.

8. **Ruby-topaz Hummingbird** *Chrysolampis mosquitus* p. 227
   Bill short, straight. Open areas, cultivation.
   a. Male. Dark rufous, iridescent head and breast; tail rufous.
   b. Female. Bronze green above, gray below; black throat line.

9. **White-tailed Goldenthroat** *Polytmus guainumbi* p. 230
   Bill longish, slightly decurved, reddish below. Seasonal; marshy savannahs.
   a. Male. Generally pale golden green; facial markings; tail tipped white.
   b. Female. As male, but more buff below.

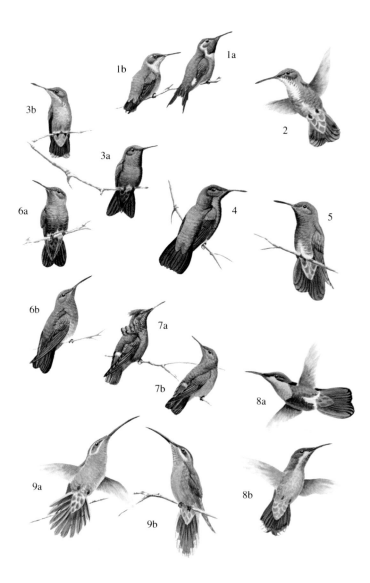

1b   1a
3b
3a
2
6a
4   5
6b
7a
7b
8a
9a   9b   8b

Plate 12: Trogons, Jacamar, Kingfishers and Bellbirds

1. **Violaceous Trogon** *Trogon violaceus* p. 236
   Smaller than 3.
   a. Male. Head, breast blue; lower underparts yellow; tail barred.
   b. Female. Upperparts, breast gray; eye-ring whitish.

2. **Collared Trogon** *Trogon collaris* p. 235
   Female. Head, breast, upperparts brown; lower underparts reddish.

3. **White-tailed Trogon** *Trogon viridis* p. 234
   Larger than 1.
   a. Male. As 1a, but tail broadly tipped and edged white.
   b. Female. As 1b, but eye-ring pale blue. Size and calls diagnostic.

4. **Rufous-tailed Jacamar** *Galbula ruficauda* p. 242
   a. Male. Metallic bronze-green; white throat; lower underparts rufous.
   b. Female. As male, but throat rufous.

5. **Black-tailed Tityra** *Tityra cayana* p. 309
   Female. Head, wings, tail black; bill, face red; rest whitish streaked black.

6. **Bearded Bellbird** *Procnias averano* p. 269
   Female. Olive green, with yellowish underparts streaked green. (See Plate 29(2) for male.)

7. **Pygmy Kingfisher** *Chloroceryle aenea* p. 239
   Tiny.
   a. Male. Dark green above, rufous below, abdomen white.
   b. Female. As male, but green band across breast.

8. **Green Kingfisher** *Chloroceryle americana* p. 239
   Fairly small (cf. Amazon Kingfisher). The commonest kingfisher.
   a. Male. Dark green above, wing-spots white; below white with rufous band.
   b. Female. As male, but below buffy white with two green bands.

9. **White Bellbird** *Procnias alba* p. 268
   a. Male. All white with black wattle. Extremely rare visitor.
   b. Female. Resembles Bearded Bellbird.

Plate 13: Woodpeckers and Woodcreepers

1. Olivaceous Woodcreeper *Sittasomus griseicapillus* p. 252
Small; generally grayish olive with rufous wings, rump, tail.

2. Red-rumped Woodpecker *Veniliornis kirkii* p. 249
Small.
  a. Male. Crown, rump red; upperparts brown, barred below.
  b. Female. As male, but crown brown.

3. Red-crowned Woodpecker *Melanerpes rubricapillus* p. 248
  a. Male. Crown, nape red; upperparts chequered; rump white.
  b. Female. As male, but crown brown, nape pinkish.

4. Plain-brown Woodcreeper *Dendrocincla fuliginosa* p. 251
Medium-sized; all brown with rufous wings, tail; bill straight.

5. Straight-billed Woodcreeper *Xiphorhynchus picus* p. 252
Larger than 4; dark brown, spotted and streaked buff; wings, tail rufous; bill straight, pale. Mangroves.

6. Buff-throated Woodcreeper *Xiphorhynchus guttatus* p. 253
As 5, but much more widespread, and slightly larger; bill longer, slightly decurved, black.

7. Chestnut Woodpecker *Celeus elegans* p. 246
Fairly large, crested; generally rufous with yellow rump. Forests.

8. Streaked-headed Woodcreeper *Lepidocolaptes souleyeti* p. 254
Medium-sized; head, underparts streaked; back, wings, tail chestnut; bill slender, decurved, pale. Uncommon.

O'Neill
72

Plate 14: Small Antbirds and Ovenbirds

1. **White-flanked Antwren** *Myrmotherula axillaris* p. 263
   a. Male. Black with concealed white flank-patch; white wing-spots.
   b. Female. Brown above, buffy below; wing-spots buff.

2. **White-fringed Antwren** *Formicivora grisea* p. 264
   a. Male. White superciliary; below black outlined with white; white wing-bars.
   b. Female. As male, but underparts buff, streaked dark.

3. **Streaked Xenops** *Xenops rutilans* p. 257
   Very small; streaked brown with rufous rump, tail; bill short, upturned. Arboreal; creeps.

4. **Stripe-breasted Spinetail** *Synallaxis cinnamomea* p. 255
   Dark reddish brown, streaked below; tail graduated. Forests, undergrowth.

5. **Plain Antvireo** *Dysithamnus mentalis* p. 262
   a. Male. Slate gray with dark mask. Forests, low levels.
   b. Female. Olive brown with rufous crown.

6. **Pale-breasted Spinetail** *Synallaxis albescens* p. 254
   Resembles 4, but dull brown with chestnut crown and shoulders. Scrub. Call diagnostic.

7. **Yellow-throated Spinetail** *Certhiaxis cinnamomea* p. 256
   Resembles 4, but bright rufous above, white below. Marshes.

Plate 15: Larger Antbirds and Leaftosser

1. **Black-crested Antshrike** *Sakesphorus canadensis* p. 260
   a. Male. Black head, breast; back brown. Mangroves, marshy scrub.
   b. Female. Chestnut crown.

2. **Great Antshrike** *Taraba major* p. 259
   a. Male. Large; black above, white below; eye red. Undergrowth.
   b. Female. Rich brown above.

3. **Barred Antshrike** *Thamnophilus doliatus* p. 261
   a. Male. Dumpy; chequered black and white. Scrub.
   b. Female. Rufous; face streaked.

4. **White-bellied Antbird** *Myrmeciza longipes* p. 265
   a. Male. Rufous above; face and breast black. Forests. Terrestrial.
   b. Female. Lacks male's black markings.

5. **Gray-throated Leaftosser** *Sclerurus albigularis* p. 257
   Dark brown; rump rufous, tail black. Forests. Mainly terrestrial.

6. **Silvered Antbird** *Sclateria naevia* p. 265
   a. Male. Grayish brown, streaked and spotted with white. Streamsides.
   b. Female. Browner.

7. **Black-faced Antthrush** *Formicarius analis* p. 266
   Walks rail-like on forest floor. Diagnostic call.

8. **Scaled Antpitta** *Grallaria guatimalensis* p. 267
   Large; faintly scaled; "tail-less". Terrestrial. Extremely rare.

Plate 16: Manakins, Vireos, Gnatwren and Wren

1. **Golden-headed Manakin** *Pipra erythrocephala* p. 271
   a. Male. Unmistakable. Sharp, explosive display calls. Forests.
   b. Female. Green, paler below; legs pink; bill horn brown.

2. **Scrub Greenlet** *Hylophilus flavipes* p. 333
   Brownish olive above, yellowish below; legs pale. Tobago.

3. **Golden-fronted Greenlet** *Hylophilus aurantiifrons* p. 332
   Resembles 2, but crown tawny, underparts buffy yellow. Small flocks.

4. **Long-billed Gnatwren** *Ramphocaenus melanurus* p. 328
   Tiny; bill very long; tail often cocked, or loosely wagged.

5. **White-bearded Manakin** *Manacus manacus* p. 274
   a. Male. Black and white; orange legs. Leks on forest floor.
   b. Female. Darker green than 1b; legs longer, orange.

6. **Blue-backed Manakin** *Chiroxiphia pareola* p. 273
   a. Male. Sky blue mantle, scarlet crown; pale orange legs. Tobago.
   b. Female. Olive green, paler below.

7. **Rufous-browed Peppershrike** *Cyclarhis gujanensis* p. 329
   Stocky, stout-billed; head gray, eyebrow rufous. Constantly repeated song.

8. **Rufous-breasted Wren** *Thryothorus rutilus* p. 318
   Speckled face, rufous breast. Melodious song. Forest undergrowth.

1a

1b

2

3

4

5a

5b

6a

6b

7

8

O'Neill
72

Plate 17: Larger Flycatchers

1. **Boat-billed Flycatcher** *Megarhynchus pitangua* p. 284
Massive bill, upperparts olive brown, little rufous in wings and tail.

2. **Great Kiskadee** *Pitangus sulphuratus* p. 286
Bill slimmer than Boat-billed, wings and tail much more rufous.

3. **Variegated Flycatcher** *Empidonomus varius* p. 283
Streaked below, wings edged white; tail edged rufous, short bill. Rare.

4. **Bright-rumped Attila** *Attila spadiceus* p. 277
a. Greenish phase. Sometimes streaked below; yellow rump.
b. Rufous phase. Otherwise resembles a. Penetrating call.

5. **Sulphury Flycatcher** *Tyrannopsis sulphurea* p. 282
Resembles 9, but stockier, darker above; sides of breast faintly streaked.
Moriche palms.

6. **Piratic Flycatcher** *Legatus leucophaius* p. 283
As 3, but smaller and lacks rufous; prominent eye-streak. Monotonous
call.

7. **Fuscous Flycatcher** *Cnemotriccus fuscatus* p. 293
Generally brownish; wing-bars buff; whitish superciliary. Undergrowth.

8. **Streaked Flycatcher** *Myiodynastes maculatus* p. 285
Kiskadee-sized; heavily streaked above and below; tail rufous; heavy bill.

9. **Tropical Kingbird** *Tyrannus melancholicus* p. 280
Gray head, upperparts tinged green. Open country. Abundant.

10. **Bran-colored Flycatcher** *Myiophobus fasciatus* p. 294
Reddish brown; wing-bars; streaked below. Scrub, undergrowth.

11. **Brown-crested Flycatcher** *Myiarchus tyrannulus* p. 288
Head brown, breast gray, lemon yellow below; tail with rufous inner
webs. Common in scrub.

12. **Dusky-capped Flycatcher** *Myiarchus tuberculifer* p. 290
As 11, but smaller and head much darker. Melancholy whistle.

13. **Venezuelan Flycatcher** *Myiarchus venezuelensis* p. 289
As 11, but tail with narrow rufous outer webs. Call as 12. Tobago forest.

14. **Swainson's Flycatcher** *Myiarchus swainsoni* p. 289
As 11, but no rufous in tail. Mandible brown. Rare southern visitor.

Plate 18: Medium-sized Flycatchers

1. Forest Elaenia *Myiopagis gaimardii* p. 302
Above olive green; yellowish wing-bars; crown-patch usually concealed; narrow bill (cf. *Tolmomyias*). Call: *pitch-weet.*

2. White-winged Becard *Pachyramphus polychopterus* p. 308
 a. Male. Black with white wing-edging; tail graduated, edged white.
 b. Female. Olive brown above; wing and tail edgings buff.

3. Scrub Flycatcher *Sublegatus modestus* p. 302
Supra-loral streak whitish; gray throat sharply demarcated from yellow abdomen.

4. Yellow-bellied Elaenia *Elaenia flavogaster* p. 299
Conspicuous crest. The largest and by far the commonest elaenia.

5. Tropical Pewee *Contopus cinereus* p. 291
Dark brown above; sides of breast brownish, throat and mid-breast pale. Forest edge; perches on open branches.

6. Slaty-capped Flycatcher *Leptopogon superciliaris* p. 305
Crown and ear-patch slaty; above olive green. Forest, in low and middle levels.

7. Small-billed Elaenia *Elaenia parvirostris* p. 300
Resembles 4, but noticeably smaller; crest less pronounced. Rare southern migrant.

8. Euler's Flycatcher *Empidonax euleri* p. 292
Above brown tinged olive; buffy wing-bars. Forest, in low and middle levels; inconspicuous.

9. Pied Water-Tyrant *Fluvicola pica* p. 276
Both sexes white with black mantle, wings and tail. Open areas near water.

10. White-headed Marsh-Tyrant *Arundinicola leucocephala* p. 277
 a. Male. Black with white head and neck.
 b. Female. Gray above; face and underparts white.

1

2a

2b

3

4

5

6

7

8

9

10a

10b

O'Neill
72

Plate 19: Smaller Flycatchers

1. **Yellow-olive Flycatcher** *Tolmomyias sulphurescens* p. 295
Crown gray, whitish "spectacles", yellow wing edging, iris pale; bill broad, flat.

2. **Yellow-breasted Flycatcher** *Tolmomyias flaviventris* p. 296
Resembles 1, but wings darker, conspicuously edged yellow; below golden yellow.

3. **Mouse-colored Tyrannulet** *Phaeomyias murina* p. 303
Above brown, wing-bars pale buff; weak superciliary. Bocas islands, NW Trinidad.

4. **Southern Beardless Tyrannulet** *Camptostoma obsoletum* p. 304
Resembles tiny elaenia; forest edge, cultivation, scrub.

5. **Crested Doradito** *Pseudocolopteryx sclateri* p. 298
Tiny; bright yellow below. Very rare, marshes.

6. **Spotted Tody-Flycatcher** *Todirostrum maculatum* p. 297
Long, flat bill; throat, breast heavily streaked. SW Trinidad, mangroves.

7. **Short-tailed Pygmy-Tyrant** *Myiornis ecaudatus* p. 298
Tiny, "tail-less"; greenish, paler below. Rare in forest.

8. **White-throated Spadebill** *Platyrinchus mystaceus* p. 295
Very broad, flat bill; above brown with conspicuous face pattern. Undergrowth.

9. **Ochre-bellied Flycatcher** *Mionectes oleaginea* p. 307
Olive green above, buffy orange below. Forests, undergrowth.

10. **Olive-striped Flycatcher** *Mionectes olivaceus* p. 306
Dark olive green, below streaked yellowish; white post-ocular spot. Rare, forests.

O'Neill

Plate 20: Swallows

1. **Caribbean Martin**   *Progne dominicensis*   p. 311
   a. Male. Glossy blue-black; sharply contrasting white abdomen. Tobago.
   b. Female. Duller than male; breast grayish brown.

2. **Gray-breasted Martin**   *Progne chalybea*   p. 312
   Resembles 1, but a bit smaller; anterior underparts grayish brown. Trinidad.

3. **White-winged Swallow**   *Tachycineta albiventer*   p. 310
   Glossy blue-green; rump, wing-edging, underparts white. Near water.

4. **Southern Rough-winged Swallow**   *Stelgidopteryx ruficollis*   p. 314
   Above brown with pale rump; tawny throat, yellowish white below.

5. **Blue-and-white Swallow**   *Notiochelidon cyanoleuca*   p. 313
   Blue-black above, all white below. Southern visitor. Gregarious.

1a

1b

2

3

4

5

O'Neill
72

Plate 21: Thrushes and Mockingbird

1. **Yellow-legged Thrush**   *Platycichla flavipes*   p. 323
   a. Male (Tobago). All black; bill, eye-ring and legs yellow.
   b. Female. Olive brown, paler below. Mountain forests.

2. **Tropical Mockingbird**   *Mimus gilvus*   p. 320
   Pale gray with white superciliary and underparts; long, white-tipped tail.

3. **White-necked Thrush**   *Turdus albicollis*   p. 327
   Dark olive brown above, gray below; throat white with dark streaks.
   Forests.

4. **Orange-billed Nightingale-Thrush**   *Catharus aurantiirostris*   p. 322
   The smallest resident thrush; bright brown above, bill and legs orange.
   Mountain forests.

5. **Bare-eyed Thrush**   *Turdus nudigenis*   p. 326
   Somewhat resembles 3, but warmer brown above; conspicuous golden
   eye-ring. Non-forest areas.

6. **Cocoa Thrush**   *Turdus fumigatus*   p. 324
   Rich brown, slightly paler below. Forest and cultivation.

1a 1b

2

3

5

4

6

O'Neill
72

Plate 22: Icterids

1. **Red-breasted Blackbird** *Sturnella militaris* p. 344
   a. Male. Unmistakable. Grassy savannahs.
   b. Female. Heavily streaked, brownish; underparts sometimes reddish.

2. **Moriche Oriole** *Icterus chrysocephalus* p. 341
   Black with golden hood, rump and shoulder. Rare. Moriche palms.

3. **Yellow Oriole** *Icterus nigrogularis* p. 342
   All yellow with black throat, tail and wings (edged white).

4. **Giant Cowbird** *Scaphidura oryzivora* p. 335
   All black glossed purple. Male larger, with ruff. Iris red.

5. **Yellow-rumped Cacique** *Cacicus cela* p. 338
   Black with yellow rump, wing-patch, under-tail; bill whitish. Gregarious.

6. **Shiny Cowbird** *Molothrus bonariensis* p. 334
   a. Male. Shiny blue-black, glossed purple. Much smaller than 4.
   b. Female. Dull brown, paler below; conical bill.

7. **Carib Grackle** *Quiscalus lugubris* p. 339
   a. Male. Glossy black with long, keel-shaped tail; iris white. Gregarious.
   b. Female. Duller with shorter tail. Immature brownish.

Plate 23: Honeycreepers and Warblers

1. **Bicolored Conebill** *Conirostrum bicolor* p. 359
   a. Adult. Blue-gray above, buffy below. Mangroves.
   b. Immature. Greener than adult, yellowish below.

2. **Tropical Parula** *Parula pitiayumi* p. 347
   a. Male. Blue-gray above tinged green; lores black; white wing-bars; golden below.
   b. Female. As male, but without black lores; less golden below.

3. **Bananaquit** *Coereba flaveola* p. 356
   Black above, white superciliary; rump and most underparts yellow.

4. **Green Honeycreeper** *Chlorophanes spiza* p. 362
   a. Male. Shining bluish green; head black; mandible yellow.
   b. Female. All grass green.

5. **Masked Yellowthroat** *Geothlypis aequinoctialis* p. 353
   a. Male. Yellow-green above, crown gray, black mask; yellow below.
   b. Female. As male, but without mask. Savannahs, marshes.

6. **Golden-crowned Warbler** *Basileuterus culicivorus* p. 355
   Grayish green above, yellow below; black, gray and orange crown-stripes. Forests.

1a

1b

2b

2a

4b

3

4a

5a

6

5b

Plate 24: Euphonias and Honeycreepers

1. **Violaceous Euphonia**   *Euphonia violacea*   p. 365
   a. Male. Bluish black above; forehead and entire underparts golden yellow.
   b. Female. Olive green above, yellowish below. Often found in pairs.

2. **Golden-rumped Euphonia**   *Euphonia cyanocephala*   p. 363
   a. Male. Crown, nape bright blue; throat, upperparts black; rump, underparts yellow.
   b. Female. Olive above with blue hood, yellowish below. Very rare.

3. **Trinidad Euphonia**   *Euphonia trinitatis*   p. 364
   a. Male. Resembles 1a, but yellow crown-patch more extended, and throat bluish black.
   b. Female. As 1b, but lower breast, abdomen pale gray. Diagnostic call.

4. **Purple Honeycreeper**   *Cyanerpes caeruleus*   p. 360
   a. Male. Violet; lores, wings, tail black; legs bright yellow.
   b. Female. Green, streaked below; face, throat buff with blue moustachial.

5. **Red-legged Honeycreeper**   *Cyanerpes cyaneus*   p. 361
   a. Male. Resembles 4a, but crown turquoise, wing-linings yellow; legs red.
   b. Female. Green, faintly streaked below; legs dull red.

6. **Blue Dacnis**   *Dacnis cayana*   p. 363
   a. Male. Turquoise blue; throat, tail black; wings black edged blue.
   b. Female. Green with blue head. Bill shorter than in 4 and 5.

1a

2b

2a

1b

3b

4a

3a

4b

6b

5b

5a

6a

O'Neill
72

Plate 25: Larger Tanagers

1. **Blue-gray Tanager** *Thraupis episcopus* p. 369
Grayish blue, brightest on wings. Semi-open areas.

2. **Swallow-Tanager** *Tersina viridis* p. 358
   a. Male. Generally blue; face, throat black; flanks barred black.
   b. Female. Green; flanks barred yellow. Mountain forests.

3. **Blue-capped Tanager** *Thraupis cyanocephala* p. 371
Above olive green with dark blue head; grayish blue below. Mountain forests.

4. **Palm Tanager** *Thraupis palmarum* p. 370
Dull olive with darker tail; wings "two-toned". Semi-open areas.

5. **Speckled Tanager** *Tangara guttata* p. 366
Yellowish green edged with black; "speckled" effect. Mountain forests.

6. **Turquoise Tanager** *Tangara mexicana* p. 367
Mainly dark blue with turquoise shoulder; lower underparts yellow. Small flocks.

7. **Silver-beaked Tanager** *Ramphocelus carbo* p. 372
   a. Male. Velvety black tinged crimson; enlarged bill silvery.
   b. Female. Dull reddish brown, brighter on rump, underparts. Forest edge, scrub.

1

2b

3

2a

4

5

6

7b

7a

O'Neill
72

Plate 26: Tanagers and Large Finches

1. **White-shouldered Tanager**   *Tachyphonus luctuosus*   p. 377
   a. Male. Black with conspicuous white shoulder. Mainly forest.
   b. Female. Above olive green with gray head; underparts yellow.

2. **White-lined Tanager**   *Tachyphonus rufus*   p. 376
   a. Male. Black with (usually concealed) white wing-linings.
   b. Female. Rufous. Usually in pairs.

3. **Red-crowned Ant-Tanager**   *Habia rubica*   p. 375
   a. Male. Dull red, brighter below; scarlet crown-stripe. Forest undergrowth.
   b. Female. Olive brown, paler below. Small groups.

4. **Red-capped Cardinal**   *Paroaria gularis*   p. 380
   Above black, below white, with mainly red head. Rare, swamps.

5. **Streaked Saltator**   *Saltator albicollis*   p. 379
   Olive green, streaked below; white superciliary. Bocas islands and NW Trinidad.

6. **Grayish Saltator**   *Saltator coerulescens*   p. 379
   Dark gray above, paler and buffier below; superciliary and chin white, throat bordered by black.

1a

2b

1b

2a

3b

4

3a

6

5

O'Neill
72

Plate 27: Finches

1. **Large-billed Seed-Finch**   *Oryzoborus crassirostris*   p. 391
   a. Male. Black with white speculum; massive, pale bill.
   b. Female. Dark brown, buffy brown below. Extremely rare.

2. **Lesser Seed-Finch**   *Oryzoborus angolensis*   p. 391
   a. Male. Upperparts and breast black; lower underparts dark chestnut.
   b. Female. As 1b, but richer brown and smaller. Very rare.

3. **Yellow-bellied Seedeater**   *Sporophila nigricollis*   p. 389
   a. Male. Head, upper breast black, upperparts olive, rest pale yellow.
   b. Female. Olive brown above, buffy brown below. Rare.

4. **Ruddy-breasted Seedeater**   *Sporophila minuta*   p. 390
   a. Male. Blue-gray above, rump and underparts chestnut. Tiny.
   b. Female. As 3b, but smaller. Rare.

5. **Blue-black Grassquit**   *Volatinia jacarina*   p. 383
   a. Male. Glossy blue-black, axillars white. Common, open areas.
   b. Female. Resembles 4b, but underparts streaked.

6. **Sooty Grassquit**   *Tiaris fuliginosa*   p. 385
   a. Male. Sooty black, tinged olive. Forest edge, second growth.
   b. Female. As 3b, but dingier.

7. **Black-faced Grassquit**   *Tiaris bicolor*   p. 384
   a. Male. Olivaceous gray; head and breast black.
   b. Female. As 6b, but greener. Tobago and Bocas islands.

1a

2a

1b

2b

3a

3b

4a

5b

4b

5a

6a

7a

6b

7b

O Neill
72

Plate 28: Finches

1. **Gray Seedeater** *Sporophila intermedia* p. 386
   a. Male. Gray, paler below; small white speculum; pinkish bill; legs black.
   b. Female. Brown above, paler below. Rare; scrub.

2. **Slate-colored Seedeater** *Sporophila schistacea* p. 386
   a. Male. As 1a but darker. Orange-yellow bill; legs greenish gray.
   b. Female. As 1b, but darker. Rare; forest edge.

3. **Orange-fronted Yellow-Finch** *Sicalis columbiana* p. 392
   Small, canary-like with orange fore-crown. Extremely rare.

4. **Variable Seedeater** *Sporophila americana* p. 387
   a. Male. Head, upperparts, breast-band black; throat, wing-edgings, underparts white.
   b. Female. As 2b. Rare; Tobago.

5. **Lesson's Seedeater** *Sporophila bouvronides* p. 388
   a. Male. Head, throat, upperparts black; moustachial, speculum, underparts white.
   b. Female. As 2b. Rare; second growth, marsh edge.

6. **Saffron Finch** *Sicalis flaveola* p. 393
   a. Adult. As 3 but larger. Locally common; gregarious.
   b. Immature. Streaky gray; collar and under-tail-coverts tinged yellow.

7. **Red Siskin** *Spinus cucullatus* p. 394
   a. Male. Red; head, wings, tail black. Probably extirpated.
   b. Female. Duller than male; whitish lower underparts.

1a

1b

2a

2b

3

4b

5a

4a

5b

6a

7a

6b

7b

O'Neill
72

Plate 29: Toucan, Bellbird, Guan, Ibis, Hawks and Woodpeckers

1. **Channel-billed Toucan** *Ramphastos vitellinus* p. 243
   Mainly black; throat, breast white and yellow; massive bill.

2. **Bearded Bellbird** *Procnias averano* p. 269
   Adult male. White with brown head and black wings; wattled throat.

3. **Common Piping-Guan** *Aburria pipile* p. 113
   Crested; eye-ring, throat and wattle blue; white wing patch.

4. **Scarlet Ibis** *Eudocimus ruber* p. 69
   Adult. Scarlet with black wing-tips. Gregarious.

5. **Zone-tailed Hawk** *Buteo albonotatus* p. 95
   Adult. Black with whitish bands on long tail; legs and cere yellow. In flight resembles Turkey Vulture.

6. **Gray Hawk** *Buteo nitidus* p. 98
   Adult. Pale gray above, finely barred white below; tail banded.

7. **Lineated Woodpecker** *Dryocopus lineatus* p. 246
   a. Male. Prominent crest and malar stripe red; *narrow* white streak from bill to neck; white scapular stripes do *not* meet.
   b. Female. As male, but no malar stripe and forehead black.

8. **Crimson-crested Woodpecker** *Phloeoceastes melanoleucos* p. 249
   a. Male. Resembles 7, but head mostly red with white cheek-patch and white at base of bill; throat black; white scapular stripes usually meet on back.
   b. Female. Forehead black; *wide* white stripe from bill to neck.

PORTRAITS

by Don R. Eckelberry

I

Rufous-breasted Hermit
(Glaucis hirsuta)
Arima Valley, Trinidad
Don R. Eckelberry

II

Collared Trogon ♂
(Trogon collaris)
Arima Valley, Trinidad
Don R. Eckelberry

III

Blue-crowned Motmot
(Momotus momota)
Aruma Valley, Trinidad
Don R. Eckelberry

IV

Golden-olive Woodpecker
♂ (*Piculus rubiginosus*)
Arima Valley, Trinidad
Don R. Eckelberry

V

Black-tailed Tityra ♂
(Tityra cayana)
Arima Valley, Trinidad
—Don R. Eckelberry

VI

Yellow-legged Thrush ♂
(*Platycichla flavipes*
melanopleura) ♂♂♀
Arima Valley, Trinidad

VII

Crested Oropendola
(Psarocolius decumanus)
Arima Valley, Trinidad
—Don R. Eckelberry

VIII

Yellow-hooded Blackbird
(Agelaius icterocephalus)
Arima, Trinidad. ORTE

IX

Bay-headed Tanager
(Tangara gyrola)
Arima Valley, Trinidad
Don R. Eckelberry

ALCEDINIDAE: Kingfishers

These birds have short necks and legs, rather short, rounded wings, large heads and massive, sharp-pointed bills. Five of the 6 American species have been recorded in Trinidad, where they are always associated with water. A kingfisher is usually seen perched upright on a branch overhanging water, from which it plunges headlong after a fish, or flying rapidly and directly up a river or stream. The nest is made in a hole in a riverbank; both parents incubate and care for the young. (5)

Ringed Kingfisher: *Ceryle torquata*
Great Ringed Kingfisher; Great Grey Kingfisher

Habitat and status. A rare visitor to Trinidad, occasionally nesting, usually found by reservoirs or the larger rivers; recent records are mostly between March and June, but 4 birds were seen between 4 December and 31 January; presumably migratory. (Specimen: PSM, also collected by Léotaud.)

Range and subspecies. Extreme S USA south to Tierra del Fuego, also on Lesser Antilles; the nominate race ranges S to Peru and N Argentina (excluding Lesser Antilles).

Description. 16 in. *Male:* crested head and upperparts generally blue-gray with white collar; most of underparts chestnut, lower abdomen whitish; in flight shows white edges to wing and tail-feathers; bill very large, mostly black with pale base to mandible. *Female:* as male but with blue-gray band across upper breast.

Voice. A loud, harsh rattling series, *kitti-kitti*, etc.

Food. Fish. The bird may dive direct from a perch or hover first while locating the prey.

Nesting. Breeding recorded in Trinidad only by B/S, who found a single egg on 8 April in a nesting tunnel in the bank of the Caroni River. The nesting tunnel may be up to 6 ft long; there are sometimes several grouped together. The egg measured 43.4 × 34.1mm. In the Orinoco area the breeding season is June–August (Cherrie 1916); nesting may be colonial, up to 150 pairs being found nesting in the high bank of a river. In Central America Skutch (1945b, 1957) found 8 eggs averaging 45.4 × 32.6mm. The adults incubated alternately for approximately 24-hr sessions. Clutch is 3–5; 2 recorded fledging periods were about 34 and 37 days.

Behaviour. At Pointe-a-Pierre the bird rests for lengthy periods during the day quite high up on the branches of bamboo or *Cecropia* trees. It is usually rather wary.

Belted Kingfisher: *Ceryle alcyon*

Habitat and status. A regular and fairly common visitor from the north to both islands, frequenting the coast, reservoirs, swamps and the larger rivers. Recorded at Pointe-a-Pierre in all months from 18 October to 22 April. In Tobago frequently seen between December and April; on Little Tobago Dinsmore had November and June records. (No specimens, but collected by Léotaud.)

Range. Breeds in North America, wintering S to Panama and the West Indies; there are a few records from Colombia, Venezuela and Guyana.

Description. 13 in. *Male:* generally resembles male Ringed Kingfisher, but smaller, and underparts *white* with broad grayish blue breast-band. *Female:* as male, but also has a *narrow* chestnut band across abdomen, and flanks are streaked with chestnut.

Voice. A harsh rattle.

Food. Fish. Usually hovers over water before diving.

Behaviour. A solitary and wary bird which will fly in stages for hundreds of yards along a river in front of a boat rather than double back. In Florida Meyerriecks and Nellis (1967) found these kingfishers associating, while feeding, with foraging egrets, hovering above the latter and diving as they disturbed the fish.

Amazon Kingfisher: *Chloroceryle amazona*
Great Green Kingfisher

Habitat and status. A rare visitor to Trinidad, recorded only by Léotaud, who collected a specimen, and Smooker, who found a breeding pair on the Madamas River amidst deep forest. (No extant specimens.)

Range. Mexico S through Central and most of South America.

Description. 11 in. *Male:* head and upperparts generally glossy dark green with a very few white spots and a white collar; breast chestnut, lower underparts white. *Female:* as male, but underparts white with *narrow green breast-band* and some green streaks on flanks. (See Green Kingfisher.)

Voice. A loud, frog-like rattle; also short, harsh *chrrt*.

Food. Small fish and crustaceans.

Nesting. Breeding recorded by B/S in May. The nest tunnel was 3 ft long in a riverbank; 4 white eggs av. 33.6 × 26.5mm. Skutch (1957) records an incubation period of 22 days for the Costa Rican race. Both parents incubated during the day, the female alone at night. There was no nest sanitation, so that the nest chamber became foul with the remains of fish.

Green Kingfisher: *Chloroceryle americana*
Little Green Kingfisher; "Fisherman" **Plate 12(8)**

Habitat and status. A fairly common resident in both islands, frequenting forest streams and mangrove swamps, occasionally the seacoast. (Specimens: AMNH, ANSP, YPM, LM, CM, BM, TRVL.)

Range and subspecies. S USA south through Central and South America to Bolivia and Argentina; *C. a. croteta* (Wetmore), which has a larger and heavier bill, is confined to Trinidad and Tobago.

Description. 7.5 in. *Male:* very similar to male Amazon Kingfisher, but much smaller and with conspicuous white spots on wings and tail. *Female:* as male, but underparts white suffused with buff with 2 green bands across breast.

Measurements. Wing: 7 males 76–81mm (78); 7 females 78–81mm (79.7). Weight: 8 males 28–32.5gm (30.3); 5 females 30–36.5gm (33.8).

Voice. A prolonged and harsh, chirping rattle.

Food. Mainly fish; I have also observed birds picking what were probably aquatic insects off vertical cliffsides by waterfalls.

Nesting. Breeding recorded in Trinidad (B/S) between March and October; in Tobago recorded in April. Moult recorded August–November. The nest is at the end of a tunnel, up to 3 ft long, usually in a riverbank, sometimes partly concealed by vegetation. The same nest tunnel is used repeatedly. The clutch is normally 3 eggs, sometimes 4, the average size of an unspecified number being 23.3 × 17.8mm. Once this species took over a nest tunnel of the Pygmy Kingfisher, removed its eggs and enlarged the tunnel for its own use.

Behaviour. Found singly or in pairs, this kingfisher is seen on low perches beside rivers, occasionally on the pebbly bed of a shallow forest river or stream. As one approaches, it flies off along the waterway but will soon double back, flying a little way into the forest to avoid contact. As it perches, it often twitches its tail and bobs its head.

Pygmy Kingfisher: *Chloroceryle aenea*
Plate 12(7)

Habitat and status. A rather uncommon resident in Trinidad, found mainly in mangrove swamps but also up the lower stream valleys of the Northern Range. (Specimens: AMNH, YPM, LM, BM, TRVL.)

Range and subspecies. Mexico S to Bolivia and Brazil; the nominate race ranges from Costa Rica south.

Description. 5.5 in. *Male:* generally dark green, glossed blue, on head and upperparts, with a few white spots on the wings; underparts *mainly rich chestnut,* centre of abdomen white. *Female:* as male, but also has greenish breast-band.

Measurements. Wing: 8 males 55–61mm (57.4); 2 females 56, 58mm. Weight: 4 males 14–17.5gm (14.9); 1 unsexed 14.5gm.

Voice. A high-pitched but distinct *djeet.*

Food. Small fish and aquatic insects; flying insects are also caught on the wing.

Nesting. Breeding recorded from May to September. The nest tunnel is about 1 ft long, with the chamber at one side, and is not always located near water but in any available earth bank. The clutch is 3 or 4 white eggs, av. 19.3 × 15.2mm (11).

Behaviour. This species is found singly or in pairs and appears less wary than others in its family, perhaps because it more easily escapes notice through its small size and habit of perching low in shady undergrowth beside water. It flies and dives with extreme rapidity, feeding sometimes in shallow, muddy puddles.

MOMOTIDAE: Motmots

Most members of this family are fairly large, strikingly coloured birds with strong bills and long, graduated tails, the elongated central feathers ending in a racquet tip. Motmots are found in deep forest perched amidst the taller undergrowth, or they may occur in more open second growth, sitting on an exposed but shaded branch, from which they swoop out to pluck a berry or seize an invertebrate. With their soft hooting calls and quiet disposition they may easily be overlooked. Nests are made in a hole in a bankside, where both parents share the care of the young. (1)

Blue-crowned Motmot: *Momotus momota*
Swainson's Motmot; Blue-diademed Motmot; "King of the Woods"; "Bouhoutou"; "Wutetetoo"   **Portrait III**

Habitat and status. A fairly common resident in both islands. In Trinidad not commonly seen, as it frequents heavily shaded parts of the forest at all levels; in Tobago much commoner, being found also in more exposed situations, cocoa plantations, even sandy beaches and pasture land with large trees. (Specimens: AMNH, ANSP, CM, YPM, LM, BM, TRVL.)

Range and subspecies. Mexico S to Bolivia and Argentina; *M. m. bahamensis* (Swainson) is confined to our islands, being distinguished by its deep cinnamon rufous underparts.

Description. 18 in. Upperparts green; centre of crown and broad streak through eye black, broad circle around crown turquoise in front, brilliant dark blue behind; underparts rufous with short black streak, edged blue, on breast; tail blue, the long central feathers with racquet tips; iris reddish; bill black. *Immature:* lacks breast-streak.

Measurements. Wing: 5 males 133–138mm (135.2); 7 females 133–142mm (137.9). Weight: 6 females 99–133gm (111); 133gm was weight of egg-laying bird); 9 unsexed 89–130gm (111.7).

Voice. A soft, deep, hooting note, sometimes double, *whoop* or *whoo-hoop;* often longer notes are uttered, with a roll or ripple in the tone. Nestlings make a low rattling call within their tunnel.

Food. Berries of forest plants, including *Sloanea;* mainly large invertebrates, including beetles, cockroaches, centipedes, stick-insects, millipedes and scorpions; occasionally small reptiles or even birds. Semi-tame birds in Tobago take soaked bread, cheese, etc., from feeding tables.

Nesting. Breeding recorded in Trinidad during April and May (9 nests) and in Tobago from March to July (many nests). Moult recorded in Trinidad between June and October; it is a slow process, lasting at least 4 months. The unlined nest is in a tunnel, made usually a few feet up in a high bank; the tunnel, which may be 5–14 ft long (not always in a straight line), is excavated well in advance of egg-laying and is often used more than once. The clutch is 3 white eggs, av. 33.4 × 27.4mm (6). In Costa Rica Skutch (1964a) found that incubation (by both parents) lasted about 3 wk, and that the young, which hatch naked, fledged when aged 29–32 days. The young are fed a varied diet.

Behaviour. Usually solitary, though mated pairs evidently stay together for some time, if not permanently. Though Skutch (1964a) did not find this, I suspect that nest tunnels are used for roosting outside the breeding season; I have seen pairs going into the tunnels at dusk. When excited, a perching motmot swings its tail from side to side like a pendulum or holds it stiffly out to one side. In flight it is swift and silent, but in Tobago at least it seems often incredibly tame as it sits by a roadside while people pass at close quarters. It sometimes takes a dust-bath in the middle of a road. In an apparent courtship display involving up to 10 individuals at once, motmots hold leaves or twigs in their bills, but these materials are not used for nesting.

Notes. The strange adornment of the racquet-tipped tail of several species of motmots is caused by the weak attachment of the original barbs to the feather shaft at that part of the feather. At maturity these barbs drop off through abrasion against leaves, etc., as the bird moves about. In a few birds the feather vanes remain intact. There is no evidence that the motmot "deliberately" creates the racquet tip by trimming its own feathers.

GALBULIDAE: Jacamars

Members of this family of slender, medium-sized birds with brilliant, irides-cent plumage and long, thin bills resemble enormous hummingbirds. Like the latter, they are birds of excitable temperament and intense vitality. Usually found on an exposed perch amidst second growth or in forest clearings at lower levels, jacamars hawk gracefully for the larger flying insects in the manner of flycatchers, returning with their prey to the same perch, where they batter it vigorously against the branch, thus removing the wings. They nest in holes, usually in banks, both parents sharing the nesting duties. (1)

Rufous-tailed Jacamar: *Galbula ruficauda*
"King Hummingbird"   **Plate 12(4)**

Habitat and status. A fairly common resident of both islands, especially Tobago, frequenting dense second growth, including bamboo patches, as well as clearings and forest edges at lower levels; in Tobago commonly found on roadsides in forest and cocoa plantations at all levels. (Specimens: AMNH, ANSP, CM, LM, YPM, BM, TRVL.)

Range and subspecies. Mexico S to Ecuador, Bolivia and N Argentina; the nominate race ranges from N Colombia and Venezuela to the Guianas and N Brazil.

Description. 10.5 in. *Male:* upperparts and a band across upper breast iridescent golden green; throat white, rest of underparts chestnut; tail long (5 in.), outer feathers chestnut. *Female:* as male, but throat buff. Bill black, long (1.75 in.), straight and very thin.

Measurements. Wing: 8 males 81–87mm (84.4); 8 females 81–86mm (83.6). Weight: 7 males 25–28gm (26.1); 7 females 24–33.5gm (26.9); including one egg-laying; 3 unsexed 19*, 24*, 28gm.

Voice. A high-pitched, single note, often repeated, sometimes in an acceler-ating series, e.g., *pee-pee-pee*, etc., rising in pitch at the end.

Food. Insects, including flies, beetles, bees, dragonflies and butterflies, some of the latter quite large. Usually prey is caught in the air and brought to a perch, where it is battered to death.

Nesting. Breeding recorded in Trinidad from February to June, especially March and April; in Tobago many nests recorded from February to July; moult is in August. The unlined nest is in a short tunnel, up to 18 in. long, usually in a sandy bank, sometimes in a termites' nest, a few feet above ground, or even in the earth round the roots of a fallen tree. Clutch is 2–4, usually 3, white eggs, av. 22.5 × 19.1mm (13). (A few lightly spotted eggs have been found.) In Costa Rica Skutch (1963b) found that both parents incubated alternately during the day, the female at night; the incubation period was 19–23 days.

Newly hatched birds are covered with white down and soon call (sounding very much like the adults) from the nest tunnel. The nestling period of this race in Venezuela (Skutch 1968) was 18 or 19 days, less than in Costa Rica.

Behaviour. Jacamars are found in pairs throughout the year, so the pair bond may be permanent. During courtship the male feeds the female with insects, after first stripping off the wings. Gilliard (1959a) saw these jacamars defending their nest tunnel from Rough-winged Swallows, which are probable competitors. Even near the nest they are quite unwary of man or other predators; as one approaches, the bird may call shrilly or swoop with graceful, undulating flight to a new perch. They may frequently be seen dust-bathing on gravel roads.

RAMPHASTIDAE: Toucans

Members of this family are unmistakable with their enormous, disproportionate bills. The single species in Trinidad frequents tall forest trees, where it feeds in the canopy on fruits, and nests in tree-holes. Mostly located by its loud, high-pitched call, the toucan in flight swoops and glides swiftly from tree to tree; with its powerful legs it hops about the branches with great dexterity. (1)

Channel-billed Toucan: *Ramphastos vitellinus*
Sulphur-and-white-breasted Toucan; "Tocan"; "Tia Poco"
Plate 29(1) and Figure 34

Habitat and status. Common in forest at all levels in Trinidad, where it usually keeps to the higher branches. (Specimens: AMNH, ANSP, CM, YPM, LM, BM, TRVL.)

Range and subspecies. Colombia S to Ecuador and Bolivia; the nominate race ranges from Venezuela to the Guianas and N Brazil.

Description. 20 in. Generally black; breast-band, upper- and under-tail-coverts red; sides of neck and throat white, upper breast orange-yellow; most of bill black, the base and bare face-patch light blue. Sexes similar, but male slightly larger.

Measurements. Wing: 5 males 180–190mm (186); 6 females 180–186mm (182.3). Bill (chord); 5 males 120–138mm (128.4); 6 females 100–121mm (111). Weight: 2 males 358, 423gm; 3 females 298, 315, 387gm. (Data mostly from Surinam, in Haverschmidt 1952.)

Voice. A high-pitched single note, e.g., *pyok*, repeated at intervals of a few seconds; at a distance resembles the yelping bark of a puppy.

Food. Highly nutritious fruits of forest trees, sometimes picked up from the

Figure 34. Channel-billed Toucan

ground; insects are also fed to the young. In Brazil the diet is known to include nestlings of the kiskadee (Schubart et al. 1965).

Nesting. Breeding recorded from March to June. The nest is unlined, in a tree-hole, 12–18 in. deep, often at a considerable height above ground, but occasionally as low as 3 ft (Lill 1970). Regurgitated seeds may cover the floor of the nest chamber. The clutch is 2–4 white eggs, av. 35.7 × 28.8mm (4). Incubation (by both parents) was thought by Chenery (1956) to last 4.5 wk, while the fledging period was 46 days; Lill found one fledging period to be 44–51 days. The young are fed most irregularly, once 29 times during the day, whilst another time 9 hr elapsed without a single parental visit.

Behaviour. Gregarious in small flocks, but often seen in pairs or singly. The flight is undulating, but toucans rarely fly long distances. During courtship the male feeds the female, handling berries in its ungainly bill with remarkable dexterity. Toucans of other species are known to rob birds' nests, but this has not yet been proved of this bird in Trinidad; however, smaller birds show great alarm when a toucan is near their nests. I once saw one of a pair of toucans sitting on an open high branch after a rain shower with its huge bill agape. Chenery saw one drinking water from a bromeliad. Lill saw a pair near their nest mobbing a 6-ft-long tree boa (*Boa enydris*) on the ground; this tree-climbing snake may well be a predator of the toucans' eggs or young.

Notes. This toucan is occasionally kept as a pet with great success, and it is a rewarding and amusing pet; in captivity it eats baby mice voraciously. Though legally protected, it is occasionally shot for food in Trinidad.

PICIDAE: Woodpeckers

This well-known family, locally called carpenter birds, is represented in our area by birds ranging in size from quite small to large. Woodpeckers live, feed and breed typically in trees, where they climb on the trunk or larger branches, usually in a vertical attitude, supported by their stiff tail-feathers. Their flight is short and undulating. Nests are made in tree-holes, and both sexes care for the eggs and young, the male alone incubating at night. The eggs are white. (6)

Golden-olive Woodpecker: *Piculus rubiginosus*
Green Woodpecker; Blue-headed Woodpecker   **Portrait IV**

Habitat and status. A common resident in both islands, especially Trinidad, frequenting forests and cultivated areas with trees at all levels. (Specimens: AMNH, ANSP, CM, YPM, LM, BM, TRVL.)

Range and subspecies. Mexico S through Central and South America to Venezuela, Guyana, Bolivia and N Argentina; *P. r. trinitatis* (Ridgway) is confined to Trinidad; it is smaller and has a less heavy bill than *P. r. tobagensis* (Ridgway), which is confined to Tobago.

Description. 7.5 in. *Male:* upperparts generally golden olive, under-tail-coverts and outer tail barred; fore-crown dark grayish blue, hind-crown and moustachial streak red; broad stripe across face yellowish white; underparts barred blackish and yellow; bill black. *Female:* as male but without red moustachial streak. *Immature:* resembles adults.

Measurements. *P. r. trinitatis.* Wing: 9 males 102–106mm (104); 7 females 99–107mm (102.9). Weight: 14 males 51–68gm (56.2); 9 females 51–61gm (55.4). *P. r. tobagensis.* Wing: 2 males 109, 112mm; 1 female 109mm. Weight: 2 males 59*, 69gm; 1 female 55gm.

Voice. Normally a loud, sharp, single note, *wheep;* also a sharp, rather high-pitched trill and a subdued *wit-wit* or *woit-woit,* uttered by 2 birds together.

Food. Mostly insects, especially the larvae of wood-boring beetles, and ants, sometimes taken from the ground; also berries and fruits.

Nesting. Breeding recorded in Trinidad from March to June (8 nests); moult in August and September. The unlined nest is in a tree-hole 4–60 ft above ground. Clutch is 2–3 white eggs, av. 24.3 × 18.5mm (6). In the Costa Rican highlands Skutch (1956a) found a clutch of 4 eggs, of which only 1 fledgling survived. The parents alternated at incubation during the day. The young, which hatch naked, were fed by regurgitation at a very slow rate, visits averaging about once per hour. Nest sanitation was neglected as soon as the young could be fed at the mouth of the nest-hole. A fledged bird flew (when disturbed) at the age of 24 days.

Behaviour. Usually found singly or in pairs, though young birds accompany their parents for a while after leaving the nest. Adult birds roost in tree-holes, sometimes old nest holes. They do not always forage on tree trunks, but may be seen pecking about on horizontal limbs and epiphytes, preferring to explore soft green wood.

Notes. In the past this species was considered by some farmers to be a pest that attacked cocoa pods, and was accordingly designated as vermin by the authorities. There is controversy, however, over whether the birds are attacking already infested pods and eating injurious insects, thus outweighing the harm they otherwise might do. An impartial study is necessary.

Chestnut Woodpecker: *Celeus elegans*
Yellow-crested Woodpecker; Pale-crowned Crested Woodpecker
Plate 13(7)

Habitat and status. A fairly common resident of forests in Trinidad at all levels. (Specimens: AMNH, ANSP, CM, YPM, LM, BM.)

Range and subspecies. Colombia S and E to Ecuador, Bolivia, the Guianas and N Brazil; *C. e. leotaudi* (Hellmayr) is found only in Trinidad and is distinguished by being smaller, paler and brighter than the nominate race.

Description. 11 in. *Male:* generally rich chestnut brown with yellow rump and flanks; pronounced tawny crest, yellowish at the tip; tail black; malar stripe crimson; bill yellowish white. *Female:* lacks the crimson malar stripe.

Measurements. Wing: 5 males 139–154mm (145.4); 5 females 133–145mm (140.6). Weight: 6 males 112–129gm (120.3); 9 females 93.5–139gm (115.6).

Voice. A harsh, disyllabic squawk, more reminiscent of a chicken or parrot than a woodpecker; also drums loudly.

Food. Insects; also known to take fruit, including *Cecropia,* in Brazil (Schubart et al. 1965).

Nesting. Breeding recorded in April and May (5 nests); moult from July to November (taking well over 4 months to complete). In the Arima Valley drumming recorded from November to February. The nest-hole, about 2 in. in diameter, is usually in the trunk of a dead tree, with the bottom of the nest chamber 6–12 in. below the entrance. The clutch is 3 white eggs, av. 27 × 21.8mm (6).

Behaviour. This noisy species is often seen in small parties of up to 5 individuals; they frequent mainly the lower branches of forest trees.

Lineated Woodpecker: *Dryocopus lineatus*
Plate 29(7) and Figure 35

Habitat and status. A widely distributed, but not common, resident in Trinidad, found in forests and second growth at all levels up to 2000 ft; also

Figure 35. Lineated Woodpecker

seen in isolated large trees on the edges of savannahs. (Specimens: AMNH, ANSP, BM, TRVL.)

Range and subspecies. Mexico S to Peru, Paraguay and N Argentina; the nominate race ranges from Colombia south to Argentina, and east to the Guianas.

Description. 13 in. *Male:* upperparts black, with white stripe down scapulars; crown, crest and nape scarlet; *cheeks blackish,* bordered by narrow white line from base of bill to sides of neck; crimson malar streak; *throat heavily streaked black,* breast black, lower underparts barred blackish and buff; bill whitish; iris white. *Female:* lacks malar streak, and forehead is black. (See also Crimson-crested Woodpecker.)

Measurements. Wing: 1 male 188mm; 4 females 180–185mm (182.5). Weight: 4 males 206–217gm (210.5); 1 female 158gm. (Data from Surinam [Haverschmidt 1948].)

Voice. Utters a loud, ringing series of notes, *wic-wic-wic,* etc.; also gives a short, sharp *keek* followed by a harsh trilling note. Both sexes also drum—a long, rolling tattoo.

Food. Insects, especially ants living on *Cecropia* trees, and the larvae of wood-boring beetles; also seeds, e.g., *Heliconia.*

Nesting. Breeding recorded between December and April (6 nests). The nest is in a tree-hole, usually in a dead tree, 20–65 ft above ground. The clutch is 2–3 white eggs, av. 34.3 × 25.6mm (5). The young are fed by regurgitation at a very slow rate.

Behaviour. An energetic, rather wary bird, easily noticed because of its loud calls and resonant drumming. Skutch (1945b, 1969b) describes how this woodpecker in Central America exploits *Cecropia* trees, using its bill to pierce the slender branches and extract the pupae of the ants which swarm on these trees. Since these ants form an important part of its diet, it is an advantage to feed the young by regurgitation rather than with individual particles (ants), which would necessitate many more feeding visits. In courtship behaviour the pair touch bills or wave them from side to side, and flash their wings (Kilham & O'Brien 1979). One pair fought with Pygmy-Owls for possession of a nest-site.

Red-crowned Woodpecker: *Melanerpes rubricapillus*
Bonaparte's Woodpecker; Wagler's Woodpecker;
Little Red-headed Woodpecker; *Centurus rubricapillus*   **Plate 13(3)**

Habitat and status. A common resident in Tobago, where it frequents second growth and semi-open cultivated areas below 1000 ft. Not recorded from Trinidad, but common on the Venezuelan island of Patos in the Bocas. (Specimens: AMNH, LM, BM.)

Range and subspecies. S Costa Rica through Panama to Colombia, Venezuela and the Guianas; *M. r. terricolor* (Berlepsch) is found in Tobago, Margarita Island and NE Venezuela; it is larger than the nominate race and has a darker chin and breast.

Description. 7 in. *Male:* upperparts and wings barred black and white, rump white; crown bright red, nape reddish; forehead, face and underparts generally olive-brown, abdomen reddish; tail black, barred with white at tips. *Female:* as male, but crown buffy, nape reddish. *Immature:* red areas of the head duller than in adult, the nape being pale yellow in newly fledged birds.

Measurements. Wing: 9 males 106–111mm (108.7); 4 females 101–107mm (104.2). Weight: 3 males 50, 54, 64gm; 2 females 45, 46.5gm.

Voice. A shrill, rattling trill, *krrrrrt*, sometimes repeated several times; also a light *whick;* drums rapidly.

Food. Mainly insects, especially ants, but also berries. Semi-tame birds also take sugar, soaked bread and citrus fruit from feeding tables.

Nesting. Breeding recorded from March to July (9 nests); moult August to November. The nest is in a hole, usually in a dead tree, up to 40 ft above ground. A clutch in Panama (Wetmore 1968) was 2 eggs, av. 23.7 × 17.6mm. In Costa Rica (Skutch 1945b, 1969b) the male incubates and broods at night, sharing the duties with the female by day. The young are fed frequently (up to 9 times per nestling per hr). Fledging is at 31–33 days.

Behaviour. A very conspicuous, noisy and excitable species, often seen in pairs or family groups. It often moves about tree foliage in a manner quite unlike a woodpecker, though it also climbs tree trunks and fenceposts. Wetmore (1968) describes how in Panama males in display follow the females in flight; on alighting they raise the stiffly spread wings at a 45° angle while they call their high-pitched *whick* note repeatedly. When nervous, this species constantly "feints" from side to side. When entering a roost hole, it usually goes in tail first. Kilham (1972a) suggests that this is because there is little room to turn round inside a narrow cavity; nesting holes are usually in wider cavities, and these are entered normally.

Red-rumped Woodpecker: *Veniliornis kirkii*
Kirk's Woodpecker   **Plate 13(2)**

Habitat and status. A fairly common resident in both islands, occurring in forest, cultivated areas with trees and semi-open woodland; occasionally found on the edge of mangrove swamps. (Specimens: AMNH, ANSP, CM, YPM, LM, BM, TRVL.)

Range and subspecies. Costa Rica through Panama and Colombia to Ecuador and Venezuela; the nominate race is found in NE Venezuela, Trinidad and Tobago.

Description. 6.5 in. *Male:* upperparts generally golden brown, tinged olive, wings spotted with pale buff, rump bright red; head mainly dusky brown, the feathers of crown tipped red, nape streaked and tipped yellow; tail dark brown, outer feathers barred with buff; underparts finely barred dark brown and buff; bill black. *Female:* as male, but crown dark brown, nape orange-brown.

Measurements. Wing: 8 males 86–95mm (90.1); 8 females 89–92mm (91.1). Weight: 4 males 32–37gm (35.1); 5 females 33–42gm (36.9).

Voice. A repeated *quee-quee-quee*, sounding more urgent and louder towards the end; also a single note, *keer*. It also drums rapidly.

Food. Insects.

Nesting. Breeding recorded (5 nests) from December to March and in June; moult in June and September. The nest is in a tree-hole 10–25 ft above ground; a clutch of 3 eggs av. 23 × 17.5mm.

Behaviour. Usually found singly or in pairs. When feeding, this species pecks deliberately and loudly at a branch, and is often located by this noise.

Crimson-crested Woodpecker: *Phloeoceastes melanoleucos*
Black-and-white Woodpecker; Malherbe's Woodpecker
Plate 29(8) and Figure 36

Habitat and status. A rather uncommon resident in Trinidad, occurring in lowland forest and open areas with large trees. (Specimens: AMNH, LM, BM, TRVL.)

Figure 36. Crimson-crested Woodpecker

Range and subspecies. Panama and Colombia S to Ecuador, Peru, Bolivia and Argentina; the nominate race ranges from Colombia E to the Guianas and S to Peru and Paraguay.

Description. 14 in. In most respects resembles the Lineated Woodpecker, but has a black (*not* streaked) throat; cheeks are white (*not* black), prolonged into a white line down the sides of the neck; white stripes down the back converge (almost always) into a V. *Male:* entire crown, crest and malar patch red. *Female:* lacks the malar patch, and forehead is black. Bill whitish; iris bright yellow.

Measurements. Wing: 1 male 202mm; 3 females 200, 201, 205mm. Weight: 1 female 279gm*.

Voice. Usual call a loud, sharp, grating note of 2 or 3 syllables; also a higher-pitched chattering and a soft, musical rattle. Both sexes drum loudly in a typical rhythm: a single strong blow followed by a weaker, rolling series.

Food. Insects, including caterpillars and larvae of wood-boring beetles; also berries.

Nesting. Breeding recorded in December and April (2 nests). The nests were in tree-holes about 30 ft above ground; 2 white eggs av. 35.5 × 26mm.

Behaviour. These birds are found singly or in pairs. Their flight over any considerable distance is strongly undulating. Kilham (1972b) describes mated pairs in Panama "drum-tapping" and touching bills during courtship.

DENDROCOLAPTIDAE: Woodcreepers

The members of this family (sometimes known as woodhewers) superficially resemble woodpeckers in that they habitually climb tree trunks, supported by their stiff tails. Instead of boring holes, however, they explore the wood for insects with their long, slightly curved bills; some species in Trinidad follow army ants. Generally brown in colour and with streaked heads, these obscure-looking birds draw attention to themselves by their penetrating calls. They inhabit forests, including mangroves, and nest in tree-holes, where they lay white eggs. Much still remains to be discovered about their life-history. (5)

Plain-brown Woodcreeper: *Dendrocincla fuliginosa*
Ochreous-bellied Woodhewer; Little Cocoa Woodhewer   **Plate 13(4)**

Habitat and status. A common resident in Trinidad, less common in Tobago (where ant swarms are rare), frequenting forests and cocoa plantations at all levels. (Specimens: Trinidad, AMNH, ANSP, CM, YPM, LM, BM, TRVL; Tobago, AMNH.)

Range and subspecies. Honduras S through Central and South America to Peru, Bolivia, Paraguay and N Argentina; *D. f. meruloides* (Lafresnaye) is found in N Venezuela and on our islands.

Description. 8.5 in. Generally brown with rufous wings, upper-tail-coverts and tail; *no noticeable streaks;* bill fairly long (1 in.), dark above, lower mandible pale; iris brown (in *immature* gray).

Measurements. Wing: 2 males 99, 105mm; 10 females 93–101mm (95.6). Weight: 1 male 41gm*; 10 females 30–38.5gm (34.1), 1 female (probably egg-laying) 46gm; 98 unsexed 31–54.5gm (38.7).

Voice. Varied; utters a rather low-pitched but vigorous, uneven trilling; a harsh, scolding but not loud, single note, *waaa*, repeated at intervals; a soft *poo;* a short churr; also, rarely, a short, decelerating cadence, reminiscent of *Myrmeciza* but less ringing.

Food. Insects, including cockroaches, beetles and ants, and spiders; also, in Panama, grasshoppers, moths, centipedes and *Anolis* lizards (Willis 1972).

Nesting. Breeding recorded from May to November, especially the earlier months; regular calling begins in February. Moult recorded from June to December, especially last 3 months. The nest is situated in a tree-hole up to 30 ft above ground, or in a hollow in a dead stump; it is made of leaves, stalks and plant-down. The clutch is 2 eggs, av. 27.9 × 21.1mm (4). The female alone incubates and cares for the young.

Behaviour. This species is almost always found in association with columns of army ants (*Eciton* and *Labidus*), either singly or in loose groups. I have found 10 birds together in one spot. As the marching ants flush large numbers of arthropods, these woodcreepers, along with various other birds from several families, prey upon them (and sometimes upon the ants). This species may be found feeding on the ground or near it, or may move to less productive feeding areas on tree trunks and lower branches when some larger, dominant species is present (Willis 1966a, 1972).

Olivaceous Woodcreeper: *Sittasomus griseicapillus*
Caribbean Woodcreeper   **Plate 13(1)**

Habitat and status. A fairly common resident in Tobago, where it occurs mainly in hill forest but is recorded also from second growth at lower levels; keeps to the lower parts of the trees. (Specimens: AMNH, BM.)

Range and subspecies. Mexico S through Central and South America to Bolivia, Paraguay and N Argentina; *S. g. griseus* (Jardine) is found in N Venezuela and Tobago.

Description. 6 in. Head, underparts and upper back grayish olive, with wings, upper-tail-coverts and long tail light chestnut; bill rather short for a woodcreeper. A very slim bird.

Measurements. Wing: 3 males 81, 82, 85mm; 4 unsexed 68–74mm (71). Weight: 3 males 15–16gm; 4 unsexed 12–14gm (13).

Voice. A rapid, high-pitched trill, rising and falling in pitch.

Food. Insects.

Nesting. No definite breeding record, but a bird was seen to enter a narrow crevice 15 ft up in the trunk of an immortelle tree during early April. Moult August–October. In the Costa Rican mountains Skutch (1967) found a bird carrying dead leaves into a crevice 40 ft up in a palm. Only one adult apparently was concerned with incubation, so the eggs were left unattended while the sitting bird left the nest for intervals of up to 25 min.

Straight-billed Woodcreeper: *Xiphorhynchus picus*
Picine Woodhewer; Mangrove Woodhewer   **Plate 13(5)**

Habitat and status. An uncommon resident in Trinidad, confined to mangrove swamps. Recent records only from Caroni swamp. (Specimen: LM.)

Range and subspecies. Panama E and S to the Guianas, Peru and C Brazil; *X. p. altirostris* (Léotaud) is confined to Trinidad, distinguished by larger size, larger and heavier bill, and more definite light spots on the underparts.

Description. 9 in. Very like the Buff-throated Woodcreeper but smaller, and the bill is shorter, straighter and whitish in adult birds; the throat is also whiter.

Measurements. Wing: 1 female 108mm. Weight: 1 female 51gm*.

Voice. A high-pitched trill, rapid at first, then decelerating; also, in alarm, an excited *pik-pik-pik*.

Food. Spiders; also insects (cockroaches, beetles, etc.) and lizards in Surinam (Haverschmidt 1968a).

Nesting. The only breeding record to date is of a nest I found on 28 July 1964, in the centre of the Caroni swamp. It was unlined, in the hollow of a dead mangrove (*Avicennia*) 6 ft above ground and contained 2 well-grown young which had gone by 9 August. The young answered their parents' calls from within the hollow. The eggs of the nominate race in Surinam measured 25.4 × 19.6mm (Haverschmidt 1968a).

Buff-throated Woodcreeper: *Xiphorhynchus guttatus*
Cocoa Woodhewer   **Plate 13(6)**

Habitat and status. A common resident in both islands, occurring in forests, cultivated areas with trees, even on the edge of mangrove swamps. (Specimens: AMNH, ANSP, CM, YPM, LM, BM, TRVL.)

Range and subspecies. Guatemala S through Central and South America to Bolivia and Brazil; *X. g. susurrans* (Jardine) occurs in our islands and is also recorded from the adjoining Paria peninsula of Venezuela, but not from the Bocas Islands.

Description. 10 in. Head and neck dark brown, spotted and streaked with pale buff; upper back liver brown, lower back, wings and tail rufous; underparts olive brown, breast streaked with buff; bill black, long (1.5 in.) and slightly decurved with a pronounced hook at the tip.

Measurements. Wing: 14 males 102–115mm (107.9); 9 females 90–105mm (97.4). Weight: 14 males 43–58gm (51.2); 12 females 41–49gm (45.2); 25 unsexed 36.5–59gm (49.2).

Voice. Usually a series of loud notes, *kew-kew-kew,* etc., typically introduced by 2–3 fainter notes; the series tends to fade away with a single, lower-pitched note. Also utters a single note, a loud, twanging *kew,* especially when about to roost.

Food. Insects, including beetles and cockroaches, and spiders.

Nesting. Breeding recorded from March to July (6 nests); calling begins in January and continues until early October, while moult has been recorded from June to January. The nest is in a tree-hole or hollow stump and is made of bits of bark, or sometimes dead leaves and plant-down. The clutch is 2 eggs, av. 30 × 22.8mm (4). B/S remark that this family appears to utilize existing natural holes, frequently of large diameter, rather than create holes for themselves like woodpeckers.

Behaviour. Usually solitary, but small groups gather to exploit the food at army ant swarms, where they may feed on the ground or the lower branches of trees. When climbing a tree, members of this family habitually move up the trunk in a spiral from near the bottom. On reaching the first major intersection of branches, they fly off with a short undulating flight to the next tree and start again.

Streaked-headed Woodcreeper: *Lepidocolaptes souleyeti*
Souleyet's Woodhewer; Thin-billed Woodhewer   **Plate 13(8)**

Habitat and status. A rather uncommon and local resident in Trinidad, frequenting forest edges and second growth, usually near water. (Specimens: AMNH, YPM, TRVL.)

Range and subspecies. Mexico S to Ecuador, Peru and N Brazil; *L. s. littoralis* (Hartert & Goodson) ranges from NE Colombia to Venezuela, Guyana and N Brazil.

Description. 7.75 in. Head and neck dark brown, streaked with buff; upper back olive brown; wings, rump and tail bright chestnut; underparts olive brown streaked with buff; bill quite long (1 in.), slender, decurved and whitish.

Measurements. Wing: 3 males 88, 90, 90mm; 2 females 84, 87mm.

Voice. A thin, high-pitched trilling series, *chi-chi-chi,* etc., sometimes with downward inflection.

Food. Feeds on insects and spiders found by probing the bark of tree trunks.

Nesting. Breeding recorded in April and May (B/S). A nest was found in a knothole on an immortelle tree, 10 ft from the ground; it was made of weed stems and plant-down, but nests in Central America were all constructed of pieces of bark (Skutch 1969b). The clutch is 2 eggs, av. 26.2 × 19.2mm (4). In Costa Rica Skutch found the incubation period to be 15 days, and the fledging period 19 days. Both parents shared in duties at the nest.

FURNARIIDAE: Ovenbirds

Most members of this family are small, brown birds, usually with some rufous colouring in their plumage. Those few species occurring in our islands are most diverse in habitat and habits. The 3 spinetails inhabit country ranging from hill forest to mangrove swamps and forage on the ground or amidst undergrowth; they nest in large, complicated structures built of sticks. The xenops resembles a tiny woodcreeper or nuthatch but has a short, wedge-shaped bill. The leaftosser behaves and looks more like a small forest thrush, but it nests in holes made in banks. (5)

Pale-breasted Spinetail: *Synallaxis albescens*
White-throated Spinetail; Pale-breasted Castle-builder   **Plate 14(6)**

Habitat and status. A fairly common and widely distributed resident in Trinidad, occurring in semi-open scrub and cultivated areas, especially in the lowlands; also known in the Bocas Islands. (Specimens: AMNH, CM, LM, BM, TRVL.)

Range and subspecies. Costa Rica S through Panama and South America to Bolivia and Argentina; *S. a. trinitatis* (Zimmer) occurs also in Venezuela.

Description. 6.5 in. Generally dull brown above with chestnut crown and wing-coverts; paler below; tail fairly long, graduated. *Immature:* lacks chestnut patches.

Measurements. Wing: 7 males 55–59mm (56); 4 females 53–56mm (55). Weight: 2 males 12.5, 13gm*; 1 female 12.5gm*; 1 unsexed 15.5gm.

Voice. A persistent double note, *wer-choo,* the second sharper and higher than the first; also a long rattle.

Food. Insects and spiders.

Nesting. Breeding recorded from December to September, with no apparent peak; moult recorded in August. The nest, located in trees at heights varying from 2 to 30 ft, is a large, round mass of twigs with a narrow horizontal passage leading from the base; the small egg chamber is floored with a pad of plant-down. Sometimes a few pieces of snakeskin are placed in the entrance passage. Two or 3 white eggs are laid, av. 20.5 × 15.5mm (6). Both sexes share nesting duties; incubation lasts about 18 days, fledging 16 days. The Striped Cuckoo often parasitises this species.

Behaviour. Usually found in pairs, this species skulks in the undergrowth, rarely flying more than a few yards.

Stripe-breasted Spinetail: *Synallaxis cinnamomea*
Cinnamomeous Spinetail   **Plate 14(4)**

Habitat and status. A fairly common resident of hill forest in Trinidad; in Tobago widespread at all levels in both forest and second growth. (Specimens: Trinidad, AMNH, CM, LM; Tobago, AMNH, LM, BM.)

Range and subspecies. Colombia and Venezuela; *S. c. carri* (Chapman) is confined to Trinidad and is darker than the nominate race and has a few pale streaks on the upper breast; *S. c. terrestris* (Jardine) occurs only in Tobago and is larger and paler, with more pronounced pale streaks on the breast.

Description. 6 in. Head and upperparts dark reddish brown, wing-coverts chestnut; throat black streaked with white, rest of underparts brown, streaked with buff; tail fairly long and graduated.

Measurements. *S. c. carri.* Wing: 4 males 56–59mm (57.8); 2 females 55, 56mm. Weight: 5 males 15.5–18gm (17.0); 2 females 17, 17.5gm*; 4 unsexed 18–19gm. *S. c. terrestris.* Wing: 2 males 61, 61mm; 3 females 55, 58, 60mm. Weight: 2 males 16.5, 20gm*; 3 females 16.5, 16.5, 19.5gm*; 10 unsexed 17–23gm (20.2).

Voice. Usually a plaintive, disyllabic call, rendered sometimes as *me-too* or *keep going*, the last note with rising inflection. This is sometimes followed by a series of the *keep* notes, getting softer. Also utters a rather querulous *chew* or *tui*, which in alarm sharpens to a quick *chee-chee-chee;* also a short, repeated *mik, mik.*

Food. Apparently small insects and spiders taken from among the leaf litter on the ground; also seen leaping up into the air to take flying ants.

Nesting. Breeding records in Trinidad (7 nests) scattered in February, May, September, November and December; in Tobago recorded March–August; moult September. The nest and eggs resemble those of the Pale-breasted Spinetail; 6 from Trinidad av. 19.0 × 14.8mm, while 1 Tobago egg measured 21 × 16.5mm.

Behaviour. Though it tends to skulk in undergrowth, I have found this species surprisingly confiding on occasion. Once, when I stood near their nest in the Pigeon Peak forest of Tobago, a pair hopped all around me within a few feet without displaying any alarm.

Yellow-throated Spinetail: *Certhiaxis cinnamomea*
"Marsh Giouiti"; "Rooti"   **Plate 14(7)**

Habitat and status. A common resident in Trinidad, occurring in marshes and the edges of mangrove swamps. (Specimens: AMNH, ANSP, YPM, LM, BM, TRVL.)

Range and subspecies. Colombia S to Argentina and Uruguay; the nominate race occurs from Venezuela S and E to the Guianas and NE Brazil.

Description. 6 in. Head and upperparts generally rich chestnut brown; throat pale yellow, rest of underparts whitish; tail long, graduated, the bare shafts protruding.

Measurements. Wing: 2 males 58, 60mm; 1 female 57mm. Weight: 4 males 13–15.5gm (14); 2 females 12.5, 13.5gm*; 3 unsexed 12, 13, 15.5gm.

Voice. A shrill, rattling series of notes, lasting several seconds.

Food. Small insects, including froghoppers, beetles, dragonflies, caterpillars and ants, and spiders.

Nesting. Breeding recorded from June to October. Birds begin building in May or even April, but most eggs are laid in June (16 of 31 recorded clutches). Moult is recorded in November and February. The nest is located in a small clump of mangrove or marsh plants, often at ground level, sometimes at considerable height, up to 30 ft. It resembles the large stick nest of the other spinetails, but the narrow entrance tunnel (which is added last) stretches from the base at one side almost vertically to the roof. There are 3, sometimes 4, eggs in the clutch, av. 18.8 × 14.5mm (10). Frequently this species is parasitised by the Striped Cuckoo, which lays 1 or 2 eggs. It is not known how the cuckoo enters the nest, or how the young spinetails are ejected.

Behaviour. An extremely noisy and conspicuous species. Even during the breeding season the birds appear to be quite unwary of humans. Often, as I have been investigating the contents of a nest by making a small hole in the side, the parent birds have come right to the nest, where they have immediately begun to repair the damage even before my departure.

Streaked Xenops: *Xenops rutilans*
Xenops rutilus   **Plate 14(3)**

Habitat and status. A fairly common resident of forests in Trinidad, occurring at all levels, mostly in lower branches. (Specimens: AMNH, ANSP, CM, YPM, LM, BM, TRVL.)

Range and subspecies. Costa Rica S to Bolivia and N Argentina; *X. r. heterurus* (Cabanis & Heine) ranges from Costa Rica to Ecuador, Colombia and Venezuela.

Description. 5 in. Head dark brown with superciliary and malar streaks whitish, forming a sort of crescent; upperparts brown, rump and tail rufous with some black on middle tail-feathers; wings dark brown with buff bar at base of primaries; underparts olive brown with pale streaks; bill short, wedge-shaped, slightly upturned, lower mandible whitish.

Measurements. Wing: 6 males 64–65mm; 2 females 62, 63mm. Weight: 4 males 14–16gm (14.8)*; 2 unsexed 13gm each.

Voice. A quick succession of shrill twittering notes rising to a climax and then tailing off, sometimes with a final distinct note.

Food. Insects, including the larvae of wood-boring beetles; typically feeds by searching in bark or along thin, bare twigs and gleaning prey.

Nesting. Breeding recorded in February, April and May; moult in May. The nest is made of a few leaf stems and roots placed in a natural tree cavity 8–15 ft above ground. The clutch is 2 white eggs, av. 20.8 × 16.2mm (4). Both sexes incubate.

Behaviour. This species, usually found singly, climbs tree trunks and branches at all angles, but without using its tail as a prop. It often pecks noisily at some rotten stub, exposing the insects within. While calling, the bird may raise and flap its wings at the spluttering climax, thus displaying the buff wing-bar conspicuously.

Gray-throated Leaftosser: *Sclerurus albigularis*
Gray-throated or White-throated Leafscraper   **Plate 15(5)**

Habitat and status. A common resident of forests and mature second growth on Trinidad. Formerly also on Tobago (Kirk), but no recent records. (Specimens: AMNH, ANSP, CM, LM.)

Range and subspecies. Costa Rica through Panama and South America to Ecuador, Peru and NW Bolivia; the nominate race ranges from E Colombia to N Venezuela and Trinidad and Tobago.

Description. 6.5 in. Upperparts brown with chestnut rump and black tail; throat pale gray, breast rufous, lower underparts brown; bill strong, fairly long (0.75 in.).

Measurements. Wing: 5 males 83–89mm (86); 10 females 82–87mm (84.2). Weight: 1 male 32.5gm*; 5 females 33–36.5gm (33.9)*; 7 unsexed 33–37.5gm (35.1).

Voice. Usually a 5-syllable phrase; first a rather soft note, then 2 loud, higher notes, then 2 less loud but shorter and sharper notes; this is repeated persistently in early morning and late afternoon. Also, in alarm or excitement, a sharp *chick,* repeated at intervals.

Food. Small insects and spiders found amidst the leaf litter on the forest floor, where the bird scratches about like a short-legged thrush, tossing the dead leaves aside as it searches for food.

Nesting. Breeding recorded in Trinidad from October to May with a peak in December–February, when song is most prominent. Nests reported from Tobago require corroboration. The nest is made at the end of a short tunnel excavated in a bankside, often by a path, a few feet from the ground; the tunnel often curves to one side, leading to a nest chamber floored with a few leaves. There are 2 white eggs, av. 24.8 × 19.8mm (10). It is suspected that the female alone excavates the tunnel and cares for the eggs and young (Junge & Mees 1958).

Behaviour. This nondescript, thrush-like bird is not easy to see in the dim light of the forest understory, and it is normally rather wary of intruders. However, its behaviour on being disturbed from its nest-hole is almost invariable. Flying out as one approaches, it perches at some point opposite and below the path, sometimes clinging to a tree trunk or branch in full view, more often just out of sight, where it scolds harshly. If followed, it quickly disappears and eventually slips quietly back to the nest. Presumably this performance is a form of distraction display.

FORMICARIIDAE: Antbirds

This family is represented by a variety of species, which may be found in every type of habitat in our islands. Most species are small, many are crested; the sexes are usually dissimilar, males tending to be black or gray, patterned with white, while females are often rufous brown and white. Several species with long legs and short tails are mainly terrestrial; the remainder live in under-growth or the lower branches of trees. Some antbirds associate with army ants and are often found in small groups; others occur singly or in pairs. They are almost entirely insectivorous. Generally skulking in habit, they attract attention with their chuckling or high-pitched whistling calls. These calls serve to maintain contact between pairs amidst thick undergrowth and are heard in all months of the year. The nests of most species are flimsy hammocks slung from low branches; both parents share the nesting duties in those cases covered by our present scanty information. (10)

Great Antshrike: *Taraba major*
"Cou-cou"   **Plate 15(2)**

Habitat and status. A common resident in Trinidad, frequenting second growth in cocoa and citrus plantations, and occasionally forests, at all altitudes; a bird of thick undergrowth. (Specimens: AMNH, ANSP, CM, YPM, LM, BM.)

Range and subspecies. Mexico S to Argentina and Uruguay; *T. m. semifasciatus* (Cabanis) ranges from Colombia and Venezuela to the Guianas and N Brazil.

Description. 8 in. *Male:* upperparts black, with 2 white wing-bars and (usually concealed) white dorsal patch; underparts white; bill heavy, strongly hooked, black; prominent red iris. *Female:* as male, but rich reddish brown above instead of black. *Immature male:* as adult, but with rufous wing-coverts.

Measurements. Wing: 10 males 89–98mm (94.1); 6 females 90–97mm (93.8). Weight: 4 males 50–58gm (55); 1 female 67.5gm* (probably egg-laying).

Voice. Usual call is a series of 30–40 quite musical notes, *pook-pook-pook,* etc., speeding up and ending with a snarl (which may be double). Less usually, a series of louder and less musical notes, starting with a rapid burst and slowing down at the end. Also utters a harsh, scolding churr.

Food. Insects, including beetles, grasshoppers and bees, mostly gleaned from understory foliage; also known to take lizards, seeds and occasionally small mammals.

Nesting. Breeding recorded in March and May–July. The nest is a deep but rather flimsy hammock of dried grass and roots, 3 in. in diameter at the top, 2.5 in. deep, unlined, slung by its rim from a lateral fork up to 8 ft from the ground. Central American nests (Skutch 1969b) have been even larger, and lined with a few leaves. There are 2 or 3 eggs, white covered with gray scrawls and blotches and sometimes a few brown lines, av. 27.8 × 21.7mm (6). Both adults incubate and brood the young. In Costa Rica Skutch found an incubation period of 17 or 18 days, and a fledging period of 12 or 13 days.

Behaviour. This very shy, skulking species is almost always found in pairs and is much more commonly heard than seen. Chapman (1894) describes the threat display of a male, posing with bill pointing vertically up, crest raised and the normally concealed white dorsal patch fully evident. At the Nature Centre a pair has often been found sleeping at night, tucked inside foliage overhanging a path and apparently unconscious of human attention.

Black-crested Antshrike: *Sakesphorus canadensis*
Plate 15(1)

Habitat and status. A common resident in Trinidad, frequenting undergrowth and middle tree levels in mangrove swamps, swampy forests such as Bush-Bush and lowland scrub, usually near water; also common on Gasparee, Monos and Huevos. (Specimens: AMNH, ANSP, YPM, LM, BM, TRVL.)

Range and subspecies. Colombia to Peru, N Brazil and the Guianas; *S. c. trinitatis* (Ridgway) occurs also in NE Venezuela and Guyana.

Description. 6.5 in. *Male:* head and prominent crest black, back brown with mantle rather rufous; wings black with white edges forming bars, short tail black, throat and breast black, rest of underparts gray; bill short, rather stout and hooked. *Female and immature male:* head and crest chestnut, the cheeks barred black and white, upperparts as male but duller; breast dull buff, finely streaked with black; tail browner, tipped white.

Measurements. Wing: 5 males 73–78mm (75); 6 females 68–75mm (71). Weight: 6 males 23.5–26gm (24.9); 8 females 20.5–29.5gm (24.2).

Voice. The song is a regular series of musical notes, usually about 8 in 3 sec, moving up in pitch and gently accelerating. Also heard is a scolding churr and, possibly in alarm, a chuckling series of notes of the same pitch.

Food. Mainly insects, including beetles, plant-bugs and caterpillars, and spiders. Also known to take small lizards and berries.

Nesting. Breeding recorded in May and July (5 nests); moult in November. The nest is a deep but flimsy hammock, usually made of black fibres, slung below a laterally forked branch or vine, often a few feet from the ground, sometimes as high as 36 ft. There are 2 eggs, white with purple spots and lines, av. 22.8 × 17mm (4). Both sexes incubate. In Surinam Haverschmidt (1953b) found breeding in most months of the year; both sexes shared in nest-building, incubating and care of the young. The 2 eggs were laid 2 days apart, the incubation period being 14 days. The eggs were practically never left uncovered, both birds sitting for long periods, the female always during the night. The young, which hatch naked, were fed mostly on insects brought one at a time. The adults carried out nest sanitation.

Behaviour. Frequently found in pairs, mostly in the lower branches of trees. While singing the bird raises its crest, and both head and tail bob in time to the notes. Occasionally the singing is performed as a duet. Haverschmidt (1953b) noticed courtship feeding by the male, followed by copulation.

Barred Antshrike: *Thamnophilus doliatus*
White-barred Bush-shrike; "Pintade"; "Guinea Bird"   **Plate 15(3)**

Habitat and status. A common resident in both islands, frequenting especially semi-open secondary growth, gardens, mangroves and forest edge; on Tobago also found commonly in rain forest up to 2000 ft. (Specimens: Trinidad, AMNH, ANSP, CM, YPM, LM, BM, TRVL; Tobago, AMNH, LM, BM.)

Range and subspecies. Mexico S through Central and South America to Bolivia, N Argentina and Paraguay; *T. d. fraterculus* (Berlepsch & Hartert) occurs in E Colombia, Venezuela and Trinidad; *T. d. tobagensis* (Hartert & Goodson) is confined to Tobago, where the males are whiter below and the females darker.

Description. 6 in. *Male:* black, barred all over with white; crest white tipped with black; iris yellow. *Female:* upperparts chestnut brown, crest chestnut; sides of head and neck buff streaked with black, underparts brownish buff. *Immature:* in changing plumage crown and wing-coverts are the first to show adult feathers. Even in the nest juvenile birds show sex distinctions in plumage.

Measurements. *T. d. fraterculus.* Wing: 25 males 68–77mm (71.2); 17 females 66–73mm (68.5). Weight: 21 males 25–30.5gm (28.0, S.D. 1.5); 11 females 26–30.5gm (27.8). *T. d. tobagensis.* Wing: 5 males 71–77mm (73.6); 6 females 68–75mm (71.5). Weight: 6 males 22–28gm (25.9); 6 females 24.5–30gm (26.6).

Voice. A chuckling series of rather unmusical clucks, *ka-ka-ka,* etc., accelerating rapidly at the end; pairs often duet; alarm call a deep caw; also calls a halting series of 5–6 querulous, semi-musical notes, *kiaw, kiaw,* etc. During the main call the bird bows and bobs its head up and down, keeping it low, and simultaneously wags its tail rapidly.

Food. A large variety of invertebrates, from very small to quite large species, and including ants; also small lizards and berries (11 species recorded). Foraging methods and locations are particularly diverse, enabling considerable habitat niche expansion, especially on Tobago (Keeler-Wolf 1986). Since the 1963 hurricane some birds have occasionally taken soaked bread from feeding tables.

Nesting. Breeding recorded in Trinidad during almost all months with no apparent peak (24 nests); moult also recorded in 10 months. In Tobago breeding recorded from April to August (13 nests); moult June–September; breeding possibly stimulated by locally favourable conditions. The nest is a deep cup of grasses or plant-fibres, suspended by the rim from a lateral fork, usually at a low height but sometimes as high as 30 ft. There are 2, rarely 3, eggs, creamy white marked variously with purple and sometimes pale gray; 7 eggs from Trinidad av. 22.8 × 16.9mm (1 extra long measured 25.1mm). Both sexes incubate. Haverschmidt (1968a) records an incubation period in Surinam of 14 days, and a fledging period of about 12 days (as also in Costa Rica [Skutch 1969b]), but in Trinidad a single nestling left the nest aged 16 days.

Behaviour. These birds are usually found in pairs, and their regular calling in duet through the year suggests a lengthy pair bond, possibly permanent. The male feeds the female during courtship. Generally rather skulking in habits, frequenting low undergrowth, incubating birds sit very tight at the nest, only leaving at the last moment.

Notes. D. W. Snow and Snow (1964) pointed out the high percentage of trapped birds of this species undergoing wing-moult. In addition, the sequence of wing-moult was somewhat irregular.

Plain Antvireo: *Dysithamnus mentalis*
Bush-bird   **Plate 14(5)**

Habitat and status. A common resident of forests at all altitudes in Trinidad, at higher altitudes in Tobago; frequents the lower branches of trees below the canopy. (Specimens: Trinidad, AMNH, ANSP, CM, LM, TRVL; Tobago, AMNH, USNM, FMNH, LM.)

Range and subspecies. Mexico S to Bolivia, N Argentina and Paraguay; *D. m. andrei* (Hellmayr) occurs in NE Venezuela and Trinidad; *D. m. oberi* (Ridgway) is confined to Tobago; the female of the latter race has the lower underparts more yellowish.

Description. 5 in. *Male:* head and upperparts slate gray with blackish cheek-patch and white tips to wing-coverts, forming inconspicuous wing-bars; underparts pale gray, abdomen whitish; bill black. *Female:* crown rufous, upperparts olive brown with wings and tail rufous, the coverts tipped whitish; underparts pale olive. *Immature male:* as adult male, but with flight feathers edged with brown, rump tinged olive, and abdomen yellowish.

Measurements. *D. m. andrei.* Wing: 7 males 58–66mm (62.4); 4 females 60–63mm (61.2). Weight: 9 males 12.5–14.5gm (13.1)*; 5 females 11.5–13gm (12.3)*. *D. m. oberi.* Wing: 10 males 63–66mm (63.5); 6 females 60–63mm (61.7). Weight: 2 males 11, 12.5gm*.

Voice. Song is a series of musical piping notes, accelerating and dying away, the rhythm reminiscent of a bouncing ball coming to rest. Also utters a plaintive piping, *pu-pu,* repeated at intervals, and a deep churring.

Food. Small insects and spiders taken mostly from foliage, less often from open branches; typically gleans like a vireo, but sometimes accompanies army ant swarms.

Nesting. Breeding recorded in Trinidad from April to August (12 nests), but song persists until November. The nest is a small, fairly deep cup slung in the lateral fork of a sapling in the forest a few feet above the ground; it is constructed of stems and a few leaves and tendrils, lined with finer stems and decorated outside with moss, which often hangs down forming a ragged tail. The clutch is 1 or 2 eggs, white marked with cinnamon mainly at the larger end, av. 18.6 × 14.1mm (4). Both sexes share the nesting duties (Lill & ffrench 1970). The young hatch naked. In Costa Rica the incubation and fledging periods are 15 and 9 days, respectively (Skutch 1969b).

Behaviour. Usually found in pairs or small groups foraging in the understory. An incubating or brooding bird, when flushed, usually drops steeply to the ground and flutters conspicuously along in a distraction display. Sometimes during this performance (Skutch 1969b) it reveals a white or, in the female, buff shoulder stripe, which is normally concealed.

White-flanked Antwren: *Myrmotherula axillaris*
White-flanked Ant-bird   **Plate 14(1)**

Habitat and status. A common resident in Trinidad, occurring in primary and secondary forest, where it keeps to the lower branches of trees and saplings. (Specimens: AMNH, ANSP, CM, LM, BM, TRVL.)

Range and subspecies. Honduras S to Bolivia and Brazil; the nominate race ranges from E Venezuela and the Guianas S to Peru, Bolivia and N Brazil.

Description. 4.25 in. *Male:* upperparts dark gray with black wings, the coverts tipped white, appearing as bars of white spots; underparts black, flanks and underwings white with long silky feathers. *Female and immature male:* upperparts brown, wings rufous with indistinct bars on coverts; underparts yellowish buff, flanks white.

Measurements. Wing: 6 males 52–55mm (53.7); 5 females 52–55mm (53). Weight: 10 males 6.5–9.5gm (7.7); 7 females 6.5–9gm (8).

Voice. A somewhat irregular trilling; also utters a querulous *cheew-cheew* and a higher, sharper *queep.*

Food. Small insects, including caterpillars and flies, and spiders.

Nesting. Breeding recorded April–August (5 nests); moult in May, September and October. The nest is a tiny basket of black fibres, decorated with a few dead leaves, slung from a forked twig usually 1.5–4 ft (once 10 ft) from the ground. There are 2 eggs, white scrawled and blotched purple, especially at the larger end, av. 17.8 × 12mm (3). Both adults incubate. Skutch (1969b) records an incubation period of 16 days in Panama.

Behaviour. This species is usually seen in small parties of up to 6 individuals, often associated with other species, travelling restlessly through the middle or lower branches of forest trees. While foraging, this antwren rarely stays still, but flicks its wings constantly, showing little flashes of its contrasting white flanks. It moves rapidly among the leaves and vines like a warbler, searching for tiny insects; sometimes it flies a few feet to seize an insect in mid air. Occasionally a bird holds its wings aloft for a moment in what may be a threat display. Wiley (1971b) suggests that the contrasting plumage may provide a visual signal which maintains the cohesion of the flock.

White-fringed Antwren: *Formicivora grisea*
Black-breasted Antwren; Allied Antwren   **Plate 14(2)**

Habitat and status. A common resident in Tobago, also occurring on Chacachacare and Huevos islands; especially frequents dense second growth, but is also found in forest up to 1800 ft; keeps mostly to undergrowth but also seen foraging to middle levels. (Specimens: Chacachacare, BM; Tobago, LM, BM.)

Range and subspecies. Colombia SE to the Guianas and Brazil; *F. g. intermedia* (Cabanis) occurs in NE Colombia, Venezuela and on Huevos and Chacachacare islands; *F. g. tobagensis* (Dalmas), which is larger, is confined to Tobago.

Description. 5 in. *Male:* crown and upperparts grayish brown, wing-coverts black tipped white, forming 2 wing-bars; tail longish, black tipped white, outer feathers edged white; lower face and underparts black, white stripe from above eye to sides of breast and flanks. *Female:* upperparts as male, white superciliary, underparts buff with dark streaks.

Measurements. *F. g. intermedia.* Wing: 9 males 54–57mm (55.9); 3 females 50–52mm (51.0). Weight: 9 males 9–10gm (9.2); 3 females 9–10.5gm (9.5). *F. g. tobagensis.* Wing: 10 males 50–57mm (54.9); 6 females 53–58mm (55.8). Weight: 10 males 9–14gm (11.2); 6 females 10–12gm (10.7); 9 unsexed 9.5–12.5gm (11).

Voice. Utters a single whistle, *tu,* followed by a soft trill. Also an incisive *tu-ik,* repeated at first slowly, then faster. Sometimes one call merges into the other.

Food. Small insects and spiders gleaned from foliage and twigs.

Nesting. Breeding recorded on Chacachacare and Huevos from June to August; moult in August and September. In Tobago there are 3 nest records in April and August, moult in August and September. The nest is a flimsy hammock of grasses slung in a lateral fork, usually very close to the ground, sometimes as high as 10 ft. There are 2 eggs, creamy marked with purple, especially at the larger end. Two eggs from Chacachacare av. 17.3 × 13.5mm, 4 from Tobago av. 18.4 × 12.7mm. Both sexes incubate.

Behaviour. Frequently found in pairs at all times of the year, and fairly confiding.

Silvered Antbird: *Sclateria naevia*
Stripe-breasted Antwren   **Plate 15(6)**

Habitat and status. A fairly common but local resident in Trinidad, particularly in Nariva, also recorded in mangroves at Caroni and Los Blanquizales; it is also found among streams in parts of the Northern Range, such as Paria and Cumaca; largely terrestrial. (Specimens: AMNH, LM, BM, TRVL.)

Range and subspecies. Colombia to Peru, Bolivia and C Brazil; the nominate race ranges through E Venezuela, the Guianas and NE Brazil.

Description. 6 in. *Male:* upperparts dark grayish brown, wing-coverts tipped with white; throat white with a few dark streaks, rest of underparts gray streaked and spotted with white; tail short; bill long (1 in.), fairly thin, black; legs long. *Female:* as male but browner instead of gray, wing-coverts tipped with buff.

Measurements. Wing: 5 males 67–72mm (69.2); 6 females 68–72mm (69). Weight: 1 male 23gm; 1 female 22gm*.

Voice. A regular, rapid, high-pitched trill, *pi-pi-pi-pi,* etc., sometimes going up or down in pitch.

Food. Insects, including beetles and cockroaches, and spiders.

Nesting. No definite breeding records, but the species' sedentary nature implies local breeding. Calling regular in May.

Behaviour. Usually found skulking in pairs on the ground or low in the thick undergrowth beside streams.

White-bellied Antbird: *Myrmeciza longipes*
Swainson's Ant-wren; "Mad-bird"   **Plate 15(4)**

Habitat and status. A common resident in Trinidad, found in forest at all levels, also in second growth, keeping to the ground or low undergrowth. (Specimens: AMNH, ANSP, CM, LM, BM.)

Range and subspecies. Panama E to Guyana and N Brazil; the nominate race occurs also in NE Colombia and N Venezuela.

Description. 6 in. *Male:* crown and upperparts chestnut brown, sides of head gray, chin, throat and breast black, rest of underparts white; tail short; bill fairly long and thin, blackish; legs long, pink. *Female:* upperparts as male, face gray with darker cheeks, most of underparts whitish with buff throat.

Measurements. Wing: 8 males 64–70mm (66.9); 5 females 62–69mm (65). Weight: 4 males 24.5–28.5gm (26.4)*; 3 females 22.5*, 23, 27gm.

Voice. Usually a loud, ringing series (reminiscent of a woodcreeper), slowing down and ending in several deliberate and less musical notes; also, possibly in alarm, a rapid, rather liquid trill; also a hard, short *chuck* or *cherk*.

Food. Small insects, including beetles, cockroaches, moths, also spiders. Often feeds at army ant swarms, picking up prey mostly from the ground. At other times feeds among dead leaves on the ground, tossing them aside as it forages.

Nesting. Recorded in September and December (Snow, 2 nests). Song recorded throughout the year. Details mistakenly given by B/S for this species probably refer to the Red-crowned Ant-Tanager. Nests of 4 other members of this genus on the mainland of Central and South America are open cups made of dead leaves and roots, lined with fine rootlets and placed on or very near the ground. Eggs are creamy streaked with purplish brown, and clutch size is 2 eggs.

Black-faced Antthrush: *Formicarius analis*
"Cock-of-the-Woods"; "Coq Bois"   **Plate 15(7)**

Habitat and status. A common resident in Trinidad, frequenting forests and second growth, especially in the Northern Range; essentially terrestrial. (Specimens: AMNH, ANSP, CM, LM, BM, TRVL.)

Range and subspecies. Mexico S through Central and South America to Bolivia and C Brazil; *F. a. saturatus* (Ridgway) is found in N Colombia and Venezuela.

Description. 8 in. Upperparts dark brown with rump rufous; face and throat black with conspicuous whitish eye-ring; sides of neck rufous, breast gray, abdomen paler, under-tail-coverts chestnut; tail short, held erect while walking; bill stout, fairly long, black; legs long, plumbeous. Sexes similar.

Measurements. Wing: 12 males 91–96mm (94.3); 6 females 89–93mm (91.8). Weight: 5 males 58–62gm (59.3)*; 1 female 64gm*; 6 unsexed 57–66gm (61.8).

Voice. Typical call is a high, sharp whistle followed by 2–5 more notes descending in pitch; occasionally the first note is followed by a long series of rapid notes, gradually descending in pitch. Also, in alarm, 2 or 3 ringing, explosive notes, *prook,* etc., or a long series of these notes in the form of a trill.

Food. Mostly insects taken from the forest floor, often in association with army ants. In other parts of its range known to take snails, small lizards and snakes.

Nesting. Breeding recorded in March and September (3 nests); moult in November; calling continues throughout the year. The nest of dead leaves and stalks is situated in a hollow treestump. There are 2 white eggs with some variation in size, one clutch av. 27.6 × 21.6mm, another 31.7 × 24.2mm. In Costa Rica Skutch (1969b) found that both sexes of this species incubated and that the young hatch with a considerable covering of dark gray down. Incubation lasts 20 days and fledging 18 days.

Behaviour. Found singly or in groups attending army ants. This rail-like bird rarely leaves the forest floor, but walks briskly about, perching briefly on fallen branches or stumps. If surprised, it flies rapidly for a short distance. It is attracted by an imitation of its call and will approach very close to a quiet observer. Skutch (1969b) records that it flies into its nest-hole in one continuous motion, without the careful inspection of the cavity and its surroundings practised by other hole-nesting birds.

Scaled Antpitta: *Grallaria guatimalensis*
Trinidad Antpitta   **Plate 15(8)**

Habitat and status. A very rare species in Trinidad forests, known from 17 specimens collected high on Aripo by Klages in 1912 and a sight record of 2 birds by Smooker on the Heights of Oropouche in 1925. One good sight record at Springhill on 4 January 1981 (P. Hall). Other possible records from El Tucuche and Matura forest. (Specimens: AMNH.)

Range and subspecies. Mexico S through Central and South America to Ecuador, Peru and N Brazil; *G. g. aripoensis* (Hellmayr & Seilern) is confined to Trinidad; it is smaller than the nominate race, the underparts are brighter and deeper chestnut, and the black markings on the back are larger.

Description. 7.5 in. Crown slate, forehead spotted with buff, upperparts olive brown, the feathers of crown, nape and back edged with black, giving a scaled appearance, wings brown, the secondaries tinged with rufous; face dark gray streaked pale rufous; throat pale rufous, edged black; rest of underparts bright rufous with a few black edges on upper breast; tail very short; legs long; bill stout. A robust bird with apparently no tail.

Measurements. Wing: 11 males 101–105mm; 6 females 98–105mm.

Voice. Unrecorded in Trinidad; in Venezuela a low, resonant series of hoots, lasting about 4 sec and accelerating.

Food. Unrecorded. Probably insects.

Nesting. No definite record, but Smooker suspected that a cup nest of twigs, roots and fibres, placed on dead leaves in an epiphyte 8 ft from the ground, was of this species; the eggs of the Mexican race are pale blue (Edwards 1967).

Behaviour. Essentially a terrestrial species, occasionally flying to a low branch. In Costa Rica Slud (1964) describes its progress as by "leaping, springy hops".

COTINGIDAE: Cotingas

This family consists of birds of varying appearance and size, though most members are characterised by their rounded wings, short legs and broad bills slightly hooked at the tip. In several species there are unique, bizarre features; the bellbirds, for instance, have fleshy wattles protruding from the head or throat. One characteristic behaviour shared by many cotingas is their habit of turning their heads curiously from side to side while otherwise motionless on a perch. The call-notes are diverse, ranging from loud, explosive notes to musical whistling. Nests, too, are of very differing types; in some species the males assist in feeding the young, while in others there is no pair bond. Their food includes both fruits and insects; the lives of many species are spent in the canopy of forest trees. (2)

White Bellbird: *Procnias alba*
Plate 12(9)

Habitat and status. An extremely rare visitor in Trinidad, inhabiting the forest of the Northern Range. Definite records are of male birds, one collected by Léotaud, one by Downs in July 1954; also, birds were seen in Arima Valley in April 1969 and July and September 1989, at Caura in September 1980 and at Hollis Dam in June 1990. Since there has never been evidence of lek formation in Trinidad, these records are presumably of wandering individuals. (Specimen: TRVL.)

Range. Venezuela and the Guianas to N Brazil.

Description. 12 in. *Male:* plumage all white; there is a single wattle, black, up to 3 in. long, which hangs down from the base of the upper mandible. *Female:* upperparts yellowish green, underparts white, the feathers edged with green; no wattle.

Measurements. Wing: 1 male 158mm.

Voice. Two distinct, very loud, calls, both ringing and bell-like in quality. One consists of 1 or 2 similar musical notes, *ding-ding*, resounding for about 1 sec; the other consists of 2 distinct notes, the first lower than the second, *aahn-king*, together lasting perhaps 3 sec.

Food. In Guyana known to eat fruit (Lauraceae).

Behaviour. The male calls for long periods during the day while perching on bare, horizontal branches high in a forest tree. B. K. Snow (1961) observed that in Guyana the bird moved sharply on its perch from right to left while making the *ding-ding* call; as it made this rapid turn, the wattle flew out at an horizontal angle; the wattle was always positioned to the right of the bill before the call was made. Once the bird jumped 2 ft to the left while calling, in what may have been a stereotyped courtship manoeuvre. After calling, as the bird prepared to leave the perch, its wattle contracted to a third of its former length.

@ O'Neill - 1990

Figure 37. Bearded Bellbird (male)

Bearded Bellbird: *Procnias averano*
Mossy-throated Bellbird; Black-winged Bellbird; "Campanero";
"Anvil-bird"   **Plates 12(6) and 29(2), and Figure 37**

Habitat and status. A fairly common resident in Trinidad, frequenting forests and second growth on the edge of forest at all levels up to 2000 ft. (Specimens: AMNH, ANSP, YPM, CM, LM, BM.)

Range and subspecies. NE Colombia, Venezuela, Guyana and N and E Brazil; *P. a. carnobarba* (Cuvier) occurs throughout the range except for E Brazil.

Description. 11 in. *Male:* generally whitish with coffee brown head and black wings; bare throat with numerous black, string-like wattles hanging down. *Female and immature male:* upperparts olive green, underparts yellowish streaked with green, throat gray with fine pale streaks.

Measurements. Wing: 6 males 158–166mm (160); 3 females 137, 145, 154mm; 1 immature male 135mm; 4 unsexed in immature plumage 133–138mm (135.2). Weight: 1 male 178gm*; 1 female 126.5gm; 1 immature male 114gm; 5 unsexed 111–130gm (119.9).

Voice. The male gives 2 distinct calls. One is a very loud, explosive, single note, *bock,* uttered at intervals of a few seconds. The other is a more musical series of similarly pitched notes, resembling the regular blows of a hammer on an anvil, *tonk-tonk-tonk* . . . , uttered at the rate of 1–2.5 notes per sec. Females apparently do not call. In Venezuela the species also makes a musical disyllabic *kay-kerong;* this call is never heard in Trinidad nowadays, though it is likely that 100 yr ago it was (Brewster and Chapman 1895).

Food. Fruit, taken on the wing; 20 families of plants (mostly trees) have been recorded (B. K. Snow 1970), but most important are the Lauraceae and the Burseraceae, of which the pericarps are especially rich in protein and fat. Mostly drupes are taken, the large seed being regurgitated. The nestling is fed on regurgitated fruit, especially *Ocotea oblonga* and *Cinnamomum elongatum,* both Lauraceae of high nutritive value.

Nesting. There are 7 breeding records from April to August and 1 each in October and November. Moult must occur from August to mid-October, the only time when males do not call from their territories. The nest is situated in a variety of trees, 8–50 ft above ground, usually in a semi-open area near forest. It is an inconspicuous, flimsy-looking structure of twigs with a main platform about 7 in. in diameter, made mostly of the white olivier (*Terminalia obovata*), and a central cup 2 in. in diameter, made of twigs of the ti-fay (*Maprounea guianensis*). The female, who carries out all nesting duties, takes about 5 days to build the nest, grasping the interlocking twigs with her feet and forcing them into shape with her breast. The clutch is 1 egg, light tan mottled with brown, 1 measuring 40.3 × 28.4mm. Incubation lasts for 23 days, the female spending up to 87% of daylight hours at the nest. The only nestling ever studied (B. K. Snow 1970) hatched with a covering of thick, whitish down. Except at the beginning, the female hardly brooded the nestling by day, and for 23 days it stayed remarkably motionless and silent even during feeding. The female carried out nest sanitation and removed regurgitated seeds. At 33 days old the nestling flew, having spent the last few days perched beside the nest. Adult male plumage is not attained for about 2.5 yr, and the adult call is not fully developed till about 2 yr old.

Behaviour. Since the females alone look after nesting, adult males are free to be polygamous. They own permanent calling territories within forest below 2000 ft, in groups of 3 or 4 birds. Here the male spends up to 87% of the daylight hours throughout the whole year, except for the period of moult, during which time immature males may temporarily take over the territory. The calling takes place either on understory saplings 20–30 ft high with a series of long slender side-branches or on a high perch above the forest canopy with a clear view round about. From the latter the male calls especially the far-carrying *bock* call, regularly turning to face a new direction, and he tends to call here when a neighbour is nearby. When visited by another bellbird, the male in a ritualized display shows off his black-and-white plumage and wattles by jumping from branch to branch of the understory sapling and posturing with fanned tail and wattles pushed forward by his erect breast feathers. He also display-preens, showing off his brown crown and a patch of bare skin on the thigh. As the display proceeds, the bird moves steadily down the sapling, the position of dominance being the lowest. If a male visitor persists, the displaying male finally leaps along the branch towards him making the *bock* call, which causes the other to go. A similar procedure occurs with a female visitor, which may then culminate in mating if the female does not leave. It seems that the female visits all the calling males in a group one after the other (B. K. Snow 1970).

PIPRIDAE: Manakins

Members of this family are small forest birds usually with short wings and tails, and short, broad-based bills. While females are predominantly dull green, the males are usually black with patches of brilliant colours. They feed mainly on fruits taken on the wing. The ready availability of fruit year-round in the tropics enables manakins to spend much time on other activities (D. W. Snow 1985a). Manakins are notable for their elaborate courtship displays, which vary considerably within the family; most of these involve assemblies of male birds sometimes known as "leks". The nest is a flimsy hammock built onto a low sapling or fern, often near water; the female alone cares for the eggs and young, as far as is known, and there is no pair bond. Their call-notes take the form of abrupt chirps and whistles, hardly qualifying for the title of song, but several species also produce bizarre sounds mechanically. Recapture data on marked birds have revealed that the annual survival rate is high, as much as 89% in *Manacus;* individuals have been found with a *minimal* age of 14 yr (*Manacus*) and 12 yr (*Pipra*) in Trinidad (D. W. Snow & Lill 1974), while I have recorded a male *Chiroxiphia* aged at least 15 yr on Tobago. (3)

Golden-headed Manakin: *Pipra erythrocephala*
Plate 16(1)

Habitat and status. A very common resident in Trinidad, frequenting forests and second growth, mostly in the middle or lower branches of trees. (Specimens: AMNH, ANSP, CM, YPM, LM, BM, TRVL.)

Range and subspecies. Panama and E Colombia south to N Peru, the Guianas and Brazil; the nominate race ranges from N Brazil and the Guianas northwards.

Description. 3.5 in. *Male:* all black with a golden orange cap, thighs white with lower edge red; bill yellowish; iris white. *Female and immature male:* generally olive green, paler below; bill horn brown; iris dark or spotted with white; legs of both sexes pink. (There is a considerable variation in plumage, apart from occasional albinism. Both females and immature males regularly have a few male-type feathers in head or body; some adult males have a few female-type feathers.)

Measurements. Wing: 183 adult males 52–60mm (56.7 S.D. 1.2); 19 immature males 56–60mm (58.6); 46 females 54–62mm (58.7, S.D. 1.5). Weight: 291 adult males 10.5–17gm (12.8, S.D. 0.97); 9 immature males 12–13.5gm (12.7); 214 females 12–16.5gm (14.1, S.D. 0.97). (The greater weights were recorded mainly in the breeding season and were probably of egg-laying birds.)

Voice. Various sharp, buzzing trills and whistles. Just before display, males call *pu*, or a trill flanked by sharper notes, *pir pir prrrrr-pt-pt*. During various displays males call a sharp *zit zit, kew kew* or *zeek*.

Food. The small berries of many forest plants (43 species recorded), especially Melastomaceae; also insects, including beetles, flies and caterpillars, and spiders. Both insects and fruit are taken from the foliage by birds in flight. One male watched for a whole day (D. W. Snow 1962c) spent no more than 11% of the daylight hours feeding.

Nesting. Breeding extends from January to August, though occupied nests have been recorded only in January, March (2), June (4), July (5) and August; peak of breeding activity April–June; annual moult August–November (3 months for each bird). The nest is a shallow cup (less than 3 in. diameter) slung between the lateral fork of a sapling or branch, 4–35 ft above ground, probably high as a general rule. It is constructed of rootlets and fibres and often has a few leaves, etc., hanging beneath. The clutch is 1 or 2 eggs, yellowish, thickly spotted and streaked with brown at the thicker end, av. 19.3 × 14.7mm (2). There is a 2-day gap between the laying of the eggs, the female incubating alone for 16 or 17 days. Rate of nest failure is high (D. W. Snow 1962c).

Behaviour. The males spend most of their time, except during the moult, displaying at traditional display "grounds" in groups of 6–12 birds. Each male occupies a particular perch, 20–40 ft above ground, usually a small horizontal branch under the tree canopy. Display movements and postures are very diverse (D. W. Snow 1962c); they include darting rapidly to another perch and back, facing about with a flick of wings, moving (or "sliding") sideways or backwards very rapidly along the perch with tail raised, raising the wings horizontally or vertically above the back and jumping up from the perch with wings fluttering. In a display flight the male leaves his perch for another and returns to it very fast with an S-shaped trajectory, sometimes following this with the backward "slide". Most of these movements are accompanied by stereotyped calls. In an aggressive pose directed at an intruder a male holds for some seconds a statuesque upright posture with head pointed upwards, bill slightly open and pupils greatly contracted. When not actually displaying, two neighbouring males often sit side by side on a "neutral" perch. When a female visits the display ground, an outburst of display ensues; occasionally mating takes place on the perch. Sometimes birds in immature plumage (probably males) are seen performing somewhat incomplete and uncoordinated displays away from the traditional grounds.

Notes. Junge and Mees (1958) described the birds of this species in Trinidad as a separate race, *flavissima,* on the basis of larger size and the fact that the female-plumaged birds are more yellow on the underparts and more yellowish green on the upperparts than the nominate race. However, their distinctions seem too slight and their sample too small to warrant this separation.

Blue-backed Manakin: *Chiroxiphia pareola*
Tobago Manakin; "Weeks"　　**Plate 16(6)**

Habitat and status. A fairly common but local resident in Tobago, inhabiting forest mainly at higher altitudes, but also found in secondary growth near sea level. (Specimens: AMNH, LM, BM.)

Range and subspecies. Colombia and Venezuela S to the Guianas, Bolivia and Brazil; *C. p. atlantica* (Dalmas) is confined to Tobago; it is larger than the nominate race and the bright colours of the crest and mantle are more extensive.

Description. 5.5 in. *Male:* all black with scarlet V-shaped patch on crown and sky blue mantle; legs pale orange. *Female:* olive green, lower underparts yellowish; legs yellow. *Immature males:* resemble females, but older birds begin to show red on crown and some blue on back.

Measurements. Wing: 15 males 74–81mm (78.2); 5 females 73–77mm (75.8). Weight: 10 males 20–24.5gm (22.5); 2 females 22, 24gm.

Voice. Frequently a soft chirrup. Various other calls are associated with display (D. W. Snow 1963); they include a sharp, high-pitched single or double note, *whee* or *whee-whew,* a rolling churr, followed by an abrupt *chup,* often repeated 2 or 3 times, sometimes uttered by 2 males in synchrony, and a vibrant buzzing or twanging note, repeated by the males while displaying and ending with one or more sharper notes; rather rarely, a low, musical double note, *coo-ee,* is uttered.

Food. Berries, including *Norantea;* also insects.

Nesting. Only one record, in July 1974 at Grafton, but courtship display is common from early in the year. The nest was a deep but flimsy cup of rootlets with a base of dead leaves, saddled in a lateral fork about 6 ft above ground. The clutch was 2 eggs, dull ivory spotted with dark brown, av. 24.5 × 18.1mm (2).

Behaviour. The males perform a remarkable joint display (D. W. Snow 1963). They use for a display perch a bare stick, horizontal or sloping, a few feet above ground in the forest. These perches are traditional and may be in small groups; the birds clear the leaves from branches in the vicinity of the perches. On the perch one male may be dominant, but the group of display perches seems to be the common property of a group of males, which move from one perch to another (Gilliard 1959b, D. W. Snow 1971, 1977). From a high branch nearby 1 male calls to another; the 2 males perch side by side and utter the *chup* calls in unison (1 bird in fact calling about 0.05 sec later than the other). Sometimes, after the synchronized calling, the 2 males jump up and down alternately on the display perch, uttering the buzzing note; when a female comes to the perch, the 2 males continue their alternate jumping, facing the female, but now the joint movement becomes circular as the perching bird moves forward under the jumping bird, which moves backwards in flight before landing. Occasionally immature males join the display or take the place of the female, intently watching the performers. As many as 8 males may be involved in a group of 3 display perches. The end of a bout of jumping is usually signalled by one or more very sharp notes, following which the birds disperse. While these various joint displays serve the purpose of attracting females to the display perch, another display preceding copulation is performed by 1 male only, who crosses and recrosses the perch with a buoyant, bouncing flight, occasionally uttering a low twanging note, while the female watches, continually turning to face the male. Sometimes the male crouches, head down, displaying his red cap and blue mantle. As he takes off, his wings apparently make a soft, mechanical click, but it is not known how this is done.

White-bearded Manakin: *Manacus manacus*
Black-and-white Manakin; "Casse Noisette"; "Stickman"   **Plate 16(5)**

Habitat and status. A common resident in Trinidad, inhabiting forests, second growth and cocoa or citrus estates; keeps to undergrowth and lower branches. (Specimens: AMNH, ANSP, CM, YPM, LM, BM, TRVL.)

Range and subspecies. Colombia and Venezuela S to Bolivia, N Argentina and Paraguay; *M. m. trinitatis* (Hartert) is confined to Trinidad, being a little larger than the nominate race, while the female has yellower underparts.

Description. 4.5 in. *Male:* crown, upper back, wings and tail black; lower back gray; rest of head, neck and underparts white; legs orange. *Female and immature male:* generally olive green, darker than the female Golden-headed Manakin; legs *orange*. In flight the wings whirr audibly, especially the adult male's. Immature males moult into adult plumage in June–September of the year following their year of birth.

Measurements. Wing: 63 adult males 51–55mm (52.4, S. D. 1.1); 41 immature males 52–57mm (54.9, S.D. 1.2); 82 females 53–57mm (54.7, S.D. 0.95). Weight: 191 adult males 16–23gm (18.5, S.D. 1.3); 58 immature males 14–19.5gm (17.3, S.D. 1.2); 344 females 14–21.5gm (16.8, S.D. 1.3). (All female weights of 19.5gm upwards were recorded in the breeding season, and many were known or suspected to be egg-laying.)

Voice. Usually a musical *peerr,* slightly trilled. In display males make a variety of sounds, including a loud, high *chwee,* and *chee-poo;* they also produce a sharp snap or rapid series of snaps by means of their highly modified secondaries.

Food. Fruit, mainly small berries of Melastomaceae (66 species of plants recorded by D. W. Snow [1962a]), which are taken in flight; also insects, including beetles, flies and flying termites, especially in the breeding season.

Nesting. Breeding recorded from December to September, but the beginning of the season varies from year to year, with the peak normally in May and June. D. W. Snow (1962a) recorded 272 nests as follows:

I	II	III	IV	V	VI
9	23	19	27	46	69

VII	VIII	IX	X	XI	XII
37	35	6	—	—	1

Annual moult recorded between July and December (individuals taking about 80 days to moult). The nest is a flimsy, shallow cup of rootlets lined with fine panicles of a melastomaceous herb, slung between the forked branches of a sapling or on a fern, a few feet above ground, often beside a stream. The clutch is 2 eggs, rarely 1, dull white with brown streaks mainly at the larger end, av. 21×15.7mm (2). Incubation lasts 18–19 days, and fledging 13–15 days. The young are fed, by regurgitation, on fruit (mainly) and insects. A female may nest 2–4 times in a season, the interval between broods being at least 3 wk.

Behaviour. The males spend much of their time (90% of daylight hours for one individual) displaying at communal display grounds. D. W. Snow (1962a) found that display at these traditional grounds continued all year but was reduced during the moult; display goes on all day, with peak periods soon after dawn and in early afternoon. Each male clears a "court" on the forest floor, 1 or 2 ft square, and displays on the small saplings bordering it; the court is a patch of bare earth with all leaves and small twigs removed. The number of courts in one display ground varied from a few to 70; these leks are larger in Trinidad than among mainland populations (Olson & McDowell 1983). The various display movements include leaping from one perch to another with a loud wing-snap, leaping from a perch to the ground and back again, fanning the wings, and "sliding" headforemost down a vertical sapling. All these movements are extremely rapid and most are accompanied by stereotyped mechanical sounds made by the wings. Though all the display postures and movements occur without the presence of a female, when a female does appear there is a frenzy of activity as several males compete for her attention. Copulation is usually preceded by a regular sequence of display by both birds. No pairs are found, both males and females copulating apparently indiscriminately, though certain individual males seem to be more successful then others. Neighbouring males tolerate each other on neutral ground, but each fiercely defends his court. Established males are rarely dispossessed, and vacant courts are the subject of keen competition; it may take many months for a young male to obtain a court at a regular display ground, and some birds display intermittently at separate "practice" courts. The females visit the display grounds in small groups at the beginning of the season, when display is rather confused and copulation rare. Later the females visit singly and coordinated displays are common.

TYRANNIDAE: Tyrant Flycatchers

This family is represented in our area by a larger number of species than any other, and these show great diversity in habitat and habits. Most species are of medium or small size with rather nondescript plumage in dull green, brown or yellow, the sexes being similar. Many are crested, with concealed crown-patches, while eye-stripes and wing-bars are common. Bills vary considerably, but many are broad at the base and flattened, with prominent rictal bristles. Members of this family may best be recognised by their upright, alert posture at a perch and by the habit, well-developed in many species, of flying from the perch to seize an insect in mid air and returning to the same perch. Flycatchers also often feed on fruit, and some include in their diet reptiles, rodents or small birds. Their song is not very developed, but distinctive call-notes are often the best means of identifying the more confusing species. Nests are of many kinds, including cups, balls with side entrances and nests in holes. Both parents share in the nesting duties, some species being fiercely territorial. Though most species in our area are sedentary, several others migrate from North or South America. (39)

Pied Water-Tyrant: *Fluvicola pica*
White-shouldered Water-tyrant; "Washerwoman"; "Nun"   **Plate 18(9)**

Habitat and status. A common resident of Trinidad, inhabiting the edges of mangrove swamps and marshy savannahs, occasionally ponds and reservoirs; some local movement indicated by the occurrence of an individual on Soldado Rock in August. (Specimens: AMNH, ANSP, CM, YPM, LM, TRVL.)

Range and subspecies. E Panama and Colombia S to Bolivia and Argentina; the nominate race ranges as far south as N Brazil and the Guianas.

Description. 6 in. *Adult:* generally white with black wings, tail, nape and mantle. *Immature:* as adult but dark brown instead of black. Bill black. The male is slightly larger.

Measurements. Wing: 7 males 64–68mm (66.1); 7 females 59–66mm (61.1). Weight: 3 males 12, 12, 12.5gm*; 3 females 11, 11.5, 11.5gm.

Voice. A metallic, nasal, buzzing note, *djweeoo.*

Food. Insects, including froghoppers, caterpillars and small beetles; usually feeds amongst vegetation at water's edge, but occasionally catches tiny insects by hovering just above the water.

Nesting. Breeding recorded from June to October (12 nests) and once in January, but birds may be found in the vicinity of nests in most other months;

moult recorded in June and November–January. The nest is an oval ball of dried grass, plant-down (often *Gossypium*) and leaves, lined with feathers, usually white ones; the opening is at one side near the top. It is placed in a conspicuous spot at the end of a branch, on a stump, or in a small bush. Most nests are low, often over water, others may be as high as 30 ft. The clutch is 2 or 3 eggs, white with a few brown spots at the larger end, av. 17.2 × 13.3mm (8). Both sexes build the nest, incubate and attend the young. The species is sometimes parasitised by the cowbird *Molothrus*.

Behaviour. Usually found singly or in pairs, this species is seen feeding in ditches or on low vegetation, often mangroves. When perched or on the ground, it bobs up and down conspicuously and does not seem very wary. In display makes a "butterfly" flight with rounded wings and fanned tail.

White-headed Marsh-Tyrant: *Arundinicola leucocephala*
"Widow"; "Nun"   **Plate 18(10)**

Habitat and status. A common resident in Trinidad, found on marshy savannahs, reed-beds and the edge of mangrove swamps. (Specimens: AMNH, ANSP, YPM, LM, TRVL.)

Range. Colombia and Venezuela S to Bolivia, Argentina and Paraguay.

Description. 5 in. *Male:* all black, with entire head and neck white; bill fairly short, lower mandible yellow. *Female and immature male:* upperparts ash gray with dark brown wings; forehead, sides of head and underparts white.

Measurements. Wing: 6 males 59–66mm (63); 5 females 55–62mm (58.8). Weight: 1 male 13gm; 2 females 12, 12.5gm*.

Voice. Usually silent; call-note a very high-pitched single note, *tzeek*.

Food. Insects, including dragonflies, grasshoppers, froghoppers (*Tomaspis*) and beetles.

Nesting. Breeding recorded from January to April (6 nests) and July to October (8 nests). The nest resembles that of the Pied Water-Tyrant in location and appearance, but always has a "porch" over the opening, obscuring the entrance. The clutch is 2–4 creamy white eggs, av. 19.2 × 14mm (8). Both sexes build the nest and attend the eggs and young. The cowbird *Molothrus* commonly parasitises this species.

Behaviour. Usually seen singly or in pairs, perching conspicuously on a low branch. Rarely seen on the ground like the Pied Water-Tyrant.

Bright-rumped Attila: *Attila spadiceus*
Polymorphic Attila   **Plate 17(4)**

Habitat and status. A rather uncommon and local resident in Trinidad, inhabiting forests, cocoa plantations and second growth both in the Northern Range and Bush-Bush swamp forest. (Specimens: AMNH, YPM, TRVL.)

Range and subspecies. Mexico S to S Brazil; the nominate race ranges from E Colombia, Venezuela and the Guianas S to Peru, Bolivia and N Brazil.

Description. 8 in. Plumage varies. Upperparts either greenish or rufous brown, the wings edged olive or chestnut, *rump bright yellow or buff;* underparts pale buff or greenish, sometimes streaked with brown; tail short; bill black. This species resembles a *Myiarchus* flycatcher with a large head.

Measurements. Wing: 1 female 90mm.

Voice. Usually a loud, penetrating sequence of whistles, possibly rendered *twick, tweed-it, tweed-it . . . tweed,* rising in pitch slightly and getting louder. Also heard are a quick succession of full, loud whistles, followed by a pause, then a softer double note, *weep-weep-weep-weep, weetoo.* The last double note may be uttered by itself, sometimes *weetootoo.* Also a bubbling, flute-like sequence, *too-i, too-i, too-i,* etc., and a rapid, woodpecker-like rattle, *kikikikiki.*

Food. Recorded in other parts of its range are insects, including butterflies, small lizards and frogs; feeds among upper or middle branches.

Nesting. Breeding recorded in March and April (2 nests). Calling regularly heard except July–September. One nest was placed in a tree-hole and was constructed of stems and small twigs; another was 3 ft up on the side of a low bank, constructed of moss and lined with black rootlets. The clutch is 2–4 eggs, creamy white heavily marked with purple brown, av. 23.7 × 17.2mm (2). In Costa Rica only the female incubates (Skutch 1971), but the male attends nearby and escorts her to the nest. Incubation lasts at least 18 days and fledging a similar time. Newly hatched nestlings are covered with dark gray down.

Behaviour. An active and noisy species, which keeps hidden in thick cover; usually solitary.

Fork-tailed Flycatcher: *Tyrannus savana*
"Scissors-tail"; "Swallow"; *Muscivora savana;*
Muscivora tyrannus   **Figure 38**

Habitat and status. The nominate race is an abundant visitor to Trinidad, frequenting savannahs and foothills of the Northern Range, roosting in mangroves; regularly present in large numbers June–September, earliest 5 May, latest 10 October, a few individuals 5 and 12 April and 16 November. Also regular in Tobago. (Specimens: AMNH, ANSP, YPM.) *T. s. monachus* (Hartlaub) occurs in much smaller numbers in similar habitat in Trinidad from November to February. It is possible that it is present in other months but escapes notice. (Specimens: LM, TRVL.)

Range and subspecies. The nominate race breeds in Argentina and Chile, migrating north to N South America, including offshore islands, vagrants

Figure 38. Fork-tailed Flycatcher

reaching Grenada and Barbados; *monachus* breeds in Central America from Mexico S and in Colombia and Venezuela; it is also known from the Guianas and N Brazil; a third race occurs in Colombia. *T. s. monachus* may be distinguished from the nominate race by its much paler gray back with a whitish collar; in addition, only the outer 2 primaries of the adult male are deeply notched (whereas in *tyrannus* the outer 3 are notched; see Zimmer 1937).

Description. 12–16 in. Head black with concealed yellow crown-patch, back gray with rump and tail black, wings brown; underparts white. Very long outer tail, *male:* 11 in., *female:* 7 in. Bill black, medium-sized. Many birds are seen during June–September in heavy moult without the long tail.

Measurements. *T. s. tyrannus.* Wing: 1 female 112mm; 3 unsexed 108, 112, 115mm. *T. s. monachus.* Wing: 1 male 106mm; 1 female 99mm. Weight: 1 male 30gm*; 1 female 29.5gm*.

Voice. Rather silent usually; sometimes utters a sharp *tick*.

Food. Insects, especially froghoppers (*Tomaspis*), beetles, mole crickets, termites, caterpillars and flying ants, and millipedes; also berries and seeds.

Nesting. No records in Trinidad, but Friedmann and Smith (1955) recorded a nest of *monachus* during May in NE Venezuela, where apparently the breeding season extends to September.

Behaviour. During the day this species feeds in loose flocks, perching on posts, wires and other lookout positions on the savannah, frequently also on the ground. It hawks for prey like a typical flycatcher or seizes it amidst the grass. It is extremely aggressive, harassing a variety of other species, including the Osprey, Scarlet Ibis, Striated Heron, Wattled Jacana and Purple Gallinule. In the evening it gathers in traditional roosts, which may be in mangroves (both Caroni swamp and Monkey Point are well known) or in the forest at Arena and in the Caura Valley (Herklots). Flocks fly to the roosts during the last hour of daylight, radiating inwards from a large area. The birds fly steadily in extended formation with several yards between each individual, in this way filling the sky as far as an observer can see. Very large numbers inhabit each roost. Birds making for Monkey Point from the Oropouche Lagoon fly over the sea for a considerable distance. If caught by a heavy rain shower they settle temporarily in the nearest cover.

Notes. Friedmann and Smith (1955) state that in Venezuela both races are present from May to October, but that *tyrannus* is mainly found in open country in the vicinity of woods, while *monachus* prefers open savannah. However, they and Haverschmidt (1968a) in Surinam have found mixed flocks. Thus there is the unusual situation of an abundant species with 2 similar races in the same area during the breeding season of one of them. Though the species has not been found to breed in Trinidad, the possibility is not at all remote. Further studies on the distribution and ecology of the different races of this species should prove very interesting.

Tropical Kingbird: *Tyrannus melancholicus*
Lichtenstein's Kingbird; Yellow Kingbird; Grey-headed Kiskadee;
"Yellow-belly"   **Plate 17(9)**

Habitat and status. A common resident in both islands, inhabiting semi-open areas with trees, gardens and roadsides, also edges of mangrove swamps. (Specimens: AMNH, ANSP, CM, YPM, LM, TRVL.)

Range and subspecies. S USA south to N Argentina; *T. m. chloronotus* (Berlepsch) ranges from Mexico S through Central America to Panama, N Colombia and Venezuela and offshore islands, including Curaçao and Grenada.

Description. 8.5 in. Head gray with concealed orange crown-patch and blackish eye-streak; upperparts gray tinged green, wings and tail brown; throat whitish, breast greenish yellow, rest of underparts lemon yellow; bill black, fairly stout. *Immature:* has wing-coverts conspicuously edged with pale buff. (See also Gray Kingbird.)

Measurements. Wing: 4 males 112–116mm (113.5); 5 females 107–115mm (111). Weight: 2 males 37, 39gm*; 4 females 31.5–37.5gm (34.2)*; 4 unsexed 35–44.5gm (39.1).

Voice. A high-pitched, twittering trill; at dawn the male sings a series of thin, single notes, *pit-pit-pit*, etc., interspersed with short trills, *tsirrr*.

Food. Mainly flying insects, including beetles, flies, bees and wasps, dragonflies, locusts, butterflies and moths, termites; also caterpillars, cicadas and plant-bugs; berries.

Nesting. Breeding recorded from January to August, with 33 of 44 recorded nests in Trinidad found from April to July; in Tobago nesting recorded in February, June (4) and July (5); moult recorded in August and October. The nest is a rather flimsy, shallow cup of twigs, lined with rootlets and sometimes grass, placed conspicuously in a tree at any height from 3 to 70 ft (usually 8–20). Recorded clutches are 2 (× 14) or 3 (× 5) eggs, creamy white boldly marked with reddish brown spots and streaks, av. 23.3 × 16.1mm (10). The incubation period is 16 days. In Central America (Skutch 1960) only the female builds the nest and incubates, attending the eggs for about 66% of the daylight hours. The male assists in feeding the young, which fly after 18 or 19 days.

Behaviour. Though occasionally seen in loose flocks, this species is usually found in pairs sitting on conspicuous perches, from which it sallies out after prey or to harry another species, usually larger. I have known it to attack a Magnificent Frigatebird, Gray Hawk and Aplomado Falcon, also numerous smaller species, which however it rarely seems to harm. In courtship display birds call shrilly and persistently from a perch, flapping their wings with head lowered and bill pointed towards the ground. Both species of kingbirds and the Fork-tailed Flycatcher have been seen drinking in flight from the surface of ponds and lakes, often in small flocks.

Gray Kingbird: *Tyrannus dominicensis*
White-breasted Kingbird

Habitat and status. A rather uncommon and local resident in Trinidad, frequenting the edges of savannahs and marshes where there are tall trees. Increased records from September to April indicate migration from the north. In Tobago also resident, seemingly more common and in a broader habitat overlapping that of *T. melancholicus*, numbers increasing similarly. (Specimens: AMNH, LM.)

Range and subspecies. Extreme SE USA south through the West Indies and Central America to Colombia, Venezuela and the Guianas; the nominate race breeds in USA, the Greater Antilles, N Colombia and Venezuela, including offshore islands; the more northern birds winter on the Caribbean coast of Central America, both coasts of Panama and in N South America; *T. d. vorax* (Vieillot) breeds in the Lesser Antilles, some migrating S to the Guianas; some of this race are to be expected here.

Description. 9 in. Resembles Tropical Kingbird, but larger with a *heavier bill;* upperparts gray with dark brown wings and tail, underparts *white* with gray breast.

Measurements. Wing: 2 males 113, 116mm. Weight: 3 females 40.5, 42.5, 46gm*; 2 unsexed 43, 46gm.

Voice. A shrill, rolling trill, *pipiri pipiri,* louder and harsher than Tropical Kingbird.

Food. Mainly insects, including beetles and dragonflies. On Bonaire (Voous 1957) it feeds also on cicadas, wasps, grasshoppers and caterpillars; also on lizards, berries, big seeds and even small fish.

Nesting. Breeding recorded in Trinidad between May and September (4 nests, B/S), in Tobago May–July (4 nests); moult in July. The nest resembles that of the Tropical Kingbird, being placed in a tree 6–20 ft above ground. The clutch is 2 eggs, pinkish cream, with longitudinal markings in 2 shades of reddish brown forming a ring at the larger end, av. 25.9 × 18.6mm (6).

Behaviour. Almost all records of birds seen outside the breeding season are of single birds; a few are of small groups of up to 5 individuals.

Sulphury Flycatcher: *Tyrannopsis sulphurea*
Plate 17(5)

Habitat and status. A rare and local resident in Trinidad, found on savannahs where moriche palms (*Mauritia*) grow, as on Aripo Savannah, Erin, near La Brea, also Bush-Bush Forest. (Specimen: AMNH.)

Range. Locally in Colombia, Venezuela, the Guianas, Ecuador, Peru and Brazil.

Description. 7.5 in. Rather similar to Tropical Kingbird, but shorter and more heavily built. Head and neck *dark gray,* with concealed yellow crown-patch; back dull olive, wings and tail brown; throat grayish white, breast greenish yellow, rest of underparts bright yellow; bill black, *broad* and *shorter* than that of kingbird.

Measurements. Wing: 1 female 106mm. Weight: males 52–61gm; females 52–59gm. (From Haverschmidt 1968a, in Surinam.)

Voice. A very noisy, confused squealing note, *jweez* or *jweez-y-jweez.*

Food. Insects and berries.

Nesting. Breeding recorded in April (B/S). The nest is an open cup of sticks placed in the leafy crown of a *Mauritia* palm. The clutch is 2 eggs, creamy buff heavily blotched with umber brown and clouded with pale violet, av. 25.2 × 19mm (2).

Behaviour. A noisy, conspicuous species, often found in small groups and keeping mainly to the tops of the palms.

Variegated Flycatcher: *Empidonomus varius*
Varied Flycatcher   **Plate 17(3)**

Habitat and status. An uncommon visitor to Trinidad, recorded by Roberts (4 specimens) near Brighton in August 1931, and by Plowden-Wardlaw at Cocos Bay in August 1950; also occasionally seen in Arima Valley and Waller Field at forest edge. (Specimens: ANSP, YPM.)

Range and subspecies. Colombia S to Paraguay and Argentina; *E. v. septentrionalis* (Todd) ranges from E Colombia to N Venezuela; a southern race migrates to N South America.

Description. 7 in. Crown dark brown with concealed yellow crown-patch, prominent white superciliary streak above dark eye-streak; back brown, wings darker, the primaries edged rufous, rest of wings and coverts edged with white; rump and tail dark brown, *edged with rufous;* underparts pale brown, becoming yellow on abdomen and breast and flanks streaked blackish; bill black. (See also Piratic Flycatcher.)

Voice. Usually quiet in Trinidad; in Guyana utters a rather harsh *chee-chee-chu,* the final syllable prolonged, or a high, thin *zree* (Snyder 1966).

Food. In Surinam mainly insects, also berries (Haverschmidt 1968); in the Orinoco region berries and small fruits (Cherrie 1916).

Piratic Flycatcher: *Legatus leucophaius*
Black-banded Petchary   **Plate 17(6)**

Habitat and status. A fairly common breeding bird in Trinidad, found in semi-open country with large trees, cultivated areas with shade trees, forest clearings and edges up to 1000 ft; apparently absent from N Trinidad from October to January (February or March arrival dates in Arima Valley [D. W. Snow]; leaving in September), but I have December and January records; probably some birds migrate to the mainland. Also visits Tobago, recorded in March–April at Charlotteville, Hillsborough and Bloody Bay; all were associating with Crested Oropendolas. (Specimens: AMNH, ANSP, CM, YPM, TRVL.)

Range and subspecies. Mexico S to Bolivia and Argentina; the nominate race ranges from Nicaragua southwards.

Description. 6 in. Similar to Variegated Flycatcher but smaller; also *lacks the rufous edges* to primaries, rump and tail; tail shorter; bill black, short and broad at base.

Measurements. Wing: 3 males 83, 87, 88mm; 4 females 73–82mm (77). Weight: 1 male 21gm; 1 female 22gm.

Voice. Usually a double call consisting of a penetrating whistle, *pee-yee*, followed a second later by a tittering *pe-de-de-dee;* also utters a monotonous, repeated *weep weep weep,* etc.

Food. Mainly berries; also insects, including dragonflies.

Nesting. Breeding recorded from February to August (11 nests). This species does not build its own nest but uses those of other species, usually dispossessing the builders as soon as the structure is complete. The hosts include *Psarocolius, Cacicus* and *Icterus nigrogularis;* in other parts of its range also *Pachyramphus, Myiozetetes, Pitangus, Tolmomyias, Rhynchocyclus* and *Phacellodomus.* All these species build domed or enclosed nests. The Piratic Flycatchers accomplish the eviction of the rightful owners by sheer persistence, repeatedly entering the nest, ultimately causing abandonment, and then removing the eggs. They rarely attack their opponents, but provoke attack; while one of the pair engages the attention of both the owners, the other enters the nest. After successfully appropriating the nest, the flycatchers sometimes add a bed of loose bits of leaf. The clutch is usually 2, occasionally up to 4, eggs, brown with a few blackish spots and fine black lines mainly at the larger end, av. 22.5 × 16mm (2). In Costa Rica Skutch (1960) found that the female alone incubated for a period of 16 days. The young, covered with tawny down when hatched, are fed by both parents, brooded by the female and fly after 18–20 days.

Behaviour. This species is conspicuous during the breeding season, when its song is uttered persistently through the day, delivered from a high perch, often near its nest. At this time 1 or 2 birds are the most ever seen in one area. The lack of records during the off-season may be due to its silence and inconspicuousness at that time rather than to its absence.

Boat-billed Flycatcher: *Megarhynchus pitangua*
Broad-billed Kiskadee   **Plate 17(1)**

Habitat and status. A common and widespread resident in Trinidad, occurring at forest edges and clearings up to over 2000 ft, cocoa plantations and semi-open areas with large trees, usually well up in the trees. (Specimens: AMNH, ANSP, YPM, CM, LM, TRVL.)

Range and subspecies. Mexico S to Bolivia and Argentina; the nominate race ranges from Colombia southwards.

Description. 9 in. Head black with concealed yellow crown-patch, a broad white superciliary streak meeting at nape; upperparts olive brown, wings brown with narrow rufous edges (not very noticeable in the field), tail brown edged rufous, underparts yellow, throat white; bill black, massive, very broad. (See also Great Kiskadee.)

Measurements. Wing: 5 males 112–118mm (115.2); 8 females 106–118mm (112.5). Weight: 3 females 53, 56, 58gm*; 2 unsexed 63, 65gm.

Voice. A strident, harsh, rolling trill, given in bursts; also a less harsh *waaa-waaa-waaa;* I have also heard groups of this species uttering shrill parrotlet-like calls, *pee-a-wit,* etc.

Food. Insects, including cicadas, which are found among the upper foliage of trees rather than in mid air; also berries.

Nesting. Breeding recorded from February to June (14 nests). The nest is a large, open saucer of sticks, lined with tendrils and usually placed in an exposed situation in a tree high above ground, occasionally as low as 20 ft. The clutch is 1–3 eggs, dull white thickly marked with streaky blotches of dull brown and pale gray, av. 29.7 × 21.5mm (3). In Costa Rica Skutch (1960) records a 2- or 3-day interval separating the laying of the eggs; the female alone builds the nest and incubates for over 75% of the daylight hours, the male guards the nest in the female's absence; the incubation period is 17–18 days and the fledging period 24 days.

Behaviour. This species is often found in family parties after the breeding season, foraging mainly beneath the tree canopy among the larger branches and trunks. It is fairly excitable but not so aggressive as the very similar Great Kiskadee.

Streaked Flycatcher: *Myiodynastes maculatus*
Plate 17(8)

Habitat and status. A fairly common resident in Trinidad, less common in Tobago, frequenting the edges of forest and cocoa plantations with tall shade trees, also deciduous woodland, as on Monos and Huevos. (Specimens: AMNH, ANSP, CM, YPM, LM, TRVL.)

Range and subspecies. Mexico S to Bolivia and Argentina; *M. m. to-bagensis* (Zimmer) ranges through Venezuela and Guyana; Haverschmidt (1969) reported an individual of the race *solitarius* (Vieillot) on a ship travelling from Surinam to Trinidad on 15 April at a point some 250 miles from Trinidad. *M. m. solitarius,* which has black (not brown) streaks on upper- and underparts, breeds in S South America, migrating N to Venezuela and the Guianas, where it has been recorded from March to September. A bird found on a rig off Galeota Point in June was probably this race.

Description. 9 in. Head brown with concealed yellow crown-patch, black eye-streak and pale superciliary streak; back brown, streaked dark brown, wings brown edged rufous and whitish; rump and tail broadly edged chestnut;

underparts yellowish white, with conspicuous brown streaks on breast and flanks; bill black, fairly heavy.

Measurements. Wing: 6 males 110–115mm (111.7); 5 females 103–110mm (107.2). Weight: 5 males 46.5–49gm (47.8); 5 females 43–50gm (46.4; also 1 egg-laying 68gm).

Voice. An incisive *chip chip chip,* etc., repeated about once a second or quicker; in excitement this becomes *chipper-chipper,* etc., and louder; also a stereotyped phrase, sung from a treetop, usually at dawn or dusk, *scree-per-cher-wee,* the middle notes sometimes doubled, and often followed by a typical rattling note; tone similar to that of Kiskadee.

Food. Insects, including cicadas, beetles and locusts, also berries; in Panama (Gross 1950) small lizards also.

Nesting. Breeding recorded in Trinidad from March to July (6 nests). The nest is an open cup of twigs and grass, usually placed in a tree hollow, sometimes on a large bromeliad, quite high in a tree. One nest on Huevos Island was in an almond tree on the seashore. The clutch is 2 or 3 eggs, whitish covered with reddish brown markings, av. 24.4 × 19.0mm (5). In Central America Skutch (1960) found that the eggs were laid at 1- or 2-day intervals; the female alone built the nest and incubated, spending 66% of the daylight hours on the nest, the incubation period being 16 or 17 days. Both parents fed the young, which became very noisy as they grew older. The fledging period may be from 18 to 21 days.

Behaviour. This rather noisy and conspicuous species is usually found perching quite high in trees, from where it makes short sallies like a typical flycatcher after its prey. It is frequently found in pairs or small family parties during the breeding season.

Great Kiskadee: *Pitangus sulphuratus*
Derby Flycatcher; "Keskidee"   **Plate 17(2)**

Habitat and status. A common resident in Trinidad, frequenting semi-open areas, including urban and suburban districts, cultivated estates and the edge of forest up to well over 2000 ft; fairly common on all of the Bocas Islands. Birds at Speyside, Tobago, were introduced about 1970. Quesnel (1956) found 20 pairs occupying a favourable area of 44 acres in Port of Spain. (Specimens: AMNH, ANSP, YPM, CM, LM, TRVL.)

Range and subspecies. S USA through Central and South America to Bolivia and Argentina; *P. s. trinitatis* (Hellmayr) ranges from E Colombia to NE Venezuela and N Brazil.

Description. 9 in. Very similar to Boat-billed Flycatcher, but back earth brown and wings more broadly edged with rufous (conspicuous in the field); bill black, fairly long, heavy, but not so broad as in Boat-billed. Voice diagnostic.

Measurements. Wing: 8 males 108–115mm (112.2); 7 females 102–114mm (108.3). Weight: 5 males 53–67gm (60.3); 2 females 53.5*, 63gm; 7 unsexed 57–64gm (59.4).

Voice. Usual call an exuberant phrase, from which the standard English name has been taken, originally expressed in the French, "Qu'est-ce qu'il dit?", often repeated, sometimes just the first syllable, and a variety of similar raucous cries. At dawn often sings another distinct phrase, consisting of 3 or 4 double syllables, *kayeer,* followed by a raucous trill and ending sometimes with a lower-pitched *kweer.* As with parrots, it is easy to ascribe intelligent meaning to the varied, boisterous cries of this species!

Food. Apparently omnivorous; recorded food includes insects, mostly large beetles, grasshoppers, mole crickets, caterpillars, bees and butterflies; berries, including fruits of palms, peppers (*Capsicum*) and the parasitic *Phthirusa;* lizards; mice; fledgling birds (*Coereba*); fish and offal from the seashore; also scraps of many kinds from garbage dumps, beaches, feeding tables, etc.

Nesting. Breeding recorded in all months except September, especially February–May, 52 nests distributed as follows:

I	II	III	IV	V	VI
3	9	7	8	14	3

VII	VIII	IX	X	XI	XII
1	2	—	1	2	2

Moult recorded in June, August and November. The nest is a large, untidy, dome-shaped structure of grasses, with bark, stems and other material often intermingled, and lined with fine grass, the entrance at the side near the top; a few examples of cup-shaped nests with no roofs have been found in South America (W. J. Smith 1962). The nest is placed usually in an exposed position high in a tree (rarely as low as 6 ft) or wedged against a telephone pole beside the wire; one on Monos Island was placed on an isolated pile at the end of a broken-down jetty 60 yd out from the shore. Nests may be used several times, after repairs. Recorded clutches are 2 (× 6), 3 (× 13) and 4 (× 1) eggs, cream with scattered markings of dark brownish red, mainly at the larger end; size range: 25.5–31.1 × 20–21.6mm, av. 28.2 × 20.8mm (12). The species has been parasitised by the Shiny Cowbird (*Molothrus*) in Surinam (Haverschmidt 1968b). Both adults build the nest and feed the young, but only the female incubates, while the male characteristically perches on guard nearby. There are often 2, perhaps 3, broods in the season.

Behaviour. An extremely pugnacious and conspicuous species, strongly territorial, driving other species, especially larger ones, away from the vicinity of its nest. Smaller species, however, are usually tolerated, and some even nest nearby, possibly gaining protection as a result of the Kiskadees' presence. The Kiskadee is one of the earliest birds to call at dawn, well before sunrise. When calling, it frequently flaps its wings and raises its crest. Its typical method of foraging is to sit, shrike-like, on a perch, diving down to pick up its prey often near or on the ground, whence it returns to the perch and proceeds to batter its victim to death.

Brown-crested Flycatcher: *Myiarchus tyrannulus*
Rusty-tailed Petchary; Wied's Crested Flycatcher   **Plate 17(11)**

Habitat and status. A fairly common but local resident in Tobago, much less common in Trinidad, frequenting deciduous forest and the edges of mangrove swamps; particularly common on outlying islands such as the Bocas, Little Tobago, etc. (Specimens: Trinidad, AMNH, CM, LM; Tobago, AMNH, LM.)

Range and subspecies. SW USA and Mexico S to Bolivia and Argentina; the nominate race ranges through South America from NE Colombia, Venezuela and Trinidad S to Argentina; *M. t. tobagensis* (Hellmayr & Seilern), which is larger and darker above, is confined to Tobago.

Description. 8.5 in. Upperparts olive brown, head browner with slightly erectile crest; wings brown with pale edges forming 2 wing-bars on coverts, primaries narrowly edged rufous, long tail dark brown, *inner webs broadly edged rufous* (conspicuous when spread); throat and breast pale gray, lower underparts lemon yellow; bill black, base of mandible pinkish. (See also Venezuelan Flycatcher and Swainson's Flycatcher.)

Measurements. *M. t. tyrannulus.* Wing: 2 males 95, 99mm; 5 females 88–96mm (91.2). Weight: 2 males 28gm each*; 5 females 25.5–31gm (28.9)*; 12 unsexed 27–36.5gm (30.7). *M. t. tobagensis.* Wing: 1 male 96mm; 5 females 93–95mm (93.8). Weight: 1 male 30.5gm*; 5 females 27.5–30.5gm (28.8)*; 8 unsexed 27–32gm (29).

Voice. Most commonly a quick, light *whip,* often repeated; also a penetrating *weep-weep,* a grating, wheezing *djeer,* reminiscent of an elaenia, and a quick splutter.

Food. Mostly insects, including caterpillars, butterflies, froghoppers and wasps; in other areas known to take beetles, grasshoppers and cicadas; also berries, e.g., *Bursera,* and seeds.

Nesting. Breeding recorded in Trinidad and on Monos in April, May, June and October (5 nests). Tobago nests recorded in January and February. Moult recorded from July to September (both races). The nest is situated in a tree-hole, broken bamboo stump, or even in a scaffolding pipe, 6–20 ft above ground; it is made of roots, grass, moss and bark, and lined with plant-down; often a discarded snakeskin is incorporated. The clutch is 2 or 3 eggs, creamy white heavily marked, especially at the larger end, with dark purple and lavender, av. 22.6 × 17.5mm (5). Both parents feed the young, which are liable to infestation by the parasitic fly *Philornis* (ffrench 1965a).

Behaviour. A rather skulking species, found singly or in pairs on low branches or amidst undergrowth, occasionally higher, where it feeds like a typical flycatcher, making short flights and returning to the same perch. On the perch it appears restless, flicking its tail and glancing around frequently.

Venezuelan Flycatcher: *Myiarchus venezuelensis*
"Short-crested Flycatcher"; "Fierce Flycatcher"   **Plate 17(13)**

Habitat and status. A fairly widespread resident of forest and deciduous woodland in Tobago. Previous published records of *M. ferox* from Tobago refer to this species (fide W. E. Lanyon), while records of *ferox* from Trinidad probably refer to Swainson's Flycatcher. (Specimens: AMNH, BM.)

Range and subspecies. NE Colombia, N Venezuela and Tobago; *M. v. insulicola* (Hellmayr & Seilern) is confined to Tobago. It is doubtfully separable from the mainland population (Lanyon).

Description. 8 in. Rather similar to Brown-crested and Swainson's flycatchers. *Adult:* in fresh plumage shows pronounced but narrow rufous edges to outer web of primaries and tail; bill *all black. Immature:* has broader rusty edgings.

Measurements. Wing: 5 males 90–94mm (92.0); 5 females 87–91mm (88.4).

Voice. Most commonly a whistle, very similar to *M. tuberculifer* but more drawn-out; also utters some shorter, sharper notes.

Food. Mostly insects taken amidst upper branches.

Notes. This species has long been considered a race of *M. ferox*, but W. E. Lanyon (in unpublished MSS) has found it to be sympatric with the latter in Venezuela. He considers the two forms specifically distinct, since they differ strikingly in voice and considerably in morphology.

Swainson's Flycatcher: *Myiarchus swainsoni*
Plate 17(14)

Habitat and status. A visitor (during the Southern Hemisphere winter) to Trinidad, where recorded only by Smooker, Roberts in August 1931 at Oropouche, and Mees (Junge & Mees 1958), who obtained a good series from July to September in forest N of Tacarigua and in bamboos at Orange Grove. This species has probably been overlooked. (Specimens: ANSP, LM, BM.)

Range and subspecies. Throughout the tropical zone of South America; the nominate race breeds in S Brazil, Argentina, Paraguay and Uruguay, migrating N to Colombia, Venezuela and Guyana.

Description. 8 in. Very similar to Venezuelan Flycatcher, but lower underparts paler yellow; in *adult* wings and tail *not* edged rufous, but some rufous edges in *immature;* bill usually black above, flesh or reddish brown below, but sometimes all black. Some individuals doubtfully separable in the field from *M. venezuelensis* or *M. ferox,* except by voice.

Measurements. Wing: 6 males 86–95mm (90); 2 females 84, 85mm. Weight: 5 males 18–26gm (22.8)*; 2 females 21, 24.5gm*.

Voice. Not recorded in Trinidad. On its breeding grounds the calls resemble those of *M. tuberculifer,* being musical whistles of medium pitch with a somewhat hoarse, wheezing quality, e.g., *whee-oo* or *jee-a.* Some notes are more prolonged and trilled, with occasionally a short, sharper note, *whit.*

Behaviour. Mees (1958) remarks that the birds he saw in Trinidad were silent and indolent. They were, of course, undergoing their post-breeding moult.

Dusky-capped Flycatcher: *Myiarchus tuberculifer*
Dark-capped Petchary; Olivaceous Flycatcher   **Plate 17(12)**

Habitat and status. A fairly common resident in Trinidad, frequenting forest at all levels, most commonly seen low down on edges of clearings. My Tobago records reported in Herklots (1961) refer to *M. venezuelensis.* (Specimens: AMNH, ANSP, LM, TRVL.)

Range and subspecies. S USA and Mexico S through Central and South America to Argentina; the nominate race ranges from E Colombia, Venezuela and Guyana S to Bolivia and Paraguay.

Description. 7 in. Similar to Brown-crested, Venezuelan, and Swainson's flycatchers, but *smaller;* head blackish, underparts brighter yellow, wings and tail edged paler, lacking any rufous; bill black. *Immature:* has rusty edges to wings and tail. Voice diagnostic. Lanyon (1963) points out that the differences in voice form the basis of species discrimination where different members of this genus are sympatric.

Measurements. Wing: 9 males 80–84mm (81.9); 2 females 75, 76mm. Weight: 9 males 17.5–21mm (19.1)*; 1 female 15gm*; 1 unsexed 22gm.

Voice. Usually a single, slightly hoarse, melancholy whistled note, *whee-er,* rising and falling a little in pitch; sometimes following the last note is a double *pipyoo* accompanied by a high-pitched, sharp, rasping *peez.*

Food. Insects, including flies, damsel-flies and beetles; also seen feeding on berries.

Nesting. Breeding recorded in Trinidad only by B/S in April and June, the same nest location being used after a 10-month interval. The nest was of dried weed stems and moss lined with fine black fibres; it was placed in a hole in a dead stump 15 ft above ground. The clutch is 3 eggs, buff heavily marked with dark brown and lavender, especially at the thick end, av. 23.6 × 17.7mm (6). These eggs are somewhat larger and darker than those of the Guatemalan race found by Skutch (1960). Both parents attend the nest; when disturbed, the Guatemalan young flew at the age of 13 days.

Behaviour. Found singly or in pairs, this flycatcher makes typical darts from a mid-level perch after its prey, returning to the same perch. One bird near the rest-house on the El Tucuche trail was remarkably tame, flying down almost to the feet of campers and carrying off pieces of eggshell and silver paper, presumably as nest material; this was on 24 May, soon after the first heavy rains.

Olive-sided Flycatcher: *Nuttallornis borealis*
Contopus borealis

Habitat and status. A rather uncommon winter visitor from the north to Trinidad, found mostly in clearings amidst hill forest where it perches on the bare tops of tall trees. First recorded by R. Weston on 9 April 1951 (specimen taken), then by Mees on 20 January 1954, both in Arima Valley. Since then I have collected 45 sight records between 14 October and 26 April, mostly from January to March. (Specimen: LM.)

Range. Breeds in N Canada and USA, migrating S to South America and wintering from Colombia and Venezuela to Peru and NE Brazil.

Description. 6.25 in. A stocky flycatcher with a large head and bill and rather short tail; upperparts olive brown, with inconspicuous whitish wing-bars and white tufts which often protrude from beneath the closed wing at the sides of the rump; throat, mid-breast and abdomen whitish in contrast to darker olive sides; bill black, yellowish below.

Measurements. Wing: 1 male 108mm. Weight: 1 male 31.5gm*.

Voice. Song a stereotyped, 3-syllable whistle, often written *whip-three-beers;* also frequently a light *pip-pip-pip* and *tu-ee*. (Tape-recordings made in Trinidad by Snow were identified at Cornell University as the typical utterances of *western* Olive-sided Flycatchers.)

Food. Typically feeds by making sallies, sometimes quite long, from a high perch after flying insects. Food in North America comprises mainly flying ants and bees (Bent 1942).

Tropical Pewee: *Contopus cinereus*
Caribbean Pewee   **Plate 18(5)**

Habitat and status. A common resident in Trinidad, inhabiting forest edges, clearings, cultivated areas with tall trees and second growth; perches both high in trees and at lower levels near the ground. (Specimens: AMNH, ANSP, CM, YPM, LM, TRVL.)

Range and subspecies. Mexico S through Central and South America to Bolivia, Paraguay and Argentina; *C. c. bogotensis* (Bonaparte) ranges from E Colombia to Venezuela and NE Brazil.

Description. 5.5 in. Crown blackish, *upperparts dark brown,* wing-coverts pale-edged forming 2 *whitish wing-bars;* throat and mid-breast whitish, sides of breast and flanks grayish brown, abdomen pale yellow; bill short, black above, *orange under mandible.*

Measurements. Wing: 11 males 73–82mm (76.4); 11 females 70–75mm (72.3). Weight: 10 males 10.5–13gm (12.1)*; 11 females 8.5–13.5gm (11.1)*.

Voice. Normally a trilling *threeee;* also utters a single, clear *weet,* which may be repeated every few seconds.

Food. Flying insects.

Nesting. Breeding recorded in March and May–July (10 nests); moult in September. The nest is a small, compact saucer of fine fibres and grass stems lined with fine grass and decorated on the outside with gray lichen, placed in lateral fork or saddled on a horizontal branch, often quite exposed, 7–60 ft above ground. The clutch is 2 eggs, cream marked with reddish brown and lavender mainly at the larger end, there being only a few spots scattered over the rest; av. 17.8 × 13.6mm (7). In Costa Rica Skutch (1960) found that the eggs were laid at intervals of 1 or 2 days, and the female alone incubated, the period being 15–16 days; the male was attendant during nest-building but did not help to build the nest; he did, however, feed his mate while she incubated. The nestlings are covered in thick, whitish down and have bright yellow gapes.

Behaviour. A quiet, unobtrusive species, usually seen singly outside the breeding season. It feeds like a typical flycatcher, making short sallies after flying insects. On return to the same perch it usually quivers its tail up and down for a while. It can be quite aggressive in defence of the nest, attacking other species as large as a Kiskadee with a noisily snapping bill.

Euler's Flycatcher: *Empidonax euleri*
Lawrence's Flycatcher   **Plate 18(8)**

Habitat and status. A common resident in Trinidad, frequenting forest and cocoa plantations mostly in hilly areas. My Tobago records quoted in Herklots (1961) refer to the Fuscous Flycatcher. (Specimens: AMNH, ANSP, CM, LM.)

Range and subspecies. Colombia and Venezuela S to Bolivia and Argentina, also on Grenada; *E. e. lawrencei* (Allen) ranges from Colombia to Venezuela, with one record from Surinam.

Description. 5.25 in. Upperparts brown tinged olive, wings darker with 2 *dull buff wing-bars;* throat pale gray, breast brownish olive, abdomen pale yellow; eye-ring whitish, but *no eye-stripe;* bill short, broad-based, black above, below whitish with pink streaks.

Measurements. Wing: 6 males 64–68mm (66.2); 6 females 59–63mm (61.8). Weight: 5 males 9.5–12.5gm (11.5)*; 6 females 10.5–12gm (11.2)*; 17 unsexed 11–14gm (12.5).

Voice. Usually a rather loud, slightly hoarse series of notes, the first loudest and most prolonged, followed after a slight pause by a diminishing series of quick notes, run together, e.g., *chee, chi-wi-wi-wi-wi,* etc.; also a drawn-out *peer, peer-wheer.*

Food. Insects.

Nesting. Breeding recorded from May to July; moult in August and October. B/S describe the nest as a deep cup of grass and leaves, or of moss lined with black fibres, placed in a lateral fork or in the knothole of a tree, 4–15 ft above ground. The clutch is 2 or 3 eggs, cream marked with reddish brown spots and blotches, chiefly at the larger end, av. 17.3 × 13.5mm (5).

Behaviour. Generally solitary, this species often sits on an exposed perch quite low, from which it makes little sallies after insects, not necessarily returning to the same perch; it frequently flicks its tail up and down with a jerky motion.

Fuscous Flycatcher: *Cnemotriccus fuscatus*
Léotaud's Dusky Flycatcher   **Plate 17(7)**

Habitat and status. An inconspicuous but locally common resident of both islands, in Trinidad mostly found in the dry deciduous forests of the NW peninsula and on the Bocas Islands; in Tobago more widespread, occurring in hill forest as well as more low-lying scrubby country, also Little Tobago and St. Giles Islands. (Specimens: AMNH, LM.)

Range and subspecies. Colombia and Venezuela S to Bolivia, Paraguay and Argentina; *C. f. cabanisi* (Léotaud) ranges from N Colombia to N Venezuela.

Description. 6.25 in. Upperparts grayish brown, wings darker with 2 *buff wing-bars;* a *conspicuous whitish superciliary streak;* tail long; breast brownish, lower underparts pale yellow; bill all black.

Measurements. Wings: 41 unsexed 62.5–71.5mm (66.3). Weight: 41 unsexed 12–16gm (13.6).

Voice. Call-note a light *chip* or *chooee;* song on mainland *chip, weeti-weeti-weetiyee* (Hilty & Brown 1986); dawn song is an explosive series, *pit-pit-peedit.*

Food. Insects, taken amidst foliage.

Nesting. Breeding in April and May (Abbott, in Herklots); 3 Tobago nests in February (2) and July; moult August–October. The nest is made of twigs and bark lined with black fibres, about 12 ft above ground in the crotch of a small tree. The clutch is 3 eggs, white with black markings mainly at the larger end.

Behaviour. A rather quiet, unobtrusive species which keeps mainly to low undergrowth, where it sallies out to catch small insects close to the ground.

Bran-colored Flycatcher: *Myiophobus fasciatus*
Stripe-breasted Petchary   **Plate 17(10)**

Habitat and status. A widespread resident in Trinidad, not uncommon in semi-open savannahs, second growth and in deciduous forest on the Bocas Islands, especially Chacachacare. (Specimens: AMNH, ANSP, CM, LM, TRVL.)

Range and subspecies. Costa Rica S through Panama and South America to Bolivia, Argentina and Uruguay; the nominate race ranges from E Colombia to N Venezuela, the Guianas and Brazil.

Description. 5 in. Head and upperparts warm brown, with a concealed orange or yellow crown-patch and 2 pale buff wing-bars; underparts whitish with *dark streaks on breast and flanks,* lower underparts pale yellow; bill black, lower mandible pale brown. *Immature:* lacks coronal patch.

Measurements. Wing: 4 males 57–61mm (59.5); 2 females 55, 55mm; 6 unsexed 54–64mm (57.5). Weight: 5 males 10–10.5gm (10.2); 4 females 8.5–10gm (9.2); 11 unsexed 9–12gm (10.0).

Voice. In alarm, a rather weak, trilling twitter; also, in Costa Rica, the male utters a low, full whistle, whilst in Ecuador a dawn song consists of a soft but full whistled monosyllable, repeated once per second for long periods (Skutch 1960).

Food. Small insects and berries.

Nesting. Breeding recorded from March to August (12 nests), also once in November; moult recorded in March, October and December; the season appears to be extended. Two broods are recorded (Mees), with an interval of less than 2 wk. The nest is a deep, neat cup of stems, bark, bamboo sheaths and cobweb lined with fine fibres or plant-down, the rim sometimes decorated with moss; the exterior appears rough and unfinished, often with material hanging down in a tail. The nest is suspended by the rim to a lateral fork, usually 5 or 6 ft from the ground in scrubby savannah country; B/S record a nest at 30 ft. The clutch is 1 or normally 2 eggs, cream with red brown spots forming a wreath, av. 17.7 × 13.2mm (16). This species is parasitised by the cowbird *Molothrus.* In Costa Rica Skutch (1960) found that the nest is built within about 9 days, then a few days elapse before the first egg is laid, the second following after an interval of 1–3 days. The female alone builds the nest and incubates, sitting in many short sessions, for 17 days. The male attends nearby but does not share the incubation. Both parents feed the young, which hatch with some gray down. They fly at 15–17 days old.

Behaviour. This small flycatcher is unobtrusive, keeping to the lower levels of vegetation, amongst which it flits about with quick darts as it feeds. When excited it displays its bright yellow crown-patch.

White-throated Spadebill: *Platyrinchus mystaceus*
Little Broadbill; Tobago Flatbill   **Plate 19(8)**

Habitat and status. A rather uncommon and inconspicuous resident of both islands, but widespread in both hill forest and second growth, where it inhabits undergrowth. (Specimens: AMNH, CM, LM, TRVL.)

Range and subspecies. Mexico S through Central and South America to Bolivia, Argentina and Paraguay; *P. m. insularis* (Allen) occurs also in Venezuela.

Description. 4 in. Crown dark brownish olive with a concealed yellow crown-patch, *long yellowish superciliary streak* curving down behind *blackish ear-coverts,* eye-ring yellow, malar streak blackish; upperparts olive brown, *tail very short;* throat white, rest of underparts buff; bill *very broad* and flat, black above, pale brown below.

Measurements. Wing: 4 males 55–60mm (57.5); 1 female 51mm; 9 unsexed 50–58mm (54.6). Weight: 2 males 9, 9.5gm*; 1 female 9gm*; 20 unsexed 7.5–11gm (9.8).

Voice. An incisive *chweet* or *wick,* sometimes repeated once or twice; also, in Costa Rica, a trill like that of a gnatwren (Slud 1964).

Food. Insects taken low down in swift darts.

Nesting. Breeding recorded May–July (3 nests); in Tobago 1 June record; moult in September. The nest described by B/S is probably that of another species. Snow found 2 nests, placed 1.5 and 2 ft above ground in the fork of a sapling; the nest is a deep cup of dead grasses and pale fibres bound with cobweb, the inside lined with black fibres.

Behaviour. A quiet, solitary species, which, however, moves rapidly through the lower undergrowth with rather sudden flights. Slud (1964) found that in Costa Rica the calling male exposes the concealed crown-patch, spreading it like a fan.

Yellow-olive Flycatcher: *Tolmomyias sulphurescens*
Sulphury Flatbill   **Plate 19(1)**

Habitat and status. A fairly common resident in Trinidad, inhabiting forests and second growth, where it keeps high in the trees; confused with the Yellow-breasted Flycatcher by several observers, e.g., B/S, Herklots. (Specimens: AMNH, ANSP, CM, LM, TRVL.)

Range and subspecies. Mexico S through Central and South America to Bolivia, Argentina and Paraguay; *T. s. berlepschi* (Hartert & Goodson) is confined to Trinidad, having more green and less gray in the crown.

Description. 6 in. Crown gray, tinged olive, upperparts olive green, wings and tail darker, edged greenish yellow; whitish "spectacles"; *throat, breast and flanks grayish green,* abdomen pale yellow; iris pale gray; bill black above, pinkish white below. (See also Yellow-breasted Flycatcher.)

Measurements. Wing: 4 males 68–70mm (69.5); 3 females 65–68mm (67). Weight: 3 males 15, 15.5, 16.5gm*; 3 females 16, 17.5, 18.5gm*.

Voice. Usually a well-spaced *chip, chip, chip,* the number of *chips* varying somewhat.

Food. Insects, taken amidst foliage rather than in mid air; also berries.

Nesting. Breeding recorded in April, June and July (7 nests); regular singing May–August; moult in October. The nest is retort-shaped with the entrance tube pointing vertically downwards; it is made of tough, fine rootlets or black fungal hyphae, sometimes mixed with grass and cobweb. This structure, measuring 10 in. long × 5 in. wide, is suspended from a branch 8–40 ft above ground, usually below 20 ft, well away from other foliage. B/S describe clutches of 2 or 3 eggs with widely differing colours: deep pink with dark markings merging, or pinkish buff, marked clearly with red and lavender, or whitish with scattered markings in violet; the size varied little, av. 22.0 × 14.8mm (11). In Costa Rica Skutch (1960) found that nest-building, by the female alone, took 2–3 wk; eggs were laid at intervals of 1 or 2 days, and incubated by the female alone for 17–18 days; the young, which hatch naked, were fed by both parents but brooded by the female only; the fledging period was 22–24 days. After the departure of the young the female continued to sleep in the nest. The toughly constructed nests are sometimes used by other birds, including *Legatus,* after the owners have left.

Yellow-breasted Flycatcher: *Tolmomyias flaviventris*
Yellow-vented Flatbill   **Plate 19(2)**

Habitat and status. A common resident of both islands, inhabiting forests and second growth, also edges of mangrove swamps; usually keeps to the upper branches. (Specimens: AMNH, ANSP, CM, YPM, LM, TRVL.)

Range and subspecies. Colombia S to Peru, Bolivia and SE Brazil; *T. f. collingwoodi* (Chubb) ranges from E Colombia and Venezuela to the Guianas and N Brazil.

Description. 5 in. A little *smaller* than Yellow-olive Flycatcher. Head and upperparts yellowish olive green, wings and tail darker edged yellow or yellowish green; lores, eye-ring, *throat and breast golden yellow,* lower underparts duller yellow; bill flat, black above, whitish below.

Measurements. Wing: 10 males 57–62mm (59.6); 4 females 57–60mm (58.7). Weight: 8 males 10–13gm (11.5)*; 3 females 12, 12, 14.5gm*; 13 unsexed 9.5–14gm (12.4).

Voice. Usually a loud, penetrating, high whistle, *peeeet* or *peee-it*, typically in sequences of three in Tobago, two in Trinidad; also uttered singly at long intervals.

Food. Insects, including moths and small beetles, taken high in trees; also berries.

Nesting. Breeding recorded in Trinidad in May and July–September (5 nests); May and June records from Tobago; singing regular from April to December. The retort-shaped nest resembles that of the Yellow-olive Flycatcher, being usually made of black fibres and suspended from a branch from a few to 40 ft above ground. The clutch is 2 or 3 eggs, creamy white spotted with deep violet mainly at the larger end, av. 19.9 × 13.8mm (6). Very frequently the nest is located near a wasps' nest. Haverschmidt (1968a) in Surinam found that one parent, probably the female, built the nest and incubated; nest-building might take 5 wk; eggs were laid on alternate days and were incubated for 17 days; both parents fed the young.

Spotted Tody-Flycatcher: *Todirostrum maculatum*
Spotted Tody-tyrant   **Plate 19(6)**

Habitat and status. A rare resident of mangroves in SW Trinidad, first recorded in May 1957 (Herklots); locally not uncommon at Icacos and Los Blanquizales. (Specimens taken by Herklots.)

Range and subspecies. Peru and Venezuela S to Bolivia and N Brazil; the nominate race ranges from Venezuela and the Guianas to Brazil.

Description. 4 in. Head slate gray, lores whitish; upperparts grayish green, wings brown edged with yellowish green, tail brown; *throat white, breast yellow, both heavily streaked with black,* mid-abdomen plain yellow; iris orange-yellow; bill longish, flat, black above, paler below.

Voice. A surprisingly loud *chee* or *tee-dee.*

Food. Insects.

Nesting. Recorded in mangroves near Icacos, where an elliptical pouch of dry grass, leaves and down was found on 23 May 1982, slung from a thin branch 8 ft above ground. Both parents attended. In Surinam the eggs are white spotted with red (Haverschmidt 1968a).

Behaviour. This species frequented low trees and shrubbery at the edge of and within the mangrove swamp. It is rather a confiding bird.

Short-tailed Pygmy-Tyrant: *Myiornis ecaudatus*
Plate 19(7)

Habitat and status. An uncommon species in Trinidad, probably resident but easily overlooked owing to its small size and habitat mostly in the foliage below the forest canopy, occasionally lower; recorded in various parts of Trinidad up to 500 ft. (Specimens: AMNH, CM, BM.)

Range and subspecies. Costa Rica S through Panama and South America to Peru, Bolivia and Brazil; *M. e. miserabilis* (Chubb) ranges from Colombia to Venezuela and the Guianas.

Description. 3 in. Head gray with whitish superciliary and eye-ring; upperparts yellowish green, wings and tail blackish edged green; underparts whitish, flanks pale yellow; tail very short indeed. A tiny flycatcher.

Measurements. Wing: 1 male 35mm; 2 females 35, 35mm. Weight: 1 male 4.8gm; 1 female 4.5gm.

Voice. A very thin note (resembling an insect or treefrog), rather incisive, *chi* or *tzee*, often repeated.

Food. On the mainland small beetles, cockroaches, bugs and spiders.

Nesting. Recorded at Talparo in January (V. Quesnel). Builds a purse-shaped nest with a side entrance, made out of dry leaves, moss, stems and fine roots, suspended from a branch 6–10 ft above ground. In Brazil the clutch is 2 eggs, white or yellowish with reddish brown spots mainly at the larger end, the size approximately 13 × 10mm (Pinto 1953). Both parents feed the young, but probably only the female incubates (McNeil & Martinez 1968).

Behaviour. Usually found singly, this species forages amidst foliage, flitting suddenly at a leaf to pick off an insect; at other times it perches quietly and would pass unnoticed were it not for its cricket-like call.

Crested Doradito: *Pseudocolopteryx sclateri*
Sclater's Sharp-winged Tyrant   Plate 19(5)

Habitat and status. Very rare in Trinidad marshes, but recent records suggest it to be resident, or, alternatively, a breeding visitor from the south, since breeding birds were collected by B/S in June 1928 and by Roberts in July–August 1931; the species was next recorded in June–July 1979 (T. Manolis), February 1983 and March 1984 (G. White), and June–September 1984 (R. Andrews), all in freshwater marshes bordering Caroni swamp; also reported from NE coast in hills around Salybia (Murphy 1986). (Specimens: AMNH, ANSP.)

Range. Venezuela (recent records from Falcon and Apure states), Guyana south to N Argentina and N Paraguay; the scattered records in N South America indicate migration from the south.

Description. 4 in. Crown crested, blackish with some orange edging, head and neck blackish, upperparts olive brown with 2 pale rufous wing-bars, *underparts bright yellow.* Some birds with duller yellow underparts, browner faces, and distinct buffy or whitish superciliary stripes may be females. Bill black, some with pinkish lower mandible. *Immature:* also has superciliary, and entire underparts buffy. Appearance and behaviour suggest a wood warbler or a kinglet (*Regulus*); frequently cocks or flicks its tail.

Measurements. Wing: 1 male 41mm.

Voice. Call-note is a thin, high and very soft *sik,* also a sharp *kip.* Song is thin and squeaky, *tsik, tsik, tseee-lee.*

Food. Insects gleaned from low foliage (*Cyperus,* etc.) or taken from short, upward sallies.

Nesting. Recorded by B/S in June, also Roberts collected males in breeding condition in July–August. Andrews and Manolis found a juvenile with a female on 26 July, and a nest with eggs on 17 August. The nest is a deep, open cup made of grass, weed stems and plant-down, and attached to marsh-plants 2–4 ft above ground which may be flooded. The 2 eggs are creamy buff with no markings, av. 16.1 × 12.9mm.

Yellow-bellied Elaenia: *Elaenia flavogaster*
Common Elaenia; "Top-knot"; "Jay"; "Cutterhead"   **Plate 18(4)**

Habitat and status. A common resident on both islands, frequenting semi-open areas with trees, gardens, cultivated areas, second growth and forest edges; also all outlying islands with scrub and trees. (Specimens: AMNH, ANSP, CM, YPM, LM, TRVL.)

Range and subspecies. Mexico S to Argentina; the nominate race ranges from Colombia E and S to Venezuela, the Guianas, Peru, Bolivia, Argentina and Paraguay; also Grenada and St. Vincent.

Description. 6.5 in. *Prominent crest,* often seeming 2-horned, with white crown-patch (concealed when crest not raised); head and upperparts grayish olive brown, wings brown with 2 white wing-bars, tail brown; throat whitish, breast grayish yellow, lower underparts pale yellow; bill black above, whitish pink below. *Immature:* lacks crown-patch. The largest elaenia in the area.

Measurements. Wing: 18 males 73–84mm (78.7); 6 females 74–78mm (75.7). Weight: 14 males 22.5–27.5gm (24.6); 4 females 23.5–25gm (24.1); 46 unsexed 21–29gm (24.9).

Voice. Usually a long-drawn-out, rather hoarse, nasal whistle, *zheeer,* sometimes with an extra shorter syllable, *zheeer-chu,* and repeated several times; also a short, *Myiarchus*-like *weep.* Dawn song, delivered before sunrise, is a persistent, urgent-sounding *wee-chuhu,* or a repeated wheezing phrase, *zhu-zhee-zhu-zhee.*

Food. Predominantly berries and small fruits; also insects, including ants, beetles and plant-bugs, taken both in flight and amidst foliage.

Nesting. Breeding recorded from February to July, with a decided peak from April to June, also November and December (45 nests); B/S, without giving details, say that nesting is earlier at higher altitudes, adding that they had found nests with eggs from February to October. June and July records (4) from Tobago. Moult recorded from August to November. The nest is a shallow cup of roots, bark and grass, decorated with lichen and cobweb and lined with feathers; it is saddled on the lateral fork of a branch 12–50 ft above ground, occasionally only a few feet (where large trees are unavailable). The clutch is 2 (exceptionally 1 or 3) eggs, cream marked deep red and lavender, the marks usually concentrated at the larger end in a wreath, av. 22.2 × 16.1mm (14). Incubation, by the female only, lasts 16 days, and fledging 15–17 days. In Costa Rica Skutch (1960) found that both parents build the nest, the female incubates for about 66% of the daylight hours, while the male sometimes guards the nest in her absence. Two days elapse between the laying of the 2 eggs. Both parents feed the young; the female alone broods, by day fairly constantly for the first 6 days, much less thereafter, by night until 2 or 3 nights before fledging. A second brood may be attempted.

Behaviour. This noisy and conspicuous species appears to live in pairs even outside the breeding season. When calling, it raises its crest, but this crest is frequently raised at other times; in fact, it is only occasionally seen with the feathers flattened, most often during incubation. It is one of the earliest birds to start calling in the morning. Mated birds often take part in a rather confused duet, but this is in no way stereotyped.

Small-billed Elaenia: *Elaenia parvirostris*
Plate 18(7)

Habitat and status. A rare migrant to Trinidad, recorded only 3 times: 2 individuals were taken by Mees on 30 July and 3 August in second growth near Tacarigua, the other was captured on Chacachacare Island on 30 May in deciduous forest (ffrench 1967a). (Specimens: LM.)

Range. Breeds in Bolivia, S Brazil, Paraguay, Uruguay and Argentina, migrating N during the southern winter to Colombia, Venezuela, including Margarita Island and the Guianas.

Description. 6 in. Smaller and much slighter than the Yellow-billed Elaenia, fairly similar to Lesser Elaenia. Head and upperparts uniform olive green, with a concealed pale lemon crown-patch, distinct yellowish eye-ring, wings with 2 whitish wing-bars; *underparts mainly white,* lemon yellow only on flanks and under-tail-coverts; bill short, narrow, black above and tip of mandible, of which the base is pinkish orange. Difficult to identify in the field; in the hand its measurements are diagnostic.

Measurements. Wing: 1 male 75mm; 2 unsexed 71, 72mm. Weight: 1

male 16gm*; 2 unsexed 12.5*; 15.5gm. (In Venezuela birds arriving in mid-May have a high fat level [McNeil & Carrera de Itriago 1968] but have not started to moult. Our May bird had not moulted and weighed 15.5gm; the other 2, taken within 4 days 2 months later, had nearly finished moult, but the weight discrepancy is considerable.)

Voice. In Guyana a brief, hard *tuk;* from Argentina a brief, fairly high but throaty *tchk-too, preech-tuk* is reported (Snyder 1966).

Food. Insects, including caterpillars, in Venezuela (Friedmann & Smith 1950).

Lesser Elaenia: *Elaenia chiriquensis*
White-crowned Flycatcher; Chiriqui Flycatcher; Bellicose Elaenia

Habitat and status. A rather rare and local resident in Trinidad, found in savannahs with small trees and bushes; possibly migrant, since all records are from March to August; there may be confusion with the Small-billed Elaenia. (Specimen: ANSP.)

Range and subspecies. Costa Rica S to Bolivia and Paraguay; *E. c. albivertex* (Pelzeln) ranges in South America from Colombia S to Bolivia and Paraguay.

Description. 5.25 in. Head (with occasionally raised crest) and upperparts dull grayish olive, with a concealed white crown-patch and whitish eye-ring, wings and tail darker, edged pale lemon, showing as 2 dull white wing-bars; throat white, *breast and flanks grayish,* rest of underparts pale lemon; bill short, blackish above, lower mandible light pinkish, tipped blackish. See also Small-billed Elaenia.

Measurements. Wing: 1 unsexed 68mm. Tail: 1 unsexed 57mm. Weight: 1 unsexed 18gm.

Voice. Usually a light but insistent, clear whistle, *weep;* also, in Costa Rica, a 2-syllabled *wee-ur,* the second syllable lower-pitched and buzzy (Slud 1964); the song, uttered at dawn and more rarely at dusk, is a rapid, unmusical phrase, often repeated, *a-we-d'-de-de* (Skutch 1960).

Food. Berries and seeds; also small insects, taken in flight and amidst foliage.

Nesting. Breeds from April to June (about 20 nests) according to B/S. The nest resembles that of the Yellow-bellied Elaenia but is deeper and more loosely built, with no lichen and few if any feathers lining it; it is placed quite near the ground in the upright fork of a small tree. The clutch is 2 eggs, light cream or dull brown marked with 2 shades of red-brown, av. 19.2 × 15mm (8). Skutch (1960) found that in Central America only the female builds the nest, incubates, and broods the young; 1 or 2 days' interval elapses between the laying of the 2 eggs; incubation lasts 14–15 days. The female, a restless sitter, incubates for 50–75% of the daylight hours; both parents feed the young, which hatch with sparse, gray down; the young fly after 15 or 16 days; occasionally there is a second brood.

Behaviour. This is a rather shy species, difficult to observe because of its habit of remaining within the foliage of the dense bush or trees in its habitat. Skutch (1960) found it extremely pugnacious in defence of its small territory. Within a dense population in Costa Rica numerous fights occurred, both intra- and inter-specific. At dusk the male sang a song, similar to the dawn song, while flying steeply and erratically up to 100 ft or so, reaching an apex and darting back down into cover.

Forest Elaenia: *Myiopagis gaimardii*
Gaimard's Elaenia   **Plate 18(1)**

Habitat and status. A fairly common resident in Trinidad, inhabiting forests and second growth, mostly in the treetops, also edges of mangrove swamps. (Specimens: AMNH, ANSP, CM, YPM, LM, TRVL.)

Range and subspecies. Panama and Colombia S through South America to Bolivia and Brazil; *M. g. trinitatis* (Hartert & Goodson) is confined to Trinidad, being somewhat larger than continental forms and with duller, less greenish upperparts.

Description. 5 in. Crown blackish with a large, partly concealed, white or pale lemon crown-patch; whitish superciliary and eye-ring; upperparts *olive green*, wings brown edged *yellowish*, showing 2 wing-bars; throat whitish, breast greenish yellow, lower underparts pale yellow; bill black, lower mandible pinkish orange at base.

Measurements. Wing: 6 males 59–65mm (62.8); 9 females 57–62mm (60.0). Weight: 1 male 13.5gm*; 5 females 9.5–12.5gm (11.7)*; 7 unsexed 12.5–14gm (13.2).

Voice. A regular, loud *pitch-weep,* repeated at intervals; also a sharp titter, *pipipipip* (Snow); Mees describes an 8-syllabled song, while Chapman (1894) mentions "a soft *pee-a-wee*".

Food. Insects and berries, usually taken in upper branches.

Nesting. Breeding recorded in February (Downs) and September (B/S). The former nest was at 10 ft in a pomerac tree (*Eugenia*), the latter in a mangrove 15 ft above the water. The nest resembled that of the Yellow-bellied Elaenia but was smaller and unlined. There were 2 eggs, pale cream marked with deep red-brown and lavender at the larger end, av. 17.5 × 14.0mm.

Scrub Flycatcher: *Sublegatus modestus*
Smooth Flycatcher   **Plate 18(3)**

Habitat and status. An inconspicuous but locally common resident in

Trinidad, inhabiting mangrove swamps and, more especially, dry deciduous forest and scrub on the Bocas Islands (ffrench 1967a). (Specimens: AMNH, ANSP, YPM, LM.)

Range and subspecies. Costa Rica and Panama S through South America to Paraguay, Argentina and Uruguay; *S. m. glaber* (Sclater & Salvin) ranges from Colombia to Venezuela (including Margarita and Patos islands), and Surinam. (See Notes below.)

Description. 5.75 in. Head dark brown, slightly crested, but *no crown-patch;* lores and eye-ring whitish; *upperparts grayish brown,* wings edged pale, forming 2 whitish wing-bars; *throat and breast gray,* lower underparts yellow; bill blackish horn above and below. Somewhat suggests a small *Myiarchus.*

Measurements. Wing: 2 females 68, 70mm; 27 unsexed 65–72mm (68.4). Weight: 2 females 11.5, 13gm*; 29 unsexed 10.5–15gm (12.3).

Voice. A clear whistle, *pfeee;* song recorded in the Curaçao group of islands (Voous 1957) was a high-pitched, thin rattle, *pee-wee-reeree.*

Food. Mainly insects, especially ants and small beetles, in Curaçao (Voous 1957) and Surinam (Haverschmidt 1968a); also berries.

Nesting. Breeding in Trinidad recorded in May and June (2 nests), though B/S ascribe a March nest to this species; moult in August and September. I found a nest in the Caroni swamp saddled on the lateral fork of a mangrove at 5 ft; it was a shallow cup of leaves; B/S's nest was similarly placed in a hog-plum tree (*Spondias*) at 20 ft, being made of fibres, leaves and grass, decorated with pieces of bark. A nest in the Orinoco region (Cherrie 1916) was lined with a few feathers. The clutch is 2 eggs, white marked with dark brown at the larger end, av. 19.1 × 13.7mm (2). Incubation lasts at least 14 days. The incubating bird, probably the female, is fed on the nest by her mate.

Behaviour. A bird of extremely quiet habits, usually seen singly; it forages near or on the ground with short sallies after insects.

Notes. Haverschmidt (1970a) remarks on the fact that different subspecies of *S. modestus* are found in the same area in various parts of NE South America; also that the species in Surinam and Guyana is found in two different habitats (as is the case in Trinidad). It may be that different species are involved, with very inconspicuous morphological differences.

Mouse-colored Tyrannulet: *Phaeomyias murina*
Mouse-coloured Flycatcher   **Plate 19(3)**

Habitat and status. Common on Chacachacare Island, where it frequents undergrowth and bushes in dry deciduous forest, probably resident, recorded in April, May, August–October; also recorded rarely from Monos Island, and in Trinidad near Tacarigua. (Specimens: AMNH, LM.)

Range and subspecies. Panama and Colombia S to Argentina; *P. m. incomta* (Cabanis & Heine) ranges from Panama E to Venezuela.

Description. 4.75 in. Head and upperparts grayish brown with a distinct *dull white superciliary streak* and 2 pale buff wing-bars; throat gray, breast and lower underparts pale yellowish; bill black above, *pinkish orange below.* Distinctly smaller and drabber than the Scrub Flycatcher.

Measurements. Wing: 15 unsexed 55–62mm (57.8). Weight: 37 unsexed 8–12gm (10.0).

Voice. A thin *peeet* or *czert,* or a quick chatter.

Food. In Surinam berries (of Loranthaceae) and small beetles (Haverschmidt 1968a).

Nesting. No definite breeding record, but B/S had a May record of a possible nest, a moderately deep cup of leaves lined with fine fibres set in an upright fork of cactus at 12 ft. I found in September recently fledged birds on Chacachacare, also adults starting to moult. Nests in Venezuela (Cherrie 1916) and Surinam (Haverschmidt 1970b) are small cups of fine grass, sometimes mixed with moss or spiderwebs and lined with feathers; they are set in tree forks up to 20 ft above ground. Two different races in Ecuador and Surinam lay a clutch of 2 pale cream or white eggs (Marchant 1960, Haverschmidt 1970b). The eggs are laid with a 2-day interval; incubation, by the female alone, lasts 14 days in Surinam, 16–17 days in Ecuador. On the other hand, fledging took 17 days in Surinam and 14–15 days in Ecuador. Both parents feed the young, which hatch in whitish down and are brooded until 8 days old.

Behaviour. An extremely unobtrusive species, but very aggressive in defence of the nest.

Southern Beardless Tyrannulet: *Camptostoma obsoletum*
Ridgway's Tyrannulet; Temminck's Tyrannulet   **Plate 19(4)**

Habitat and status. A common resident in Trinidad, frequenting light deciduous forest, the edges of montane forest, cultivated areas and gardens with trees. (Specimens: AMNH, ANSP, CM, YPM, LM, TRVL.)

Range and subspecies. Costa Rica and Panama S through South America to Bolivia, Argentina and Paraguay; *C. o. venezuelae* (Zimmer) occurs only in Venezuela, including Patos Island, and Trinidad, including Monos Island.

Description. 4 in. Head dark brown, with crest often raised, no crown-patch, pale superciliary streak; *upperparts grayish green,* paler on rump; wings and tail brown, wing-coverts edged pale yellow, showing 2 wing-bars; throat grayish, breast yellowish, abdomen yellow. With crest raised resembles a miniature Yellow-bellied Elaenia.

Measurements. Wing: 6 males 52–55mm (53.5); 4 females 47–50mm (48.2). Weight: 4 males 6.5–8gm (7.4)*; 4 females 6–7.5gm (7.0)*.

Voice. Usually a sharp, high-pitched whistle, 1 loud note often followed by several quicker, softer notes in a falling, melancholy cadence, *tleee-tee, tee, tee;* also a short *zick-zick, chi-chi-chi* or *queek;* in excitement, as during courtship, the high notes are repeated several times, often followed by a short churring note, *pee-chrr-pee-chrr,* etc.

Food. Small insects and spiders; also berries.

Nesting. Breeding recorded in February–April, July, October and November (6 nests); moult in May. The nest described by B/S is of another species. Snow records a nest placed 25 ft up beside the fork of a tree, supported by a few twigs; it was domed with a small entrance near the top, made of rootlets and lined with feathers. Nests of 2 different races in Surinam and Ecuador are little balls of dead leaves and fibres with side entrances, and lined with plant-down (Haverschmidt 1954b; Marchant 1960). The nest is often located near a wasps' nest; it is built by the female alone, usually 4–12 ft above ground; the clutch varies from 1 to 3 eggs, white with markings of red-brown and lilac at the larger end; eggs are laid with a 2-day interval, incubation lasting 14–15 days and fledging about 17 days; both parents feed the young.

Behaviour. An active little bird which feeds restlessly like a warbler, flitting among the foliage at all levels. During courtship birds constantly flirt and fan their tails, raising their crests and calling excitedly. Sometimes a pair fly up together into the air, meet for a moment and fly down again.

Slaty-capped Flycatcher: *Leptopogon superciliaris*
Venezuelan Leptopogon; Gray-capped Leptopogon   **Plate 18(6)**

Habitat and status. A rather uncommon but widely distributed resident in Trinidad, mainly found in forests of the Northern Range at all elevations. (Specimens: CM, LM.)

Range and subspecies. Costa Rica and Panama through Colombia and N Venezuela to Ecuador, Peru and N Bolivia; *L. s. pariae* (Phelps & Phelps) is confined to Trinidad and the extreme E of the Paria peninsula in Venezuela.

Description. 5 in. *Crown dark gray,* face and superciliary streak whitish, *crescent-shaped blackish patch over ear-coverts;* upperparts olive green, wings darker edged and tipped yellowish forming 2 wing-bars; throat whitish, breast greenish yellow, lower underparts yellow; bill black, lower mandible pale pinkish at base.

Measurements. Wing: 2 males 68, 69mm; 5 females 62–65mm (63.6); 4 unsexed 63, 68, 69, 69mm. Weight: 3 males 9.5*, 11.5*, 13gm; 5 females 9.5–11.5gm (10.5)*; 22 unsexed 9.5–13gm (12.0).

Voice. Usually an incisive *switch-you;* also a single metallic note, *choop* or *check,* which may become a chatter, both delivered with wide-open bill; also a thin, squeaky note, apparently used for contact.

Food. Insects taken in the air and among foliage.

Nesting. Breeding recorded from February to July (12 nests), with moult in August, September, December and January. The nest is a round, compact ball of various plant materials decorated with cocoons and lined with soft fibres; the side entrance is sometimes sheltered by a porch. The structure is suspended from a short root or tendril and located in some dark situation such as a rocky cleft, or very often under the fringe of vegetation at the top of a bank where earth has fallen away. The clutch is 2 white eggs, av. 19.5 × 14.1mm (6). The fledging period is 20 days.

Behaviour. This species is usually seen singly or in pairs; it does not seem shy as it perches on an exposed branch fairly low in a tree to sing its penetrating song. In excitement it flicks one wing upwards, like *Mionectes oleaginea.*

Olive-striped Flycatcher: *Mionectes olivaceus*
Venezuelan Mionectes   **Plate 19(10)**

Habitat and status. A rare species, possibly resident, in Trinidad, found in forest mainly in the Northern Range. (Specimens: LM.)

Range and subspecies. Costa Rica and Panama through Colombia to Ecuador and C Peru; *M. o. venezuelensis* (Ridgway) also occurs in N Venezuela.

Description. 5 in. Head and body dark olive green, with small, whitish post-ocular spot; yellow streaks on upper breast and flanks; bill blackish above and tip of lower mandible, of which the pale yellow base is conspicuous in the field. *Adult male:* differs from female and immature in extremely narrowed and club-tipped ninth primary.

Measurements. Wing: 1 male 66mm; 1 female 65mm; 1 unsexed 72mm. Weight: 1 male 13gm; 1 female 15gm*; 2 unsexed 16, 18gm.

Voice. Undescribed.

Food. Insects taken from amidst foliage; also occasionally berries.

Nesting. No certain record, since B/S, who describe nests and eggs, seemed to find difficulty in distinguishing this species from *M. oleaginea* both in appearance and in nesting.

Behaviour. A quiet and unobtrusive species which forages fairly low in trees and perches sometimes quite openly.

Ochre-bellied Flycatcher: *Mionectes oleaginea*
Oily Flycatcher; Pale-bellied or Oleaginous Pipromorpha;
Pipromorpha oleaginea **Plate 19(9)**

Habitat and status. A common resident in both islands, especially Trinidad, frequenting forests usually in undergrowth near streams. (Specimens: AMNH, ANSP, CM, YPM, LM, TRVL.)

Range and subspecies. Mexico S through Central and South America to Bolivia and S Brazil; *M. o. pallidiventris* (Hellmayr) also occurs in NE Venezuela.

Description. 5 in. Head and upperparts olive green, wings brown, edged buff showing 2 indistinct wing-bars; *underparts mainly dull orange-buff,* upper breast tinged green; bill black, base of mandible yellowish. *Adult male:* differs from female and immature in its considerably emarginated outer primary; the male is also slightly larger.

Measurements. Wing: 24 males 62–68mm (64.5); 6 females 57–61mm (58.7). Weight: 12 males 11.5–14gm (12.5)*; 7 females 10–11.5gm (10.9), and 1 egg-laying 15.5gm; 242 unsexed 9–15gm (12.1).

Voice. A series of several high-pitched squeaky notes, *wick-wick-wick,* etc., followed by 2 or 3 louder, lower-pitched but penetrating notes, each almost disyllabic, *chiu-chiu.* Also, during a flight-chase, an excited chittering.

Food. Berries and seeds, especially *Alchornea, Trema, Miconia* (B. K. Snow & Snow 1979); also insects and spiders taken amidst foliage.

Nesting. Breeding recorded in Trinidad from March to September, with a decided peak in May and June (61 nests), regular singing February–July; moult May–October, especially the last 3 months. Though the start of breeding varies annually according to climate and food availability, individual moulting periods hardly vary at all (D. W. Snow & Snow 1964). In Tobago breeding recorded in March, April and June. The nest is a ball of green moss lined with fine black fibres, with a side entrance, sometimes screened by a porch. It is usually suspended from a liana or root, often above a stream, 1–2 ft above the water, or hung from the side of a bank, rock or fallen tree. Of 28 clutches, 22 had 3 eggs, while 6 had 2, 4 or 5 eggs, pure white, av. 18.7 × 14.5mm (7). The eggs are laid at 2-day intervals. Incubation lasts 18–20 days and fledging 19 days. All parental activities at the nest are performed by the female; no pair bond is formed. Newly hatched young are covered sparsely with gray down, and are fed through regurgitation.

Behaviour. An inconspicuous and solitary species, most noticed when the males sing during the breeding season. While calling, the male flits about, flicking his wings upwards one at a time. Skutch (1960) in Costa Rica found males owning "territories" up to 100 ft in diameter, in which they stayed during most of the breeding season, calling and displaying. Occasionally rival males chased each other excitedly through the undergrowth. This dispersed lek behaviour and the emancipation of the male from nesting duties is probably connected with the ready availability of a fruit diet (B. K. Snow & Snow 1979).

White-winged Becard: *Pachyramphus polychopterus*
Kaup's Becard   **Plate 18(2)**

Habitat and status. A fairly common but local resident in both islands, found in light forest, second growth and the edge of mangrove swamps. (Specimens: AMNH, ANSP, CM, LM, BM, TRVL.)

Range and subspecies. Guatemala S through Central and South America to Argentina, Paraguay and Uruguay; *P. p. tristis* (Kaup) ranges from E Colombia through Venezuela to the Guianas.

Description. 6 in. *Male:* head and upperparts black, wing-coverts tipped white, forming 2 prominent wing-bars; underparts dark gray, tail tipped white. *Female and immature male:* head gray-brown, upperparts olive green, wings broadly edged buff; underparts mainly yellowish, outer tail broadly tipped buff. Distinguished by its large head and habit of cocking it sideways and peering.

Measurements. Wing: 6 males 74–80mm (77); 9 females 69–73mm (71.8). Weight: 3 males 17.5, 19, 21.5gm; 4 females 18.5–23gm (20.9).

Voice. A flute-like warbling, usually including a plaintive *tior-tior-tior-tior;* also some chattering notes.

Food. Insects and berries.

Nesting. Breeding and regular singing recorded in Trinidad from March to September (7 nests); moult in March. In Tobago nests may be built as early as January. The nest is a very large mass of material (perhaps 2 ft long, 1 ft broad) placed quite high in a tree, often near a wasps' nest. It is constructed by the female alone of material ranging from dead leaves, twigs, roots and vines to grass and bits of bark; some nests in Tobago were mainly composed of white cotton fibre taken from wild *Gossypium* bushes. The opening to the nest chamber is at the side near the top; sometimes there are 2 chambers, lined with dead leaves. There are usually 3 eggs, pale grayish brown heavily marked, especially at the thicker end, with dark brown, av. 20.4 × 15.3mm (8). In Costa Rica Skutch (1969b) records an incubation period of 18–19 days. The female alone incubates, but the male guards the nest and sometimes escorts the female to and from the nest. Both adults feed the young, which are fledged after about 21 days.

Behaviour. This species, usually found singly or in pairs, is somewhat sluggish, as it sits for longer periods in the middle or upper branches of a tree,

O'Neill
73

Figure 39. Black-tailed Tityra (male)

peering about for prey. Occasionally it will make a sudden foray to flutter briefly at a leaf, picking off an insect from the underside.

Black-tailed Tityra: *Tityra cayana*
"Benedictin"; "Frog-bird"   **Plate 12(5), Figure 39, and Portrait V**

Habitat and status. A fairly common resident in Trinidad, frequenting the edges of forest, second growth and shade trees in cocoa plantations. (Specimens: AMNH, ANSP, YPM, LM, BM, TRVL.)

Range and subspecies. Colombia S to Argentina and Paraguay; the nominate race ranges from E Colombia and Venezuela to the Guianas and N Brazil.

Description. 9 in. *Male:* upperparts whitish, but with head, wings and tail black; underparts white; bare skin around eye and base of bill red, tip of bill black. *Female:* as male, but darker gray above, with fine black streaks on back and breast.

Measurements. Wing: 2 males 120, 129mm; 2 females 120, 123mm. Weight: 2 males 76, 78gm*; 2 females 77.5, 78.5gm*.

Voice. Typically a rather weak, single, buzzing or grunting note; when excited, this is extended to a double call, *beeza-buzza.*

Food. Usually medium-sized tree fruits of various kinds, especially those with high nutritious value (not soft berries as a rule); also seen to take a large green grasshopper from among foliage.

Nesting. Breeding recorded in February, March and November (3 nests); moult in May. The nest is in a tree-hole, often an old woodpecker hole, or at the top of a dead coconut palm, into which the adults carry a mass of dry leaves. The eggs are laid among the leaves, where they remain hidden in the absence of the female. Those of this race are undescribed, but eggs of the Brazilian race are buff marked with brown, av. 30.5 × 22.4mm (2). In a study of the related *T. semifasciata* in Costa Rica, Skutch (1946) found that the female alone incubated, both parents fed the young, the fledging period was at least 3 wk, and 2 broods were reared in one season.

Behaviour. This species is often seen in groups of several individuals, mostly males, or in pairs. They keep high in the tree canopy, frequenting clearings especially, flying rapidly and directly to a new perch. An apparently rather aggressive species, from which other birds move away.

HIRUNDINIDAE: Swallows

The members of this well-known family are characterised by their short necks, slender bodies and long, pointed wings; most species are quite small, and many have forked or notched tails. Swallows inhabit open country, where they feed entirely on insects caught on the wing. Migrants from both North and South America visit our islands during their off-season. Several species are gregarious, roosting and breeding in colonies. Nests are usually built in natural cavities or tunnels, in cliffs, banks or man-made structures. Both parents care for the young, though normally only the female incubates. Swallows are often found perching in large numbers on wires, which they seem to prefer to trees. (8)

White-winged Swallow: *Tachycineta albiventer*
Plate 20(3)

Habitat and status. A very local resident in Trinidad, not uncommon at Pointe-a-Pierre, also seen at various points of the W and S coasts from Chaguaramas to Erin, and at Navet Reservoir; usually found near water, especially reservoirs. (Specimens: AMNH, LM.)

Range. South America from Colombia and Venezuela to N Argentina and Paraguay.

Description. 5.5 in. *Adult:* head and most of upperparts blackish glossed blue-green; rump white, wing-coverts and inner secondaries broadly edged white; underparts white. *Immature:* upperparts grayish brown with almost no blue-green; rump and underparts white.

Measurements. Wing: 1 male 100mm; 1 female 98mm. Weight: 1 male 17gm*.

Voice. A shrill, grating *chirrup.*

Food. Small insects taken low over water or grassland.

Nesting. Breeding recorded from April to August (7 nests). The nest is a cup of grass stems lined with feathers; it is sometimes placed in a natural cavity in a treestump or between boulders; at Pointe-a-Pierre several nests have been made in open scaffolding pipes just above water. The clutch is 3–6 white eggs, av. 19.3 × 13.3mm (11).

Behaviour. Less gregarious than other swallows, this species is often seen singly or in small groups, rarely up to 20 together. It flies low with fast wing-beats, frequently gliding; occasionally it turns suddenly to take an insect. It perches on wires, projecting twigs or poles, buoys in water and sometimes on sand or shingle. It seems fairly tolerant of human disturbance. Occasionally I have seen small numbers bathing in reservoirs, dipping briefly before flying on.

Caribbean Martin: *Progne dominicensis*
"Purple Martin"; Snowy-bellied Martin; Antillean Martin;
"Rainbird"   **Plate 20(1)**

Habitat and status. Regularly found in open areas and locally a common breeding bird in Tobago, especially near steep coasts, cliffs and islands, and over ridges in the hilly areas; also Hillsborough Dam; records mostly between January and October (earliest 10 January) indicate migration, probably to the continent, outside the breeding season. (Specimen: AMNH.)

Range and subspecies. The nominate race is known from Jamaica E through the Antilles and S to Tobago, casual in Bermuda; another race occurs in W Mexico; a Cuban form, lacking visible white on the underparts, is considered conspecific by some authors.

Description. 7.5 in. *Adult male:* generally glossy blue-black, appearing black at a distance, with conspicuously contrasting white lower underparts from mid-breast to vent. *Female and immature:* duller than adult male; upper breast and sides grayish brown, rest of underparts white. Second-year males are in intermediate plumage. Females and immatures are probably not separable in the field from Gray-breasted Martins, but are larger, with grayish brown more sharply demarcated from white of underparts. Tail forked; wings broader than those of other swallows.

Measurements. Wing: 1 male 142mm; 1 female 143mm; 5 unsexed 133–141mm (136). Weight: 1 male 38gm; 4 unsexed 39–42gm (40).

Voice. A liquid, twangy *chew.*

Food. Small flying insects, including butterflies.

Nesting. Breeding recorded in June and July (8 nests), and probably from April onwards; some moult observed in July and August. The nest is a few sticks placed loosely in a rock crevice, often in seacliffs, or in old woodpecker holes in dead palms. All observed clutches were 2 eggs; but clutch size reaches 6 elsewhere in the West Indies.

Behaviour. Fairly gregarious, especially in the evening. The species spends much time soaring on the updraughts over cliffs or ridges. At Hillsborough Dam many congregate on the overhead wires, feeding over the water and occasionally bathing.

Gray-breasted Martin: *Progne chalybea*
White-bellied Martin; "Swallow"; "Rainbird"   **Plate 20(2)**

Habitat and status. A common resident in Trinidad, most commonly seen along the W and N coasts and on Soldado Rock, but also found inland over the Northern Range and other areas, especially over reservoirs, as at Navet, Pointe-a-Pierre and Valencia; also common over urban areas. (Specimens: AMNH, ANSP, CM, TRVL.) Also once recorded in Tobago (Hellmayr 1906). Some migration is possible, but the population at Soldado Rock remains constant in numbers through the year.

Banding status. Twelve birds were banded in July 1964 on Soldado Rock; one of these was retrapped in June 1966 at the same locality.

Range and subspecies. The nominate race ranges from Mexico S through Central and South America to Ecuador, Peru and C Brazil; another race, ranging farther S to Paraguay, Argentina and Uruguay, migrates N in the southern winter as far as Venezuela and Surinam (Eisenmann & Haverschmidt 1970).

Description. 7 in. *Adult male:* similar, though smaller, to adult male Caribbean Martin, but throat, breast and sides grayish brown, *not* dark blue. *Female:* duller than male; throat and breast paler, less sharply demarcated from lower underparts than in Caribbean Martin. *Immature:* upperparts dull brown, *not* dark blue. Tail forked.

Measurements. Wing: 5 males 128–137mm (132.4); 1 female 127mm. Weight: 115 unsexed 36–48gm (42.9). Large samples weighed in January, June and October showed little variation in mean weight.

Voice. Normal call very similar to that of Caribbean Martin. The song, often heard at dawn on Soldado Rock, is a high-pitched musical warble, reminiscent of the Skylark (*Alauda arvensis*), sung high in the air.

Food. Small flying insects, including moths, dragonflies, bugs, bees, ants and termites; also seen to take large grasshoppers occasionally.

Nesting. Breeding recorded from April to July, most of 26 nests in May and June; adult moult recorded in October, first-year birds in December/January. The nest is a loose cup of sticks or stems, placed in a rock crevice (the natural site) or in a variety of man-made structures such as the scaffolding, sometimes the pipes, of a bridge, jetty or even in holes in the structure of an oil refinery, as at Pointe-a-Pierre; also under the eaves of buildings. The clutch is 2–4 white eggs, av. 22.8 × 16.2mm (7). Incubation, in Guyana (Bent 1942), lasts 15–16 days; fledging period about 22 days.

Behaviour. Essentially gregarious, both in nesting and at the roost. Large numbers congregate on overhead wires at Pointe-a-Pierre, especially in the evening. Sometimes they indulge in communal bathing in the water of a reservoir, flying down, dipping briefly, then proceeding up and round again; occasionally numbers of martins perch on sandy beaches or the dry mudbanks of reservoirs, but they normally perch on wires, pipes and the thin, bare branches of trees. When feeding, these martins scatter, but they are usually found in groups flying high above the ground. In the evening they move in loose flocks of up to 2000 to a roost, which may be along a pipeline at Pointe-a-Pierre or among rocky cliffs at Soldado Rock. Except during the breeding season, martins are largely absent during the day at Soldado Rock, crossing at least 7 miles of sea to feed over land. Leaving the island within 1 hr of sunrise, they return between 5:00 and 6:00 P.M. to roost.

Blue-and-white Swallow: *Notiochelidon cyanoleuca*
Plate 20(5)

Habitat and status. A locally common visitor to savannahs in C and S Trinidad, where it is found regularly over canefields at McBean and pastures at Orange Grove between June and September. Arrival from the mainland usually coincides with the first heavy rains (between 23 May and 11 June for the 10 yr 1962–1971), earliest date 30 April, latest departure date 29 October. (Specimens: ANSP, LM.)

Range and subspecies. Mexico south to S South America; *N. c. patagonica* (Lafresnaye & d'Orbigny) breeds in S South America, migrating N to Panama, Colombia, Venezuela, Trinidad and the Guianas, occasionally as far as Mexico; it is larger than the nominate race, which ranges from Costa Rica S to Argentina; reported breeding of the species in Trinidad presumably refers to the latter race, but no specimens exist.

Description. 5 in. *Adult:* upperparts blue-black, wings and tail black; underparts white from throat to abdomen, under-tail-coverts blackish, flanks brown. *Immature:* brown above with a few blue-black feathers, throat and breast mottled. Tail slightly forked.

Measurements. Wing: 1 male 102mm; 1 female 102mm. Weight: 1 male 15.5gm*; 1 female 16gm*.

Voice. A light *chit* or *chree.*

Food. Small flying insects, including froghoppers, flies, bugs, ants and beetles.

Nesting. Breeding recorded only by B/S in late March. A nest of grass, lined with feathers, was placed in a cavity in an old bridge and contained 3 white eggs, av. 16.7 × 12.7mm. In Costa Rica (Skutch 1960) nests are placed in cavities in a variety of sites: trees, buildings, banks, etc. Clutch size is 2–4, the eggs being laid on consecutive days. Incubation period is 15 days, fledging 26–27 days, the young becoming fully independent about 2 wk later. The nest is used for sleeping both before and after breeding, and the young fledged birds may share it with their parents even while a second brood is being raised.

Behaviour. Generally gregarious, these birds forage low over the savannahs, twisting and turning rapidly in the manner typical of swallows. They often rest in long lines on the telephone or electricity wires which form the only convenient perching site across the wide savannah.

Southern Rough-winged Swallow: *Stelgidopteryx ruficollis* Plate 20(4)

Habitat and status. A fairly common resident in Trinidad and the Bocas islands, frequenting open areas and forest clearings; some sight records from Tobago in April (A. Spaans) and August. (Specimens: AMNH, ANSP, CM, LM, TRVL.)

Range and subspecies. Honduras S to N Argentina and Uruguay, some races being migratory; *S. r. aequalis* (Bangs) ranges from Colombia to Venezuela and Trinidad.

Description. 5.5 in. Upperparts brown with *pale grayish rump,* wings and tail blackish; throat and lower face pale chestnut, lower underparts yellowish white.

Measurements. Wing: 5 males 100–109mm (104.2); 3 females 103, 104, 106mm. Weight: 1 male 15gm; 6 unsexed 14–16gm (15.1); 7 immatures 12.5–15.5gm (13.9).

Voice. A rather unmusical *chirrup,* the pitch rising slightly.

Food. Small flying insects, including ants, bees, bugs, flies and beetles.

Nesting. Breeding recorded in April and May (5 nests); moult in August. The nest is in a cavity in a bank, wall or cliffside, occasionally the disused nest tunnel of a kingfisher or jacamar, and is lined with dead grass; the birds are not known to dig their own tunnels. The clutch is 3–6 white eggs, av. 18.5 × 12.8mm (3). In Central America Skutch (1960) found that eggs were laid on consecutive days and incubated by the female alone for 16–18 days; the young are fed by both parents, and, though fully feathered after 13 days, do not fly before 20–21 days. Much comparative information is given on USA birds by Lunk (1962).

Behaviour. Usually not gregarious, this swallow is notable for its slow, deliberate flight quite near the ground, coursing frequently over the same area; it seems to be a distinctly sedentary species. I have noticed small loose flocks gathering in the evening to roost, and Skutch (1960) in Costa Rica found large numbers roosting communally in sugarcane patches in a manner most reminiscent of wintering Dickcissels in Trinidad (ffrench 1967b).

Notes. The origin of the English name for this species lies in the serrated edge of the outer primary. Various speculations have been made as to the function of this, one of the most plausible being that of Lunk (1962), that it may produce a faint high-pitched sound in flight, of possible importance in aerial display.

Bank Swallow: *Riparia riparia*
Sand Martin

Habitat and status. A rather uncommon passage migrant in Trinidad, where I have sight records from savannahs and the seashore on 28 December, 26 January, 1 March and 24 April; sight records of 2 birds in Tobago in April (A. Spaans). (No specimens, but the species has been identified by several experienced observers.)

Range. Breeds in North America and the N Palearctic region, wintering in our area S to Argentina.

Description. 5 in. Upperparts brown; underparts white with a brown band across the breast; tail shallow-forked. A bird seen in company with Barn Swallows and a Cliff Swallow was distinguished by its many glides and long flittering flights upwind.

Barn Swallow: *Hirundo rustica*
Swallow (in Europe)

Habitat and status. A common visitor to both islands, frequenting savannahs, swamps and coastal areas; in Trinidad present from late August (earliest date 17 August) to May (latest date 28 May, many birds), but numerous only locally, e.g., Oropouche Lagoon, Caroni marshes, Piarco savannah. (Specimens: ANSP, LM.)

Range and subspecies. Worldwide in distribution; *H. r. erythrogaster* (Boddaert) breeds in North America S to Mexico, wintering S to Chile and Argentina.

Description. 7 in. *Adult:* upperparts glossy steel blue, *forehead chestnut;* white spots on tail, of which the very long, narrow outer feathers form a *deep* *fork; throat chestnut,* partial blue-black collar extending down to sides of breast, lower underparts pale chestnut. *Immature:* as adult, but tail less deeply forked, and chestnut of underparts paler, sometimes almost white.

Measurements. Wing: 1 male 116mm; 2 unsexed 111, 114mm. Weight: 1 male 17gm*; 4 unsexed 16, 17.5*, 18, 19.5gm*.

Voice. A light, metallic *chik.*

Food. Small flying insects, including dragonflies, flies, beetles and ants. Feeding flocks often concentrate at insect swarms found over manure or sugarcane refuse (bagasse) heaps, rubbish tips, etc.

Notes. Two birds trapped on 11 January were moulting wing- and tail-feathers (D. W. Snow & Snow 1963a).

[Cliff Swallow: *Petrochelidon pyrrhonota*]

Habitat and status. Two sight records only, at Nariva on 1 March 1959 and at Port of Spain sewage ponds on 25 January 1988 (D. Fisher). (No specimens.)

Range. Breeds in North America, wintering S to Argentina and Uruguay; a rare transient in the West Indies (Bond 1960), but small numbers regular on autumn and spring passage through Barbados.

Description. 5.5 in. Upperparts dark glossy blue with whitish forehead and *pale chestnut rump;* sides of head and throat chestnut, rest of underparts buff; *tail square* or hardly forked. Flies higher than Barn Swallow, with which it commonly associates.

MOTACILLIDAE: Pipits and Wagtails

This family of slender, long-tailed birds is found mostly in the Old World but is represented in America by a few species, usually inhabiting open areas. Mostly terrestrial, wagtails feed on insects, walking or running about busily, bobbing their heads and frequently wagging their tails. Their flight is strong and undulating. (1)

White Wagtail: *Motacilla alba*

Habitat and status. A single record only, of a bird seen (and photographed) by many people at Waller Field agricultural station between 26 December 1987 and 2 January 1988 (F. Oatman). Accidental vagrant from Old World. (No specimen.)

Range. Breeds in Europe and Asia, wintering S to Africa, the far eastern population extending into Alaska, casual down W coast of North America; 1 recent record from Costa Rica.

Description. 7 in. *Adult (breeding):* hind-crown, upperparts black (or back pale gray in some races), wings edged white; forehead, sides of head and lower underparts white, throat and breast black; tail long, edged white. *Non-breeding birds:* have white throat with crescentic black bib, upperparts less dark. Bill short.

Voice. A light *chizzik*.

* * *

[Greater Bird-of-Paradise: *Paradisaea apoda*]

Although this species does not properly belong to the avifauna of Trinidad and Tobago, I include a note on its status partly because many people would be surprised to see it omitted, and partly to clear up a few general misunderstandings.

This species, one of the family of birds-of-paradise (Paradisaeidae), is a native of the Aru Islands off the coast of New Guinea. When the plume trade brought threats of extinction to several members of the family, the late Sir William Ingram captured and transported a large number of immature Greater Birds-of-Paradise. In September 1909 about 48 birds were released on the island of Little Tobago (sometimes known as Bird-of-Paradise Island), with the object of preserving the species for posterity in the wild state. It appears that the distance of 1 mile from the main island of Tobago effectively prevented the birds, which are heavy fliers, from leaving Little Tobago.

A reliable census of the numbers of surviving birds was not made until 1958, when E. T. Gilliard spent 3 wk on the island, estimating a minimum of 15 birds and a maximum of 29. Evidently the birds had bred on the island, though a nest has never been found. In 1965–66 J. J. Dinsmore spent nearly 10 months studying the ecology and behaviour of the species, then reduced to a maximum of 7 birds (Dinsmore 1967, 1969, 1970). It was concluded that the island could support up to 25 birds, as the species had shown itself able to adapt to the conditions on Little Tobago. But the remaining birds gradually died out, the last reliable sighting being on 25 February 1981. Meanwhile, with the diminution of the plume trade, Greater Birds-of-Paradise still flourish on the Aru Islands.

TROGLODYTIDAE: Wrens

These birds are small and cryptically coloured, with short, rounded wings, stumpy tails and slender, straight or slightly curved bills. In our islands they inhabit undergrowth and low vegetation, and with their skulking habits are more commonly heard than seen, for their song is highly developed. The House Wren, however, is frequently found near human habitation. Wrens are insectivorous, foraging among foliage, on the ground and around buildings. (2)

Rufous-breasted Wren: *Thryothorus rutilus*
Speckled Wren; Bush Wren; "Jungle Wren"   **Plate 16(8)**

Habitat and status. A common resident of Trinidad, less common in Tobago, frequenting undergrowth and dense thickets in forests and second growth. (Specimens: Trinidad, AMNH, ANSP, CM, LM, TRVL; Tobago, AMNH, LM.)

Range and subspecies. Panama and W Costa Rica east to Colombia, Venezuela, Trinidad and Tobago; *T. r. rutilus* (Vieillot) ranges from E Colombia to Venezuela and Trinidad; *T. r. tobagensis* (Hellmayr) is confined to Tobago, being slightly larger and darker below.

Description. 5 in. Upperparts grayish brown, tail barred blackish; *throat and sides of face conspicuously speckled black on white;* breast reddish orange, abdomen brownish white, flanks brown.

Measurements. *T. r. rutilus*. Wing: 18 males 55–64mm (61.0); 6 females 57–59mm (58.0). Weight: 6 males 14–17gm (16.3); 3 females 14, 14, 15gm, 1 egg-laying 20gm; 21 unsexed 13.5–18.5gm (16.9). *T. r. tobagensis*. Wing: 5 males 61–65mm (63.0); 6 females 59–65mm (62.5). Weight: 6 unsexed 15.5–20gm (17.2).

Voice. Song is a musical whistle of 6–10 clear notes, varying considerably but usually ending with a flourish of quicker notes; this is often performed antiphonally by a mated pair, more rarely in unison. Other calls include a sharp, high-pitched *chweep,* like a diminutive sneeze, a double *chupeek,* very sharp at the end, and a short trill, rising in pitch. Immature birds call a high-pitched double squeak.

Food. Insects taken amongst foliage, especially tangled vines, or on the ground, also centipedes. Sometimes exploits army ant swarms.

Nesting. Breeding recorded in Trinidad from January to July (17 nests); song recorded in all months; moult in March, August and October. Five Tobago records, in January, March, June (2) and July. The nest is a fairly large sphere, loosely built of bamboo leaves, grass and other leaves, lined with fine grass or plant-down; there is a wide side entrance. The nest is often situated in a tangle of vines, in ferns or in a thicket 1–5 ft above ground but I have seen a nest as high as 40 ft situated in a bromeliad on a tree-trunk. The clutch is 2–4 eggs, white with spots and blotches of reddish brown, av. 18.9 × 14.1mm (3). The species is parasitised by the cowbird *Molothrus,* which also deposits eggs in the sleeping nests of the wren. In Costa Rica, Skutch (1960) found that both parents build the nest and feed the young, but the female alone incubates. The young, which hatch naked, are fledged after 16 days.

Behaviour. Extremely skulking; the loud song is given by a mated pair every few seconds during the daylight hours in the breeding season. This enables them to maintain contact as they work their way through dense undergrowth.

House Wren: *Troglodytes aedon*
"House Bird"; "God-Bird"; "Cucurachelle"

Habitat and status. A common resident of both islands, including the larger offshore islands, frequenting gardens in urban areas, cultivated areas, secondary scrub and forest clearings, especially at lower levels; also recorded near houses up to 2000 ft. (Specimens: Trinidad, AMNH, ANSP, YPM, CM, LM, TRVL; Tobago, AMNH, LM.)

Range and subspecies. Throughout America from Canada to Tierra del Fuego. *T. a. albicans* (Berlepsch & Taczanowski) ranges from E Colombia to Venezuela, Trinidad and the Guianas, also S from Ecuador and Peru to C Brazil; *T. a. tobagensis* (Lawrence) occurs in Tobago only; it is larger and much paler below. Some authors consider the Neotropical forms of the House Wren a separate species, *T. musculus,* the Southern House Wren.

Description. 5 in. Crown and upperparts mouse brown, rump reddish brown, wings and tail barred with blackish; superciliary streak, sides of head, throat and abdomen whitish; breast, flanks and under-tail-coverts buff; bill light brown.

Measurements. *T. a. albicans.* Wing: 14 males 52–56mm (54.0); 4 females 53–54mm. Weight: 2 males 13, 14gm; 2 females 13, 13.5gm; 27 unsexed 12.5–17.5gm (14.4). *T. a. tobagensis.* Wing: 3 males 55, 59, 60mm; 3 females 56, 58, 59mm. Weight: 6 unsexed 14.5–17gm (15.8).

Voice. Song variable; a brilliant, loud, warbling series, usually with a trill in the middle and ending with a rise in pitch, e.g., *tsee-tsee-toodle-oodle-tooee;* it is often prolonged by several more chattering notes, which, along with scolding churrs, are also heard separately. This species is one of the first to sing at dawn and will sing at night if disturbed. The female twitters weakly in answer to her mate. I once found a bird calling a strange, plaintive note when a coral snake (*Micrurus lemniscatus*) was nearby.

Food. Small insects, including caterpillars and ants, and spiders, gleaned from crevices and foliage; often forages around windows of houses.

Nesting. Breeding recorded in Trinidad (102 nests) throughout the year, as follows:

I	II	III	IV	V	VI
6	5	2	9	17	14

VII	VIII	IX	X	XI	XII
7	4	7	14	8	9

Snow's records in Arima Valley show distinct peaks in May and October–November; singing is regular through the year; moult in August. Breeding in Tobago recorded from March to December. The nest is a large, untidy saucer of twigs lined with feathers, down, snakeskins or soft fibres, placed often on a beam beneath the roof of a house, or in some hole between masonry, in the cleft of a tree, in a bromeliad fairly high in a tree or in the abandoned nesting cavity of another species. The clutch is 3–6 eggs, usually 3 or 4, pale cream marked with 2 shades of red, especially heavy at the larger end; 8 eggs (from Trinidad) av. 18.2 × 13.6mm. They are laid on consecutive days. The cowbird *Molothrus* especially victimises this species, up to 9 eggs being added to the wren's clutch. Both parents build the nest and feed the young, but the female alone incubates, for a period of 14–15 days. The young are fledged after 16–19 days. A pair may breed (or attempt to breed) 2 or 3 times a year, the interval between successful broods being at least 6 wk. In Costa Rica, Skutch (1960) found much shorter intervals between broods, and also that young birds of one brood sometimes helped to feed the nestlings of the next brood.

Behaviour. Often a very confiding species. In a commonly seen display both members of a pair vibrate their wings while the male sings; sometimes he points his head up almost vertically while singing.

MIMIDAE: Mockingbirds

This family, confined to the New World, consists of thrush-like birds with long tails and rounded wings; the bill is fairly long and usually slightly decurved. The song is conspicuous and usually musical, and is much used in aggressive territorial display. Mockingbirds feed on or near the ground, taking insects and small fruits. The single species recorded in our islands is most commonly found near human habitation. (1)

Tropical Mockingbird: *Mimus gilvus*
Southern Mockingbird; Graceful Mockingbird; "Day-clean"; "Paraulata"   **Plate 21(2)**

Habitat and status. A common resident in both islands, being widespread in every habitat except thick forest in Tobago; in Trinidad apparently a recent arrival, mainly found in gardens and scrub near human habitation. In 1931 it was restricted to St. Augustine (Roberts 1934); by 1956 it was common at Piarco, Port of Spain and in oil company residential areas in S Trinidad; it can now also be found a few miles up the valleys of the Northern Range, on the E coast as far as Toco, on savannahs at Caroni, Oropouche, Cumuto, and on the Bocas Islands W to Chacachacare. (Specimens: both islands, AMNH, ANSP, LM.)

Range and subspecies. Through the Lesser Antilles and from Mexico S through Central America to Colombia, Venezuela, the Guianas and N Brazil; *M. g. tobagensis* (Dalmas) is confined to Trinidad and Tobago and has darker gray upperparts with more extensive white on wing-coverts and tips of outer tail-feathers.

Description. 10 in. Head and upperparts gray, wings darker edged with white, forming wing-bars; *tail long, blackish, broadly and conspicuously tipped white;* broad streak through eye blackish, superciliary streak whitish; underparts mainly white with more or less gray on throat and breast; bill black; iris yellow.

Measurements. Wing: 7 males 105–113mm (109.7); 7 females 102–111mm (107.4). Weight: 1 male 56gm*; 2 females 51, 56gm*; 30 unsexed 43–67gm (51.1).

Voice. Song extremely varied and mostly musical. A typical burst of song lasts several seconds and includes whistled notes of different pitches and cadences, the phrases often being repeated once or twice. Sometimes one bird imitates precisely the phrases being sung by a rival on a neighbouring territory. Rarely are the calls of other species incorporated. Song is occasionally heard at night. Apart from the musical notes, a variety of clucks and wheezes are heard; one alarm note is a sharp, metallic *cheer*, often repeated.

Food. Insects, including beetles, caterpillars, flying termites and wasps; also spiders; also often berries and fruits, including mango, sapodilla, pawpaw; in the Dutch Leeward Islands reported to take lizards and birds' eggs.

Nesting. Breeding in Trinidad (86 nests) recorded in all months except August and December, as follows:

I	II	III	IV	V	VI
11	10	11	13	19	5

VII	VIII	IX	X	XI	XII
2	—	5	4	3	—

Moult recorded from August to October. Fewer records for Tobago cover February–July. The nest is a rough cup of twigs lined with rootlets, placed usually fairly low in a tree or shrub, often quite conspicuous. The clutch is usually 3, occasionally 2 or 4, grayish green or blue eggs spotted or blotched with reddish brown, av. 27 × 19.4mm (10). Incubation, by the female alone, lasts for 13–15 days; both parents feed the young, which hatch sparsely covered with black down; Snow and I have recorded 6 fledging periods of 13–15 days and one other of 18–19 days. In N Venezuela Skutch (1968) found a pair which nested 3 times between March and June, successfully at least twice. The young flying birds associated with their parents during later broods and roosted near the nest.

Behaviour. Usually found in pairs or family groups, this species defends its territory with aggressive zeal, attacking not only other birds but also large lizards, e.g., *Iguana* and *Ameiva*, mongooses and dogs. One conspicuous habit is that of lifting and half-spreading its wings, "wing-flashing", often while foraging on the ground. The function of this habit is not clear, but by analogy with the northern *M. polyglottos* it may be associated with food-getting (by flushing out insects); it may be an expression of wariness; or it may be an extension of a balancing movement (Horwich 1965).

TURDIDAE: Thrushes

These are medium-sized birds with fairly long, sharp bills and generally sober plumage. In our area 3 species are mainly terrestrial, hopping or running on the ground and feeding on insects and other invertebrates, while 2 others are arboreal; berries are also an important part of their diet. The songs of several species are conspicuously musical. Territories are held, but our thrushes do not seem to be as aggressive as mockingbirds. Nests are usually built of moss and roots, often lined with mud, and are well concealed in trees or banks. (7)

Orange-billed Nightingale-Thrush: *Catharus aurantiirostris*
Birchall's Catharus   **Plate 21(4)**

Habitat and status. A rather rare resident in Trinidad, confined to the higher parts of the Northern Range, mostly above 2500 ft, where it inhabits undergrowth. (Specimens: CM, LM.)

Range and subspecies. Mexico S to Panama, Colombia and N Venezuela; *C. a. birchalli* (Seebohm) occurs also in NE Venezuela.

Description. 6.5 in. Upperparts bright brown, underparts gray becoming white posteriorly; narrow eye-ring conspicuously orange; *bill bright orange;* legs long, orange-yellow. *Immature:* has buff centres and dark tips to feathers on head, upper back, breast and flanks.

Measurements. Wing: 8 males 77–82mm (79.5); 3 females 73, 76, 76mm. Weight: 2 males 21.5, 25.5gm*.

Voice. Song is a short, loud but musical phrase, often repeated and stereo-typed but varying for individuals; the phrase normally includes 2 or 3 higher-pitched, emphatic notes among several lower, chuckling notes. One alarm call (Junge & Mees 1958) is a loud *charrrr*, another is a low *chuck,* followed by a nasal wheeze.

Food. Insects; I once watched a bird feeding at an army ant trail. In other areas known to take fruit also.

Nesting. The only breeding record is by B/S, who record a pair building a nest in May; song occurs in all months from December to August. In Costa Rica (Skutch 1960) this species builds a fairly large, cup-shaped nest of moss and plant stems, lined with fine roots and situated in a bush or thicket a few feet above ground. The 2 or 3 eggs are blue or greenish spotted and blotched with reddish brown. The female alone incubates for 13–15 days; both parents feed the young, which are fledged at 13–17 days old.

Behaviour. An extremely secretive species; hard to observe in the field. The conspicuous song is delivered from a low perch, usually amidst undergrowth.

Gray-cheeked Thrush: *Catharus minimus*
Hylocichla minima

Habitat and status. A rare visitor to Trinidad, 4 records only, once when a freshly dead bird was found beside the plate-glass door of a building in Port of Spain on 1 November 1963 (Worth & Aitken 1965); also sight records at Springhill on 25 March 1972 and 19 December 1989, and at Aripo on 23 January 1988. (Specimen: TRVL.)

Range and subspecies. Breeds in NE Siberia and N North America, wintering south to N South America; the nominate race winters S (from September to May) to Ecuador, Peru, Colombia, Venezuela, Guyana and NW Brazil. Rare in the West Indies.

Description. 6.25 in. A small grayish olive thrush with gray cheeks, an inconspicuous eye-ring and pale underparts, the *breast spotted with black.*

Measurements. Wing: 1 male 104mm.

Voice. The call-note is a nasal *vee-a* or *quee-a* (Peterson 1947).

Veery: *Catharus fuscescens*
Hylocichla fuscescens

Habitat and status. A rare visitor to Trinidad, recorded twice in forest: an immature bird was trapped at St. Pat's on 19 April 1975, and another was seen at Springhill on 15 October 1982.

Range. Breeds in North America, wintering S from Central America to N South America. Rare transient in West Indies.

Description. 6.5 in. Upperparts warm brown, pale tips to wing-coverts in *immature,* underparts white, throat and upper breast buff lightly spotted with brown.

Measurements. One unsexed bird. Wing: 99mm; weight: 45gm.

Yellow-legged Thrush: *Platycichla flavipes*
Black Thrush; Black-and-grey Thrush   **Plate 21(1) and Portrait VI**

Habitat and status. A fairly common but local resident of both islands, inhabiting mountain forest, in Trinidad mostly above 1800 ft, occasionally descending lower to feed and ranging widely; in Tobago mostly above 1000 ft. Herklots' record (1961) of an all-black thrush on Morne Bleu in November 1954 was probably a colour variant. (Specimens: Trinidad, AMNH, CM, YPM, LM, BM; Tobago, AMNH, CM, BM.)

Range and subspecies. Colombia E and S to Venezuela, Brazil, Paraguay and NE Argentina; *P. f. melanopleura* (Sharpe) occurs in Trinidad, NE Venezuela and Margarita Island; the adult male is generally black, with dark gray back, flanks and lower underparts. *P. f. xanthoscelus* (Jardine) is confined to Tobago, is larger, and the male is all black.

Description. 8.5 in. *Adult male:* all black or generally black with dark gray back, flanks and lower underparts; narrow eye-ring, bill and legs yellow. *Female:* upperparts olive brown, underparts ochreous brown; bill yellow or blackish, legs yellow-brown. *Immature:* as adult, but feathers on crown and upperparts with buff tips, throat and breast mottled and barred black and yellow.

Measurements. *P. f. melanopleura.* Wing: 20 males 105–118mm (111.2); 5 females 103–113mm (107.4). Weight: 14 males 52–67gm (59.0); 4 females 55–66gm (62.1). *P. f. xanthoscelus.*Wing: 9 males 112–121mm (116.3); 2 females 106, 111mm. Weight: 2 males 59, 66.5gm.

Voice. The song, delivered from a high perch, is remarkably musical and varied, rivalling even those of European thrushes in beauty. Repeated phrases figure prominently, and in Tobago imitations of manakins and spinetails are sometimes included. Alarm note a typical thrush-like cluck.

Food. Small fruits, including those of the matchwood (*Didymopanax*), *Myrcia* and *Sloanea;* also insects.

Nesting. Breeding recorded in Trinidad during March–July (6 nests); moult in August; song heard in both islands from January to August. Three nests found by B/S resembled those of other Turdidae but were a little shallower. They were constructed of roots mixed with mud and coated with moss, lined with fine roots; the situation was in a niche on a bank, or a rock at the side of a ravine. Each clutch was of 2 eggs, pale blue or greenish blue marked with reddish brown, av. 29.2 × 20.4mm (6).

Behaviour. This arboreal species is rather shy and is usually located by its song, so that females are rarely seen.

Cocoa Thrush: *Turdus fumigatus*
Sabian Thrush; Pale-vented Robin (Thrush)   **Plate 21(6)**

Habitat and status. A common resident in Trinidad, frequenting forest and cultivated areas with large trees up to altitudes of 2000 ft; its habitat overlaps those of the Bare-eyed and White-necked thrushes. (Specimens: AMNH, ANSP, CM, YPM, LM, TRVL.)

Range and subspecies. Colombia and Venezuela E and S to the Guianas, Bolivia and Brazil; also in St. Vincent and Grenada. *T. f. aquilonalis* (Cherrie) ranges from NE Colombia to N Venezuela and Trinidad.

Description. 9 in. Upperparts rich chestnut brown, paler brown below; bill brown. *Immature:* has buff edges to wing-coverts.

Measurements. Wing: 7 males 109–118mm (114.7); 7 females 104–119mm (112.0). Weight: 20 males 55.5–75gm (69.3); 15 females 66.5–83gm (75.1); 118 unsexed 56.5–81gm (71.0). (D. W. Snow & Snow [1963b] remark that birds from lowland regions were smaller and lighter than those in the Northern Range; but more data are needed to confirm this.)

Voice. The song is a good indicator of breeding activity; it is a series of loud, musical notes, consisting mostly of rapidly repeated short phrases, with considerable variation and quality; also a sudden and rapid series of similar notes, *wee-a-wee-a-wee-a,* etc., descending slightly in pitch; in alarm, a rapid, harsh *kik-ik-ik-ik.*

Food. Invertebrates taken on the ground, and berries. Commonly seen feeding in roadside ditches in the Northern Range.

Nesting. Breeding recorded (188 nests) in all months except September, as follows:

I	II	III	IV	V	VI
8	20	20	24	28	37

VII	VIII	IX	X	XI	XII
19	1	—	2	18	11

The moulting period is June–October, each individual taking about 90 days. Three or 4 broods may be reared in 1 yr, nests being regularly re-used if the previous brood is successful; 2 nests were used 4 times each. Intervals between successive nesting attempts vary from 6 to 199 days, the shortest occurring from April to July, the longest when moult intervenes. The nest is a bulky cup of plant material strengthened with mud and containing much moss on the exterior, lined with rootlets. It may be found up to 15 ft above ground, in niches in banks, recesses in tree trunks and branches, on stumps or tops of tree ferns, especially along roads or paths in forest or cocoa plantations. Clutch size averages 2.8 (19 × 2, 66 × 3, 2 × 4, apparently not varying seasonally); the eggs are pale greenish blue, marbled and blotched with pale reddish brown, especially at the larger end; an unspecified number averaged 28.2 × 20.4mm (B/S), 2 extra large being 32.2 and 32mm long. They are laid on consecutive days, probably in the latter half of the morning. Incubation, by the female, normally lasts 12.5–13.5 days, and fledging occurs at 13–15 days. The young, which moult their body feathers soon after leaving the nest, may be attended by parents up to 32 days after fledging. In an analysis of 57 nests

33% were successful, those in forests being less so than those in cocoa plantations. (Breeding data from D. W. Snow & Snow 1963b).

Behaviour. A sedentary species; at least occasionally, mated pairs remain together for some years. Territorial behaviour is weakly developed, and breeding birds allow others to forage close to their nest without molestation (D. W. Snow & Snow 1963b).

Bare-eyed Thrush: *Turdus nudigenis*
Bare-eyed Robin; "Goldeye Thrush"; "Big-eye Grive"   **Plate 21(5)**

Habitat and status. A common resident of both islands, including offshore islets, inhabiting semi-open savannahs, gardens, cultivated areas (citrus and cocoa), dry scrub and deciduous forests; less commonly in secondary forests up to 2000 ft. (Specimens: AMNH, ANSP, CM, YPM, LM, TRVL.)

Range and subspecies. Colombia and Venezuela S to Ecuador, Peru and Brazil; the nominate race ranges from E Colombia to Venezuela, the Guianas and N Brazil, also the Lesser Antilles from St. Lucia S.

Description. 9.5 in. Upperparts olive brown, paler below, throat white streaked brown, lower underparts whitish; bill yellowish; *large bare ring around eye golden yellow. Immature:* has buff spots on wings.

Measurements. Wing: 35 males 104–122mm (112.8, S.D. 3.9); 16 females 107–115mm (110). Weight: 25 males 55–74.5gm (61.6, S.D. 4.6); 9 females 56.5–74gm (65.6); 47 unsexed 50–75gm (61).

Voice. The song, which may be heard in any month of the year but most regularly from April to August, resembles that of the Cocoa Thrush but is more halting and less far-carrying. Call-notes include a querulous, cat-like, double note, *keer-lee*, and a more musical phrase, *chareera.*

Food. Berries and fruits, including paw-paw, guava and avocado pear; also invertebrates, including caterpillars, beetles, moths and earthworms, taken from the ground; readily takes soaked bread, etc., from feeding tables.

Nesting. Breeding recorded in Trinidad from April to September (158 nests) as follows:

IV	V	VI	VII	VIII	IX
2	54	53	34	14	1

Tobago nests recorded from May to August. Moult in August–December. Two broods, rarely more, may be reared in a season; in three cases the same nest was re-used. The nest is a cup constructed of various plant materials mixed with mud and lined with rootlets, usually not decorated with moss (like forest thrushes'). It is situated 6–25 ft above ground in the fork of a large branch or shrub. Clutch size averages 2.96 (9 × 2, 41 × 3, 7 × 4, the average decreasing later in the season). The eggs are deep blue or greenish blue, marked with deep reddish brown especially at the larger end, av. 29.3 × 19.4mm (10). The female alone incubates, but both parents attend the young. Of 21 nests, 33% were successful (D. W. Snow & Snow 1963b).

Behaviour. I have noted aggressive behaviour towards other species at feeding tables and bathing places. One bird stood for more than 2 min in a birdbath, in 3 in. of water, drinking occasionally. After leaving to feed briefly, it returned to chase off a mockingbird and bathe.

White-necked Thrush: *Turdus albicollis*
White-throated Thrush; White-necked Robin   **Plate 21(3)**

Habitat and status. A common resident in Trinidad, less common in Tobago (especially since 1963), frequenting forests mainly in hilly areas, where it occurs in undergrowth. (Specimens: AMNH, ANSP, CM, YPM, LM, TRVL.)

Range and subspecies. Mexico S through Middle and South America to Bolivia, N Argentina and Paraguay; *T. a. phaeopygoides* (Seebohm) occurs also in NE Venezuela. Some authors regard the Middle American forms as a different species.

Description. 8 in. Upperparts dark olive brown, upper throat white streaked with dark brown, lower throat conspicuously white, rest of underparts grayish becoming white posteriorly. *Immature:* has buff centres to feathers of wing-coverts and a mottled buff-and-gray breast-band.

Measurements. Wing: 6 males 107–112mm (109.7); 3 females 107, 109, 114mm. Weight: 4 males 47.5–52.5gm* (49.2); 2 females 54, 58gm*, 3 females (probably egg-laying) 66, 66.5, 70gm; 85 unsexed 45–63gm (54.0).

Voice. The song is a slow and melancholy, but tuneful, series of paired notes; this species and the Cocoa Thrush are amongst the earliest singers to be heard at dawn in the forest. Alarm note is a low cluck.

Food. Fruits of forest trees, including *Cordia, Myrcia* and *Miconia,* also invertebrates taken from the ground.

Nesting. Breeding recorded in most months with a peak from March to June (76 Trinidad nests), as follows:

I	II	III	IV	V	VI
2	6	10	10	11	20

VII	VIII	IX	X	XI	XII
3	3	—	—	7	4

Moult recorded only in May and June, but probably extends to October. One Tobago nest in April. There are probably 3 broods in a year, the intervals between breeding in 3 successively used nests being 38, 77 and 87 days. The nest resembles that of the Cocoa Thrush, but is often more exposed, and is smaller and shallower. Clutch size averages 2.08 (49 × 2, 2 × 3, 1 × 4), the eggs being blue marked with rich red-brown and underlying lavender, av. 27.6 × 20.7mm (10). They are laid on consecutive days, apparently in the morning, the female incubating for 12.5 days. Both parents feed the young. Of 35 nests, 20% were successful (D. W. Snow & Snow 1963b).

Behaviour. Though commonly seen feeding at roadside ditches in forested areas, this thrush mostly frequents undergrowth and low branches in deep-shaded forest, where it is more often heard than seen, being much more shy than its congeners. It holds rather small, permanent territories.

SYLVIIDAE: Old World Warblers and Gnatcatchers

The Polioptilinae, usually considered members of the family of Old World warblers found in the Americas, includes only 1 species inhabiting Trinidad, where it frequents the undergrowth and low branches in forest and second growth. It is a small, inconspicuous, wren-like bird with a very long, thin bill and a long, narrow tail, which it flicks loosely as it moves restlessly among the foliage somewhat in the manner of certain antbirds. Members of this family are largely insectivorous, and their songs are mostly high-pitched and somewhat monotonous trills. (1)

Long-billed Gnatwren: *Ramphocaenus melanurus*
Long-billed Antwren; Long-billed Gnatcatcher;
Straight-billed Gnatwren   **Plate 16(4)**

Habitat and status. A common resident in Trinidad, found in forest and, more especially, dense second growth, where it keeps to the undergrowth and the lower branches of trees, especially where vines are prominent. (Specimens: AMNH, ANSP, CM, LM, TRVL.)

Range and subspecies. Mexico S through Middle and South America to Ecuador, Peru and Brazil; *R. m. trinitatis* (Lesson) ranges from E Colombia to N Venezuela and Trinidad.

Description. 5 in. Upperparts grayish brown, sides of head rufous; tail blackish, outer feathers tipped white; throat whitish, rest of underparts pale, washed with buff; *bill long* (1 in.) and slender. The loosely wagging tail is a good field mark.

Measurements. Wing: 8 males 49–51mm (49.9); 8 females 46–53mm (48.5). Weight: 3 males 6, 6, 7.5gm*; 2 females 8*, 8gm; 10 unsexed 8–9.5gm (9.1).

Voice. Usual call is a monotonous trill on 1 note, usually rather deliberate and even, but occasionally varying in rapidity; also a repeated *check-check-check*, etc., and a low churring in alarm.

Food. Small insects and spiders, taken amidst foliage.

Nesting. Breeding recorded (9 nests) in February, April, June–August; moult in December. The nest is a compact, fairly deep cup about 3 in. in diameter, made of leaves, fine stems and dry grass and lined with thin, black fibres; it is situated in the fork of a small plant or attached to the branch of a sapling within a few inches, rarely up to 18 in., of the ground. The clutch is 2 white eggs, lightly spotted with pale brown, av. 17.3×13.0mm (5); 2 eggs weighed 1.5, 2gm. Both parents co-operate in all nest duties. The incubation period is 16–17 days, and the fledging period 11–12 days; the young are devoid of natal down at hatching.

Behaviour. Frequently found in pairs and small groups, it is likely that flying young birds stay with their parents for some time after leaving the nest. B/S remark that the adults are unwary while building the nest, but Skutch (1960, 1968) describes how they approach and leave the nest with elaborate caution, hopping through the foliage above it and rarely flying directly to and from it. While incubating, often with the bill protruding vertically, an adult sits very still even when threatened by humans or some predator. There is some disagreement as to whether both sexes or only the male make the trilling call.

VIREONIDAE: Peppershrikes and Vireos

Birds of this family include the typical vireos, small and extremely non-descript greenish yellow birds with rather long, slightly hooked bills; the even smaller greenlets, with thinner, sharp bills; and the robust and larger peppershrikes (often placed in a separate family, Cyclarhidae), with their large heads and powerful, hooked bills. They frequent the more open woodlands and deciduous forests, being found mainly in the lower branches of trees and in dense thickets. The song of most species is a musical but monotonous phrase, by which they can be identified more readily than by their appearance, which is well camouflaged amidst thick foliage. (6)

Rufous-browed Peppershrike: *Cyclarhis gujanensis*
Yellow-breasted Peppershrike   **Plate 16(7)**

Habitat and status. A common resident in Trinidad, found in open woodland and second growth, gardens and cultivated areas, frequenting mostly the middle and upper branches of large trees. (Specimens: AMNH, ANSP, CM, YPM, LM, TRVL.)

Range and subspecies. Mexico S through Central and South America to Argentina and Uruguay; *C. g. flavipectus* (Sclater) occurs also on the Paria peninsula in NE Venezuela.

Description. 6.5 in. Upperparts green, head mainly gray with a broad rufous superciliary streak; throat and breast yellow, abdomen whitish.

Measurements. Wing: 8 males 73–81mm (77.4); 7 females 70–77mm (73.7). Weight: 1 male 22.5gm*; 2 females 23.5, 27.5gm*; 23 unsexed 26.5–35gm (29.4).

Voice. Normal call is a melodious phrase of several quick notes with the high notes emphasised, repeated about every 5 sec; it invites rendition into English (e.g., B/S's version "D'you *wash* every *week?*"), but in fact there is no set cadence, each individual repeating a particular phrase many times. Each bird may have a repertoire of different phrases (Quesnel 1987), but it is not clear how many. Another call occasionally uttered (but never repeated soon afterwards) is a loud series of similar notes, descending in pitch and getting softer, *wyoo-wyoo-wyoo-wyoo,* etc. Alarm calls include a harsh, jay-like scolding, a penetrating *whip,* and a high-pitched, nasal note reminiscent of a toucan, but softer.

Food. Insects and spiders; large prey is held with the foot and torn into pieces by the strong bill.

Nesting. Breeding recorded (10 nests) June–November, January and February, with moult from June to October. The nest is a flimsy hammock slung, usually at a great height, in a lateral fork of a tree or in a bush; it is constructed of fine roots and moss. The clutch is 2 or 3 pinkish white eggs, spotted and blotched with brown. Both parents feed the young.

Behaviour. This species moves rather slowly and deliberately among foliage, and its weak flight covers short distances only. It is sedentary, living in pairs apparently throughout the year.

Yellow-throated Vireo: *Vireo flavifrons*

Habitat and status. A few records only, for each island; on Chacachacare one was caught, banded and released on 13 April 1960 (Snow); I trapped a bird at Las Lapas in the Northern Range on 18 April 1971; possibly the same bird was seen at the same locality on 24 May 1971; in Tobago one was watched by several observers, including myself, at close range near Pembroke on 23 December 1956. (No specimens.)

Range. Breeds in E North America, wintering S from Mexico through Central and South America to Colombia and N Venezuela; rare in the West Indies.

Description. 5 in. Upperparts olive brown, becoming gray on rump; 2 conspicuous whitish wing-bars; *prominent yellow eye-ring and lores;* throat and *breast bright yellow,* abdomen whitish.

Measurements. Wing: 2 unsexed 72, 75mm. Weight: 1 unsexed 21gm.

Chivi Vireo: *Vireo chivi*

Caribbean Vireo; "Red-eyed Vireo"; *Vireo olivaceus; Vireo virescens*

Habitat and status. A locally common breeding species in both islands, frequenting especially deciduous woodland in NW Trinidad and the Bocas Islands, but also found in lowland forest, cocoa plantations and suburban gardens with scattered trees; its status is puzzling, Trinidad populations being apparently absent from October to February; this may be merely a local movement to the continent, for Dinsmore reported the Little Tobago population to be resident throughout the year. (Specimens: AMNH, ANSP, CM, YPM, LM, TRVL.)

Range and subspecies. South America from Colombia S to Bolivia, Argentina and Paraguay; *V. c. vividior* (Hellmayr & Seilern) ranges from N Colombia through Venezuela and Trinidad to the Guianas and N Brazil; it differs from *V. c. chivi* (Vieillot), which migrates from S Brazil to Venezuela from March to August and may well reach Trinidad, by its more extensive gray crown, yellower under-tail-coverts and longer bill; *V. c. tobagensis* (Hellmayr) is restricted to Tobago; it is larger, has a duller back, heavier crown-stripes and heavier bill. All the *chivi* group are often merged in *V. olivaceus,* the northern Red-eyed Vireo, but the latter's song is more elaborate, including 3- and 4-syllabled phrases, it is larger (wing 73–85mm), and it has a distinct wing formula (see Measurements); it may occur on migration from North America between September and March.

Description. 5.5 in. *Adult:* crown gray, white superciliary stripe bordered by black above and below; upperparts yellowish green, underparts whitish, under-tail-coverts yellow; iris reddish. *Immature:* as adult, but sides of crown pale brown above superciliary stripe; also mantle, scapulars and secondary wing-coverts pale yellowish brown; iris dark brown.

Measurements. *V. c. vividior.* Wing: 4 males 72–76mm (74.7); 4 females 69–71mm (70.2); 55 unsexed 67–79mm. Weight: 66 unsexed 14–18gm (15.6). *V. c. tobagensis.* Wing: 5 males 72–81mm (76.0); 3 females 75, 76, 76mm. Weight: 7 unsexed 15.5–21gm (17.9). (*V. chivi* has its outermost, i.e., ninth, primary shorter than sixth and usually shorter than fifth; in *V. olivaceus* ninth is longer than fifth, usually longer than sixth.)

Voice. A distinctive, typically 2-syllabled chirrup, *cheep-cheup,* repeated frequently with short intervals.

Food. Small insects and spiders, taken amidst foliage of upper branches.

Nesting. Breeding recorded from April to June in both islands (5 nests in Trinidad, 2 in Tobago), when song too is most apparent; moult in August. The nest is a small cup of fine grass, often bound together outside by pieces of thin bark and spiderweb; it is slung beneath a lateral fork amidst foliage 6–40 ft above ground. The clutch in Trinidad is usually 3 white eggs, sparsely marked with brown, av. 19.6 × 14.1mm (9). The species is sometimes parasitised by the Shiny Cowbird.

Black-whiskered Vireo: *Vireo altiloquus*

Habitat and status. An uncommonly seen passage migrant through Trinidad, recorded recently in January, March, April and September, usually in forest or forest edges, frequenting large trees. (Specimen: AMNH.)

Range and subspecies. Breeds in S USA, West Indies, including the Bahamas, wintering S to Panama and NE South America; the nominate race may well occur in our islands, being known to winter from Panama E and S to Venezuela, the Guianas and N Brazil; the only specimen, however, taken on 27 March 1903, is *V. a. barbadensis* (Ridgway), which breeds in the Lesser Antilles.

Description. 6 in. Resembles the Chivi Vireo but is larger, has an *olive brown crown,* more uniform with the upperparts, and a conspicuous *black malar stripe.*

Measurements. Wing: 1 female 78mm.

Voice. Song is an abrupt, 3-syllable phrase, not very musical; it is a more elaborate phrase than that of *V. chivi.*

Food. Insects and fruits, including that of the forest tree *Ocotea canaliculata.*

Nesting. B/S's record of a nest probably refers to another species.

Golden-fronted Greenlet: *Hylophilus aurantiifrons*
Golden-fronted Wood-bird; Eastern Ochre-fronted Hylophilus
Plate 16(3)

Habitat and status. A common resident in forest and second growth at all elevations in Trinidad, mostly in the middle and upper branches of trees. (Specimens: AMNH, ANSP, CM, YPM, LM, TRVL.)

Range and subspecies. Panama E to Colombia and Venezuela; *H. a. saturatus* (Hellmayr) ranges from E Colombia to Trinidad and N Venezuela.

Description. 5 in. Upperparts greenish, wings and tail brown, forehead and sides of head yellowish buff; underparts pale yellow, tinged buff. A nondescript species which flits like a warbler amongst the foliage.

Measurements. Wing: 9 males 57–61mm (58.4); 3 females 52, 53, 54mm. Weight: 8 males 7.5–10gm (8.3)*; 3 females 8, 8.5*, 8.5gm; 13 unsexed 10–12gm (10.5).

Voice. Typical call is a double note, *chee-vee* or *choo-chwee,* with varying emphasis and quality; also a chattering or chirping note, which may be speeded up to a scolding, reminiscent of a tit or chickadee (*Parus*).

Food. Small insects and spiders, taken amidst foliage.

Nesting. Breeding definitely recorded (3 nests) in July and October, but B/S say April–August; moult recorded in September. The nest is a deep cup of leaves, stems and grass suspended by the rim from a lateral fork of a branch or a vine, 5–30 ft above ground. The clutch is 3 eggs, white sparsely spotted with brown, av. 17.6 × 13.2mm (7). Both parents build the nest. The species is parasitised by the cowbird *Molothrus*.

Behaviour. Moves restlessly about the foliage, usually in parties of several individuals. It is one of the first species to react when the call of the Ferruginous Pygmy-Owl is simulated.

Scrub Greenlet: *Hylophilus flavipes*
Tobago Hylophilus   **Plate 16(2)**

Habitat and status. A common resident in Tobago, found in semi-open savannahs, second growth, dense scrub and forest edges at all elevations. (Specimens: AMNH, LM.)

Range and subspecies. Costa Rica through Panama to Colombia and Venezuela; *H. f. insularis* (Sclater) is confined to Tobago, being larger than the nominate race, with a stronger bill; iris brown.

Description. 5 in. Head olive brown with an indistinct pale superciliary, upperparts greenish, brighter on rump and wings; underparts yellowish; bill mainly dark with some yellow at base; legs pale.

Measurements. Wing: 4 males 60–61mm; 6 females 58–61mm (59.5). Weight: 4 males 9.5–12gm (10.6)*; 2 females 11.5, 12gm.

Voice. Usually a long series of repeated, mechanical-sounding notes, *weet-weet-weet* or *weary-weary-weary,* etc., about 35 in a series, but this varies; also utters a variety of churrs and high squeaks.

Food. Insects taken from foliage of upper or mid-level branches.

Nesting. Breeding recorded (3 nests) in February, April and June, with moult in August. The nest is a deep cup made of fine grass, sometimes interwoven with plant-down, slung from a small branch at about 10 ft. The clutch is 3 eggs, white lightly spotted with brown, av. 19.7 × 13.5mm (3).

Behaviour. Usually found in pairs or singly, this species is less restless than its congener in Trinidad.

ICTERIDAE: American Orioles

These birds form a heterogeneous family, of which the most notable common characteristic is the long, conical bill. Medium to large in size, most are mainly black, often with varying amounts of yellow or red. In many species the sexes are similar in plumage, but the female is noticeably smaller. In our area the majority are savannah or marsh dwellers, but several others inhabit semi-open woodland and cultivated areas, rarely true forest. Their diet includes invertebrates, fruit and seeds. Calls are often loud or raucous but include a remarkable musical repertoire. Several species are gregarious, nesting in colonies with conspicuous nests; the nests themselves vary considerably in location and construction, ranging from simple grass nests on the ground to complicated pensile nests high in a tree. In most species the female undertakes all nesting duties, but the cowbirds are parasitic. (13)

Shiny Cowbird: *Molothrus bonariensis*
Glossy Cowbird; "Lazy Bird"; "Papa Small"   **Plate 22(6)**

Habitat and status. A common resident in both islands, frequenting savannahs and semi-open areas, including urban areas; some roost in mangroves. (Specimens: AMNH, ANSP, CM, YPM, LM, TRVL.)

Range and subspecies. Throughout South America north to E Panama; *M. b. minimus* (Dalmas) ranges through the Guianas and N Brazil; it has been spreading gradually northward through the Antilles during the last century (Bond 1956) and reached S Florida in 1985.

Description. 7.5 in. *Adult male:* entirely shiny blue-black, glossed purple; iris brown. *Adult female:* dull brown, darker on wings and tail, slightly paler below. *Immature:* as female but with yellowish superciliary and underparts, more or less streaked below. Flight faster and more swooping than grackle's.

Measurements. Wing: 4 males 91–101mm (96.5); 17 females 82–90mm (85.7). Weight: 5 males 38–41.5gm (39.5); 7 females 29.5–33.5gm (31.1).

Voice. Song is loud and musical, usually a series of piercing whistles interspersed with bubbling notes; in display it is often preceded by several wheezing notes as the male puffs himself up with head and breast feathers erected. Sometimes the bubbling notes are uttered alone by either sex.

Food. Insects, including beetles, caterpillars, moths and froghoppers; also seeds, including rice. It also takes soaked bread from feeding tables.

Nesting. Breeding recorded (111 nests) in every month from May to January, except November; moult in July. The species is a brood parasite, and 176 host species are recorded throughout its range; in Trinidad and Tobago 22 hosts are recorded, principally *Agelaius, Troglodytes* and *Sturnella* (Wiley & Wiley 1980, Manolis 1982). Some cowbirds are promiscuous, others appear to form pairs, at least temporarily; the female probably lays only 1 egg in a nest, but may lay in 5 different nests in a season. One female was seen to lay its egg in a blackbird's nest within a mere 30-sec visit. Often several females each deposit an egg in a nest, up to 14 being recorded in one nest. For survival it is important that the cowbird nestling hatch no later than the host's nestling, but if the cowbird lays in a new nest before the host does, the nest may be abandoned. Occasionally a cowbird destroys, even eats, the eggs of its host, but this is not usual, and many hosts are tolerant of the parasite. The nearly spherical eggs, which are laid before noon, vary considerably in size and colouring, av. 20.7 × 17.0mm (15). The ground colour may be white, pale green or blue, or pale pink, and there may be no markings, or spots and blotches in brown, reddish or blackish. The incubation period is 11–12 days, usually less than that of the host. Up to 3 cowbird young may survive in a nest, and frequently the host's young fledge along with the cowbird young. There appears to be no aggressive behaviour towards them by the parasite, but if competition for food occurs at a critical stage, the host's young succumb.

Behaviour. Frequently found in large flocks, especially at roosts in mangroves where the numbers may reach thousands, sometimes in association with other blackbird species. When foraging on the ground this species walks with its tail cocked up at a jaunty angle. In courtship display the male raises and lowers his bill, vibrates his wings and sings loudly. Sometimes, when the female is on the ground, the male flies in tight circles around her, 2 or 3 ft up, singing as he flies. Though apparently not territorial, male cowbirds often indulge in wild chases of each other; both sexes are promiscuous.

Giant Cowbird: *Scaphidura oryzivora*
Rice Grackle; "Jackdaw"   **Plate 22(4)**

Habitat and status. A fairly common resident in Trinidad, found outside the breeding season on open savannahs in the east, but also widespread in cultivated areas with large trees and forest edges; in Tobago its presence was first suspected by B/S (1937), and it is certainly well known now from many sight records. (Specimens: AMNH, ANSP, YPM, TRVL.)

Range and subspecies. S Mexico south to N Argentina; the nominate race ranges from Panama throughout South America to N Argentina.

Description. *Male:* 14 in. All black, glossed with purple; the neck feathers form a conspicuous ruff, giving the bird a hunch-backed appearance; iris red. *Female:* 11 in. As male, but less glossy and with less ruff; iris yellowish red. Flies with pronounced swoops.

Measurements. Wing: 3 males 171, 186, 190mm; 2 females 153, 154mm. Weight: 1 male 175gm; 1 female 144gm.

Voice. The song is a somewhat strident, trisyllabic whistle, *tew-tew-hee,* the last note much higher-pitched. Other calls are a sharp, loud, grating series, *dzt-dzt-dzt,* and a more musical *pernt,* uttered in flight.

Food. Invertebrates taken on the ground or off the hides of domestic animals; also grain, including corn and rice.

Nesting. There are 5 definite breeding records from Trinidad in January and February and 1 in May. The species is a brood parasite, using as hosts only the Crested Oropendola (*Psarocolius*) and the Yellow-rumped Cacique (*Cacicus*) in Trinidad, though other closely related icterids (not found in Trinidad) are recorded as hosts elsewhere. The clutch is not known, but up to 6 eggs have been found in one nest; they vary considerably in shape and size, av. 33.5 × 23.7mm (10). In colour they may be white or pale blue with a few black spots and lines. Haverschmidt (1967) in Surinam found that only white eggs were laid in *Psarocolius* nests, and blue eggs in *Cacicus* nests, but much more data are needed to clarify this situation. In Panama an interesting interrelationship was found (N. G. Smith 1968) between this species and its hosts, since the latter's nesting success increased substantially when the cowbird's young were present; the eggs and larvae of parasitic botflies were efficiently preened from the host's young by the young cowbirds; in their absence the botflies caused heavy mortality. In colonies where botflies themselves were absent, the hosts were less likely to accept the cowbird eggs.

Behaviour. Often associates in small flocks, especially when feeding on savannahs; roosts communally in numbers up to 250. In display (Skutch 1954) the male arches his neck and emphasises his ruff as he walks stiffly towards a female, sometimes bobbing up and down in front of her by flexing his legs. A similar posture may be adopted in a preening display, the bird soliciting preening as it tucks the bill close in to the breast (Harrison 1963).

Crested Oropendola: *Psarocolius decumanus*
"Yellowtail"; "Cornbird"; "Pogga"; *Ostinops decumanus*   **Portrait VII**

Habitat and status. A common resident of both islands, including Little Tobago and St. Giles Islands, frequenting forests and cultivated areas with large trees below 2000 ft. (Specimens: AMNH, ANSP, CM, YPM, LM, TRVL.)

Range and subspecies. Panama S through South America to N Argentina; *P. d. insularis* (Dalmas) occurs only in Trinidad and Tobago. It was separated from the nominate race on the grounds of a brighter chestnut rump, but this character is not always evident.

Description. *Male:* 17 in. Generally black with chestnut rump and under-tail-coverts; long tail mostly yellow; narrow black crest long but often not visible; bill long, whitish; iris blue. *Female:* 13 in. As male, but smaller, duller and lacks crest.

Measurements. Wing: 12 males 195–247mm (226.8); 12 females 152–173mm (163.2). Weight: 1 male 335gm; 3 females 124, 136, 157gm*.

Voice. The calls, extraordinary in their variety and quality, defy accurate description. Territorial calls often begin with a hoarse trill, rising or falling in pitch, followed by several hollow gurgling notes, which I have often found reminiscent of a steelbandsman practising. In the call which usually accompanies courtship display the male first utters 2 gurgling notes, the second higher in pitch, followed by a rattling, unmusical trill, resembling the tearing of thick paper, accompanied by loud wing-flapping and feather-rustling. Other calls include a warning *cack,* and a musical *whick,* often uttered by a flock on its way to roost.

Food. Omnivorous; often takes insects, including caterpillars, termites and beetles, or nestlings of smaller birds; also berries, blossoms, especially *Erythrina,* and fruits. The species' fondness for corn, citrus and occasionally cocoa has led to its being classed as an agricultural pest.

Nesting. Breeding recorded in Trinidad (many nests) during January to May, especially the first 3 months; in Tobago recorded from January to March. Nest-building may begin during December. Nesting is colonial, usually about a dozen nests grouped in a single tree, but the number varies considerably, up to 43 being recorded (Drury 1962), though many nests remain unoccupied. Nests are often built in immortelle trees or palms and hang from the branches at a height of 20–100 ft like long, slender bags, much narrower at the top than the bottom; the bulb-shaped egg chamber is at the bottom, but the entrance is near the top. The nest is constructed of strips of grass, sedge, vine, palm fibre or banana leaf 1–5 ft long, while the egg chamber is lined with bits of dry leaves. Drury (1962) describes the nest-building in detail, showing how the female first attaches the material to the branch and weaves it into an entrance hole, then works downwards on the sides and bottom, the completed structure being normally 4–5 ft long and 9 in. wide at the base; building takes 9–25 days. The clutch is 1 or 2 eggs, pale green or gray with blackish spots or lines, av. 35.0 × 24.1mm (10). Incubation by the female is reported to last about 15 days (Tashian 1957) or 17–19 days (Drury 1962), while the fledging period lasts 4–5 wk. The Giant Cowbird is a common brood-parasite, while the flycatcher *Legatus* sometimes appropriates the nest of this species.

Behaviour. Gregarious at all times, roosting usually in bamboos. The males are polygamous, there being a dominant male and several subordinate males at each colony (Drury 1962); the territory covers the nest tree and 2 or 3 adjacent trees, but some males hold territories in nestless trees. The females too are promiscuous, copulating both with the dominant male and with other males on other territories. Within a colony females form groups which build nests clustered together; a different group may build nests some weeks later than the main group. In courtship display the male bends forward on his perch, bowing low and extending his wings together over his back; bringing his fanned tail up at right angles to the body, he vibrates his wings rapidly while making the call described above. Some displays are performed as the male clings to the side of the nest. The male also postures with ruffled neck and rump feathers, raised crest and glaring eyes. In flight the male's wings make a resonant swishing sound which may have behavioural significance. When soliciting, the female raises her head and tail and flutters her wings.

Yellow-rumped Cacique: *Cacicus cela*
Yellow-backed Cornbird; "Cornbird"   **Plate 22(5)**

Habitat and status. A common resident in the E and S of Trinidad, rarely seen in the Northern Range W of Arima and Las Cuevas or in the Caroni plain, only occasionally at Pointe-a-Pierre; it is found in open woodland or cultivated areas with large trees, at altitudes usually below 500 ft, often near human habitation. (Specimens: AMNH, ANSP, YPM, LM, TRVL.)

Range and subspecies. Panama and northern South America S to Peru, Bolivia and C Brazil; *C. c. cela* (Linnaeus) occurs in the species' range E of the Andes.

Description. *Male:* 11.5 in. Generally black with yellow patch on wing-coverts and yellow rump, under-tail-coverts and base of tail; short, black crest; bill whitish; iris blue. *Female:* 10 in. As male, but smaller, duller and lacks crest.

Measurements. Wing: 5 males 148–160mm (155.2); 2 females 121, 127mm. Weight: 1 male 101gm*.

Voice. The male's song is a brilliant and extraordinary performance, consisting of a great variety of liquid, fluting notes interspersed with harsh cackles, clucks and wheezes. While singing, the male bows slightly, raises his yellow rump feathers and vibrates his wings. Often vocalisations of other species are imitated. The noise from an active colony is indescribable.

Food. Invertebrates, including beetles, caterpillars and thrips, spiders and small crabs; also berries and other fruit and sometimes leaves.

Nesting. Breeding recorded from December to June (many nests), but particularly in the dry season; the exposed nests tend to be destroyed by prolonged rain, but I have seen nests still in use during early August. Nesting is colonial, often in an isolated tree next to a house (in 4 known cases, a police station!); up to 105 nests may be built in one tree, attached to the extremities of the branches 15–50 ft up. The nests are placed closer together than those of *Psarocolius*, often with 2 nests in contact. In most cases there is a wasps' nest (*Polybia*) in the tree. The cacique's nest, which is built by the female, is a bag, wider at the bottom, 12–18 in. long and constructed of tough plant-fibres and vines, with the entrance hole at one side near the roofed top; it is lined with plant-down. The clutch is 2 eggs, whitish with black-and-brown spots and blotches, av. 30.6 × 19.1mm (6). The female alone undertakes incubation and feeding of the young. In one colony the different nests may be at all stages of the cycle, from fresh eggs to nearly flying young. The species is a common host of the parasitic Giant Cowbird, and its nests are sometimes taken over by the flycatcher *Legatus*.

Behaviour. Gregarious at all times. The males are polygamous, but several co-exist at one nest colony, the females outnumbering the males. Aggressive encounters between the males often take place but are seldom prolonged. At

Barro Colorado, Skutch (1954) found that courtship and mating took place away from the nest tree, even though the males sang and displayed there. Within a colony the females formed groups which built nests close together, and members of a group often left their nests simultaneously in order to feed.

Carib Grackle: *Quiscalus lugubris*
Lesser Antillean Grackle; "Blackbird"; "Boat-tail";
Holoquiscalus lugubris   **Plate 22(7)**

Habitat and status. A common resident in Trinidad, where it frequents open areas in the lowlands, especially in the vicinity of towns and villages, often roosting in mangroves; in Tobago said to have been introduced from Trinidad in 1905, now common in similar habitat. (Specimens: AMNH, ANSP, YPM, LM.)

Range and subspecies. The Lesser Antilles from Barbuda S to Grenada, E Colombia, N Venezuela and some offshore islands, the Guianas and NE Brazil; *Q. l. lugubris* (Swainson) occurs on the mainland and in Trinidad and Tobago.

Description. *Male:* 10.5 in. Entirely black, glossed purple and green; tail long, keel-shaped; bill long, decurved, black; iris yellowish white. *Female:* 9 in. As male, but duller and tail shorter and less evidently keel-shaped. *Immature:* brownish black; iris pale brown. Occasionally albino or semi-albino individuals are seen.

Measurements. Wing: 6 males 109–115mm (113.2); 3 females 95, 99, 99mm. Weight: 3 males 66*, 67, 76gm.

Voice. A variety of harsh, ringing notes, twittering squeaks and clucks is uttered, the more musical notes often repeated; the male's song is a rhythmical, rattling series, ending with a resonant bell-like note, e.g., *tickita-tick-tick-tickita-tickita-ting;* other calls include a rapid *chi-chi-chi-chi,* and separate *ticks* and clucks; the young are most vociferous just before leaving the nest, calling an insistent, repeated *chiu.* The populations on the different Caribbean islands have noticeably different song dialects, though all are alike in style.

Food. Insects, including caterpillars, beetles, grasshoppers, mole crickets, cockroaches, froghoppers and termites; also spiders, earthworms, crabs and small lizards; near houses it may become accustomed to eat scraps of all kinds, including grain, bread, sugar and meat.

Nesting. Breeding recorded in Trinidad (59 nests) during two distinct periods, as follows:

I	II	III	IV	V	VI
7	2	—	—	4	18

VII	VIII	IX	X	XI	XII
10	5	3	—	2	8

Nesting is often colonial, with 10 or more nests in a single tree, but nests are also found singly. The nest is a deep cup of grasses, coarse plants and mud lined with fine grass; it is situated in a tree, often *Lagerstroemia*, or thick bush, such as *Ixora*, 4–50 ft above ground. The clutch is 2–4 eggs, greenish blue scrawled with blackish lines, av. 27.3 × 19.8mm (10). The female incubates for 12 days, and the young are fledged after 14 days. The male attends at the nest but does not seem to take part in feeding the young. The species is sometimes parasitised by the Shiny Cowbird.

Behaviour. Though pairs and single birds are often seen, this is generally a gregarious species in feeding, nesting and roosting. Groups often band together like jackdaws to attack intruders, such as cats, dogs, mongooses or humans, fearlessly swooping at their heads. If one of their number is injured or trapped, a band of excitedly clucking grackles quickly collects nearby. During the breeding season when a pair is close together, the female almost invariably precedes the male in flight. The greater preponderance of females leads to some polygamy. In courtship display the male walks stiffly with legs wide apart beside the female and sings with his feathers ruffled, wings half-raised and quivering and tail cocked high. At other times the male stands with his bill pointing skywards in a threat display.

Yellow-hooded Blackbird: *Agelaius icterocephalus*
Yellow-headed Marsh-Blackbird   **Portrait VIII**

Habitat and status. A common resident in freshwater marshes and savannahs in Trinidad, roosting in mangroves or in tall grass and sugarcane on the edge of marshland; occasional at Pointe-a-Pierre reservoirs. (Specimens: AMNH, ANSP, YPM, LM, TRVL.)

Range and subspecies. Colombia, Venezuela, the Guianas, N Brazil and NE Peru; *A. i. icterocephalus* (Linnaeus) occurs throughout the range except C Colombia.

Description. 7.5 in. *Male:* all black, except for bright yellow head, throat and upper breast; lores black. *Female:* upperparts blackish brown with yellowish edges to feathers; sides of face and throat dull yellow, rest of underparts brown tinged with yellow.

Measurements. Wing: 25 males 82–91mm (87.0, S.D. 2.4); 12 females 70–81mm (76.6). Weight: 27 males 31.5–40gm (35.4, S.D. 2.0); 17 females 24–31gm (26.6).

Voice. A noisy, rather unmusical species, uttering clucking and wheezing notes, e.g., *check* and a long-drawn-out *tzee*.

Food. Insects, including beetles, dragonflies, froghoppers, mole crickets, butterflies and moths; also seeds, especially rice.

Nesting. Breeding recorded (230 nests) from May to November, principally

June–August; moult in January and June; occasionally large colonies with hundreds of nests are formed. The nest is a deep cup of reeds or grasses slung between several water-plants, e.g., *Eleocharis* or *Cyperus,* rice-plants or water-hyacinth in shallow water; sometimes nests are built in small trees or mangroves up to 20 ft above ground. The male builds the nest in his territory, which may be up to 50m in diameter, within which he may have several females nesting, the different nests being occasionally only 2m apart. The female may add a little material to line the nest; the clutch is 3, occasionally 4, pale blue eggs speckled or scrawled with blackish markings, av. 23.6 × 16.4mm (10). Although the nest-site is defended by the male, there is much brood parasitism by the Shiny Cowbird; this does not seem to seriously affect the nesting success, which, although low, is limited rather by losses from predation or bad weather. Incubation by the female is 10–11 days, and the young, which fledge at about 12 days, are fed principally by the female (Wiley & Wiley 1980, Manolis 1982).

Behaviour. An extremely gregarious species, especially at the roost or nest. It associates commonly with grackles and cowbirds at their mangrove roosts. In display the male calls his wheezy note and ruffles the feathers of his bright yellow hood.

Red-winged Blackbird: *Agelaius phoeniceus*

Habitat and status. A single record only, of a male (northern race) seen on many occasions between 26 June 1980 and mid-1981 in marshes bordering Caroni swamp (ffrench & Manolis 1983). J. Bond (in litt.) suggested it may have been transported by boat.

Range. Breeds in North and Central America S to Costa Rica and Cuba; northern populations migrate S to Texas and California.

Description. 9 in. *Male:* Glossy black with *red shoulder patch,* tipped broadly with buffy yellow. *Female:* dark brown, upperparts edged buff and chestnut, heavily streaked below.

Voice. Call-note, *check.* Song a strident 3-syllable *ko-low-ee,* the last note trilled.

Behaviour. Often gregarious outside breeding season. The visitor described above held a territory adjoining Yellow-hooded Blackbirds during two seasons.

Moriche Oriole: *Icterus chrysocephalus*
"Moriche"   **Plate 22(2)**

Habitat and status. A rather rare resident in Trinidad, mainly in the east and south, inhabiting swampy forests, especially among *Mauritia* palms, though often seen at forest edges; since it is a favourite cage-bird, escaped individuals undoubtedly occur. (No specimens, but recorded in every month of the year.)

Range. E Colombia, Venezuela, the Guianas, E Ecuador, NE Peru and N Brazil.

Description. 9 in. All black, but crown, nape, patch on bend of wing, rump and thighs golden yellow; bill black, long and slightly decurved.

Voice. The song is a long series of musical whistles and squeaks, somewhat resembling a finch's song; also utters single notes typical of *Icterus* spp.

Food. Mainly berries; also (in Surinam) beetles.

Nesting. One breeding record in February near Vega de Oropouche. The nest was basket-shaped, made of grasses and plant-fibres, with the entrance at the top, and was fastened to a palm leaf at 35 ft. The clutch was 2 eggs, pale blue spotted with black.

[Troupial: *Icterus icterus*]
"Turpial"

Habitat and status. Individual birds have been seen at Mount Hope in June 1932 (B/S), on numerous occasions between September 1964 and December 1966 at Pointe-a-Pierre and in Port of Spain in March 1965, all in suburban areas; since this is a popular cage-bird, it is likely that all are records of escaped cage-birds; but the plumage of the birds has been richly coloured, suggesting that these were visitors from the mainland. (No specimens.)

Range. E Colombia, Venezuela, S Guyana, E Ecuador, Peru, NE Bolivia, Paraguay and Brazil.

Description. 10 in. Head, mantle, upper breast and tail black; wings black with broad white stripe and yellow lesser coverts; nape, lower back and underparts bright orange-yellow; bill black, gray at base; iris whitish; naked area around eye. (See also Northern Oriole.)

Voice. Commonest note is an extremely loud, musical cadence of 2 notes, the second several tones lower in pitch, e.g., *whee-a,* sometimes varied to a similar, trisyllabic *choop-ee-a,* the notes run together; also a ringing, musical series of 10–12 similarly pitched notes, *wee-wee-wee-wee,* etc.

Food. Invertebrates and small fruits.

Yellow Oriole: *Icterus nigrogularis*
"Cornbird"; "Golden Oriole"; *Icterus xanthornus*   **Plate 22(3)**

Habitat and status. A common resident in Trinidad, found in open woodlands, semi-open savannahs, suburban areas and gardens, also mangrove swamp edges. (Specimens: AMNH, ANSP, CM, YPM, LM, TRVL.)

Range and subspecies. Colombia, Venezuela (including offshore islands), the Guianas and N Brazil; *I. n. trinitatis* (Hartert) is confined to Trinidad and the Paria peninsula of Venezuela.

Description. 8 in. *Adult:* generally yellow, the head golden; lores, throat, upper breast and tail black; wings black edged white. *Immature:* dull yellow; wings and tail brownish black.

Measurements. Wing: 4 males 94–102mm (98.0); 10 females 81–92mm (87.8). Weight: 3 males 46, 49, 50gm; 5 females 39–50gm (44.1).

Voice. The song is a musical, flute-like phrase, usually 3 or 4 notes, the first slightly separated from the others and much higher-pitched; also utters a harsh *cack,* sometimes repeated.

Food. Mainly invertebrates, including beetles, caterpillars, froghoppers, grasshoppers, cicadas, flies and spiders; also berries, such as the fruit of the golden palm (*Chrysalidocarpus*), and blossoms of trees (e.g., *Sesbania*). Though the species is often accused of eating citrus fruit, it has not been established whether such fruit was already infested with insects, which form its staple diet.

Nesting. Breeding recorded in all months from January to August (30 nests), principally April–July; moult in August and September. The nest is a slender bag about 18 in. long, attached by the rim to a small twig at the extremity of a branch or palm-leaf, 7–30 ft above ground; it is constructed of grass or palm fibres, usually pale in colour, and is lined with fine grass; entrance is at the top. Nests are usually found singly; if two are close together, they have probably been built by the same pair. Clutch is 2–4, usually 3, whitish eggs marked with dark brown spots or lines, av. 27.1 × 17.9mm (10). Both parents feed the young. Nests are sometimes appropriated by the fly-catcher *Legatus;* abandoned nests are also used by the Saffron Finch.

Behaviour. Generally solitary or in family units; occasionally several groups collect to exploit an unusual food supply. I once found 14 orioles, including 8 young, excitedly feeding on insects at a newly dug shallow trench about 8 yd long.

Northern Oriole: *Icterus galbula*
Baltimore Oriole

Habitat and status. There are 5 sight records, all of males, from Maraval and Pointe-a-Pierre in December 1963, January 1970 and March 1981; and from Hillsborough Dam, Tobago, in February 1957. (No specimen.)

Range. Breeds in C and E North America, wintering from Mexico S to Panama, N Colombia and NW Venezuela; a rare transient through the W West Indies.

Description. 6.5 in. *Adult male:* head, neck, upper breast and upper back black; lower back and lower underparts bright orange; wings black with orange bar on bend of wing, greater coverts edged white, appearing as white bars; tail black, outer feathers broadly tipped orange. (Troupial is much larger and has broad orange collar at nape.) *Female:* upperparts olive brown, wings darker with two white wing-bars; yellowish below.

Voice. A low, double whistle.

Food. In Tobago seen feeding among immortelle blossoms; at Pointe-a-Pierre ate the fruit of the golden apple (*Spondias cytherea*). Wintering birds in Costa Rica (Timken 1970) fed mainly on insects, especially caterpillars and beetles, and only a little on plants.

Red-breasted Blackbird: *Sturnella militaris*
Red-breasted Marshbird; "Soldier Bird"; "Trinidad Robin";
Leistes militaris   **Plate 22(1)**

Habitat and status. A common resident in open grassland, savannahs and marshes in Trinidad; first recorded from Tobago at Lowlands in November 1974; records from W Tobago up to 1990 indicate that the species may be becoming established on the island. (Specimens: AMNH, ANSP, YPM, TRVL.)

Range and subspecies. Panama south to S Peru, Argentina and Uruguay (this includes the southern form *superciliaris,* possibly a distinct species); *L. m. militaris* (Linnaeus) ranges from Panama south to NE Peru and C Brazil.

Description. 7 in. *Adult male:* upperparts, wings and lower underparts black, edged with buffish brown (which wears off in full breeding plumage); throat, breast, upper abdomen and edge of lesser coverts bright red. *Adult female:* upperparts blackish broadly edged with buffish brown; buff streaks through crown and above eye; tail barred with grayish brown; underparts buff tinged with more or less red, flanks streaked. *Immature:* as female but paler, and underparts pale brown with no red. (See also Bobolink.)

Measurements. Wing: 6 males 92–95mm (94.0); 2 females 83, 84mm. Weight: 3 males 43.5*, 43.5*, 48gm; 1 unsexed 38.5gm.

Voice. The male utters a short *chip* followed by a high-pitched wheezing note in the course of a display flight, in which he climbs steeply to about 25 ft above ground, calls and with folded wings dives steeply down, giving a rattling trill as he does; also utters light chirping notes.

Food. Insects, including beetles, caterpillars, crickets, froghoppers and grasshoppers; also rice and grass seeds.

Nesting. Breeds from March to December, especially May (B/S). The nest is a deep, open cup of grass lined with fine grass, sometimes with plant-down, placed on the ground amidst long grass; sometimes there is a tunnel through the grass at one side, formed by the adult bird approaching the nest that way (thus avoiding direct flight to the nest). The clutch is 2–4 eggs, deep cream densely marked with pale reddish brown blotches, av. 23.6 × 17.4mm (10). The species is often parasitised by the Shiny Cowbird.

Behaviour. Though not gregarious, several individuals may associate in one area. The male tends to prefer a conspicuous perch on a post or tuft of grass, whilst the nondescript females skulk in the long grass. In Surinam Haverschmidt (1968a) suspected that males were polygamous.

Bobolink: *Dolichonyx oryzivorus*

Habitat and status. Three sight records only: an adult male at Oropouche, Trinidad, on 14 June 1965 (C. L. Stoute), and immatures at Friendship and Pigeon Point, Tobago, on 17 February 1974 and 31 October 1982. Usually frequents grasslands. (No specimen.)

Range. Breeds in N North America, migrating through the West Indies and Central America and wintering in S South America. A few records of transients from N South America, including islands off Venezuela. Latest spring date in West Indies 23 May (Bond).

Description. 6 in. *Male: (breeding plumage)*: black with broad golden buff patch on nape, brown spots on mantle, whitish lower back and white bar on scapulars. *Female, immature and male in winter plumage:* upperparts and wings buff brown streaked with black; buff streaks through crown and over eye; flanks streaked black, underparts yellowish brown; resembles immature *Leistes* but has plain, unbarred tail with pointed feathers.

Voice. A musical *pink*.

Behaviour. Often found in large flocks on migration.

PARULIDAE: Wood Warblers

Only 3 representatives of this family of small, thin-billed birds breed in our area; many species have been recorded on migration from North America during their winter months, but several of these are known here only from occasional sight records. There are reports of additional species, such as Cerulean and Yellow-throated warblers, which, however, have not been in my view adequately documented so as to warrant full treatment in the text. Most species are found in woodland high in the trees, but others are confined to open country and marshland, one being mainly terrestrial. Most warblers flit restlessly about the outer branches of trees, feeding on small insects or berries; their song is rather limited, while the calls of the migrants are confined to sharp single notes. In breeding plumage many warblers are brilliantly patterned, mostly in yellow, black or white, but the winter plumage of most of the visitors is somewhat drab. (23)

[Golden-winged Warbler: *Vermivora chrysoptera*]

Habitat and status. Two sight records only: a female on 29 December 1976 beside the Arima-Blanchisseuse road (Brewer 1977), and a male on 22 January 1988 at the Aripo road (B. Cassie). (No specimen.)

Range. Breeds in North America, wintering S to Colombia and N Venezuela.

Description. 5 in. *Male:* gray above with black throat and ear-patch bordered in white; crown and wing-patch golden yellow, underparts grayish white. *Female:* similar but duller.

Black-and-white Warbler: *Mniotilta varia*

Habitat and status. Many sight records from Trinidad, indicating that the species regularly winters in small numbers; earliest date 20 October; records mostly from rain forest in Arima Valley, but also high on El Tucuche; 2 records from Tobago on 7 and 31 January. (No specimen.)

Range. Breeds in C and E North America; winters from Florida and Mexico through the West Indies and Central America to Panama, N Colombia, Venezuela and E Ecuador.

Description. 5 in. *Adult male:* head and upperparts streaked black and white; white streaks through crown and over eye, cheeks black; underparts white with black streaks on breast and flanks. *Female and immature:* as male but with white cheeks; underparts almost all white.

Behaviour. Creeps on branches and trunks of trees. Along with other birds one of this species was attracted when I simulated a Pygmy-Owl call.

Prothonotary Warbler: *Protonotaria citrea*

Habitat and status. An uncommon visitor to both islands during the northern winter, frequenting the vicinity of water, such as mangrove swamps and, occasionally, light woodland, usually near the ground; a male caught on Little Tobago on 24 October (Dinsmore); also many sight records from Tobago January–March; on Trinidad records from Caroni, Nariva and Pointe-a-Pierre November–January; also high in the Northern Range on 27 March 1970, presumably on migration (J. Satterly and others). (No extant specimens, but collected by Léotaud.)

Range. Breeds in USA, wintering from Florida and Mexico S to Panama, N Colombia and Venezuela, and Surinam; rare transient in West Indies.

Description. 5.5 in. *Adult male:* head and underparts bright golden yellow, mantle olive green; lower back, wings and tail bluish gray. *Female:* as male, but duller, with olive green crown.

Northern Parula: *Parula americana*
American Parula

Habitat and status. Three records from Tobago: 1 female trapped at Grafton on 19 December 1974, another seen there on 18 January 1985 (D. Fisher) and 1 on Little Tobago on 1 November 1977 (G. Blidberg). (No specimen, but photographic evidence.)

Range. Breeds in North America S to Florida. Winters S to Costa Rica and West Indies; a regular if rare winter visitor to Lesser Antilles.

Description. 4 in. Very similar to Tropical Parula but distinguished by a distinct white eye-ring and broader white wing-bars; also *male* has dark breast-band and *less* black in face, *female* has whitish lower underparts.

Measurements. One female: wing: 55mm; weight: 7gm.

Tropical Parula: *Parula pitiayumi*
Olive-backed Warbler; *Compsothlypis pitiayumi*   **Plate 23(2)**

Habitat and status. A fairly common resident in Trinidad, frequenting forests, especially deciduous woodland on the Bocas Islands; also recorded from Tobago (Hellmayr 1906) but no recent records. (Specimens: AMNH, CM, YPM, LM.)

Range and subspecies. S USA and Mexico S through Panama and N South America to Peru, Bolivia, N Argentina and Uruguay; *P. p. elegans* (Todd) ranges from Colombia E to Guyana and N Brazil; some authors consider it conspecific with the Northern Parula (*P. americana*).

Description. 4 in. *Adult male:* head and upperparts generally blue-gray, mantle olive green, wing-coverts tipped white forming 2 wing-bars, lores blackish; throat and upper breast orange-yellow, lower underparts yellow. *Female:* as male, but lacks black lores, and entire underparts yellow. *Immature:* upperparts entirely blue-gray, no wing-bars, underparts yellow with gray band across upper breast.

Measurements. Wing: 10 males 50–56mm (53.3); 2 females 50, 56mm. Weight: 6 males 6.5–7.5gm (7.3); 1 unsexed 8.5gm.

Voice. Song is a very high-pitched trill, accelerating and descending in pitch, and ending with a sharp *weet;* also a light, sharp *tip,* and, from newly fledged birds, a repeated *pitchew.*

Food. Small insects and berries taken from the canopy or just below.

Nesting. Breeding recorded only by B/S, who found nests with eggs in June and July. Song recorded in all months, especially March–July. I have found newly fledged young on Chacachacare in late August; moult recorded in September. The nests were domes of green moss with a side entrance, placed

348 WOOD WARBLERS

among epiphytes on silk-cotton trees about 30 ft high. The clutches were of 2 eggs, white marked with deep chestnut, av. 17.4 × 13.0mm (4).

Yellow Warbler: *Dendroica petechia*
"Trinidad Canary"; *Dendroica aestiva*

Habitat and status. A common winter visitor to both islands, frequenting mangroves, marshland, savannahs with trees and bushes, suburban areas; regularly present mid-September–late March, earliest 7 September, latest 3 April. (Specimens: AMNH, YPM, LM, TRVL.)

Banding status. Forty birds banded during September–March 1959–68 at Oropouche Lagoon, Caroni and once in the Northern Range (23 March); no recoveries, but 1 bird was retrapped in the same locality 8 days later.

Range and subspecies. Breeds from Alaska and Canada S through North and Central America to Peru, Colombia, Venezuela (including offshore islands) and the West Indies S to St. Lucia and Barbados; *D. p. aestiva* (Gmelin) breeds in North America, wintering S to Peru, Colombia, Venezuela, the Guianas and N Brazil. Trinidad birds belong to the North American populations, *aestiva* group, formerly regarded as a species distinct from the Caribbean islands' *petechia* group (with chestnut cap), often called the Golden Warbler.

Description. 4.5 in. *Male:* head yellow, upperparts yellowish green, wings darker edged yellow, tail brown edged yellowish; underparts bright yellow, more or less streaked with chestnut. *Female:* as male but greener and without chestnut breast-streaks.

Measurements. Wing: 7 males 60–65mm (62.8); 8 females 57–62mm (59.2). Weight: 10 males 8.5–10gm (9.1); 15 females 7.5–9.5gm (8.6). No significant weight change from September to March.

Voice. An incisive *chip.* Full song begins in early March.

Food. Small invertebrates, mainly beetles, taken amidst foliage of trees and small shrubs. I have found up to 30 together, exploiting a rich food supply amidst pigeon peas and ochroes.

[Magnolia Warbler: *Dendroica magnolia*]

Habitat and status. Two sight records only: a male in breeding plumage at Speyside, Tobago, on 22 April 1967 (J. C. Ogden) and an immature bird on the edge of the Nariva swamp on 21 December 1966 (W. C. Baker). (No specimen.)

Range. Breeds in Canada and USA S to Virginia; winters S from Mexico to Panama and the N West Indies, casual in Colombia and Lesser Antilles.

Description. 4.5 in. *Male (breeding):* crown and nape bluish gray with white streak behind eye; upperparts black, but rump yellow; *tail black with broad white band;* wing-coverts white; underparts yellow with black streaks on breast and flanks. *Adult (winter) and immature:* crown and nape gray, upperparts olive green, rump yellow; 2 white wing-bars; otherwise similar to breeding male, but duller.

Cape May Warbler: *Dendroica tigrina*

Habitat and status. A rare winter visitor to Tobago, recorded between 1 January and 2 April by various observers; 1 sight record from Nariva, Trinidad, on 16 February (Satterly); frequents mangroves and suburban woodlands. (Specimen: BM.)

Range. Breeds in Canada and N USA, wintering south to N West Indies; rare in S West Indies and casual in Central America S to Panama.

Description. 4.5 in. *Male (breeding):* crown blackish, *cheeks chestnut,* upperparts olive streaked black, *rump yellow;* large white patch on wing-coverts; sides of neck yellow, underparts yellow streaked black. *Adult (winter) and immature:* upperparts dull grayish green, rump yellowish, 2 white wing-bars; *sides of neck yellowish,* underparts pale yellowish *finely streaked* black.

[Black-throated Blue Warbler: *Dendroica caerulescens*]

Habitat and status. One sight record only of an adult male seen at close quarters amidst cocoa trees at Springhill estate, Trinidad, on 27 March 1966 (T. Hake). (No specimen.)

Range. Breeds in Canada and USA S to Georgia, wintering S to Greater Antilles; casual visitor to Mexico, Guatemala and Colombia, accidental in Venezuela.

Description. 4.5 in. *Male:* upperparts blue-gray, white patch on wing; cheeks, throat and sides of breast black, rest of underparts white. *Female:* upperparts olive brown, narrow white superciliary streak, small white patch on wing, underparts dull yellowish olive.

[Yellow-rumped Warbler: *Dendroica coronata*]
Myrtle Warbler

Habitat and status. Two records only of birds seen at Turtle Beach and Buccoo, Tobago, in April–May 1975 and January 1985.

Range. Breeds in North America, wintering S to Panama and through West Indies to Barbados; casual in Colombia and Venezuela.

Description. 5 in. *Male (breeding):* upperparts gray streaked black, crown and rump yellow; underparts white with black breast and sides, with prominent yellow patch on each side of breast; two white wing-bars and some white in tail. *Female:* similar but brown rather than gray. *Immature:* brown above streaked black, rump yellowish.

[Black-throated Green Warbler: *Dendroica virens*]

Habitat and status. Two sight records only in Trinidad: a male seen at Arena Forest on 8 December 1968 (T. Davis) and a male at La Laja on 6 April 1969 (Satterly). A woodland species. (No specimen.)

Range. Breeds in Canada and USA S to Georgia; winters from S USA and Mexico S to Panama and Greater Antilles; casual in Colombia, Venezuela and Lesser Antilles.

Description. 4.5 in. *Male (breeding):* upperparts green, wings and tail blackish, 2 white wing-bars; *sides of head and neck golden yellow,* throat and breast black, rest of underparts white. *Female:* as male but duller, and throat is mottled with blackish. In *winter* both sexes have only indefinite blackish markings on the underparts.

[Prairie Warbler: *Dendroica discolor*]

Habitat and status. One record only, of an immature bird seen on 21 March 1978 in scrub at Laventille Marsh (Keith 1979). (No specimen.)

Range. Breeds in E North America, wintering S to Costa Rica and West Indies, where recorded from Martinique and Aruba; casual in Colombia.

Description. 5 in. *Male:* olive above, faintly streaked chestnut, with 2 dull wing-bars; sides of head and underparts yellow, boldly streaked black on face and flanks. *Female and immature:* duller. Often flicks tail.

[Blackburnian Warbler: *Dendroica fusca*]

Habitat and status. Four records from Trinidad: males at Springhill and La Laja on 3 January, 14 February and 31 March, and a female at Andrews Trace on 24 April. (No specimen.)

Range. Breeds in North America S to Georgia; winters from Guatemala S to Ecuador, Peru, Colombia and Venezuela; a rare transient in West Indies; 1 record from Grenada.

Description. 4.5 in. *Male (breeding):* upperparts black with white stripes on back and white patch on wing; crown, superciliary stripe and sides of neck orange-yellow, throat and breast orange; lower underparts white, flanks streaked black. *Female and winter male:* upperparts brownish gray streaked black, 2 white wing-bars; head and neck pattern as breeding male but yellow, especially dull in *immatures.*

[Chestnut-sided Warbler: *Dendroica pensylvanica*]

Habitat and status. Five records from Trinidad, of birds seen in the Northern Range and at Aripo Savannah in late December and March–April. (No specimen.)

Range. Breeds in North America S to Georgia; winters in Central America S to Panama, casual in Colombia and Venezuela, rare transient in West Indies.

Description. 4.5 in. *Male* (*breeding*): crown yellow, upperparts greenish streaked black, 2 whitish wing-bars; black streaks through and below eye, underparts white with chestnut flanks. *Female:* as male but duller. *Adults* (*winter*) *and immature:* upperparts plain yellowish green, 2 white wing-bars, narrow white eye-ring, underparts white.

[Bay-breasted Warbler: *Dendroica castanea*]

Habitat and status. Six records in Trinidad from Northern Range and Arena Forest between 12 December and 10 April, and 1 from Grafton, Tobago, on 11 November. (No specimen.)

Range. Breeds in North America S to New York; winters from Panama S to Colombia and Venezuela, migrating through Central America and the West Indies from Jamaica west.

Description. 5 in. *Male* (*breeding*): crown, throat, breast and sides chestnut, face black, upperparts grayish olive streaked black, 2 white wing-bars; sides of neck and lower underparts buff. *Female:* much duller than male but similar in pattern. *Winter adults and immatures:* upperparts green streaked black, 2 white wing-bars; underparts buff with more or less chestnut on sides; resembles immature Blackpoll but under-tail-coverts buff and legs black.

Blackpoll Warbler: *Dendroica striata*
Dendroica breviunguis

Habitat and status. A rather uncommon passage migrant through both islands, recorded in every month from October to April, more than half of over 40 records occurring in the second half of October, only 6 from December to February; earliest date 6 October, latest 5 April; most records were from low trees at forest edges; definitely more common some years than others. (Specimens: LM, TRVL.)

Banding status. One bird banded at Springhill Estate in November 1964. No recovery.

Range. Breeds in North America S to New York; winters in South America from E Colombia S to Peru and N Brazil, migrating through the West Indies.

Description. 4.5 in. *Male* (*breeding*): crown black, cheeks white, upperparts grayish olive streaked with black, 2 white wing-bars; underparts white, flanks streaked black. *Female and winter adults:* upperparts greenish, streaked more or less with black, 2 white wing-bars; underparts whitish (or yellowish in winter), sides faintly streaked, *under-tail-coverts white; legs buff.*

Measurements. Wing: 2 males 74mm; 1 female 71mm. Weight: 1 unsexed (in October) 9gm.

Ovenbird: *Seiurus aurocapillus*

Habitat and status. One male was taken at Waller Field on 19 January 1971 (Tikasingh); also 2 sight records from Little Tobago Island, 1 in November 1966 and another in March 1967 (Dinsmore). (Specimen: TRVL.)

Range. Breeds in North America, wintering S to Central America, Colombia, N Venezuela and the Greater Antilles, more rarely the Lesser Antilles.

Description. 5 in. Crown-stripe orange bordered by black, white eye-ring, upperparts olive green; underparts white heavily streaked and spotted with black. Terrestrial.

Measurements. Wing: 1 male 67mm.

Northern Waterthrush: *Seiurus noveboracensis*

Habitat and status. A common winter resident in both islands, frequenting mangroves, rivers and streams, especially where there is thick cover, also gardens and cultivated areas near water; regularly present from last week of September to first week of May (earliest date 31 August, latest 24 May), many individuals probably only transient. (Specimens: AMNH, LM, TRVL.)

Banding status. Over 160 birds were banded between 1958 and 1970 in various parts of both islands. None has been recovered, but several have been recaptured in subsequent winters at the same localities.

Range and subspecies. Breeds in North America south to West Virginia; winters from S USA through Central America and the West Indies to Ecuador, N Peru, Venezuela and the Guianas; *S. n. noveboracensis* (Gmelin) breeds in E North America, wintering in the range of the species.

Description. 5 in. Upperparts olive brown with a yellowish superciliary stripe; underparts whitish to yellowish tinged buff, *heavily streaked* (including throat) with dark brown. Mainly terrestrial, walking with a constant bobbing motion, similar to Spotted Sandpiper.

Measurements. Wing: 5 males 75–79mm (76.8); 9 females 71–75mm (73.1). Weight: 72 unsexed 12.5–22gm. The average remains at about 15.5gm from October to February, rising to 16.5gm in March, 17.9 in April and 19.5gm in May.

Voice. A penetrating, metallic single note, *tink;* in excitement repeated frequently.

Food. Invertebrates taken from the ground, especially in damp areas. The bird frequently tosses aside leaves while foraging.

Behaviour. Mostly solitary, though several individuals, probably transients, associate loosely at the beginning and end of the season. In mangrove areas birds apparently roost communally, beginning to gather about 1 hr before sunset. In the Botanic Gardens of Caracas, Venezuela, Schwartz (1964) found winter residents holding territories averaging half an acre, which they inhabited and defended individually for about 6 months, and to which they returned in subsequent winters. Territory owners intimidate intruders with calls, chases or by walking towards them in a crouched attitude, occasionally fighting.

Notes. The Louisiana Waterthrush (*S. motacilla*) winters in much the same area as this species, though it is rare in the West Indies E of Puerto Rico. Where the 2 species occur together, they occupy different habitats, the Northern preferring mangrove swamps and the Louisiana freshwater streams (Bond 1960). Street (1946) claimed 6 sight records for Trinidad of the Louisiana Waterthrush, but these records have not been substantiated. Though I have repeatedly looked for the latter species in freshwater habitats, and often trapped birds at forest streams, all records are of the Northern Waterthrush.

[Common Yellowthroat: *Geothlypis trichas*]

Habitat and status. A male in winter plumage was reported to have been taken by Kirk in Tobago (B/S); this may be identical with the undated specimen of a female or young male stated under the authority of Jardine (1846) to have come from Tobago; the confused evidence does not seem to me to warrant its full inclusion on the check-list. No other confirmed records, but the species was reported from the Laventille marsh, Trinidad, on 6 March 1965 (Gochfeld 1973). (Specimen: BM.)

Range. Breeds in North America, wintering S to Panama and Greater Antilles.

Description. 5 in. *Male:* similar to male Masked Yellowthroat but crown brown, *not* gray, and black mask bordered with white above; upperparts browner. *Female:* resembles Masked Yellowthroat but is browner above, with buffish flanks.

Masked Yellowthroat: *Geothlypis aequinoctialis*
South American Yellowthroat; "Manicou Bird"   **Plate 23(5)**

Habitat and status. A locally common resident in Trinidad, frequenting savannahs and freshwater marshes with small bushes, also canefields; skulks mainly in long grass; Herklots collected a specimen in a clearing high in the

Northern Range, but this seems unusual. (Specimens: AMNH, ANSP, CM, YPM, LM, TRVL.)

Range and subspecies. W Panama and Colombia S to Bolivia, Argentina and Uruguay; *G. a. aequinoctialis* (Gmelin) occurs from E Colombia through Venezuela and Trinidad to the Guianas and N Brazil.

Description. 5 in. *Adult male:* crown gray, upperparts yellowish green, broad black mask from forehead through eye to ear-coverts, underparts bright yellow. *Female and immature:* as male but duller below and lack black mask.

Measurements. Wing: 7 males 60–64mm (61.9); 4 females 57–60mm (58.2). Weight: 4 males 12.5, 14, 14.5*, 14.5gm; 2 females 11.5, 14gm*.

Voice. The song is a high-pitched, rapid series of similar notes, up to about 14, *weechu-weechu-weechu,* etc., dropping slightly in pitch; it is one of the first birds to sing at dawn; also utters a plaintive, liquid single note, *chiew.*

Food. Small insects, including froghoppers, caterpillars, beetles and grasshoppers.

Nesting. Breeding recorded in February, May, August and October, while song is heard virtually through the year. The nest is a deep cup of coarse grass, lined with finer materials and placed near the ground amidst rank grass or sugarcane. The clutch is 2 eggs, dull white marked with reddish brown and underlying lavender, variable in shape, av. 19.3 × 14.8mm (6).

[Hooded Warbler: *Wilsonia citrina*]

Habitat and status. One sight record only for Trinidad, an adult male at Waller Field on 17 December 1967 (Worth 1969). (No specimen.)

Range. Breeds in E North America from Iowa S to the Gulf states, wintering from Mexico S to Costa Rica and occasionally Panama; a rare transient in the West Indies, recorded in Martinique.

Description. 4.5 in. *Male:* crown, nape, sides of neck, throat and breast black, forehead and face yellow; rest of upperparts olive green, underparts yellow; prominent white patches on outer tail. *Female:* as male but lacking the black markings.

American Redstart: *Setophaga ruticilla*

Habitat and status. A common winter resident in both islands, frequenting mangroves and forests at all levels; birds found in more open areas with scattered trees, gardens, etc., are probably transients; regularly present from mid-September to early April, earliest date 26 August, latest 19 April. (Specimens: AMNH, YPM, LM, TRVL.)

Banding status. Two birds were banded in 1966, and 1 in 1975, near Arima. No recoveries.

Range and subspecies. Breeds in North America from Alaska and Canada S to Louisiana and Georgia, wintering from Mexico and the West Indies S to Ecuador, Colombia, Venezuela, the Guianas and NW Brazil; *S. r. ruticilla* (Linnaeus) breeds in E North America, wintering S to Guyana and Ecuador.

Description. 4.5 in. *Adult male:* head, breast and upperparts black, with salmon pink patches on sides of breast, wing and sides of tail; abdomen white. *Female and immature:* head gray, upperparts greenish brown, underparts white, patches on breast; wing and tail similar to adult male but yellow (or pale orange in immature male).

Measurements. Wing: 12 males 63–67mm (64.7); 3 females 60, 61, 62mm. Weight: 9 males 7.25–8.5gm (7.6); 2 females 7.5, 7.5gm. Birds caught in all months from October to February showed no appreciable difference in weight.

Voice. A light, incisive *chip.*

Food. Small insects caught on the wing in flycatcher fashion or taken from foliage.

Behaviour. An extremely confiding species which often approaches and forages close to an observer. It responds to the call of the Pygmy-Owl, joining other small birds to mob the intruder.

Golden-crowned Warbler: *Basileuterus culicivorus*
Chapman's Warbler; Olivascent Warbler   **Plate 23(6)**

Habitat and status. A fairly common resident in Trinidad, where it inhabits forests at all elevations, second growth and cultivated areas with dense thickets, being found mostly near the ground; also known from all the Bocas Islands. (Specimens: AMNH, LM.)

Range and subspecies. Mexico S through Central and E South America to NE Argentina and Uruguay; *B. c. olivascens* (Chapman) is restricted to Trinidad and NE Venezuela, being distinguished by its larger bill and grayer upperparts.

Description. 5 in. Head grayish with black eye-stripe, white superciliary stripe and orange crown-stripe bordered on either side with black; upperparts grayish green, underparts bright yellow. Sexes similar.

Measurements. Wing: 8 males 59–63mm (61.1); 5 females 56–60mm (57.8). Weight: 22 unsexed 9.5–12gm (10.5).

Voice. Song is an abrupt, short series of sharp, whistled notes, *see-see-see,* etc., moving down in pitch; the usual call-note is a loud, sharp *chip,* reminiscent of the waterthrush's note but less metallic; also utters a loud scolding, probably in alarm.

Food. Small insects gleaned from understory foliage.

Nesting. Breeding recorded from March to June (21 nests) predominantly in May; B/S report later nesting in the NW peninsula. The nest is a dome made of grass and other vegetation, with a wide entrance, usually placed in a niche low on a bankside, often by a path in the forest. The clutch is 2–4 eggs, white marked with reddish brown mainly at the larger end, av. 17.5 × 13.6mm (6).

Behaviour. Normally a rather shy, skulking species; however, it performs an elaborate distraction display when flushed from its nest, dragging its wings along the ground, fluttering and chirping plaintively at a distance of only a few feet.

COEREBIDAE: Bananaquits

With the recent transfer of many species formerly in this family to the tanagers, there remains only the Bananaquit, considered by some authors to be a wood warbler. I prefer to treat it separately, partly because of its morphology, and also because of various aspects of its behaviour, especially its unique nesting habits. With over 30 races, it is found in a variety of habitats over a wide area. Its short legs and strong toes enable it to cling to vegetation at any angle, often hanging upside down to feed, probing into flowers for nectar or piercing both flowers and fruit with its sharp, slightly decurved bill. An energetic and extremely active species. (1)

Bananaquit: *Coereba flaveola*
"Sugar-bird"; "Sucrier"   **Plate 23(3)**

Habitat and status. An abundant resident in both islands, including off-shore islets, occurring in every habitat with trees or bushes from sea level to the highest mountains, less common in mangroves, and not occurring in open savannah. (Specimens: AMNH, ANSP, CM, YPM, LM, TRVL.)

Range and subspecies. SE Mexico south to N Argentina and Paraguay, also in the West Indies; *C. f. luteola* (Cabanis) ranges through N Colombia and Venezuela to Trinidad and Tobago. There is considerable variation in the plumage of the various subspecies.

Description. 4 in. Head and upperparts black with white superciliary streak, a white patch at the base of the flight feathers, and yellow rump; chin and throat gray; rest of underparts yellow; outer tail tipped white; bill black, rather short, slender and slightly decurved. *Immature:* as adult but dingy, with yellowish superciliary.

Measurements. Wing: 63 males 54–61mm (57.7, S.D. 1.4); 48 females 50–59gm (54.2, S.D. 1.6). Weight: 34 males 9–12gm (10.5, S.D. 0.69); 24 females 9–11gm (9.9, S.D. 0.64). These measurements are all from the island of Trinidad. Significant weight differences have been found on birds from the

Bocas Islands (D. W. Snow & Snow 1963a; ffrench 1965a, 1969a); 25 unsexed adults from Monos averaged 9.9gm, while 73 from Chacachacare, trapped in 4 different months, averaged 9.25gm. This compares with an average of 10.6gm for 305 birds of both sexes from Trinidad, and 10.45gm for 98 Tobago birds.

Voice. The song of the male is a rapid, high-pitched and variable chatter, interspersed with sibilant squeaks and wheezes; both sexes utter the high squeak separately. There is a noticeable variation between the songs of different subspecies.

Food. Mainly nectar, taken from a large variety of flowers (50 species were recorded by B. K. Snow and Snow [1971], especially large trees such as *Erythrina poeppigiana* and *Symphonia globulifera,* but also vines and herbaceous plants [Feinsinger et al. 1985]); feeds especially at plants with clusters of small flowers, but obtains nectar from large flowers by piercing the base of the corolla; in times of nectar shortage also takes small fruits, usually chewing or sucking the pulp, and forages amongst foliage for small insects; occasionally takes protein corpuscles from the tree *Cecropia peltata.* It readily takes sugar or syrup from feeding tables or bottles and can become very tame.

Nesting. In Trinidad breeding has been recorded (83 nests) as follows:

I	II	III	IV	V	VI
25	13	16	10	7	4

VII	VIII	IX	X	XI	XII
—	1	—	1	1	5

Regular singing throughout the year; moult between April and November; in Tobago breeding records from November to August. A pair may nest successfully 3 times within 6 months, using the same nest. The nest is an oval structure of grass, leaves and stems (occasionally feathers or paper) lined with finer materials and domed, with the porched, downward-pointing entrance near the top on one side. It is situated 2–30 ft above ground in a shrub or on the extremity of a branch; many nests are found in artificial situations, e.g., amidst ornamental plants, on wires, even in houses. Though the species is not colonial, I have found 2 occupied nests within 20 ft; Gross (1958) in Tobago found 54 nests within a radius of 0.5 mile. Both parents build the nest (in fact the male starts the building process) and feed the young by regurgitation, but only the female incubates. Gross recorded incubation periods of 12 days (as have others on the continent), but I have recorded periods of 13 and 14 days in Trinidad, with fledging periods of 15–17 days. The eggs are laid on consecutive days. The clutch is usually 2, sometimes 3, cream or buff eggs, densely marked with brown especially at the thick end, av. 17.2 × 12.8mm (10). Adults also construct separate roosting nests, which are smaller, more roughly made and tend to have the entrance nearer the bottom.

Behaviour. A very confiding species which lives in pairs and is mainly sedentary. When feeding it moves rapidly from flower to flower, perching and clinging effectively to all kinds of surfaces. In display birds bow and bob from side to side, bringing into prominence the raised yellow rump feathers.

TERSINIDAE: Swallow-Tanagers

Though superficially resembling a tanager, the single species of this family is characterised by its short legs, long wings and short, wide, flat bill. It feeds partly on fruit but also on insects, catching them in rapid flight like a swallow. In Trinidad it is confined to mountainous areas and may be migratory. (1)

Swallow-Tanager: *Tersina viridis*
Swallow Fruit-eater   **Plate 25(2)**

Habitat and status. A rather rare and local breeding species in Trinidad, known only in the Northern Range above 800 ft, mostly 2000–3000 ft, frequenting clearings in forest; records, predominantly March–June, indicate probable migration, but there are a few records from November–February. In Venezuela it is known to move during the dry season to more humid, lower elevations. (No specimens, but collected by Léotaud.)

Range and subspecies. E Panama and Colombia S to Paraguay and N Argentina; the Trinidad subspecies is probably *T. v. occidentalis* (Sclater), which ranges from Panama through Colombia, Venezuela and the Guianas to N Brazil.

Description. 6 in. *Adult male:* generally purplish blue, glossed greenish in bright light, with black forehead, lores and throat; wings and tail black, broadly edged blue; abdomen white, flanks barred black; bill black. *Female:* grass green, with gray face and throat; abdomen yellow, flanks barred green and yellow. *Immature male:* green mottled with more or less blue according to age; black face markings develop slowly through a mottled gray stage. Full adult plumage reached after 3 or 4 yr, but males breed in their first year.

Measurements. Wing: 2 males 81, 83mm; 2 females 86, 88mm. Weight: 2 males 28, 30gm; 2 females 31.5, 32gm.

Voice. An abrupt, unmusical squeak, *tswis,* also a disyllabic *sieee;* the male's song is a pebbly twitter of up to 7 syllables.

Food. Berries and small fruits of various trees, especially Lauraceae: also small flying insects, which form an important part of the diet of fledglings (Schaefer 1953). Fruit is usually taken from a perched position, though I have seen birds hovering and plucking berries. Instead of swallowing the entire berry, the bird revolves it in its bill and drops the seed after scraping off the pulp. Food is occasionally stored, by both adults and young, for some hours in throat-pouches.

Nesting. Breeding recorded (11 nests) from April to June, mostly before 10 May. The nest is a cup of roots and fibres lined with fine palm fibres and placed at the end of a horizontal tunnel up to 18 in. long, usually in a bank 3–6 ft above ground. In Venezuela (Schaefer 1953) many nests are built in artificial holes in walls. The solidity of the nest depends on climatic factors associated with altitude; at higher elevations larger nests are built. The clutch is 2 or 3 glossy white eggs, av. 25.6 × 18.5mm (3). The eggs are laid on consecutive days, and incubation, by the female, lasts 13–17 days, beginning usually after the first egg is laid. The female sits for very lengthy periods, and usually the male keeps no contact with her during incubation. The female also does most of the nest-building. Hatching takes place on consecutive days, and the fledging period is 24 days. The male helps to feed the young. Occasionally there is a second brood, especially if the first nesting was unsuccessful.

Behaviour. A social species, especially outside the breeding season, when loose flocks are formed which do not associate with other passerines. Breeding birds hold territories, and in courtship the male feeds the female or displays with a stalk in his bill. In a common display (Schaefer 1953) 2 birds, facing each other, bow and jerk upward in alternate movements many times. Sometimes several birds perform this display together.

THRAUPIDAE: Honeycreepers and Tanagers

These small to medium-sized birds are notable for their brightly coloured plumage (in most species); honeycreepers have comparatively slim, often decurved, bills, suitable for taking nectar, while the generally larger tanagers have fairly stout bills and feed largely on fruit, though insects are also taken. The song is poorly developed in most species. They are widespread in forest (mostly in the canopy) and second growth, also occasionally in cultivated areas and savannah edges, often associating in small, loose flocks, and with birds of other families. Most species build cup-shaped nests, constructed by the female. The euphonias make covered nests, which are usually built by both sexes, though only the female incubates. (21)

Bicolored Conebill: *Conirostrum bicolor*
Grey Dacnis; Blue-grey Honeycreeper; *Ateleodacnis bicolor*
Plate 23(1)

Habitat and status. A fairly common but local resident in Trinidad, including Monos Island, occurring mainly in mangrove swamps and neighbouring woodland. (Specimens: AMNH, ANSP, YPM, LM.)

Range and subspecies. Colombia and Venezuela E and S to the Guianas, NE Peru and Brazil; *C. b. bicolor* (Vieillot) occurs in Venezuela, Trinidad, the Guianas and E Brazil.

Description. 4.5 in. *Adult:* upperparts grayish blue, primaries brown edged bluish; underparts gray tinged with creamy buff. *Immature:* greenish above with pale yellow underparts. Some birds breed in immature plumage.

Measurements. Wing: 6 males 59–64mm (60.8); 1 female 57mm. Weight: 1 male 10.5gm*; 1 female 10.5gm*.

Voice. A feeble, high-pitched *tseep.*

Food. Small insects, including caterpillars and beetles; also eats small seeds in Venezuela (Friedmann & Smith 1955).

Nesting. Breeding recorded (7 nests) from March to July, principally July. Nesting details in B/S are wrong. Two similar occupied nests I have found at Caroni were small, compact, deep cups of grasses, liberally mixed with heron feathers and lined with feathers, one about 12 ft up in a mangrove (*Avicennia*), the other only 1 ft above water level, woven about the crotch of a small mangrove (*Rhizophora*). One clutch was of 2 eggs, pale buff ovals with dark brown blotches concentrated mainly at the thick end, 1 egg measuring 19.0 × 13.8mm; also in the nest were 3 eggs of the cowbird *Molothrus,* which is evidently a common parasite, for at 2 other nests cowbirds were being fed. Both parents feed the young.

Purple Honeycreeper: *Cyanerpes caeruleus*
Yellow-legged Honeycreeper; "Yellow-legged Grampo"   **Plate 24(4)**

Habitat and status. A common resident in Trinidad, inhabiting mostly forest, also cocoa and citrus cultivation, especially noticeable in the canopy, feeding on flowering trees such as immortelles; I have seen a few individuals (possibly introduced) in Tobago. (Specimens: AMNH, ANSP, CM, YPM, LM, TRVL.)

Range and subspecies. Colombia and Venezuela S to Peru, Bolivia and C Brazil; *C. c. longirostris* (Cabanis) is restricted to Trinidad, and is distinguished by its longer bill.

Description. 4.5 in. *Adult male:* generally violet blue with black lores, throat, wings and tail; bill black, strongly decurved and fairly long; legs bright yellow. *Female and immature:* upperparts green, lores and throat pale chestnut with a blue moustachial streak; underparts yellowish green streaked with darker green; legs greenish.

Measurements. Wing: 14 males 56–60mm (58.6); 10 females 55–58mm (56.4). Weight: 27 males 10–14gm (12.6); 17 female-plumaged, including several probably egg-laying females 11–15gm (12.7).

Voice. A thin, high-pitched note.

Food. Small insects and spiders, obtained mostly from the undersides of small twigs, also from amongst foliage and in flowers, occasionally by hawking; also small fruits such as *Miconia* spp. and *Trema micrantha,* and the juice of citrus and other fruits, which it pierces and sucks; nectar is also regularly taken. Most feeding occurs between 25 and 50 ft above ground, but occasionally birds come to the ground for fallen fruit.

Nesting. Breeding recorded only in April and June (4 nests); moult from August to November. One nest was a small cup of moss lined with dark rootlets, set in the hollow of a small stump 5 ft above ground (Snow); 2 eggs from Brazil (Pinto 1953) were white spotted with dark brown and averaged 17.5 × 13.0mm. The male helps in feeding the young.

Red-legged Honeycreeper: *Cyanerpes cyaneus*
Blue Honeycreeper; "Red-legged Grampo";
"Grimpeur Pattes Rouges"   **Plate 24(5)**

Habitat and status. A fairly common resident in Trinidad, sharing much the same habitat as the Purple Honeycreeper, but also found on the Bocas islands in deciduous forest; also occurs quite commonly in Tobago, mostly in hilly districts; wanders widely outside the breeding season. (Specimens: both islands, AMNH, LM: Trinidad only, ANSP, YPM.)

Range and subspecies. Mexico S to Peru, Bolivia and C Brazil, also Cuba; *C. c. cyaneus* (Linnaeus) ranges from E Venezuela and Trinidad S to the Guianas, E Peru, Bolivia and Brazil; *C. c. tobagensis* (Hellmayr & Seilern) is restricted to Tobago, being distinguished by its slightly larger size.

Description. 5 in. *Adult male:* generally dark violet blue with black lores, mantle, wings and tail; crown turquoise; underwing and inner webs of flight feathers lemon yellow (only visible in flight); bill black, slightly decurved, not as long as in Purple Honeycreeper; legs red. After the breeding season the male moults into an "eclipse" plumage, generally greenish with black wings and tail. *Female and immature:* greenish, paler below with obscure streaks; legs reddish brown, or dusky in juveniles.

Measurements. Wing: *cyaneus,* 12 males 63–68mm (65.4); 6 females 61–63mm (62.5); *tobagensis,* 7 males 68–71mm (69.3); 3 females 67, 67, 68mm. Weight: *cyaneus,* 7 males 13–15gm (14.2); 10 female-plumaged 12.5–16gm (14.0); *tobagensis,* 1 male 13.5gm*.

Voice. A thin, high-pitched note, *tsip;* in alarm utters a pebbly *chink,* more metallic than Bananaquit's note.

Food. Small insects taken from amongst foliage and underneath fine twigs, or frequently while hovering or hawking; small fruits, including several *Miconia* spp. and the fleshy arils of trees such as *Sloanea* and *Cupania* and the vines *Doliocarpus* and *Norantea;* more rarely takes nectar from a variety of flowering plants, mostly trees.

Nesting. Breeding recorded in Trinidad (3 nests) in March, June and July.

The account by B/S of this species building a purse-shaped nest with blackish eggs is mistaken (Eisenmann 1953), determined by comparison with nests from Trinidad (Snow), Brazil (Pinto 1953) and Costa Rica (Skutch 1954). The nest is a flimsy cup of rootlets and grass, or of moss with a few fungus-covered twiglets, lined with blackish fibres and fastened by cobweb to the fork of a slender branch 10–15 ft above ground. The clutch is 2 eggs, white spotted with brown mainly at the thick end; 4 eggs of this race from Brazil averaged about 16.5 × 12.5mm. In Costa Rica the female performs most of the nesting duties, but the male helps to feed the young. Incubation lasts 12–13 days, and fledging takes place at 14 days.

Behaviour. An excitable species which gathers in small, loose flocks outside the breeding season. It is one of the first species to be attracted by the call of the Pygmy-Owl. In display males posture at each other for long periods, bowing, flicking their wings and turning from side to side. Birds also perch quietly for long periods on the bare twigs of tall trees.

Green Honeycreeper: *Chlorophanes spiza*
Black-crowned Honeycreeper   **Plate 23(4)**

Habitat and status. A common resident in Trinidad, found in forest and second growth with large trees, frequenting mostly the canopy. (Specimens: AMNH, ANSP, CM, YPM, LM, TRVL.)

Range and subspecies. Mexico S to Bolivia and Brazil; *C. s. spiza* (Linnaeus) ranges from NE Venezuela and Trinidad through the Guianas and N Brazil.

Description. 5.5 in. *Adult male:* generally glossy green, tinged blue, with black crown, nape and cheeks; iris red; bill black above, yellow below. *Female and immature:* generally grass green with yellowish throat. More like a tanager than a honeycreeper in build, with a fairly wide-based bill.

Measurements. Wing: 31 males 71–77mm (73.2); 11 females 65–72mm (70.2). Weight: 36 males 17–21gm (18.7); 20 female-plumaged 15–22gm (18.6).

Voice. An incisive, warbler-like *chip*, often repeated.

Food. Mostly fruit, 22 species being recorded (B. K. Snow & Snow 1971), especially *Miconia* spp., *Trema micrantha* and *Ficus* spp.; most fruit is taken from a perched position and eaten whole; some nectar is taken, usually from flowering trees, e.g., *Eugenia, Calliandra,* which attract insects; here small insects are taken in flight.

Nesting. Breeding recorded (4 nests) from May to July; moult records from February, April and September. The nest is a small cup of dead leaves and rootlets lined with finer materials and situated in a fork 20 ft above ground (B/S); the clutch is 2 eggs, white spotted with dark brown, av. 19.6 × 13.6mm (2). The female alone builds the nest, attended by the male, who sometimes feeds her. In Costa Rica (Skutch 1962) the incubation period is about 13 days; the male may help in feeding the young.

Behaviour. Frequently forages in small parties, often in association with other species; it is quickly attracted by the call of the Pygmy-Owl.

Blue Dacnis: *Dacnis cayana*
Turquoise Honeycreeper (or Dacnis)   **Plate 24(6)**

Habitat and status. A fairly common resident in Trinidad, frequenting forest edges and second growth, occasionally even savannahs with trees. (Specimens: AMNH, ANSP, CM, YPM, LM, TRVL.)

Range and subspecies. Nicaragua S to Bolivia and N Argentina; *D. c. cayana* (Linnaeus) ranges from E Colombia, Venezuela and Trinidad through the Guianas to C Brazil.

Description. 5 in. *Adult male:* generally bright turquoise blue with black forehead, throat and mantle; wings and tail black edged with turquoise. Bill shorter than most honeycreepers', resembling tanagers'. *Female and immature:* generally *green with blue head,* underparts paler; wings brown edged green.

Measurements. Wing: 8 males 62–65mm (62.6); 4 females 60–61mm. Weight: 10 males 12–15gm (13.5); 8 female-plumaged 12–15.5gm (13.9).

Voice. A thin, high-pitched *tsip.*

Food. Small insects, including caterpillars and aphids, taken from amongst foliage mostly above 10 ft from the ground; it also probes bromeliads and flowers for insects, but rarely takes nectar; fruit of many species is taken, especially of Euphorbiaceae and Melastomaceae (B. K. Snow & Snow 1971), mostly swallowed whole.

Nesting. Breeding recorded in March, June and July (7 nests); moult from June to September. The nest described by B/S is of another species. In Costa Rica, Skutch (1962) describes the nest of this species as a deep cup of fine fibres, plant-down and secondary rachises of *Mimosa,* suspended between a lateral fork 18–25 ft above ground. The female builds the nest, attended by the male, who feeds her while she incubates; the male helps to feed the young; the clutch is 2 eggs, and the fledging period is about 13 days.

Behaviour. Often forages in small parties composed mostly of birds in female plumage.

Golden-rumped Euphonia: *Euphonia cyanocephala*
Black-necked Euphonia; Blue-hooded Euphonia; "Tête bleu";
Tanagra musica; Euphonia musica   **Plate 24(2)**

Habitat and status. A rare resident in Trinidad, found in hilly areas of forest and cultivation; small flocks are rumoured by bird-catchers to be locally common in September and October. (No specimens, but collected by Léotaud.)

Range and subspecies. Colombia and Venezuela E to Trinidad and S to Paraguay and N Argentina; *E. c. intermedia* (Chubb) ranges in the north S to the Guianas and N Brazil. Closely allied forms *E. musica* and *E. elegantissima* from the West Indies and Central America have recently been considered to be separate species.

Description. 5 in. *Male:* crown and nape light blue; rest of head, neck and upperparts black glossed violet, but rump golden yellow; breast and abdomen yellow. *Female and immature:* generally greenish with small golden patch on forehead; crown and nape blue as in male. All euphonias have short tails and stubby bills.

Voice. Undescribed from Trinidad; in Venezuela the call-note is a soft, musical chirp.

Food. Berries, especially of mistletoe (Loranthaceae).

Nesting. One nest with eggs recorded by B/S in July. It was globular with a side entrance, made of dried grass and moss, lined with fine fibres, placed in the outer branches of a small tree 6 ft from the ground. There were 2 pale cream eggs, marked with pale brown with some black lines mainly at the thicker end, av. 16.6 × 12.9mm.

Trinidad Euphonia: *Euphonia trinitatis*
"Cravat"; *Tanagra trinitatis*   **Plate 24(3)**

Habitat and status. A rather uncommon but widespread resident in Trinidad, inhabiting mostly second growth and cultivated areas with large trees, usually keeping to the treetops; a sight record from Tobago (Pilling & Trowern 1964) was probably of an escaped cage-bird. (Specimens: AMNH, LM.)

Range. N Colombia, N Venezuela and Trinidad.

Description. 4.5 in. *Male:* head and upperparts black glossed blue, crown bright yellow; *throat black glossed blue;* rest of underparts yellow; outer tail-feathers white on inner web. *Female and immature:* olive green above, yellowish olive below with centre of breast and abdomen pale gray; under-tail-coverts bright yellow. Slimmer than the Violaceous Euphonia, and with a finer bill.

Measurements. Wing: 2 females 54, 54mm. Weight: 1 female 14gm*.

Voice. A high-pitched, plaintive and penetrating whistle, *pee,* usually double but also heard 3–5 times, once heard in a long series of perhaps 20 notes; also a rapid, double note, *puwee* or *cooleee,* the second note higher than the first. The female answers the male with a call similar but shorter and less penetrating.

Food. Berries, especially of mistletoe (*Loranthus*) and the "bird-vine" (*Phthirusa*), which are usually found rather high in trees; also forages for insects (B. K. Snow & Snow 1971) by searching the undersides of fine twigs.

Nesting. Breeding recorded (5 nests) in February and March. The nest is a ball of dry grass and stems lined with finer materials, with a side entrance. B/S found a nest situated near the end of the branch of a small tree 7 ft from the ground; but 3 nests in a hog-plum tree (*Spondias*) at Pointe-a-Pierre have been 40 ft up, 2 in a large bromeliad, the other in a hollow, horizontal stump. B/S record 4 eggs, pale cream marked with deep brown, av. 17.7 × 12.9mm. Both sexes build the nest and feed the young, but only the female incubates.

Behaviour. The species appears to remain in mated pairs throughout the year. In courtship display both members of a pair flick their wings and flirt from side to side, frequently bowing low, the male showing his bright crown.

Violaceous Euphonia: *Euphonia violacea*
"Semp"; *Tanagra violacea*   **Plate 24(1)**

Habitat and status. A common resident in Trinidad, inhabiting forest and second growth, including cocoa and citrus estates, with large trees. (Specimens: AMNH, ANSP, CM, YPM, LM, TRVL.) In Tobago much less common but widespread in hilly areas. (No specimens.)

Range and subspecies. E Venezuela, Trinidad, Tobago and the Guianas S to Brazil, Paraguay and N Argentina; *E. v. violacea* (Linnaeus) occurs in the range south to N Brazil; *E. v. rodwayi* has been separated on the grounds of larger size and more violaceous upperparts, but these characters do not hold consistently.

Description. 4.5 in. *Adult male:* head and upperparts black glossed blue; forehead and entire underparts golden yellow; some white on inner webs of flight feathers and base of tail, visible mainly in flight. *Female and immature:* olive green above, yellowish olive below. Young males often show traces of the golden forehead first.

Measurements. Wing: 45 males 56–62mm (58.6); 15 females 54–60mm (57.5). Weight: 65 males 12.5–17gm (14.6); 12 females 13.5–16.5gm (15.1); 1 egg-laying female 19gm.

Voice. Song is an extremely varied series of musical notes interspersed with chatters and squeaks; often included are imitations of the calls of other species, e.g., in Trinidad the alarm notes of *Formicarius, Turdus nudigenis, T. fumigatus* and *Troglodytes,* the calls of *Touit, Xiphorhynchus guttatus* and *Megarhynchus,* and in Tobago *Turdus nudigenis, Formicivora* and *Tyrannus melancholicus.* The usual alarm note is a loud *cheep,* often repeated with snatches of song. In addition, I have invariably found that the male, on release from capture, utters a loud chatter as he flies away; a similar chatter is often made by the female as she leaves the nest when disturbed.

Food. Almost entirely small fruits, especially of epiphytes, e.g., the bromeliad *Aechmaea nudicaulis,* the mistletoes and the cactus *Rhipsalis;* a large variety of fruits has been recorded (B. K. Snow & Snow 1971), the feeding being at all levels in trees and shrubs; rather rarely takes insects.

Nesting. Breeding recorded in Trinidad (25 nests) in all months from January to August, mainly May–July; moult recorded July–September. The nest is a ball of dead leaves, rootlets and moss, lined with ferns and grass, with a side entrance. Typically it is situated at the top of a bank overlooking a path; other nests are placed on stumps or in tree cavities, usually amidst epiphytes or other vegetation. The clutch is usually 4, sometimes 3, whitish eggs marked with red, especially at the thick end, av. 18.0 × 12.1mm (4). Only the female incubates, but both parents feed the young. A nest may be used more than once.

Notes. All 3 euphonia species are prized as cage-birds, though the first 2 are rarely seen in cages. This species may be the only one in Trinidad and Tobago whose repeated trapping has not yet endangered its existence on the islands, due to its choice of a comparatively inaccessible habitat. Unfortunately aviculture in Trinidad and Tobago is almost entirely limited to the trapping process. Except for a very few enthusiasts, no attempt is made to breed cage-birds, females are kept only for use as decoys, and the knowledge of a bird's diet and hygiene is generally non-existent. Most "semps" are fed nothing but banana, with no water provided, and in spite of legal requirements many cages are far too small. It is not surprising that most cage-birds die after a short period of captivity.

Speckled Tanager: *Tangara guttata*
Spotted Tanager; Yellow-browed Tanager; *Tangara chrysophrys*
Plate 25(5)

Habitat and status. A fairly common resident in Trinidad, frequenting forest and second growth mainly above 1800 ft. (Specimens: AMNH, CM, LM.)

Range and subspecies. Costa Rica, Panama, Colombia, Venezuela, Trinidad and N Brazil; *T. g. trinitatis* (Todd) is restricted to Trinidad, being distinguished by the brighter and more extensive yellow about the head and the more conspicuous spots on upperparts and breast.

Description. 5.5 in. Upperparts yellowish green, the feathers with black centres appearing as spots; fore-crown and face yellowish, lores black; wings and tail blackish edged green; underparts bluish white with conspicuous black spots. Sexes similar.

Measurements. Wing: 5 males 68–71mm (70.0); 4 females 69mm each. Weight: 22 unsexed 15–20.5gm (18.4).

Voice. Utters a rather weak metallic chirping, usually only in flight.

Food. Mostly small fruits taken from forest trees and shrubs, especially Melastomaceae and Euphorbiaceae; insects are also taken, mostly from below leaves which the bird examines while clinging upside down to the branch.

Nesting. Breeding recorded (4 nests) in January, June and July; moult in March, April and August (see *T. gyrola*). The nest is a small, compact cup of leaves and rootlets interwoven with fungal hyphae. In Costa Rica, Skutch (1954) found clutches of 2 eggs, laid on consecutive days; they were white, heavily mottled with brown, 1 measuring 20 × 15.1mm. Both sexes build the nest, and though only the female incubates, she is fed by her mate at this time, and both parents feed the young. Incubation lasts about 13 days, and fledging takes 15 days.

Behaviour. This species is rarely seen singly. Mated pairs stay together throughout the year, and often small parties of 6 or 8 birds forage together, frequently in company with *T. gyrola* or some honeycreepers.

Turquoise Tanager: *Tangara mexicana*
Blue-and-yellow Tanager; "Mexican" Tanager;
"Sucrier Martinique"   **Plate 25(6)**

Habitat and status. A common resident in Trinidad, found in forest edges, open woodland, cultivated area with trees, and not uncommon in gardens near human habitation; rare above 1800 ft. (Specimens: AMNH, ANSP, CM, YPM, LM, TRVL.)

Range and subspecies. Colombia and Venezuela S to Bolivia and Brazil; *T. m. vieilloti* (Sclater) is restricted to Trinidad, having more vivid yellow underparts and darker blue head and breast than the nominate form.

Description. 5.5 in. Fore-crown, face and breast dark blue, lores black; hind-crown, back, wings and tail black, rump blue; *patch on lesser wing-coverts turquoise;* sides dark blue spotted with black, lower underparts pale yellow. Sexes similar.

Measurements. Wing: 4 males 73–77mm (75.0); 4 females 70–73mm (71.2). Weight: 2 females 20.5, 21gm; 17 unsexed 18–23.5gm (20.5).

Voice. A light, high-pitched and squeaky chatter, usually heard from several birds together.

Food. Fruit of many trees and shrubs, taken at all levels from the ground to above 50 ft, especially *Miconia* spp., *Ilex, Chiococca alba* and *Cecropia peltata;* unlike other *Tangara* spp. (B. K. Snow & Snow 1971) feeds on mistletoes and also pecks pieces out of larger fruits; also feeds on insects, foraging mostly on fine twigs (including dead twigs).

Nesting. Breeding recorded from April to October (10 nests fairly evenly distributed); moult from June to September (see Bay-headed Tanager). A nest was a deep cup of moss and roots decorated with lichen and leaves, and lined with fine rootlets; it was set in the fork of a tree 20 ft above ground. The clutch was 3 grayish green eggs, marked unevenly with rich brown, av. 19.5 × 14.4mm. D. W. Snow and Collins (1962) found groups of 4 and 5 adults attending young at the nest and feeding them after fledging; the nest, however is built by 1 bird only.

Behaviour. Highly social, living in groups usually of 4–7 birds, rarely more; birds are hardly ever seen feeding singly.

Bay-headed Tanager: *Tangara gyrola*
Red-headed Tanager; Blue-rumped Green Tanager; "Tête Cacao"; "Worthless"   **Portrait IX**

Habitat and status. A common resident in Trinidad, frequenting forest and second growth at all levels, but more common in wetter areas. (Specimens: AMNH, ANSP, CM, YPM, LM, TRVL.)

Range and subspecies. Costa Rica and Panama S to Bolivia and Brazil; *T. g. viridissima* (Lafresnaye) is confined to NE Venezuela and Trinidad. There is considerable geographic variation in the plumages of the various subspecies.

Description. 5.5 in. Generally green with chestnut head, narrow collar of gold behind head; upperparts are tinged with gold, and some specimens show some bluish tinge on the underparts. *Immature:* has no sheen, and the head is green with flecks of chestnut.

Measurements. Wing: 9 males 71–76mm (73.7); 4 females 70–72mm (70.8). Weight: 128 unsexed 17.5–26.5gm (20.5).

Voice. Song is a rather slow 5-note sequence, *seee, seee, seee, tsou tsooy,* the last 2 notes lower in pitch; also twitters in flight and when feeding, like other *Tangara* species, and calls a single metallic note.

Food. Mostly fruit taken from a wide variety of trees, shrubs, vines and epiphytes (33 species, B. K. Snow & Snow 1971), including especially *Miconia* spp., *Cecropia peltata* and *Ficus* spp. Fruits are usually swallowed whole, but occasionally it pecks at larger fruit; sometimes fruit is taken on the wing in the manner of a manakin. Insects are also taken, almost always from the underside of a branch, which it examines from first one side, then the other; in this respect differs from the Turquoise Tanager by foraging higher in trees and on thicker branches.

Nesting. The few breeding records (11 nests) are widely scattered from January to August, with moult recorded in all months from February to September (see below). The nest is a compact cup of moss and other vegetation, thinly lined with fine roots or grass; on two occasions it was placed in a fork near the top of a small tree about 15 ft above ground. In Costa Rica Skutch (1954) found that nests were mainly built by the female, with occasional help from the male. Clutch size was 2 eggs, laid on consecutive days, being whitish marked with brown mainly at the thick end. Incubation, by the female alone, lasted 13–14 days, and fledging 15–16 days. Both parents fed the young. Up to 3 broods may be reared in one season, the interval between broods being as little as 18 days.

Behaviour. Highly social, like the other *Tangara* species.

Notes. The wing-moult of this species and its congeners shows some surprising departures from that of other tanagers. First, records are spread over a long period of the year; in each individual moult develops very slowly, the feathers being replaced one at a time rather than 2 or 3 adjacent feathers growing simultaneously; also there is evidence of arrested moult. It may be that breeding (e.g., with a second or third brood) occurs during the moult, and that during this time the moult process is arrested. More data are needed on the rate of wing-moult in individuals and its correlation with breeding. Also it is not known whether other members of this genus share *T. mexicana*'s habit of communal feeding of young, and whether this or some other aspect of their breeding biology may affect the moult schedule.

Blue-gray Tanager: *Thraupis episcopus*
Blue Tanager; "Bluebird"; "Blue Jean"; *Thraupis virens*   **Plate 25(1)**

Habitat and status. A common resident in Trinidad and Tobago, including offshore islands, frequenting open woodland and cultivated areas with trees and bushes, gardens and urban areas. (Specimens: Trinidad, AMNH, ANSP, CM, YPM, LM, TRVL; Tobago, AMNH, LM.)

Range and subspecies. Mexico south to NW Bolivia and N Brazil; *T. e. nesophila* (Riley) ranges from E Colombia, extreme N Brazil and NE Venezuela to Trinidad; *T. e. berlepschi* (Dalmas) is confined to Tobago and is brighter and darker blue on rump and shoulder patch.

Description. 7 in. Generally grayish blue, brighter blue on rump and upperparts, with a patch of vivid violet blue on wing-coverts. Sexes similar.

Measurements. *T. e nesophila.* Wing: 8 males 89–96mm (91.1); 12 females 85–92mm (88.5). Weight: 1 male 33.5gm; 1 female 35gm; 47 unsexed 31–45gm (37.0). *T. e. berlepschi.* Wing: 1 male 93mm; 1 female 92mm; 27 unsexed 87–96mm (91.4). Weight: 25 unsexed 30–36gm (32.9).

Voice. Song is an extremely high-pitched, squeaky, sibilant series of about 10 drawn-out notes, delivered rather deliberately and without a recognisable pattern; single squeaks are also uttered by both sexes.

Food. Fruit, taken from a variety of trees and shrubs, especially the matchwood (*Didymopanax*) and *Cecropia peltata;* it is known to feed at a number of commercially grown fruits and vegetables; it frequently pecks at larger fruits, and always eats while perched. Sometimes feeds on the nectar of flowering trees, especially the yellow poui. It also takes insects, hawking for some, e.g., termites, and searching the flowers of trees; more commonly it forages amidst foliage, examining leaves and the undersides of branches and darting forward to seize its prey as it attempts to escape.

Nesting. Breeding recorded in Trinidad (128 nests) in the following months:

I	II	III	IV	V	VI
8	5	10	34	31	20

VII	VIII	IX	X	XI	XII
11	4	—	3	1	1

Moult in May to August, especially the latter. In Tobago the few records of nests and moult indicate a similar situation. The nest is a deep cup of leaves, stems, grass and sometimes moss, situated either amidst foliage near the end of a branch or wedged in a fork quite close to a tree trunk, 10–60 ft above ground; sometimes the bases of palm fronds are used as sites. The clutch is 1 to 3, usually 2, eggs, laid on consecutive days; they are grayish green or cream heavily marked with sepia, sometimes with black lines; often the eggs of a clutch differ in their markings considerably; 10 from Trinidad av. 24.1 × 16.9mm. Both sexes build the nest and feed the young, but only the female incubates, for a period of about 14 days; fledging takes 17 days. The species is occasionally parasitised by the cowbird *Molothrus*. In Costa Rica (Skutch 1954) and Surinam (Haverschmidt 1954c) 2 or more broods in a season are recorded.

Behaviour. A restless, noisy and excitable species, usually found in pairs, occasionally in larger parties. It is aggressive towards other species and is known to appropriate the nests of smaller birds. It is not very shy of humans, and breeds in gardens and forages at comparatively low levels near houses.

Palm Tanager: *Thraupis palmarum*
"Palmiste" **Plate 25(4)**

Habitat and status. A common resident in Trinidad, frequenting forest edges, second growth and cultivated areas, including gardens and urban districts; shows a decided preference for palm trees. Since 1982 recorded from various parts of Tobago. (Specimens: AMNH, ANSP, CM, YPM, LM, TRVL.)

Range and subspecies. Nicaragua S to Bolivia, Paraguay and S Brazil; *T. p. melanoptera* (Sclater) occurs from E Colombia and Ecuador through Venezuela, Trinidad and the Guianas to Peru, Bolivia and N Brazil.

Description. 7 in. Generally dull olive green, paler and brighter on crown; wing-coverts and base of primaries yellowish green, contrasting with blackish primaries and appearing as a *pale wing-bar in flight;* tail blackish edged green.

Sexes similar. Wild hybrids occur between this species and the Blue-gray Tanager.

Measurements. Wing: 12 males 95–103mm (97.5); 8 females 87–95mm (91.5). Weight: 4 males 35–37gm; 3 females 35.3, 37.5, 38gm; 48 unsexed 32–47gm (38.6).

Voice. Song is similar in quality to Blue-gray Tanager, but the notes are mostly shorter and more rapid with a staccato pattern; the single call-note is a penetrating *weest*.

Food. Fruit of a variety of trees and shrubs, including *Didymopanax, Cecropia peltata* and some palms, especially those with small fruits, e.g., the introduced golden palm (*Chrysalidocarpus*); also feeds on the nectar of flowering trees, e.g., immortelles and pouis; insects are frequently taken, especially caterpillars; most commonly it forages among large leaves, clinging to the leaf upside down or vertically, head downward; also hawks for termites.

Nesting. Breeding recorded in every month (126 nests) as follows:

I	II	III	IV	V	VI
4	4	21	21	16	25

VII	VIII	IX	X	XI	XII
17	12	1	3	1	1

Moult recorded in almost every month from May to December. D. W. Snow and Snow (1964) found at one site an almost continuous breeding season with up to 4 broods in a year, interrupted only by the moult. There was usually a quick succession of nesting attempts from March to August, with often another nest in October. Intervals between broods were usually 11–25 days, but sometimes over 6 wk. The nest resembles that of the Blue-gray Tanager, but is usually sited in a palm tree at the base of the fronds; it also nests under the eaves of houses. The clutch is often 2, sometimes 3, creamy eggs spotted with sepia, av. 24.0 × 17.7mm (10). The female incubates for 14 days, and fledging takes 17–20 days. Both parents build the nest and feed the young.

Behaviour. A social species, often seen in pairs, but also banding into parties of 6 or 7, especially in the evening, when many birds congregate in high branches prior to roosting, in association with various other species. Excitable and nervous, it resembles the Blue-gray Tanager in general habits.

Blue-capped Tanager: *Thraupis cyanocephala*
Blue-headed Tanager; Ashy Tanager; "Blue Mantle"   **Plate 25(3)**

Habitat and status. An uncommon and local resident in Trinidad, frequenting forest, especially clearings, and cultivated areas, mostly above 2000 ft. (Specimens: AMNH, CM, LM.)

Range and subspecies. Trinidad, N Venezuela and the Colombian Andes S to Peru and NW Bolivia; *T. c. busingi* (Hellmayr & Seilern) is restricted to Trinidad and the Paria peninsula of Venezuela; it is darker gray below with a more prominent loral streak.

Description. 7.5 in. Crown and face bright dark blue, lores black, pale moustachial streak; upperparts olive green, underparts mostly bluish gray, under-tail-coverts and under-wing yellowish; bill black, base of mandible pale gray.

Measurements. Wing: 6 males 78–86mm (81.8); 3 females 80, 80, 85mm. Weight: 1 male 28gm*; 1 unsexed 31.5gm*.

Voice. A weak twittering, reminiscent of *Tangara* spp.

Food. Berries, including those of Melastomaceae and (Junge & Mees 1958) coffee; also invertebrates.

Nesting. Breeding recorded only once by B/S, who found a nest on 5 June in the crotch of a tree, 25 ft above ground, near a roadside on Morne Bleu. It was a deep cup of stems, fibres and moss, with some bits of bark outside and lined with soft fibres. There were 2 pale greenish blue eggs, marked with sepia, av. 25.2 × 17.2mm. Moult recorded in August and September.

Behaviour. Always seen in pairs or larger parties, often gathering to feed at a tree. It is attracted by the call of the Pygmy-Owl.

Silver-beaked Tanager: *Ramphocelus carbo*
Silver-beak; Silver-billed Tanager   **Plate 25(7)**

Habitat and status. A common resident in Trinidad, frequenting light woodland and semi-open areas with thickets, also cultivated estates and forest edges up to 2000 ft; keeps closer to the ground than most other tanagers. (Specimens: AMNH, ANSP, CM, YPM, LM, TRVL.)

Range and subspecies. Colombia and Venezuela S to Bolivia, Paraguay and C Brazil; *R. c. magnirostris* (Lafresnaye) is confined to Trinidad and the Paria peninsula of Venezuela.

Description. 7 in. *Male:* generally velvety black, tinged with crimson; throat and upper breast deep crimson; upper mandible black, lower mandible much enlarged at base and pale bluish, appearing silvery in the field. *Female and immature:* dull reddish brown, rump and underparts dull maroon red; bill black.

Measurements. Wing: 87 males 76–85mm (80.9, S.D. 1.8); 43 females 72–80mm (77.1, S.D. 1.8). Weight: 111 males 24.5–37.5gm (29.5, S.D. 2.2); 23 females 23.5–31gm (27.4, S.D. 2.1).

Voice. Song, often heard at dawn, is a series of 2–5 2-syllabled phrases, *kick-wick* or *che-wa,* deliberate and rather thrush-like in tone, but thinner; this is often followed by a lower-pitched, creaky *weer;* the whole series is repeated many times, with some variation. Usual call-note is a sharp, metallic *chip,* also occasionally a quickly repeated *wek-wek-wek.*

Food. Fruit, and occasionally nectar, of many different plants (40 species recorded by B. K. Snow & Snow 1971), including especially Melastomaceae, e.g., *Clidemia,* and other small shrubs; also the fruits of various bromeliads; most feeding is below 25 ft, much of it below 10 ft. Insects, including caterpillars, beetles and butterflies, are also taken in low foliage or on the ground; the bird hops about rapidly on top of the foliage, darting forward to seize its prey; rather rarely hawks for flying insects.

Nesting. Breeding recorded (163 nests) as follows:

I	II	III	IV	V	VI
33	14	15	19	20	35

VII	VIII	IX	X	XI	XII
14	9	1	—	—	3

Regular song January–July; moult from May to December, especially August and September; indications are that individual moult may take up to 4 months. The nest is a deep cup of dead leaves and grass, mixed with fibres and rootlets and lined with a few fibres. It is situated usually in a bush 3–8 ft up, but may be low down in a tuft of grass or on a stump, or 25 ft up in a bushy tree. Fifty-three recorded clutches (Snow) were 2 × c/3, 49 × c/2, 2 × c/1, but often only 1 chick survived. The eggs, laid on consecutive days, are bright greenish blue, marked with blackish brown, av. 22.8 × 16.8mm (10). On nearby South America (Haverschmidt 1968a, Skutch 1968) only the female builds the nest and incubates, for a period of 12 days; the young fledge after 11–12 days. Sometimes the male helps to feed the young. The nest may be used for a second brood. The species is sometimes parasitised by the cowbird *Molothrus.*

Behaviour. Moves around in pairs or parties of 6–8, mostly birds in female plumage. There is an apparent lack of territoriality; in Venezuela, Skutch (1968) found 2 occupied nests 3 ft apart. In display the male points his bill skywards, showing the bright lower mandible. Like other tanagers, this species frequently flicks the wings and tail when about to fly.

Hepatic Tanager: *Piranga flava*
Caribbean Red Tanager; Toothed Tanager

Habitat and status. A rather uncommon resident in Trinidad, confined to forest and second growth in the Northern Range above 1000 ft. Confusion with the Summer Tanager by Herklots (1961) and other observers may have been based on the belief that this species has a *black* bill, which in Trinidad it does not. (Specimens: AMNH, FSM.)

Range and subspecies. SW USA south through Central and South America to C Argentina; *P. f. faceta* (Bangs) ranges from N Colombia through N Venezuela to Trinidad.

Description. 7 in. *Male:* all brick red, paler below; ear-coverts brownish but often not noticeable in the field; bill blackish only at base, ridge and tip of upper mandible, lower mandible and rest of upper mandible pale horn, appearing almost yellowish in the field; in the hand the "tooth" on upper mandible is diagnostic. *Female and immature:* greenish olive above, wings and tail dark edged olive; lower half of eye-ring and underparts yellow; upper mandible dark horn, lower pale gray. An immature male in changing plumage was seen on 26 April.

Measurements. Wing: 6 males 86–90mm (87.8); 2 females 82, 88mm. Weight: 3 males 31.5, 35.5, 36gm; 2 females 31, 40gm.

Voice. Call-note an incisive and abrupt *chup* or *choop,* repeated often; also a creaky *weez.* A recently fledged bird begging from its parent uttered a high-pitched *eeeooo.*

Food. Berries and insects, including butterflies; sometimes forages in clearings quite close to the ground.

Nesting. Breeding recorded in February, July and October, and possibly December. One nest was made of dry grass and situated amidst the sprouting vegetation of a trimmed forest tree at the edge of a clearing, 20 ft above ground. The 2 eggs were greenish, spotted with brown. Both parents fed the young.

Behaviour. Seen in pairs at all seasons. In display the male points his bill up, showing the bright throat, and moves his head from side to side. The species is attracted to the call of the Pygmy-Owl and seems quite unwary of man.

Summer Tanager: *Piranga rubra*

Habitat and status. An uncommon winter visitor to Trinidad, recorded in all months from October to March (earliest 25 October, latest 19 March), mostly in Northern Range forest, but also at Pointe-a-Pierre in light woodland. Herklots (1961) had trouble distinguishing between this species and the Hepatic Tanager (ffrench & ffrench 1966). (Specimens: AMNH.)

Range and subspecies. Breeds in North America from California to Delaware, wintering S through Central America to Ecuador, Bolivia, Brazil and Venezuela; *P. r. rubra* (Linnaeus) breeds in E USA, wintering in the southern part of the range; casual in West Indies.

Description. 7 in. *Male:* all rose red, slightly paler below; bill pale horn. *Female and immature:* upperparts yellowish olive green, dull golden yellow below; wings and tail dark, edged olive green. *Immature male:* brighter than female, often dull orange-brown above; change into adult male plumage occurs early in the year following hatching; 1 "patchy" individual seen on 6 February. (See also Hepatic Tanager.)

Measurements. Wing: 1 male 96mm; 2 females 94, 94mm.

Voice. Call-note a rapid, low-pitched *pit-tiuc-tiuc-tiuc* or *pee-ta-ta,* quite distinct from note of Hepatic.

Food. Berries and insects.

Scarlet Tanager: *Piranga olivacea*

Habitat and status. Two records from each island, all of adult males: in Trinidad from the Moruga area on 16 April 1979 and 28 April 1983; on Tobago at Crown Point on 1 May 1966 and 20 April 1978. These dates indicate spring passage migrants. (No extant specimen, but the species was reported to have been collected on Trinidad in the nineteenth century).

Range. Breeds in North America, wintering S to Bolivia.

Description. 6.5 in. *Male (breeding):* scarlet with black wings and tail. Non-breeding males show female plumage, but with black wings and tail. *Female:* above olive green, yellowish below, wings dusky.

Food. Berries, including those of *Bursera simaruba.*

Red-crowned Ant-Tanager: *Habia rubica*
Cardinal Ant-Tanager; Red Ant-Tanager   **Plate 26(3)**

Habitat and status. A fairly common resident in Trinidad, widely distributed in forests at all levels, where it keeps to the undergrowth and denser parts. (Specimens: AMNH, ANSP, CM, LM, TRVL.)

Range and subspecies. Mexico S to Paraguay and N Argentina; *H. r. rubra* (Vieillot) occurs in NE Venezuela and Trinidad.

Description. 7 in. *Male:* generally dull brownish red, brighter red below; brilliant *scarlet stripe through crown,* bordered black, forming a crest which is raised in excitement. *Female and immature:* yellowish olive brown, throat yellowish; crown-stripe as male but yellowish buff. Young male in changing plumage seen on 26 April.

Measurements. Wing: 10 males 88–96mm (91.3); 5 females 84–91mm (87.8). Weight: 20 males 29.5–35.5gm (31.8); 5 female-plumaged 26.5–32.5gm (30.4); 1 female (probably egg-laying) 37gm.

Voice. Usual call a harsh, ratchet-like rattle, often followed by a musical *pee-pee-pee;* song (rarely heard) is a desultory musical 2-syllable warble, repeated at intervals.

Food. Arthropods and berries; most foraging is done on understory branches and twigs; occasionally attends army ant swarms; larger arthropods are torn apart by the bill.

Nesting. Breeding recorded (22 nests) in the following months:

I	II	III	IV	V	VI
—	1	1	—	3	11

VII	VIII	IX	X	XI	XII
3	2	—	1	—	—

Song mostly in early months; moult from June to October. B/S were confused about this species, ascribing its nest to the antbird *Myrmeciza*. The nest is a flimsy, shallow cup of small twigs, rootlets and fine fibres, usually including some pieces covered with white fungus which project from the nest; the lining is made of black fungal hyphae. The usual site is near a stream, in a fork just below the crown of a small forest sapling or in the top of a small tree fern, 3–5 (occasionally up to 9) ft above ground. The clutch is 1–3 (nearly always 2) eggs, whitish marked with brown mostly at the thick end, av. 23.6 × 16.8mm (2). Incubation, by the female, lasts 13 days, the eggs being laid on consecutive days. The female also builds the nest and mostly feeds the young, though the male helps a little. In Costa Rica (Skutch 1954) and Belize (Willis 1961) nest predation was very high, even though the adults' journeys to and from the nest were limited in number by long periods of incubation and brooding, eggshells and fecal sacs were swallowed and large-sized food items were provided for the young; in addition, adults showed great caution in approaching and leaving the nest. Willis found the fledging period to be 10 days, but the young were still incapable of efficient flight for several days after that.

Behaviour. Usually found in pairs or small (probably family) groups of 4 or 5. It is highly vocal and reacts excitedly to human intrusion, quickly disappearing into thick undergrowth. It frequently associates with other species as part of wandering flocks of insectivorous birds; in Belize Willis (1960) found a notable association between this species and a greenlet, *Hylophilus*. In a distraction display the bird cocks up its tail and depresses its wings, then makes short fluttering flights.

White-lined Tanager: *Tachyphonus rufus*
White-shouldered Tanager; "Parson"; "Cocoa Bird";
Boddaert's Tanager   **Plate 26(2)**

Habitat and status. A common resident in both islands, including offshore islets, widely distributed in second growth, forest edges, semi-open areas and gardens, including urban districts; keeps low in vegetation. (Specimens: AMNH, ANSP, CM, YPM, LM, TRVL.)

Range. Costa Rica S to Paraguay and N Argentina.

Description. 7.5 in. *Adult male:* glossy black, except for white under-wing-coverts and a small white patch on inner upper-wing-coverts, only visible (but conspicuous) in flight; bill black with base of lower mandible bluish white. *Female and immature:* entirely rufous. It seems that some immature birds have a few adult male feathers soon after leaving the nest (ffrench 1965a). Birds in patchy plumage have been observed in August and November.

Measurements. Wing: 57 males 82–94mm (87.5, S.D. 2.2); 16 females 79–88mm (83.9). Weight: 60 males 31–40.5gm (35.2, S.D. 1.9); 25 females 31–42.5gm (36.6); 1 female (probably egg-laying) 47.5gm.

Voice. Song a deliberate repetition of a 2-syllabled musical phrase, *cheeru* or *cheep-chooi,* accented on the first syllable, at the rate of about 100 per min; usual call a short *check,* also a weak, thin *seep.*

Food. Fruit taken from a wide variety of plants (31 species recorded), including especially epiphytes, e.g., the bromeliad *Gravisia aquilega;* fruits are often taken while hovering; some nectar is taken from flowering trees, especially immortelles. Commercially grown fruits are also exploited, and this species readily takes sugar and fruit from feeding tables. Insects, including beetles and grasshoppers, are frequently taken, mostly from or near the ground, sometimes at army ant swarms. Sometimes it hovers briefly just above the ground, and also hawks for flying insects; although it forages amongst foliage for insects, it rarely examines branches or twigs closely, but moves rapidly, seizing its prey with sudden darts.

Nesting. Breeding recorded in Trinidad (23 nests) from February to August, especially May and June, with a single November record; regular song March–July; moult recorded from July to October. The nest is a bulky cup of leaves lined with thin fibres; it is situated in a bush or tree up to 40 ft above ground. The clutch is usually 3, sometimes 2, eggs, pale cream marked with blackish brown; av. 23.3 × 18.8mm (10). Only the female incubates, for 14–15 days, but both parents feed the young. Haverschmidt (1968a) in Surinam records that the male feeds the female in courtship.

Behaviour. A restless bird, but not wary of human presence; moving about low branches and bushes it often flicks a wing before flying, the male thus disclosing his white feathers. Except for family parties, which are found soon after fledging, it is seen in pairs at all seasons, one member flying behind the other rather than with it. In the late evening numbers sometimes gather in the high branches of a bare tree before going off to roost.

White-shouldered Tanager: *Tachyphonus luctuosus*
Lesser White-shouldered Tanager; "Little Parson" **Plate 26(1)**

Habitat and status. A rather uncommon resident in Trinidad, but widely distributed in forest and second growth, also cocoa plantations. (Specimens: AMNH, ANSP, YPM, LM, TRVL.)

Range and subspecies. Honduras S to Bolivia and C Brazil; *T. l. flavi-ventris* (Sclater) is restricted to Trinidad and neighbouring NE Venezuela, being distinguished by its longer wing and larger bill.

Description. 5.5 in. *Adult male:* all black, except for conspicuous white patch on wing-coverts (visible at all times) and white underwing. *Female and immature:* head and neck gray, upperparts olive green, underparts ochreous yellow. A young male on 5 March was in patchy plumage, black with olive green outer primaries, inner secondaries, outer tail, some wing-coverts and patches on head and body.

Measurements. Wing: 8 males 65–68mm (66.4); 3 females 62mm each. Weight: 8 males 12.5–15gm (13.6); 3 females 13, 13.5, 17.5gm (probably egg-laying).

Voice. A slight, unmusical *tchirrup,* or a squeaky *tswee,* often repeated.

Food. Mostly insects, including stick-insects, which it takes in foliage, often above 25 ft, picking its prey off leaves and sometimes fluttering down after it. Occasionally feeds on fruit, including the pomerac (*Eugenia malaccensis*) and *Miconia* spp.

Nesting. Breeding recorded only by B/S (2 nests) in April and May, and once in September (Gibbs); moult recorded September–November. The nests were fairly deep cups of dried grass lined with fine fibres and placed in low vegetation within a few feet of the ground. The clutches were 3 eggs, varying in colour, av. 19.5 × 16.1mm (6); one set were rich buff marked with reddish brown, mainly at the thick end; the others were pale cream, sparsely marked with blackish brown.

Behaviour. Usually found in small groups, associating in flocks with other small insectivorous species and wandering restlessly through the lower levels of the more open forest.

FRINGILLIDAE: Finches, Seedeaters and Grosbeaks

Apart from the larger saltators, members of this family are small (4–6 in.) birds, mostly nondescript, the males being somewhat more brightly coloured than the generally brown females. The bill is short and conical, adapted to the main diet of seeds. The song of many species is attractive and musical, leading to a great demand locally for the best songsters as cage-birds. Mostly occurring in the more open areas and light woodland, they are fairly conspicuous, and several species habitually flock together. Most species build small cup-shaped nests; the female builds, incubates and broods, but the male always helps to feed the nestlings. (20)

Notes. I have followed Meyer de Schauensee (1966) in keeping, for ease of reference, to the traditional arrangement of the various branches of this family. Numerous proposals have recently been made, dividing the family into Fringillidae and Emberizidae, rearranging the order of various "sub-families" and moving certain genera to the Thraupidae or Icteridae.

Grayish Saltator: *Saltator coerulescens*
Grey-breasted Saltator; "Pitch-oil"   **Plate 26(6)**

Habitat and status. A common resident in Trinidad, including offshore islets, frequenting light woodland, semi-open areas, including savannahs with dense thickets, edges of mangroves and cocoa estates, also gardens in suburban areas. (Specimens: AMNH, ANSP, CM, YPM, LM, TRVL.)

Range and subspecies. Mexico S to Costa Rica, and Colombia south to N Argentina and Uruguay; *S. c. brewsteri* (Bangs & Penard) ranges from E Colombia through Venezuela to Trinidad.

Description. 9 in. *Adult:* upperparts dark gray, white superciliary streak; underparts paler gray, chin whitish bordered by a short black line on each side, lower underparts buff; bill heavy, black. *Immature:* olive green above, yellowish superciliary, yellowish green below; resembles adult Streaked Saltator but is larger.

Measurements. Wing: 9 males 96–103mm (99.1); 7 females 94–100mm (98.4). Weight: 5 males 48.5–56gm (52.3); 1 female 51.5gm.

Voice. Song is a series of several abrupt, squeaky notes, with 1 or 2 notes much higher-pitched than the others, the syllables vaguely resembling *pitch-oil-pitch-oil;* also utters a less musical chatter.

Food. Berries and soft fruits; I have often seen it eating leaves and blossoms of various garden plants, e.g., bougainvillaea, hibiscus and the climber *Clitoria;* also known to take insects, including ants and weevils.

Nesting. Breeding recorded from March to October (33 nests), especially May, moult in August and October–January. The nest is a deep cup of twigs, leaves and grass, lined with fine fibres and situated in a tree or bush up to 12 ft above ground. The clutch is 2, occasionally 3, blue eggs marked with black scrawls and blotches only at the thick end, av. 26.6 × 18.9mm (4); 1 extra large measured 30 × 21mm. In Honduras (Skutch 1945) the fledging period is 15 days.

Streaked Saltator: *Saltator albicollis*
Stripe-breasted Saltator   **Plate 26(5)**

Habitat and status. A common resident on all the Bocas Islands from Gasparee to Chacachacare, also known on the NW peninsula of Trinidad, frequenting deciduous woodland and dry coastal scrub; on the islands more common than its congener. (Specimens: AMNH, CM, LM.)

Range and subspecies. Costa Rica S to Ecuador, Peru, Colombia, Venezuela and Trinidad, also the Lesser Antilles from Guadeloupe to St. Lucia; *S. a. perstriatus* (Parkes) ranges from NE Colombia through Venezuela to Trinidad.

Description. 7.5 in. Upperparts olive green, rump grayer, short whitish superciliary stripe; underparts whitish conspicuously streaked with olive green; bill black, with orange-yellow tip and gape. A much slimmer bird than the Grayish Saltator.

Measurements. Wing: 10 males 91–98mm (93.5); 16 unsexed 86–95mm (89.5). Weight: 25 unsexed 30–44gm (36.9).

Voice. Song is a regular phrase of 3–5 musical notes, almost of mockingbird quality but varying slightly according to individuals, e.g., *tchew-tchew-tcheeoo* or *tchyaw-tchair-tchaw-tchaw;* sometimes the long note is lengthened at the end and terminated abruptly with a short metallic note. The song is delivered from an exposed perch. It also utters a weak, single note.

Food. Small berries and seeds.

Nesting. Breeding recorded (2 nests) in May on Chacachacare; moult from July to September. The nest is a small but deep cup of twigs and leaves lined with fine twigs and set in a fork about 6 ft above ground. The clutch is 2 or 3 eggs, resembling those of the Grayish Saltator but smaller, av. 24 × 18.2mm (2). In Costa Rica (Skutch 1954) only the female incubates, but the male may feed her on the nest or guard the nest in her absence. Both parents feed the young, which are fledged after 13 days.

Red-capped Cardinal: *Paroaria gularis*
Black-eared Cardinal; Black-faced Cardinal; *Coccopsis gularis*
Plate 26(4)

Habitat and status. A rather rare resident in Trinidad, found only in mangrove swamps and neighbouring marshes. (Specimen: BM.)

Range and subspecies. Colombia and Venezuela S to Bolivia and C Brazil; *P. g. nigrogenis* (Lafresnaye) ranges from E Colombia through N Venezuela to Trinidad; it is distinguished from the nominate subspecies by a broad black cheek-patch and by the red (not black) lower throat.

Description. 7 in. Crown and deep V on throat scarlet, broad black patch from lores to ear curving downwards; sides of neck and rest of underparts white, upperparts glossy black; bill black, lower mandible whitish at base. *Immature:* brown on head and upperparts, a little red on head.

Voice. A sharp *tchep.*

Nesting. One breeding record (B/S) in September from Caroni swamp. The nest was a shallow cup of fine stems and bits of bark, lined with similar materials and decorated outwardly with spiderweb; it was situated in the fork of a mangrove 10 ft above water. The 2 eggs were pale cream, profusely marked with olive brown, forming a cap at the thick end, av. 20.9 × 14.5mm. There was also an egg of the cowbird *Molothrus*.

Behaviour. Often seen in pairs. It seems a restless species, darting about in the mangroves or on the earth banks, even bathing in the swamp-edge. I have twice seen it quarrelling with small flycatchers.

[Rose-breasted Grosbeak: *Pheucticus ludovicianus*]

Habitat and status. Two records only from Trinidad, of birds seen on 20 April 1982 at the Nature Centre (S. Higginbotham) and on 28 November 1986 (G. Upton); also at Crown Point, Tobago, on 5 December 1981 (J. Wunderle). (No specimen.)

Range. Breeds in North America, wintering S to Peru, Venezuela and the Guianas. Probably overlooked previously.

Description. 7.5 in. *Male (breeding)*: black above with white wing-patches, rump and lower underparts; throat black, breast red. Non-breeding males more or less streaked brown or buff. *Female and immature:* above brown with dark streaks, pale crown-stripe, superciliary and wing-bars; below pale streaked brown. Bill stout, whitish.

[Blue-black Grosbeak: *Cyanocompsa cyanoides*]
Guiana Blue Grosbeak

Habitat and status. Recorded only by Beebe (1952), who includes it without comment among birds of the Arima Valley in Trinidad. Without question a mistake.

Range. S Mexico south to Bolivia and Brazil.

Description. 6 in. *Male:* dark blue with brighter blue on head and wing-coverts; bill very thick. *Female:* smoke brown, darker on wings and tail.

Voice. A very musical, warbling series.

Dickcissel: *Spiza americana*
"Venezuelan"; "Rice-bird"

Habitat and status. A common winter visitor to Trinidad, concentrated mainly in rice-growing areas, especially Oropouche Lagoon and Nariva, but wandering also in the neighbouring foothills amongst cultivated lands and rough scrub (ffrench 1967b); normally present in many thousands December–mid-April (earliest date 3 December, latest 2 May), but in some years not present in numbers before mid-January, in others (e.g., 1972–81) apparently completely absent. (Specimens: LSUM, TRVL.)

Range. Breeds in C North America S to Texas; winters mostly from Mexico S through Central America to Colombia, Venezuela and Trinidad; casual in Ecuador, Guyana and Cayenne.

Banding status. A total of 2888 birds were banded in SW Trinidad between January 1959 and April 1966; one was retrapped in the same place 3 days later, another almost 1 yr after being banded at a roost 2 miles away; otherwise no recoveries or retraps. Males outnumbered females by 2 to 1.

Description. 6 in. *Adult male:* crown and upperparts olive brown, upper back streaked black; wings warmer brown with conspicuous chestnut patch on lesser coverts; sides of head and neck gray with yellow superciliary and malar stripes; chin white, large black throat patch, sides of breast and mid-abdomen bright yellow, lower underparts and flanks whitish. *Adult female:* rather similar to male, but upperparts paler, the black streaks more conspicuous by contrast; chestnut wing patch less conspicuous; superciliary duller, *black* malar stripe bordering white or yellowish throat. A few females have small black throat patches. *Immature:* generally duller than adult; lesser-wing-coverts dull brown or olive. Young males often show spotty black throat patches.

Measurements. Wing: 141 males 77–89mm (82.8, S.D. 2.03); 74 females 71–80mm (74.7, S.D. 1.66). Weight (December–late March): 326 males 26–35.5gm (30.5); 153 females 22–29gm (25.7). From the last days of March up to mid-April considerable increase takes place, so that from 13 to 17 April: 31 males 32–51gm (43.3); 19 females 32–42gm (36.1).

Voice. The song, occasionally heard in Trinidad, is a grating, unmusical *dick, dick, dickcissel;* other calls include the flight call, a grating *bjjt,* an incisive *chick* or *jeep,* a chattering *je-je-je,* and a sibilant *tsuilp* or *tsirrup.* The calls of many birds at a roost together take on a unified texture, resembling a highly amplified hissing. These roosting calls are given from the time the main body of birds arrives at a roost until 20 min or so after sunset. At dawn calls start about 20 min before sunrise and continue until the flocks leave. These calls are less pronounced at the beginning and end of the season.

Food. Mostly rice, taken from the ground or stacks of rice straw left after the November harvest; in some areas the species ruins rice crops, but in Trinidad the timing of harvests in November and June precludes this. Also takes grass seeds, and probably some insects (which are an important part of the diet in USA).

Behaviour. This highly gregarious species feeds in small flocks of about 25 birds. When not feeding, groups perch together singing and calling in small trees and bushes. There is often aggressive interaction among males, but no pair bonds are formed in Trinidad, nor is there any sexual grouping. Large roosts are used in sugarcane, or occasionally bamboo, mostly the same localities year after year (ffrench 1967b). Numbers in these roosts probably approach 100,000. The feeding flocks assemble about 5 P.M. and travel to the roost in large, densely packed groups of hundreds or thousands. The roost may be up to 15 miles distant from the feeding grounds; on their way to it the flocks often combine into a huge column over a mile long. Arrival at the roost is between 5 and 6 P.M., later in April, but departure, soon after sunrise, is often over within 5 min. Sometimes a population changes roosts during the season. At the roost birds perch on cane leaves, bent horizontal, about 6 ft above ground, often in close-packed groups. Predators at the roost include the Merlin and Barn Owl, once an Aplomado Falcon; occasionally they are hunted by humans. Though normally birds do not leave the roost after dark, at migration time in mid-April after a significant period of restlessness soon after 6 P.M. birds settle into silence, then bands of up to 100 set off in the dark and with hardly a sound towards the west.

Notes. Recently considered to be closer to the Icteridae.

[Indigo Bunting: *Passerina cyanea*]

Habitat and status. A single record only, of a male seen at close quarters near Las Lapas on 17 March 1977 (J. Satterly et al.). (No specimen.)

Range. Breeds in North America, wintering S to Colombia, NW Venezuela and offshore islands, Greater Antilles E to Virgin Islands.

Description. 5 in. *Male:* deep blue, darker head. *Female:* brown, paler below with indistinct darker streaks. Some females and winter males have traces of blue on wing-coverts and tail. Bill short, thick.

Blue-black Grassquit: *Volatinia jacarina*
Glossy Grassquit; "Johnny Jump-up"; "Ci-ci-Zeb"; "Black Poochi"; "Zwee"   **Plate 27(5)**

Habitat and status. A very common resident in both islands, including offshore islets, frequenting savannahs, semi-open areas with bushes and scrub, edges of mangrove, cultivated lands and gardens and sugarcane fields, in which some birds roost; even recorded at 2000 ft where forest has been cleared. (Specimens: AMNH, ANSP, CM, YPM, LM, TRVL.)

Range and subspecies. Mexico S throughout Central and South America to N Chile, N Argentina and Paraguay; *V. j. splendens* (Vieillot) ranges from Mexico S to Peru, N Brazil, Trinidad, Tobago and Grenada.

Description. 4 in. *Adult male:* all glossy blue-black, but axillaries white (sometimes visible in flight); wings and tail black. *Female and immature:* upperparts dull brown, underparts yellowish brown, breast and flanks streaked with blackish. Some males breed in mottled intermediate plumage.

Measurements. Wing: 37 males 45–51mm (48.3, S.D. 1.3); 9 females 45–48mm (46.4). Weight: 28 males 8–11.5gm (9.6, S.D. 0.70); 5 females 9–10.5gm.

Voice. The male calls, usually in display, a wheezing, drawn-out *jweee.*

Food. Seeds of grasses; also insects, including beetles and froghoppers, and spiders.

Nesting. Breeding recorded in Trinidad mainly from May to September (30 nests), also November–January (6 nests), but B/S report "occupied" nests in all months, and song is recorded in all months (though less in March); in Tobago B/S report the breeding peak in August and September, also November and December (Lill). Moult recorded from August to February. The nest is a small cup of grass, sometimes lined with plant-down or fine fibres (or rootlets in Tobago), placed from ground level to 15 ft up in a bush, most lower down. The clutch is 1–3, usually 2, pale green eggs marked with reddish brown, especially at the thick end, several av. 16.8 × 12.5mm. Both sexes incubate and feed the young. In Ecuador (Marchant 1960) the incubation period is 9–10 days and the fledging period 9 days.

Behaviour. Though frequently seen singly or in pairs, this species also forms considerable flocks, especially outside the breeding season, which feed together and move about in loose formation. Roosting is also usually communal, sometimes involving several hundred birds. In display, the male perches on an exposed branch or post and jumps up about a foot with spread tail held high and white axillaries visible, before alighting on the same perch; as he jumps he utters his wheezing note. Such jumps may be made every few seconds over very long periods, even when no female is apparently present; though most perches are a few feet above ground, I have seen jumping on a grass lawn and on the summit of a 50-ft tree; Lill has recorded it on the roof of a house.

Black-faced Grassquit: *Tiaris bicolor*
Carib Grassquit   **Plate 27(7)**

Habitat and status. A common resident in Tobago, found in long grass and low scrub, in open areas, second growth or forest edges, especially roadsides; also found commonly on Chacachacare Island and more rarely on Huevos Island. (Specimens: Tobago, AMNH, LM.)

Range and subspecies. N coasts of Colombia and Venezuela, including offshore islands; also the West Indies (except Cuba); *T. b. omissa* (Jardine) ranges from Puerto Rico through the Lesser Antilles to Tobago, islands off Trinidad and the mainland range of South America.

Description. 4.5 in. *Adult male:* head and breast dull black, upperparts dull olive green, lower underparts pale grayish olive. *Female and immature:* head and upperparts grayish olive green, underparts browner and paler.

Measurements. Wing: 15 males 49–54mm (50.9); 9 females 49–51mm (49.8). Weight: 16 males 8.5–11gm (9.4); 10 females 9–10.5gm (9.7).

Voice. Song is a weak, buzzing series, *dik-zeezeezee*.

Food. Mostly seeds of grasses, sedges and weeds (Lill); also feeds occasionally on cactus fruits and insects.

Nesting. Breeding recorded (15 nests) in Tobago from June to November, and January. The nest is a loosely built dome of grass lined with finer grass, with a narrow side entrance near the top; it is situated in a small bush or bankside usually not far above ground, occasionally up to 45 ft (Lill). The clutch is 2 or 3 eggs, whitish marked at the thick end with pale reddish brown, av. 17.0 × 12.5mm (6). Both sexes build the nest and feed the young after fledging.

Behaviour. Often found in pairs and small groups, but roosting singly (Lill); in Curaçao (Voous 1957) recorded in larger, loose flocks and roosting communally in considerable numbers. In a display flight the male flies a short distance rather slowly with rapidly vibrating wings, uttering his buzzing call.

Sooty Grassquit: *Tiaris fuliginosa*
Plate 27(6)

Habitat and status. A fairly common resident in Trinidad, widely distributed in second growth and forest edges up to 2000 ft, also in savannahs and semi-open cultivation; there is a marked local movement towards higher altitudes during the wet season; most commonly seen on roadsides in the Northern Range. (Specimens: AMNH, LM, TRVL.)

Range and subspecies. N Venezuela and Trinidad, E and S Brazil, also recorded from Roraima and C Colombia; *T. f. fumosa* (Lawrence) occurs in Venezuela and Trinidad.

Description. 4 in. *Adult male:* head and upperparts blackish brown, tinged olive; underparts paler and grayer; bill black, gape red (showing at corner). *Female and immature:* upperparts olive brown, paler below.

Measurements. Wing: 23 males 58–63mm (60.7); 7 females 57–62mm (59.4). Weight: 12 males 11–16gm (13.4); 4 females 13–14gm.

Voice. Song is a rather faint, very high-pitched, buzzing series, tending to fade away, e.g., *tizzy-izzy-izzy-iii iii;* also utters a simple, repeated *chee*.

Food. Seeds of grasses; also some small fruits (Lill).

Nesting. Breeding recorded (10 nests) from July to December, also once in May; a moult record in June. The nest is a flimsy ball of grass and fine roots lined with fine grass, with a large side entrance; the site varies from a stump or a bankside, even the ground, to a tree up to 30 ft above ground. The male helps to build the nest and to feed the young after fledging. The clutch is 2–3, occasionally 4, white eggs marked with rich brown especially at the thick end, av. 18.1 × 13.9mm (10).

Behaviour. Occasionally found in flocks of up to 40, and sometimes roosting is communal.

Slate-colored Seedeater: *Sporophila schistacea*
Long-winged Seedeater; "Brazilian"; "Brazo"   **Plate 28(2)**

Habitat and status. Uncommon and local in Trinidad, recorded only by Mees during August–November 1953 in light second growth and cultivation bordering forest in the Northern Range; more of a woodland species, especially in bamboo, than Gray Seedeater; local bird-catchers know both species and regard them as varieties of one species. (Specimens: LM.)

Range and subspecies. Costa Rica S to Ecuador, N Bolivia and NE Brazil; also S Mexico; *S. s. longipennis* (Chubb) ranges from S Venezuela and Trinidad through the Guianas to Brazil.

Description. 4.5 in. *Adult male:* head, upper breast and upperparts dark gray, with white streaks bordering throat and white patch on wing; lower underparts white. Top of head flatter in profile than Gray Seedeater; bill orange-yellow (or dull yellow in younger birds); legs greenish gray. *Female and immature:* upperparts olive green, underparts brown tinged yellowish olive; bill gray.

Measurements. Wing: 3 males 63, 63, 64mm. Weight: 3 males 11, 12, 12.5gm*.

Voice. Song is a monotonous, high-pitched, metallic trill, usually preceded by a louder single note, far less variable than the song of the Gray Seedeater; this is the best field mark.

Food. Seeds.

Nesting. Not recorded in Trinidad, but according to bird-catchers the species is resident.

Gray Seedeater: *Sporophila intermedia*
Grey Seed-finch; "Picoplat"; "Ring-neck"   **Plate 28(1)**

Habitat and status. A formerly common (but now diminishing) resident in Trinidad, widely distributed in second growth and semi-open areas mostly in low-lying country, but also found at forest edges in foothills. (Specimens: AMNH, ANSP, CM, YPM, LM, TRVL.)

Range and subspecies. Colombia, N Venezuela, Trinidad and Guyana; *S. i. intermedia* (Cabanis) ranges eastward from N and E Colombia.

Description. 4.5 in. *Adult male:* resembles male Slate-colored Seedeater, but crown more rounded in profile, bill pink or pinkish yellow, and legs blackish; also wing shorter and tail longer. Song is diagnostic. *Female and immature:* upperparts dark brown, underparts yellowish brown; bill blackish. In a variety known locally as Ring-neck the male has a whitish band across the throat.

Measurements. Wing: 12 males 54–58mm (55.9); 11 females 52–57mm (54.5). Weight: 3 males 11, 13, 16gm; 4 females 11–13gm (11.8).

Voice. Song is a varied and attractive series of trills, whistles and chirps, including some imitations of other species; also utters individual chirps.

Food. Seeds of grasses, sedges and weeds (Lill).

Nesting. Breeding recorded June–September (11 nests), also 1 February record (Lill); moult in June, September and November–January. The nest is a flimsy cup of rootlets and tendrils lined with fine fibres and situated in the fork of a small tree or bush 6–20 ft above ground. At one nest only the female built, but at two others both sexes fed the young after fledging. The clutch is 2, occasionally 3, creamy eggs irregularly marked with dark brown, av. 18.9 × 13.5mm (10).

Behaviour. Seen in small flocks outside the breeding season.

Notes. This is probably the most popular of the small finches which are commonly trapped as cage-birds in Trinidad. In spite of official limitations, many people openly flout the law by trapping out of season, using bird-lime for trapping and keeping birds in cages that are too small. It seems that many of those in authority regard such offences as too trivial to merit more than occasional attention. Along with the constant encroachment on habitat, the unchecked trapping of male finches—both *Sporophila* and *Oryzoborus*—will undoubtedly result in the complete extinction in Trinidad within a decade or so of all these species, except perhaps *S. minuta*. The authorities should act before it is too late, by totally protecting all finches and providing adequate enforcement.

Variable Seedeater: *Sporophila americana*
Larger Black-and-white Seed-Finch; Black-and-white Seedeater; Wing-barred Seedeater; "Tobago Picoplat"   **Plate 28(4)**

Habitat and status. A rather uncommon and local resident in Tobago, occurring in semi-open areas, cultivated lands and forest clearings in hilly areas; numbers undoubtedly affected by trapping; there is a single record, of doubtful validity, of a caged-bird said to have been taken on Chacachacare Island in 1934. (Specimens: AMNH, LM.)

Range and subspecies. S Mexico south to Ecuador, Peru and C Brazil; *S. a. americana* (Gmelin) ranges from Venezuela and Tobago through the Guianas

388   FINCHES, SEEDEATERS, GROSBEAKS

to N Brazil. Some authors treat the *S. aurita* (Bonaparte) group of Middle America and NW South America as a distinct species and call *S. americana* of E South America the Wing-barred Seedeater.

Description. 4.5 in. *Adult male:* head, sides of face, upper back, wings and tail black; lower back gray, wing-coverts tipped white, appearing as 2 short wing-bars; throat and sides of neck white, narrow blackish band across lower throat, rest of underparts pale gray. *Female and immature:* upperparts buffish brown, paler below. Bill dark, fairly thick.

Measurements. Wing: 8 males 56–61mm (58.9); 5 females 55–58mm (56.2). Weight: 5 males 12.5–14gm (13.3); 3 females 12*, 13, 14.5gm.

Voice. Song is a pleasant, musical series of considerable length but little intensity, consisting of rapid twitters, trills and isolated whistled notes, tapering off to a chatter; also utters a single musical note.

Food. Seeds of grasses and sedges.

Nesting. Breeding recorded in January (Lill). Two nests resembled those of *S. intermedia,* made mostly of stems and tendrils with a definite "wreath" at the rim and lined with fine black fibres. One was 4 ft up in the crotch of a cocoa sapling, the other 45 ft up in the fork of an immortelle tree. Only the female built and incubated. In Costa Rica (Skutch 1954) and Surinam (Haverschmidt 1968a) the eggs are laid on consecutive days and incubated by the female alone for 12 days; the male may feed his mate on the nest, and he helps to feed the young by regurgitation; the fledging period is 11–13 days. Two broods may be reared in one season.

Behaviour. Not gregarious.

Lesson's Seedeater: *Sporophila bouvronides*
Black-and-white Moustache-Finch; Lined Seedeater;
White-cheeked Seedeater; "Chat"   **Plate 28(5)**

Habitat and status. Formerly a locally common resident in both islands, also Monos, occurring in light woodland and second growth, edges of swamps and marshes and semi-open cultivated areas. The population has been much reduced by trapping. A noticeable movement of this species (and other finches) towards higher altitudes takes place at the beginning of the wet season; it is probably migratory. (Specimens: ANSP, CM, YPM, LM, TRVL.)

Range. Colombia and Venezuela S to the Guianas, Brazil and E Peru. Formerly considered conspecific with the Lined Seedeater (*S. lineola*).

Description. 4.5 in. *Adult male:* head and upperparts black, rump and small wing-patch white; cheeks white, throat and line alongside neck black, rest of underparts white. *Female and immature:* upperparts olive brown, yellowish buff below, lower underparts paler. Bill blackish above, yellowish lower mandible. Some males breed in this plumage.

Measurements. Wing: 15 males 55–59mm (57.3); 5 females 53–56mm (53.8). Weight: 11 males 7.5–12gm (9.8); 2 females 8.5, 8.5gm; 13 female-plumaged 9–11gm (9.9).

Voice. Song is a long rolling trill, followed by a formless chattering; also utters a warbler-like *chip.*

Food. Seeds, mostly of grasses.

Nesting. Breeding recorded in Trinidad from June to August (13 nests), but B/S report nests from April to September, and in Tobago up to October. Regular song recorded May–September. The nest is a flimsy cup of roots and grass lined with fine black fibres; it is situated in the crotch of a sapling or in the outer branches of a larger tree, 2–30 ft above ground. The clutch is 2 or 3 whitish eggs, profusely marked with brown and blackish brown, av. 18.2 × 12.8mm (10). Both parents feed the young.

Yellow-bellied Seedeater: *Sporophila nigricollis*
"Silverbeak"; "Ringneck"   **Plate 27(3)**

Habitat and status. Formerly a common resident in both islands, including offshore islets; rather more local in Trinidad, where it has been reduced by excessive trapping; frequents semi-open cultivated areas and gardens, forest edges and light second growth up to 2000 ft; there is a considerable movement to higher altitudes during the wet season. (Specimens: AMNH, ANSP, CM, YPM, LM.)

Range and subspecies. Costa Rica S through most of South America to NE Bolivia, N Argentina and C Brazil, also the southern Lesser Antilles; *S. n. nigricollis* (Vieillot) occurs through most of the range.

Description. 4.5 in. *Adult male:* head, neck and upper breast blackish, upperparts dull olive, rest of underparts pale yellow; bill pale blue-gray, appearing whitish in the field. *Female and immature:* upperparts olive brown, yellowish buff below, abdomen paler; bill dark.

Measurements. Wing: 12 males 53–56mm (54.8); 5 females 51–54mm (52.8). Weight: 8 males 8.5–9.5gm; 1 female 8.5gm.

Voice. Song is a fairly short, monotonous but musical series, with considerable dialect variation (Lill); it is delivered from an exposed perch, often a telephone wire; also utters a single *cheep* and a slight chittering when excited.

Food. Seeds, principally of grasses; also caterpillars and spiders, and is known to visit feeding tables for bread.

Nesting. Breeding recorded in Trinidad (9 nests) from June to November (the usual song period), and 2 nests (August) in Tobago; B/S report May nests in Trinidad, and June–September in Tobago, where Lill also has an October record. The nest is a deep but flimsy cup of grass or roots situated in a small tree or shrub. One pair nested twice in a garden fern-basket (ffrench 1965c), using mostly coconut fibre from husks. The nest takes 5–12 days to build, the female doing most of the building, attended but not always helped by the male. The clutch is 2, occasionally 3, pale blue-green or buff eggs marked with chocolate brown and black, mainly at the thick end; eggs av. 17.0 × 12.0mm (13); 6 weighing 1.25gm each. Only the female incubates, for up to 80% of daylight hours, over a period of 12 days, the eggs being laid on consecutive days (once 2 days apart). Both parents feed the young, mostly by regurgitation of seeds, but also with insects. The fledging period is 10 days. The nest for a second brood was begun 8 days after the first brood fledged.

Behaviour. Except during the breeding season, when birds form pairs and hold territories, the species is inclined to move around in loose flocks of up to 50 individuals and often roosts communally (Lill). In Trinidad rarely are so many present in one area because of trapping.

Ruddy-breasted Seedeater: *Sporophila minuta*
Small Red-bellied Finch; Ruddy Seedeater; "Robin"   **Plate 27(4)**

Habitat and status. Formerly a common resident of both islands, frequenting open savannahs and marshes, waste ground with scattered bushes and thickets, cultivated areas and gardens, including suburban districts; now quite scarce, since numbers have been decimated by trappers; locally distributed in Tobago, mostly in the west. (Specimens: AMNH, ANSP, CM, YPM, LM, TRVL.)

Range and subspecies. Mexico S to Bolivia, N Argentina and Paraguay; *S. m. minuta* (Linnaeus) ranges from Ecuador, Colombia and Venezuela through Trinidad and Tobago to the Guianas and N Brazil.

Description. 4 in. *Adult male:* head and upper back bluish gray, wings and tail dark brown edged gray, with small white patch on wing; lower back and underparts chestnut. *Female and immature:* head and upperparts dull brown tinged olive; underparts buffish brown, abdomen paler. Some males breed in this plumage.

Measurements. Wing: 28 males 47–51mm (48.8, S.D. 1.1); 13 females 46–50gm (48.2). Weight: 10 males 7–9gm (7.9); 5 females 7–8gm.

Voice. Song is a short series of high-pitched, rather deliberate, musical whistles; also utters individual whistles.

Food. Seeds of grasses, sedges and weeds, occasionally small fruits (Lill); rarely takes small insects, sometimes (Junge & Mees 1958) in the air.

Nesting. Breeding recorded in Trinidad from May to July (11 nests), once in September, and in November–December (3 nests); regular song from May to December; moult records scattered in February, June, August and December. B/S report Tobago nests from July to September. The nest is a small, deep cup of grass, notable for stiff pieces of grass which project out from the rim. The site varies considerably from low down in grass tussocks, shrubs and bushes to

8 ft above ground in a small tree; garden plants and ornamental fern-baskets are also used. The clutch is 2 eggs, varying from cream to greenish blue, marked with dark brown or chestnut, mostly at the thick end, av. 15.6 × 12.6mm (10). The female alone incubates, with the male attending nearby, and usually both parents feed the young, which are fledged after 11 days.

Behaviour. Commonly seen in considerable flocks when not breeding, and roosting communally.

Notes. It is significant that this small *Sporophila* species was for long the most common in Trinidad, being rarely caged, but as the larger species became scarce, it too began to be persecuted. Only a change in public attitude will save these finches from local extinction.

Large-billed Seed-Finch: *Oryzoborus crassirostris*
Larger Thick-billed Finch; "Twa-twa"   **Plate 27(1)**

Habitat and status. An extremely rare species in Trinidad, nearly extirpated; formerly resident, inhabiting semi-open areas and thickets on the edge of marshes and savannahs, especially in the east of the island; often imported as a cage-bird. (Specimen: AMNH.)

Range and subspecies. Nicaragua locally S to Bolivia and SE Brazil; *O. c. crassirostris* (Gmelin) ranges from E Colombia and Venezuela to Trinidad, the Guianas, NE Peru and N Brazil.

Description. 6 in. *Adult male:* black, with large white wing-patch; bill massive, whitish to bluish horn. *Female and immature:* upperparts brown, rufous brown below; bill dark.

Measurements. Wing: 1 male 75mm.

Voice. Song is an exceptionally rich and mellow musical whistling, with considerable variation and beauty.

Food. Seeds and insects.

Nesting. Breeding recorded in May (B/S), and a possible September record (Williams 1922). The nest is a well-made but thin cup of grass and stalks lined with plant-down; one had green moss about the rim; it is situated fairly low in a bush. The clutch is 2 or 3 eggs, cream marked with dark brown, av. 22.7 × 15.3mm (8). In captivity (Deane 1967) the incubation period was 12 days for each of 3 clutches; the female alone incubated but both parents fed the young; 3 broods were reared within 5 months.

Lesser Seed-Finch: *Oryzoborus angolensis*
Chestnut-bellied Seed-Finch; Thick-billed Seed-Finch; "Chickichong"; "Bullfinch"   **Plate 27(2)**

Habitat and status. A rare resident in Trinidad, formerly widespread but numbers much depleted by trapping; inhabits forest clearings and edges, deciduous forest and second growth; a few sight records in Tobago since 1966 may have been escaped cage-birds. (Specimens: AMNH, ANSP, CM, YPM, LM, TRVL.)

Range and subspecies. Mexico S to Bolivia, N Argentina and Paraguay; *O. a. torridus* (Scopoli) ranges from Ecuador, Peru and E Colombia to Venezuela, Trinidad, the Guianas and N Brazil. Some authors consider *O. funereus* of Middle America and NW South America to be a distinct species; on that basis *O. angolensis* is called the Chestnut-bellied Seed-Finch.

Description. 5 in. *Adult male:* head and upperparts black, with a little white, often hidden, at the base of primaries; breast black, abdomen and under-tail-coverts dark chestnut; bill thick, black. *Female and immature:* upperparts dull brown, underparts cinnamon brown.

Measurements. Wing: 8 males 58–61mm (59.6); 5 females 55–58mm (56.6). Weight: 4 males 12.5–14.5gm (13.4); 2 unsexed 12.5, 12.5gm.

Voice. Song is a fairly long, musical series of clear whistled notes, tending to drop in pitch and often repeated immediately, sometimes interspersed with a few chattering notes; call-note is a single, liquid whistle.

Food. Seeds and insects.

Nesting. Breeding recorded (2 nests) in June and September, but B/S report "eggs from February to August". The nest is a flimsy but deep cup of fine reddish grass with seed-heads attached, situated amidst thick grass or vines, usually fairly near the ground. The clutch is 2, sometimes 3, creamy eggs, profusely marked with dark brown, av. 19.0 × 13.8mm (7). In captivity the female incubated for 12 days, and the male helped to feed the young.

Behaviour. Not gregarious. Though the male is often to be seen perched on an exposed branch when singing, the female is rarely noticeable as she skulks in thickets.

Orange-fronted Yellow-Finch: *Sicalis columbiana*
Venezuelan Yellow Finch; Orange-fronted Grass-Finch   **Plate 28(3)**

Habitat and status. Recorded only by Smooker in 1926 near San Juan in Trinidad in grassland; several birds were seen. (Specimens: BM.)

Range and subspecies. E Colombia, Venezuela, E Peru and Brazil; *S. c. columbiana* (Cabanis) ranges from E Colombia through Venezuela to Trinidad.

Description. 5 in. *Male:* Upperparts greenish yellow, the feathers with olive green centres; fore-crown bright orange, wings and tail brownish edged yellow; underparts dull yellow. *Female:* upperparts brownish, wings and tail edged yellow, underparts grayish white. Distinctly smaller than Saffron Finch.

Measurements. Wing: 1 male 62mm.

Nesting. One breeding record in September 1926 (B/S). The nest was a cup of roots and grass stems situated in a hollow at the end of a broken branch 12 ft above ground. There were 3 pale green eggs, marked with olive brown, especially at the thick end, av. 16.8 × 13.1mm. Cherrie (1916) in Venezuela records 2 similar nests, one in a wall crevice, the other near the mouth of an abandoned kingfisher nest-hole; there were 3 clutches of 4 eggs.

Saffron Finch: *Sicalis flaveola*
"Trinidad Canary"   **Plate 28(6)**

Habitat and status. A locally common resident in Trinidad, frequenting savannahs and open country, especially where the grass is kept short, as in housing estates. In Tobago a few birds were introduced at Charlotteville in 1958. (Specimens: LM, BM.)

Range and subspecies. Throughout South America from Colombia to Argentina and Uruguay; also introduced to Panama and Jamaica; *S. f. flaveola* (Linnaeus) occurs from N Colombia E through Venezuela and Trinidad to the Guianas.

Description. 5.5 in. *Adult male:* similar to *S. columbiana,* but larger and underparts bright yellow. *Female:* as male, but less bright; orange *crown less extensive,* but this is indistinguishable in the field. *Immature:* head gray, upperparts grayish brown, tinged yellow and streaked blackish; underparts pale gray with some dark shaft streaks; under-tail-coverts yellow; in older birds there is a pale yellow band around nape and across upper breast.

Measurements. Wing: 6 males 68–74mm (71.3); 2 females 69, 70mm; 9 unsexed 68–72.5mm (70.5). Weight: 1 male 23gm; 9 unsexed 20–24gm (21.2).

Voice. Song is a loud, musical phrase of 3–4 incisive, pebbly notes, often repeated; the notes are mostly of similar pitch, except for 1 high note near the end of each phrase; another song is much softer, a thin, repetitive warble; call-notes a pebbly *chink* and a querulous *chooee.*

Food. Seeds of grasses, sedges, weeds and trees (Lill).

Nesting. Breeding recorded (17 nests) in most months from April to January, with 1 moult record in October. The nest in Trinidad is almost always in the abandoned nest of the Oriole (*Icterus nigrogularis*), to which some material is added, but some nests have been cups of dead leaves and other materials placed in natural hollows in trees. The species takes readily to artificial sites such as scaffolding pipes, roof eaves or nest-boxes, especially where there is shelter. The clutch is 2–4 creamy eggs, marked with purplish brown, av. 19.8 × 15.2mm (5). Both parents feed the young, but the female alone incubates.

Behaviour. After the breeding season this species becomes very gregarious, feeding and roosting in flocks of up to 50, mostly consisting of birds in immature plumage. Often a flock is predominantly immature, with 2 or 3 adults in attendance.

Red Siskin: *Spinus cucullatus*
"Colorado"   **Plate 28(7)**

Habitat and status. A very rare species, possibly formerly resident, in Trinidad; the records are on Monos in May 1893 (Chapman, 3 specimens), on Gasparee Island in November 1921 and at Carenage in June 1926 (Smooker, sight) and at Diego Martin in August 1926 (Smooker, possible nest); the only recent record is of 2 birds seen in a treetop at 500 ft in Arima Valley in May 1960 (B. K. Snow). I have only seen the species in a cage (said to be of Venezuelan origin). (Specimens: AMNH.)

Range. NE Colombia, N Venezuela and Trinidad.

Description. 4.5 in. *Male:* red with black head, wings and tail; 2 red wing-bars. *Female:* brownish red with dark gray head, wings and tail; wing-bars orange; breast reddish orange, lower underparts and flanks whitish.

Measurements. Wing: 2 males 62, 67mm; 1 female 57mm.

Voice. A raspy *jut-jut.*

Food. The fruit of cactus (Chapman 1894).

Nesting. B/S report a possible nest in August. It was a deep cup of dried grass and moss lined with plant-down and situated in the fork of a tree 12 ft above ground. There were 3 pale greenish white eggs, unmarked, av. 16.6 × 13.0mm.

Appendix I

Species Recorded on Tobago (total of 210)

*Least Grebe
Pied-billed Grebe
Audubon's Shearwater
*Wilson's Storm-Petrel
Leach's Storm-Petrel
Red-billed Tropicbird
*White-tailed Tropicbird
Brown Pelican
Red-footed Booby
Brown Booby
Anhinga
Magnificent Frigatebird
Great Blue Heron
*White-necked Heron
Great Egret
*Little Egret
Snowy Egret
Little Blue Heron
Tricolored Heron
Green-backed Heron
Cattle Egret
Black-crowned Night-Heron
Yellow-crowned Night-Heron
*Jabiru Stork
*Scarlet Ibis
*Glossy Ibis
*Roseate Spoonbill
*Fulvous Whistling-Duck
Black-bellied Whistling-Duck
*Green-winged Teal

American Wigeon
White-cheeked Pintail
Blue-winged Teal
*Lesser Scaup
*Masked Duck
*Swallow-tailed Kite
Broad-winged Hawk
*Short-tailed Hawk
*Swainson's Hawk
*Gray Hawk
*Common Black Hawk
*Great Black Hawk
*Ornate Hawk-Eagle
Osprey
*Yellow-headed Caracara
Peregrine Falcon
Merlin
Rufous-vented Chachalaca
*Spotted Rail
Sora
Common Gallinule
Purple Gallinule
*Caribbean Coot
*American Coot
*Wattled Jacana
*American Oystercatcher
*Southern Lapwing
Black-bellied Plover
Lesser Golden Plover
Semipalmated Plover

*Species is very rare, possibly extirpated or of dubious status. See main text for clarification.

*Snowy Plover
Collared Plover
*Killdeer
Ruddy Turnstone
Solitary Sandpiper
Lesser Yellowlegs
Greater Yellowlegs
*Greenshank
*Spotted Redshank
Spotted Sandpiper
Willet
Least Sandpiper
White-rumped Sandpiper
Pectoral Sandpiper
Semipalmated Sandpiper
Western Sandpiper
Sanderling
Stilt Sandpiper
*Ruff
Buff-breasted Sandpiper
*Upland Sandpiper
Whimbrel
*Eskimo Curlew
*Marbled Godwit
Short-billed Dowitcher
Common Snipe
*Black-necked Stilt
*American Avocet
*Parasitic Jaeger
*Lesser Black-backed Gull
*Ring-billed Gull
Laughing Gull
*Black-headed Gull
Common Tern
Roseate Tern
Bridled Tern
Sooty Tern
Least Tern
Royal Tern
Sandwich Tern
Brown Noddy
*Fairy Tern
Pale-vented Pigeon
Eared Dove
Ruddy Ground-Dove
White-tipped Dove
Lined Quail-Dove

Green-rumped Parrotlet
Orange-winged Parrot
Yellow-billed Cuckoo
*Mangrove Cuckoo
Smooth-billed Ani
Barn Owl
Striped Owl
Common Potoo
Lesser Nighthawk
*Common Nighthawk
*Nacunda Nighthawk
White-tailed Nightjar
*White-collared Swift
*Black Swift
Gray-rumped Swift
Short-tailed Swift
Rufous-breasted Hermit
*White-tailed Sabrewing
White-necked Jacobin
Black-throated Mango
Ruby-Topaz Hummingbird
*Blue-chinned Sapphire
Copper-rumped Hummingbird
Collared Trogon
Belted Kingfisher
Green Kingfisher
Blue-crowned Motmot
Rufous-tailed Jacamar
Golden-olive Woodpecker
Red-rumped Woodpecker
Plain-brown Woodcreeper
Olivaceous Woodcreeper
Buff-throated Woodcreeper
Stripe-breasted Spinetail
*Gray-throated Leaftosser
Barred Antshrike
Plain Antvireo
White-fringed Antwren
White-winged Becard
Blue-backed Manakin
Fork-tailed Flycatcher
Tropical Kingbird
Gray Kingbird
Piratic Flycatcher
Streaked Flycatcher
Brown-crested Flycatcher
Venezuelan Flycatcher

Fuscous Flycatcher
White-throated Spadebill
Yellow-breasted Flycatcher
Yellow-bellied Elaenia
Ochre-bellied Flycatcher
Caribbean Martin
*Gray-breasted Martin
*Southern Rough-winged Swallow
*Bank Swallow
Barn Swallow
Rufous-breasted Wren
House Wren
Tropical Mockingbird
Yellow-legged Thrush
Bare-eyed Thrush
White-necked Thrush
*Yellow-throated Vireo
Chivi Vireo
Scrub Greenlet
Shiny Cowbird
Giant Cowbird
Crested Oropendola
Carib Grackle
*Northern Oriole
*Red-breasted Blackbird
*Bobolink
*Black-and-white Warbler
*Prothonotary Warbler

*Northern Parula
*Tropical Parula
Yellow Warbler
*Magnolia Warbler
*Cape May Warbler
*Yellow-rumped Warbler
*Bay-breasted Warbler
Blackpoll Warbler
*Ovenbird
Northern Waterthrush
*Common Yellowthroat
American Redstart
Bananaquit
*Purple Honeycreeper
Red-legged Honeycreeper
Violaceous Euphonia
Blue-gray Tanager
Palm Tanager
*Scarlet Tanager
White-lined Tanager
*Rose-breasted Grosbeak
Blue-black Grassquit
Black-faced Grassquit
Variable Seedeater
Lesson's Seedeater
Yellow-bellied Seedeater
Ruddy-breasted Seedeater

Appendix II

Tobago Species Not Recorded on Trinidad (total of 22)

Wilson's Storm-Petrel		
White-tailed Tropicbird		
Jabiru Stork		
Swainson's Hawk		
Rufous-vented Chachalaca	B	
American Coot		
Snowy Plover		
Spotted Redshank		
Fairy Tern		
Striped Owl	B	
White-tailed Sabrewing	B	
Red-crowned Woodpecker	B	(Patos Island)
Olivaceous Woodcreeper	B	
White-fringed Antwren	B	(Bocas islands)
Blue-backed Manakin	B	
Venezuelan Flycatcher	B	
Caribbean Martin	B	
Scrub Greenlet	B	
Northern Parula		
Yellow-rumped Warbler		
Black-faced Grassquit	B	(Bocas islands)
Variable Seedeater	B	

B signifies breeding.

Bibliography

Alvarez de Toro, M. 1971. On the biology of the American Finfoot in southern Mexico. *Living Bird* 10: 79–88.

American Ornithologists' Union. 1957. *Check-list of North American Birds.* 5th ed., Baltimore: Lord Baltimore Press. 691 pp.

Ashmole, N. P. 1963. The biology of the Wideawake or Sooty Tern on Ascension Island. *Ibis* 103b: 297–364.

Ashmole, N. P., and H. Tovar. 1968. Prolonged parental care in Royal Terns and other birds. *Auk* 85: 90–100.

Barlow, J. C. 1967. Autumnal breeding of the Paraguay Snipe in Uruguay. *Auk* 84: 421–22.

Baudouin-Bodin, J. 1960. Des hèrons cendrés bagues au lac de Grand-Lieu repris aux Antilles. *Oiseau Rev. Fr. Ornithol.* 30: 270.

Beard, J. S. 1944. The natural vegetation of the island of Tobago, British West Indies. *Ecol. Monogr.* 14:135–63.

———. 1946. *The natural vegetation of Trinidad.* Oxford Forestry Mem. 20. Oxford: Clarendon Press. 152 pp.

Beebe, W. 1952. Introduction to the ecology of the Arima Valley, Trinidad. *Zoologica* 37: 157–83.

Belcher, C., and G. D. Smooker. 1934–37. Birds of the colony of Trinidad and Tobago (in 6 parts). *Ibis* (13)4: 572–95, *et seq.*

Bent, A. C. 1929. *Life histories of North American shorebirds, II.* U.S. Natl. Mus. Bull. 146. 412 pp.

———. 1942. *Life histories of North American flycatchers, larks, swallows and their allies.* U.S. Natl. Mus. Bull. 179. 555 pp.

Berlioz, J. 1962. Notes critiques sur quelques espèces de Trochilidés. *Oiseau Rev. Fr. Ornithol.* 32: 135–44.

Birkenholz, D. E., and D. A. Jenni. 1964. Observations on the Spotted Rail and Pinnated Bittern in Costa Rica. *Auk* 81: 558–59.

Blake, E. R. 1950. Birds of the Acary Mountains, southern British Guiana. *Fieldiana Zool.* 32(7): 419–74.

Blokpoel, H., R. D. Morris and G. D. Tessier. 1984. Field investigations of the biology of Common Terns wintering in Trinidad. *J. Field Ornithol.* 55: 424–34.

Bond, J. 1956. *Checklist of birds of the West Indies.* Philadelphia: Acad. Nat. Sci.

———. 1958. *Third supplement to the checklist of birds of the West Indies.* Philadelphia: Acad. Nat. Sci.

———. 1960. *Birds of the West Indies.* London: Collins. 256 pp.

———. 1961. *Sixth supplement to the checklist of birds of the West Indies.* Philadelphia: Acad. Nat. Sci.

———. 1966. *Eleventh supplement to the checklist of birds of the West Indies.* Philadelphia: Acad. Nat. Sci.

———. 1970. *Native and winter resident birds of Tobago.* Philadelphia: Acad. Nat. Sci. 30 pp.

———. 1979. Derivations of Lesser Antillean birds. *Proc. Acad. Nat. Sci. Phila.* 131: 89–103.

———. 1985. *Birds of the West Indies.* 5th ed. London: Collins. 280 pp.

Bosque, C. 1986. Actualizacion de la distribucion del Guacharo (*Steatornis caripensis*) en Venezuela. *Bol. Soc. Venez. Espeleol.* 22: 1–10.

Bosque, C., and R. Ramirez. 1988. Post-breeding migration of Oilbirds. *Wilson Bull.* 100: 675–77.

Bostic, D. L., and R. C. Banks. 1966. A record of stingray predation by the Brown Pelican. *Condor* 68: 515–16.

Brewer, D. 1977. Golden-winged Warbler. *J. Trin. Tob. Field Nat. Club,* p. 11.

Brewster, W., and F. M. Chapman. 1895. Notes on birds observed in Trinidad. *Auk* 12: 201–11.

Brosset, A. 1964. Les oiseaux de Pacaritambo (Ouest de l'Ecuador). *Oiseau Rev. Fr. Ornithol.* 34: 1–24.

Brown, L. 1947. *Birds and I.* London: Michael Joseph.

Brown, L., and D. Amadon. 1968. *Eagles, hawks and falcons of the world.* 2 vols. Middlesex: Country Life Press. 945 pp.

Buchanan, O. M. 1971. The Mottled Owl *Ciccaba virgata* in Trinidad. *Ibis* 113: 105–6.

Buckley, F. G., and P. A. Buckley. 1968. Upside-down resting by young Green-rumped Parrotlets. *Condor* 70: 89.

Bull, J. 1978. Palearctic waders and larids in the southern Caribbean. *Ardea* 66: 121–23.

Bundy, C. F. 1965. A new Floridian. The Scarlet Ibis. *Audubon Mag.* 67: 84–85.

Chapman, F. M. 1894. On the birds of the island of Trinidad. *Bull. Am. Mus. Nat. Hist.* 6:1–86.

———. 1895. Further notes on Trinidad birds, with a description of a new species of *Synnallaxis. Bull. Am. Mus. Nat. Hist.* 7: 321–26.

Chenery, E. M. 1956. The Sulphur and White-breasted Toucan. *J. Trin. Field Nat. Club,* pp. 4–11.

Cherrie, G. K. 1906. A collection of birds from Aripo, Trinidad. *Brooklyn Inst. Bull.* 1(8): 188–91.

———. 1908. Further notes on a collection of birds from Trinidad. *Brooklyn Inst. Bull.* 1(13): 353–70.

———. 1916. A contribution to the ornithology of the Orinoco region. *Brooklyn Inst. Bull.,* pp. 133–374.

Collins, C. T. 1968a. The comparative biology of two species of swifts in Trinidad, West Indies. *Bull. Fla. State Mus.,* 11(5): 257–320.

———. 1968b. *Notes on the biology of Chapman's Swift,* Chaetura chapmani. Am. Mus. Novit. 2320. 15 pp.

———. 1969. A review of the shearwater records for Trinidad and Tobago. *Ibis* 111: 251–53.

———. 1974. Survival rate of the Chestnut-collared Swift. *West. Bird Bander* 49: 50–53.

Coltart, N. B. 1951. Nests of the Orange-breasted Falcon. *Oologists' Rec.* 26: 43.

Conway, W. G. 1962. The weights of eleven living eagles and vultures at the New York Zoological Park. *Auk* 79: 274–75.

Cory, C. B. 1893. A list of the birds collected on the island of Tobago, West Indies, by W. W. Brown during April and May 1892. *Auk* 10: 220.

Darnton, I. 1958. The display of the manakin, *Manacus manacus*. *Ibis* 100: 52–58.

Davis, D. E. 1940. Social nesting habits of the Smooth-billed Ani. *Auk* 57: 179–218.

Davis, L. I. 1962. Acoustic evidence of relationship in *Caprimulgus*. *Texas J. Sci.* 14: 72–106.

Davis, T. A. W. 1952. An outline of the ecology and breeding seasons of the birds of the lowland forest region of British Guiana. *Ibis* 95: 450–67.

———. 1961. Nests of *Empidonomus varius, Pitangus lictor,* and *Myiozetetes cayanensis*. *Auk* 78: 276–77.

Deane, R. S. W. 1967. Breeding of Twa-Twa in captivity. *J. Trin. Field Nat. Club,* pp. 9–10.

de Dalmas, R. 1900. Note sur une collection d'oiseaux de l'ile de Tobago. *Mem. Soc. Zool. France* 13: 132–44.

Devas, R. 1950. *Visitor's book of birds. Trinidad and Tobago.* Port of Spain: Muir Marshall.

Dinsmore, J. J. 1967. Ecology and behavior of the Greater Bird-of-Paradise on Little Tobago island. M.S. thesis, Univ. of Wisconsin.

———. 1969. Dual calling by birds of paradise. *Auk* 86: 139–40.

———. 1970. Courtship behavior of the Greater Bird of Paradise. *Auk* 87: 305–21.

———. 1972. Avifauna of Little Tobago Island. *Q. J. Fla. Acad. Sci.* 35(1): 55–71.

Dinsmore, J. J., and R. P. ffrench. 1969. Birds of St. Giles Is., Tobago. *Wilson Bull.* 81: 460–63.

Dorward, D. F. 1962a. Comparative biology of the White Booby and the Brown Booby *Sula* spp. at Ascension. *Ibis* 103b: 174–220.

———. 1962b. Behaviour of Boobies *Sula* spp. *Ibis* 103b: 221–34.

Downs, W. G. 1959. Little Egret banded in Spain taken in Trinidad. *Auk* 76: 241–42.

Drury, W. H. 1962. Breeding activities, especially nest-building, of the Yellowtail (*Ostinops decumanus*) in Trinidad, West Indies. *Zoologica* 47: 39–58.

Dusi, J. L. 1967. Migration in the Little Blue Heron. *Wilson Bull.* 79: 223–35.

Eastman, W., and K. Eastman. 1959. Bird observations on Tobago. *Fla. Nat.* 32. 8 pp.

Eckelberry, D. R. 1964. Bird painting in a tropical valley. *Audubon Mag.,* pp. 284–89.

———. 1967. My Eden. *Audubon Mag.,* pp. 44–53.

Edwards, E. P. 1967. Nests of the Common Bush-Tanager and the Scaled Antpitta. *Condor* 69: 605.

Eisenmann, E. 1953. What bird lays black eggs? *Auk* 70: 362–63.

———. 1963. Is the Black Vulture migratory? *Wilson Bull.* 75: 244–49.

———. 1971. Range expansion and population increase in North and Middle America of the White-tailed Kite. *Am. Birds* 25: 529–36.

Eisenmann, E., and F. Haverschmidt. 1970. Northward migration to Surinam of South American martins (*Progne*). *Condor* 72: 368–69.

Erwin, R. M., G. J. Smith and R. B. Clapp. 1986. Winter distribution and oiling of Common Terns in Trinidad. *J. Field Ornithol.* 57: 300–308.

Escalante, R. 1968. Notes on the Royal Tern in Uruguay. *Condor* 70: 243–47.

Feinsinger, P. 1980. Asynchronous migration patterns and the coexistence of tropical hummingbirds. Pp. 411–19 *in* A. Keast and E. S. Morton (eds.), *Migrant birds in the Neotropics: ecology, behavior, distribution and conservation.* Washington, D.C.: Smithsonian Institute Press.

Feinsinger, P., and R. K. Colwell. 1978. Community organization among Neotropical nectar-feeding birds. *Am. Zool.* 18: 779–95.

Feinsinger, P., and L. A. Swarm. 1982. "Ecological release", seasonal variation in food supply, and the hummingbird *Amazilia tobaci* on Trinidad and Tobago. *Ecology* 63: 1574–87.

Feinsinger, P., L. A. Swarm and J. A. Wolfe. 1985. Nectar-feeding birds on Trinidad and Tobago: comparison of diverse and depauperate guilds. *Ecol. Monogr.* 55: 1–28.

Feinsinger, P., J. A. Wolfe and L. A. Swarm. 1982. Island ecology: reduced hummingbird diversity and the pollination biology of plants, Trinidad and Tobago, West Indies. *Ecology* 63: 494–506.

ffrench, R. P. 1961. The Red-billed Tropicbird. *J. Trin. Field Nat. Club*, pp. 9–10.

——. 1963. Bulwer's Petrel in Trinidad, West Indies. *Auk* 80: 379.

——. 1965a. Notes on the avifauna of Grand Fond, Monos. *J. Trin. Field Nat. Club*, pp. 28–50.

——. 1965b. Some unusual habits of Little Blue Herons. *Caribb. J. Sci.* 5: 89.

——. 1965c. The nesting behaviour of the Yellow-bellied Seedeater. *Caribb. J. Sci.* 5: 149–56.

——. 1967a. The avifauna of Chacachacare Island. *J. Trin. Field Nat. Club*, pp. 45–46.

——. 1967b. The Dickcissel on its wintering grounds in Trinidad. *Living Bird* 6: 123–40.

——. 1969a. Further notes on the avifauna of Chacachacare Island. *J. Trin. Field Nat. Club*, pp. 10–11.

——. 1969b. The avifauna of Saut d'Eau Island. *J. Trin. Field Nat. Club*, p. 16.

——. 1969c. Conservation News. *J. Trin. Field Nat. Club*, pp. 22–24.

——. 1973. Dubious bird records for Trinidad and Tobago. *J. Trin. Field Nat. Club*, pp. 74–79.

——. 1975. Some noteworthy bird records from Tobago. *J. Trin. Tob. Field Nat. Club*, pp. 5–11.

——. 1977. Some interesting bird records from Trinidad and Tobago. *Living World (J. Trin. Tob. Field Nat. Club)*, pp. 9–10.

——. 1978. More records of rare birds in Trinidad and Tobago. *Living World (J. Trin. Tob. Field Nat. Club)*, pp. 25–26.

——. 1981. Some recent additions to the avifauna of Trinidad and Tobago. *Living World (J. Trin. Tob. Field Nat. Club)*, pp. 35–36.

——. 1982. The breeding of the Pearl Kite in Trinidad. *Living Bird* 19: 121–31.

——. 1983. Further notes on the avifauna of Trinidad and Tobago. *Living World (J. Trin. Tob. Field Nat. Club)*, pp. 32–34.

——. 1985a. Additional notes on the birds of Trinidad and Tobago. *Living World (J. Trin. Tob. Field Nat. Club)*, pp. 9–11.

——. 1985b. Changes in the avifauna of Trinidad. Pp. 986–91 *in* P. Buckley et al.

(eds.), *Neotropical ornithology*. Ornithol. Monogr. 36. Washington, D.C.: American Ornithologists' Union.

———. 1989. The birds and other vertebrates of Soldado Rock, Trinidad. *Living World (J. Trin. Tob. Field Nat. Club)*, pp. 16–20.

———. 1991. Synchronous breeding and moult in the Brown Noddy tern on Soldado Rock, Trinidad. *Living World (J. Trin. Tob. Field Nat. Club)* (in press).

ffrench, R. P., and C. T. Collins. 1965. Royal and Cayenne terns breeding in Trinidad, West Indies. *Auk* 82: 277.

ffrench, R. P., and M. ffrench. 1966. Recent records of birds in Trinidad and Tobago. *Wilson Bull.* 78: 5–11.

———. 1978. The birds of Grafton Estate, Tobago. *Living World (J. Trin. Tob. Field Nat. Club)*, pp. 19–24.

ffrench, R. P., and F. Haverschmidt. 1970. The Scarlet Ibis in Surinam and Trinidad. *Living Bird* 9: 147–65.

ffrench, R. P., and T. Manolis. 1983. Notes on some birds of Trinidad wetlands. *Living World (J. Trin. Tob. Field Nat. Club)*, pp. 29–31.

Finsch, O. 1873. Notes on a collection of birds from the island of Trinidad. *Proc. Zool. Soc. London*, pp. 552–89.

Fisher, D. J. 1978. First record of Black-headed Gull *Larus ridibundus* and third record of Herring Gull *L. argentatus* for South America. *Bull. Br. Ornithol. Club* 98: 113.

Foster, M. S. 1971. Plumage and behaviour of a juvenile Gray-headed Kite. *Auk* 88: 163–66.

Friedmann, H. 1929. *The cowbirds*. Springfield, Ill.: Charles C Thomas.

Friedmann, H., and F. D. Smith. 1950. A contribution to the ornithology of northeastern Venezuela. *Proc. U.S. Natl. Mus.* 100: 411–538.

———. 1955. A further contribution to the ornithology of northeastern Venezuela. *Proc. U.S. Natl. Mus.* 104: 463–524.

Gibbs, R. G., and K. Gibbs. 1975. Observations at a Gray Hawk's nest. *J. Trin. Tob. Field Nat. Club*, pp. 2–5.

Gilliard, E. T. 1959a. *Notes on some birds of Northern Venezuela*. Am. Mus. Novit. 1927. 33pp.

———. 1959b. *Notes on the courtship behavior of the Blue-backed Manakin*. Am. Mus. Novit. 1942. 19 pp.

Gochfeld, M. 1973. Observations on new or unusual birds from Trinidad, West Indies, and comments on the genus *Plegadis* in Venezuela. *Condor* 75: 474–78.

Greenlaw, J. S. 1967. Foraging behavior of the Double-toothed Kite in association with White-faced Monkeys. *Auk* 84: 596–97.

Gross, A. O. 1950. Nesting of the Streaked Flycatcher in Panama. *Wilson Bull.* 62: 183–93.

———. 1958. Life history of the Bananaquit of Tobago island. *Wilson Bull.* 70: 257–79.

Hagar, J. A. 1966. Nesting of the Hudsonian Godwit at Churchill, Manitoba. *Living Bird* 5: 5–43.

Harris, M. P. 1969. Food as a factor controlling the breeding of *Puffinus lherminieri*. *Ibis* 111: 139–56.

Harrison, C. J. O. 1963. Interspecific preening display by the Rice Grackle *Psomocolax oryzivorus*. *Auk* 80: 373–74.

Hatch, D. E. 1970. Energy conserving and heat dissipating mechanisms of the Turkey Vulture. *Auk* 87: 111–24.

Haverschmidt, F. 1947. Field notes on the Black-bellied Tree-Duck in Dutch Guiana. *Wilson Bull.* 59: 209.

———. 1948. Bird weights from Surinam. *Wilson Bull.* 60: 230–39.

———. 1952. More bird weights from Surinam. *Wilson Bull.* 64: 234–41.

———. 1953a. Notes on the life-history of *Columbigallina talpacoti* in Surinam. *Condor* 55: 21–25.

———. 1953b. Notes on the life-history of the Black-crested Antshrike in Surinam. *Wilson Bull.* 65: 242–51.

———. 1954a. Evening flights of the Southern Everglade Kite and the Blue and Yellow Macaw in Surinam. *Wilson Bull.* 66: 264–65.

———. 1954b. The nesting of the Ridgway Tyrannulet in Surinam. *Condor* 56: 139–41.

———. 1954c. Zur Brutbiologie von *Thraupis episcopus* in Surinam. *J. Ornithol.* 95: 48–54.

———. 1955. Beobachtungen an *Tapera naevia* und seine Wirte in Surinam. *J. Ornithol.* 96: 337–43.

———. 1958. Notes on the breeding habits of *Panyptila cayennensis*. *Auk* 75: 121–30.

———. 1961. Der Kuckuck *Tapera naevia* und seine Wirte in Surinam. *J. Ornithol.* 102: 353–59.

———. 1962a. Beobachtungen an der Schleireule, *Tyto alba*, in Surinam. *J. Ornithol.* 103: 236–42.

———. 1962b. Notes on some Surinam breeding birds. II. *Ardea* 50: 173–79.

———. 1962c. Notes on the feeding habits and food of some hawks of Surinam. *Condor* 64: 154–58.

———. 1966. The migration and wintering of the Upland Plover in Surinam. *Wilson Bull.* 78: 319–20.

———. 1967. Additional notes on the eggs of the Giant Cowbird. *Bull. Br. Ornithol. Club* 87: 136–37.

———. 1968a. *Birds of Surinam*. Edinburgh: Oliver and Boyd.

———. 1968b. Great Kiskadee parasitized by Shiny Cowbird in Surinam. *Auk* 85: 325.

———. 1969. A Streaked Flycatcher at sea. *Bull. Br. Ornithol. Club* 89: 166.

———. 1970a. Are there two species of Shrub Flycatcher (*Sublegatus*)? *Auk* 87: 358.

———. 1970b. Notes on the life-history of the Mouse-colored Flycatcher in Surinam. *Condor* 72: 374–75.

———. 1972. Notes on the Yellow-billed Tern. *Bull. Br. Ornithol. Club* 92: 93–95.

———. 1974. Notes on the Grey-breasted Crake *Laterallus exilis*. *Bull. Br. Ornithol. Club* 94: 2–3.

Heatwole, H. 1965. Some aspects of the association of Cattle Egrets with cattle. *Anim. Behav.* 13: 79–83.

Hellmayr, C. E. 1906. On the birds of the island of Trinidad. *Novit. Zool.* 13: 1–60.

Hellmayr, C. E., and B. Conover. 1942. *Catalogue of birds of the Americas and adjacent islands*, vol. I. Chicago: Field Mus. Nat. Hist. 636 pp.

Herklots, G. A. C. 1961. *The birds of Trinidad and Tobago*. London: Collins, 287 pp.

Hilty, S. L., and W. L. Brown. 1986. *A guide to the birds of Colombia.* Princeton: Princeton Univ. Press. 836 pp.

Holt, D. W., et al. 1986. First record of Common Black-headed Gulls breeding in the United States. *Am. Birds* 40: 204–6.

Horwich, R. H. 1965. An ontogeny of wing-flashing in the Mockingbird with reference to other behaviors. *Wilson Bull.* 77: 264–81.

Hoy, G., and J. Ottow. 1964. Biological and oological studies of the Molothrine cowbirds (Icteridae) of Argentina. *Auk* 81: 186–203.

James, C., and G. Hislop. 1988. *Status and conservation of two cracid species, the Pawi or Trinidad Piping-Guan* (Pipile pipile) *and the Cocrico* (Ortalis ruficauda) *in Trinidad and Tobago.* For. Div., Min. of Food Prod., Forestry and Environment, Trinidad.

Jardine, W. 1846. Horae Zoologicae, No. VIII. Ornithology of the island of Tobago. *Ann. Mag. Nat. Hist.* 18: 114–21.

Jenni, D. A. 1969. Diving times of the Least Grebe and Masked Duck. *Auk* 86: 355–56.

Johnson, R. E. 1937. The nest of the Common Potoo. *Illustrated London News,* March 13, p. 436.

———. 1956–57. Trinidad birds (in 4 parts). *Shell Trin. Mag.* (various issues).

Junge, G. C. A., and G. F. Mees. 1958. *The avifauna of Trinidad and Tobago.* Zoologische Verhandelingen 37. Leiden. 172 pp.

Junge, G. C. A., and K. H. Voous. 1955. The distribution and relationship of *Sterna eurygnatha. Ardea* 43: 226–47.

Kahl, M. P., and L. J. Peacock. 1963. The Bill-snap reflex: a feeding mechanism in the American Wood Stork. *Nature* (Lond.) 199: 505–6.

Keeler-Wolf, T. H. 1982. Reduced avian densities in Tobago lower montane rain forest: a resource-based study. Ph.D. diss., Univ. of California, Santa Cruz. 305 pp.

———. 1986. The Barred Antshrike (*Thamnophilus doliatus*) on Trinidad and Tobago: habitat niche expansion of a generalist forager. *Oecologia* 70: 309–17.

Keith, A. R. 1979. Prairie Warbler at Trinidad. *Am. Birds* 33: 745.

Kelso, E. H. 1936. A new owl in a collection from Tobago. *Auk* 53: 82.

Kielhorn, W. V., et al. 1963. Bathing behavior of frigatebirds. *Condor* 65: 240–41.

Kilham, L. 1972a. Shortness of tail in Red-crowned Woodpeckers and their habit of entering roost holes backward. *Condor* 74: 202–4.

———. 1972b. Habits of the Crimson-crested Woodpecker in Panama. *Wilson Bull.* 84: 28–47.

Kilham, L., and P. O'Brien. 1979. Early breeding behavior of Lineated Woodpeckers. *Condor* 81: 299–303.

Kirk, J. 1883. List of birds in L. G. Hay's Tobago handbook. N.p.

Lancaster, D. A. 1970. Breeding behavior of the Cattle Egret in Colombia. *Living Bird* 9: 167–94.

Lanyon, W. E. 1963. *Experiments on Species Discrimination in* Myiarchus *Flycatchers.* Am. Mus. Novit. 2126. 16 pp.

Lapham, H. 1970. A study of the nesting behaviour of the Rufous-vented Chachalaca (*Ortalis ruficauda*) in Venezuela. *Bol. Soc. Venez. Cienc. Nat.* 117: 291–328.

Léotaud, A. 1866. *Oiseaux de l'île de la Trinidad.* Port of Spain: Chronicle Press. 560 pp.

Lill, A. 1969. Allopreening in the dove *Geotrygon montana. Condor* 71: 72.
——. 1970. Nidification in the Channel-billed Toucan in Trinidad. *Condor* 72: 235–36.
Lill, A., and R. P. ffrench. 1970. Nesting of the Plain Antvireo *Dysithamnus mentalis andrei* in Trinidad, West Indies. *Ibis* 112: 267–68.
Loftin, H., and E. L. Tyson. 1965. Stylized behavior in the Turkey Vulture's courtship dance. *Wilson Bull.* 77: 193.
Lowe-McConnell, R. H. 1967. Biology of the immigrant Cattle Egret *Ardeola ibis* in Guyana, South America. *Ibis* 109: 168–79.
Lunk, W. A., 1962. *The Rough-winged Swallow,* Stelgidopteryx ruficollis. *A study based on its breeding biology in Michigan.* Nuttall Ornithol. Club 4. 155 pp.
Luthin, C. S. 1984. I.C.B.P. Report no. 2, World Working Group on Storks, Ibises and Spoonbills. W. W. Brehm Fund for International Bird Conservation, Walsrode, Germany. 20 pp.
McKelvey, M. 1965. Unusual bathing habits of the Turkey Vulture. *Condor* 67: 265.
McNeil, R., and M. Carrera de Itriago. 1968. Fat deposition in the Scissor-tailed Flycatcher and the Small-billed Elaenia during the austral migratory period in N. Venezuela. *Can. J. Zool.* 46: 123–28.
McNeil, R., and A. Martinez. 1968. Notes on the nesting of the Short-tailed Pigmy-Tyrant in N.E. Venezuela. *Condor* 70: 181–82.
Manolis, T. 1981. First sight-record of South Polar Skua *Catharacta maccormicki* for Trinidad, West Indies. *Am. Birds* 35: 982.
——. 1982. Host relationships and reproductive strategies of the Shiny Cowbird in Trinidad and Tobago. Ph.D. diss., Univ. of Colorado, Boulder. 136 pp.
Marchant, S. 1960. The breeding of some S.W. Ecuadorian birds. (2 parts) *Ibis* 102: 349–82, and 584–99.
Marshall, R. C. 1939. *Silviculture of the trees in Trinidad and Tobago.* London: Oxford Univ. Press. 247 pp.
Mayr, E. 1966. Hummingbird caught by Sparrowhawk. *Auk* 83: 664.
Meanley, B. 1963. Pre-nesting activity of the Purple Gallinule near Savannah, Georgia. *Auk* 80: 545–47.
Metcalf, W. G. 1966. Observations of migrating Great Shearwaters *Puffinus gravis* off the Brazilian coast. *Ibis* 108: 138–40.
Meyer de Schauensee, R. 1966. *The species of birds of South America and their distribution.* Wynnewood, Pa.: Livingston Pub. Co. 577 pp.
Meyer de Schauensee, R., and W. H. Phelps. 1978. *A guide to the birds of Venezuela.* Princeton: Princeton Univ. Press. 424 pp.
Meyerriecks, A. J. 1960. *Comparative breeding behavior of four species of North American herons.* Nuttall Ornithol. Club 2. Cambridge. 158 pp.
Meyerriecks, A. J., and D. W. Nellis. 1967. Egrets serving as "beaters" for Belted Kingfisher. *Wilson Bull.* 79: 236–37.
Miller, A. H. 1947. The tropical avifauna of the upper Magdalena Valley, Colombia. *Auk* 64: 351–81.
Morris, R. D. 1984. Breeding chronology and reproductive success of seabirds on Little Tobago, Trinidad. *Colon. Waterbirds* 7: 1–9.
Moynihan, M. 1962. *Hostile and sexual behavior patterns of some South American and Pacific Laridae. Behaviour,* Suppl. 8.
Mrsovsky, N. 1971. Black Vultures attack live turtle hatchlings. *Auk* 88: 672–73.
Murphy, R. C. 1936. *Oceanic birds of South America.* 2 vols. New York: Amer. Mus. Nat. His.

Murphy, W. L. 1986. *A birder's guide to Trinidad and Tobago.* College Park, Md.: Peregrine Enterprises. 124 pp.

——. In press. Second record of Baird's Sandpiper (*Calidris bairdii*) for Trinidad, with notes on its occurrence in the Caribbean Basin. *Am. Birds.*

Murphy, W. L., and S. Fried. In press. Little Egret (*Egretta garzetta*): second and subsequent records for Trinidad, and first record for Tobago, with notes on its status in the Caribbean region. *Am. Birds.*

Murphy, W. L., and W. Nanan. 1987. First confirmed record of Western Reef-Heron *Egretta gularis* for South America. *Am. Birds* 41: 392–94.

Nelson, J. B. 1969. The breeding behaviour of the Red-footed Booby. *Ibis* 111: 357–85.

Olson, D. H., and M. K. McDowell. 1983. A comparison of White-bearded Manakin (*Manacus manacus*) populations and lek systems in Surinam and Trinidad. *Auk* 100: 739–42.

Orians, G. H., and D. H. Paulson. 1969. Notes on Costa Rican birds. *Condor* 71: 426–31.

Owen, D. F. 1959. Mortality of the Great Blue Heron as shown by banding recoveries. *Auk* 76: 464–70.

Palmer, R. S. (ed.) 1962. *Handbook of North American birds,* vol. I. New Haven: Yale Univ. Press.

Peters, J. L. 1931 and later. *Checklist of birds of the world.* Cambridge: Harvard Univ. Press.

Peterson, R. T. 1947. *A field guide to the birds.* Boston: Houghton Mifflin. 290 pp.

Pinto, O. 1953. Sobre a coleçao Carlos Estavao de peles, ninhos e ovos das aves de Belem (Para.). *Pap. Avulsos Dep. Zool. (São Paulo)* XI, no. 13:111–222.

——. 1965. The fruit of the palm *Elaeis guineensis* in the diet of *Cathartes aura ruficollis. Hornero* 10: 276–77.

Post, P. W. 1967. Manx, Audubon's and Little shearwaters in the N.E. North Atlantic. *Bird-Banding* 38: 278–305.

Quesnel, V. C. 1956. The density of the population of breeding Kiskadees in Port of Spain. *J. Trin. Field Nat. Club,* pp. 24–25.

——. 1977. Stay-at-home Starthroat. *Living World (J. Trin. Tob. Field Nat. Club),* p. 11.

——. 1985. Why do Nightjars sit on the road at night? *Living World (J. Trin. Tob. Field Nat. Club),* pp. 19–23.

——. 1987. The songs of the Rufous-browed Peppershrike, *Cyclarhis gujanensis. Living World (J. Trin. Tob. Field Nat. Club),* pp. 43–46.

Ramo, C., and B. Busto. 1987. Hybridization between Scarlet Ibis (*Eudocimus ruber*) and White Ibis (*E. albus*) in Venezuela. *Colon. Waterbirds* 10: 111–14.

Rand, A. L. 1966. A display of the Boat-billed Heron. *Auk* 83: 304–6.

Ridgely, R. S., and G. Tudor. 1989. *The birds of South America,* vol. 1. Oxford: Oxford Univ. Press. 516 pp.

Roberts, H. R. 1934. List of Trinidad birds with field notes. *Trop. Agric. Trin.* 11(4): 87–99.

Robertson, W. B. 1964. The terns of the Dry Tortugas. *Bull. Fla. State Mus.* 8(1): 1–95.

Rooks, D. 1983. First record of the Double-striped Thick-knee in Trinidad, West Indies. *Living World (J. Trin. Tob. Field Nat. Club),* p. 3.

——. 1987. Bird observations in Tobago, December 1985 to November 1987. *Living World (J. Trin. Tob. Field Nat. Club),* pp. 41–42.

Rowley, J. S. 1966. Breeding birds of the Sierra Madre del Sur, Oaxaca, Mexico. *Proc. West. Found. Vert. Zool.* 1: 107–204.

Rowley, J. S., and R. T. Orr. 1965. Nesting and feeding habits of the White-collared Swift. *Condor* 67: 449–56.

Ruschi, A. 1967. Some observations on the migration of hummingbirds in Brazil (in Portuguese). Bol. Mus. Biol. Prof. Mello-Leitao, Zool. 28: 1–5.

Saunders, J. B. 1956. The Scarlet Ibis. *Trin. Regent News* 6(4): 10–12.

———. 1957. Bird life on Soldado Rock. *Trin. Regent News* 7(3): 4–7.

Schaefer, E. 1953. Contribution to the life history of the Swallow-Tanager. *Auk* 70: 403–60.

Schönwetter, M. 1961. *Handbuch der oölogie,* part 3. Berlin: n.p. 184 pp.

Schubart, O., A. C. Aguirre and H. Sick. 1965. Contribuiçao para o conhecimento da alimentaçao das aves brasileiras. *Arq. Zool. (São Paulo)* XII, no. 1: 95–249.

Schwartz, P. 1964. The Northern Waterthrush in Venezuela. *Living Bird* 3: 169–84.

Sick, H. 1958. Distribution and nests of *Panyptila cayennensis* in Brazil. *Auk* 75: 217–20.

———. 1959. Notes on the biology of two Brazilian swifts, *Chaetura andrei* and *C. cinereiventris. Auk* 76: 471–77.

Sick, H., and J. Ottow. 1958. Vom brasilianischen Kuhvogel, *Molothrus bonariensis,* und seinen Wirten, besonders dem Ammerfinken, *Zonotrichia capensis. Bonn. Zool. Beitr.* 1: 40–62.

Siegfried, W. R. 1966. Age at which Cattle Egrets first breed. *Ostrich* 37: 198–99.

Skutch, A. F. 1945a. The most hospitable tree. *Sci. Monthly* 60: 5–17.

———. 1945b. Incubation and nestling periods of Central American birds. *Auk* 62: 8–37.

———. 1946. Life history of the Costa Rican Tityra. *Auk* 63: 327–62.

———. 1949. Life history of the Ruddy Quail-Dove. *Condor* 51: 3–19.

———. 1952. On the hour of laying and hatching of birds' eggs. *Ibis* 94: 49–61.

———. 1954. *Life histories of Central American birds I.* Pac. Coast Avifauna 31. 448 pp.

———. 1956a. Roosting and nesting of the Golden-olive Woodpecker. *Wilson Bull.* 68: 118–28.

———. 1956b. A nesting of the Collared Trogon. *Auk* 73: 354–66.

———. 1957. Life history of the Amazon Kingfisher. *Condor* 59: 217–29.

———. 1959. Life history of the Blue Ground-Dove. *Condor* 61: 65–74.

———. 1960. *Life histories of Central American birds II.* Pac. Coast Avifauna 34. 593 pp.

———. 1962. Life histories of honeycreepers. *Condor* 64: 92–116.

———. 1963a. Life history of the Little Tinamou. *Condor* 65: 224–31.

———. 1963b. Life history of the Rufous-tailed Jacamar in Costa Rica. *Ibis* 105: 354–68.

———. 1964a. Life history of the Blue-diademed Motmot. *Ibis* 106: 321–32.

———. 1964b. Life histories of hermit hummingbirds. *Auk* 81: 5–25.

———. 1964c. Life histories of Central American pigeons. *Wilson Bull.* 76: 211–47.

———. 1965. Life history notes on two tropical American kites. *Condor* 67: 235–46.

———. 1966. Life history notes on three tropical American cuckoos. *Wilson Bull.* 78: 139–65.

——. 1967. *Life histories of Central American highland birds.* Nuttall Ornithol. Club 7. 213 pp.

——. 1968. The nesting of some Venezuelan birds. *Condor* 70: 66–82.

——. 1969a. Notes on the possible migration and the nesting of the Black Vulture in Central America. *Auk* 86: 726–31.

——. 1969b. *Life histories of Central American birds III.* Pac. Coast Avifauna 35. 580 pp.

——. 1971. Life history of the Bright-rumped Attila. *Ibis* 113: 316–22.

Slud, P. 1964. *The birds of Costa Rica.* Bull. Am. Mus. Nat. Hist. 128, 430 pp.

Smith, N. G. 1968. The advantage of being parasitized. *Nature* 219: 690–94.

Smith, W. J. 1962. The nest of *Pitangus lictor. Auk* 79: 108–10.

——. 1965. *Dendroica pensylvanica* in Trinidad. *Auk* 82: 279.

Smithe, F. B., and R. A. Paynter. 1963. Birds of Tikal, Guatemala. *Bull. Mus. Comp. Zool. Harv. Univ.* 128(5): 245–324.

Snow, B. K. 1961. Notes on the behavior of three Cotingidae. *Auk* 78: 150–61.

——. 1970. A field study of the Bearded Bellbird in Trinidad. *Ibis* 112: 299–329.

——. 1973. Social organisation of the Hairy Hermit *Glaucis hirsuta. Ardea* 61: 94–105.

——. 1974. Lek behaviour and breeding of Guy's Hermit *Phaethornis guy. Ibis* 116: 278–97.

——. 1977. Comparison of the leks of Guy's Hermit hummingbird *Phaethornis guy* in Costa Rica and Trinidad. *Ibis* 119: 211–14.

Snow, B. K., and D. W. Snow. 1971. The feeding ecology of tanagers and honeycreepers in Trinidad. *Auk* 88: 291–322.

——. 1972. Feeding niches of hummingbirds in a Trinidad valley. *J. Anim. Ecol.* 41: 471–85.

——. 1979. The Ochre-bellied Flycatcher and the evolution of lek behavior. *Condor* 81: 286–92.

Snow, D. W. 1961. The natural history of the Oilbird, *Steatornis caripensis,* in Trinidad, West Indies. Part I. *Zoologica* 46: 27–48.

——. 1962a. A field study of the Black and White Manakin in Trinidad. *Zoologica* 47: 65–104.

——. 1962b. Notes on the biology of Trinidad swifts. *Zoologica* 47: 129–39.

——. 1962c. A field study of the Golden-headed Manakin in Trinidad. *Zoologica* 47: 183–98.

——. 1962d. The natural history of the Oilbird, *Steatornis caripensis,* in Trinidad, West Indies. Part II. *Zoologica* 47: 199–221.

——. 1963. The display of the Blue-backed Manakin in Tobago. *Zoologica* 48: 167–76.

——. 1965a. The breeding of Audubon's Shearwater in the Galapagos. *Auk* 82: 591–97.

——. 1965b. The breeding of the Red-billed Tropicbird in the Galapagos islands. *Condor* 67: 210–14.

——. 1968. The singing assemblies of Little Hermits. *Living Bird* 7: 47–55.

——. 1971. Social organization of the Blue-backed Manakin. *Wilson Bull.* 83: 35–38.

——. 1977. Duetting and other synchronised displays of the blue-backed manakins *Chiroxiphia* spp. Pp. 239–51 *in* B. Stonehouse and C. Perrins (eds.), *Evolutionary ecology.* London: Macmillan.

——. 1978. The nest as a factor determining clutch-size in tropical birds. *J. Ornithol.* 119: 227–30.

——. 1985a. *The web of adaptation: bird studies in the American tropics.* Ithaca: Cornell Univ. Press. 192 pp.

——. 1985b. Affinities and recent history of the avifauna of Trinidad and Tobago. Pp. 238–46 *in* P. Buckley et al. (eds.), *Neotropical ornithology.* Ornithol. Monogr. 36. Washington, D.C.: American Ornithologists' Union.

Snow, D. W., and C. T. Collins. 1962. Social breeding behavior of the Mexican Tanager. *Condor* 64: 161.

Snow, D. W., and A. Lill. 1974. Longevity records for some Neotropical land-birds. *Condor* 76: 262–67.

Snow, D. W., and B. K. Snow. 1963a. Weights and wing-lengths of some Trinidad birds. *Zoologica* 48: 1–12.

——. 1963b. Breeding and the annual cycle in three Trinidad thrushes. *Wilson Bull.* 75: 27–41.

——. 1964. Breeding seasons and annual cycles of Trinidad land-birds. *Zoologica* 49: 1–39.

——. 1973. The breeding of the Hairy Hermit *Glaucis hirsuta* in Trinidad. *Ardea* 61: 106–22.

Snyder, D. E. 1966. *The birds of Guyana.* Salem: Peabody Museum. 308 pp.

Stager, K. E. 1964. *The role of olfaction in food location by the Turkey Vulture, Cathartes aura.* Los Ang. Cty. Mus. Contrib. Sci. 81. 63 pp.

Stensrude, C. 1965. Observations on a pair of Gray Hawks in southern Arizona. *Condor* 67: 319–21.

Stiles, F. G., and A. F. Skutch. 1989. *A guide to the birds of Costa Rica.* Ithaca: Cornell Univ. Press. 523 pp.

Stonehouse, B. 1962. The tropicbirds (genus *Phaethon*) of Ascension Island. *Ibis* 103b: 124–61.

Storer, R. W. 1961. Observations of pellet-casting by Horned and Pied-billed grebes. *Auk* 78: 90–92.

Street, P. B. 1946. Some notes on Trinidad birds. *Auk* 63: 369–78.

Tashian, R. E. 1957. Nesting behavior of the Crested Oropendola (*Psarocolius decumanus*) in northern Trinidad. *Zoologica* 42: 87–98.

Taylor, E. C. 1864. Five months in the West Indies. Part I. *Ibis* 6: 73–97.

Teal, J. M. 1965. Nesting success of egrets and herons in Georgia. *Wilson Bull.* 77: 257–63.

Temple, S. A. 1972. Systematics and evolution of the North American Merlins. *Auk* 89: 325–38.

Thomas, B. T. 1987. Spring shorebird migration through central Venezuela. *Wilson Bull.* 99: 571–78.

Timken, R. L. 1970. Food habits and feeding behavior of the Baltimore Oriole in Costa Rica. *Wilson Bull.* 82: 184–88.

van Tyne, J. 1950. Bird notes from Barro Colorado island, Canal Zone. *Occas. Pap. Mus. Zool. Univ. Mich.* 525: 1–12.

Vaurie, C. 1967. *Systematic notes on the bird family Cracidae.* No. 7: *The genus Pipile.* Am. Mus. Novit. 2296. 16 pp.

Verner, J. 1961. Nesting activities of the Red-footed Booby in British Honduras. *Auk* 78: 573–94.

Vesey-Fitzgerald, D. 1936. Further notes on the food and habits of Trinidad birds with special reference to common canefield birds. *Trop. Agric.* 13: 12–18.

Voous, K. H. 1957. *The birds of Aruba, Curaçao, and Bonaire.* Studies Fauna Curaçao Caribbean Islands 7, no. 29. The Hague: Martinus Nijhoff. 260 pp.

Wetmore, A. 1965 and 1968. *The birds of the Republic of Panama.* Parts I and II. Washington: D.C.: Smithsonian Institute Press. Part I: 483 pp. Part II: 605 pp.

White, G. 1987. Noteworthy bird records. *Living World (J. Trin. Tob. Field Nat. Club),* p. 42.

Wiley, R. H. 1971a. Song groups in an assembly of Little Hermits. *Condor* 73: 28–35.

——. 1971b. Cooperative roles in mixed flocks of antwrens. *Auk* 88: 881–92.

Wiley, R. H., and M. S. Wiley. 1980. Spacing and timing in the nesting ecology of a tropical blackbird: comparison of populations in different environments. *Ecol. Monogr.* 50: 153–78.

Williams, C. B. 1922. Notes on the food and habits of some Trinidad birds. *Bull. Dep. Agric. Trin. Tob.* 20: 123–85.

Williams, T. C. 1985. Autumnal bird migration over the Windward Caribbean Islands. *Auk* 102: 163–67.

Williams, T. C., J. M. Williams, L. C. Ireland and J. M. Teal. 1977. Bird migration over the western North Atlantic Ocean. *Am. Birds* 31: 251–67.

Willis, E. O. 1960. Red-crowned Ant-Tanagers, Tawny-crowned Greenlets, and forest flocks. *Wilson Bull.* 72: 105–6.

——. 1961. A study of nesting ant-tanagers in British Honduras. *Condor* 63: 479–503.

——. 1966a. Interspecific competition and the foraging behavior of Plain-brown Woodcreepers. *Ecology* 47: 667–72.

——. 1966b. A prey capture by the Zone-tailed Hawk. *Condor* 68: 104–5.

——. 1966c. Competitive exclusion and birds at fruiting trees in western Colombia. *Auk* 83: 479–480.

——. 1972. The behavior of Plain-brown Woodcreepers, *Dendrocincla fuliginosa. Wilson Bull.* 84: 377–420.

Witherby, H. F., et al. 1952. *The handbook of British birds.* London: H. F. & G. Witherby.

Wolfe, L. R. 1962. Food of the Mexican White Hawk. *Auk* 79: 488.

Worth, C. B. 1969. Hooded Warbler in Trinidad, West Indies. *Wilson Bull.* 81:215.

Worth, C. B., and T. H. G. Aitken. 1965. First record of Gray-cheeked Thrush in Trinidad, West Indies. *Auk* 82: 109.

Young, C. G. 1928 and 1929. A contribution to the ornithology of the coastland of British Guiana. *Ibis* Series XII(4): 748–81; and Series XII(5): 1–38, 221–61.

Zahl, P. A. 1950. Search for the Scarlet Ibis in Venezuela. *Natl. Geogr. Mag.* 97: 633–61.

Zimmer, J. T. 1937. *Studies of Peruvian birds.* Am. Mus. Novit. 962. 10 pp.

Index

SCIENTIFIC NAMES